# THE BRITISH RAJ

## VOLUME II
## DECAY

**ELISABETH BECKETT**
**Edited by John Wrake**

Copyright © 1989 – 2011 Elisabeth Beckett & John Wrake

All Rights Reserved

ISBN: 1466369663

ISBN 13: 9781466369665

LCCN : 2011960032

# CONTENTS

| | |
|---|---|
| **Illustrations** | v |
| **Editor's Note** | vii |
| **Introduction** | 1 |
| **The Myth** | 9 |
| **Part 1. Malice** | **13** |
| Chapter I. Conspiracy | 13 |
| Chapter II. Congress | 31 |
| Chapter III. Rowlatt | 39 |
| Chapter IV. Ghadr | 47 |
| Chapter V. Khilafat | 61 |
| Chapter VI. Afghanistan | 77 |
| Chapter VII. Militarism | 95 |
| Chapter VIII. German Schemes | 101 |
| Chapter IX. Infiltration | 109 |
| Chapter X. Peshawar | 127 |
| **Part 2. The Mahatma** | **133** |
| Chapter I. Agitate | 133 |
| Chapter II. The Fuze | 147 |
| Chapter III. Timing | 153 |
| **Part 3. Mobs** | **165** |
| Chapter I. Delhi | 165 |
| Chapter II. Ahmedabad | 173 |
| Chapter III. Viramgam | 181 |
| Chapter IV. Lahore | 185 |
| Chapter V. Kasur | 189 |
| Chapter VI. Amritsar | 191 |

**Part 4. The Man** — **203**
    Chapter I. Life & Career — 203
    Chapter II. The Sarhad Campaign — 213
    Chapter III. Grip — 237
    Chapter IV. Dyer At Thal — 253

**Part 5. The Minister** — **261**
    Chapter I. Ambition — 261
    Chapter II. Ignorance & Superstition — 271
    Chapter III. Visiting — 281
    Chapter IV. The Hunter Inquiry — 307
    Chapter V. Hunter Evidence — 317
    Chapter VI. The Indemnity Debate — 327
    Chapter VII. The India Act — 351
    Chapter VIII. Montagu's Speeches — 373
    Chapter IX. The Final Debate — 387

**Part 6. The Aftermath** — **401**
    Chapter I. The Outcome — 401
    Chapter II. The Implications — 411
    Chapter III. The Lessons — 421

**Appendix I Rowlatt Acts** — **427**

**Appendix II Blackwoods Article** — **443**

**Appendix III Mrs. Wathen Diary** — **449**

**Appendix IV District Reports** — **459**

**Appendix V Glossary Of Indian Words** — **469**

**Bibliography Notes** — **473**

**Bibliography** — **477**

# ILLUSTRATIONS

Illustrations have come from various sources. Some consist of photographs freely available on the internet in websites such as Wikipedia, Wikimedia. Others come from private individuals who have allowed access to family collections of photographs. Numbers of these were taken by individuals who were present in Amritsar and the Punjab in the years between 1919 and 1921.

I am particularly grateful to Simon Parker-Galbreath of St. Helens, Tasmania, who hosts a website devoted to the 1/25th London Regiment and Amanda Stacey here in England who has given permission to use photographs dating from April 1919 taken from Percy Chisnell's album.

The photograph of the Punjab Rifles Armoured Train Section was provided by courtesy of the North Western Railway website hosted by Terry Case. The site was discovered due to a memento bearing the legend North Western Railway made by Corporal Harry Simpson from the propeller of the plane of 20 Sqn. R.A.F. which crashed on the North West Frontier of India while being flown by Flt. Lt. later Marshal of the Royal Air Force Sir John Slessor. Harry Simpson's family kindly provided the Bristol F2B photograph and others taken in 1921.

A major source has been Elisabeth's family.

Illustrations in the book will be found facing pages viii, 106, 232 and 312.

# EDITOR'S NOTE

This book of two volumes is built upon a manuscript written by Elisabeth Beckett, as the result of a lifetime's research into the origins and end of 'The British Raj', Britain's involvement in the History, Life and Government of the Indian Sub-Continent, from its inception at the beginning of the 17$^{th}$ Century, until the Declaration of Independence of India and the birth of Pakistan in 1947.

Volume I, entitled THE BRITISH RAJ –GROWTH, records the story of the men and women who made British India a reality and through the course of three Centuries, transformed the lives of all India's inhabitants.

This Volume II, entitled THE BRITISH RAJ – DECAY, is chiefly concerned with events which occurred during the early years of the Twentieth Century, focussing on a particular incident which took place at Amritsar in the Punjab on the 13$^{th}$ April 1919.

This incident has been named as the cause of the ending of the greatest Empire which the world has seen.

Elisabeth wrote her manuscript from a width and depth of knowledge and experience which is truly staggering. From the records of her parents, who were present at that event, conversations with their friends who were also there, from her own intimate knowledge of the land of her birth and its people and language, from her experience as the wife of a District Officer up to 1947, from her many Indian friends and from her wide contacts and reading, she gathered together the facts which display a very different picture from the manufactured story of that event and its outcome.

I should explain how I come to be involved with the book.

About ten years ago, Mrs. Peggy Fraser, a neighbour, passed me a manuscript which she had received from a friend, who, like her, had been the wife of a District Officer in India before Independence, asking for her comment. Knowing nothing of military matters, Peggy felt out of her depths, but knowing of my military service and interest in history, she asked me to look at it and send any comments to the author. The author was Elisabeth and my comments to her began a friendship which I value very highly.

I found her manuscript totally fascinating, for it told me a great deal about international affairs of which I was ignorant and made sense of events which had puzzled me.

From my military training, I was able to throw some light on one aspect of her account of the firing which took place at Amritsar, for which, she was grateful. I was bold enough to suggest that the facts which she had uncovered should be made more widely available, but that the MS was unsuitable for publication as it was. I even suggested an alternative layout.

Other matters demanded her attention and the possibility of a book took a back seat.

Having found her growing increasingly frail in 2008, aged 84 and suffering from leukemia, the book was not mentioned and I was saddened to be told of her death in February 2009.

Elisabeth's campaign against the loss of British Sovereignty to the European Union, stemming from her knowledge of Constitutional Law, had won her wide support. Speaking with some of her other friends, I discovered that I was not alone in thinking that her life of service to this Country was deserving of some form of memorial and it seemed to me that it would be fitting to attempt publication of her manuscript.

Consequently, a year after her death, I contacted two of her children, to ask for their views. Sabrina and William expressed agreement in principle and were ready to make the manuscript available for a rewrite, if an editor could be found.

The upshot of our conversation was a request that I might undertake this, since I was familiar with the material. I agreed, somewhat reluctantly, since I have limited experience.

Elisabeth's manuscript falls naturally into two parts. Though the climax of the first part is the.Mutiny of 1857, that event did not mark the end of growth, any more than Amritsar in 1919, the focus of Volume II, ushered in decay. Political India describes the Mutiny as 'The First War of Independence', suggesting an earlier start to the decay of the British Raj, despite the fact that the Mutiny was not India-wide. In the same way, growth may be said to have continued after 1919. Nevertheless, changes occurred in the latter half of the Nineteenth Century which make Elisabeth's division sensible.

This second volume of her account is the result.

Square brackets [] indicate notes by the author.

Italic text is used for extracts from original documents and direct quotations.

*John Wrake.*

**ELISABETH BECKETT WITH HER MOTHER AND ELDER SISTER
AND THE FAMILY'S BEARER, M. ASHRAF KHAN, ABOUT 1926.**

**R.B. BECKETT, ESQ., B.A., I.C.S., SECRETARY, MUNICIPAL COMMITTEE, LAHORE, WITH HIS STAFF IN 1924.**

**R.B. BECKETT ON TOUR IN 1920 PRESIDING AT A POLLING STATION AT KOTLI.**

# INTRODUCTION

Two things have to be said in introducing this book. The first is that I am a 'child of the Raj'. My father was a member of the Indian Civil Service, going out to India in 1914 before Delhi (the New Delhi) was built. To him, it was little more than a village when he arrived in India. Only a short while before, under Lord Curzon, it had been made the capital of India, and fixed as a concept by the Durbar in 1901. For those who know the saying "Divide and Rule" it may be of interest to know that it was the division of Bengal, also decided by Lord Curzon, that was the origin of this phrase. Far from dividing in order to rule, in India, we endeavoured to hold together, help relationships and understandings. That effort is epitomised in the construction of the Indian Railways – a network which still holds India together. It was an inevitable part of the Pax Britannia that gave India peace for the first time probably since the time of the Great Emperor Akbar. We amalgamated, protected, ensured stability and prevented the endless incursions from other countries such as France, Afghanistan and in this book, the Germans. Because of our peace making gifts, we were given the title that Indians give to their rulers, 'heaven born'; people ploughing fields would greet us with 'may your rule be long'. We made the deserts to flower, particularly in the Punjab, by our systems of canals and the resultant increase in productive land. In this way, we achieved an enormous growth of food which helped to reduce famine, until 1947, when India was divided; the Indians were given the Ferozepore headworks on the River Ravi and stopped the flow of water, leaving Pakistan with corn wilting in the fields and threatened famine. This is the story about an earlier time, for that tragedy came not under British rule, but Indian.

In modern times, it is extremely difficult to see through the mirage that various writers, with acrid thoughts and subconscious angers, have broadcast about the British in India. One of the most famous incidents so portrayed is the 1919 rebellion, in which General Dyer fired at Amritsar on a 'vast and hostile crowd' estimated at over 25,000 – and since the mobs that had devastated Amritsar earlier were estimated at 75,000 in the record of at least one policeman, the crowd might have been indeed

75,000. The place where this vast gathering accumulated is about the size, or rather more, of Trafalgar Square, without the lions and the traffic! (about eight acres).

It is about India at that time and about General Dyer that this book is written.

The second thing to be said is that it so happened that in 1919, my parents were in Amritsar during the Rebellion. My father was City Magistrate, my mother a bride newly out from England. This has meant that I have an exceptional knowledge of what went on, from the people who were there and who were my parents' friends. They had married on November 12th 1918, the day after the Armistice. They had reached Amritsar early in 1919. By April, the time when the Rebellion began, the hot weather was starting. The Deputy Commissioner of Amritsar, Miles Irving, had to come to the Magistrate's Courts to tell my father to go to the point, the Hall Bridge, where the night before it had been decided that he should provide the legal requirement for the guard on the Civil Lines in case there was any trouble. The reason that Miles Irving had to come and tell my father that a crowd had started gathering, instead of telephoning, was that in concert with the pre-arranged conspiracy, the telephone lines were cut as soon as the mob began to collect. My father went on horseback. He was not armed, being a civilian.

That first event was the beginning of mayhem, arson and murder, which Gandhi and his Congress Report claimed was provoked by my father firing. The description in the Report and in countless plagiarized versions, described a crowd of peaceful people, bareheaded, (a rare sight in those days) bare footed, carrying no sticks, asking for the whereabouts of their loved ones. Any claim by me that the Congress Report was, almost throughout, inaccurate and sometimes sheer balderdash, would have been challenged simply because I am my father's daughter and people who believe Gandhi to have been truthful, prefer to believe him rather than me, or my father.

For this reason, as I intended to write objectively of the historic events of that time, I had to do a great deal of research and check the facts. This took time and led to my discovery that Gandhi was habitually the most fearsome liar, troublemaker, and a man who regularly provoked appalling violence. So what was intended as a brief story about an important event for my children to read, has led to a book of some six parts and hundreds of pages, which still only gives a glimpse of the events that took place in 1919 and of the Rebellion which General Dyer, a great, brave and humble man reduced to failure at one stroke.

If I had not lived in India myself as the daughter of a High Court Judge, travelling into far off areas when he went on circuit, and if I had not been the wife of a Deputy Commissioner, a District Officer, who himself travelled throughout his District, which was the size of Wales, I could not have written this book, nor would I have had the interest or grasp to do the research and correlate the information.

Some of my friends who knew something about India and who took an interest in my magnum opus, told me that I was wrong, that I had got hold of the wrong end of the stick, because the propaganda launched against the British at that time and continued since then, against Dyer and in favour of Gandhi, the subject of astonishingly inaccurate propaganda, has been accepted as true. It is not true as the following pages show, but almost completely false. Nonetheless, it was the story that helped to bring down one of the most wonderful Empires that ever existed. You will see why the factual description of events and of my father's involvement is important as a matter of historical accuracy and as a true image of how we lived and worked and of how, by lies and falsehood, the tales of Gandhi and his echelon were spread.

Forgive the length of this book. I found that due to the false image of our period in India, the mere statement of the facts had to be backed up. In the process of turning round the false image so much encouraged by the political left, I had to go into far greater depth than should have been necessary, to show clearly the intricate and serious situation which ended up with the division of India into several parts again.

The main strength of the propaganda, was in the words used to convey images that were almost entirely spurious. The Bagh in which the crowd gathered and on which General Dyer fired, had a main gate, which the leaders of the Rebellion had locked so that the crowd could not escape. The result was that the firing is referred to, not as a firing on a crowd to disperse it, which it was, but as a massacre. The number of people killed and wounded was claimed to be many hundreds, amounting to about 1500. In fact, the rebels and their friends themselves provided these figures, which were accepted by Government without thought. The actual numbers were less than 100 killed and more than 100 wounded. Since exceptional compensation was offered, it being India, where names and addresses are not as fixed as in Britain, the numbers were considerably inflated and still only about 1% of the numbers killed under Mrs Gandhi in the Golden Temple in 1984. In the case of the appalling tragedy of Amritsar in 1984, the Sikhs say that the official numbers were far less than what they actually know to have been the case. The British after 1919 sent round a proclamation offering compensation and asking for names and numbers. The Hunter Committee accepted the figures collected by Gandhi's friend, Swami Shraddanand, hardly very satisfactory; as it was found that the names of people allegedly killed had never been known in their villages. That the British would use such figures in the first place is quite extraordinary, but it was the alleged figures that led to the claim of "Massacre", not the real ones. Those have never been given publicity, to my knowledge.

Whether it was the inflation of the numbers, or the description of the crowd, or the locking of the gate, which was used to turn dispersal into massacre, the propaganda worked.

I was in India in 1942, when Gandhi was organizing his Quit India movement to hold up all food, ammunition, reinforcements and medical supplies going into Burma to stop the Japanese advance. The behaviour of the Quit India people was the same as that of the Amritsar Rebels. Telegraph lines and railway lines were cut and all communications were stopped and for a while, Bengal, through which all supplies had to go, was cut off from the rest of India. Britons were lynched and in one case that I know of, an airman's body was carried through the town as an exhibition.

In 1919, the conspirators were very much in touch with the Amir of Afghanistan, already moving troops up to the Indian Frontier. If Amritsar had fallen to the rebels, the supply of troops to the Frontier would have been cut off in just the same way. Dyer's act was not only a defence of the women and children in the Fort and of his own troops, but of the railway centre which distributed the life blood of troops up to Peshawar and the Afghan border. The Third Afghan War is omitted from the image of the Amritsar incident, but by the end of April/beginning of May, Thal in British India was under siege by the Afghans with British troops running out of water and in great danger.

I have chosen the following construction. Part 1 records the stirring towards rebellion and the Government realization that anti-terrorist legislation must be brought in – the Rowlatt Bills - and an explanation. It records the German endeavour to take over India, starting at the beginning of the last century, and the schemes involving members of the Oriental Desk in Berlin and their move to Moscow after 1918; the infiltration of German subjects and propaganda into Afghanistan; the control of Turkey by Parvus; the effect of the valiant revolt in the desert of the Hejaz in which Lawrence took part and which probably as much as anything, saved Muslim India, and the tragedy of Kut.

Part 2 is concerned with Gandhi, from his early days in South Africa, to his malign influence on Indian affairs over the half Century after his return in 1915, during which, under the pretence of "peace and love", he fostered and directed rebellion by violence and lies.

Part 3 records the outbreaks of violence across India under the guise of non-co-operation with the Rowlatt legislation, with particular reference to the Punjab.

Part 4 gives some idea of the character and activities of General Dyer, from his childhood and his Army career. It illustrates his immense courage, his popularity and quick thinking and a little about his relationship with his family.

Part 5 is concerned with Edwin Montagu, the brash young Liberal politician, who, as Secretary of State for India, ignored those with experience of Indian affairs and set out to change how India was governed, in accordance with his liberal views and the wishes of his nationalist friends. His speech in the Commons on the Amritsar incident is a classic case of political backstabbing.

Part 6 is concerned with the outcome of the rebellion and the change of attitude of the British Government towards those involved, showing a weakness which encouraged exploitation. This weakness encouraged the nationalists to continue their pressure for Home Rule, their campaigns of violence and non-co-operation, up to and including World War II and ending with Independence in 1947, Partition and the massacre of millions. It points up the real lessons from Amritsar, subversion, the power of propaganda and the manipulation of facts, from which our country still suffers.

I add a final personal note. Not only were many of the people mentioned known to me personally, but wherever I have looked at evidence, reports or notes, or at the speakers in debates, if I have not known them personally, I have known them as it

## Introduction

were second hand through friends. I was at a school started by Miss Hilda Martin, the governess of the Miles Irving children, to which went many of the children of the people who were involved in the Amritsar incident. We did not have government payments for our passages to Britain and it was therefore common for us to go to schools where we could stay during the holidays. I, for instance, went to this school at the age of just four. I remember Miles Irving, the Depute Commissioner of Amritsar clearly, as a gentle man and his children were and are my friends. My mother was half French and she did not fill her house with other people except when she gave parties, but of those whom she knew intimately, the bulk were Indian, particularly the wives and families of other High Court Judges. As a result I knew Indian girls well; I had fewer friends among British girls.

Our relationships were intricate. While Diwan Chaman Lal, a friend of Nehru and previously of Jinnah, was in prison for some political law breaking, his pony was leant to me to exercise and yet my father, as a High Court Judge before whom Chaman Lal might appear, was not able to speak to him in public. My father had been friendly with the early leaders of the Congress, people like the Tyabjis, whose son Din went into the I.C.S., and others. As a lonely young man in Jullunder District, he had been a member of the Indian Club as well as the British Club, but went more to the former because of the greater intellectual involvement. The acrid racist propaganda of Forster or of Scott is wildly separate from what our lives were really like. To read Martin Gilbert's "Servant of India" about a cousin, is to see something of an integration of relationships which the 1919 Rebellion completely altered. After that, the attitude to the British became more polarized.

A word has to be said about the story having been accepted in various serious historical works. Men who came out to India after the Rebellion, people like Penderel Moon and Philip Mason, knew little or nothing about the Rebellion and accepted the then-current invented story. The officials were not allowed to publish their experiences by the Terms of their contracts– my mother writing for Blackwoods for instance, wrote anonymously - nor was the Incident widely discussed. Philip Mason made a comment to me, which qualified his and Penderel's attitude. *"It is time to stop researching and start writing."* Any historian has to begin from something of the given story, and these men came out to India as first generation people, who had not taken in, by a sort of osmosis, India as she really is. Dyer was what we call 'country bred'; the son of English people who had been in India for several generations and his knowledge of India and Indians was deep and comes out in the following pages.

Under us there was an encouragement to racial pride and respect for the rulers - the men who as Deputy Commissioners spent their time walking or riding through the villages, speaking to the people, sorting out problems – which was in the tradition leading to one Indian Civil Servant describing their constant, close relationship and their use of horses as *"Their involvement was so constant that the dung from their horses never dried."* - From that closeness, this book shows Gandhi making the first steps of separation; a separation which was built on hatred, not affection and respect.

Where those of an older generation, who are proud to meet us and to introduce us to their friends, or as I found in Madras from an atypical young man in the seventies: *"We look back on British Rule as a Golden Age"*, and then slamming the table when I smiled, *"I mean it, we look back on British Rule as a Golden Age,"* the modern view, in India and here, is of the imperious British exploiting the peaceful, trusting Indian.

The next step when we left was for the schoolbooks to be printed and presumably written in Russia. The result is, that with the young, knowing nothing, we are met with fearsome inventions and reiterated claims of 'Imperialism' - even at an august scientific meeting, the scientist lecturer, an Indian, interspersing an interesting lecture with the word Imperialism. One young man to whom I have spoken, described the Jallianwalla Bagh incident as similar to Tiananmen Square, apparently having no inkling of the truth of the history of India in which we took part. Such ignorant attitudes are far from unique, but it is a pity when a proud people take on an attitude, which leads them into anger and distress.

The question has to be asked: Why did it take seventy years for someone to point out that the propaganda story was wrong? The answer has to lie firstly, in the restrictions on the officials about relating their experiences. My mother's account in Blackwoods was anonymous because of her husband's position, (entirely blowing away the images in the Attenborough film 'Gandhi', which is so relied on). One or two other reminiscences about Dyer himself in Blackwoods, relating to his actions in the Sarhad, came out at the time, but the only books that seriously dealt with the true story were Sir Michael O'Dwyer's 'India as I Knew It' which was not published until 1927 and Ian Colvin's book 'The Story of General Dyer' which was not published until 1929. By the time these books had been published, the consequences of Edwin Montagu's Reforms (1919) and his speech in the Commons (1920) had so persuaded people going out to India, such as Philip Mason and Penderel Moon, that they were under the impression that the new policy was friendship with Indians and in such a friendship, the propaganda story had to be accepted if the so called friends were not to be regarded as liars.

This is a difficult point, but it is mentioned in Philip Mason's 'The Guardian'. Much as no one believes that Russia was a much better place before Bolshevism took over, or France before the revolution (for which I lean on the diary of the Marquis de Boufflers and, to an extent, Shama's 'Citizens') no one remembers the relations between Britain and India prior to the Bolshevik claims which guided Labour Members of Parliament in Britain. Underlying much of Martin Gilbert's 'Servant of India' there is a great deal of this background, as in my father's autobiography. A relationship, which was not, contrary to the claims of racism, racist, but merely discriminatory, in the terms that some people, one did not like, or did not trust. Nirad Chaudhuri gave some idea about that earlier time. It became an idea of the British, just as it did with Chamberlain in his relationship with Hitler, that one had to get on with the people one met, regardless of their awful behaviour. My endeavour has simply been to give some indication, both of what India was like, and how salient to India's future was the action of that brave man, General Dyer, whose dispersal of a violent mob suppressed the incipient nation-wide Rebellion, integrated with the Third Afghan War, which would have killed many thousands and possibly millions of people and left India in the hands of a most unpleasant and ruthless regime.

So long has it taken to complete this book, that most of those Old India hands who have helped and encouraged me, have passed on and few people now have the India of this book in their blood. I have realized that a potted history is needed for background; one young friend whose grandparents were in India remarked to me that she did not approve of our 'just taking India over', a common thought among those who do not know the history of our acquisition of India.

Let me end this introduction with two quotations – the first by Mohammed Ali Jinnah, the founder of Pakistan, in a speech given in 1916 when he was thirty-six:

*"There is first the great fact of British rule in India with its Western character and standards of administration, which, while retaining absolute power of initiative, direction and decision, has maintained for many decades unbroken peace and order in the land, administered even-handed justice, brought the Indian mind, through a widespread system of Western education, into contact with the thoughts and ideals of the West, and thus led to the birth of a great and living movement for the intellectual and oral regeneration of the people."*

The second quotation comes from the Report of the Rowlatt Committee.

*"Our study and examination of the cases have impressed us with the correctness of the conclusions arrived at in their Report by the Sedition Committee 1918 presided over by Mr Justice Rowlatt, as to the alliance and interconnection of all the groups, forms into one revolutionary movement with one common object, viz the overthrow of His Majesty's Government in India by force. All the individual cases stand so closely interconnected as parts of one whole that they form both as to the personnel and acts of crime, one continuous movement of revolution which must be regarded as living and prolonged in all its parts until the movement is completely extinguished."*

# THE MYTH

On April 13th 1919, General Dyer, with fifty riflemen, entered the Jallianwalla Bagh in Amritsar and ordered firing on the vast and hostile crowd gathered there. His action has been remembered to this day as a massacre. It has led to claims about the British Rule that have caused ripples throughout the world. It has been said that it caused the destruction of the Empire. The number of men killed was rather less than one hundred, the number wounded rather more. It is now known that many of the people who died were crushed to death, rather than killed by rifle fire, because the main gate had been locked by the rebel leaders to prevent the people leaving. As a result, they either had to pull themselves over a five foot wall, or get out through much smaller entrances, taking time to do so, for the mass of people were estimated by some, to number 30 or 40 thousand. Among them, were no women and no children. At least one man later gave evidence to the Congress Committee, that he had escaped by lying underneath a large number of people - he was not wounded or harmed in any way.

The actual facts have been distorted by various tales. In the present, the main distortion has come from the film 'Gandhi', made by Sir Richard Attenborough and paid for by the Government of India when under the rule of Indira Gandhi, whose father and grandfather were involved with the event. The story which Sir Richard Attenborough portrayed is factually incorrect. His portrayal of Gandhi behind bars, is Attenborough's way of picturing the man whom he worships, being turned back from the borders of the Punjab. Gandhi himself described this event as follows:

*"Before the train reached Palwal railway station, I was served with a written order to the effect that I was prohibited from entering the boundary of the Punjab ... but what do you want to do with me? I asked Inspector Bowring of the Indian Police. He replied that he did not know, but was awaiting further orders. For the present, he said, I am taking you to Bombay."* Gandhi had just set out from Bombay, where he sometimes lived.

If this little glimpse of the inaccuracy of the Attenborough story indicates the film's exaggeration, it also makes clear the possibility that the rest of that story, including the imagery of General Dyer and the firing, is also untrue.

The portrayal of the firing, the appearance of Dyer, the presence of women in the Bagh, the later pictures of Dyer as a stupid man without feeling or sense, are predictable. The questions asked by the Indian members of the Hunter Committee in the film, were in the main, not asked. Dyer therefore did not respond as he is depicted as doing. The firing had been notified and was expected; the crowd was not peaceful but excited; listening to poems and incitement to murder; the men were armed with lathis (described as lethal weapons in the criminal code of the time) and some of them had axes. Only one accurate fact is depicted - that the gate was locked. It had been locked by the rebel leaders themselves, in order to support the picture which they were trying to present, that the British were brutal and murderous. The Deputy-Commissioner, walking back to the headquarters in the Ram Bagh, saw to his horror the pile of bodies at the locked gate. Nehru later had the gate bricked up.

The lies are perpetuated, whether by Attenborough with his questionable saint, or such people as Peter Jay, whose series on the radio about the Empire, used young men who were not born when we (the British) were there, to claim *"How we hated them"*. That is in direct contradiction to our own experiences when we go back to India and are told: *"We look back on British rule as a Golden Age"* or *"We never wanted you to leave, it was only the politicians"*, or are asked, as was Mark Wathen, (who had been a boy of eight at the time of the firing) *"When are you coming back?, We trust you"*, or Bill Kennedy's experience when, as Deputy Commissioner of Gurdapur in 1947, the village headman came in to see him, weeping and saying *"Sahib, why are you leaving us, what have we done wrong?"* or again, the member of the Indian Civil Service from Bihar, who wished to go back with his family to show them his old District, and who wrote to the Manager of the town hotel asking for rooms and received in reply, the offer of rooms as long as he wished to stay and he would not be charged, for it would be an honour to have him and his family there. The result was the astonishment of his daughter, who had been brought up with the Peter Jay type of imagery and could not believe that we were popular, loved and trusted.

For those of us who were there, the films and stories that have been told since are fantasies; without relevance to those years of hard and constant work or the knowledge of what really did happen.

The firing took place as the hot weather was beginning. Nine days later, on April 22nd, the Government of India, always running on a shoestring, would permit the use of fans in Government offices. On the 14th, Elinor Astbury was being driven in her father's motorcycle sidecar through Amritsar, on her way to the Hills, for the better climate in the hot weather. The town was absolutely quiet, the streets empty, despite the outbreak of arson, murder and violence, which had taken place only days earlier. Her father was an engineer in the Public Works Department and she later married Phillip Tolinton, who was in the Indian Civil Service. In 1919, she was a little girl aged five.

The streets were quiet - a relief from the tension of the past months, a tension that was typical of India when gathering to rebellion: Linlithgow was to feel it in 1940 when Gandhi was fasting; it had warned people of the Mutiny in 1857 and in 1919, army officers slept with revolvers under their pillows.

## The Myth

The change in Amritsar after the firing was felt by everyone. My father, R B Beckett, I.C.S., City Magistrate of Amritsar, walking to work, was spoken to by an Indian couple whom he had not known before, who told him that they were grateful for what had happened since it had stopped the rising. They said that their son had been killed in the firing, and that they had told him not to go to the meeting, but nonetheless they were glad it was over and peace had been restored. At the Ram Bagh, the Company Garden, men and women were queuing to thank General Dyer for his action.

*"The prevailing sentiment of gratitude at being delivered from the tyranny of the mob"* wrote Dyer's biographer, Ian Colvin, *"was expressed by the Raises and Chowdhris and citizens, who came to see General Dyer all together soon after the 13th, thanked him for his action and said that his action had saved Amritsar and other cities in the Punjab from a general plunder ... in the compound, the Company Garden, also known as the Ram Bagh, large, even for India and yet insufficient to contain the crowd which clamoured to see the General Sahib and thank him for saving their women folk and their goods. Captain Briggs (General Dyer's Brigade Major) tried to satisfy the crowd with messages but in vain, in the end the General was dragged out and acclaimed the saviour of Amritsar."*

All over India there were sighs of relief. Little May Bristow (later Kennedy) [1] remembered Indian solders being billeted in her parents' large bungalow in Ambala where her father was the bank manager.

Colonel Stead of the Punjab Frontier Force was in Jullundur, General Dyer's Brigade Headquarters in 1919. He was then a twenty four year old subaltern, recently returned to India from fighting in France and remembered his bearer bringing to him his morning cup of tea: *"The hot weather came in early and I was sleeping outside my quarter, when my bearer woke me with early tea on 14th April. He normally placed the tray on my bedside table saying 'Salaam, Sahib' and touching his forehead with one hand, but on this occasion he repeated the 'Salaam Sahib' several times, bringing both his hands up to his forehead; so much so that I asked him what on earth was the matter. He replied 'There is good news Sahib, the General Sahib has shot many people in Amritsar yesterday. Now thank God, we will have some peace'."*

The pretence that all India was against the British was not true at that period, or later. Indians, like Germans or Dutch in the last war, did not dare to stand up to their leaders when they had sufficient strength; still less when they were afraid that the leaders would murder them, burn their houses down over their heads, prevent them arranging marriages for their children, spreading rumours about them that would ruin their businesses or their careers or generally tyrannize them. The dominance of the political leaders has already been indicated by the mob at Amritsar going to the Jallianwalla Bagh in the teeth of ample warning that if they did they would be

---

1 Mrs Kennedy, on reading the first draft of this book commented *"This is the story I always knew was true but I thought it would never be written"*

fired on. They went in the teeth of a parade throughout the town of the Deputy-Commissioner, a General and one of the senior policemen in a car, British troops marching with police and the Town Crier reading to them in Urdu and in Punjabi the proclamation that this was so. A number of people were allowed to collect at the stopping points in the city and had the matter explained in both Urdu and Punjabi. So determined is the prejudice in this matter, than a man writing to a newspaper in 1997 claimed that the Town Crier spoke in English! Not only did he not read English, he could not even understand it. In the Hunter Committee hearing, a translator was needed to tell the Committee members what he was saying and enable him to understand their questions.

In the following chapters, the evidence of the conspiracies and of the influence of the politicians and the fear of their pawns, becomes clear, which led to the need for an Act, the Rowlatt Act, to replace the Defence of India Act which had been passed in 1915 and was to be in force only until the War ended.

The Rowlatt Act was a much less strong Act than the Defence of India Act (1915), which had been put forward by Sir Michael O'Dwyer, Lieutenant-Governor of the Punjab, who was at that time dealing with one of the worst of the conspiracies instigated and partly funded by the Germans, called the Ghadr movement, (see Chapter IV - Ghadr meaning Mutiny).

The conspiracies depended largely on insidious and false claims which spread throughout India. At the time of the passing of the Rowlatt Act, a provision for emergencies, of the sort that is on the statute books of most countries, the false representations about it were used to persuade people that to rise against it was reasonable. The anger and indeed, fury, whipped up by lies, was displayed by people who had resisted the blandishments of the Ghadr in previous years.

This Act was planned to counteract the continuing conspiracies that were on the brink of destroying India. Gandhi, who led the rising, wrote describing his decision to organise resistance to it in his autobiography 'Some of my Experiments with Truth'.

*"The recommendations of the Rowlatt Committee seemed to me to be altogether unwarranted by the evidence published in its report, and were, I felt, such that no self-respecting people could submit to them."*

And on that he had decided to organise resistance. He had already been waiting in the wings to try out his passive resistance, and it was generally accepted that this was Gandhi's opportunity. In Jullundur, on the other hand, where the leadership of subversion, if it did exist, was less overt, Colonel Stead's description of the way people behaved to him after the firing, shows another attitude.

*"On biking down to parade that morning, I saw a Tonga coming towards me. The driver, seeing me, took the Tonga into the dust at the side of the road and the two passengers got out, one of them, who was using an umbrella, folded it and they salaamed deeply as I passed. This sort of thing had not been seen since the days of the East India Company nearly 100 years ago."*

# PART 1:
# MALICE

## Chapter I
## CONSPIRACY

How comes this difference between the observations of the time and the tale portrayed in the Attenborough film? Whence comes this extraordinary disparity between the event and the portrayal?

The time was the end of the First World War; the Germans had been beaten and reduced to accepting defeat, which for that proud nation was, in itself, the prelude to a determination to rise and attack again. Writing about the magnificent response by the Empire to the threat of the war, John Buchan wrote *"But it was the performance of India, which took the world by surprise and thrilled every British heart – India, whose alleged disloyalty was a main factor in German calculations"*. (from 'The British Conquest and Dominion of India' by Penderel Moon: Duckworth 1989).

During the War, more than half a million men fought from India – 365,000 being recruited during the War itself. In terms of the size of India, this may seem very little, but the soldiers who fought were volunteers and had families who were left behind them and the numbers of those were far larger. Today, the Indian and Pakistan armies are still in touch with their old officers, constantly writing for photographs and inviting them to come to Regimental reunions. Of those soldiers from the whole of India as it was then, one half were Punjabi Mussulmans, showing exceptional loyalty, since the British were fighting the Turks (nominally leaders of Islam) and the Germans were fighting on the side of the Turks.

For those who knew something of the conspiracy which lay behind the Rebellion which Dyer's action put down, it appeared that the centre of the rebellion being placed in Amritsar, was at least in part, to destroy the fine reputation of the Punjabis.[2]

---
2  Details of Army numbers from Sir Michael O'Dwyer's 'India as I Knew It', Constable 1925. Opinion about the centring of the rebellion in the Punjab from Captain Blacker's 'On Secret Patrol in High Asia', John Murray 1922.

In addition, Amritsar was the rail centre for the frontier and the centre of Bolshevik activity. This rebellion was not, as Attenborough and the inventors of his story portrayed, a mere gathering of simple folk collected together for a fair, but a rebellion well grounded in an India-wide conspiracy, intended to bring the whole of India into a maelstrom of violence and hatred and to a large extent, inspired and funded firstly by the Germans and then by the Bolsheviks. India, like Russia, was an autocracy; whereas the British method of rule is from the people, India, with her caste system, keeps the lower orders in subjection, subject to the higher caste at the top.

One of the most prestigious leaders of the Punjab, a man loyal to the Raj, which he believed to be essential for the peace of the endlessly warring element of India, was Sir Umar Hayat Khan. He lived in, and owned vast territories in the North-West of the Punjab, in Shapur and Montgomery and as an Honorary Major, had fought in France and Mesopotamia. He was a Tiwana and there was a Tiwana Regiment, so he was in a position to know a great deal that was going on which the Government might not have known. His comment on the firing, made in reply to a question by a member of the Hunter committee, the Honourable Mr. W. F. Rice, C.S.I., I.C.S. (Additional Secretary to the Home Department of the Government of India) was that if the disturbances were not stopped, they would first spread to the villages and later, affect the fathers and brothers of the soldiers, who would then have joined in.

Rice asked *"Do you think the people in the neighbouring districts kept quiet by hearing what had happened at Jallianwalla Bagh?"*

In the same vein as before, Umar Hayat Khan replied: *"Yes. After April, troop trains passed. Various detachments were sent because it was considered a better thing to split the army in smaller portions and keep them going, so that people who wanted to get at them could not do so."*

Q. *"Do you think that if there had not been firm measures taken, there might have been a really big outbreak and serious danger to everyone?"*

A. *"It was of course very big. It was stopped. It was a really big thing"*.

Umar Hayat Khan pointed out that there was a conspiracy, as at the time of the Mutiny. *"No Sahibs knew about it until they were killed at Meerut in 1857. The thing is, it is so cleverly arranged. They are clever like they were at the time of the Mutiny."*

He was asked *"They want the British Government to go out and they want to put themselves in their place?"* and his reply was a clear *"Yes"*. In so many words, it is rebellion.

Both Sir Umar Hayat Khan's father and uncle had fought to suppress the Mutiny and he saw the parallels in the 1919 rising clearly in those terms, as well as in those of his personal knowledge.

As General Dyer said later, *"It would have become a mutiny. Since the Amir had been petitioned by Hindus and Muslims from the plains to invade India, the invasion could not then have been stopped. Later on, the whole Punjab would have been against the Government and then other places like the United Provinces might have joined and later on, the whole of India would have been in opposition. In the villages in the Punjab the villagers were very excited, I had been to other Districts, to Jhang, Gujranwala, Gujrat and Jullundur."*

The firmness that Umar Hayat Khan applauded was the wish of everyone who was loyal to the Sirkar; Umar Hayat Khan himself had been the Chairman of a Committee of Hindus, Muslims and Sikhs who went to the Chief Secretary of the Punjab Government, J. P. Thompson, on the 6th April, when the first processions and strikes had taken place in the Punjab and asked that the Government should be firm. Again, he went to the Governor, Sir Michael O'Dwyer, who said he would take on board their suggestions and advice. They all knew the matter was serious and potentially dangerous. Each of them was jeered at and threatened by the crowds, largely led by students and Umar Hayat Khan was called 'Uncle'[3], a taunt that would have been obvious, for he was not an 'Uncle', not by any means. He was a member of the Legislative Council and put forward his criticisms of government, for example, against the Colony Bill and the Land Alienation Act. The first was withdrawn by the Government and refused signature by the Viceroy. Umar Hayat Khan put in constant reports to the various officials and did not spare his words when he felt them to be necessary but, as a landowner, he felt that the stability that the British gave to the country was as beneficial as any form of Government could be. For him, as for many others, loyalty was deserved by a Government, which he could openly criticise if he wished and his feelings were the same as those of the mass of the people. Those who were against the Government were the educated or semi-educated middle classes, the disaffected intelligentsia, as in Russia, who were discontented at not getting the jobs for which they felt their education fitted them, not counting the few who could have been appointed to replace the 900 British members of the Indian Civil Service who were the men who ruled India (the remaining 300 being Indian).

There was a definite division between the townspeople (incited, so he said, by newspapers such as 'The Tribune') and the country people, who barely read them. It was from the country that recruits for the Army were drawn, and the feeling was strong that the country provided the defence for India and had given men who risked their lives during the war, where the townsfolk gave no recruits and yet wished to rule the nation and in the present dangers, spread rumours which were completely untrue, to stir up the country people to be used as 'dupes' by them. It was an accurate picture. When Nehru, a townsman, wrote of his experiences later ('Personal Experience and The Conquest and Dominion of India', Moon; Duckworth 1990) he wrote of his ignorance of the country people and described them as 'Khaira'. They were the nobodies, whom the politicians were stirring up to stop paying their taxes.

The whole Government of India, always constrained by shortage of cash, depended on its taxes to exist and one of the main thrusts of the incitement by the conspirators was that, if they took over India, they would stop demanding Land Tax (which has

---

[3] The word in Urdu is 'Cha-Cha' and can be affectionately applied to family friends, but also used as a form of patronising insult.

since been done). Gandhi's Salt March was another instance of an attempt to reduce or remove the essential funds for the machinery of Government. The Salt Tax was a few pence for a mound, and was one of the lightest methods of taxation, continued from the days of the Moghuls and costing the family little, the collection being also cheap. In 1942, Lord Wavell was still being nagged by Gandhi to remove the tax which paid for the defence of India, in the sense that it paid for the armed forces.[4]

The intention of the rebellion was to paralyse Government by destruction of the railways, cutting of telegraph wires, by the refusal to obey laws and through violence, leading to the arrest of people in such numbers that the prisons could not hold them. On the surface, the Satyagraha movement was named as the initiator of the unrest, but underneath, there was widespread conspiracy of great depth and countrywide, which had been waiting for years to come to fruition.[5]

Its strength lay in its ruthless treatment of anyone who got in its way; people were killed if they stood as witnesses or if they tried to prevent its noxious policies being taught in the schools. The police and the C.I.D. were unable to bring the terrorists to court, even when they found evidence, through the suborning of witnesses by violence, blackmail, threats of theft and actual theft. All these activities were part of the gradual development of a system which was sometimes overt, like the propaganda in America, which led to the Ghadr movement leasing of the Komagatu Maru, a ship which brought a large number of Indians from the United States, with the intention of taking over India. Armed and determined, they and others coming to India in the same manner, were in the main interned, many in villages, where they waited ready to join in with the rebels if the rebellion prospered. The main sanction preventing them spreading their noxious and violent plans was that the villagers among whom they lived when they were not imprisoned, disliked them and would by no means agree to join their movement.[6]

The initiators of that movement were the Germans, working with Har Dayal Parma Nand and others. Parma Nand was the Principal of the Arya Samaj College in Lahore. He was sentenced to death for his part in the Ghadr Rebellion, although later amnestied. This highlights a further aspect of the conspiracy movement. The Arya Samaj was a Hindu movement, which believed in teaching students about the Golden Age, which could be recovered, if the Hindus were to rule again. By its very doctrine, it was inherently anti-Muslim as well as anti-British. Parma Nand looked to yet another link in the chain, namely India House in London, which printed and distributed anti-British literature, which Parma Nand was applying for in order to

---

[4] Wavell: the 'Viceroys Journal', Edited by Penderel Moon; Constable 1973

[5] 'Gandhi and Modern India', Moon; 'The Life of Mahatma Gandhi', Louis Fischer, Jonathan Cape 1951; M. K. Gandhi 'An autobiography or The Story of My Experiments with Truth' vol. 1 and vol. 2, published 1927 and 1929 respectively, Penguin 1983. Bardoli - Evidence of the Government of Bombay and of Ahmad Abed under the Bombay Presidency.

[6] Sir Michael O'Dwyer, ibid; My father's unpublished autobiography; the Rowlatt Report; Moon, 'Conquest and Dominion';. Sir Umar Hayat Khan; 'Secret Evidence before the Hunter Committee.

indoctrinate his students. From India House came propaganda which even incited to murder[7] and which led to the killing of Sir Curzon Wylie, the political A.D.C. to the Secretary of State for India. India House was a hostel for Indian students in London, run by a man called Krishnavarma, who, like so many of the leaders of the movement, had been educated in Britain, did brilliantly at Balliol and was also a student of Madame Blavatsky's Theosophy, as was Nehru. Krishnavarma commented in his monthly journal that 'Political assassination was not murder' and when the young assassin of Sir Curzon Wylie, a young man from a devoted and loyal family was hanged, he called it 'an example of heroic courage'. All this was in 1909, an earlier manifestation of the conspiracy that, with the threat of the Rowlatt legislation, would lead to rebellion in 1919. It was one of the underlying problems of the Government of India.

Madame Blavatsky, the Russian Theosophist, had founded the Theosophical Society with an American, W. S. Olcott, in 1875. Annie Besant, who had been married to an English clergyman, succeeded Blavatsky. She founded, with Tilak, the great leader of the Nationalist movement in India, a society for Home Rule. In 1918 she had just been released from prison for encouraging murder in much the same terms as did Krishnavarma. The Theosophical Society had formulated a new approach to psychology as well as being involved in the occult and had a wide following. Among those involved, although not directly involved with India, was Rudolf Steiner, the Austrian philosopher and educationalist, close to Jung.[8] The successive leaders of the Theosophical Society were Socialists to an extent where General Sir Bindon Blood believed Blavatsky to be a Communist Spy![9]

Theosophy was one of the descendants of Illuminism. Historically, it had similarities to the megalomaniac behaviour of the Illuminati and the Masons who organised and inspired the French Revolution.[10]

In the present day, we have the Bilderberg Group, which so sinisterly moves towards World Government, meeting perhaps more overtly than the India conspiracy, but in locations surrounded by security guards or troops, in order to keep out the Press and maintain the secrecy of their proceedings.

The Congress, a further extension of the movement to press for 'self determination' (the Bolshevik term) was also closely connected with the Socialists in Britain

---

7  'Servant of India' Martin Gilbert Longman's Green, 1966

8  Rudolf Steiner parted company with the Theosophists when they claimed that Krishnamurti, an Indian child adopted by Annie Besant, was a reincarnation of Christ Jesus.

9  'Servant of India' ibid; 'A Treatise on the Seven Rays' 5 vols. Alice Bailey, Lucis Publishing Ltd 1953; General Sir Bindon Blood.

10  Nesta H. Webster 'The Surrender of an Empire', 'The French Revolution', 'World Revolution'; 'Secret Societies and Subversive Movements', Boswell Printing and Publishing Co. 1926; The Rowlatt Committee 1918 Report; Sir Verney Lovett 'A History of the Indian Nationalist Movement' published February 1920, republished Frank Cass & Co 1968; Simon Sharma 'Citizens' published by Penguin Group 1989; Intelligence Reports and others.

and in 1919, Congress voted £10,000 to go to the Socialist newspaper, the 'Daily Herald', seemingly frequently short of funds and a little later the recipient of £75,000 derived from the sale of Tsarist jewels, in Hatton Garden, brought over by a Bolshevik delegation from Russia.[11]

The relationship lasted throughout the rest of our years in India and in the Debate in the Commons on the 'Punjab Disturbances' in June 1920, every man jack of the Labour Party voted in line with Congress claims. One or two Labour M.P.s joined with Sarojini Naidu (Gandhi's great friend and one of the first signatories of the Satyagraha pledge) on the platform at Caxton Hall, supporting the unfounded rumours about the rape of Sikh girls at Amritsar, which she declaimed in flowery and untruthful language. (Hansard Commons Debates July 1920).Mrs. Naidu was the sister of Chattopadhya, who was earlier on the Oriental Desk in Berlin, but moved to Moscow.

Labour, being prepared to expound any anti-British propaganda put forward by a tiny fraction of the population of India, supported the attitudes which finally left India in the hands of that very Brahmin oligarchy which still rules today. Violent disturbances are endemic in India - even in the elections of 1998, at least 150 were killed in electioneering ('Time Magazine', 21st March, 1998). In 1919, at the time of the new reforms, the British were endeavouring to expand the Legislative Council into an elected Legislative Assembly and to expand the Provincial Assemblies and increase democracy, to see that everybody, each group, every religion and caste, should have a voice. While India's political voice, loudly shouted throughout the countries of the world, was claiming repression, violence and massacre, in India itself, the Government of India, unable to use the same mechanisms and unwilling to propagandise in a country where impartiality was essential, was doing its best to hold to law and order and give the country the peace it needed if it was ever to understand what democracy was about.

Conspiracy was clearly inferred by the behaviour of people obeying orders and in the overt propaganda which followed the passing of the Rowlatt Bills through the Legislative Council to the tune of speeches of such vehemence and irrelevant vituperation, that they themselves were an influential part of the propaganda which led to less prestigious persons believing that the legislation was wrong. Sir Michael O'Dwyer observed that many of those who voted against the Bills were personally in favour of them but did not dare say so. Until 1919, The Legislative Council could still pass Acts without a majority. When the Reforms became law, a definite step of certification by the Viceroy became necessary when the Assembly voted against the interests of government.

---

11  Evidence of the Government of the Bombay Presidency, Hunter Committee Evidence vol. 11; 'Daily Herald', September 10th 1920; Papers of Lord Davidson, House of Lords Record Office; 'Daily Herald', previously known as The Herald – Letters of Leonard Woolf, ed. Frederick Scotts Bloomsbury, first published 1990; Nesta Webster 'Surrender of an Empire' ibid.

Thus Lord Findlay could say *"A conspiracy is always inferred from the acts of people who are obviously acting in concert. It is very seldom that you can get any evidence of a conspiracy except from such action and anyone who looks at the evidence of things in the Punjab must, I submit, come to a very different conclusion on this matter from that to which Lord Hunter's Commission came."* They had said in their Report on the Disturbances that no evidence had been brought before them sufficient to establish a conspiracy to overthrow the British Government.[12]

The actions that led to the inference were clear and beyond them there were the transcripts of the conspiracy cases (which the Hunter Committee did not read). There was the ample evidence of conspiracy from the events in Peshawar, which showed the involvement of the people in the plains with the Afghans, the Frontier Tribes and the Afghan postmaster. Those were only mentioned in the secret evidence and when Mr. Thompson, the Secretary to the Government of the Punjab, asked whether the Committee wanted more information, the Indian member who was a personal friend of Gandhi, Pandit Jagat Narayan, said that, no, he did not wish to hear any more. For some reason that remains unfathomable to this day, Peshawar had been left out of the list of cities which were to be investigated to find if there had been any conspiracy. Edwin Montagu, the Secretary of State for India did suggest that perhaps there had been no Martial Law there, after Sir Michael O'Dwyer made some comment on Peshawar being left out, but even that was incorrect, so we are left only with the evidence from which the Hunter Committee came to their conclusions and which was the subject of the Debate in the Lords.[13]

The second point made in the Lords was the widespread nature of the rising, from Ahmedabad and Bombay to Calcutta in the East, along the lines followed during the Mutiny. The Punjab was undoubtedly in the eye of the storm.

A continual stream of people of some wealth moving in cars (in those days very rare), not by rail, since the lines were liable to be pulled up, went to Peshawar for meetings and then to Afghanistan - some of them even to Kabul to see the Amir. Some of them had with them a petition signed by Hindus and Muslims, asking the Amir to invade India. Although much of this information comes from Major Sir Umar Hayat Khan, some of it comes from the Intelligence Service, and there was some

---

12  Lord Findlay, opening in the Debate on the case of General Dyer. Hansard 19th July 1920. Sir Michael O'Dwyer 'India as I knew It' ibid; Umar Hayat Khan in the secret evidence before the Hunter Committee.

13  Volumes 5 & 6 of the Hunter Committee, Secret Evidence. Government of the Punjab; Unpublished Diary of Mrs. Gerard Wathen, wife of the principal of the Khalsa College, with kind permission of the family; Montagu papers in Trinity College, Cambridge, with kind permission of Mr Montagu's daughter; various letters by Sir Michael O'Dwyer; 'Times and Morning Post' late 1919 and 1920; Peshawar Conspiracy; Life of General Dyer, Ian Colvin 1928; Commander-in-Chief's Dispatch, Afghan Campaign; Public Records Office, Kew - various research at Kew, finding that the details of the people involved between the Hindus and Muslims from the Plains and the conspiracy for the Third Afghan War generally are on the secret list under the 250-year rule; Hansard, House of Lords' Debate 15th July 1919.

mention of the Amir in the Delhi evidence (Vol. 1. Hunter Committee Evidence). Umar Hayat Khan mentioned some of the names of these emissaries. The inference for the conspiracy was made clear in the destruction of railway lines, particularly in the Punjab and particularly on the routes to the Frontier. Amritsar was a centre for travel to the Frontier and the Ghurkhas who fired in the Bagh later, were en route for Peshawar when they were taken off the train at Amritsar to help with the situation. The Deputy-Commissioner, Miles Irving, had written two days previously to the Chief Secretary, J. P. Thompson, and told him of the threat. The letter was before the Hunter Committee, in which he had pointed out that there was no way that he could hold the City and the Civil Lines with a *"Company of British Infantry and half a company of Garrison Artillery"*. The words that Miles Irving actually used were *"It is absurd"*. Though the letter was addressed to Mr. Kitchin, the Commissioner, in the way in which India was run, the copy was sent to the Chief Secretary and by the Sunday, had drawn a reply from the Government of the Punjab, with instructions to deport the two leaders who had taken Gandhi's Satyagraha vow, to Dharamsala in the Hills. Under the Defence of India Act – an Act passed in 1915 at the time of the Ghadr invasion - wide powers were authorised to deal with difficulties during the War and it allowed judges, in specific political cases, to sit without juries and gave provincial governments powers of internment.[14] It was replaced by the Rowlatt Acts, about which so much agitation was made, although their provisions were considered by the Legislators to be less strong and wide, but which formed the essential basis for emergency action to deal with attempts to overthrow Government.

Of Dr. Kitchlew, Miles Irving wrote: *"Kitchlew himself I regard as the local agent of very much bigger men. Who those are can only be guessed from their rage at the Rowlatt Acts, which strike at the root of organised anarchic crime"* and later, *"I was wrong in thinking I could influence Kitchlew – he is too deep in. I possibly may get hold of some of the outer circle (the Congress Party people)*[15]*, but I have not much hope from them."* He spoke of the soil being prepared for local revolution and, as did Umar Hayat Khan, remarked that the hartals were a preparation for much more that was to come. The first hartal in the Punjab was to be on the 6th April, following the first on 30th March in Delhi. The Amritsar hartal was called after a meeting for Honorary Magistrates had been held at Miles Irving's bungalow, at 3 p.m. on Saturday the 5th. The hartal had been called off, but by 5 p.m. he was told by Kitchlew that the hartal was now on. *"It is said that this was a consequence of the belief that the meeting of Honorary Magistrates at my house had promised to stop the hartal, and was intended to show that they could do nothing."* This intricate and devious behaviour was central to the undermining of the British and loyal Indian element of Government, shown by

---

14. Sir Percival Griffith 'To Guard My People' History of the Indian Police, Ernest Benn 1971; O'Dwyer 'India as I Knew It' and the secret evidence of the Hunter Committee; Oxford History of Modern India 1740-1947 OUP 1965.

15. Kitchlew, who had been educated at Cambridge with Nehru and in Germany, was probably part of the German scheme.

the attitude to the Rowlatt legislation in the Legislative Council and it also indicates the desire to humiliate the British, so typical of the rebel party. It was Nehru who said, *"the reason we liked the Germans was a desire to humiliate the British."*

These intricate moves, both in the background and the foreground, were evident to the Hunter Committee and much the same was said in all the secret evidence. Evidence was given of the Bolshevik involvement; of funds and propaganda flowing in from High Asia, from Stockholm and from other sources. The Lahore Conspiracy cases were put before them and they most certainly knew that *"all reasonable men"* in Umar Hayat Khan's words, knew that there was a conspiracy, but the secret evidence was not put before Parliament.

In the account of the deportation of Kitchlew and Satyapal to Dharamsala, given in the open evidence, is recorded how the various officials met at Miles Irving's house and were given positions for defending the Civil Lines and the railway, in case there was to be a rising the following day. The deportation took place and within half an hour, one of the policemen stated that a crowd of 75,000 had collected in Aitchison Park. Its members then ran to positions which were too precise to be entirely spontaneous. First, they went towards the Civil Lines where the officials, their families and some wealthy Indians lived [the officials lived in bungalows that belonged to Indians, for we could not buy our property], the intention apparently being to loot and murder British wives and children. The story told by the crowd was that they wished to speak to the Deputy Commissioner and ask where Kitchlew and Satyapal had been taken. A policeman in plain clothes in this crowd heard people saying they would tear the Deputy Commissioner to pieces and when Miles Irving arrived, the crowd threw stones at him. The claim that the crowd was innocent was not demonstrated by its behaviour which was violent, even hysterical, and my father described it as mischievous, when he arrived at the bridge over which it was coming, in the order of 30,000 men. The wild behaviour of the crowd was clearly evidenced; its stone-throwing tactics were clear, the hitting of the muzzles of the horses with sticks, which led to the little posse of three artillerymen and my father being driven back. Though the missionary, Miss Sherwood, did not give evidence to Hunter, she later supported this in letters to the Press, describing the mass of people running through the city and tearing down the awnings or anything else to get weapons and sticks. The Gandhi/Congress propaganda later claimed that the crowd was peaceful and bare-headed and without shoes in mourning for their loved ones. The stone-throwing was so constant and violent that finally, a young subaltern was given permission by another Magistrate [not my father] to fire.

When the crowd found they could not get any further towards the Civil Lines, elements turned and went to the Telegraph Office and endeavoured to murder the officer in charge. Another part went to the Railway Station.

My father later wrote; *"It turned out a broiling hot day. I went to court after breakfast while my wife drove out to see Mrs. Wathen at the Khalsa College. Kitchlew and Satyapal were arrested according to plan and sent off to some hill station with the Superintendent of Police. I might have been working for half an hour, or an hour, ready in my riding kit for anything that might happen, with my mare ready saddled outside and only needing the girths to be tightened, when Miles Irving, the Deputy Commissioner, came into my Court. There seemed to be trouble in the city but all the telephone wires had been cut. Would I please go to the Hall Bridge as once and take up my place if the report was true?"* - an extract which clearly does not support the claim that the firing was the cause of the rioting.

All over India, telegraph wires were cut. Umar Hayat Khan said that this was due to the fact that the telegraph had been the method of knowing where the mutineers were in 1857/8. In Simla, the Government of India was cut off and Lord Meston later said in the Lords' Debate, that they thought they might be the only white men alive in India. When it came to sending the confirmation for Martial Law in the Punjab, the Government had to use a small wireless station which was working very badly because of a serious thunder storm and they were afraid the message might not get through at all, since telegraph and telephones were not working.

There is evidence of people cutting the lines in Ahmedabad, Delhi, Lahore and Amritsar, as well as other places not dealt with by Hunter.

There was evidence of people getting together in massive numbers with no apparent warning and coming pretty smartly to the various points of attack.

If there was no conspiracy, how did this come about? It was also strangely coincidental that, at the Railway Stations in Lahore, Ahmedabad and Delhi, the sweetmeat-sellers, who worked on a Government contract, were attacked by growing crowds because they would not obey the hartal, since they did not wish to break their contracts. In each case, the violent gatherings effectively seized up the railway stations and all travel.

That these incidents (apart from Delhi) should all take place on 10th April is more than coincidental. The Lords were right to decide that there had been evidence of conspiracy.

In the Secret Evidence, Intelligence had found that Gandhi and Moti Lal Nehru had spent some hours in discussion. Gandhi had claimed that they had the clerks and the servants to the British under their hands and since Gandhi moved in time to be turned back on the 10th, the date that Kitchlew and Satyapal were deported, it seems probable that his visit was made to coincide with the deportation. This would have married up the background conspiracy to fit in with the outer expression.[16]

Further evidence of the torn-up railway lines and the cut telegraph-wires is written in the report of Captain Briggs, General Dyer's Brigade Major. He gives a description of the difficulties getting troops to Amritsar, messages about their arrival and messages to and from General Beynon, the Divisional Commander at Lahore.

---

16 Miss Sherwood's letters from 'The Globe'; 'The Challenger'; from Sir William Joynson-Hicks' speech in the debate in the Commons. The evidence is in Volume II of the Hunter Evidence; from Volume I Delhi; from Volume 2 Ahmedabad; House of Lords Debate ibid; Unpublished autobiographical notes R. B. Beckett I.C.S. Secret Evidence and Hunter Report.

## Conspiracy

Since the telegraph wires were cut, messages had to be carried by the engine-drivers of the trains and men going to Amritsar were armed with orders to requisition any transport they might need if the broken tracks made rail travel impossible. Umar Hayat Khan emphasised the dreadful situation that would arise if ammunition and reinforcements had not been able to get through to the Frontier due to the destruction of the railway lines mentioned in the Secret Evidence. Briggs' report was not put into the Hunter evidence, because by the time that Hunter came to sit in Lahore to take the Amritsar evidence, Briggs was dead. He had been murdered on the Frontier by being given powdered glass. In the subsequent questioning, General Dyer showed his distress having just recovered from extreme exhaustion after the punishing campaign which he had conducted on the Frontier, where he had forced the Afghans to retreat. Possibly worse of all was the death of his dear friend and comrade, without whose assistance he would not have had the necessary papers and whose death came as a shock and a surprise just before coming into the Hunter Inquisition.[17]

Briggs' statement contained much importance evidence, but in this section on conspiracy, his evidence of having gone down to the Railway Station with General Dyer at the request of the Station Master to see the bundles of lathis awaiting collection, is of the greatest importance.

*"On or about the 29th April, the Station Master at Amritsar called me up on the telephone and said a very exceptionally large amount of sticks (lathis) were arriving and he asked for orders as to their disposal. I told him not to deliver them to consignees but wait for orders. The General Officer Commanding and myself went down to the Station that day to see them. One large storehouse was full up to the roof with them and there were many more in trucks...*

*By obtaining statistics from the Station books, it was found that in 1918, 12 bundles had arrived in March and April where in March and April this year, 1056 had arrived. These sticks were very thick and very heavy and a blow from them in a vital spot could kill a man at once. We were very pleased at capturing what was evidently the enemy's arsenal".*

This information became available in General Dyer's statement to the Army Council in England when he got home, but even that was only brought into the House on the night prior to the Debate in the Commons. It is dated 3rd July. Winston Churchill and Edwin Montagu had done a good deal to delay the Hunter evidence getting to Dyer in time for him to write his statement and get it sent in on time. In their speeches, Churchill and the Secretary of State for India claimed (like Attenborough) that Dyer had fired on an unarmed peaceful crowd.

This phenomenal haul of lathis could have been read about in Dyer's (written) statement for the Hunter Committee and could also have been seen by the handful of people who saw his statement in the Commons. Whether the addition was made or not, the 'unarmed peaceful crowd' at the Bagh was referred to by General Dyer

---

17  Captain Briggs' Statement; Umar Hayat Khan ibid; Colvin, 'Life of General Dyer'.

as 'The Danda Fauj' (the bludgeon army) two weeks before the store of lathis was found. There had been posters put up telling people to join the Danda Fauj and these had been mentioned in the Hunter evidence. Lord Meston, who had been Governor of the United Provinces, commented that he had never seen a crowd of that sort that did not have lathis. Colonel Smith, the Indian Medical Service Civil Surgeon, who was carrying out a cataract operation when he heard the first shots, believed that it was the white man, root and branch which the mobs and their leaders intended to destroy.

It was not merely the white man - it was his religion. India was known for an eclectic approach to other religions, except in the troubles between Muslim and Hindu, but the Mission School and Book Shop were burnt down and over 200 Mission children, Indians, and their teachers, were brought into the fort for their protection, with the English women and children. The Roman Catholic Church and the Mission Church were both destroyed. The target appears to have been the white man and his religion also.[18]

Umar Hayat Khan pointed out that there were no guns in the crowds because licences were mainly given to landowners, who were not involved in the conspiracy. The claim of peaceful non-co-operation and Satyagraha would have been negated by the use of firearms, but although lathis were classed in the Criminal Code as lethal weapons, it could be claimed that the use of lathis was not the same as the use of guns, since in the former case, there was no need for licences.

Then we come to the divisions between different elements in society. For the people working for a 'Hindu Raj', it was important to bring in the Muslim community, both as cannon fodder and to establish the image of unity. The Mosques were widely used for political meetings, as they are still used. In order to bring the Sikhs in, the Golden Temple was suggested for the meeting that took place in the Jallianwalla Bagh, but Sundar Singh Majithia, the priest in charge of the Golden Temple, refused to allow it to be used for such a meeting. The purpose in using both the Golden Temple and the mosques was to provoke the British to fire on them and thus confirm the integration of these two great communities into the rebellion and show the British as barbarians.

Dyer, knowing India and Indians well, being a friend of Indians and refusing (with his wife) to become members of the Jullundur Club when Indians were not allowed to become members, knew, as he had warned his wife, that *"Hindus and Muslims have joined against us"*. What extra encouragement had been needed to inspire this amalgamation of the two great religions of India?

From Hunter we get the evidence of Charlie Donald, then in charge of the Fisheries in the Kangra district, of the effect of the propaganda against the new Rowlatt legislation. He had driven down from Dharamsala to Lahore for a minor operation and as he went by car, he had to stop to fill up his radiator with water quite frequently,

---

18  General Dyer's statement to the Army Council, 3rd July 1920 – National Archives and Montagu papers from Trinity College Cambridge; volume 3 Hunter Committee Evidence, Amritsar

particularly in view of the heat. Whenever he stopped, he talked to the people in the villages. Being what we called 'country bred', like General Dyer (British born in India), he could speak the local dialect as well as Urdu, the 'lingua franca' of the Punjab and much of Northern India, unlike the Indians on the Hunter committee, who would not in those days have been able to communicate with the villagers, since they would not have spoken the same language. He had stopped for breakfast with Malcolm Darling[19] at Gurdaspur and this being the 11th, he had heard of the troubles at Amritsar on the 10th. *"I was told"* he said, *"that there was trouble in Amritsar and I questioned anybody that I saw as to what the trouble was and there I had certain misrepresentations. The information was varied, but it was more or less on the same lines. I heard rumours to the effect that two or three people collected together would be arrested by the police, that nobody could get married without paying a tax of Rs.5 to the Government, that if a man died, before his relatives could bury him they would have to pay Rs. 5 to the Government and finally that people must realise that crops belong to the Government as well as the land and that Government could commandeer any part of the crop. There are variations, but this was the general trend."*

Lord Hunter, questioning him asked, *"Did people believe these representations were the result of the Rowlatt legislation?"*

Donald replied that they did, and was questioned further on the effect on the peasants of these beliefs; *"They were agitated and extremely angry"* was his reply.

In reply to questions from an Indian, Sir Chiminlal Setalvad, Donald told him that he stopped at three or four villages.

Q. *"And how many people did you speak to?"*
A. *"I am not quite sure. I mean my questions were aimed at whoever happened to be there".*
Q. *"Hindus or Mohammedans?"*
A. *"Probably Hindu. There was one Sikh, I did not know what the others were. I did not notice them particularly."*
Q. *"Can you talk their language?"*
A. *"Yes".*
Q. *"Did you talk to them in their language?"*
A. *"Yes"*

The questioning in the way of the Indian Members was always lengthy and repetitive. My father and Percy Marsden both commented that they were cross-examined as though they were criminals – both of them being magistrates knew what this meant. Thus I paraphrase much of the rest of the evidence.

---

19 Malcolm Darling was the channel for the information about the English women at Amritsar in great fear and misery, not knowing whether their husbands in the city had been killed or not, which E. M. Forster changed into the club scene in 'A Passage to India'.

He asked what the trouble was about; they told him of the trouble in Amritsar; the peasants told him it was caused by the 'naya ganun' meaning, new laws, that the new law, the Rowlatt Law was the cause of the trouble at Amritsar and that its provisions were as he had already told the Committee. Repeatedly asked, he said that it was not he who told the peasants, but they who told him, that the cause of the trouble at Amritsar was the new law. Then, more questioning on the class of people; some of the people had come from Amritsar and were wandering about and in filling up his car with oil and water he spoke to the people who, in the manner typical of India, gathered around him. He had not stopped specifically to speak to them. He did try also to find out what was going on for his own edification and was told that Europeans had been killed and some people shot. He did not know if the people had been eyewitnesses: *"they may have been, but they would not have told me if they were.*

*One man went so far as to say 'Sade Gale Jal de' the new ganun is burning in my throat. May I tell you a little part of what I actually spoke to them about? When I heard their versions of the new ganun, I said to the fellows, look here, do you believe in the representations of the Rowlatt Act that you have heard? I know nothing about that because I am not a lawyer, but do you believe these representations of the Rowlatt Act to be genuine? Their reply was when the whole country is speaking of it, it must be true. I said, never mind if the whole country is speaking of it, I asked them if, with their knowledge of the British in India all these years, individually or collectively, they thought the British Government was capable of doing the things that were misrepresented to them. They said no. Then I replied, I am not saying my exact words – but this was the general trend of my argument – I said if this was intended to be brought in, would it not have been brought in after the mutiny; was there any necessity to bring in a rule like this when hundreds of people were fighting side by side with ourselves? Then they said "Sade Gale Jal de"* (that is burning in my throat).

> Q. *"Did they tell you who told them these things?"*
> A. *"No; I asked them first of all who started those rumours. One old fellow turned round to me and said, 'You ought to know'. I said if I knew I would not have asked him. Then I asked who started this thing and they said it was all over the country. I asked them can you give me an idea who started it? They said 'No'. So I said look here, there are three people in India who are concerned with law. The ordinary people know absolutely nothing about it and the three people are (1) judges, (2) policemen and (3) pleaders. I said is it possible – I know nothing about it – but is it possible that one of these has started it? It is not to the interest of policemen or magistrates to start these rumours, but there may be some discontented pleaders without a brief who may have started it. Thereupon one man said 'Ghatl vakil hua' (a no-good pleader). I said again, There are three people who know the law. may it be one of these? I wanted to get some information".*

> Q. *"Did you ask them as to who the pleader was, who started these rumours; who was the pleader?"*
> A. *"I was only asking him for information."*

This was surely evidence of widespread conspiracy to inflame the people. Donald had pinpointed the class of person who Sir Umar Hayat Khan had also said were responsible for much of the trouble - the unsuccessful barristers. The rumour (so it was remarked in the House of Lords) had spread or been spread from the Himalayas to Cape Cormorin. The alleged clauses of the Bills were quoted to the Amir of Afghanistan by people going up to Afghanistan from the plain. The claims about the Rowlatt Act were overt anti British propaganda, combined with the allegations made in the speeches of the Legislative Council, which, although they did not make such ludicrous claims, inspired India with feelings of dread and hatred. The intention of the Act was to stop the conspirators in their tracks. It had to be published in the Gazette of India if there was to be any need to invoke it and as Sir Percival Griffiths remarked, it was an Emergency Act, such as is on the Statute Books of most countries.

For the middle classes, the rumour, also untrue, was a little phrase *"Na dalil, Na Vakil, Na Appeal" (No Argument, No Lawyer, No Appeal)"* The phrase was spread to pervert men's minds and in such a way that rebellion against the Government could be the only outcome.

The story told by Colonel Stead in the Frontier Force Magazine, the 'Piffa', gives much the same information. Stead was sent by Dyer round the villages with a company of troops after the firing. Dyer himself also went round, holding durbars with the Sikh leaders to allay people's fears and make sure that the stories told by the conspiracy were refuted with authority. The village to which Captain Stead referred, was Jandialla. Cavalry were to join him on the road.

*"I was only 24 years of age and had no experience of duties in aid of the Civil Power. My only military experience had been advancing across the open flat plains of Mesopotamia and being shot at and shelled by the Turks in the process. Dyer had no responsible officers available and my selection for this job proves this point.*

*We arrived the following morning at Jandialla Station which had been well burnt and then marched the mile or two to the town, leaving the machine guns to guard the train. On reaching the town, I did a foolish thing which was to order bayonets to be fixed. My idea was to create an impression, but what I succeeded in doing was to clear the town of its inhabitants, and we had considerable difficulty in collecting a crowd to be addressed by the Junior Indian Civil Service Officer who accompanied us for this purpose. I thought his few words were very ineffective, so I got up on a bullock cart and spoke myself ... I told them that if they burnt Government property then it would be quite fair if the nearest town or village was burnt in return. I then asked them what their grievances were and got the reply 'The Rowlatt Act'. Now this was an Act that had recently been passed by the British-Indian Government to curb sedition and forbade, I think, the assembly of more than five persons. I asked them what they knew about the Act and the reply that has really stuck in my memory was from the man who said: 'We all know about the Rowlatt Act. It lays down that if a man has more than one daughter the Government will take the rest.'*

*On being asked what the Government was going to do with all these girls, they shouted 'Put them in brothels for British troops of course'.*

*I said Ahsti, Ahsti (slowly, slowly). I know the British soldier is the finest and most capable in the world but I doubt if he would be able to deal with (thinking quickly) some 700-1000 girls.*

*At this there was a roar of laughter and the whole attitude of the gathering changed. I then told them that the Sirkar (the British-Indian Government) for many years had given them peace, which they had not had in the olden times, with regular invasions over the passes of the North West and that their own late Maharajah, Ranjit Singh, had not been above pinching good looking girls for his harem.*

*It was then that a Sikh notable, a grand old man, came up to me and said: 'May I have a few words?' He then told them: 'Every word that the Sahib has said is absolutely true, he had confirmed all that my father and my grandfather told me about the rape and pillage that used to take place before the Sirkar came'. He sent for chairs and he and I sat down and talked for quite a time. He said 'These disturbances are not directed against the Government, but against the conditions that a long and protracted war have brought about, and these, not even the Government, but only time will change ... The Babu-log (semi educated office workers) have seized the opportunity and played on this discontent in their lust for power. You have heard the silly stories about the Rowlatt Act that they have spread. The old Sikh went on: 'There is much such unfairness in the world, my sons have been killed in the war, one with the Australians at Gallipoli and the other with the Indian Army in France. The Indian Army boy was a good boy but the Australian one was a wastrel. They have both left widows whom I look after. The Indian widow gets a mere pittance as a pension whilst the Australian one gets a good deal' and with this, he pulled out several Australian cheques from his pocket. All I could say was, 'Probably, an Australian Captain gets twice my pay but I do not let it worry me'."*

Stead's tale is so evocative of the closeness and humour that existed among the Indians and British working in India. The young Assistant-Commissioner was a man called Abdul Huq, a senior man when the author was in India in the 1940's. The elder was possibly not a Sikh but a Hindu called Lala Tek Chand Jaini, who was one of the men who gave evidence to the Hunter Committee. Of the firing at Amritsar he commented that it was necessary - he had seen a crowd of people going to Amritsar; asked why, they said they were going to loot; - this was on the 10$^{th}$. On the 12$^{th}$, he heard of more men going to Amritsar and they were sharpening their axes before they went.

Not only did Lala Tek Chand Jaini know from his parents of the troubles before the British came. Durga Das, the Reuters journalist from the Punjab, in his book 'India from Curzon to Nehru and Beyond' wrote: *"Viewing things objectively, the very early years of the 20$^{th}$ Century formed the golden period of the British Raj. People enjoyed* *peace and contentment in a climate of social security. To the intelligent and adventurous, opportunity beckoned with open arms. Anyway, I cannot recall a single reason for being dissatisfied with the conditions of my childhood. My father's standing in the village was high. In the schoolroom, he often spelled out the blessings of the Raj. My grandmother appeared to hold the alien ruler in the same high regard. Many of her bedtime stories revolved around Sikh Shahi (Sikh misrule) and the Mutiny of which we now speak as the First War of Independence. She was all praise for the Ram Raj of Malka, Queen Victoria."*

The change of attitude towards British rule demonstrated by the actions of the crowds in 1919 was not confined to the Punjab. Some would have us believe that it was a spontaneous outbreak of revulsion at foreigners' wicked new laws, but 'spontaneous' action covering the whole of India is about as likely as spontaneous combustion of every Indian's house. Investigation of suspicious fires usually uncovers a hidden hand with a match.[20]

There were clear indications of inflammatory hands at work in 1919. To whom did they belong?

---

20 Personal remarks and information from Colonel Eric Helby and others' opinions on Dyer's actions and his words in evidence to the Hunter Committee, Punjab Evidence vol. 111; Rowlatt Report, "The Committee to investigate and report on the nature and extent of criminal conspiracies connected with the revolutionary movement in India."; Sir Verney Lovett, 'A History of the India Nationalist Movement' ibid; Speech of Dr. Ansari to the Muslim League 1919; Delhi Evidence vol. 1 Hunter Committee. Sir Michael O'Dwyer; 'Revolt in the Desert' and other books by T. E. Lawrence or about him.
R. B. Beckett unpublished autobiography; Moon 'British Conquest and Dominion of India' ibid.; Amritsar Evidence Vol. 111; Piffa Magazine; Hunter Secret Evidence; Griffiths 'To Guard my People'; Durga Das, 'India from Curzon to Nehru and Beyond' Collins 1969; Edwin Montagu; 'An Indian Diary' edited Venetia Montagu Heinemann 1930; Montagu Papers, Trinity College Library; Coupland; 'India a Restatement' OUP 1945; Hansard Debates on India in the House of Lords, 1917 – 1920 (Reforms); Report of the Montagu-Chelmsford Reforms, Government Paper 1918; Field-Marshal Lord Roberts 'Forty Years in India'; Corelli Barnet; Malcolm Darling was the man who arranged for Forster to come to India as tutor to the Maharaja of Devas.

# Chapter II
# CONGRESS

In Bengal, Congress had been referred to with disparagement. In the 'Jugantur' newspaper, Arabindra Ghosh had written of the 'smallness and lowliness of Congress', the organisation which, first formulated by Octavian Hume in the previous century, was the political organisation expected to bring Indians in to the forefront of political position and power. Its annual meetings were, in the beginning, an opportunity for Indians to praise the British and the favours of British rule. The first speakers to the first resolution put forward, that the basis of government should be widened and that the people should have their natural legitimate share therein, was Subramania Aiyar of Madras who said:

*"By a merciful dispensation of Providence, India, which was for centuries the victim of external aggression and plunder, of internal civil wars and general confusion, has been brought under the dominion of the great British power."*

In 1885, the Indians were still nervous of further invasions, but as that fear receded, due to the security afforded by the Indian Army and the British battalions serving in India, revolutionary politics began to spread its wings.

Probably the most active samiti (association) in Bengal was the Anusilan, whose tentacles as a Hindu revivalist society spread all over India and initiated many of the crimes in a similar way to the Arya Samaj, in the Punjab. Part of the wide-spreading tentacle nature of the samiti was shown in the Muzaffarpur murders in April 1908, when Mrs. and Miss Kennedy were killed by a bomb thrown in the dark into the carriage in which they were driving.

In the subsequent trial it was shown that the murders were carried out by two youths deputed by the Anusilan Samiti and were a mistaken attempt against a magistrate, obnoxious to the revolutionaries, who had been transferred from Calcutta to Muzaffarpur.

The judge in the Alipore conspiracy case, who dared to criticise the Bengali youth who had carried out the murder, used words of the literature being published in relation to the Muzaffarpur murders, quoted later by Sir Lawrence Jenkins, the Chief Justice of England, saying: *"They exhibit a burning hatred of the British race, they breathe revolution in every line, they point out how revolution can be effected. No calumny and no artifice is left out which is likely to instil the people of the country with the same idea or to catch the impressionable mind of young."* This was in 1908, Gandhi having written his racist book in 1907. These were the words to which Edwin Montagu, as Under-Secretary for India, objected and which, with no background knowledge, moved him to suggest that judges should be supervised – a suggestion which was soon sat on.

In July 1907, Bal Gangadur Tilak, publishing in his journal 'Kesari' an incitement to murder by claiming it as magic, had been imprisoned for six years. Tilak's subtle encouragement took place in the Bombay Presidency, but in a sense it was the same approach as that of the conspirators in Bengal. The further belief of the conspirators there was that it would be possible to get arms or learn to make them and they observed that it did not take strength to kill Europeans. It had been easy for Shivaji to kill Afzal Khan, the 18th Century Mogul General, by doing so as he was making obeisance to the Mogul General and in the same way, it would be easy to kill the hated Feringhi. Tilak's approach was through violence. He had started by causing trouble with loud music and processions outside Muslim mosques and trouble between the two religious groups then followed, but this time the hostility had turned towards the British.

It was because they knew of the widespread conspiracy that the Germans believed it would be a simple matter to suborn India.

These were not the only publications intended to incite violence. Mazzini, the Bhagavad Gita with its encouragement to kill the enemy, Hind Swaraj, Ruskin, Thoreau, Garibaldi and such principles as the religious principle of absolute surrender to the divine will, were employed by designing and unscrupulous men as potent means to influence and unbalance the weak minded and thus ultimately, bend them to become instruments in 'the commission of nefarious crimes from which they might otherwise recoil with horror', in the words of Mr Justice Mukharji.

Three more books were being circulated: 'The Bhawani Mandir', (Bhawani being Kali; Goddess of Destruction), to promote moral, physical and spiritual strength, described worship in powerful and moving terms, using religion for political purposes. This was very similar to Gandhi's later use of his volunteers, shown in the film 'Gandhi', burning to death twenty-two policemen at Chauri Chaura. Gandhi is later portrayed in the film as fasting because of this incident, putting forward a concept of sincere apology, unlikely to have been sincere in view of his attitude later to the horrors inspired by him in the Malabar Rebellion (which the film omits). Kali was the Goddess of the Thugs.

Secondly, the book 'Bartaman Rananiti' (The Art of War). This incorporates various violent methods of achieving the aims of those involved in these movements. It was believed that Sakti, the divine energy would, develop young men who involved themselves in violence, so that they would become fearless and expert in swordplay and develop heroic qualities.

The third of these books was 'Mukti Kon Pathe?' (What is the path of salvation?). This book was a collection of articles from the 'Jugantur' and justified dacoity (gang robberies) on their own countrymen, an extension of the conspiracies and by these, claiming to show love for their country.

The object of a further revolutionary, Barindra, in Bengal, was to persuade the English-educated young of Bengal that the British Government was 'founded on fraud and oppression', a concept that it still alive in Bengalis to this day.

The trial also brought out the fact that the Alipore conspiracy case disclosed a connection between Deoghar in the Santhal Parganas of Bihar and some of the other conspirators. Deoghar is a health resort and a place of pilgrimage.

The family involved in the murder had lived at Deoghar for several years; Barindra Ghosh belonged to a Society called the Golden League, the objects of which were to forward the Swadeshi (indigenous products and boycott agitation). Another Bengali, a printer, together with other revolutionaries, lived on a farm nearby. A house called Sil's Lodge at Deoghar was used for the training of others and for bomb-making. Bombs were found there as late as 1915 and in the Alipore bomb trial, a copy of the newspaper Bande Materam was found, which bore the name of one of the Muzaffarpur murderers. Bande Materam was the name of a seditious newspaper, first published by Har Dayal in Geneva, but subsequently continued elsewhere. It was also the name of a revolutionary song and was deeply significant to these young Indians who were being trained with a ruthless and inhumane approach to life that could even persuade them to murder those belonging to a calling reverenced by Hindus. The murder of Gandhi himself was carried out by a Bengali activist of this type.

At Amritsar in 1919, the incited mob callously endeavoured to burn a Mission School over the heads of the inmates, virtually all of whom were Indian. The Bengal incitement to robbery and homicide spread far beyond Bengal, to an extent where those bitten with the propaganda would ignore all thought of profession, religion or patriotism, their minds becoming almost totally dehumanised. <u>Much of the propaganda stemmed from Britain and Europe in the first place</u> (author's underline), but in the matter of the botched attempt on the Chief Presidency Magistrate of Bengal, Mr. Kingsford, the insidious effect spread further, through Lajpat Rai to Ramsay Macdonald and thence to the Under Secretary of State, Edwin Montagu. The perversion of Montagu's mind led him to side with the rebels in the Amritsar Debate and use material against the British derived, not from the Hunter Majority Report, not even from the Hunter Minority Report (in which Pandit Jagat Narayan had used every shred of convertible material he could to damn the British), but from the Congress Committee Report which was produced by Gandhi and the politicised barristers who were involved in the rebellion themselves. Such an attitude of mind had also led Montagu, on his travels through India to write the Reform proposals, refusing to go into the Districts and see how India was governed, before he put forward the legislation that was intended to alter the way of government. Umar Hayat Khan was shocked at the pro-urban legislation that was to come out of the report and affect the Reforms.

The Rowlatt report puts the responsibility for the upheavals in the United Provinces on the shoulders of the Bengalis. Bengalis, who were going into schools and giving lessons on the wickedness of the British [still repeated by Bengalis in England today] who had, according to them, caused disease, famine and poverty in India. Scientific evidence was irrelevant, statistics proved the contrary, and in the Swadeshi movement, the claim was that the British had exploited India. The example given was the claim that India was being flooded with British cotton – in fact, the cotton grown in India was short staple and unsuitable for the fine yarn used for shirts, grown in other countries and processed and woven in Britain. The growing prosperity of India had been enhanced in the War, when factories for the production of uniforms and armaments were set up.

Except in Government department statistics, which were not widely available, there was little attempt made to refute the claims that people of reason and experience knew to be untrue.

Among the revolutionaries, the only scientific education given by their centres was in bomb-making. The disciplines were clearly in keeping with the Russian methods, where centres in which people were involved knew nothing of other centres. The conspirators were told to join other organisations as well as their own. Death was a penalty for disobedience and once having taken the oath, a man could not leave the organisation, since he had always to give his change of address to the leader of his cell who sent it to the organiser higher up.

Disciplines included swordplay or lathiplay, with lathis used as swords and people becoming extremely dextrous. The Chauri Chaura use of lathis a few years later comes to mind; also the use of lathis at Amritsar and at Delhi in 1919, when a soldier on duty with a rifle was disarmed by a boy with a lathi. The aim was to collect as many students and young people as possible - a point made by Sir Umar Hayat Khan in the Secret Evidence.

Beyond all the oaths to Kali, the laying of revolvers at her feet and humbly promising eternal loyalty, there was the more sinister underhand determination to suppress all moderate thought and traduce Indians in responsible positions. When the people of some standing in later times dared not say anything that would put them in a vulnerable position, it was the continuation of the threats of violence, which they knew to be a real possibility, which closed their mouths.

By 1911, Nationalists were working with the Germans for invasion on the East coast of India and with the same people for invasion from Persia and Afghanistan. The change was in the attitude of Indians, living no longer under the Marquis of Dufferin and Ava as in 1885, but under Lord Minto (a bomb was thrown at him in

Ahmedabad), Lord Hardinge (bomb thrown at him in Delhi) and Lord Chelmsford. Change of attitude had also changed their words.

That same Subramania Aiyar of Madras, who in the first Congress Resolution had paid tribute to the benefits of British rule, wrote to President Wilson during the War: *"...you and the other leaders have been kept in ignorance of the full measure of misrule and oppression in India."* Disregarding the fact that British officials spoke the local language up to interpreter level, with many dialects as well, he wrote *"Officials of an alien nation, speaking a foreign tongue, force their will upon us."* Bearing in mind the disparity of numbers, (there being around 900 British administrative officers throughout India at that time, to 350,000,000 Indians) and that we walked or rode among the people with ease and friendship, this was hardly an accurate description of us. Further, *"They grant themselves exorbitant salaries and large allowances."*

The salaries and allowances were so mean, that the cost of sending families (or oneself) home on leave, was not covered by them. Kipling tells the story, and my father told a similar one, that it was impossible for people, if they fell ill, to go home with their families, for although an official's fare was paid with his vacation salary, it was for one month in 22 months and the fare of his wife and children had to be saved out of his pay. In this matter, it is perhaps relevant that an official, having to have a car or horses to tour his large District (in the case of myself and my husband, our District was the size of the whole of Wales) and the servants to look after them and us (in a country where caste caused demarcation lines between types of service unknown in Britain), his salary was Rs. 300 a month (£300 a year). This Indian claim of affluence was as inaccurate as the rest. An Indian barrister (pleader) drew an enormous amount more than an official and there were many Hindu and Muslim judges, for the top administrative jobs were not reserved for the British. Indians such as Sachendra Sinha, later the Under Secretary of State, could not afford to give up their prosperous positions to take up Government careers. Sinha lost a great deal financially when he became a member of the Viceroy's council.

*"They refuse us education"* – absolutely untrue – from the days of Lord Wellesley, education had been available. Private schools were also set up and are referred to in the Rowlatt Report. People who are wishing to indoctrinate children do not stop at going in to the Government Schools. Sir Michael O'Dwyer mentions that the politicians stopped him opening schools.

*"They sap us of our wealth"* – far from it. As he wrote, India was more prosperous than ever before.

*"They impose crushing taxes without our consent."* During the war, new taxes had been imposed, largely because of the great increase in wealth which brought a lot of people into a tax bracket which previously they would not have attained, but these were discussed and voted on in the Legislative Council.

It is interesting to note that one of the concerns about the new extension of the representation system was that it would put up the cost of government, which the low pay of officials and their clerks had kept down. By the end of the war, the treatment of the services in salaries, pensions and other service requirements had become so bad, that Lloyd George had to go into Parliament and alter the system in order to get more recruits. Aiyar's last claim was that thousands of political people, to him 'patriots', were put into prison for nothing and that the prisons were filthy. In those days they may have been. It is relevant to note this patriot's opinion of patriotism, which will gain further weight in the ensuing pages.

Congress became such a powerful force that it is hard to believe that in order to achieve the first meeting, Surendranath Banerjee, a journalist and politician who had previously been in the Indian Civil Service, toured Northern India in the year prior to the meeting to drum up interest. Octavian Hume, an ornithologist and an employee of the Provincial Civil Service, first of the Company and then of the Government, having ornithological friends all over India, set up committees in principal cities which were to be the foundation of a nationwide organisation. Even so, at the first meeting, there were only 70 delegates from among those who had been pressed to come.

By the annual meeting in December 1919, the thousands of delegates meeting at Amritsar were to turn down the Reform proposals which had by that time been formulated by the Viceroy and the Secretary of State on a formula to which many Indians had put their opinions. That meeting was held under the Presidency of Moti Lal Nehru, the father of Jawarharlal. In the interim, in 1907, the Moderates were still in control under Gokhale although the extremists under Tilak endeavoured to press their point that the Congress should act as the men of violence demanded, the Moderates won their view that 'This Congress is of the opinion that the system of Government obtaining in the self governing British colonies should be extended to India and as steps leading to it, urges that the following reforms should be carried out.'

The Extremists had tried to carry out their resolution by force and the President, Dadabhai Naoroji, a one time Member of Parliament in Britain, commented that *"Agitation is the life and soul of the whole political, social and industrial history of England ..."* Sir Verney Lovett's comment was apposite to the ongoing history of India at the time: *"Mr. Naoroji ignored the important fact that agitation in homogeneous England does not mean the exacerbation of colour feelings, of religious jealousy and hatred. In India it is generally carried on by methods that mean this"*. He might have added, in view of the nature of the political violence of that time, it also meant hatred and violence towards Moderates and this continued to the end of our time. When, in 1944, some Indians speaking to two non official Britons, commented on their fear of what would happen to India and to Indians if Gandhi got power, they spoke in fear, stressing that their listeners must not mention their names. Most Moderates spoke like this, risking Gandhian retribution if it were to be known.

Sir Verney added *"...those leaders of the Congress movement who had not become intoxicated with excitement and racial animosity had, before this meeting, begun to see that things were going too far. It is probable, too, that some, at least, were becoming aware that behind all the whirlwind of passion in Bengal, behind the schools and colleges which were developing into seedbeds of sedition, behind the pamphlets and newspapers which were disseminating hatred and bitterness far and wide, the ground was being prepared for even more serious doings by fanatics inflamed with the purpose of gradually organising a bloody revolt. This, the Government was slow to realise. Its friends in England persistently misunderstood the movement. It had not touched the fighting races or the fighting castes and the main grievance was sentimental. Few anticipated that it would lead to actual bloodshed.*[21]

*Fewer dreamt that it would bring forth an unending series of violent crimes or that, in a country where sons closely adhere to the occupations of their fathers, the sons of clerks, lawyers and schoolmasters, would, under the influence of racial sentiment and vague idealism, abjure the ambitions of their class and drill with daggers and pistols and indeed, it is certain that had more of these young men and boys ever known firm discipline and intelligent supervision in and out of study hours, they would not have fallen so easy a prey to the plots of unscrupulous revolutionaries."*

Among those 'friends' in England were the Under Secretary of State and Mr. Ramsay Macdonald.

Members of the Congress Party cannot be absolved from the responsibility for their encouragement of extremism, nor can those British politicians who did not restrain them.

---

21  A loyal Bengali gentleman once told Sir Verney that he was so amazed by the first outrages that he refused to credit them.

## Chapter III
## ROWLATT

There is no doubt that the revolutionary conspiracies and the German/Indian propaganda were in the ascendancy. In the judgements of the cases on which Rowlatt and his committee had to rest their claims, it was clearly stated that even when those who committed violence, murder, robbery and blackmail were arrested, it was impossible to get at those in the background, manipulating the criminal actions from behind the scenes.

The Defence of India Act, had, as a Wartime Emergency Act, simplified the committal proceedings, normally long drawn out and obscuring the facts. Indian pleaders were notoriously long-winded and the bulk of the pleaders, if not complicit with the revolutionary movement, had sympathy with it.

The difficulties were severe; the Committee describing them under the heading 'Statements'.

*"Lastly we have had placed before us a great number of statements. In some cases these have been made by approvers, who have been willing to give evidence, but in most cases they were made by persons in custody who are not so disposed. There are a very few statements (and those only as to particular incidents) made by police agents and members of the public. The great mass of the statements is by persons in custody other than approvers, and as to these, we must offer some comment and explanations. Unfortunately with few exceptions, we have felt bound to treat these statements as confidential. By the Indian Evidence Act, a confession by a person in police custody is not evidence against him unless made before a magistrate with certain formalities laid down in the Code of Criminal Procedure. No statement made by an accused to a police officer is admissible, except insofar as it distinctly refers to some fact deposed to, as discovered in consequence of that statement. This has induced a great candour in speaking to the police, but if statements made under*

*such circumstances were made public we are satisfied that it would be a breach of a well understood though often unexpressed condition. What compels us to be particularly careful in this respect is that the deponents would, in our judgement, certainly be exposed to the vengeance of their associates.*

*The above considerations have hampered us considerably in fortifying, by way of reasoning upon evidence disclosed upon the face of this report, the conclusions at which we have arrived. They have robbed us of the power to cite particular deponents by name, to set forth the circumstances of the making of statement, to discuss his means of knowledge and the corroboration, which he receives from independent statements or ascertained facts. We have however been able to use extracts from statements where the identity of the deponent is not directly or indirectly alluded to.*

*The statements in question have been made at various times, from 1907 down to the date of the sittings of this Committee (19th July 1918 – October 1918). They are not copious in the latest period, when police action under the Defence of India Act broke the morale of the conspirators. At this time the leaders, when arrested, sometimes after a long period in hiding, have in many though not in all cases, been ready to tell the whole story freely. Some speak under the impulse of a feeling of disgust for an effort which has failed. Some of a different temperament, are conscience-stricken. Others speak to relieve their feelings, glad that the life of a hunted criminal is over. Not a few speak only after a period of consideration during which they argue with themselves the morality of disclosure. We have not failed to bear in mind that information of this kind is not blindly relied upon, least of all in India. But we have had remarkable facilities for testing these statements. The fact that they are exceedingly numerous, that they have been made at different dates and often in places remote from one another, gives an opportunity for comparison far more useful than if they were few and connected.*

*But this is not all. In numerous instances a deponent refers to facts previously unknown: to revolutionary haunts not yet suspected or person not yet arrested. Upon following up the statements the facts have been found to have occurred, the haunts are found in full activity, persons indicated have been arrested and in turn have made statements, or documents have been unearthed and a new department obtained for further investigation. This class of research has been particularly successful in the years 1916 and 1917, and a network of information has been obtained which leaves no escape from the general conclusions which we shall record. The fatal precision of the information given by persons arrested was only too well appreciated by those who remained at large. A revolutionary and undoubted murderer, since arrested, thus writes in a letter dated 2nd January, found in January 1918. 'One gives out the names of ten others and they in turn give out something. By this process we have been entirely weakened. Even the enemy don't consider that they who remain are worth taking'."*

For those interested in reading the document, these indications will be seen clearly; the author has in the main paraphrased the incidents leaving out the details, but in paragraph 170, there are some illustrations of the intricate ways in which information fell into place.

*"... the case of the Armenian Street dacoity committed in Calcutta at about 9 p.m. on the 7<sup>th</sup> May 1917. This case possesses many features favouring the discovery of the crime, and its ruthless cruelty should make it probable that any that could assist the police would come forward to do so. It will be remembers that five eyewitnesses of the occurrence survive, namely the two servants (both wounded) of the proprietors, who were both killed, and two women and one Mohammedan who were in the shop as customers. Further, the dacoits went away in a taxi-cab from which, after going some distance, they took out one of their number who had been badly wounded, shot him and left his body upon the ground. These are, therefore important clues. Now we have carefully examined the materials collected by the police and what is available. A neighbour from his own village has independently identified the murdered dacoit. From papers and statements obtained by the police in searches in connection with the investigation of a previous crime, it was known that he belonged to a certain gang, but the documents and statements cannot be made legal evidence against the individuals in the gang on a charge of committing dacoity. Ten members of this gang have by degrees been arrested and all except three have admitted their guilt to police officers of standing. Two of those who have made no statements however, have wounds upon them described by other prisoners as received by them in the course of the dacoity. The taxi driver came forward but, though he admits to witnessing the murder of the dacoit and washing blood from the car, he said nothing about it for a week and spoke only when he thought he might be found out. His story varies and he obviously was an accomplice. He was identified as one of the dacoits, by one of the prisoners in custody who, as above mentioned, has made no statement, but at the same time he identified as another dacoit, a perfectly innocent member of the public brought in for the purposes of identification.*

*The taxicab was engaged by a man who has also been found. This man was in the car throughout and is also an accomplice, though he did not take part in the actual dacoity. He says he recognised the photograph of the murdered dacoit and also that of another member of the gang. He was employed to hire the car by another man, who admits that he procured the engagement of the car knowing it was for dacoity. The two wounded servants at the shop and the three customers say they could not identify any of the dacoits. It will be remembered that two of the customers fled, the other, a woman, hid under a bench and the two servants fell wounded at the commencement of the attack. One of the servants however, thinks he recognises the photograph of the murdered dacoit as that of a young man who was loitering near the shop earlier in the day. The upshot of the whole matter is that there is no untainted evidence against anyone.*

*Bhowanipore Murder. A senior Deputy Superintendent of Police and his orderly, a head constable, were proceeding home on bicycles near the Presidency Hospital when five youths armed with pistols attacked them in broad daylight. At that time in the evening, the roads of that neighbourhood are filled with traffic, although the particular crossroad of about a quarter of a mile in length on which the murder was actually committed carries comparatively little. On one side of this crossroad is an open plot of land on which a crowd of Bengali youths were playing football. The scene of the crime is only about 100 yards from one of the main thoroughfares.*

*The Deputy Superintendent was shot dead with nine wounds on his person, one of which was in the head. The head constable was seriously wounded and subsequently succumbed to his injuries in hospital. Both the Deputy Superintendent and his orderly were armed, but the suddenness of the attack afforded them no opportunity of using their weapons as they were cycling at the time.*

*After the outrage, the culprits escaped in the direction of the main thoroughfare to the East of the scene. They were challenged by a constable on point duty in the vicinity and fired at him. They then escaped through a small byelane into a thickly populated Indian quarter. They were dressed in ordinary clothes as worn by average Bengalis of that class and there was therefore nothing by which to identify them after they had got clear away from the vicinity of the crime.*

*The police investigation on the spot gave no hope of identifying the culprits. The only evidence was that of the wounded head constable who stated in hospital that he would be able to identify two of the youths, whom he described as wearing respectively a white shirt and a striped coat.*

*The nature of the crime itself provided no clue to the particular section of the revolutionary party responsible, as many sections were known to have conspired or attempted to murder this officer previously.*

*The general statements of individuals arrested in Bengal shortly after the outrage showed clearly that this crime was the work of the Dacca Anusilan Samiti, without however indicating the particular persons responsible for it.*

*If the above synopsis is closely followed, it will be seen that of the five persons captured at different times each states that he and the other four were the actual murderers and there is a good deal of concurrent information as to some at any rate of their confederates. Still there is no evidence justifying prosecution*

*The two crimes we have just dealt with occurred in 1916 and 1917 respectively, when the police had the experience of ten years behind them. Both crimes were committed in the streets of Calcutta."*

The next example is one of terrorism. The Alipore murders of the two Kennedy ladies took place in April 1908; the approver involved in that trial was killed before the trial, and at that, killed in prison before he could give evidence. The comment in 'Swadhin Barat' was as follows: *"When coming to know of the weakness of Narendra [Narendra Goshin the approver] who, roused by a new impulse, had lost his self-control, our crooked-minded merchant rulers were preparing to hurl a terrible thunderbolt upon the whole country and when the great hero Kanailal, after having achieved success in the effort to acquire strength in order to give an exhibition of India's unexpected strength, wielding the terrible thunderbolt of the great magician and making every chamber in the Alipore jail quake, drew blood from the breast of the traitor in his country, safe in a British prison, in iron chains, surrounded by the walls of a prison, then indeed the English realised that the flame which had been lit in Bengal had at its root a wonderful strength in store ..."*

'Bande Materam' in its edition of 12th September 1908, wrote:

*"Kanai has killed Narendra. No more shall the wretch of an Indian who kisses the hands of his companions reckon himself safe from the avenging hand. The first of the Avenger's history shall write of Kanai and from the moment he fired the fatal shot the spaces of his country's heaven have been ringing with the voice 'beware the traitor's fate."*

In a subsequent trial, on 2nd June 1910, the commitment order runs as follows:

*"The fear shown by the majority of the witnesses was one of the notable features of the case. It was obvious that many of them only spoke with reluctance, while a considerable number showed such extreme nervousness at the sight of the accused when shown them for identification, that they made not the faintest effort to identify any of them and exhibited only a great anxiety to escape at the earliest possible moment. The demeanour of the witnesses was a striking testimony to the terror which the gang had inspired."*

Lord Sydenham, in the Debate in the House of Lords, told of an example of a man's feeling of conscience after committing a crime in October 1917. The Debate was on the intended visit of the Secretary of State, Edwin Montagu, to India and his influence in the release of Annie Besant from her internment under the Defence of India Act, consequent on her articles in her paper 'New India'. She appeared anxious to imitate the most dangerous language in which the India Press had indulged. He was warning the Government of the likely exacerbation of the situation in India if Annie Besant, living comfortably and freely in Ootacamund with her friends, with freedom in every way except to leave 'Ooty' or publish more incitement to 'excitable young Indians', was freed. He was endeavouring to make clear that to let her go would be read as weakness and make things worse and not make for Montagu's imagined 'better atmosphere'.

*"All political agitation in India, from the first, has been accompanied by assassination and in many cases the assassins themselves have named the newspapers and speakers from whom they drew the inspiration of murder. Mr. Jackson, a most valued Indian civilian, a student of Indian languages and literature and devoted to the people, was shot at an entertainment given to him by Indians and the young assassin in his trial made this confession. He said – 'I read of many instances of oppression in 'Kesari', the 'Rashtramat', the 'Kalifand', other newspapers. I think that by killing Sahibs, we people can get justice. I never got justice myself, nor did anyone I know. I now regret killing Mr. Jackson. I killed a good man causelessly'."*

In 1908, the Government became convinced that the law needed strengthening, and the Criminal Law Amendment Act was brought in, together with the Newspapers (Incitement to Offences Act). Lord Minto, speaking on the Bill said *"The seeds of its wickedness have been sown amongst a strangely impressionable and imitative people – seeds that have been daily nurtured by a system of seditious writing and seditious speaking of unparalleled violence, vociferating to beguiled youth that outrage is the evidence of patriotism and its reward, a martyr's crown."*

The report gives a further example of the effects on youth, in the voluntary confession made to the Chief Presidency Magistrate in Calcutta. *"I was introduced to a gentleman named Jatindra nath Mukharji of 275, Upper Chitpur Road, by a boy named Janendra nath Mitra in the month of September. By reading the 'Jugantur', I got a very strong wish to do brave and violent works and I asked Jatin Mukharji to give me work at 275, Chitpur Road. He told me about the shooting of Shamsul Alam, Deputy-Superintendent, who conducted the bomb case and he ordered a boy named Satish Chandra to make arrangements for this case. I asked Jatin for such works, and he asked me whether I shall be able to shoot Shamsul Alam. I answered that I will be able."* Deponent went on to describe the murder and ended: *"I make this statement so as not to injure Jatin, but as I have come to understand that anarchism will not benefit our country, and the leaders who are blaming me now thinking the deed that of a head-cracked boy, to show them that I alone am not responsible for the work. There are many men behind me and Jatin, but I do not wish to give their names in this statement. The leaders who are now blaming me should be kind enough to come forward and guide boys like me in good ways."*

In this situation, the Committee looked at the possible way of securing the punishment of seditious crime. They came to the conclusion that (a), change in the general law of evidence or procedure which, if sound, would be advisable in regard to all crime, and (b), changes in the substantive law of sedition or modifications in the rules of evidence and procedure in such cases designed to deal with the special features of that class of offence, would help.

The Committee, after lengthy comments on the law and its effects, came to the Emergency Provisions for Trials. They had already dealt with the method of notification of the implementation of the Bills by the Governor-General in Council.

*"Emergency Provisions for Trials: Coming now to the measures themselves, we are of the opinion that provision should be made for the trial of seditious crime by Benches of three Judges without juries or assessors and without preliminary commitment proceedings or appeal. In short, the procedure we recommend should follow the lines laid down in Section 5.9 of the Defence of India Act. It should be made clear that section 512 of the Code of Criminal Procedure (relating to the giving in evidence under certain circumstances of depositions taken in the absence of an absconding accused) applies to these trials, it having, we understand, been questioned whether Section 7 of the Defence of India Act has this effect. We think it necessary to exclude juries and assessors mainly because of the terrorism to which they are liable, but terrorism apart, we do not think they can be relied on in this class of case. They are too much inclined to be affected by public discussion. We could give instances which have come before us, where we think there have been miscarriages of justice owing*

*to the causes above mentioned. We may further point out that the trial of such cases without jury or assessors was introduced by the Criminal Law Amendment Act 1908. As regards the procedure and absence of right of appeal, we think it essential that the delay involved in commitment proceedings and appeal be avoided. It is of the utmost importance that punishment or acquittal should be speedy both in order to secure the moral effect which punishment should produce and also to prevent the prolongation of the excitement which proceedings may set up. Furthermore, the delays involved by commitment proceedings and the double examination of witnesses increase the chance of witnesses being intimidated, add to the hardships involved in their attendance, with the consequence of making them less ready to come forward and also afford time for them to forget the facts.*

*We think however, there is one important amendment to be made in the procedure. Under the temporary scheme now in operation, charges are formulated after the evidence for the prosecution has been closed. In our opinion some expedient must be found for defining the issues and communicating them to the accused a reasonable time before he has to meet or rebut them. We do not apprehend how an accused can deal relevantly either in cross examination or by preparation with a case not formulated."*

The concern for justice and for the protection of the accused, who was to be placed under the Protection of the Court, i.e. the Superintendent of the prison rather than under police protection, was evidence of this. The Rowlatt Act was beneficial, despite being used as a useful target for attack.

The Bills themselves will be found in APPENDIX I, ROWLATT LEGISLATION.

So far, apart from one or two passing references, I have written of the conspiracies within India arising from the evident malice towards Government of shadowy and unnamed individuals in the sub-continent, encouraged and perhaps led by the Congress Party, whose activities culminated in rebellion in 1919.

But malice and plotting was not confined to India.

# Chapter IV
# GHADR (MUTINY)

The Ghadr movement was, in the main, a Sikh movement and posed a particular threat to the stability of India because Sikhs have their home in the Punjab with their religious centre, The Golden Temple, at Amritsar. Sikhs formed a large part of the Indian Army, in the Punjabi and Sikh regiments.

In the aftermath of the Hunter Inquiry, one of the main charges levelled against General Dyer was that he had said that in firing, he had wished to affect the morale of the country people outside the town. People who did not recognise the sound basis of his remark had held this against him. That remark was based on his position in charge of the Jullunder area, which included Amritsar and the country around it, containing many of the villages where Ghadr members had been interned. The fear that the internees might join in the rebellion at Amritsar was one of General Dyer's concerns and on the 12th April 1919, the day before the firing, news had come of a meeting being held in Amritsar with various explicit intentions. As General Dyer put it, *"Telegraphic and telephonic communications had been cut and trains could no longer proceed in safety in various directions from Amritsar. The inhabitants of the surrounding villages who had been told that the British Raj was at an end were coming into Amritsar in increasing numbers with the objective of swelling the ranks of the mob. A Danda Fauj was to be formed so numerous that with 'slaps' it was said they could drive the British out of the country. Arrangements had been made to arm the Danda Fauj with sticks and large consignments of these sticks were coming into Amritsar".*

What was the background?

In 1914, a Tamil named Champakaram Pillai, President of a body in Zurich called the International Pro-India Committee, applied to the German consul in Zurich to obtain permission to publish anti-British literature in Germany. In October, he left for Germany to work under the Foreign Office in Berlin, where he established the

'Indian National Party' attached to the German General Staff. Among its members were the ubiquitous Har Dayal, Taraknath Das, Barkatulla, C.K. Chakrabarti and Heramba Lal Gupta (two of the accused in the German/Indian conspiracy trial in San Francisco). In the main, their duties were the writing and dissemination of anti-British propaganda. Pillai was the one in charge of the German codes and the instructing of at least one agent, who was going to Bangkok to start a printing press, to smuggle propaganda over the Siamese-Burmese border; Heramba Lal Gupta was for a time the Indian agent of Germany in America and arranged with Captain Boehm that he should go to Siam and train men for an attack on Burma. Boehm was also involved with Irish conspiracies and was later arrested and tried in connection with the case at San Francisco, but his activities did not end on the borders of Siam. A letter from the then German Foreign Secretary, Alfred Zimmerman, a Social Democrat (as opposed to Monarchist) and later a proponent of the U-boat war which brought America into the fight against Germany, directed Chakrabarti to replace Gupta when he left on a more active duty. The letter is dated February 4$^{th}$ 1916, is from Berlin and is addressed to the German Embassy in Washington.[22]

The Rowlatt Report stated that the German General Staff had 'definite schemes' against India. These schemes were in the main dependent on the non-Mohammedan population. Mohammedan schemes were based on the North-West Frontier of India, whereas the Ghadr party of San Francisco were based in Bangkok and Thailand, also centres for the Bengali revolutionaries. Both the schemes were under the general direction of the Consul General for Germany at Shanghai, acting under orders from the German Embassy in Washington.

British Intelligence supported the belief, shared by the French, that there was evidence that a rebellion was expected. The French derived their belief from Indians in Europe and the British gave sound grounds for this belief.

In November 1914, a Maratha named Pingle and a Bengali named Satyan Sen arrived in India from America in a ship, the S.S. Salamis. Pingle went up country to organise rebellion there and Satyan remained at 150, Bow Bazaar at Calcutta. Pingley or Pingle went to Amritsar where, with the Bengali, Rash Behari, he organised the Ghadr movement in the Punjab and brought up bomb-making equipment and know-how from Bengal. They were the brains behind the attempts to enlist the troops into their schemes. In January and February 1915, their emissaries were tampering with troops at Jhelum in the North and as far South as Benares. They had met with some success in certain battalions returned from the Far East and also in a Sikh squadron of cavalry in Lahore. The Punjab Government got wind of the incitement and information that a general rising had been planned for the night of February 21$^{st}$, when various cantonments in Northern India would be the scene of mutiny and the murder

---

22    *"In future all Indian affairs are to be exclusively handled by the Committee to be formed by Dr. Chakrabarti, Birendra Sarker and Heramba Lal Gupta, which latter person has meantime been expelled from Japan, thus cease to be independent representatives of the Indian Independence Committee existing here"*. Sd. Zimmerman

of their British officers, combining with Ghadr supporters from outside. It was envisaged that these would seize the magazines, arms and ammunition and bring about a general rising.

The plan had spread down to Bengal and to disaffected elements at Dacca. From the Sikh squadron at Lahore which was thoroughly disaffected, twelve men were seconded to the guard of the Lieutenant-Governor, Sir Michael O'Dwyer. The information which had alerted him was naturally secret and he refused to get rid of the men despite the danger, nor would this brave man get the troopers transferred, in case it alerted the conspirators. On February 19th, 1915, the C.I.D. and Sir Michael got news that Pingle and Rash Behari had moved their headquarters to Lahore and, suspecting that there had been some leakage of their plans, they had brought the date of the rising forward to the 19th. They had sent messengers to various selected sites including several cantonments, to tell them to act accordingly. Sir Michael and his staff realised they must act at once.

In four separate houses in Lahore, raids were carried out that very afternoon by the brave and able policeman, Khan Lyakat Hayat Khan and Lionel (later Sir Lionel) Tomkins, the head of the C.I.D. In this raid, thirteen of the revolutionaries were captured, together with arms, bombs and bomb-making materials and revolutionary literature.

Unfortunately, Pingle and Rash Behari escaped. Pingle was arrested a few weeks later in the lines of the 12th Cavalry at Meerut with a collection of bombs brought up from Bengal - sufficient, so experts said, to blow up an entire regiment. Pingle, with one of his friends was arrested, tried and hanged. His co-conspirator, Parmanand, had his sentence commuted by the Viceroy to transportation for life, but he was later released. The trial took place under the Defence of India Act and was the first Lahore Conspiracy case, one of several that the Hunter Committee refused to read or consider in their investigation into whether or not there was any evidence of conspiracy for the 1919 rebellion. The Ghadr movement was still alive and active in 1919 and was one of the main concerns in Dyer's action at Amritsar. His reasoned fear was that if the rebellion at Amritsar was not put down promptly, the Ghadr Sikhs might join in. They would undoubtedly have taken the opportunity, had the unrest spread.

Sir Michael was inclined to think that Pingle, a brave man, who did not hesitate to take part in the actions he advocated, was more to be admired than Rash Behari, who had kept out of danger himself, while advocating his followers to act in a manner that could, and in some cases did, lead to their deaths.

Action was not only taken at Lahore. Coded telegrams were sent to various cantonments that were known to be involved - Sialkot, Ferozepore, Rawalpindi and others. At the Lahore and Ferozepore cantonments, the Ghadr party had already gathered in order to join in as had been planned. Sir Michael then added the comment, which soldiers will recognise as being an honest observation on actions by authorities in times of war: *"The tainted Sikh squadron was sent to the Front soon after with the rest of the regiment; for in time of war it was not thought advisable by the military authorities to have a court-martial which would make public the mutinous preparations. The Depot was moved to a distant station and when it was detraining, some of the bombs which had been secreted for months after 19th February, exploded. A Court-Martial could not now be avoided. The result was that eighteen men of the regiment were sentenced to death and twelve were actually executed."*

Although most of this took place in what today is Pakistan, though India in 1915, a success such as had been achieved by the C.I.D. and the military with the Punjab Government, immediately weakened those who might have joined the rebellion. It is a characteristic of Indians and Pakistanis to this day that nothing succeeds like success, but a failure will frequently lead to even one's own followers leaving. Benazir Bhutto mentioned this in writing of her experiences. Just as the early success of the rebels at Amritsar in April 1919 led to the spread of further risings through the surrounding district, the rebellion, using the widespread conspiracy to achieve yet more, could have spread throughout India if nothing had been done to make clear that the rebels would not be allowed to succeed in their aims. Just so, Dyer's action made clear that a strong Government was in control, and thus stopped the rot. People hanging out of trains yelled to trains coming in the other direction *"The Sahibs are shooting"* and with that and other such claims, the rebellion died.

In the Ghadr Mutiny, this was not the case. With the leaders, the mutinous troops and also the Ghadr groups getting ready to join in arrested, the Ghadr movement suffered a serious setback, but those who had not been caught took refuge in the United Provinces, from whence they carried out a campaign of assassination and outrage for some months. Part of that campaign was to continue to try to arouse the Indian troops and it was in tracking these men down that Pingle was caught. In the Punjab, the agents found tampering with the 22nd Cavalry were seized and given up to the authorities by the Sikh officers themselves.

Towards the end of 1914, a group of Hindu Bengalis had schemed with others to keep a cloth shop in Calcutta, in which arms could be hidden and provided for the revolutionaries. In 1915, a further group of Bengali revolutionaries, with German help, conspired to organise the revolution in Siam and other places in Bengal. They decided that funds would be raised by dacoities; in January and February, Rs. 40,000 were raised that way. Bholanath Chatterjee, had already been sent to Bangkok to get in touch with the conspirators there; Jitendranath Lahiri arrived in Bombay from Europe in March, bringing with him offers of German help and inviting the conspirators to send an emissary to Batavia to co-operate. At the meeting that was then held, it was decided that Naren Battacharaya should go to Batavia to discuss plans with the Germans. Taking the name of C. Martin, he set off in April, while another of the group, Abani Mukherjee, a Bengali, was sent to Japan. The leader, Jatin Mukherjee, went into hiding at Balasore, as he realised the police investigation was getting too close, in relation to the dacoities which had taken place in January and February.

In the same month of April, the S.S. Maverick set sail from San Pedro in California. Martin, on his arrival at Batavia, promptly got in touch with the German Consul who introduced him to one Theodore Helfferich, who informed him of a cargo of arms about to arrive at Karachi to assist the revolution. Martin then insisted on the arms coming round to Bengal having discussed it with the German Consul-General at Shanghai. The 'Maverick', however, failed to contact the schooner 'Annie Larsen' with its cargo of weapons and in consequence, never arrived in India.

Not only was Martin a bogus name, but a firm called 'Harry and Sons' was also invented as a contact. In June, Harry and Sons (in reality a business run by a well known revolutionary) wired to Martin for funds and from then on, Helfferich in Batavia sent remittances to Harry and Sons of Rs. 43,000 in various amounts between June and August 1915. When the amount had reached Rs. 30,000, the authorities discovered what was going on.

The Maverick's cargo of arms was meant to be divided between East Bengal: (actually to Hatia, to be worked by the Barisal Party); to Calcutta and to Balasore.

Up to that point, it might have appeared that the conspiracy between the Germans and the Bengalis smacked of a schoolboy escapade, but then it became more serious. Content that they had enough military strength to deal with the troops in Bengal, the conspirators were still apprehensive that reinforcements might come from outside, so they decided to cut the three main railways into Bengal by blowing up the principal railway bridges. Jatindra was to deal with the railway from Madras at Balasore, Bolanath Chaterjee, the Nagpur to Bengal railway at Chakradharpur and Harikumar Chakrabarti, the Eastern Bengal District. In Chakrabarti's case, he was told to go to Hatia where a large force was to collect arms and then march on Calcutta. The Calcutta party, under Naren Battacharaya and Bipin Ganguli, were then to take Fort William and after that, take Calcutta itself. The German officers in the Maverick were to raise and train armies, they themselves remaining in Eastern Bengal.

The planned unloading of the Maverick also required extreme secrecy.

Jadu Gopal Mukherjee apparently made contact with a zaminder at Rai Mangal to help with the unloading; the man promised to arrange men and lighters and to be ready for the boat, which would be hung with a string of lights - she would be arriving at night. It was hoped that the first distribution of arms would take place on 1$^{st}$ July 1915. Men sent to Atul Ghosh arrived to help, but the Maverick did not appear. They stayed for about ten days but still there was no news of her, nor did any news arrive from Batavia.

In the meantime, a Bengali arrived from Bangkok on 3$^{rd}$ July, with a message from Atmaram, a Punjabi, that the German Consul in Siam was sending a boat with a consignment of 5,000 rifles and ammunition and a lakh of rupees to Rai Mangal. Thinking that this was a substitute for the Maverick, the conspirators persuaded the Bengali to return to Bangkok via Batavia and tell Helfferich that the consignment of arms could be landed at Hatia (Sandwip), or Balasore in the Bay of Bengal, or Gokarna on the West coast of India, South of Karwar, but in July, Government learnt of the proposed landing of arms at Rai Mangal and took precautions. On 7$^{th}$ August, police searched Harry and Sons and made several arrests. The conspirators sent a warning telegram to Helfferich and Martin and a friend set off to discuss things with Helfferich in person. Their apprehensions were sound; the next police step was to search a branch of Harry and Sons at Balasore, and a revolutionary retreat at Kaptipada about 20 miles away. In the search, a map of the Sunderbans was found, together with a cutting from a Penang newspaper mentioning the 'Maverick'. A gang of Bengalis was rounded up; a fight ensued in which Jatin Mukharji who was the leader and Chittapraya Ray Chauduri were killed (the latter being the murderer of the police inspector who had been involved previously in arresting and giving evidence about other revolutionaries).

No more was heard of Martin for the rest of that year, but things had been so bad that the revolutionaries decided it was more sensible to go to Goa to telegraph Batavia. Even there the long arm of the C.I.D. stretched and the telegram to Martin was spotted on 17th December 1915. 'How doing – no news – very anxious – B Chatterton'. A search followed in Goa, which discovered two Bengalis one of whom was Bolanath Chaterjee. He killed himself in Poona Jail on 27th January 1916.

In Singapore, the Muslim part of a Regiment (in India, in an endeavour to help the different religions to live together, the British had mixed Regiments) mutinied, murdered their officers, ran amok in Civil Lines and were finally defeated and rounded up by a mixed team of volunteers and Naval blue-jackets. This was apparently yet another of the results of the Ghadr conspiracy in 1915.

As well as the the Illuminati inspiration in Germany, there was a similar Islamic conspiracy, Roshaniya, which may have been involved.

There were a number of ships in these German-linked schemes; belonging to Germans, chartered by them, or in some way linked to Germany, of which the 'Maverick' has been mentioned. She was a retired oil tanker of Standard Oil and belonged to a German firm, F. Jebson and Co. of San Francisco. She sailed with 25 officers and crew from San Pedro towards the end of April 1915 without cargo. There were also five 'Persians' signed on as waiters who were in reality Indians, shipped in by von Brincken, the German Consul at San Francisco and Ram Chandra, the successor to Har Dayal of the Ghadr, by then in Germany. One of the men, Hari Singh, a Punjabi, had quantities of Ghadr literature packed in trunks.

The Maverick's first stop was San Jose del Cabo, where she got clearance for Anjer in Java. The next step was to be the island of Socorro, 600 miles West of Mexico, where they intended meeting the schooner 'Annie Larsen' to tranship the armaments she had on board to the Maverick. The meeting was never effected and after a few weeks the Maverick sailed for Java via Honolulu. In Java she was searched by the Dutch authorities and found to be empty. The 'Annie Larsen' eventually arrived at Hoquiam in Washington State, where her cargo was seized by the United States authorities. The ship itself was also seized and claimed by Count von Bernstorff, the German Ambassador to Washington, but the claim that she was German property was disallowed by the United States Government.

Helfferich took care of the crew of 'Maverick' and finally sent them back to America, Martin being substituted for Hari Singh. On his arrival, the United States authorities arrested him.

A further ship involved in the Indo-German plot was the 'Harry S.', a schooner with an auxiliary crew. She intended sailing from Manila for Shanghai with a cargo of arms and ammunition, but the arms were discovered by the Customs authorities who made the master unload before sailing. Her destination then changed to Pontianak, but her engine broke down and she put into port in Celebes. On board were the two Germans, Captain Boehm and Wehde who, together with Hari Lal Gupta, were to have trained Indians for an invasion of Burma. All three men were sent to a State trial in Chicago in November 1917 (by which time the Americans had joined the war, although not by then with troops). The particular mission for Wehde was to convey $20,000 of German money to the Indian revolutionaries in India. Captain Boehm was shown to have been involved in Indian and Irish sedition together with two men on Count Bernstorff's staff, von Skal and von Igel, who had, amongst their duties, employed the Irish dissident John Devoy to work as a link between Ireland, Sinn Fein and Germany. These men were also in touch with the Indian revolutionaries.

The general intention seems to have been that the 'Harry S.' should go to Bangkok and land some of her arms which were to be hidden in a tunnel at Pakoh, on the Siam-Burma border, while Boehm got on with the training for the proposed invasion of Burma. Boehm had obeyed orders from Haram Lal Gupta in Chicago and was further instructed by the German Consul at Manila to see that 500 revolvers were landed at Bangkok and the rest of the consignment of 5,000 would be landed at Chittagong. The revolvers also had rifle stocks and were presumed to be Mauser pistols.

With the loss of 'Maverick', things became even more intricate. More steamers with arms were to be sent to the Bay of Bengal with money and arms, but the destination, on Martin's advice, was altered from Rai Mangal to Hatia. The ships were to be sent by the German Consul-General at Shanghai. The cargoes were to be, firstly, 20,000 rifles and 8,000,000 cartridges, 2,000 pistols, hand grenades and explosives and two lakhs of rupees. The other ship was to carry 19,000 rifles, 1,000,000 cartridges, hand grenades and explosives. The plans were discussed with Helfferich and the decision finally made was, that the steamer for Balasore would set out from Shanghai and go direct, while the second steamer would be a German ship lying in a Dutch port and would pick up its cargo at sea, giving sufficient arms and munitions to equip the Singapore mutineers, who would be at the Andaman Islands to capture Port Blair, pick up anarchists and convicts and other rebels, and then go on to Rangoon and raid that city. In order to assist the conspirators in Bengal, 66,000 Guilders were given by Helfferich to a Chinaman, with a letter for a Bengali at Penang, or at one of two addresses in Calcutta. The Chinaman was arrested and the money taken from him in Singapore.

The Bengali who had accompanied Martin was then sent to Shanghai to confer with the German Consul-General there, and was to return in the ship bound for Hatia, but he reached Shanghai with difficulty and was arrested there.

The Rowlatt Committee Report written on the investigation by three Indian and three British lawyers or judges, was completed on 15th April 1918, although not published in India until July and in Britain in October. Further outbreaks in and around Bengal, where the conspirators had fled to Chandergore, still went on. It is not surprising that when the Hunter Committee sat, Calcutta, where there had also been a rising in 1919, was not mentioned. It would be impossible, I believe, in the face of the trials in Lahore and in the United States in 1917, to claim that there was no evidence of conspiracy in Calcutta, Bengal and indeed all over India.

The comment of the writers of the Report was that *"Our examination of the German arms schemes suggests that the revolutionaries concerned were far too sanguine and that the Germans with whom they got in touch, were very ignorant of the movement of which they attempted to take advantage."*

This is an accurate description of the tendency of the Indian revolutionary conspirators to look at their own power using the magic so central to Indian thought, to persuade themselves that everyone was on their side, whereas most people, out of fear would agree with them if pressed, but the tendrils of conspiracy, although present and capable of movement, were not widely popular. With the War in progress, it was natural that the Germans would seek to exploit the opportunities offered by revolution in India, but they seem to have accepted the revolutionaries' assessment of their own capabilities too readily. This German-inspired movement was based on Berlin, where the leaders were paid conspirators on the Oriental Desk of the German High Command, including such men as Chattopadya, who was among that first small group of the Gandhi inspired Satyagraha movement which was foremost in the agitation that led up to the rebellion. As Michael O'Dwyer wrote *"The Germans had made their preparations with their characteristic thoroughness. Bernhardi in his book, 'Germany and the Next War', published towards the end of 1911, had described the revolutionary movement among the Hindus of Bengal and the growth of the Pan-Islamic agitation among Indian Mohammedans, a combination between which might, in his opinion, shake Britain's position throughout the East. In March 1914, the 'Berliner Tagblat' showed an uncanny knowledge of the secret organisations that were spreading in India with help from outside and had referred in particular to the Ghadr in California."*

Sir Michael put it clearly, *"The Germans in Berlin, and through their diplomatic, consular, and other more secret agencies in America and the East, were, as the evidence in the Lahore conspiracy case proved, in touch with these revolutionary organisations, directed or encouraged their activities and supplied them with funds and sometimes even arms. They directly assisted the Mohammedan movement from Kabul, which took shape in the 'Silk Letter' and other conspiracies* [see Chapter V – KHILAFAT] *and the Hindu-Sikh Ghadr movement from the Pacific and the Far East.*

*The latter was by far the most serious attempt to subvert British rule in India. It took many forms. One was to stir up rebellion in Bengal, the leaders, arms and ammunition being imported through Batavia and Siam. Another was to start a rising in Burma (then almost denuded of British troops and guarded mainly by Sikh military police, who were to be incited to revolt) by returning Ghadr emigrants from America, working into Burma through Siam. Both of these conspiracies were carefully planned under the direction of the German Consul-General at Shanghai, but both were frustrated by the vigilance of the Indian authorities ..."*

Today, we are met on our own television and radio programs with stories that are as simplistic and as rigorously anti-British as those of the First World War, and with a similar delight in believing any propaganda against the British of that time, however inaccurate or plain silly, like the 'Jewel in the Crown' or 'Gandhi' films. Looking deeper into the background and discovering the truth of the matter, is less palatable to the Germans and to the producers and writers of the present day, than the claims of Indians, frequently themselves with no more knowledge than the gullible acceptance of propaganda tales. The mass of evidence in the Rowlatt Report, covered in the same detailed way the difficulties of dealing with the widespread dacoities, threats of blackmail, murders (not just murders of policemen, but of witnesses, judges, people such as school masters endeavouring to prevent the indoctrination of children to the conspiracy attitudes), also the numberless criminal acts which had to go unpunished because, although there was evidence, no witnesses dared come forward.

The impetus for the Bengali involvement was the division of Bengal by Lord Curzon in 1905 and, almost worse for the proud Bengali, the removal of the seat of Government to Delhi from Calcutta. Part of the great Presidency had gone to Bihar, part to Assam, only the truncated part remaining as Bengal. From the 18th Century, the Bengal Presidency had been superior to Bombay and Madras and had been the seat of the decision-makers. Since the building of Fort William and then the building by the British of the magnificent town of Calcutta, founded by Job Charnock in 1690, Calcutta had taken pride of place in the East India Company and had been the seat of the Government of India. Its history was interlinked with that of the British development and unification of India, with its patchwork quilt of Princely States and of provinces under direct rule. To break this involvement with all the business, Governmental relationships and historical traditions and transfer Government to Delhi, may have been administratively sound, as Curzon seemed to think, but in terms of human feelings, it was most certainly not sound. A people prone to thoughts of grievance, involved previously in the conspiracy of the Mutiny, were easily activated to its continuation.

Delhi had been the capital of the Moghul Emperors. It was little more than a village in 1914, still with the Moghul buildings, the Jama Musjid, the Red Fort, and the old city, much as they had been when Taylor, in disguise, went into Delhi to open the gates and John Nicholson gave his life to win it back from the mutineers.

In 1911, when Lord Hardinge, the Viceroy, had gone in elegant procession on an elephant in Delhi and had been shot by the conspirators, it was still not the city we know today which was not completed until shortly before the official inauguration in 1931.

Today, the reason given for the change of capital is that Calcutta was too peripheral, geographically, but the change, remedied to an extent in 1911, was clearly in the historic sense Muslim-centred, so the new choice caused great anger and removed from Hindus much of their pride of place. It was, arguably, the moment when India (although always unruly) woke up.

In 1911, the waking-up had been due to the British vacillation in restoring the bulk of Bengal to its previous position. This time, since the areas brought back were to a large extent the Muslim East Bengal (roughly speaking, the present Bangladesh), Muslim sentiment was affronted. This attempt to remedy an unwise action caused more trouble, since in waking up the people of India, *"it seriously disturbed Indian belief in the ability of the British Government to adhere to a declared resolution"* (Sir Verney Lovett 'A History of the Indian Nationalist Movement' ibid p.88). The stability of the British Government up to then had been intrinsic to the British prestige and sense of security of the people.

The German involvement spread across India. One of the incidents which gives this support, is the cow killing riots which took place in the district surrounding Arrah in Bihar in 1917.

There had been rioting by Hindus in the area against the Muslim killing of cows for sacrifice at the time of the Muslim festival of Bakr-Id before, but by and large, they had been sorted out with the help of the District Officer involved. The Muslims, where agreements were not worked out, were subjected to violence on some occasions, as has been the case throughout India since the time of the Muslim incursions, on the receiving end of attacks by Hindus of low caste, incited and directed by higher caste men. In 1911 and 1912, there had been some outbreaks but the authorities had dealt with them and by 1915, precautions were relaxed. Again, a crowd of 5,000 armed Hindus appeared at a village; on this occasion, the authorities persuaded the Muslims to sell the cows to the Hindus and abandon their sacrifices, but the Hindus plundered another village. The following year, meetings were arranged at which the riots were carefully organised and although troops had been drafted into Patna district before the Bakr-Id festival, an armed mob of Hindus, in formation, attacked the military police at Kachanpur, where the police were compelled to open fire to protect the Muslim population. In another incident, 8,000 Hindus collected from 40 villages besieged the village of Jadapur, seized the cows and dispersed them. The Hindus thought that if they terrorised the Muslims and forced them to desist from their sacrifices, the Government would not intervene, provided that the public peace was not disturbed.

In 1917, careful precautions were taken but no information was received to suggest that the district of Shahabad would be affected. This secretiveness was similar to the Mutiny, and was started in, and largely affected, this area, where no cow-killing riots had taken place for a quarter of a century, but this district was to become the site of riots beside which the earlier ones were insignificant. The Government of Bihar and Orissa resolution passed on 18th June 1918 commented:

*"To find any parallel to the state of turmoil and disorder which then ensued, it is necessary to go back over a period of sixty years to the days of the great Mutiny."*

The first outbreak was at Ibrahimpur, south of Arrah, information being received of a dispute by District Officers at Arrah on 22nd September. The Muslim Sub-Divisional Officer and a Hindu landowner had arranged a compromise by which, goats as well as cows were to be sacrificed - some of the goats to be provided by the Hindus and some other concessions. (It should be made clear that the bulk of Hindus do in fact eat meat, frequently goat meat.) On the morning of the 28th, a large mob of Hindus, defying the agreement, appeared and attacked Ibrahimpur and two neighbouring villages (where cow sacrifice had been made without any problem before), and plundered the Muslim houses. As the Hindus had violated the agreement, the authorities allowed the Muslims to sacrifice the cows. Hindus in other villages acquiesced, but in order to avoid wanton offence, these sacrifices were performed in private. On the 30th, Ibrahimpur was attacked again by a large Hindu mob, houses were plundered, before armed police drove off the mob. Exceptionally, the Commissioner and the Deputy Inspector-General arrived - quiet prevailed for a time, but the air resounded with rumours and the Muslims were in a state of terror. Two days later, rioting took place again, this time covering an area of 40 miles, which came into the hands of the mobs. Every Muslim village or house which the mob could reach was attacked. Indian and British cavalry, in conjunction with British infantry, was moved in to protect the affected villages. Rioting continued for some time, with Arrah itself threatened with attack.

In most cases, Muslims fled when the mobs came near, but in two villages where they were more numerous, the Muslims attempted to defend themselves. They repeatedly beat off attacks although hopelessly outnumbered but finally they were overpowered.

By 7th October, 129 villages had been plundered in Shahabad district alone. Finally, troops established 13 posts in the area, connected by roads with cavalry and motorised vehicles and the rioting ceased, but the country remained in a state of ferment.

On 8th and 13th October, 30 villages were plundered in and around Gaya. With the mobs in control, Muslim suffering was beyond what can be described. Six days had elapsed before the local officers were able to get complete control. The police were inadequate, as were the troops, of which there was only a small body, which could only be obtained from a distance and in detachments. In such a wide area with bad communications, it was difficult to move soldiers, who were up against rioters knowing all the little dykes and paths which are like an intricate puzzle, the clue to which was unavailable to anyone but the inhabitants, who disappeared before they could be caught. This was an area of rice fields and small areas under cultivation which could not be ridden over or driven across, made up of waterlogged fields and narrow embankments along which the rioters could effectively melt away as the troops approached. There was something of a nightmarish quality about the situation which it was almost impossible to control, while the feeling of the troops attempting to protect the Muslims, and the Muslims themselves, was almost sinister in its uncontrollable menace.

Needless to say, the Muslims of Patna and Gaya were near to panic and, as at Amritsar in 1919, there is no doubt that if the rioting had gone on much longer the whole Province of Bihar would have been ablaze and the Eastern Districts of the United Provinces would also have been affected.

It needs to be realised that the disturbances had been carefully and skilfully organised. The religious differences had been settled and nowhere had the Muslims offered any provocation, but (again as in the Mutiny, though then it was chapattis that were used) snowball letters inciting the Hindus to loot certain villages on fixed dates came to light and there was evidence that rioters had operated on a definite plan. Further, they had been instructed on the lengths to which they should go. Murder was not included except to overcome resistance. Once again telegraph wires were cut in order to make intelligence reports impossible; damage to Government property was avoided (unlike in 1919), Post Offices, canal headquarters and other places where money was kept were not affected (unlike the conspiracies in Bengal and the Ghadr movement in the Punjab). It was deduced that the object was to show that the movement was purely religious and anti-Muslim. The main idea was to weld together the Hindus by the emotive issue of cow-killing which the rioters were led to believe they could stop by behaving as they did. They felt safe in their behaviour because of the War and because British rule was so weak as a result. Some of the snowball letters gave assurance that German and Bengali succour would arrive and the rioters of Piru attacked with cries of 'British rule is gone'. As in Amritsar a couple of years later, it was believed that the troops would be unable to suppress them and that they had no ammunition or had been forbidden to fire. To the people going to the meeting at Jallianwalla Bagh, much the same was said.

Throughout Northern India, the sufferings of the Muslims caused widespread and deep feeling. These people had not been politically motivated previously, but this was the beginning of what was shown in the Ram Lila and Moharrum festivals in the United Provinces.

In 1943, in the District of Kangra, my life and that of my husband was threatened because my husband, in order to solve the cow-killing problem, licensed an abattoir, so that cows could be bought, with the result that the Hindus would find this profitable, rather than the animals being removed from the streets without payment. The threats continued for some months, stemming from a Hindu Association in Bengal (Anyar Sang). When the British left India, pockets of Muslims, as in Bihar, were brutally slaughtered; bodies being pushed into wells or indiscriminately got rid of.

In Kangra District, all the Muslims were collected in safety - the following morning they had all been killed.

Revolutionary crime in Bihar and Orissa had been going on since 1906. The Arrah cow-killing riots were only a part of the movement; interesting because they indicate the link between German influences and the existing conspiracy movement. Bihar and Orissa had been incorporated into Western Bengal, but it was not an action of the British at their wisest, since the two provinces did not speak the same language and did not have the same traditions. Bengalis, intellectually superior, tended to get the Government posts as pleaders and in offices of all kinds and there were a number living in Bihar and Orissa. However, with the King's speech in December 1911, they had been separately constituted.

As to cow-killing in India today, half-starved cattle no longer needed are driven many miles to a festival where cow-killing is allowed and the skeletons of those cattle too weak to complete the journey litter the roadsides.

## Chapter V
## KHILAFAT

Sir Michael O'Dwyer had been appointed Lieutenant-Governor of the Punjab, following Sir Louis Dane, in 1912. His popularity with the Princes (he had been at Hyderabad for some years) and among the ordinary people, was secure. He was an outspoken Irishman brought up on a farm in Tipperary, one of a family of nine sons and five daughters. To the end of his life, he spoke with an Irish accent and *"my heart has always gone out to those who live and die by the land."* He was a Catholic, but nonetheless *"the atmosphere I was brought up in, though essentially Irish, showed no signs of racial or religious feeling."* In fact, the divisions that have continued to this day in Ireland are as politically motivated, and as little based in Irish society, as the feelings that overwhelmed India. The political propaganda increased in India during his lifetime, not only from 1912 to 1919 when he retired, but to the end of his life, for he lived in India after his retirement. His father had been shot dead by what they then called 'hooligans' - what we now call the Real I.R.A.

The majority of rural Mohammedans in the Punjab and their leaders took little interest in any but local politics, being chiefly concerned to protect themselves against exploitation by the more astute urban Hindus. Some Mohammedans had, however, as the result of the propaganda of the Sultan Abdul Hamid, and later of Enver Pasha, become imbued with Pan-Islamic aspirations.

The neutral attitude of Great Britain in the Turco-Italian and Balkan Wars of 1911-13 had caused some resentment and a speech by Prime Minister Asquith in November 1912 was interpreted as showing British hostility to Turkey and Islam. The views of this section of opinion were expressed in a very fiery newspaper 'Zamindar', edited by a notorious firebrand.

Zafar Ali Khan had started subscriptions for the Turkish Red Crescent in 1912, and had himself gone to Constantinople to present the Grand Wazir with some of the money collected. On his return, the tone of his paper became more and more anti-British, and in 1913, after many warnings, he was compelled to forfeit the Security Deposit under the Press Act. Higher Security was demanded and furnished; the paper reappeared, but again indulged in disloyal and inflammatory articles, which led to the confiscation not only of the Security, but also of the press. The Chief Court upheld this order. Early in 1914, the Turkish Consul-General came to Lahore to present the Badshahi (Imperial) Mosque with a carpet sent by the Sultan of Turkey as a mark of his gratitude.

A few weeks later, he was followed by two Turkish doctors of the Red Crescent Society. Thus <u>up to the opening of the war</u> (author's underlining, to make absolutely clear the fact that the insidious German-Turkish misinformation was already in place by 1914) there were intrigues going on between Turkey and a small but bitter and unscrupulous Pan Islamist faction in Northern India. The leaders of this anti-British section in the Press were Zafar Ali Khan of the 'Zamindar' at Lahore, Muhammad Ali Khan of the 'Comrade' and his brother Shauket Ali at Delhi; and they made no secret of their sympathy with Turkey both before and after the outbreak of the War. The great mass of intelligent Mohammedans realised from the start that Turkey, by joining our enemies, would bring about her own ruin and at the same time create a very difficult situation for Indian Mohammedans.

John Buchan had pinpointed the plans emanating from Constantinople, from the vast Turkish Empire of Mesopotamia, Egypt, Syria, Arabistan and Armenia in 'Greenmantle'. *"There is a dry wind blowing through the East, and the parched grasses wait the spark. The wind is blowing towards the Indian frontier ... I have reports from agents everywhere."*

So said Sir Walter Bullivant, the Buchan character of the book written in 1916, since Bullivant was the Head of Intelligence. Previously, when Parvus was working in Constantinople from 1910 to 1915, various intrigues had occurred which led to the Pan-Islamic movements working with Parvus, with the Sultan and the Community of Union and Progress (the Young Turks) of which Parvus was also a member, Pan-Islam and the infiltration of arms into India.

Where did the immediate Turkish subjection to Germany come from? Not only was Parvus (of whom, much more, later in this book – the man who was the pattern for 'Ivery' in Buchan's 'Greenmantle') involved, being in Turkey from 1910 to 1915, but Enver Pasha, one of the triumvirate who started the Young Turks (with all its ramifications as the C.U.P. in 1908), was military attaché in Berlin in 1909-11, having taken up his pro-German stance prior to 1905. Having deposed the Sultan in 1909 and after fighting in the Italo-Turkish war at Benghazi in 1912, he became a Lieutenant-Colonel in 1913, and in June 1913, forced the (by then) ex-Sultan, to hand over power to the Young Turks; by January 1914 he was Minister for War. If we take the times that we know Parvus was in Turkey, we find that they overlapped there.

Parvus was becoming 'extremely rich' during his time in Turkey. It is likely that he and Enver Pasha were working hand in glove and, since he is referred to as Parvus of Wilhelm II and the Sultan, it is probable that the Sultan, Abdul Hamid, was kept in position because of his use as a propaganda figure with which to stir up the Muslim world.

Asquith's speech in November 1912 had been interpreted as showing British hostility to Turkey. Though the Caliphate was no longer the spiritual centre of Islam, it was still the head of the Islamic political world.

In the Punjab, the steady men of loyalty and discretion, men like Sir Umar Hayat Khan, realised as soon as Turkey entered the war on the side of the enemies of Britain, that she would suffer for her foolishness, but India, with what is now Pakistan, was likely to behave in the way that countries will, whose characters tend towards excitableness. Mohammed and Shaukat Ali Khan began to act strongly and noisily.

When, In January 1920, Churchill was accused by the maverick Lloyd George of having 'driven Turkey into the war by seizing the German ships and later by bombing the Dardanelles forts' Churchill refuted it. He said, *"It is of course, true that the Turkish ships were taken over, as our margin of superiority was so small that we could not afford to do without them. Still less could we afford to see them transferred to a potentially hostile power."* The explanation continued, *"British and German fleets would have been within one or two of each other"*. The following telegram, now in our possession, sent by the German Admiralty to the 'Goeben' at Messina on the 4th August, 1914, ran as follows: *"An alliance has been signed with Turkey proceed at once to Constantinople."*

The Young Turks, or the Committee for Union and Progress which the movement was also called, started in 1900; the main membership was from the higher echelons of the army in which were many of the leaders of the Arabs who then developed their own movement. Among these was Feisal, Lawrence's most admired friend. There is no doubt that the Young Turks saw their future with the Germans; reinforced when war started, for Russia was attacking Turkey in the North and the British were on the side of the Russians. Enver Pasha, the Commander in Chief of the Turkish Army, a Pole, was close to the Germans, spoke German well enough to translate for the Kaiser when he came to visit Turkey, and worked happily with an army, officered to a large extent by the Germans, who also armed it.

The Arab rebellion against the Turkish overlord was legitimate in the sense that it was a necessary and responsible action if it were to achieve independence from a fairly brutal power – much as today most of us would think of Kurdistan - a reasonable aim. The Indian movement was something different, in that the British rule was Indo-British and the aim had been developed hand in hand; the aim was already there when Queen Victoria made her speech after the Mutiny.

Turkish rule, as Lawrence put it in 'Seven Pillars of Wisdom', was '*gendarme* rule', the hierarchic conceptions of Islamic and the Pan Islamic theories of the old Sultan, Abdul Hamid. His fall and the Young Turk movement altered this and made the revolts of the Arabs possible - possible, but not united. So, at a time when Western Europe was beginning to climb out of xenophobic nationality into internationality and to rumble with wars far removed from race, Western Arabia began to climb out of Catholicism into national politics, and to dream of wars for self-government and self-sovereignty, instead of for faith or dogma.

Lawrence and the Arab Revolt become even more important to Britain in the courting of Islam, but in the propaganda of today, it is typical that Lawrence should have been made out a homosexual. In real life, writing to Graves about his rape, he said that he felt his integrity had been harmed – he was noticeably broken by it as one might expect. Thus, in terms of Enver Pasha and the C.U.P. it is clear that, just as with the conspiracy in India, everything was in place for Turkey's entry into the War. Churchill's pragmatic actions were important, but not direct causes.

The British were not entirely ignorant of the dangers. They attacked the Dardanelles, intending not only to let the Russians have their access to the warm water seas, but to stop the German incursion through Turkey to move through Mesopotamia to the South. The Indian Army was therefore sent up through the Persian Gulf, whose egress is so close to Karachi, to attack Baghdad. The attack was unsuccessful and the army had to retire to Kut, where it was hemmed in under siege.

The siege of Kut was a catastrophe. From 5th December 1915 to 29th April 1916, it continued; food ran out, the river rose in its usual flood time and the city was inundated. Arabs arrived and were drafted in to help digging a mud wall to prevent the river running over the town, but the troops were reduced to eating their animals. Various efforts at relief were made – the 29th Punjabis were nearly successful. The 13th Division under Major General Maude came near to relief, seeing off some of the Turks. General Gorringe approached across open ground with infantry under heavy fire, but was twice unsuccessful; the Royal Navy endeavoured to approach through the difficulties of the floods, but the Arabs, said that they knew that Kut would not be relieved, that the garrison would fall and knowing the methods used by the Turks against those who helped the British, began to disappear.

It was known that the Turks were themselves in some difficulty, as their home province of Anatolia was under threat from the Russians, who had just then taken Erzerum, the capital of Kurdistan (with some involvement by Lawrence, as Graves puts it in his biography of Lawrence, *"Colonel Buchan's novel 'Greenmantle' has in it more than a flavour of truth"*). Another 'arrangement', as Graves puts it, was planned in the hope that Lawrence would be able to bribe the Turks to allow the British Army to withdraw. Said Lawrence: *"Bribes would be useless for they would merely encourage the Turks and the chief Young Turk being a nephew of Enver Pasha was not short of money"*. Lawrence had plans of his own, for already the Arabs were beginning to revolt. He hoped to get in touch with the Ruwala tribe in Northern Syria, hold up river traffic and raid supply columns, until the Turkish army before Kut was itself under siege and cut off. The inflexible attitude of the British Generals meant that they would not help and Lawrence was unable to carry out his offensive.

It was at this moment that Lawrence was asked to intervene with a suggestion of bribery. *"Meanwhile our government had relented, and for reasons not unconnected with the fall of Erzerum, sent me to Mesopotamia to see what could be done by indirect means to relieve the beleaguered garrison. The local British had the strongest objection to my coming; two of their Generals were good enough to explain to me that my mission (which they did not really know) was dishonourable to a soldier (which I was not)."* Liddell Hart (Lawrence's biographer) asked Lawrence in 1932 how this came about: *"I had put the Grand Duke Nicholas in touch with certain disaffected Arab officers in Erzerum; did it through the War Office and our Military Attaché in Russia. So the War Office thought I could do the same thing over Mespot. and accordingly wired out to Clayton (Lawrence's Chief in Cairo)".*

Halil Pasha, the Turkish Commander, was offered one million Sterling in silver if it would help the negotiations for the surrender of Kut, whose garrison by then were starving.

A letter to Halil Pasha was passed across the lines from Townsend, which told the Turkish Commander-in-Chief that he had been authorised to negotiate the surrender of Kut, asking for six days armistice and permission to receive supplies of food from downstream. Supplies were needed for the 19,000 military and the civilian population, 15 of whom were dying every day from starvation. Halil Pasha had already commented on his respect for the courage of the garrison in their defence of Kut. Townsend asked for permission for the British and Indian troops to leave for India.

Halil Pasha replied with a repeated agreement that the troops had carried out their duties heroically, but that the garrison would be treated as prisoners-of-war and would be given food and transport to Baghdad. They would also get the pay of prisoners-of-war. He himself was leaving at once by motorboat and suggested that Townsend should join him to discuss the arrangements for surrender. Townsend, on leaving by motorboat, was fired on and returned to Kut. Information having been sent to Halil Pasha, Townsend and the other officers left by motorboat again the following morning. Townsend had already informed Sir Percy Lake, Chief-of-Staff to Beauchamp Duff, the Commander-in-Chief of the Indian Army, that he did not think the negotiations should be conducted by himself but by Lake. Lake's reply was that, as the man on the spot, Townsend should carry on.

The negotiations continued over several days while people were dying of starvation – when the Turks produced food it was simply biscuit. A further million was added to increase the offer for the release of the garrison, whose wounded and sick were handed over to the British after examination by a Turkish doctor. Artillery requested by one of the Turkish officers produced some ire, since it had already been destroyed.

The deaths in the siege amounted to: killed 537, died of wounds 488, died of disease 721, 247 Arabs had been killed and 633 wounded inside the town, but the numbers rose on the march into captivity. A total of 5,746 of the Garrison died in the siege or afterwards in captivity. Among the negotiators were Lawrence and A. P. Herbert the Member of Parliament. The furore it caused in Britain roused Lord Northcliffe and Lord Bentinck to start and fund a Committee for the Prisoners-of-War in Turkey;

in terms of ill-treatment, it was considered in much the same way as the Japanese prisoners of war in the Second World War although the prisoners were not forced to build a railway; Lord Hardinge, retired from his Viceroyalty, explained in the House of Lords that the commitment of the Government of India to other war zones was the reason for the necessary effort and supplies not being sent to Kut. Two people who had been involved in the Prisoners of War Committee were later to be present in Amritsar – my mother as an unmarried girl, my father, invalided home from India. The author's father-in-law, an officer of the Queens Own Royal West Kents, was in such poor condition after the armistice that he had to be driven back across Europe in an ambulance. He did survive but it took over a year for him to recover.

At the time of the surrender, the strength at Kut amounted to 13,309, of whom 3,248 were Indian non-combatant camp-followers; a total of about 12,000 British and Indian troops were taken into captivity where over 4,000 of them died. Of the British rank and file, 1,700 or seventy per cent died or were never heard of again. Of the Indian rank and file, 1300 are known to have died in captivity. Officers had been separated from their soldiers, with the resulting loss of morale. Exact statistics of Indian survivors are not available, but in 1924, Indians were still turning up in their villages.

Aubrey Herbert asked for a date for a debate on the Mesopotamian campaign and reluctantly, a Commission was set up. One important point later made in the House of Lords' Debate on the Treatment of General Dyer was that representation was provided for all the officers involved in the Kut disaster. The Hunter Commission did not insist on representation for General Dyer. The Debate giving rise to the Kut Commission took place in 1916, just prior to Edwin Montagu going to India to give her what he believed to be the wish of Indians, a further step in the loosening of the ties by which the British ruled India and the further involvement of Indians in the Governing of India.

This defeat had a painful and disastrous influence on the army of India, affected always by defeat to an extent which the more phlegmatic British are not and was to weaken trust in the British. In terms of propaganda, Kut was a serious matter for the Indian Army. Barkatulla, on the Oriental Desk in Berlin, was inventing propaganda with the intention of undermining faith in the British Government among Indian prisoners-of-war; and among the papers left at Kut was an example – it may not have been written by Barkatulla, but many similar papers were written by co-workers. The intention was to spread the claims already made in the Punjab and down in Meerut by Pingle and Rash Behari, to undermine the Army of India.

Oh Dear Indian Brethren

You understand the fact well that God had created this war for setting India free from the hands of the cruel English. This is the reason why all the Rajas and Nawabs, with the help of brave Indian soldiers are at present creating disturbances in all parts of India and forcing the English out of the country. Consequently not one Englishman is to be seen in the North West Frontier of

Indian districts of Saad, Chakdara, Kohmond and Kohat. Brave Indians have killed several of their officers at Singapore, Secunderabad and Meerut cantonments. Many of the Indian soldiers have on several occasions joined our allies the Turks. Germans and Austrians are merely fighting for the freedom of our country from the English and you, being Indian are fighting against them and causing delay.

On seeing your degraded position one feels blood in the eyes that you have not got tired of their disgraceful conduct and hatred for you. You should remember how cruelly Maharajah Ranjit Singh of the Punjab and Sultan Tip were treated by the British Government, and now when our beloved country is being released from their cruel clutches, you should no longer delay the freedom of your country and try and restore happiness to the souls of your forefathers as you come from the same heroic generation to which the brave soldiers of the Dardanelles and Egypt belong. You must have heard of the recent fighting in the Dardanelles when Lord Howard was wounded and the cowardly Lord Kitchener ran away at night taking only the British soldiers with him and leaving the Indians behind. The Indian soldiers on seeing this murdered all their British officers and joined the Turks. Nearly everywhere we are finding that our Indian soldiers are leaving the British. Is it not a pity that you still go on assisting them? Just consider that we have left our homes and are fighting for only fifteen or twenty rupees a subaltern of only twenty or twenty five years old is drawing a handsome amount as salary from Indian resources while our old Risalder and Subadar majors are paid nothing like him – and even a British soldier does not salute them. Is that all the respect and share of wealth we should get for the sake of which we should let them enjoy our country? For instance see how many of you Indian soldiers were killed during the battle of Ctesiphon and there is nobody to look after the families of the dead and wounded. Brothers, just compare the pay that a British soldier draws with that which you get. Bulgaria gave them several defeats; Ireland and the Transvaal have left them but you will already know this. H.M. the Sultan's brave Turkish forces which were engaged on the Bulgar frontier before are now coming over to this side in large numbers for the sake of setting the Indians at liberty. We were forced by the British to leave our beloved country and to live in America, but on hearing the news that our country was being freed from English hands, we came over here via Germany – and found our Indian brethren fighting against our friends the Turks. Brethren, what is done is done, and now you should murder all your officers and come over and join H M Sultan's Army like our brave soldiers did in Egypt. All the officers of this force and Arabs have received orders from H. M. Sultan that any Indian soldiers irrespective of any caste, Sikh, Rajput, Mahratta, Ghurkha, Pathan, Shiah or Syed, who comes to join the Turks should be granted handsome pay and land for cultivation if he would like to settle in the Sultan's territory. So you must not miss the chance of murdering your officers and joining the Turks to help them to restore their freedom."

This Turkish/German pamphlet linked into the conspiracies; the claim against the Princes was the reverse of the truth since many of them were raising and training corps to fight on the side of their Government. Most Indians were on the side of their Government and wholeheartedly endeavoured to defend the country from the Germans.

Anyone who knows about the First World War will know that, like the Attenborough film 'Gandhi', almost the entire leaflet from Kut was untrue. Kitchener did not abandon the Indian troops at the Dardanelles, where Ataturk, with a German technical adviser, had beaten back the Allied forces. In fact, everyone was removed safely, with the exception of one wounded man. At Meerut the mutiny had been scotched; at Singapore it was true that there had been a mutiny of Muslim soldiers who acted on the Ghadr claims and killed their officers, but it had been put down.

Yet there was potential for trouble in India. Mohammed Ali Khan, through his newspaper 'The Comrade', made no secret of the brothers' sympathy with Turkey and many men of the Indian Army were Punjabi Muslims. The influential Mohammedans did what they could to influence Turkey against joining the war, but they were seeking to fight the influence of Germany and the clever agent Parvus. No persuasion was of any use. India was to be racked by Pan-Islam to a varying extent throughout the war years and until the Turkish Treaty was finally settled in 1922, when Kemal Pasha took over.

The British Government gave assurance that the Holy Places, Mecca and Medina, would be safe and that it was the Muslims' duty as loyal subjects of the King Emperor to help in the struggle with his enemies, but once again the insidious destruction of patriotism and loyalty, by the Socialist Internationals or the Peace Movement and Pan-Islam demanded a greater loyalty which obliterated the loyalties of nation and birth.

Despite the assurance, the Pan-Islamist section of the population of India and particularly the Punjab continued its intrigues with Turkey, Arabia, Germany and Afghanistan, endeavouring to stir up rebellion amongst Indian Muslims and mutiny amongst Muslim soldiers by fanatical appeals. Finally, when the Central Powers were defeated, they joined hands with the Hindu-Mohammedan Entente – as exemplified in the 1919 rebellion.

So far as Turkey was concerned, Enver Pasha was still continuing with the activities which he had undertaken over the previous years. He commanded the Turkish (German) Army in the Caucasus from 1915 to 1916 and then fled via Odessa to Germany in 1918. He was back again in 1919, fighting with General Denikin, the White Russian, against the Bolsheviks. He then moved to the Asian Bureau in Moscow, to which the Indian politicians also moved when they left the Oriental Desk in Berlin. The sinister underlying conspiracies went on and he was killed in 1922, fighting for

Pan-Turanianism, a Turkish movement supporting Pan-Islam, the German-Turkish plan for the take over of India and Asia using the extended Constantinople-Baghdad-Mosul Railway.

However, the British efforts which finally defeated Turkey also defeated the Pan-Islamic conspiracy and after these schemes had been brought to naught by the defeat of the Central Powers, the seditionists joined hands with the Hindu revolutionaries in a so-called Hindu-Mohammedan Entente. This temporary union led to a last desperate effort to shake the British power in the East. It led to the Punjab and Bombay outbreak of April 1919, and to the more serious Moplah Rebellion of 1921–1922, but after spreading disorder and bloodshed for years, it speedily collapsed when the Indian Government at last allowed the law to take its course.

The protagonists of the Entente, Gandhi and the Ali brothers, were sentenced in 1921 and 1922 to long terms of imprisonment for the sedition and incitements to rebellion in which they had openly gloried.

Sir Michael wrote: *"How much bloodshed and misery would have been saved if this step had been taken three years earlier, when the simultaneous outbreaks in the Punjab, Bombay, Calcutta, and Peshawar showed how deep-seated was the conspiracy and how wide its ramifications! But firm action at that time might have disturbed the 'peaceful atmosphere' which Mr. Montagu and Lord Chelmsford were then hoping to create for the successful launching of their scheme of diarchy. Moreover from 1919 to 1922, Gandhi and the Khilafat were the two bogies, of which the Indian authorities were in mortal terror. Yet the 'bogies' vanished on the first contact with a Court of Justice.*

*The removal of the leaders gave an opportunity for the traditional hostility between Hindu and Mohammedan 'hating one another for the love of God,' to reassert itself in an acute form, and, as the authority of Government has been steadily sapped – or openly defied - the tension has within the last two years, caused widespread disorder and bloodshed. The prevention of communal strife is now the most serious problem of the Indian Government.*

*The summary action of the new Turkish Republic in deposing the Sultan, abolishing the Khilafat, and sending the last of the historic house of Osman to wander, a penniless fugitive in foreign lands, has given the final blow to the Pan-Islamist Movement in India; and those who so long made use of it for their own selfish ends are now being called on to give an account of their doubtful stewardship of the funds collected from the Faithful. To these, Muhammad Ali has recently given the assurance that the accounts will be rendered in Heaven!*

*Thus ends the movement that for a dozen years had been a 'bogy' to the Government of India. But during the war one had to take it seriously, and one of the first measures I took in the Punjab was to restrict Zafar Ali Khan to his native village, and to keep him there till the end of the War.*

*About the same time, the Government of India, on my representation and that of other Heads of Provinces, similarly restricted the Ali brothers to a place near Delhi, and when they abused such liberty as was left to them by seditious incitements in the troubles of 1919, they were interned far from their homes.*

*Such executive measures were not only justified by the state of war, but as events proved, were in the interests of the person concerned. Zafar Ali Khan, after his release, resorted to his old methods and in 1920, was sentenced to five years' imprisonment for the most flagrant incitements to rebellion. Perhaps he will find comfort in the fact that the Punjab Legislature has recently carried, against official opposition, a resolution for his release. He is now at liberty once more, but is a spent force.*

*Muhammad Ali, in September 1921, after the outbreak of the Moplah rebellion, was similarly convicted and sentenced to two years imprisonment. He is again at large, but his efforts to galvanise the dead and buried Khilafat agitation into new life have fallen hopelessly flat. I knew both men personally. Indeed, Muhammad Ali, in 1911 at Indore, consulted me, being also a son of Oxford, as to whether he should take up a post in a Native State under my jurisdiction, or start his paper, the 'Comrade'. As he had practically arranged with some friends about the latter project, I advised him to persevere with it. At first the tone was extremely humorous, but not anti-British. It was probably the reversal in December 1911, of the partition of Bengal, in deference to Bengali Hindu agitation that drove him and other young Mohammedans into opposition to a Government that they thought had played them false. It was the irony of fate that I was subsequently one of the chief objects of his journalistic attacks.*

*Both he and Zafar Ali Khan were born journalists and brilliant masters of that frothy oratory that appeals to an Indian audience. Your Indian, unfortunately, cannot escape being drawn into the vortex of politics, and lacking balance and self-restraint, his eager ambition to make his mark, leads him in journalism into reckless attacks on the Government and often into seditious incitements. This is also good business for, as a friend wrote to me from India the other day 'It pays to go to jail, and you can't sell a newspaper which doesn't throw mud at Government and its officials.'*

*The prompt action taken against seditious propaganda in the Press or on the platform, and the hearty co-operation of leading Mohammedans, urban and rural, such as Nawab Bahram Khan and Sir Fateh Ali Khan (both since dead), Sir Umar Hayat Khan and Sir Khuda Bakhsh Khan Tiwana, Maulvi Sir Rahim Bakhsh, Chief Minister of the Bahawalpur State, Sayed Sir Mehdi Shah, and the great Pirs or religious leaders of the North and West Punjab, kept the Punjab Mohammedans as a whole steady and enabled us to recruit 180,000 Mohammedans for the Army from 1915 onwards. The main trouble was from the Pan-Islamists from outside the Province.*

*In the Christmas week of 1914, soon after Turkey had entered the War, a Mohammedan Educational Congress was held at Rawalpindi. Certain Mohammedan firebrands attended this from down country, Abul Kalam Azad, Muhammad Ali and others; but their efforts to push their violent propaganda were frustrated by the sensible and loyal men of the Punjab. Some of them went to Peshawar, others stopped at Lahore on their way back and lectured to young and impressionable Mohammedans, students at tea parties in some of the Lahore Colleges. We only heard of this visit after they had left.*

*A few weeks later, in February 1915, fifteen young Mohammedan students, many of them sons of men of staunch loyalty and good position, disappeared from Lahore, and at the same time some Frontier students also disappeared from Peshawar and Kohat. The Punjabis made their way by devious routes, with the assistance of the secret Pan-Islamic organisation, to the Wahabi[23] sect of the Mujahaddin, known as the Hindustani Fanatics, beyond the North West Frontier, which for nearly one hundred years has been receiving funds and recruits from India and in return has inspired many local risings against the infidel British Government and many murders of British officials. The Amir of the Fanatics after a time passed on the students to Kabul. There they were first imprisoned, but afterwards on the strong representations of Sirdar Nasrullah, the Amir's brother, and the anti-British section at Kabul, they were released and given allowances. They soon got in touch with the Indian revolutionary leaders, Mahendra Pratap and Barkatulla, the joint Presidents of the 'Provisional Indian Government,' who, with German help, had found their way to Kabul and were using it as an advanced base to foment trouble for the British in India.*

*Mahendra Pratap was a wealthy landowner in the United Provinces and brother-in-law of a loyal Sikh Maharaja in the Punjab. He had gone to Europe just after the outbreak of the War; had there fallen under the influence of Har Dayal, so successful in corrupting others, and through him had obtained an interview with the Kaiser who, impressed by a megalomania akin to his own, had sent him with Barkatullah on a mission to Kabul. Mahendra Pratap on arrival at Kabul, claimed to have had interviews not only with the Kaiser, but also with the Sultan, the ex-Khedive, Enver Pasha and with them 'To have set right the problems of India and Asia!' With the same ends, a combined Turco-German Mission arrived in Kabul about the same time. The runaway students bringing news of the state of affairs in the Punjab, which they represented as in the throes of the Ghadr rebellion, were made much of by these anti-British plotters. In fact they were described as 'the moving units of this work'. A few of them died a miserable death in Kabul; others were sent on dangerous missions to Central Asia, Japan and Persia. Three of the latter, together with the notorious Sikh revolutionary, Dr. Mathra Singh, afterwards hanged for rebellion and murder, fell into the hands of our Russian allies on the Persian borders, and were made over to the local British authorities. Mathra Singh and one of the students were on a mission to China and Japan; the other two were the bearers of letters to the Sultan of Turkey.*

*Of these, one was, I think, shot for treason and espionage by order of a local Court Martial in Persia, and two were brought back to Lahore early in 1917. Men have been hanged for less than they were guilty of; but more out of regard for their friends than for themselves, I gave these men a conditional pardon. The information*

---

23  This sect is the root of the Taliban and possibly of the Roshaniyah.

*they gave of their wanderings in the prosecution of Pan-Islamic, German and Afghan intrigue was most useful and threw light on the 'Silk Letter' plot.*

The Silk Letter plot became overt in 1916, though it arose out of the steps being gradually put into place before the war. It was uncovered through the affection felt for Sir Michael O'Dwyer, the Lieutenant-Governor.

A servant who was with two young men in Kabul, the sons of a fine Mohammedan Khan, kept coming and going and aroused the suspicions of the old man who was a friend of Sir Michael. The Khan questioned the servant, who admitted that he brought something secret from Kabul and produced the famous 'silk letters', written neatly in Persian on lengths of yellow silk and sewn inside his garment. *"The coat"* wrote Sir Michael, *"had been left for safety in a Native State. It was produced under the Khan's threats. The Khan cut out the 'silk letters'. Not being a Persian scholar he could not make much of them, but realising that they concealed some inner meaning, he took them to the Commissioner of the Division. The latter sent them on to me, saying he thought they were utter nonsense.*

*I did not grasp their full meaning at first, but understood enough to satisfy myself that they revealed a plot with wide ramifications. I passed them on to the Criminal Intelligence Department, where Sir Charles Cleveland speedily unravelled the whole mystery. The letters were communications from two Maulvis, Obeidullah and Ansari, who had filled important posts in the Deoband (United Provinces) School of Theology, had preached and written there and in Delhi in favour of Jihad (Holy War), and to realise that object, had gone to Kabul in 1915, visiting the Hindustani Fanatics on the way. At Kabul they were well received, got in touch with the Turco-German Mission, with the Indian revolutionaries, Mahendra Pratap and Barkatulla and set the wires working. Ansari had already gone to Arabia and returned to Kabul. The silk letters were dated July 1916, and were addressed to a trustworthy agent in Sind, who was enjoined to send them on by a reliable messenger, or to convey them in person to a famous Mohammedan religious leader, Mahmud Hasan who had already gone from Deoband to Mecca to promote the conspiracy there."*

The letters described the progress of the movement in Kabul and India, the arrival of the German and Turkish Mission, the departure of the former, the formation of the 'Provisional Government' and the activities of the students. They then outlined the plan for forming the 'Army of God', to drive out the British through an alliance of all Islamic rulers.

The Provisional Government had, earlier in 1916, gone so far as to dispatch a Mission with letters signed by Mahendra Pratap, to the Russian Governor-General in Turkestan and even to the Tsar (this letter was engraved on a gold plate) urging Russia to throw over her alliance with Britain and assist in the invasion of India – for a consideration. This Mission was turned back by the Russian Imperial Government, but the Bolshevists, when they rose to power in 1917, were quick to grasp the value of this means for giving Britain a stab in the back and have since employed it with great persistence and some success.

Prior to this, the German Government in Berlin, with the assistance of its expert staff of Indian traitors, had addressed similar letters written in faultless Urdu, sumptuously bound and signed by the Imperial Chancellor (von Bethmann-Hollweg) to the leading Indian Princes, promising them wonderful concessions if they shook off the yoke of Great Britain. Many of these letters, which we saw later, were intercepted by us when a German Mission was captured in North Persia, and doubtless they now form interesting historical documents in the archives of the Indian Foreign Office.

These intrigues show what strenuous attempts were being made by the 'Provisional Government' in Kabul and their allies to prepare the way for the 'Army of God'. The Great Mohammedan Maulvi from India to whom the 'silk letters' were addressed, in Mecca had already got in touch with the Turkish General in the Hejaz (Ghalib Pasha) and obtained from him, (as Ghalib Pasha subsequently admitted when he was our prisoner of war in Egypt), a declaration of Jihad (Holy War) against the British. Copies of this, known as the Ghalib Nama, had been distributed in India among the Frontier tribes. The 'silk letters' urged the Maulvi to carry the movement a stage further, to secure the active co-operation of the Turkish Government and of the Sharif of Mecca, who had not yet revolted against the Turks when the letters were written. This part of the scheme was ingeniously constructed and by no means impossible of execution in the circumstances then existing.

The letters went on to describe the constitution of the 'Army of God' and here the scheme appeared to be completely unreal. The headquarters were to be at Medina, and the great Maulvi was to be the Commander-in-Chief!

There were to be separate but subordinate Commands in Constantinople, Tehran, and Kabul, and the writer and arch-plotter, Obeidullah, was to have the Kabul command. The letters gave the names of three patrons, of 12 Field-Marshals, (of whom one was the Sharif of Mecca), and many other commanders. The Lahore runaway students were not forgotten. One was to be a Major-General, one a Colonel, and six were to be Lieutenant-Colonels.

As for the plans for the take over of India by the 'Army of God', as Sir Michael wrote: *"All this part of the scheme only existed on paper, but it gave us valuable information as to its sympathisers in India and enabled us to take necessary preventative measures. In the Punjab, these did not go beyond the internment of a dozen or so of those who were known to be the most active pro-Turkish adherents"*.

While this was going on, Gandhi was endeavouring, with the Maulvi Abdul Bari, to work out a plan for altering the entire religious traditions of Islam.

*"I think now,"* wrote Sir Michael in 1925 *"we perhaps treated the matter too lightly; for its centre, the 'Provisional Government' remained firmly rooted in Kabul, whence it continued to encourage seditious agitation in India and hostile action by the Frontier tribes during the War. After the War and the murder of our faithful ally, the Amir Habibullah in February 1919, it threw all its influence into promoting rebellious outbreaks in India in April 1919, in linking them up with Afghan and tribal*

*aggressions, and in precipitating the latter against Northern India in May, 1919, fortunately too late to be effective."*

For those who do not remember or have not read about the Royal family of the Prophet in the Hejaz, Hussein was the father of Ali, Abdullah, Feisal and Zeid. He had educated them all in Constantinople. Feisal was the leader of the Arab revolt. However the Turks, in the person of Abdul Hamid, the Sultan, in their co-operation with the Germans, were determined to keep control of the family of the Prophet and of his sons. It was for this reason that the 'pilgrim railway' was built by the Germans; a number of Hussein's family were kept as hostages in Constantinople, and some, including the later leader Feisal, were given high positions in the army so that they were effectively under supervision and held by Arab tradition to honour their loyalty to the Sultan. An example came at Medina, where Hussein had ordered Feisal to take the first step of rebellion; but because Enver Pasha and other important Turks came down for a military inspection and were his guests, he felt he could not order their deaths and the first stage of the revolt was postponed with tragic results.

During that inspection, Enver turned to Feisal and asked; *"Are these all volunteers for the Holy War?" "Yes,"* said Feisal, with another Holy War in mind. *"Willing to fight to the death against the enemies of the faithful?" "Yes"* said Feisal again. The Arab chiefs came up to Feisal whispering *"My Lord, shall be kill them now?"* and Feisal answered *"No, they are our guests."*

If that action had been taken, the war might have been ended with two blows, but Feisal stood by what he believed to be the behaviour and honour of the Arabs. In fact, he had to walk among the chiefs, just out of Enver Pasha and Hamal Pasha's hearing to plead for the lives of his uninvited guests - 'monsters who had already killed his best friends.'

The suspicions of Enver and Jamal had however been aroused and they wanted to keep Feisal a prisoner in Damascus, but a telegram from Medina arrived asking for Feisal's return, since the situation there was so threatening. It could be said that his chivalry which allowed the Turks to fill Medina, had nearly ruined him. However, he went out into the desert to take refuge with one of the chiefs and there raised the banner of the Arab revolt.

The first attempt was disastrous; the Arabs were poorly armed and Medina was full of Turks armed with German weapons. The Arabs broke and ran, the Turks firing on them with artillery and machine guns, while the Arabs were firing with muzzle-loaders. The Turks ordered a conference with the Arab chiefs and while the conference was in progress, the Turkish troops were ordered to assault the suburbs and massacre every living creature in them. These Turks - this same General and these same troops - had previously carried out the appalling massacres of men, women and children in Armenia – virtually genocide – because the Armenians were Christians.

The massacre at Medina was in exact contradiction to Arab tradition; it was the first rule of Arab war that women and children too young to fight must be spared and that property that could not be carried off in raiding should be left undamaged.

Feisal's men and Feisal himself knew that the Turks (together with the Germans) would stop at nothing and the massacre left them honour bound to carry out reprisals for it. It was then that Lawrence took the step of leaving the Turkish garrison of Medina alone and concentrating on the railway line that would supply the troops, effectively reversing the siege.

Sultan Abdul Hamid had intended taking over the Holy places himself, thus seriously contravening the accepted rule of Islam that the family of the Prophet should be in charge of Mecca and Medina. Sharif Hussein at Mecca did rather better than Feisal, for all Feisal's superior military knowledge, albeit hampered by his remarkable chivalry. Hussein captured Mecca in the first rush, but it was some days before the Turkish forts that overlooked the city could be silenced. The Turks then showed their true selves by shelling the Holy Mosque, the focus for all Islam in the annual pilgrimage. The Mosque held the Kaaba, the black stone that predates Islam and which was the one exception to Mohammed's edict against idolatry which he felt he could not set aside. It is probably a meteorite. Several people praying before the Kaaba were killed in the Turkish bombardment. Jeddah, the port for Mecca, was captured with the assistance of the British Navy and the whole province, excepting Medina, was cleared of Turks.

The details of this onslaught show the lying nature of the claims of the Khilafat movement and Pan-Islam. It was in the name of the Khilafat that the Muslims were roused to fight the British in India, and yet, despite the leaders' claims to support Islam, the Holy Places of their faith had been attacked and their destruction attempted.

The 'Provisional Government' and the 'Army of God' and the Holy War were all a part of this movement which, although it may have persuaded some ignorant Muslims, was another of the campaigns set up and used to achieve destabilisation in India with German or Bolshevik support. For those who have observed young people dreaming dreams when they smoke hashish or bhang, the imagery and plans are quite understandable; the trouble with this and the other plots and plans of megalomaniac dictators is that they do not end in real achievement, but like the Hashashim of an earlier time, they are so affected, that they end up in fights and wars and unnecessary suffering of the innocent.

The main reason for not taking the 'Silk Letter' conspiracy more seriously was that the revolt of the Sheriff of Mecca against the Turks in 1916 divided Islam and knocked the bottom out of the project for combined Muslim action against British India.

To give an example of the insanity that Pan-Islam had instilled into the Muslim population of India: in 1927, when Lawrence as an aircraftman was posted to India, years after the Revolt in the Desert, an old fakir, sitting on the Lahore War Memorial, was lynched by a mob who believed him to be 'Aurens' in disguise.

You do not laugh at someone with whom you are trying to work, with the intention of handing over to them the responsibility for a great nation. That was the British intention.

On the Revolt in the Desert, Sir Michael said *"I have always thought that the valuable results of the Sheriff's actions at a critical time – among others, he arrested and handed over to us the great Maulvi and other Indian conspirators – have not been fully appreciated.*

*The Government of India at the time appeared to be unduly nervous that the revolt would antagonise Indian Mohammedans and thus cause serious trouble in India. I never held that view. The small but seditious Pan-Islamic section doubtless resented the Sheriff's action and, if allowed, would have used it as a basis for anti-British agitation. One such meeting was in fact held at Lahore, attended by only a dozen or so. It was a ballon d'esai – the first; and I took care it should be the last. The Government of India made it clear that they would not tolerate any condemnation of the Sheriff, who had declared himself to be the ally of the British Government and was freeing his own people from Turkish oppression."*

Sir Michael, who was a sufficient friend of the Amir of Afghanistan to get his help despite the wishes of the sons of the old Khan, commented on the Amir himself in these terms, on the German pressure to enter the war. *"The fidelity to his treaty with us of the Amir Habibullah throughout the war was an asset of enormous value. The Amir could not afford openly to oppose the strong section among his Sirdars and officials who urged him to throw in his lot with Turkey and Germany, whose agents were in his capital, and declare a Holy War which would bring in Afghanistan, the frontier tribes and the small but actively seditious Mohammedan element in India.*

*He temporised very adroitly, and is reported to have said to the Turco-German Mission, that when they could show him an army of 100,000 men at Herat, he would begin to think they meant business."*

In 1919, as the Indian politicians began to take action to bring to a head the rebellion that they had been preparing, Habibullah was murdered in his tent while out shooting. His son, Amanullah, always a friend to the Germans, realised that the time had come to act. With his father alive, he would not have been able to help them.

# Chapter VI
# AFGHANISTAN

The belief, as Sir Umar Hayat Khan made clear, that Germany was going to win the War, was central to the concept of the rebellion which had been so carefully planned, not only by the Germans, but by the Indian politicians, with the network of Ghadr, Silk Letter, Pan-Islam and the other Germanic-inspired societies. We have touched on some of the infiltrations into Afghanistan from India, but these were not the only attempts to involve Afghanistan in the German plan to destabilise British India. Though Habibullah, the Amir, held out against the German attempts at dissuading him from continuing on his path of friendship with India and the British, he was not going to hand over his country, as had the Turks, for his own army to be led by Germans against his friends. However, there were German sympathizers in Afghanistan who were prepared to welcome money and arms entering the country through the porous border with Baluchistan (then in India) and Persia, guarded only by a string of small, widely-separated military outposts. German agents were active in the Sarhad, a desolate area of South-East Persia, where they persuaded the local tribes to help them with money, promises and lies.

The parties working actively against the Allied interest in Persia, therefore, were these adventurous Germans, bound for Afghanistan across Persia, and their dupes – the 'piratical' ruffians intent on reward and the spoils of raiding our supply convoys.

Captain James wrote of events: *"I believe that one tribe was won over to the hostile cause by a German officer with his little party who told its members of Germany and the War, and of Britain, and who actually had the cheek to rig up with poles and boxes an imitation wireless station, pretend he was in communication with the Kaiser himself, and mention unheard of rewards; also that the Kaiser had become a Mohammedan. He got away with it, gallant chap! Later on I met several of these officer agents."*

Captain James, promoted to Major in 1919, was an Officer in the Indian Cavalry who served in the Sarhad Campaign of 1916 and wrote of his experiences there and of the deep mutual affection between the British and Indian soldiers which he enjoyed. This mutual affection between the British and the Indian soldier had been established over many years. Even in the Mutiny in 1857, it was Indian troops, mainly Ghurkhas and Punjabis, Sikhs and Muslims who saved India for the Company.

James wrote of the southernmost part of the East Persia cordon, describing the sort of country and weather they encountered in the Lut Desert: *"Over the Lut, tall, whistling columns of sand were constantly travelling, pillars rising in the sky. One of these drifted towards our camp where I was sitting in my bivouac tent on my sleeping bag. On it came, just missing my horse lines, straight at me, lifted my little tent instantly, ropes, pegs and all, carried it hundreds of yards over the desert, leaving me clutching what I could of my belongings in the open and my cheery Rajputs had great fun chasing my scattered treasures.*

*The raider trouble had become so acute that a General Officer had been sent out to Robat with orders to deal with these tribes. The Cordon had been formed to prevent the German parties crossing into Afghanistan, and we must not be distracted by these tribesmen."*

In that harsh climate and under appallingly difficult circumstances, the Germans were beaten back from the Persian/Baluchistan border into which they had infiltrated and had attracted the support of the Ismailzais, the Gamshadzais and the Yarmohammedzais, together with other smaller tribes, under the main leader, Jiand Khan. These tribes attacked the caravans of supplies on which the British outposts depended, on the route between Nushki, where the railway ended and the border outposts, where groups of ten or 20 soldiers were living along a line of some hundreds of miles, guarding India. The area is still desert today, with blowing sand and some steep mountains and gorges. Loss of essential supplies threatened the survival of the outposts. The General of James' record was really Colonel Dyer, who had set out for the Sarhad with his bearer and his driver to do something which probably no other man could have done. He was later to be described as 'an Outram' after the Mutiny General, but his intelligence, which saved India at that time from the German infiltration, was more the brilliance of Lawrence of Arabia, with the experience of a soldier.

James' contemporary notes run thus: *"This General Officer was Dyer, one of the finest soldiers I have ever known, hail fellow well met with all ranks and fearless to a degree, the man whose name became associated after the war with the Amritsar incident, the man who saved countless lives there, faced by a situation which would have daunted a weaker character. Like the sportsman he was, he made his way over the desert in a motorcar! At Robat he collected a few men with his car and a host of camels, he bluffed his way two hundred miles south of Robat right to the raiders' stronghold, the fort at Khwash and occupied it ...*

*There, with a tiny force, he was surrounded by thousands of well armed tribesman. Every available man and horse was under orders to get down to Khwash as soon as possible before his bluff was called. He had cowed these brigand leaders by sheer courage. 'Where was this white chief's army?' they were saying. So from all directions we were converging on Khwash as fast as we could. As luck would have it we were just in time.*

*Tied down to the pace of our food carrying convoys we made the best speed we could. As regards distance, it was merely the customary ride of a hundred miles or so, through nothingness, as usual, and terrific heat. At Robat on the way, I joined up with the remainder of the Rajput squadron and another of our squadrons from Seistan, bound as I was for Khwash, the centuries old fort and stronghold of Jiand Khan, lord and chief of all the Sarhad tribes, surrounding the intrepid Dyer with his handful of men. With the squadron were officers of my regiment who had been north of Bandan and Neh, and it was good to meet again for the first time since 1914* [He had been in France in the intervening period].

*Through this Dante's Inferno we moved, the twin peaks of the volcano Koh-I-Taftan ever in sight, a story book setting reminding one of Alan Quartermain and here may be told the story of the capture of the German officer Winckelmann, just as J. told it to me during the journey towards Khwash. The squadron ahead – a cloud of dust; the one behind us a line of extended horsemen; the sharp sound of an occasional hoof striking a rock; the sun catching now and again the lance points; such was the setting of his adventurous tale.*

*J. was in command of a post at Neh, when a spy reported that a party of twenty men, three of whom were Europeans, had arrived at a little known oasis known as Deh Salem (the village of Peace) fifty five miles South-West, well out in the formidable Lut. Farther west from Deh Salem lies an absolutely waterless region stretching to Khabis, whose snow-capped mountains can just be seen in winter, a hundred miles distant.*

*Setting out with two troops at midday, by nightfall, J. had reached a water hole twenty miles on his way, where another of our spies confirmed the news.*

*Nobody can cross this country without halting at these widely separated wells, and from North to South of the Cordon, each well had its spy, so that even in this vastness, one or more of our posts would gain news of strangers and take suitable action.*

*There were still twenty miles to be covered, but by hard riding, J. and his men at dawn were within a mile of Deh Salem. Extending in two lines, the troops galloped straight through the little oasis but found no enemy - the birds had just flown and were making for some hills about three miles away. A race ensued but our horses were exhausted after their forty-mile forced march and it was impossible to cut the enemy off before they reached a commanding position in the hills.*

*'For action dismount' Deducting his horse holders, J. had but twenty men, so after the first exchange of fire he decided to split up his command, surround the raiders and deprive them of access to water.*

*The day passed, and at night the separate posts were drawn in closer, but the German party had managed to worm their way through in the darkness by one of the ravines in the hill. Enemy reinforcements were reputed to be arriving; J. and his men, who had been without food or water for a day and a night, therefore put Deh Salem into a state of defence having sent work back to Neh. The report however, proved to be false. The next night, one of our sentry groups saw a man approaching stealthily. After a struggle he was overpowered and turned out to be a German – Winckelmann. He owed his capture to having stayed behind to cover the retreat of his comrades. Lost in the darkness, he was creeping in, exhausted, for water. The remainder of his party, with the exception of one or two casualties from our rifle fire, were known later to have gone all the way back over Lut to Kerman (in Persia) which they reached in an absolutely beaten condition, suffering severely from thirst and exposure.*

*Winkelmann claimed to be a Lieutenant of the Potsdam Guards Artillery. At any rate, he was a sportsman; and that is how his war ended.*

*That was an enjoyable march down to Khwash. We knew that the news of our move in that direction, followed in a day or so by what infantry could be spared, was being passed with lightning speed from 'watcher' to 'watcher', to Jiand Khan and his braves. Needless to say, our own spies were spreading rumours of great armies coming to support Dyer. A moving speck in the far distance would mean an enemy camel scout, lost in a few minutes as he wheeled to carry the tidings.*

*J. was accompanied, as was typical of the extraordinary things that occurred in India, by a syce whom he called Suleiman; this man had in the first instance appeared on the Frontier and insisted on working for him and for no one else. He went with J. to France, but was later with many of the non-combatants, sent back to India. He had again appeared at Nasratabad a year later, 'An unexpected meeting, one especially pleasant to me occurred here. As I rode into the horse lines and dismounted, out ran a little figure with a wizened smiling face and short, grey, pointed beard, his eyes beaming under his wisp of turban. He held my horse with one hand and with the other wrung mine until I thought it was coming off. This was Suleiman Khan, a character known to all of us as old man syce'. Like Sinbad, he seemed a living character from a fairy story."*

J. claims that most syces were low caste, but we in India had a magnificent Baluchi syce, a man of great ability and dignity from Dera - Ghazi Khan. Syces were not always low caste; but also the extraordinary way in which Suleiman had attached himself to J. was not dissimilar to Mohammed Ashraf Khan who, when his very superior employers were about to retire and return to England, despite their warnings that my father would not be able to pay him the salary he was getting from them, insisted on being given a recommendation to my father, for whom he worked for some twenty nine years. Close admiration and the affection thus engendered, both in the army and in personal services, was a part of the richness of our lives in India, and completely contrary to the claims made by the propagandists. That loyalty and respect was mutual and, as in England, descended to later generations.

To return to James' narrative, *"Old Suleiman, old man syce, had met me again at Robat, coming along with the squadron from Seistan. That wrinkled little grey-bearded face wreathed in smiles at the idea of accompanying me again. Riding along with the transport on my second charger, smoking a cigarette, with a joke and a laugh for everyone, he might have been on his way to the polo ground in cantonments. My horse and saddle, mysteriously, were perfectly groomed and cleaned.*

*At last, passing through a winding defile, in the distance in the middle of a wide valley, we saw the turrets of Khwash fort and the green of the oasis. An hour over this level plain, and the two squadrons were watering their horses in the delightful fresh stream below the fort; our great camel convoy coming on in the distance. Over the lower slopes of the Koh-i-Taftan, the water is particularly loathsome, tasting and smelling of sulphur; it can be imagined how we revelled in this freshness, and how eager animals rushed to its luxury.*

*Dyer was delighted to see us as we were to find him and his little force upholding their bluff. Spies and watchers had cowed Jiand and his ruffians – but only for the time; one could almost sense the unseen ones from behind the rocks of the hills to the East and West; could picture their nightly conclave, their disputes as to whether this little force was to be attacked before reinforcements arrived. Dyer, however, was under no illusion about this.*

James realised, as his book 'A Far Away Campaign' makes clear, that in addition to the preparations made by Germany before the war, over and beyond the insidious propagandising of the Sikhs, the Nationalist politicians (in the main, Hindu), and through them the cities, there had been plans to incite the Muslim population throughout the Middle East and India, which had included all that might induce Mohammedan States to become her allies. What better then, encouraged by her success with Turkey, than to turn especial attention to Afghanistan, thereby pinning down in India a great number of British troops? Not too easy a task with Russia on the North, South and East. The neutral country of Persia, therefore represented the only way open, and the railway that branched to Medina, went on to Mosul on the Persian border with Turkey.

Directly Britain entered the war, German agents of first class ability already in Persia, began dealing blows at British prestige and attempting to force themselves or their emissaries into Afghanistan.

James continues: *"It was a queer situation. The tribesmen under their various leaders, had been gathering behind the hills that commanded Khwash , with every intention of saving their faces by an overwhelming night attack, realising now that Dyer had marched right through their country with a tiny force, but with camels carrying as much rations and forage as could be collected at Robat and reputed by spies of ours to be almost an army, Two squadrons of cavalry had arrived and, as they well knew, further reinforcements of infantry were following. The defeat of Jumna Khan's lashkar (greatly exaggerated of course, as regards casualties), made them think. A kind of checkmate followed – a temporary lull, a calm that could not last.*

*Dyer played the first card. Envoys were sent to the tribal leaders summoning them to a durbar (tribal council). This they agreed to, and on the following day, in they came, each with his respective 'staff'. Mounted on the most beautiful trotting camels, armed to the teeth, with bandoliers, modern rifles, and jewelled swords and daggers, they came from round the hills and over the horizon.*

*Inside the three sides of a square formed by our own men they squatted down, a semi circle of eagle eyed, hawk faced villains, as picturesque a gathering as one could wish. The fourth side of the square was formed by the British officers of our force, and in the centre General Dyer faced this most Biblical looking assembly."*

As will be shown later, this was an extremely brave move on Dyer's part. In a sense it was as brave as what he did at Amritsar, where he went in similarly with only 50 rifles to deal with a mob of 30-40,000 men armed with lathis who could easily have overrun his little troop – strategically, the two actions were similar. If he had allowed the crowd at the Bagh to move to the murder and mayhem which they were intending, despite his warning, these people would have taken the opportunity and in every town and village throughout India, the conflagration and destruction would have run like a forest fire; uncontrollable and disastrous. With his small band of soldiers, he took what he regarded as the opportunity that had been given him, to make it clear that the Raj, the Sirkar, still ruled and would impose the strength of responsible government on terrorists. The fact that the propagandists turned the thing round and that no-one employed by Government could publish their own accounts while so employed, played into the rebel leaders' hands.

Back to James: *"With the gravest attention they listened to what Dyer had to tell them, interpreted through the medium of his personal political agent, a Baluchi, whose services were invaluable to us. The import of his message was that we had no intention of interfering with them; that they had brought upon themselves, as the dupes of Germany, the casualties they had suffered; that it would be to their advantage, and to ours, to help us by refusing those German parties passage through their country. In short, he persuaded them to throw in their lot with the British Raj, emphasising the financial appeal, and not allowing them to lose sight of the fact that refusal would mean that we should most certainly wipe them off the map."*

The claim that Dyer would wipe them off the map made James smile. *"I wondered whether the minds behind those inscrutable, handsome faces realised that they could eat us in one mouthful. I wondered whether they believed that a host of British troops could possibly be spared from faraway India, as that wily Baluchi told them, to appear on the instant as if by rubbing the magic ring, and perform this 'wiping off the map'.*

*Yet after the time allowed for deliberation, one by one they salaamed Dyer and swore on the Koran to be our allies; swore by their forebears, their fathers and mothers, never to raise a hand against us. Never should a hostile party cross their territory. Could they provide forage for our horses? In short, everything that was their's, was our's. One of them, a spare well-knit man, who had been eyeing me through this ceremony, came up, salaamed, and held out his hand.*

*'Sahib', he said, 'I am Jumna Khan'.*

*He told me that the arrival of A. and myself on the scene was a complete surprise on that early morning, and inquired with great interest of what our force consisted.*

*I told him. He cursed himself when he knew, and said he would have done for us all; but in his way he was a good fellow, Jumna Khan, however many his crimes.*

*In the battle on the way to Khwash, there had been an old man who sat on the higher slope of the hill, dressed in white, urging on the Ismailzais of Jumna Khan, and who had finally been shot. I inquired who might the patriarch be who held his arms aloft. His uncle, he said. It was all Kismet, fate, the will of Allah.*

*He told me that it was no good for British officers to think that the disguise of a turban and kurta (Indian Cavalry long coat) made them indistinguishable from their men.*

*Still smiling, the handsome villain gave me his hand again, and turned to mount his camel and trot off over the horizon with his little group of followers. And from that date, Jumna Khan and his Ismailzais never lifted hand against us.*

*One after the other, the remaining chiefs disappeared and we were left in our fortress – or rather theirs. We had every reason to think that with the assistance of our new allies, a cordon might be formed reaching southwards as far as the Persian Gulf. We could return, we thought, to our posts northwards as far as Birjand.*

*'Don't you believe it' said our wily Baluchi political.*

*Dyer certainly did not, and on the following morning, summoned his staff to discuss the future. It was too dangerous to return to our northern posts, leaving our lines of communication from Robat to India to the tender mercies of those brigands. Khwash must be occupied by a garrison and made tenable. The infantry came in, augmented by two mountain guns. After our durbar of course, the tribesmen came and went as they pleased, but there was a great deal too much 'coming'. Now, instead of the unseen watcher, there were visible watchers on all sides, armed to the teeth, ostensibly about their own business. Outwardly, peace seemed the chief note.*

*The first thing we did was to set about building a mud fort, one capable of holding us all and satisfying the needs of modern warfare. The ancient stronghold of Khwash was useless, made as it was to repel the hand-to-hand fighter and invader of olden days. This was blown to pieces by gun cotton one evening at sunset and despite the necessity, there was sadness in seeing those thick walls and turrets crumbling for the last time.*

*In our new quarters, life was reasonably pleasant; rations were good, as fresh meat and eggs were easily obtainable. I had been appointed O.C. vegetable garden, and had sent to India for a large order for seeds etc. according to a catalogue that someone miraculously found. We all had our jobs, one officer acted as architect, another organised livestock and meat, a third attended to eggs and poultry. For a time affairs went well, but it took weeks by camel for any order – if lucky – to reach India and weeks for the journey back. Transport was scarce, and soon the situation became acute as regards forage for our horses. Messengers were sent out, with the necessary payment to neighbouring oases to induce the inhabitants to collect what we wanted - in due course they returned – all was well. The forage had been collected and stacked in the oases, and we only need send our camels to collect it. It was just too easy to come bluffing our way in there and take everything for granted.*

*A sudden summons came one night! Dyer told us that the badly wanted, paid for and heaped up forage in the neighbouring oases had been deliberately burnt. The babies stopped laughing and things happened at once.*

*In addition to this, a large gathering of tribesmen at the site of the burnt forage was reported. So much for the protestations, the swearing by the Koran, by the heads of their fathers and mothers and all the rest of it. Still, having bluffed our way into that country the only thing to do was to uphold our bluff. If these oath-breakers were asking for trouble they should certainly have it. Arrangements were made then and there, for a column to proceed at dawn the following morning, leaving behind in our half finished fort, the minimum of troops to protect it. Details were worked out, and in the dark of that night we separated to give the orders to our various commands.*

*Our burnt forage heaps, so urgently needed, and paid for in good silver Persian coins, were but a few miles away. Without this, or commandeered stuff, we were checkmated; our horses and camels would starve.*

*Jiand Khan and his friends had shown their hand. Their humiliation can be easily understood. They had been tricked out of their fortress and their women-folk had taunted them with cowardice in allowing this to happen.*

*Very well then, war it was, and let the best man win.*

*At dawn the next morning, Suleiman had my horse ready outside my tent, imperturbable as ever. We might have been in the paddock of some Indian racecourse, the old man seeing me off to the post. 'Good luck Sahib!' That bearded old face creased in smiles as we moved off to see what Jiand Khan and his followers were after. Did they want to fight it out?*

*Dyer led the infantry; behind them came the two mountain guns and behind them again, the transport. The distance was not great.*

*I had a squadron out on the flank of this force to get round the enemy, if engaged, or to pursue if they broke. It was a marvellous morning, and halfway to our destination we halted; the sun by now was well up and Dyer called on the Unit Commanders. Any sign of hostility or resistance and we were to go straight for it. Good orders those! The scene was set, the enemy were but an hour's trek away. We all knew what to do.*

*On again then, as before from my point of view, a column of dust denoting the main body, the infantry on my right, and the sun glinting on the lance points of my advance and flank patrols. A few miles down the valley, turning South, we obtained a view of our objective, the oasis on a long commanding ridge. As our little force wheeled we could plainly see the place was strongly held. It was obvious too, that our being able to see this meant that, the tribesmen, despite watches and spies, had not expected us in such force or so soon.*

*Instantly our infantry deployed for attack and the guns took up positions for action. My patrols came galloping in and I was already mapping out the best route to get on the enemy's flank, when down from the ridge came a small party on trotting camels, conspicuous with white flags. From our position we could just see them ride straight up to Dyer. Followed, the 'Officers Call.'*

*I galloped across with my orderly, to find that the visitors consisted of Jiand Khan himself and one or two local chiefs.*

*Dyer was furious, and ordering a guard for these 'white flaggers', directed me to go ahead in extended line, with the infantry immediately behind, straight over the ridge, where a council could be held under the palm trees. We rode straight through, pushing ahead of us those hawk-faced rascals, who were too nonplussed to resist as their king, Jiand Khan, was riding almost hand in hand with me.*

*Over the crest, Dyer ordered the main body of the infantry and the guns to form a camp close by the water supply – good fresh water too.*

*The remainder of us made for a clump of palm trees a mile distant. Here, my men formed three sides of a square, in which seated themselves, Jiand and his chiefs. We had seen en route the burnt stacks of our promised forage. In front of us stood a large expanse of tall-uncut crops - it was a mistake to have left our main body away there to make a camp.*

*The 'white flaggers' seemed to increase in numbers.*

*Dyer dismounted, faced the assembly, and accused them directly of breaking their oath, of burning our forage and of treachery. Jiand Khan immediately lost his temper, and in a second the scene was changed. Armed men sprang from the cover of the crops - we were surrounded.*

*Without an instant's hesitation, Dyer seized Jiand Khan and forced him to the ground. In the wild scrimmage, our men grabbed as many of the tribesmen as they could, wrenched their rifles from them and forced them into the square.*

*Dyer's action saved the situation. Seeing their chief disarmed, uncertain what to do, those not yet arrested faded into the tall crops and left us with our bag, which included nearly every man of importance in the Sarhad.*

*It was a close thing. Had those tribesmen not been momentarily cowed by the humiliation of their leader, had they then and there opened fire from their cover, they could have finished off Dyer and the rest of us easily.*

*Back we went to our newly found camp with our prisoners, stripped now of their rifles, bandoliers, swords and daggers. A cavalry patrol was sent direct to Khwash to announce that we should return on the following morning and to order a suitable kraal for our captives.*

*The oasis was combed for forage. We found plenty and camels too.*

*Every possible precaution was taken that night to prevent attack by would-be rescuers. Nothing however happened, and in the morning we went slowly back to our 'Dolls House' in Khwash, armies of camels carrying forage. Our prisoners to whom we had returned their jewelled swords and daggers but not their firearms, rode with us. A most ingenious kraal had been improvised, and into it they went like so many caged hawks.*

*So far so good. We had our forage, we had the ringleaders. It was too much to imagine that this would close our troubles with the tribesmen and allow us to continue our search for those needles in the haystack, German intruders, bound for Afghanistan.*

*Messengers were sent to Robat for orders about the prisoners; all the time the men were in danger and knew that the delay was giving an impression of weakness to the tribesmen.*

*We were all in our 'Doll's House' Mess one evening, discussing the future and what orders would come from India; our orderly came in and told me that General Dyer wished to see me immediately. I found Dyer in his quarters with his staff officers and his Baluchi political agent. Orders had arrived at last from India.*

*The situation in our fort was becoming daily more acute. Our cage, containing nearly every leading man in the Sarhad, was more than a white elephant. Their followers were watching day and night from every conceivable piece of cover, and would certainly attack in masses, before long. They knew well enough what a stalemate it was, and interpreted only as weakness, our forced inaction. Forage and rations were running short. Further supplies could only be obtained by a sortie in force, and a sortie meant a weakening of our small garrison, and the enemy's opportunity to dash to the rescue.*

*Here was an end to inaction and Dyer expounded to me what had been decreed. Four hundred Hazara Pioneers, a famous corps of the Indian Army, were en route from Nushki to Robat. Dyer had been ordered to get his prisoners at all costs from Khwash to Robat, at which place, they were to be handed over to the Hazaras who would convey them back over four hundred miles of desert to India to be kept at his Majesty's expense until the conclusion of hostilities."*

James' account to this point has concentrated on the successful tactics employed by Dyer in the face of vastly superior numbers. The following pages have been included in order to show the feelings between British officers and men in the Indian Army which Attenborough, Indian, German and Bolshevik propaganda has endeavoured to deny. The relationship goes on to this day and without it, nothing that Dyer did in the Sarhad, in Amritsar, in Afghanistan, would have been possible. It was on his experience of comradeship with the Indian troops that he could dare to save, not only the Punjab but also India, from the disaster planned for 1919. Without these magnificent fighting men's courage and trust, India would have been sunk in the sort of bloodshed, arson and loot which the politicians had planned. The Indian Army (and in present day terms, Indian and Pakistan Armies) deserve our gratitude and admiration, together with Dyer and his officers, for it will be seen that the bravery and courage shown were mutual.

James continues: *"Two hundred, odd miles to Robat through this desolation those precious prisoners must be taken with what escort could be spared! There was no doubt whatsoever that this escort would be attacked. Cats and mice were nothing to this. The mouse is usually shadowed and played with by one cat; this particular mouse had to cross a kitchen inhabited by a whole feline family. I was detailed for this duty, and the maximum escort was allotted to me to carry it out. We were to march just before dawn on the following morning.*

*Dyer wished me good luck as I went to give my overnight orders to my escort. The 'watchers' watched, Koh-i-Taftan grumbled, and the mice turned in to get what sleep they could before crossing the kitchen floor.*

*At the appointed time, old man syce stood holding my horse, impassive as ever. He, of course could not accompany me. The column of camels carrying our prisoners and our rations was ready to march, the cavalry and infantry escort with them, and the advance guard had signalled all clear as far as the first ridge. Suleiman smiled and wished me good luck, which he had done before, as far as this charger of mine was concerned; when I was mounting her then for the finals of the Quetta Senior Polo Tournament early in 1914. Poor 'Strawberry'! It was a different kind of tournament now.*

*We had some twenty five miles to cover before reaching our first halt, and at the pace we were tied to, that of the camels, it was sunset before we reached that waterhole. Up to then, not one 'cat' had showed a claw, but we had definitely left the wainscoting.*

*My Second-in-Command, G. and I, selected the most favourable piece of ground for our bivouac, while the animals were being watered and our patrols watched the surrounding country.*

*Before dark we settled down. The lesser chiefs sat within a palisade of barbed wire; five infantrymen with loaded rifles and fixed bayonets guarded each fifteen-yard side of this square. Jiand Khan, his son and his uncle, (undoubtedly the biggest villains of them all) I placed in charge of the cavalry quarter guard itself.*

*Pickets were posted to command possible approaches. After their food, all the prisoners were bound hand and foot and warned that the first to try to get on his feet would be instantly killed.*

*Night fell; G. and I had our meal and sat talking, discussing our next day's trek. It was pitch dark, utterly black. A final walk around our little show to make sure that all was in order, and the sentries clearly understood that any attempts at rising on the part of the prisoners was to be instantly dealt with by the bayonets and any attack from the outside to mean the same thing. Then we lay down to sleep. The situation could hardly be called conducive to rest, but towards early morning I dozed.*

*The next thing I remember was an inferno of sounds: shouts and yells from tribesmen; rifle shots, the frantic drumming of our cavalry horses' feet in their endeavours to break their picketing ropes and stampede, the air thick with dust and sand in the blackness.*

*Seizing my revolver, I stumbled through this hellish din to where I had last seen the prisoners surrounded by barbed wire and bayonets. The shock was severe. Under cover of their voluminous garments they had managed to fumble themselves quite free of their bonds and at a pre-arranged sign, flinging those filthy robes on the wire, had crashed through it with their hellish shouting and screaming, having succeeded in stampeding the horses.*

*By now scattered far and wide in that darkness in ravines and watercourses, of which every inch was known to them, already out of range of recapture, it was utterly useless to begin to organise a pursuit. Rescuing parties hundreds strong might cover every and any exit, were they even visible.*

*I groped my way to the cavalry quarter-guard. There sat Jiand Khan and his son and his uncle, three of my men holding lances at their throats. Thank God for that at least I thought, feeling physically sick with disappointment and impotence. What had happened had happened and nothing could restore the prisoners. It meant failure, ghastly dreadful failure, nothing short of that!*

*A picket patrol of my men was sent back to Dyer with instructions to get there by hook or by crook, and go like hell, darkness or no darkness.*

*It was childish and useless to see red and relieve one's feelings on those twenty fixed bayonets who had allowed such a disaster to occur. I could only await orders, as we had only three prisoners, even if the three really important ones. We might even have to rush back to Khwash fort with our new comparatively strong escort to help against an attack. Anything, I thought, as I brooded over the position would be better than this feeling of disappointment and failure.*

*Back, post-haste, came orders from Dyer, sent by a fresh cavalry patrol. He, Dyer, was setting out at once with a small force, by a route twenty miles to the North of ours. We were to march at once with our remaining prisoners Northwards, to meet him at a small oasis being nominated as our joint camp for that following night.*

*The Sarhad was, of course, ablaze with hostility. I can remember no day in my life more heartsick than this of our Northern trek. Recriminations against that prisoner guard would never get the prisoners back. In short, I was the villain responsible for the disaster.*

*The Indian Army, as with others, contains every kind of soldier. There is the ambitious, intent on staff appointments, leading to the seats of the mighty. There are the picturesque and sociable, intent on gaining soft jobs by being A.D.C.'s to those already mighty, and in many cases, never returning to their regiments. There are the 'good boys', who cling like leeches to every rule and regulation, whose life is one long, perfectly regular horizontal line, in which is no laugh, and therefore no real camaraderie or touch with the rank and file, in short, lacking deplorably that human element without which no disciplined army can exist. There are, too, the disgruntled ones, to whom life and their seniors are very unjust. These are anathema. My mind ran on these types in my disappointment, possibly filling the hours by trying to justify my existence and find my own category. Looking back through years of peacetime service, I could remember many occasions on which I had erred, and the stern admonition of my commanding officers, while I stood trembling 'on the mat'. What good fellows they had been – Damn – I liked them and my men and my horses.*

*Most men, in Dyer's position would have made my life unbearable with recrimination, but he was not that kind. He simply sent his Staff Officer across to me with orders to push on as hard as I could with the remaining prisoners, while he demonstrated towards the enemy's hill fastness with what force he could muster. This meant my escort being cut down to one troop of cavalry and some twelve infantrymen. Dyer, with his little force, was already settled down in a perimeter (entrenched) camp. We settled down into a similar camp of our own, so situated that, in case of attack, we might cover the danger zones with our crossed fire.*

*The night passed quietly, and before the following dawn, we were again en route. We covered well over thirty miles that day, urging the camels through the defiles, and advancing by a series of moves consisting of a distance as far ahead as our cavalry point and a few infantrymen, taking successive positions on high ground on the flanks, could signal back to us the 'all clear'. Jiand Khan and his relatives rode, impassive as ever, on their camels within a ring of lances, threatened with instant death in the event of the attempted escape or rescue. We were well out of range and touch with anybody. On the morrow, we had to pass through a fearsome defile for at least twenty miles, for the most part with precipitous sides, narrow, in some places never reached by sunlight; silent, threatening and reeking with danger. That night we camped near the local water, not far from the entrance. We entrenched ourselves, every man throughout the night keeping his loaded rifle on the parapet. All conceivable precautions against surprise were taken.*

*G. and I sat talking late, taking it in turns every hour or so to go round the defences. I found myself unable to shake off a definite premonition of disaster; it seemed impossible to fight against this abominable depression. It was exactly as if someone kept saying 'It's no good; do whatever you may, you cannot overcome the impossible. How can you with your tempting bait, without miraculous luck, get through?'*

*The countryside were out, to a man, to rescue their chief and his relations. Not only the coming day, with that fearsome defile to be passed, but at least two further days to be marched after that, laid heavily on my mind.*

*Those dark thoughts quickly cleared, however, as the first rays of the sun saw us wending our way towards the danger point. We would get through alright and deliver our goods to the Hazaras, yet even that could not wipe out what had happened.*

*The defile swallowed us up; we were so small a force, compelled to regulate our pace to that of the slipping, stumbling camels. Horsemen cannot climb the sheer walls of rock that hemmed us in. Our few infantrymen were doing their best. The tribesmen, surefooted as goats, could make rings round us, and above us – unseen.*

*The high, glaring sun made the heat intense. We came to a kind of basin, an opening in the ravine about a quarter of a mile long and over a hundred yards wide.*

*The infantry were almost at the far end, and I was trotting ahead to investigate the route in front of us.*

*Suddenly, this little amphitheatre became alive with yells and shouts. Here and there white clad figures darted from rock to rock. Some of my men, as they ran to cover, collapsed and lay still. Wrenching my horse round, I galloped back towards the head of the column where the prisoners were; then came a shock, as though someone had kicked me, followed by the feeling of warmth trickling down my leg. The din was like hell let loose; in front, a confused view of struggling horses and camels. Suddenly poor Strawberry gave in – she struggled on for a few strides and over we went together.*

*Disentangling myself, I got to my feet half dazed. Instantly the shock of a terrific blow in the back spun me round like a top and hurled me to the ground – then darkness.*

*Reality returned with waves of warmth, streaming down my back which I could not see, down my sleeve, which I could. It showed red.*

*I remember looking stupidly at that sleeve, which did not seem to belong to me. The khaki was soaking it up, this red stain, and it was running down the fingers at the end. Just above the elbow was the neatest little hole. This warm sensation was going on down my legs, too.*

*I recollected what had happened, and sat up to look round. A white clad figure on the opposite slope pointed his rifle at me - the bullet hit the rock six inches away. Up the slope towards me ran the gallant G. Another bullet spat from the rifle, and round he spun, falling beside me. Again all became a blur – darkness – nothingness.*

*Later, back came reality, the whole world seemed one dull ache, the heat grew fiendish. What on earth had happened? I was behind a small tamarisk bush, there had been an ambush, but where were my men, and why couldn't I get up? My struggle to do this brought an instantaneous crack from the opposite hillside and a bullet kicked up the sand between my legs. If our prisoners had been killed nothing matters now ...*

*Thank heaven, G. must have collected the survivors, and that accounted for the shots and triumphant yells and curses further up the defile. He had vanished. These sounds died down; and then could be heard, all around, men, horses and camels dying. A terrible smell, too, of blood. Soon this ceased and something came between me and the sun – it was poor Strawberry, standing there with her stomach ripped right across by a bullet, my saddle twisted sideways, the sword hanging hilt downwards half out of its sheath. There she stood puzzled, a pitiful picture. A little later she staggered away in search of water and died.*

*This was indeed the end of the world. A violent effort to get up caused agonies of pain and a renewal of the warm sensation in my limbs. I fainted again for a time. When consciousness returned, the noise of the action continuing up the defile greeted me. It was evening, and I felt, as indeed I was, a mass of congealed blood. It served, at any rate as a kind of poultice. Once again my attentive friend across the way sent a bullet whizzing past my head. That he missed me so many times seems uncommonly lucky.*

*Silence again intervened; my thoughts wandered and sank to dull indifference. I might as well join that company of dead scattered round. As the sun descended a flapping noise attracted my attention. One by one, vultures were arriving; one loathsome bird had actually perched on a rock quite close. Even that did not matter. My little force must have been wiped out. I hoped to God the prisoners were too.*

*Another warm trickle cheered me with the thought that dying cannot go on for ever, but it might take too long. As darkness fell those tribesmen would come to mutilate the dead and torture the wounded. My right arm, unhurt, groped for my revolver which was still, luckily, in its holster. One must make every effort to keep conscious; let them come creeping up, have five shots point blank at the nearest, and save the sixth to put oneself beyond their damned torture. That is what it feels like to lie out on a hillside with death, in the back of beyond. There is nothing heroic about it at all. What seems to be the inevitable is acceptable.*

*Yet it was not inevitable after all, this time. 'Sahib, Sahib,' came a voice from behind a rock on my right. I could see the face of Dafadar (Sergeant) Sheikh Haider peering at me. A superman this, at tent-pegging and trick-riding, one of the finest types of Indian cavalry soldiers. Can you get to me he asked? Impossible I indicated. 'Sahib, I have three men here. I will order them to open fire and I will come across to carry you away'. The rifles cracked rapidly; the gallant dafadar rushed across and picked me up like a feather. The next thing I remember was finding my head on his shoulder, my trickles running over him, and that bearded face laughing down at me.*

*He carried me to a little pocket of the hills where I found G., with a gaping wound in his neck and shoulder, my Indian officer with a bullet through his leg, a few men still untouched and about a dozen horses. On the edge of this shelter were posted those who could use a rifle. In the middle, was a pool of the foulest water I ever saw – but it was fluid. Our little post was pushed out and covered the rest, who dragged in the dead, spending the night burying them.*

*At dark, the yelling tribesman closed in again, waiting for their prey. They could not get at us past those covering posts, or rather preferred to wait. (Sheikh Haider was given a commission for this action, later on).*

*The sickening truth was revealed that of the prisoners, Jiand Khan and his son, whose escort were shot dead to a man, had escaped; the third prisoner had been shot.*

*I have still to experience a more heart-breaking night than that. We had little food, Indian rations, grain and that foul water. We did our best to aid one another with first field dressings, having no doctor. Occasionally came a challenge from our posts on the skyline, a shot and a renewal of those yells, and thus, exactly, passed the following day and night.*

*By noon on the third day, the horses' feedbags were emptied – our handfuls of grain were gone. We were just about at the finish. That sickening ache and still more sickening disappointment were driving me mad. We must have been a queer looking lot, stretched out there in the sun, covered with flies and reeking with blood. The ever cheery G. and I consulted and decided that as soon as it was dark we would mount the horses and go straight for the nearest post, forty miles away, where there was a small fort garrisoned by levies. I was to be lifted on a horse with a man on each side riding close to hold me up. In case we were attacked we would just go straight through, and the lucky ones would survive.*

*Down went the sun – I felt as if I had been lying on my back all my life. Quietly, all the horses were saddled. Since midday there had been comparative peace. We were out of sight in our pocket, and well under cover. The moon came up – it was time to go. The men mounted noiselessly; the gallant Sheikh Haider lifted me on my horse. Sitting on the wounds which a bullet must make passing through one's seating accommodation, I was not happy. Two horsemen ranged themselves alongside to hold me, then came G., then the remnants of the troop.*

*Off we went at a snails pace through the end of the defile, expecting every instant a rush of the hostile tribesmen; our departure seemed to make as much noise as the 'Cheltenham Flyer' going through Reading. Gradually, as the minutes passed, we realised that the enemy must have made off, fearing reinforcements. On and on, at a crawl as it seemed, we moved while the moonlit crags and boulders swayed and swung against the starry sky, and from time to time the troopers on my right and left closed in to push me back straight in the saddle.*

*Hour after hour passed and immediate danger was over, but that terrible sense of failure haunted me. How wonderful it would have been to be still escorting the prisoners, to have won through! Here was I, with this rotten sleeve holding in a cake of blood, an arm that did not even seem to belong to me – this stupid little hole in my back – everything. It was the end of the world. I wished it had been the end of mine.*

*Centuries later, the sun rose to find us still creeping on towards a waterhole where we stopped to drink. G. lay down in the sand; I stayed stuck in my saddle not relishing being ungummed. G. was still asleep as we mustered to go on. Seventeen hours after leaving that ghastly defile we trailed into the levies' fort. Then came string beds, clean, fresh water, friends and the sleep of utter exhaustion.*

*Next morning a doctor from Robat arrived – where they had learnt by means of the inexplicable desert news transmission of our plight. Followed, a filthy period of the removal of blood caked clothes that did not want to come off. We had to get back to Headquarters at Kacha, just above Robat, thirty to forty miles away, and a hasty mustering of camels followed as soon as we had rested. One camel, equipped on each side of its hump with long coffin-shaped baskets in which a man could lie, carried G. and myself - others similarly fitted carried those who could ride no longer and so we lurched along, hanging on as best we could on those hellish rocking-horses.*

*Kacha, at last, the mud huts housing its little infantry garrison, was a welcome sign of civilisation. High above us they stood, and we were carried up on stretchers by a party waiting in readiness. Ungummings, probing and dressings were not made any more pleasant by the fact that medical supplies were woefully short. What with the pain from wounds and exhaustion, and my desperate disappointment, sleep was impossible. Those tribesmen's yells rang unceasingly in one's ears. I remember my evidence being taken down, my account of the disaster. I signed it – I was in utter disgrace.*

*Yet there is always something bright in even the murkiest situation. During those horrible nights, every one of the hundred times that I turned to see the star studded sky through the open door of the hut, there came a voice, 'It's alright, Sahib, we are here,' speaking in Hindustani. Those who were left of my men had formed a voluntary guard, taking it in turns to watch the open door of my hut night after night. Can the reader wonder at my affection for them?*

*Soon came a day when at the horrible wound dressing time, that doctor, who had trekked night and day to our help was overjoyed. My arm had come to life again; those emaciated white things that used to be fingers moved themselves; G. and I were definitely beginning to heal.*

*A camel convoy was being assembled to go back those four hundred miles to Nushki, over that raider-infested country. This was to be commanded by myself, from one side of a camel's hump in a basket, with G. balancing me on the other side. Other camels similarly burdened with wounded, and what few rifles could be spared as an escort, completed the outfit.*

*We had to march entirely by night, spending the days at waterholes as best we might. It was a horrible journey, averaging twenty miles a night at the snail's place of camels, with cheerful and repeated rumours of a raiding party ready to attack us.*

*Lying in the 'coffin', heaving unevenly in time with the slouching camel, anticipating a rush of tribesmen, one counted the minutes of those weeks. What earthly chance was there with the days in the sun and sand, dreading the thought of the coming night's jolting journey forcing one's wounds open again? Yet, as ever, the bright spot arrived.*

*During the weeks in the doctor's hands at Kacha, a convoy had arrived from Khwash, the intervening country now being clear, and in it, old man syce, with my second charger. Every night of our trek to Nushki he rode alongside my camel, his little figure outlined against the sky as I looked over the edge of my basket. Nothing was too much for him to do to make the heat of the days bearable. It seemed a lifetime, but Nushki was reached, despite rumours and alarms, without incident. Civilisation again – a railway, and goodbye to those patient but uneasy camels. To see, even to hear, an engine puffing its way up and over the mountains towards Quetta was a delightful experience.* [For the author, it is pleasing to think that my Sapper Uncle, Cecil Anderson, had helped to build that railway]. *I must confess that I felt almost done for. The last four hundred miles had been a nightmare. Everything I owned had been lost in that disastrous ambush. P and O, Fortnum and Mason,* [camels] *had been engulfed.*

*Back again then to Quetta; G. and I in a perfectly good railway carriage, old man syce in attendance. It seemed more than two lifetimes since I had come down that tortuous mountain railway to Nushki, to the adventure of being swallowed up in the Baluchistan desert. Swallowed up and thrown up again, that was what it came to. Failure is a filthy thing to bite on.*

*Back again to cantonments. No yelling raiders here - sympathetic medical officers decreed a return to England to fill out that arm and clear up those holes in a disappointed body, not to mention those in a disappointed mind. If only I could have got those prisoners through! Dyer, reinforced by four hundred Hazaras, was after the raiders through that Alan Quartermain country.*

*The Commanding Officer of my regiment, who was at the depot in Quetta, sent for me just before I was leaving for England, to say goodbye and to sympathise with me in the trouble in which I had got. He was a good chap, that Commanding Officer. He told me that I was young, and that I should live it down. I couldn't help saying that I considered myself darned lucky to be alive at all."*

There are many other tales of the experiences of Indian Army Officers and this happy comradeship with their troops, remembered to this day in the Regimental Associations in this country and the Regiments in Pakistan and India. Letters arrive in England, asking for photographs of the officers of an earlier time, to help with the memories. As those now elderly officers fall off their perches and can no longer keep up the relationship, the stories still go on. I chose to use this narrative because it links with the German ingress into India from the West and gives a vivid impression of Dyer from a man who served under him, and Dyer is the man who is the subject of this book.

At the same time, the poisonous and mendacious propaganda continued. By 1919 (the campaign in the Sarhad was in 1916), the propaganda had its effect on the troops in India, newly recruited in the ensuing years, while so many of their seniors were abroad fighting in the West, in Turkey and Persia. There is no doubt that the effect was serious and the resistance to the attempts to reduce India to anarchy could have been broken. That it was not broken, was due, in large part, to the mutual respect and affection held by Indian soldiers and the British officers of the Indian Army.

# Chapter VII
# MILITARISM

If Chapter VI drew attention to the strength of the relationship between British officers and Indian soldiers in the Indian Army, it is perhaps appropriate to contrast that with German attitudes towards their inferiors during those years.

John Buchan, in his book 'Greenmantle', wrote this: *"We call ourselves insular but the truth is that we are the only race on earth that can produce men capable of getting inside the skin of remote peoples. Perhaps the Scots are better than the English, but we are all a thousand percent better then anybody else."* That might be considered a prejudiced comment, by those whose overseas experience is limited to holidays abroad or international football matches, but it rings true for anyone who has seen British soldiers on active service in far-flung parts of the world.

The other day, some Germans said that at last they were becoming accepted. After two world wars this has taken some time in coming, but at the time of which I have written, their reputation was much as one would expect.

As an example which illustrates the British attitudes and behaviour with which they may be compared, my father, just prior to World War I, was talking to a German Rhodes Scholar, whose observations on our position in Ireland seemed worth recording. *"We do not understand your attitude to Ireland"* the Rhodes Scholar remarked, *"if we have trouble in Poland, we simply send in the Uhlans and they shoot the men and rape the women."*

A further illustration of the contrast can be found in the circumstances surrounding the building of that railway by the Germans, which would give them access to Persia.

The Constantinople-Baghdad railway was part of a German plan to establish an Eastern Empire. The Railway ran from Berlin to Constantinople and thence to Baghdad, with a link to Egypt and the Suez Canal and down to Medina. At an earlier point, at Aleppo, it branched across to Mosul on the Persian border and from there down to Basra on the Persian Gulf. The branch to Suez was to be used for an attempt to take over the Canal, which would interrupt the British connection with India and any troop movements from the Indian Army to Europe. Throughout, the British tended to look at their local positions, apparently overlooking the wider German strategy.

T. E. Lawrence acquired some experience of this before the War. He had already paid a visit to Lord Kitchener, pointing out the danger of letting the Germans get control of the port of Alexandretta, which is in the crook between Asia Minor and Syria, but Kitchener told him he knew all about it. He had repeatedly warned the British Foreign Office of the complications that would follow – the French had ambitions for the control of Syria too – but Sir Edward Gray's pacific policy allowed no alternative. Kitchener's final words to Lawrence were that within three years there would be a world war, which would settle this lesser problem with a greater, *"So run along young man, and dig before it rains."*.

About Lawrence, Graves wrote: *"He was, among other things, a student of world politics and saw that the alliance between the Turks and the Germans would have dangerous results. The Constantinople-Baghdad railway was part of the German scheme for establishing an Eastern Empire with the Turks as allies.*

*After 1911, Dr. Hogarth left the* [digging] *operations at Carchemish in charge of Mr. Leonard Woolley, who re-engaged Lawrence. Woolley and Lawrence had soon come to be on the best possible terms with their workmen, who were of mixed races; Kurds, Arabs, Turks and so on. Local brigands were working for them at the diggings, including the leaders of the two most notorious brigand bands, the Kurdish and the Arab, and the two Englishmen were so well known and respected that they were made judges of various local disputes between villages or persons. Mr. Fowle relates that Lawrence had recently been away to settle a case where a man had kidnapped a girl from her father's house, but had not been able to get the father's consent to the marriage.*

*In Woolley's bedroom was an ancient wooden chest containing thousands of silver pieces for the payment of the workmen. It was unlocked and unguarded; because if any man had come to steal, the other workmen would soon have found him out and taken matters into their own hands and probably killed the thief. Lawrence and Woolley found that the way to get the best results, was to pay the workmen an extra sum of money for any antiquity that they found, according to its actual value.*

*Lawrence himself, as Dr. Hogarth tells me, preferred sleeping outside the hut on a knoll, the ancient citadel of the city, close to the river. Here would gather the diggers and amuse him with stories, many of them scandalous, about the old Sheikh of Jerablus, the modern village on the site of Carchemish, and his young wife and about the Germans in their camp a quarter of a mile away. A railway was being made from Constantinople to Baghdad and at the site of Carchemish, the railway had to cross the Euphrates. German engineers were building a bridge. The Germans could not be bothered to get to know their workmen by name, but used numbers painted onto their coats as the quickest way of recognising them. They even allowed members of tribes who were blood enemies to work side-by-side and many deaths happened this way. The Germans envied Lawrence and Woolley because they could always get as many workmen as they wanted. On one occasion, when the Englishmen had to turn away fifty men for lack of money to pay them with, the men refused to go but stayed on without pay until money might come in again.*

*With the Germans, there was good feeling. Woolley and Lawrence gave them permission, among other things, to cart off for their new building such stones from the diggings as were of no archaeological interest. But the chief engineer, Contzen, was a difficult man to remain friendly with. He was a rough drinking fellow, the son of a Cologne chemist. The back of his neck was too thick for Lawrence's taste, it lapped over his collar. He came once to ask permission to dig away some mounds of earth which, though inside the excavation area, were close to the bridge where he wanted earth for an embankment. This was refused, because the mounds of earth were the old mud, brick and city walls of Carchemish and of great archaeological importance. He grew angry with that and breaking off all friendly relations, decided to wait until the digging season ended and the Englishmen went away. So when Woolley had gone to England and Lawrence to the Lebanon mountains, Contzen recruited local labour for digging away the walls. There was an Aleppo Arab called Wahid, the Pilgrim left in charge of the digging in the absence of the others, who, hearing what Contzen was about to do, went over to the Germans and told him, that without orders from Woolley or Lawrence, he could not allow work to begin. Contzen answered that he would start the next day and ordered Wahid to leave the camp. Wahid sent a wire to Lawrence in the Lebanon, saying that he would hold up the work until further orders. He went the next morning with a rifle and two revolvers and sat on top of the threatened wall. A hundred workmen began laying a light railway from the embankment to the foot of the wall, and Wahid addressed them, promising he would shoot the first man who drove a pick into the wall, and then would shoot any German within range. The workmen, many of whom were of the English camp but doing temporary work in the off season, stopped work and sat down at a safe distance. Contzen came up and threatened, but Wahid levelled his rifle and told him to keep his distance; Contzen did not dare to do more. All that day, the two parties sat and watched each other; and all the next day. That night the Germans began a little revolver practice in their courtyard, shooting at a lighted candle. Wahid climbed up on the wall and fired half a dozen shots over their heads, shouting to them to stop their noise and go to bed; and they obeyed.*

*Lawrence wired to Wahid to hold on, he was now in Aleppo seeing to things. Wahid wired back that the Germans were becoming dangerous, and that the next morning he was going to the camp to kill Contzen. Then he made his will, got drunk and prepared for the morning. Lawrence in Aleppo found he could do nothing with the local Turkish Officials in whose care the diggings were supposed to be, so he wired to Constantinople, and got an unexpectedly quick reply. The Turkish Education Minister was ordered to go up to Carchemish in person and stop the work. Lawrence wired an order to Wahid to offer no further resistance to the Germans. He sent the wire by the railway telegraph, and the railway people, who were naturally on Contzen's side in his embankment making, knew nothing of the orders from Constantinople to stop the work and thought the opposition was at an end. Lawrence and the Minister were given a motor trolley on which they travelled at once. Wahid, getting the wire, was deeply disappointed and went off to drown his sorrows in drink. Contzen sent his gang to work on the wall. They had hardly moved two or three feet of earth and mud-brick when up came the Minister in a fury, with Lawrence behind him and made Contzen tear up the rails and dismiss his extra workmen, abusing him for his dishonesty. Wahid was publicly congratulated.*

*After this, there was further trouble with Contzen. (Though not with the German camp as a whole. As has been said, Woolley and Lawrence kept open house and the better Germans used to visit them regularly and dine with them.) One day, Ahmed, one of the house servants of Woolley and Lawrence, on his way home from shopping in the village, met the foreman of the railway workers. The foreman owed him money and a dispute started. A German engineer came up and flogged Ahmed without inquiring into the cause of the dispute - it was enough that the railway work had been delayed. Lawrence went to Contzen, and told him that one of the engineers had assaulted his house servant and must apologise.*

*Contzen consented to make enquiries, called up the engineer, and asked him for his account of the affair. He then told Lawrence angrily, 'it is a lie, the gentleman never assaulted your servant; he merely had him flogged'.*

*'Well, isn't that an assault?'*

*'Certainly not! You can't use these natives without flogging them. We flog every day.'*

*'We have been here longer than you and have not flogged a man yet, and don't intend to let you start on them. Your engineer must come to the village and apologise to Ahmed in public.'*

*'Nonsense, the incident is closed,' and Contzen turned his back.*

*'On the contrary,' said Lawrence (one can hear his small deadly voice), 'if you do not do as I ask I shall take the matter into my own hands.'*

*Contzen turned round again 'Which means?'*

*'That I shall take your engineer to the village and compel him to apologise.'*

*'You will do nothing of the sort', said Contzen, scandalised, but then he looked at Lawrence again. In the end, the engineer came to make his public apology, to the vast satisfaction of the village.*

*Later the Germans found themselves in great trouble. They had established a local bakery to prevent their men sending parties for bread to their villages every ten days. This bread getting meant that thirty or forty men missed a day's work. The Germans let the bakery to a town bred Syrian (one of a most dishonest race), who decided to make his fortune. He used bad corn and so the bread was too sour to eat. The Germans had arranged that the money for the bread supplied should be deducted from the men's pay. When the workmen refused to eat the bread and again sent home to the villages for their own, the price of the week's bread that they had refused was deducted from their pay. Not only the bread contract, but also the contract for getting men to work on the railway had been given to adventurers, as Contzen's successor, Hoffman, discovered to his disgust. Complaints of the men not getting the money due to them were so numerous that he decided to pay them himself. Unfortunately he accepted the figures given him by the contractors, and there was trouble at once.*

*The first man who came to the pay table had been offered 15 piastres a day, which was a good wage, and he had been working six weeks; he was down in the books as entitled to only six piastres a day. After deductions for bread which he had not had, water he had got from the river himself, and so on, he was found to be owed only twenty seven and a half piastres for six weeks' work. The man protested. Hoffman's Circassian guard slashed him across the face with a whip. The man stooped to pick up a stone, his friends, who were Kurds, did the same, and the guard fired. A brisk battle started, stones and a few guns on one side, revolvers on the other. Lawrence and Woolley hearing the noise, came up to persuade the men, about seven hundred of them, to cease-fire. Lawrence has a gesture that he uses in emergencies of this kind. He lazily raises both hands, clasps them behind his head and remains silent and apparently wrapped in thought. It attracts attention more readily than any noise or violent motion, and when he has his audience quiet all about him, he says what is to be said with the gentle humorous wisdom of an old nurse subduing a noisy school-room. The Kurds ceased fire, but the seven Germans did not. They continued to use their revolvers from the hut where they had taken refuge, and the Circassian raised his gun towards Woolley and Lawrence as they came up, begging the Germans to stop. The Germans had quite lost their heads and went on firing, though the Kurds were not firing back. It was only with the help of Wahid and a former brigand chief Hamoudi, that Lawrence and Woolley prevented the whole mass of workmen rushing down to do massacre. It was more then two hours before the Kurds could be drawn off, then it was found that the Germans had only cuts and bruises to show while the Kurds had eighteen men wounded and one killed.*[24]

This extract from Graves' 'Lawrence and the Arabs' may come as a surprise to those who delight in denigrating the attitudes which built the British Empire. General Dyer was, although an Englishman, one of those who could get inside the skin of Indians and it was because he could, that he added up the signs with complete accuracy in 1919.

In 1241, the Northern cities of Germany formed themselves into a league – the Hanseatic League - which took in at its largest, about a hundred cities of the East and West of Northern Europe. The Hanseatic League had an army, navy and a great deal of power that it wielded in its claim of helping trade and protecting shipping.

---

24 This account appears in Woolley's 'Dead Towns and Living Men' the slight differences in the story are due to explanations by Lawrence – Graves' note

The men of the League behaved with arrogance and extreme self-importance towards the peoples of the member states and as trade began to spread through the Southern countries of Europe and throughout the world, they became unpopular because of the restraints and controls that they used and their behaviour. They behaved as though they were superior beings towards the local people and by their power, stopped Britain trading with other countries.

In a plan to explore and trade without the despotism of the Hanseatic League, the English formed the Company of Merchant Adventurers and began to throw off the restraints of the Germans. Queen Elizabeth I stopped the Hanseatic League trading in Britain in 1587 and gave charters to those Englishmen wishing to trade overseas. In 1599, she gave her Royal Assent and Licence to *"George, Earl of Cumberland and our other well beloved subjects... that they, of their own adventures, costs and charges, as well as for the honour of this our realm of England, might adventure forth..."*

It seems possible that if Elizabeth had not taken such a step, our trade with India might never have got going, nor would we have started as we did in India, and continued under the directions of later Governors, in the same manner as instructed to William Hawkins, that, *"when you shall water and refresh your men you shall give them severe warning to behave themselves peaceably and civilly towards the people."*

Restraint of trade was forgotten in the freedom of the seas, but one expression was left. The Hansas called their trading bases 'factories' and we, the English, taking the offer of a base at Surat, also called it a factory and continued to use the term for all the trading posts of the East India Company.

# Chapter VIII
# GERMAN SCHEMES

John Buchan was entirely correct when he wrote: *"India, whose alleged disloyalty was a main factor in German calculations"*. From Count von Bernhardi's book 'Germany and the Next War' published in 1911, we know of the intention of the Germans to shake British power in India; for by then, the Germans were already working with the Ghadr party in the States and with Indian revolutionaries in Europe. The two most influential men in the plot to kill the Viceroy in 1912, when a bomb was thrown, were Har Dayal and Krishnavarma. Both had taken Honours at English Universities. Har Dayal was, as already mentioned, the leader of the Ghadr movement in the States, linked with and mainly funded by the Germans. The men, who were hanged for the attempted murder, killed one of the Viceroy's attendants as well as wounding Hardinge himself. A further conspiracy over a bomb case in Lahore, led to the punishment of the people who attacked the Viceroy and his entourage and four people were hanged. One of these was Amir Chand, a senior teacher in the Cambridge Mission School in Delhi, where his influence was strong. Among the teachers at the Cambridge Mission was a young man named C. F. Andrews, who was later to become a great propagandist for Gandhi. The Sessions Judge described Amir Chand as *"one who spent his life in furthering murderous schemes which he was too timid to carry out himself."* Two Bengali youths, who had brought the bomb up from Bengal, appealed against their sentences and one of them, when finally realising that he would have to hang, explained that it was he who had thrown the bomb, wearing the disguise of a Mohammedan Lady in purdah, standing in front of the Punjab National Bank in the Chandni Chauk in Delhi.

Germany's interest in Empire had begun to find shape in the 1880s when she began to infiltrate her ideas into the Press of various countries. The first step would be to get an article printed in a newspaper in South Africa, or in some such other place, where it could be printed without the likelihood of its information being challenged by educated people. The next step would be to get the same information repeated in German papers as being the opinion of the country in which it was initially printed. It was a devious and clever method of spreading propaganda, which gradually influenced the world. Von Bismarck who had at first, been against Empire, moved to favour it after the taking, by the Germans, of Angra Pequeria in 1883. Angra Pequeria is on the South-West coast of Africa, near Walfisch Bay, between what was Portuguese and what was Cape Territory. The Empire-building was meanwhile going on in Germany itself, as the Princes were gradually being drawn into the network of the country that had been known as Prussia. Odo Russell, Lord Ampthill, the father of the man who was later to defend Dyer's position in the House of Lords' debates, was our first Ambassador to the German Empire. Trouble came in Egypt and the Sudan, where General Charles Gordon was killed, the reverberations affecting the Gladstone Government at home in 1885, but at that time, the more insidious move was in Central Asia, where trouble with Russia was thought to have been stirred up by the Germans. Compromise seemed to Gladstone to be wiser than opposition, on a number of issues, as his health had began to fail, but the German influence was beginning to work in a widespread and insidious way, covering areas which were to become of growing importance. The journalist Moritz Busch later wrote of being employed to write a number of attacks on this country in the weekly 'Grenzboten', on Ireland, Afghanistan, India and the Boers in South Africa. In this effort, France was not far behind.

The German ruses spread to the publication of a White Book, in which papers written to the British Government were published, showing that they had received dilatory or no replies. Some at least of these had been sent to the German Minister in Britain with instructions not to send them on.

The attacks on Britain continued in subtle ways. Gladstone, even though he knew of some of these methods, put getting on with Germany before refutation. While all this was going on, trouble with the Russians began in Central Asia, which as already mentioned was believed to be of German secret promotion. Von Bismarck's initial claim to wish to get on with Britain was swept away as anti-British xenophobia, encouraged by media claims, continued to stir the German nation.

At the beginning of the 20$^{th}$ Century, media publication of anti-British information also started in this country. By 1911, the German intention to act had become overt and the actions themselves were by then well in hand. While travelling by ship back to India from Hong Kong, a couple heard German officers discussing the war that was to take place in India. On the borders of France and Germany, General Wilson, taking his holiday abroad on a pedal cycle, toured all around the Ruhr and saw Army encampments clearly mobilising for war. [General Wilson was to become Field-Marshal Sir Henry Wilson, who, as the head of the Army Council, was to restrain the over excited Montagu and Churchill in their unjust and unwise attitudes to General Dyer when he came back from India]. In Morocco, like Angra Pequeria, the Germans claimed Agadir as a suitable harbour on the Atlantic seaboard. The Germans claimed that a German firm[25] held rights in Agadir; the French, that there were no rights and anyway, that Agadir was a sandy beach with no house, no warehouse, and no harbour. The French, recognising the advantage they might gain over Morocco, were prepared to negotiate. There was a suggestion of international inspection; the French felt that the milder climate of Morocco could reasonably be needed by the Germans in the place of more humid climes, as they continued to discuss the boundaries of the Congo. Churchill wrote later, *"Suddenly and unexpectedly, on the morning of July 1st and without more ado, it was announced that His Imperial Majesty, the German Emperor had sent his gunboat, the Panther, to Agadir to maintain and protect German interests."* This small ship was already on its way. All the alarm bells throughout Europe began to ring. France found herself unable to explain an act with an immeasurable outcome[26] and an unknown purpose. Great Britain, having consulted the atlas, began to wonder what effect a German naval base on the Atlantic coast of Africa would have upon her maritime security, observing that such a fact must be taken in conjunction with German activities at Madeira and in the Canaries and with the trade routes from South America and South Africa which converged and passed through those waters. Europe was uneasy, while France was genuinely alarmed.

Sir Edward Grey, informed by Count Metternich and realising the seriousness of the situation, brought it before the Cabinet. He told Metternich that the British Government reserved its opinion until it knew more of the German intentions. Until July 21st, there was a 'period of silence'. Was Germany about to go to war with France? If she were, the firm stand of the British would have undoubtedly affected her decision. A speech by Lloyd George, new Foreign Secretary, to the City, made clear that Britain should at all hazards retain her position in the world. Sir Edward Grey asked to see Lloyd George, who remarked; *"I have just received a communication from the German Ambassador, so stiff, that the Fleet may be attacked at any moment."* It had been believed that Lloyd George would be on the side of peace and Germany was astonished by his stand on the side of France. Count Metternich was recalled for not having predicted accurately the attitude of Britain; and the scare died down. Whether the intention was there or not, Germany in 1911 was capable of war. It was not until 1917 that Germany started her U-boat war in the Atlantic, but without a port on the Atlantic seaboard of Africa.

---

25   This firm was Manussens, International Electric and others close to the international bankers in the Second World War. They used slave labour, one of the Directors being arraigned at Nuremberg. British P.O.W.s described their treatment of labour as 'starvation and torture'.

26   U-boats had not then been used, but the strategy fitted in with what was to happen later.

In America, the Ghadr movement was starting, with funds going from Vancouver to the Indian community in the United States in San Francisco on the West coast. Har Dayal arrived in 1911, having thrown up his state scholarship at St John's College, Oxford, where he had gone in 1905. He was in Lahore staying with Lajpat Rai in 1908, preaching passive resistance and boycott as Gandhi was about to preach it in South Africa, having written his booklet, Hind Swaraj, in 1907. Back in Europe in 1908, Krishnavarma went to London, Paris and then Geneva, where he started the newspaper 'Bande Materam', leaving his followers to continue their propaganda among students coming from India to England at the Highgate Centre, India House, whence Dhingra had gone out to kill Sir Curzon Wyllie - the action that had led to Krishnavarma leaving London.

The Criminal Investigation Department in India unravelled the intricacies of the conspiracy to kill the Viceroy led by Har Dayal, Dinanath, a Punjabi, and a Bengali called Chatterji. The training of conspirators was carried on by Amir Chand at the Cambridge Mission School at Delhi with a Bengali Forest Clerk, Rash Behari; Dinanath turned informer, Amir Chand and three others were hanged and Rash Behari escaped. Rash Behari Bose was a Bengali Head Clerk in a Government office in Dehra Dun.

It was clear that Har Dayal was in the confidence of Germany, for in 1913 he told an audience at Sacramento that Germany was going to war with England and that it was time to get ready to go to India for the coming revolution.

By the time the war did break out, Har Dayal was in Berlin, attached to the Indian Section of the German General Staff. He, together with Barkatullah, C.K. Chakrabarti (Bengali), Chattopadhya (brother of Mrs. Sarojini Naidu), Pillai (Madrassi), advised and translated propaganda and worked in keeping with their society's name 'The Indian Revolutionary Society'. In the judgement given in the (third) Lahore conspiracy case put before the Hunter Committee, but disregarded in the interests of claiming that there was no evidence of conspiracy, the judge said:

*"This society, which aimed at establishing a Republic in India, held constant meetings which were attended by Turks, Egyptians, German officials and most noteworthy of all, German ex-professors and ex-missionaries who in their time had received the hospitality of the British Government in India. Har Dayal and Chattopadhya were in daily communication with the German Foreign Office. To carry out the revolution in India, there was an Oriental Bureau for translating and disseminating inflammatory literature to the Indian prisoners of war in Germany. Inflammatory letters drafted by the German Government and addressed to the Indian Princes were translated and printed, and meetings were held in which the common objects of Germany and India were dilated upon, these meetings being sometimes presided over by highly placed German officials."*

In the face of this vociferous anti-British movement, the Germans probably under-estimated the feelings of the bulk of Indian leaders, showing to an extent in the attitude of Gopal Krishna Gokhale, the moderate, who believed that progress should move forward under constitutional method. Gokhale is probably best known for his testament of advice for the alterations in British rule, left with the Aga Khan after his death in 1915 (thus showing his undivisive approach to Muslims). He was proposed as a member of the Viceroy's Council, but instead, Sachindra Sinha, a Bengali barrister was given the position by Lord Minto. Sinha's remark to Lady Minto was more in contrast with nationalist thinking: *"If the English left India today in a body, we should have to telegraph to Aden to get them to return as fast as they could, for in a couple of days India would be in chaos."*

Given the information provided by the nationalists, the Germans were optimistic and their main activity was to encourage, through their agent's funds and know-how. Gurdit Singh, a Sikh from the Punjab, as an example, decided to take Indians to Canada, to break the Canadian bar to immigrants from India, probably egged on by information provided through the German Consuls in Shanghai, Moju and at Yokohama. He tried to force his unpopular cargo onto the Canadian authorities, despite their restrictions. When they would not agree, he was faced with irritated passengers, angry at being frustrated in their plans, so he took them, filled with anti-British Ghadr literature and fury, to Calcutta. The ship he hired was the Komagatu Maru, which was arranged by the German Consul at Hong Kong. What was his true intention? The Tribunal which tried the first batch of Lahore conspirators held that Gurdit Singh's main object was to cause uproar. At intermediate ports, consignments of Ghadr newspapers had been brought onto the ship and at Yokohama, two Indian revolutionaries from the United States came on board. The ship went up the Hooghly and stopped at Budge-Budge on 29th August 1914. A train was waiting to take the passengers up to the Punjab but many of them would not go and marched on Calcutta. There was an armed conflict and many of the men escaped, including Gurdit Singh. The follow-on in the Punjab was a number of serious dacoities and hold-ups. Some of the men were tried and some interned in the villages. The plot that had started in the United States was disclosed in a trial in November 1917 at San Francisco, where it was shown that the campaign was started prior to 1911, with German agents and Indian revolutionaries in Europe. In pursuance of their scheme, they founded the Ghadr Revolutionary Party in California and it spread through California, Oregon and Washington, where the German doctrine was preached, that the Fatherland would strike England.

The Komagatu Maru was the first of a large number of ships and craft, which took 'Ghadr' Indians to India. Some went to Ceylon and others to various places on the Indian seaboard. By 1919, not only was there a widespread conspiracy but armed men ready to support it. Soldiers were to be a particular target in the conspiracy. It was held by the Bengalis that they were not being employed in the army because the British were frightened of Bengali cleverness.[27]

---

27   This was decided after the Great Mutiny. The British were indeed aware of Indian, especially Bengali, closeness; the result of that pressure was that we were forced to become honest and trustworthy since we could not compete.

But in all this, the General Principles of the conspirators were being worked out. They ran thus:
1. The organisation of a nucleus – this should include many educated people.
2. The spreading of ideas throughout the nucleus.
3. Organisation of terrorist means, military and terrorist.
4. Agitation.
5. Rebellion.

By 1919 everything was in readiness.

**COMMANDING OFFICER AND SENIOR INDIAN OFFICERS OF 25TH PUNJABIS AT THE DELHI DURBAR 1911**
**(WIKIPEDIA IMAGE)**

**KOMAGATA MARU CARRIED BACK TO INDIA 354 GHADR CONSPIRATORS AFTER THEIR UNSUCCESSFUL ATTEMPT TO LAND IN CANADA IN 1914. MOST WERE RETURNED TO THE PUNJAB, WHERE THEY POSED A CONTINUAL RISK OF INSURRECTION.**
**(WIKIPEDIA IMAGE)**

## Chapter IX
## INFILTRATION

It is fairly obvious that if the Germans were intent on destabilising British India, they would not confine their efforts to the East coast of the sub-continent and I have written of the infiltration attempts through Persia in Chapter VI.

Turkey was the jumping off point for the movement against India in Afghanistan and through Persia and Zeistan into Baluchistan. The man believed to be most responsible for the infiltration into Britain of German propaganda, particularly peace propaganda, was Alexander Helphand, usually called Parvus. The stories of John Buchan, such as 'Mr Standfast', made clear the ramifications of the peace movement, which at one point looked as though it might threaten the continuation of the First World War, or the sinister doings in Constantinople which he indicated in 'Greenmantle'. Since Buchan was the head of the Department of Information during the War, his subtle delineating of the intentions of the people behind the peace propaganda, were soundly based. Part of this so-called peace movement, still in vogue today, was that the war itself was not necessary, seriously undermining those who were at the front, and their relatives, or those of the wounded or killed. It was a subtle attack on that essence of loyalty to our own nation called patriotism, without which people would lie down and be taken over. It was accomplished during the Second War by the French under Vichy leadership, continuing today in the claims that unless we give in to Federalism in Europe, we will have war. To give in to a Federalist European Union (with Germany being the largest power in Europe), is to feed the very force that we have spent so much of our fortune and our lives to resist - a continuation of the pervasive peace movement of the 1914 war.

It may be thought that a desire for peace can only be commended, and such a desire is only a natural outcome of Christian faith in the midst of a devastating war, but calls for peace may stem from other motives. They have been used to disarm opposition, give breathing-space to a failing aggressor, conceal true intentions, confuse the simple. Calls for peace were so used in 1917.

Morel, the pacifist Labour MP, like Sir Edgar Speyer, was a naturalised Briton, originally French (his name was Eduard Morel de Ville) and was also pro-German. The Evening Standard, in those days more courageous, or more secure in the patriotism of Britain, than is the Press in the present day [when the extraordinary behaviour of M.P.s who vote to give away British sovereignty and Habeas Corpus with no apparent thought of their responsibilities to their voters, barely mention that what is going on is treason], printed an extremely accurate description of Morel's activities.

The 'Evening Standard' of 31st July 1917, wrote as follows:

*"The Committee of the Workers' and Soldiers Council is also an outcome of the 'Morel' movement, which is responsible directly or indirectly, through the parent body, the U.D.C.* [Union of Democratic Control] *for the whole of the Pacifist organisations and propaganda, through which 'Morel' is attempting, by a variety of insidious appeals, to weaken the war resolutions of the people and foment industrial troubles in order to cripple our military efforts. The same master hand has woven this network of organisations. Messrs. Philip Snowdon, Ramsay MacDonald, Ponsonby, Trevelyan are, consciously or unconsciously, all creatures of 'Morel' and quite insignificant without him. This pro-German exploits their follies and their prejudices in the same way that he uses the cowards and the shirkers and the Quakers and the Syndicalists and the elements of anarchy wherever they are to be found. He has been working cunningly and assiduously for many months to save Prussia from defeat, and he has used any instrument that came to his hand. I shall continue, therefore, to call the 'Workers and Soldiers' Council, a product of the 'Morel' movement whose founder should long ago have been deprived of his naturalisation, by Act of Parliament if necessary, and expelled the country as an undesirable alien."*

These efforts to subvert patriotism culminated in the calling of a Peace Conference at Stockholm. The Labour M.P. and Cabinet member, Arthur Henderson, wished to attend with Ramsay MacDonald, anti-war Labour politician, but the plans for the Conference fizzled out. Instead, MacDonald attempted a visit to Russia to consult with the Workmen's and Soldiers' Soviets and obtained a passport, but the National Union of Seamen refused to transport him. He it was, who advised the King not to invite the Tsar and his family to come to refuge in England on the grounds that it might encourage unrest.

Not only was Germany, and in this case Parvus, involved in the spreading of peace propaganda, but America was negotiating for peace, with the German Ambassador in Washington, even persuading President Wilson to bring in the States, to stop the War. Today, when patriotism is a dirty word, and even supposedly fascist, it may be difficult to recognise the validity of defence for good reasons; the just war as it was called. War, it is said, is so terrible, (as of course it is), that pacifism is believed to be preferable to concern for one's country and one's country's virtues. Few Prime Ministers would have gone to war over the Falklands, thus stopping the take-over of a small nation against the will of her people, but stopping such aggression is still valid. The questions so rarely asked are, 'Why did Germany go to war in the first place?' 'Why in the second?' and 'Why is expansionist so-called Euro-Federalism so important now?'

These questions have to be asked, if the strategy for world rule is to be recognised. The intention was clear, from the time of the first anti-British propaganda in the 1870s; clear with the claims for ports placed in strange remote spots, which would be important for global strategy in the long term. Did the politicians then see, when they took steps to prevent these expansions, the difference from the gradual growth of the British Empire, with its aim of developing free, democratic Dominions, or lands being ruled peacefully and prosperously in a Commonwealth of Nations? The German intention seems to have been quite different. There was not the concept of freely trading units, working towards mutual prosperity, but the abstraction of commodities for the wealth of the 'Master Race'. Bernstorff made it clear when he wrote: *"...if we show ourselves accommodating to Turkey, we shall back up the existing Cabinet which is friendly to us, and get all the economic advantages that are to be had in this country (Turkey)"* and again, mentioning the Treaty of Brest-Litovsk, in which the German behaviour was of such extraordinary rapacity to the Russians: *"I therefore take the view that we should treat with Djavid (Turkish Finance Minister) just as we did with the Bolsheviks. I would tell him that we are ready to regard the money we had given to the Turks as a subvention for the defence of the Dardanelles, on condition that the Turks on their part, brought in a Liquidation Law, handed over all the raw materials they possess, and met our other demands. They must ally themselves to us to the same extent economically as they have done politically. If they refuse, we will neither forgive them their debts nor advance them any further loans."*

The defence by the Turks of the Dardanelles prevented the flow of supplies into Russia through the Black Sea.

But just as today, spies were in place long before the war. Sir Edgar Speyer had even been appointed a Privy Councillor and would have known all the war movements and been able to report them to the Germans.

Not only India, but Ireland was co-operating with German interests, particularly in 1917 when it came to the U-boat War, which the War Party in Berlin insisted on. People such as Count Bernstorff observed it to be a mistake, for he was at that time Ambassador in the United States and saw Wilson's withdrawal from the peace plans almost immediately on the sinking of U. S. shipping.

The German people had been inspired, in much the same way as the Indians, by newspaper articles and war talk, for years before the War. Mrs. Webster wrote of walking through the streets of Wiesbaden *"an unoffending young English girl many years before the War .... Never shall I forget the insults, the yells of Verfluchte Engländerin (cursed English Woman) that pursued me as I walked alone ... and in the window of the largest bookseller's shop hung a map of the world beneath which was inscribed in large letters "Zu Deutschland gehort die Welt"*. [The World Belongs to Germany].

Sir Henry Wilson's recognition of the danger was based on observation of the growing war machine in the Ruhr. General Gordon, whom we think of as an actor in an earlier period of history, warned in 1882: *"So far as England is concerned, she need not, for the next quarter of a century, be under any apprehension of serious difficulties arising with any of her European neighbours, but in 1910 or thereabouts there will have arisen a naval Power which may prove mightier than she, and should she (Germany) gain the supremacy, England will become extinct both as a land and sea power, and all her dependencies, including India, will fall into German clutches. You may live to see this* [written to James Pardey] *I shall not, but when that time comes, remember my words."*

In 1912, Lord Roberts spoke of the illusions of peace and universal disarmament at a time when Germany was drilling 'the mightiest and most disciplined force the world has ever known', but anyone who speaks of the reality of the threat of war becomes unpopular. Thus wars take place which might have been avoided, if the threat was seen to make it necessary for us to defend our own homes, as is permitted in the Gospel. Violence begets violence, where firmness and clarity prevent it.

The concern of Henry Wilson and Lord Roberts was that there should be National Service. In Ireland, conscription was not brought in and the population which did not voluntarily join the army was left to cause the miserable chaos that the Irish made at that time. In India, the only conscription was of the British in India, businessmen, bankers, and any officials that could be spared. The effect was to weaken India just prior to the rising being planned and carried out in 1919. Percy Marsden, as an example, fighting with the East Persian Cordon, returned to Kasur just after the first day or two of the rising. Indian solders, (now Pakistani and Indian), were volunteers and the townsmen who would have gained by the discipline and experience of fighting for their country, as would the whole of India, were left to conspire against the British, later to claim that they had fought to defend the Empire and Britain, and had been given nothing in return! They clamoured with the Bolshevik cry of self-determination, which many schools of thought regarded as a cloak for annexation. In 1904, Valentine Chirol, the 'Times' correspondent who knew so much about Indian unrest, wrote of the hidden policy which Germany was then denying:

*"Though I quite understand the advantages from the German point of view of utilising the war for a rapprochement with Russia – and therefore cannot see why Berlin should be so keen to deny it – it seems to me to be carrying it to dangerous lengths to try and interfere in regard to Tibet, where it cannot be pretended that Germany has any locus stand. However I suppose that Wilhelmstrasse knows best."*

To go back a few years earlier, the Cretan Rebellion led to the action of Lord Salisbury in supporting the Turks by sending British warships to the Mediterranean, to stop help coming from Greece to help the Greeks of Crete. Turkey then had been helped by Britain, so the later action in becoming an ally of Germany did not derive from earlier anti Turkish action. The year was 1896. Churchill is recorded as having taken the attitude that Lord Salisbury was wrong. *"I look on this from the point of view of right and wrong. Lord Salisbury from that of profit and loss."*

In this attitude lay Churchill's soundness, his ability to see the true nature of Nazism in later years, what might be called a sense of morality, which, since those years, has been eroded to an extent that in modern times, morality has become an almost unrecognisable concept, moving this nation to the brink of accepting any claim that is made by foolish power-seeking leaders. Yet even Churchill, in 1920, for political reasons, accepted the false version of the actions of Dyer and the other officials in the 1919 Rebellion.

Such is the effect of distortion and lies, like the ubiquitous claim that Britain's policy in India was one of 'Divide and Rule'. Far from it! We spent our time endeavouring to develop co-existence and a sense of being Indian rather than being one of a village, district, area or religion. The phrase stems from Curzon's action in dividing Bengal and when thought of in that context is reasonable, but in historical terms it is incorrect.

The propaganda that has been indicated went on throughout the early years of the century, carefully inculcated and spread not only by the Bengalis, but by Germans and later, by Bolsheviks. It was described at the time of the rebellion by John Buchan, well-placed to know what was going on. *"They are masters of propaganda ... have you ever considered what a diabolical weapon that can be – using all the channels of modern publicity to poison and warp men's minds? It is the most dangerous thing on earth. You can use it cleanly – as I think on the whole we did during the War – but you can also use it to establish the most damnable lies. Happily in the long run it defeats itself, but only when it has sown the world with mischief. Look at the Irish! They are the cleverest propagandists extant, and managed to persuade most people that they were a brave, generous, humorous, talented, warm-hearted race, cruelly yoked to a dull mercantile England, when God knows they were exactly the opposite."*

He also wrote of the Bolsheviks at Tashkent, sending propaganda into India and *"the winter of 1917 when the Bolsheviks were making trouble in Afghanistan and their stuff was filtering through into India."*

In Britain there was also pro-German feeling. Lord Haldane declared in 1913 that our relations with Germany were twice as good as they were two years previously; in January 1914, that there was a greater prospect of peace than there ever was before. Asquith and Lord Grey were bracketed with him. Lord Roberts, telling the English to prepare, was vilified, as was to happen to Churchill 25 years later.

Trebitsch-Lincoln, a Hungarian, Liberal Member of Parliament for Darlington, was appointed as censor to the General Post Office, only to be found later to be spying for the Germans; Asquith, by 1915 was faced with the Press claims that Sir Edgar Speyer's intimate relations with him were a source of danger to the country. Asquith wrote, strongly refuting the imputation on his close friend, but in 1921 Sir Edgar's activities were investigated and he was stripped of his Privy Councillorship and his British naturalisation.

In 1915, Venetia Stanley, Asquith's long-term friend, his almost daily correspondent, married Edwin Montagu, a young Privy Councillor aged 36 at that time, with a seat in the Cabinet as Chancellor of the Duchy of Lancaster. It would not be until 1917, after Asquith's fall in December 1916, that Montagu would become Secretary of State for India.

On 4th August 1914, German troops crossed the border of Belgium. Lord Grey had warned the House of Commons that the 1839 Treaty with Belgium might force Britain into war. In the afternoon of the 3rd, he sent an ultimatum to stop the invasion within 24 hours, but the Germans did not stop, and Britain was at war. The Kaiser later spoke of his gratitude for Turkey's friendship at the terrible time when all his relatives declared war on him!

On 11th August, after being chased in the Eastern Mediterranean and the Aegean by the British, the two German warships, Goeben and Breslau entered the safety of Turkish waters. Britain, with the instructions of Churchill, blockaded the Dardanelles, since Turkey was not at war.

On 29th October, the Goeben and Breslau, having been handed over by the Germans to Turkey, bombarded the Russian Black Sea ports of Odessa, Nikolaev and Sevastopol. The British Government at once sent an ultimatum to the Turks ordering them to dismiss the German military and naval missions at Constantinople, and to remove all German personnel from the two warships. The Turks refused to do so. Learning this, Churchill asked Fisher (First Lord of the Admiralty) to look into the possibility of bombarding the outer forts of the Dardanelles.

How had this close union between Turkey and Germany come about? It was one of the fears of the Turks that Russia would take over Constantinople, and this would have encouraged a refusal to fight with the Allies, but why, it has to be asked, did they allow the Germans to leave their personnel on ships that effectively had been given to them? The action was to be typical of future German/Turkish management of their mutual forces for the next five years.

That the motivation was from Parvus – 'Parvus of the Sultan and William', as Lenin wrote - becomes clear as more research is done and written about him. Until recently, this man was only known in the pages of Mrs. Nesta Webster's research and by inference, in Buchan's 'Greenmantle'. He is now known more widely in Solzhenitzyn's 'Lenin in Zurich', in which the information is derived from books by Werner Hahlweg.[28] Solzhenitsyn gives his appreciation to these authors (as I must give mine to Nesta Webster), in the following words: *"I must express my gratitude to these writers for their close attention to events which determined the course of events in the twentieth century, but which have been carefully concealed from history, and which because of the direction taken by the development of the West, have received little attention."*

---

28   Z. B. Zerman and W. B. Scharlau: "The Merchant of Revolution", London 1965, Willi Gautschi, 'Lenin als Emigrant in der Schweis', Kiln 1973 and Fritz N Platten Jun. 'Von der spiegelgasse in den Kremlin' Volkscret.

The phrase from Aldonov's writings, quoted above continues: *"Parvus the spectacular, Parvus, who profited by the war, Parvus, who created the famous theory that from the Socialist point of view, Germany had the right to victory"*. He might have added, Parvus the Propagandist.

Parvus was born in Minsk in 1867; his name was Alexandr (Izrail) Lazarevitch Helphand and he spent his childhood in Odessa where he went to the Odessa High School in 1885 and in 1891 to Basel University. He then began a successful journalistic career in the German left-wing press (the journalistic 'revolution'); we have already seen the German inspiration for revolutionary propaganda through the Press in India, starting as far as we know with Har Dayal's Ghadr movement in the States. He also linked the Social Democrats in Russia and Germany and organised and wrote in a journal called 'Iskra' (The Spark).

As in India, the revolutionaries all knew one another and Solzhenitsyn makes Lenin envious of Parvus for his revolutionary activity and success. His journalistic activities led to his expulsion from various lands, and in 1905 he roused the revolutionaries in St Petersburg to active rebellion. It was a year after the birth of the little Prince Alexis, and the frightful discovery that he was haemophiliac. Witte, the Russian Finance Minister, had just got Russia onto the Gold Standard, had made a Peace Treaty with Britain, and as a result of the revolution, managed to bring through a constitution (30th October 1905) which promised freedom of conscience, speech, assembly and association to the Russian people. It also granted an elected Parliament, the Duma and pledged that 'no law may go into force without the consent of the State Duma'. Only the bringing in of the Semonovsky Regiment of the Guard, who cleared the streets with artillery and bayonets, crushed the Parvus/Trotsky revolution. It was clear then, as it was in later years, that the freedoms given by the Tsar were not enough to assuage the desire for totalitarian power by the Bolsheviks. Rational thought might have led to a harmonious political development for Russia, but to Lenin, Parvus and Trotsky, such reasoning was irrelevant. Power was what was wanted, not freedom. Power was the goal of the German World Policy first bruited in 1898, when Parvus has already embarked on his journalistic programme to that end.

After St Petersburg, Parvus went to Constantinople. His ability to use words gave him a position of strength. Propaganda consists of words and images; the intention of the propagandist rules their use. We have already seen the effects of the German-Indian propaganda of Har Dayal in forming the Ghadr movement, we have seen that peoples' minds can be easily twisted by journalistic expertise. It was not difficult for Parvus to manipulate minds in the direction he wished, to hand Turkish power over to Germany with the intention of affecting the Russians and their seaboard – effectively leading to the prevention of Russian shipping movement for a large part of the year, since they were closed off from the warm seas of the Mediterranean and egress to the Atlantic, except when the northern seaboard was free of ice.

As to India, the Partition of Bengal in 1904 had given force to the nationalists; in 1905, the Japanese-Russian War with the defeat of the Russians, had given to the

Indians a strong message. It was regarded as one of the most influential effects on the Indian Nationalists because it showed them that the East could beat the West. The racism of the Indian nationalists is not widely recognised today, but it is central to the whole of Indian nationalist policy. It has already been seen that hatred of the British was the motive of the 1919 rebellion – 'the white man, root and branch' as the Civil Surgeon at Amritsar described it.

In 1905, Har Dayal had only just gone up to St John's College, Oxford, on a State Scholarship. What was he doing prior to his work for the Ghadr movement in the States? His book 'Forty-four months in Germany and Turkey' makes clear the link. We know that he went to Germany and was part of that Committee which later issued orders from Berlin to him when he was in the States and ordered the armaments and ammunition that would go to India, as the Committee had also informed the Bengali revolutionaries.

After failure at St. Petersburg, Parvus moved to Turkey and by 1910 he was there as a member of the Committee of Union and Progress. We know that he attacked the German Government course of rapprochement with Russia from 1907 and we know that after 1915 when he left Turkey, he had made a fortune. In the meantime, he had acted as financial adviser to the Bulgarian and Turkish Governments. His position in Turkey was due to instructions from the German Government. He was given the funds to propagandise the Balkans, paying among others Rakovsky, who was also a German agent.

So successful had been his advice to the Bulgarian and Turkish Governments at the beginning of the war, that Germany had these nations in her power.

Although he want on to other things, it is almost impossible to believe that, given German interest in India, Parvus would not have been involved in the strategies to enter India from Turkey and Persia. When he left Turkey, he was given the contract to supply German coal to Denmark. By February 1915, he had entered into negotiations with the German Ministry of Foreign Affairs to undertake to bring Russia out of the war by starting a revolution there. At some stage he went to Geneva to start the 'Bureau of Economic Research', a euphemism for a bureau of German espionage and propaganda. Har Dayal was also in Geneva at some stage as were Amir Chand, Krishna Varma and others of the Indian revolutionary party. It is possible that the career of Parvus will never be wholly known; but it is clear that he was funded, as was Lenin, by the Germans. Under cover of his trading operations, he sent German money to the Russian revolutionaries, enabling them quickly to reinforce their membership, without which help the Bolsheviks would have been ineffectual. In 1917, he again supported the Bolsheviks in Finland between April and November. His moves were unremarked.

It is not Lenin who started this great revolutionary idea of Sovietism, which has nearly conquered the world. It is Parvus – Parvus of the Sultan and Wilhelm II, Parvus the speculator, Parvus who profited by the War, Parvus who created the famous theory that from the Soviet point of view, Germany had the right to victory.

John Buchan, writing in 1918 in 'Mr Standfast', knew clearly what Parvus had been doing in 1917 when his plan to reduce the Russian army was coming to fruition. He made his anti-hero into a German seditionist and spy called Ivery; he made clear that there were a number of people in high places all over the world who were part of the Parvus network - the people he called 'the Wild Birds'. He wrote, *"Also it was the Wild Birds that wrecked Russia. It was Ivery that paid the Bolsheviks to seduce [sic] the Army, and the Bolsheviks took his money for their own purpose, thinking they were playing a deep game, when all the time he was grinning like Satan, for they were playing his. It was Ivery, or some other of the bunch, that doped the brigades that broke at Caporetto. If I started to tell you the history of their doings you wouldn't go to bed, and if you did you wouldn't sleep ... There's just this to it. Every finished subtle devilry that the Boche has wrought among the Allies since August 1914 has been the work of the Wild Birds and more or less organised by Ivery. They're the mightiest poison merchants the world ever saw, and they've the nerve of hell ..."* In another extract, Ivery himself is quoted as saying: 'He was a German; it was through Germany alone that peace and regeneration could come. His country was purged from her faults, and the marvellous German discipline was about to prove itself in the eyes of gods and men. He told her what he had told me: Germany was not vengeful or vainglorious, only patient and merciful. God was about to give her the power to devise the world's fate and it was for him and his kind to see that that decision was beneficent. The greater task of his people was only now beginning, and again, he has sat spinning his web like a great spider, and for every thread there has been an ocean of blood spilled. It's his sort that made the war, not the brave, stupid fighting Boche. It's his sort that's responsible for all the clotted beastliness.'

Lenin, at the centre of the plan to destroy Russia, went to St Petersburg University in 1891. Like Gandhi, he completed his studies for the law and never practised, but instead became a professional revolutionary. He was arrested in 1896 and sent to Siberia and was then allowed to leave and go abroad. In 1903, at a meeting of the Social Democratic Party in London, he became the leader of the Bolshevik section, splitting from the Mensheviks. After this he lived in Russia, maintaining the Bolshevism movement by armed raids on banks and post offices, carried out by his agents. Thence to Geneva, Cracow and Galicia, where, at the outbreak of war, he was arrested by the Austrian authorities. He was freed because his value in weakening Russia was foreseen.

Seeing the marshalling of agents by Germany, he offered himself to the German Foreign Office in Berlin. At first he was refused, but the ubiquitous, powerful Parvus, from his inside position and knowledge, persuaded the Foreign Office to take him on, once again from the viewpoint of his capacity to wreck Russia. Lenin was recalled to Berlin and entrusted with the job of demoralising the French and Russian armies. He was to be given 70 million marks on the declaration of war. After that further sums would be paid directly into his account as and when needed. John Buchan must have known, since his story in 'Mr Standfast' is directly relevant to Lenin's moves, if not his finances; Lenin being directed and funded by the 'Wild Birds'. So successfully was the mission carried out that an article, written in 1920 by a Russian publicist Bortzell, says that the French Leninists recognised no such virtue as Patriotism, frankly admitted Lenin's complicity with the Germans and justified him in accepting money from them during the Battle of the Marne – meanwhile working for the destruction of the French Army.

We therefore have, as Buchan made clear, a widespread conspiracy functioning in Europe and later in Britain, from before the war, which blossomed in the move by Parvus to persuade his German leaders to send Lenin to Russia.

Parvus' plans and organisation led to the undertaking to bring Russia out of the war; his method, sending money to Russian revolutionaries under cover of trading operations - after the February revolution, exclusively to the Bolsheviks. His ability to poison with words was shown with his fierce attack on Kerensky in the German press, when Kerensky disclosed the background to the Bolshevik claims. His next step in 1917 (interestingly supported by Bernstorff's documents, although without mention of Parvus), was to obstruct concerted socialist efforts to end the war and to influence the German Government to await the total collapse of Russia, having no confidence in Bolshevik organising abilities, and condemning Lenin's concessions to peasants. The peasants themselves, at first, took less interest in Bolshevism than did other groups, in keeping with Marx and Engels Communist Manifesto.

How then did the Germans get Lenin into Russia? Churchill described it: *"Lenin was sent into Russia by the Germans in the same way that you might send a phial containing a culture of typhoid or cholera to be poured into the water supply of a great city and it worked with amazing rapidity."* Ludendorff wrote in his memoirs that by sending Lenin into Russia, our Government did assume a great responsibility, but from the military point of view, his journey was justified. The negotiator of the Brest-Litovsk Treaty, General Hoffman, described the movement as one of transporting poison gas. Indeed it was. We will see the result later in the effects on the Indian rebellion of 1919.

It was Parvus, first associated with Lenin in 1901, who inspired the revolutionary and again it was Parvus who suggested to Bethmann-Hollweg, the German Chancellor, that Lenin should be sent back to Russia (although according to Nesta Webster, the suggestion may have come to Bethmann-Hollweg through the German Minister in Copenhagen, Brockdorff-Rantzau, whose Illuminist tendencies and later connection with the Bolsheviks, make this suggestion reasonable). Lenin was sent with an entourage and £2,500,000 (more like billions in today's money). Of the 165 names published of people who were with him, only 23 were Russians. The others included 3 Georgian, 4 Armenian, 1 German and 128 Jewish. The 'Times' of 9th February 1918 quoted documentary evidence produced by 'Le Petit Parisien' to show that Lenin, Trotsky and other Bolsheviks 'have been and are' in German pay. *"These documents show that as early as March 2nd 1917, a week before the Russian Revolution, the German Imperial Bank notified its agents in Switzerland to honour all demands by Lenin, Trotsky and their associates for money for propaganda purposes in Russia ..."* The 'Times' also mentioned a well-known German Jewish banking firm which had long been engaged in furthering the German cause in Russia: *"His meeting with Protopopoff in Stockholm is a matter of history. After the overthrow of the old regime, he transferred his attention to anarchists. He was until recently in Petrograd: indeed he may still be there!"*

The German attitude, as Solzhenitsyn mentioned in his comments, was to claim that Germany herself had not been involved. There are records of the documents proving the German involvement in the Sisson Report, 'the German/Bolshevik Conspiracy', communicated by Mr. Edgar Sisson, the special representative of the American Committee on Public Information, showing German involvement in the early days of the Bolshevik regime; the Soviet leaders being absolutely controlled and even appointed by the German General Staff and financed by the Imperial Bank in Berlin. Mr. Solzhenitsyn has dug out some other documents from 1917 (Nos. 30, 31, cited by Werner Hahlweg: Lenins Ruckkehr nach Russland, 1917).

31 March, Berlin.(Memo by an official of the Foreign Ministry with the General Staff), *"...above all we must avoid compromising the travellers by excessive attentiveness on our part. It would be very desirable to have some sort of declaration from the Swiss government. If we suddenly send these restless elements to Sweden without such a declaration it may be used against us."*

31 March (Assistant Secretary of State von Stumm to Ambassador Romberg in Bern. In cipher: *"Urgent! The journey of the Russian émigrés through Germany should take place very quickly, since the Entente has already started counter-measures in Switzerland. Speed up the negotiations as much as possible".*

2 April (Count von Brockdorff-Rantzau, German Ambassador in Copenhagen, to the Ministry of Foreign Affairs, Top Secret) *"...We must now definitely try to create the utmost chaos in Russia. To this end we must avoid any discernible interference in the course of the Russian revolution. But we must secretly do all we can to aggravate the contradistinctions between the moderate and the extreme parties, since we are extremely interested in the victory of the latter, for another upheaval will then be inevitable and will take forms which will shake the Russian state to its foundations. Support by us of the extreme elements is preferable, because in this way the work is done more thoroughly and achieves its results more quickly. According to all forecasts, we may count on the disintegration being so far advanced in three months or so that military intervention by us will 'guarantee the collapse of Russian might."*

Lenin did not arrive to a loyal or law-abiding nation; on 15th March 1917. Nicholas, Tsar of all the Russias, on the advice of his generals, had resigned. In his place was little Alexis (aged 11, who was to be murdered with his parents and sisters just over a year later on 16th July 1918) who had become the new Tsar. The murder was, as with most Bolshevik actions, brutal and unnecessary. In Britain, the suggestion that the family should come into the care of their cousins, the British Royal Family, was advised against by Labour Ramsay Macdonald. Russia had effectively lost her spirit and her soul, and would remain first in the hands of fear, which Communist and Bolshevik rule ordained, and then in chaos. The anarchists, Mensheviks and Bolsheviks, who had fought so hard to achieve the degree of hatred needed to attain such a result, had drawn their strength to a large extent from the Jewish population. There was the usual jockeying for power from the aristocracy, or from the minor aristocracy, but never would such a disaster have resulted from the step toward constitutional monarchy, which, with Prince Lvov as Prime Minister and Kerensky as the liberal leader of the Duma, could have brought Russia through, if there had been loyalty and sufficient patriotism for a steady development of democratic and soundly-based government.

The British Royal Family were warned that the result of taking the Russian Royals under their wing might lead to a similar fate to that of their cousins. How, it has to be asked, had such a situation arrived? Before going further with German Bolshevik activities, something of the propaganda which had achieved 1917 unrest in Italy, France and in Britain, needs to be shown.

First there was the ideal of peace during a dreadful war, the natural desire combined with the idealistic belief that it was possible. Allied with this was the fear of standing out from a crowd, persuaded by propaganda that there was no need for war, because in a socialist world there would be no boundaries and no need to fight. The pull was a two-way one; the longing and the believing were made more attainable by the claim that, in the ideal society, a person had no rights to stand against the will of the majority.

All the ideas of individual heroes braving the world were lost, in a society that was imbued with the idea that the individual did not count and was out of date. The centuries of civilisation that had evolved a civilised society were forgotten in the theory that claimed those people who had built the past were wicked. To have admired them was to be against all the ideals of the Socialist Society, which imagined that people with no education, Rousseau's primitive man, would be better governors and anyway, had the right to govern. It seems never to have dawned on the people who imbibed this philosophy that people who know no law, have no experience or training in government, are not necessarily the best people to put into positions of power. In Britain, a mobile society had always allowed people to rise. The value of people trained for generations in responsibility and moral stability was not recognised. To aid this change, all the systems by which Russia had survived through the past hundred or so years were spoken of with disgust. The Russia in which the new leaders had grown up in freedom and with a degree of safety, was to be denied and forgotten for 70 years. Even then, when the Russians came out of their particular holocaust, the entire moral ethic had decomposed through years of atheism and fear.

Instead of the love of the almost God-like figure of the Tsar, giving an earthly polarity for the peasants and the poor people, the new replacement cry became 'Peace, Land, all Power to the Soviet' and into this turmoil, anarchy came and reigned supreme.

Robert Massie claims that the Allies played into Lenin's hands by pressing Russia to continue to fight. To fight was not beyond the reasonable power of the Great Bear, but the insidious propaganda made the Russian soldiers believe in the possibility of a life that was easy and would give them heaven on earth - the age-old image of utopia, when heaven would come without ever having to work to achieve it.

To fight would have given a polarity that might have helped them through, but the German control would see that the propaganda they had so carefully fostered would not wither and die.

That first important action, the persuading of the Tsar to abdicate, was to remove from the helm a man who could have kept the nation together. For a country such as Russia, with its ruler being part of the religion of the nation, his removal was the first irredeemable disaster. That the British Royal Family would not offer the Tsar and his family safe haven, must have removed the last thread of respect from the Russian Royal Family themselves.

The plan, the theory and the means were in place. Lenin was met with the blaring triumph due to a prophet; the Mensheviks, who had merely wanted a Duma (and the removal of the Tsar) considered that the Provisional Government could carry on with their support.

Woodrow Wilson, through his agent Elihu Root, having decided that it was no good negotiating any further with the Germans, offered $325,000,000 to the Provisional Government (even some Bolsheviks were prepared to support it). In the All-Russian Conference of Soviets in April, Lenin delivered his proposals: the overthrow of the Provisional Government; the abolition of the bureaucracy, the army and the police and, of course, an end to the war. Shouts of 'That is raving! That is the raving of a lunatic' and with Molotov and Stalin against him, his proposals had no effect. He had been away too long, living comfortably in exile on German money, and Miliukov, the Foreign Secretary, described the scene;

*"Lenin was a hopeless failure with the Soviet yesterday, he was compelled to leave the room amidst a storm of booing. He will never survive it"*. That was April 17th 1917. On May 18th, Trotsky arrived from New York and left the Mensheviks to join Lenin. Lenin continued to hammer away at the Provisional Government; Miliukov proclaimed that Russia would continue to honour her obligations and fight. The American loan had been offered on the basis 'No War, No Loan', but a massive outcry forced Miliukov from office; Prince Lvov felt he could no longer remain Prime Minister, so Kerensky took his place, and also the position of Minister of War;

The Russian troops were badly beaten, the Germans made a breakthrough, Kerensky toured the front, the breakthrough became a rout and people marched through Petrograd with banners saying 'Down with the war!', 'Down with the Provisional Government!' (Petrograd was the city that had risen to Parvus and Trotsky's earlier call). The Provisional Government crushed the rising, mainly by pointing out that Lenin was a German agent and the rising was to betray the Russians from the rear while the Germans advanced from the front. The rising was only temporarily effective. Lenin escaped to Finland disguised as a fireman on a train locomotive. Trotsky gave himself up to the police and the rising was over.

That was the July rising. Kerensky had warned Nicholas *"The Bolsheviks are after me and then they will be after you."* He tried to persuade the family to move and they began to pack in secret. 12th August was the Tsarevich's 13th birthday – the family moved to Siberia.

On 13th October 1917 Lenin returned in secret to Petrograd; on 6th November the Bolshevik attack started. We see the same methods of take-over as were to be seen in India a couple of years later – railway stations, bridges, banks, telephone exchanges, post offices and other public buildings were occupied – in India they were attacked and sometimes set on fire. One thing that was not achieved in India was action by the army, but in Russia, the Bolshevik soldiers lined the streets through which Kerensky drove to get help from the army. Firing from a ship, the Aurora, led to the Ministers sitting in the Winter Palace giving up and to the Women's Battalion surrendering. It was the November Revolution, when, with forged papers from Bruce Lockhart, Kerensky escaped as a Siberian soldier to 50 years in exile.

The Royal family continued in Tobolsk. For Nicholas, it was a sad time. Pierre Gillard, the family tutor, a Swiss, recorded the Tsar being gravely shocked as these two men, whom he regarded as unsavoury blackguards and traitors, became the rulers of Russia. *"It now gave him pain to see that his renunciation had been in vain and that by his departure in the interests of his country, he had in reality done her an ill turn. This idea was to haunt him more and more."* The calm and happiness of the family come out in the records, but the purpose of this book is to show not the happiness, followed by cold-blooded murder, but the political effects of the German plan. The family might have escaped, but, for those who have principles, it is hard to plan on the likely behaviour of those who have none.

With the fall of Kerensky, the continuation of the war was impossible; the price of Lenin's perfidy, the cost of his desire for total power, these two were the same - peace. Peace, for the Germans, meant surrender and the Treaty of Brest-Litovsk.

Three months negotiations were required before the Treaty of Brest–Litovsk was signed. The Bolshevik leaders found this period filled with constant frustration. They asked for a six-month armistice - all they could obtain was a month's respite, rescindable at a week's notice. They wished to have the negotiations transferred to a neutral capital like Stockholm; this was refused. They sought to explain with their usual volubility to the conquerors, themselves desperate, the political principles on which human society should be conducted. *"But pray, dear Sirs, what do we care for your principles."* asked the German General Hoffman. With an inconsistent flicker of good faith, they responded to an Allied request by asking that no German or Austrian troops should be transferred from East to West during the armistice. To this the Germans agreed, and at once began transporting their troops uninterruptedly to France. By the end of December, such illusions, as with singular credulity the Bolsheviks had nursed, were at an end. They found themselves confronted with force, armed and resolute; and they knew that they had rendered Russia incapable of resistance.

Nevertheless, when the meaning of the peace terms came home to this strange band of revolutionaries, a spasm of revolt, impotent but intense, shook their conclaves. The cruder spirits raved against Prussian Imperialism; the subtler, vented their bitterness in sarcastic newspaper articles. Trotsky and Zinoviev had indulged in imprudent mockery and empty threats. *"A time would come, Ha! Ha!"* etc. *"The destiny of mighty peoples."* said Trotsky, *"cannot be determined by the temporary condition of their technical apparatus."* The Germans remained rigorously impassive. They received, equally with the Bolshevik delegation, representatives of a separate Ukraine Government. Vainly the Bolsheviks protested that they and they alone spoke for all the Russias. The Germans brushed their expostulations aside. Whatever else miscarried, the Central Powers meant to have the corn and the oil of the Ukraine and the Caucasus, and elaborate agreements to secure all they required without payment were presented to the new Ministers of the Russian people.

At the end of December, the negotiations were suspended and the Bolshevik delegates returned home to consult with their confederates. Some details of this new debate in pandemonium have been preserved. Trotsky, in the role of Moloch, urged the renewal of the war and the majority of the secret Assembly seemed to share his passion. The calm sombre voice of Lenin rallied them to their duty in a Belial discourse of eighteen theses.

*"I should be much for open war, O Peers!*
*As not behind in hate ..."*

But how could they resist? The armies were gone, the Allies estranged, the fleet in mutiny, Russia in chaos! Even flight over the east spaces still at their disposal could not last long. And was not something more precious than the fate of Russia at stake? Was there not the Communist Revolution? Could they fight the Bourgeois at home if they wasted their remaining strength upon withstanding the foreign invader? Geographical boundaries, political allegiances were not so important after all to Internationalists striving for worldwide revolution. Let them make themselves supreme and unchallengeable in whatever territories might still be left to Russia, and from this as a base spread the social war through every land. The arguments of Lenin prevailed. He did not even wait to hear rejoinders, but sat, according to an English eyewitness, cool and unconcerned in an anteroom while his followers frothed and raged inside. The most that Trotsky could obtain was the formula 'No war, no peace'. The Soviets would submit, but they would not sign. On 10th February 1918, Trotsky stated by wireless *"that in refusing to sign a peace with annexations, Russia declares on its side that the state of war with Germany, Austria, Hungary, Turkey and Bulgaria has ended. The Russian troops are receiving at the same time an order for a general demobilisation on all lines of the fronts."*

But this was not good enough for the Germans. They allowed a week to pass in silence and then, on 17th February declared abruptly that the armistice was at an end and that the German armies would advance along the whole front at daybreak. Trotsky's ululation that they should have at least a further week's notice, was drowned in cannon fire. From Reval to Galat on a front of a thousand miles, the German and Austrian armies rolled forward. There still remained a ragged front of troops in various stages of decomposition and of officers, faithful to the end. All these were now swept away without the slightest difficulty. The whole front was destroyed; 1,350 guns were captured in a single day, together with masses of materiel and prisoners in a German advance of about 20 miles. The town of Dvinsk, the principal objective, was captured the same evening and on the 19th the Soviets made absolute submission. Trotsky yielded the Foreign Office to the more pacific Chicherin and on March 3rd, the peace treaties were signed.

The Treaty of Brest-Litovsk stripped Russia of Poland, Lithuania and Courland; of Finland and the Aaland Islands; of Estonia and Livonia; of the Ukraine and lastly in the Caucasus, of Kars, Erdehan and Batum.

*"This is a peace", said the Soviet wireless, "but not based upon a free agreement, but which Russia grinding its teeth is compelled to accept. The Soviet Government being left to its own forces is unable to withstand the armed onrush of German Imperialism and is compelled for the sake of saving Revolutionary Russia to accept the conditions put before her."* Lenin said some years later *"We must have the courage to face the unadorned bitter truth, we must size up in full to the very bottom of the abyss of defeat, partition, enslavement and humiliation into which we have been thrown."* It is not possible to better these descriptions of the first boon that Lenin conferred on the Russian nation. In Mr Buchan's well-weighted words *"They (the Bolsheviks) lost for Russia 26% of her total population, 27% of her arable land, 32% of her average crops, 26% of her railway systems, 33% of her manufacturing industries, 73% of her total iron production and 75% of her coal fields. So much for the policy of 'no annexation'. They had saddled themselves with a gigantic but as yet unassessed payment by way of war tributes, and had been compelled to grant free export of oil and a preferential commercial treaty. So much for 'No Indemnities'. They had placed under German rule fifty-five millions of unwilling Slavs. 'So much for self-determination'.*

*If today these consequences have been to any extent modified, and if the Soviet Republic is independent of German tutelage and systematic exploitation, it is because the democracies of the West and across the Atlantic, undismayed by Russian desertion, continued to uphold the common cause. It was upon them that the re-gathered might of Germany was now to fall".*

One thing Lenin could do. Although he had taken the inception of world revolution and his methods of destruction and rebellion from Parvus, he could forbid Parvus ever to enter the Soviet Union again. Parvus began attacking Lenin only when the Soviet Government assigned two million roubles to 'support revolution in Europe'. He thought that it would be very dangerous if the Bolsheviks made Russia a great military power. He left for Switzerland after the German revolution of November

1918 and settled in a villa by the lake in Zurich. His orgies there, together with the scandals around Sklarz in Berlin, led to the Swiss asking him to leave. Sklarz, a businessman of no particular political allegiance, was an agent of Parvus and of German Naval Intelligence, but he made big deals on his own account, including war supplies and his continued operations ruined Germany after the war. The scandal that shook the world involved the bribing of socialist politicians including Schneiderman, Noake, Ebert and high-ranking officers. Parvus, after his expulsion from Switzerland, built himself a residence on the Island of Schwanenwerder in Berlin until his death in 1924.

When news of the treaty reached Tobolsk, Nicholas was overwhelmed with grief and shame. It was, as Lenin was well aware, a total rejection of Russian patriotism. The Tsar was appalled that the Kaiser, Europe's most strident spokesman of the monarchical principle, had been willing to deal with the Bolsheviks, 'to shake hands with these miserable traitors'.

But let us make all this clear. The Treaty of Brest-Litovsk, barely mentioned today, has the seed of all such rapacity in its terms, while it is foolishly believed that the Treaty of Versailles did so much harm to Germany. No mention of the success of this step in the strategic plan of Germany, the destruction of Russia by Lenin; a success that made every following depredation possible (and indeed, if one looks at the behaviour of a nation as one looks at the behaviour of an individual, predictable).

Lenin continued with the plan he will have known from Parvus in Turkey, the attack on India. He also knew the forward posts of Tsarist Russia in the khanates of High Asia, from which propaganda, arms and funds could be sent into India and Afghanistan to help the nationalists. Just as the Germans were already helping in their conspiracies on the East Coast of India and attempts to penetrate the Persian border, Bolshevik infiltration spread into Afghanistan from the North.

# Chapter X
# PESHAWAR

I give some of the intelligence reports which were coming into India and already in the hands of the Government and Montagu, the Governor of the Punjab and the Commissioner of Peshawar and I show how Peshawar was being brought into the mainstream of the rebellion, the Bolshevik involvement and the Third Afghan War. In any understanding of the dangers as they faced Dyer, when he took his decision to fire on the mob, these things have to be in our minds also.

The flavour of the Bolshevik propaganda can be seen in the report sent out from the Wireless Station of Bolshevik Russia at the beginning of December 1918.

*"On November 25th, Indian Delegation handed a memorandum to Sverdloff, President of the Central Executive Committee of the Soviets, in the names of the people of India. This memorandum gives an exposition of the long martyrdom of India under the yoke of England, which, although it has given itself the title of a democratic country, keeps a population of 325,000,000 of the inhabitants in slavery. The Russian Revolution produced an enormous psychological impression on the Indian people. In spite of England's efforts, the principle of self-determination for the nations has penetrated into India, whose events have taken such a turn that the English Government on August 20th 1917, formulated in Parliament two principles of their Indian policy. Indian delegates wanted to explain the situation to the English public, but they could not obtain permit to go to England. In the U.S.A. and in France, Indian delegates were imprisoned. They were driven out from Japan, Switzerland and Denmark under the pressure of English diplomats."* The memorandum further says that the liberty of the world will be in danger as long as the imperialists' and capitalists' power of England exists, which power is founded upon the slavery of a fifth part of the population of the globe. The memorandum ends with an expression of confidence that the

days of England are numbered, that the Indians will rise and drive out the foreign domination and that free Russia will stretch out a fraternal hand to them.

For those who today hear of the exploitation and slavery of India, it is worth knowing that since we left, Indian school textbooks have been published in Russia.

Those of us who knew India may laugh uproariously at the idea that the Indians were slaves and exploited. If there is to be any relation to reality, for 'exploitation', read 'peace and prosperity', but this type of assertion has become, over the years, part of the accepted mores of our time.

In the later version of what happened during the rebellion, the Gandhi/Bolshevik spin was quite easily accepted. The activities of the Bolsheviks in 1918 and 1919 were sent as intelligence reports from High Asia, but were not widely available. The 'Daily Mail' however, did actively encourage the relay of information and in January 1919, an officer in Helsingfors, who had taken a particular interest in the Russian scene, wrote to the newspaper giving the information that *"The Indian Centralisation Committee which is now working at Petrograd under the Bolsheviks is composed of the same members as the Berlin Indian Committee. It is stated by the Petrograd Journal 'Krasnaja Gazeta' in the special number devoted to British India and to formation of Indian Centralisation Committee at Petrograd, that a large number of Indian Bolshevist propagandists have already been sent to India and that the power of Universal Bolshevism will soon be made known to the British Empire."*

There was news of various other activists; Narendra Battachariya (under the name of C.A. Martin and M. N. Roy), who had played a leading part in the German plots against India, was continuing to publish anti-British literature and any calumny that could be used. From another source, it was heard that Battachariya and H.L. Gupta had formed a League of Friends of India and through diplomatic circles, attempted to petition the Peace Conference for the release of India from British domination.

A Bolshevik, Carl Sandberg, arrested on arrival in the States was found to have in his possession a mass of propaganda including a book called 'India for the Indians', full of extracts from Russian official documents referring to India.

For those who determinedly claim that it was the British who were racist, this title itself shows an Indian appeal to race.

The claim was one of mutual struggle with world imperialism (so shortly to be shown up by Russian imperialism).

An Indian lawyer; Hassan Shahid Suhrawardy, a Bengali, was running the India Department of the Bolshevist Ministry of Propaganda - a man who had gained permission to go to Russia in 1916.

The Berlin Committee was apparently almost defunct, although the Indian members were paid 400 marks a month until such time as peace was signed and they could return to India or elsewhere. Although this arrangement seems to have been settled, much mystery was being made in Berlin about the whereabouts of previous committee members. Dr. Hafiz, Umrao Singh Majithia and Sen. Das Gupta had received a letter from Bhupendra Nath Dutt saying that the head of the Moscow Committee had arrived in Switzerland and all the members of the previous German Committee had turned Bolshevik. At the suggestion of the Soviet Government, they also changed the name of the National Committee.

On 31st March, the news had come in that Turkestan had been decided on for the oriental propaganda, and Tashkent was to be the city for that work. Bravan, previously consular Officer in Calcutta and then in Persia, had been chosen to lead the teamwork. Propaganda was sent from Moscow and then through the High Pamirs and Chinese territory into India.

The Turkestan pattern became clearer - there were 6,000 Indians living in Turkestan - where propaganda was carried on through the Indian Committee and Indians from Afghanistan and from India had already arrived to join. Then came the name of a Bolshevist Indian who was engaged in propaganda with the Mussulman population of India. His name was Muhammad Bak Hajilachet and as one would expect, news came in of agitators being trained in large numbers in Moscow. These men were going to Tashkent and Persia and a branch of the League of Eastern Freedom was formed in Tashkent itself. The report about the large numbers of agitators and their training arrived, obviously some time after it had been established, on 25th April 1919.

In Amritsar, Dyer, having dealt with the Rebellion, would leave for Afghanistan on 8th May. By then, Captain Blacker would be on the Afghan Frontier to the North, observing the Bolsheviks working with the Afghans for war on India. On the same date, Har Dayal had had a meeting with Lenin in Moscow. Har Dayal in Delhi had influence on the Delhi students, but by this time he was pretending to hate the Germans who had treated him badly. On the other hand, in the same report came the information that the German penetration into India had by no means been abandoned; and Har Dayal had himself become a Bolshevik. *"He is believed to be in close touch with Russian Bolshevism in Stockholm; he knows the channels of communication from England and may be expected to correspond with the Russians from India if he should be allowed to return there."*

With his unique knowledge of what was going on, Captain Blacker described the events covered in part by this chapter in his own characteristic way: *"the situation was curious all round and more still from our own particular point of view since our tiny force of only one Regular battalion, one regiment of cavalry and two somewhat 'catch-'em-alive-oh' levy corps was confronted with a whole Afghan cavalry division, scarcely ten easy marches from us, complete with a brigade of cavalry, a machinegun company, several batteries of breech loading guns and a Bolshevik alliance.*

*Needless to say, it was the Soviet who organised the third Afghan War, as well as the riots of Kamins and other non-Punjabi Dravidians, in April 1919, on our lines of communication at Amritsar.*

*These riots had a double object. The first and most important was to discredit the gallant and loyal Punjabi of whom some 50,000 or more freely offered volunteers had found distant graves in the German War and its sequels. (note - I include of course in the Punjab those few contiguous districts that are predominantly Aryan in race and so ethnically akin to it, such as Mardan, Mirpur and Garhwal.). By promoting disturbances in the slums of towns such as Amritsar it was hoped to provoke headings in the easily prostituted English Press, such as 'Rebellion in the Punjab.' This succeeded in a way that must have exceeded the wildest hopes of the 'impresarios.'*

*The Soviet could scarcely assist the Afghans in any more material way than this since they had a good deal on their own hands that soap and water could not remove.*

*The second object that the Reds' agents worked to attain in Hindustan and in the South Punjab, was the more obvious one of crippling the railway that fed our troops in the Khyber and drawing troops away from the fighting line for internal defence work.*

*"As events showed, it was the Punjabis who turned out to be the King's men in all this.*

*Not only this, but it was the Punjabis who very willingly laid finger to trigger against disloyal alien crowds who blackened their country's name.*

*The whole business was precisely similar to 'Sydney Street' and the publicity it received, parallel to the dubbing of that battle a revolution in London".* ['Sidney Street' was a siege where two armed burglars, one German and one Russian, being discovered by the police, took refuge in a house in the East End of London. Being armed with weapons with a longer range than those of the police, the Scots Guards were called in with rifles. To this Churchill, as Home Secretary, gave retrospective agreement. Crowds collected; the house was set on fire, and Churchill, who stopped the fire brigade for their safety going into the house, was claimed to be responsible for the two deaths. Wild claims were made in the Press about anarchists and so on. This was in 1911].

*"The repercussion of all this was even felt in far distant Khurasan. As far as the troops were concerned, it was even possible that we should have to retire westwards over the immense tract that separated us from Teheran and our force in Northwest Persia.*

*This would certainly have been the case had the Reds taken Merv sooner, in order to join hands with the Afghans and if the wily and volatile Afghan had scratched up any enthusiasm for Amanullah's little war. However, 'if ifs and ands were pots and pans', he did not, luckily for us, since with all his faults, the bold Afghan is a sportsman and a first class fighting man, except when he happens to be a Regular Soldier*

*My detachment was soon in the middle of it, finding out what we were up against.*

*Meanwhile the cunning commissars cajoled the wily Afghan. The Soviet/Afghan defeat in the Jallianwalla Bagh at Amritsar, on the Khyber line and in the storming of the Spin Baldak Fort by the Duke of Wellington's and the 22$^{nd}$ Punjabis, had rather disgusted our sporting Aryan cousins of Kabul and Kandahar. During late 1919 and early 1920, they mistrusted the Reds, their late allies and even threatened to attack them at Merv and on the Pamirs, where a Red detachment had mobilised for an inroad into India. Soviet diplomacy kept them quiet by promises to cede back various* *areas- but by 1920 already, Gandhi and his mates, the Ali Brothers, were threatening, with Red funds and Afghan troops, to help the rising in Malabar."*

On 9th May, a day after Dyer left Amritsar with his Brigade Major, Captain Briggs, the Battle of the Bagh took place on the Frontier. On the 4th May, the Afghan Postmaster had arrived at Peshawar with a motorcar full of propaganda printed in Kabul, announcing that the Germans had resumed the war and that India and Egypt had risen. On the 8th, the British Chief Commissioner, having been told on the previous day by an informer, surrounded the City with a cordon of British troops and captured the Afghan Postmaster and his co-plotters, his plans, silver (a lakh of rupees) and the various relevant propaganda.

The new Amir had decided on war on 14th April. Zia-ur-Rahman, one of the Silk letter conspirators at Kabul, wrote to Abdul Khair of Delhi asking for prayers and letters for Afghanistan. He was not the only Silk letter conspirator, for Obeidullah, a Sikh convert, was a signatory of the Silk letters. Zaffar Hussein, one of the Lahore students now a Lieutenant Colonel in the 'Army of God', circulated the following letter during the same period:

*"You have read of the Provisional Government of India in the Rowlatt Sedition Committee Report. This Government has been instituted in order to establish a better government in place of the present treacherous, usurping and tyrant Government. Your Provisional Government has been continuously struggling for the last four years. As soon as you determined to refuse to accept the oppressive law, the Provisional Government too, succeeded in obtaining help there and then.*

*The Provisional Government has entered into a compact with the invading forces. Hence you should not destroy your real interest by fighting against them, but kill the English in every possible way, don't help them with men and money and continue to destroy rails and telegraph wires.*

*Earn peace at the hands of the attacking armies and obtain sanads of honour by supplying them with provisions.*

*The attacking army grants peace to every Indian irrespective of caste and creed. The life and honour of every Indian is safe. He who stands against them will alone be killed or disgraced.*

*May God guide our brethren to tread on the right path*
*Sd. Obeidullah*
*Wazir of the Provisional Government of India*
*Zafar Hussain*
*Secretary of the Provisional Government of India Delhi."*

Among the leaflets and proclamations was one from the Amir's father-in-law, Muhammad Tarzi, Foreign Minister for Afghanistan, asking the envoy at Simla to obtain the allegiance both of Hindus and Muslims *"... if we get a chance get exciting articles inserted in the newspapers"*.

Sir George Roos-Keppel, the Chief Commissioner, wrote to Sir Michael O'Dwyer, *"I drew it rather fine with Peshawar city. We had the cordon round at 2.30 and we now have clear proof that the rising to burn cantonments, cut the wireless, open the jail, etc, was for that night. What a blessing you got the Punjab in hand before the show started."*

This rather scrappy synopsis of the situation is in part due to Peshawar not being included in the Hunter Inquiry. Mr. Montagu, when questioned in Parliament, said there had been no disturbance in Peshawar, and he distinctly excluded Peshawar from the ambit of the Hunter Committee, which was only authorised 'to investigate the recent disturbances in Bombay, Delhi and the Punjab, their causes and the measures taken to cope with them'.

By the exclusion of Peshawar, the Hunter Committee was able to claim that *"on the evidence before us there is nothing to show that the outbreak: in the Punjab was part of a prearranged conspiracy to overthrow the British Government by force."*

The most interesting fact that has followed from all this is that information on the links between the agitators in India and the Afghans is closed under the 250-year rule. Who, one wonders, was responsible for taking such an action?

But at Peshawar, as at Bombay, as at Delhi, as at Lahore, where was the British brutality that Gandhi was claiming? How did it compare with the Indian brutality, the barbaric behaviour of the Indians?

# PART 2
# THE MAHATMA

## Chapter I
## AGITATE

Into the maelstrom of German attempts at infiltration, nationalist plotting and the war effort, in 1915 came Mohandas Kamarchand Gandhi,[29] fresh from his fame for his work in South Africa, known to the great and the good in England for various reasons involving the legislation governing the ingress of Indians to South Africa and now, self-styled Saint. In later years, he claimed he did not like the title Mahatma, but by the time of the movement that ended in the 1919 rebellion, he was signing his own letters 'Mahatma Gandhi', (Mahatma meaning 'Great soul', effectively 'Saint').

The main result of his actions in South Africa was to stop indentured labour going there. Lord Hardinge supported this policy and the practice ended in 1915. It is interesting to look into the history of indentured labour in South Africa and to realise that, in its early days, the labourers had the vote in the same way as the Boers and other nationals.

Indentured labour was run well; it was a great help in providing the labour that was needed to develop South Africa. The labourers themselves and their families were well paid by the standards of the time - for example, an indentured labourer was better paid than a police constable in British India, plus his food, shelter and medical care, as well as being given the possibility of remaining in South Africa if he wished, for the payment of £3.

Gandhi's marches had resulted in the £3 residence payment being removed and permission being given for the indentured labourers to be married by their own rituals. Gandhi would have continued to fight for more, in the way he did in India, but Ghokale, with whom he had stayed in 1901 in Calcutta and who had gone with him to

---

29    As mentioned by Sir Penderel Moon in Gandhi And Modern India, Gandhi's policy was "agitate, agitate, agitate."

South Africa, and was, (so Gandhi claimed) his guru, dissuaded him from continuing and himself wrote to General Smuts. As Gandhi left, Smuts heaved a sigh of relief making the well-known comment *"The Saint had left our shores, I hope for ever."*

It is said that, it is not what you know, but who you know which makes for success. Gandhi arrived back in India with a label of saintliness which, despite his unreliability, his volte-face changes of activity and claims, has not left him to this day. It is significant that Attenborough's film (described to me by Nirad Chaudhuri, an Indian who knew Gandhi and was a member of the Congress Party, as *"falsehood from beginning to end"*) could not have been accurate or historically frank and have left Attenborough's audience with any such belief.

The danger of claiming sainthood for a leader is that, like the image portrayed of Stalin or Hitler, people legitimise their opinions and actions and are moved to wicked and evil behaviour in the name of their saint, which they otherwise would not have undertaken. It is possible that the greatest validation of the psychologist Jung, is his contention that our libido, our life force, tends towards a search for the saintly leader. During the period covered by this book, Lenin was an example of a Messianic leader, to whom the masses looked for spiritual direction in life, rather than to their own innate wisdom. The suppression of Gandhi's various rebellions could only have been achieved because the Indian Civil Servants and the officials generally, came through their long training extraordinarily self reliant, and became administrators of a fine integrity, not seen or credited today.

There can be no serious doubt that Gandhi was a fraud and a liar. He was also a ruthless inciter to violence, as ruthless as Stalin and more ruthless than Mussolini. He had claimed in South Africa that the Immigration Laws were so wicked as to be a Black Act. They were not. The three clauses on which he rested his case were firstly, against any but a Christian marriage, and this, the Government of South African, under that great man Jan Smuts, agreed to remove. Secondly, that thumbprints were needed on the immigration documents. This, he must have known, was the method in large parts of the world for dealing with documents where there was competition for jobs and people were illiterate. To give an example, I have evidence that all Indian workers on ships signed their contracts with their thumbs. Typically, to stir up feelings of insult, Gandhi claimed in a wily way that this was being done to insult Indians, where in reality, it was the way used to ensure jobs. The third clause was the tax of £3 if people wished, after indenture, to continue to reside in South Africa. None of this was serious, once the marriage restriction was removed, but then, even that was largely because it was not envisaged that marriages would take place other than between Christians. For this he marched and screamed out his fury and disgust at a 'Black Act', about which, most of his followers would have known nothing. His march was a confidence trick, just as later were his claims about the Rowlatt Acts.

The Pathan who had followed Gandhi on the march in South Africa and into prison, believing him to be a truthful person, knocked him down when he realised, on his release, that Gandhi had lied. He realised that the 'Black Act' had been nothing but a simple and undemanding law.

To a largely liberal-minded upper class in Britain, although if they had read the Acts they would have known that they were not 'Black', the claim was acceptable because they thought, as did Montagu, that Gandhi was a social reformer – the real hero of the settlement of the Indian question in South Africa. Though even he himself felt he had done nothing and said so, his hobnobbing with the great and the good in Britain at that time, had worked wonders for his reputation. This is to understand the superficialities of the political mind.

It seems clear that Gandhi did not consider the suffering of others in his actions. As far back as his time in South Africa, without speaking to his wife but having discussed it with friends, he decided to go in for Bramacharia, the sublimation of the sexual force. In his case, this (logically), meant ceasing to sleep with his wife. What she would not have expected, was that it also meant spending nights and days with a plethora of other women. Woodrow Wyatt described Gandhi's anger, (frightening his secretary) when he had been unable to sublimate his sexual force, even in his seventies, because the present nubile girl was too pretty. During serious political talks, (not unlike the behaviour of Mae West, who could not sit through a meal without going into another room with her current boyfriend), he would leave for 'massage' from one of the two girls who always accompanied him. Political discussion had to be interrupted frequently, as Philip Tollinton found in the North West Frontier Province. To those girls, Gandhi showed no allegiance as their physical charms faded. He is now on record as complaining of how boring was the adulation of Miriam Slade, 'Mirabhai', whose father was a British admiral, when he returned to his ashram and she met him with affection and obeisance, wishing to kiss his feet. In his autobiography, he describes in the most persuasive terms, the promises of faithfulness that he gave his wife on their marriage according to Hindu rites when he was thirteen, but he never indicates that he considered his use of other women for his sexual appetites as a betrayal of his vows. Instead he says, *"Then came the call from South Africa and that already found me fairly free from the carnal appetite"*. However little this may have been the case during the years that followed, at the age of sixteen, married for three years, he found it impossible, when sharing the nursing of his dying father with his mother and a servant, to keep his mind off sex. He left his father to the attentions of a visiting uncle, so as to go back to bed with his wife, by then heavily pregnant. Whether as a result of the ensuing activities or not, the baby that arrived shortly afterwards died after a few days. Gandhi's uncle was able to be with his father as the old man died.

This incident and his comments on his father's illness, refute the claims in his 1907 book 'Hind Swaraj', which is a diatribe against everything Western, including medicine. At that early age, he showed the absorption with sex, which continued throughout his life

Gandhi returned to India in 1915: *"I realised what a deep impression my humble services in South Africa had made throughout the whole of India,"* he said after travelling third class by train throughout India. Within months he had established his ashram, first in a village near Ahmedabad and then on the banks of the Sabarmati River, nearby. Funds were forthcoming from wealthy friends in Ahmedabad. Gokhale gave money and Gandhi's cousin, Magan Lal, who had run his Phoenix centre in South Africa, was put in control of the ashram. Already while travelling, he had discarded his ordinary clothes for the costume he would wear later and which is a part of his image today. At a fair at Harwar he gave darshan to the crowds. His simple dress, the clothing of most Indians in their own homes when relaxing, had given him the aura of a saint just as is shown in 'Kim', where Kipling gives the retired Prime Minister from an Indian State, who has become a holy saint, the simple dress which to the ordinary Indian indicated the rejection of worldly power and pursuit when worn by an educated man in public. Thus in 1915, having discarded the business suit of a lawyer, he had already shown both by his third class travel alongside persons of all castes or casteless, and by his dress, despite his fame and education, that he was a saint. He had decided to *"acquaint India with the method I had used in South Africa, and to.... test in India the extent to which its application might be possible."*

It makes little difference today that many of the rulers of other ashrams, more dedicated to the spiritual than the political, disliked, distrusted, and recognised the fundamental hypocrisy inherent in his claims to sainthood, Those men did not publish a well funded newspaper, supported by such people as G.D. Birla, the multi-millionaire businessman, nor did they write about their feelings, so their voice is no longer heard.

If Nirad Chaudhuri's comments on Gandhi are correct, that the man thought he was fighting Satanism in the form of the Government of India, (although to the British, or indeed to many Indians, this may have seemed a sign of psychological upset), then his behaviour was logical, though meretricious.

The only pity is that he never actually said that this was how he thought. If he had, less notice would have been taken of him

Gandhi on his arrival in India, was a declared follower of G.K. Gokhale, who was a great friend of Moti Lal Nehru. Gokhale was the man who had won the battle in Congress at Surat in 1907 against the Extremists. The Extremists under Lokmanya Tilak believed in violence. Congress had finally, after chair throwing and general disturbance, decided to vote in G.K. Gokhale, who believed in advance towards Independence through constitutional means, as their President. Gokhale was not altogether a meek man; he thought deeply about the reforms needed for the governing of India - of her social regeneration. The then Viceroy, Lord Minto, said that while Indians kept their women down, any regeneration of India was impossible. Moti Lal Nehru was in earlier times, also a Moderate, a successful and wealthy barrister. He had also been an Anglophile, sending his son to be educated in England (at Harrow). His home was open to English people as well as Indians, though he was a Brahmin. By 1918, Gokhale was dead; but before he died he left a testament of his proposals for Indian reforms with the Aga Khan. Much of it was adopted by the Congress in their suggestions which were given to Montagu by so many of the delegates who attended him on his tour prior to the formulation of the Reforms published in 1918, and which Moti Lal Nehru felt did not go far enough.

Gokhale, frail prior to his death in 1915, no longer influenced Gandhi, who had become a follower of Tilak. It is doubtful whether Tilak appreciated the honour, for just prior to his death in 1920 he made his opinion clear – *"what we want are majorities, not Mahatmas"*. Gokhale, who represented the Bombay non-official Members on the Viceroy's Council, was appointed to the Royal Commission on Indian Public Services in 1912. He started the 'Servants of India', which consisted of well-educated well-breeched young Indians who were dedicated to the service of India, going through the villages and helping the ordinary people, without ambition or fuss, where there were plenty of jobs and plenty of need for such employment. It was the Tilak attitude that Gandhi had taken. Moti Lal Nehru had also come over to an anti-British attitude, by the time that he and Gandhi had their discussions in Lucknow.

In these chapters I have tried to make plain that we were not racist in the present-day sense of the word. We thought that Indians, where we met them and gave or received their hospitality, were our friends. Indeed they were, but at the time of the growing rupture caused by the conspiracy, and the rebellious intent, all this changed. Moti Lal Nehru no longer welcomed Britons to his home. Gandhi had a few semi, or totally-dependent Britons as frequent visitors, of whom Miriam Slade and F.C. Andrews were two.

On his return to India, despite having promised Gokhale (who had promised Smuts that Gandhi would now leave), that he would not do anything in India to stir up trouble or make speeches until he knew more about the country he had left thirty-five years earlier, and for which he needed a year, Gandhi immediately went to a College and delivered inflammatory speeches to the students.

Already in 1918 and early 1919, he had been making trouble in Madras. By July 1920, he was again in Madras, instigating the burning down of the Mills owned by the British and the homes of those who worked for them – the British mills being much better run, the homes of the workers being far more salubrious, and the workers better paid and cared for.

He went on from that to the forcible persuasion of people not to go to Government Schools, not to take Government jobs or go in for Government work of any kind, including attending the Courts. The result, as the movement gathered momentum, was that youths leaving school were unable to get jobs because they were not properly qualified and his endeavours (after Tilak's death) to set up a Tilak Fund and start alternative schools were not successful. The funds simply did not come in as they had for the rebellion and conspiracies with the Germans and Bolsheviks.

The aim was to harm anyone who did not fit in with his dictates; anyone selling drink could have their shop burnt down or looted; the same with imported cloth; indeed, in 1921 when the Prince of Wales arrived in India and Gandhi was determined to upstage him, the vast bonfires of foreign cloth, the rioting and murders were an indication of the general trend. Women wearing saris of foreign cloth were stripped of them in the streets. People who had been buried, were dug up and their skulls kicked around the streets, to the acute distress of their relatives It is the attitude of the men whom he called 'volunteers', who, armed with lathis, were allowed to treat anyone and everyone with violence that astonishes us today.

In all these matters, Lord Chelmsford and then Lord Reading in 1921, (a close friend of Montagu's) were too weak to arrest Gandhi, or to take the necessary steps to uphold law and order. Chauri Chaura, the burning to death of 22 policemen and their helpers, in their police station was a result of police being prepared to take those steps. Gandhi, of course, fasted for the wrong done by his followers – only General Sir George Barrow (who was on the Hunter Committee) later made the point that Gandhi incited people to violence and then fasted. The extraordinary thing is that all of us, who worked in India among Indians, knew about Gandhi. Why did nobody in England do anything about him?

Chauri Chaura and the Moplah Rebellion are all of a part, together with other smaller incidents, which were reported and written up in the book 'Gandhi and Anarchy', on which, without a great deal more of detailed research, we have to rely. That book by Sir Sankaran Nair has disappeared from every library shelf except that of the Indian Institute in Oxford.

The most serious collaboration by the British came with Reading and then Halifax, both of whom allowed Gandhi to call on them and talk to them for literally hours on end. Reading, writing to Montagu, said 'I liked him', Churchill pictured Gandhi going up the steps of the Viceroy's house as the 'little fakir in a dhoti'. The point that Churchill got, but the Viceroys apparently did not, was that in India, such availability to the leader of the rebel outbreaks of 1919 and 1920-1922 (when Gandhi was finally arrested) was to give an accolade to the horrid little man, which gave him licence, literally to kill.

Gandhi was involved with the Congress during the 1919 Rebellion, working with the President, Moti Lal Nehru, in his co-ordination and secret talks just prior to the rebellion. It was not until the 1919 Congress meeting at Amritsar, that he agreed the Reforms that had just gone through Parliament, while Moti Lal Nehru and the majority of Congress voted against them. Only until after the Debates on the Disturbances in Parliament, did he adhere to this view, but as soon as they were over, he came out in his true colours, the colours of 'Hind Swaraj', written in 1907, and went directly to order his followers not to stand for the new Provincial Councils or for the Assembly. He made a collection for schools and colleges in the name of Tilak, the extremist, who died in July that year, so as to make possible the boycott of all colleges, schools, courts and government institutions. He ran the Khilafat movement, started in India by the Ali brothers, who had been in detention during the war for activities against the government and incitement against Muslims joining the army. He continued his 'non-violent, non co-operation campaign', one of such violence and cruelty that any nation encountering such behaviour must deny its leader and perpetrator. He was arrested for its continuation when he ordered the recruitment of yet more 'volunteers', the 'lathi volunteers', whose activities by that time, had carried out the purpose and provisions of the earlier boycott.

For a dictator to get power, he must, first, create fear. The rebellion did that for Gandhi, through the Government demonstrating that it would no longer be prepared to protect those ordinary people who had been threatened by mobs of ruffians, nor support those who had been loyal.

He was eventually imprisoned in 1922, but in 1924, he managed to persuade the Viceroy of India, Lord Reading, that he was too ill to remain in prison; he was released and was later elected the President of Congress.

It was the age for dictators posing as saviours and each and every dictator was portrayed in a saintly glow when in his prime, but at Gandhi's door can be laid the cruelties that took place in the Punjab in 1919, of the Malabar Rebellion, the tragedy of Cawnpore in the early 1930s, the determination to uphold racism, the destruction of British trade; the breaking of the Lucknow Pact [the 1916 agreement between Congress and the Muslim League for the share of ministries in any future independent government] in the 1937 elections, which led in turn to the divisions of India; the creeping paralysis of Congress's infiltration into the Indian States, and thus, to the prevention of a federation which could have led from British rule to Indian rule with none of the horrors of partition. While appearing to be behaving in line with the intentions of Gokhale, he in fact followed the extremist and violent behaviour of Tilak's movement.

In the underlying autocracy of Hindus with their Brahmin superiors, there was a growing divide, but even there it had not become established throughout the country. An example of the background to the completion of this ferment was the behaviour of Tilak, a Mahratta Brahmin, thought to have been the prototype of 'panditji' in the 'Lost Dominion', where the slow development of the Brahmin influence is described. Tilak attempted to ostracise the Maharaja of Kolhapur, the descendant of Sivaji the hero of Mahratta independence of an earlier time, because he strongly disagreed with Tilak's violent propaganda against the Government. The author being of a later time, imagined Panditji to be Nehru.

Probably the clearest evidence of the feelings of the people was given by Sir Michael O'Dwyer, who had himself been a Resident at Hyderabad. He wrote: *"In several States, a struggle was then going on between the Decanni Brahmins, strongly entrenched behind their hereditary, social and religious pretensions and the North-country Hindus, Khastri, Kayastha, or Baniya, who outside the office were generally the better men. The cleavage between the Mahratta Brahmins on one side and the Mahratta Princes and peasantry on the other,.... is rapidly becoming more acute. Tilak, the typical Mahratta Brahmin brought matters to a head twenty years ago by his attempt to outcast and ostracise the Maharaja of Kolhapur, the descendant of Sivaji, the hero of Mahratta independence, because the Maharaja stoutly opposed his propaganda. Since then, the Mahrattas have been striving to shake off Brahmin domination and the movement has been hastened by the Reforms Scheme, which gave undue power to the Brahmin literati in Bombay and elsewhere, a power which they are accused of using for their own selfish ends. Even in Central India in my time, the Ruling Chiefs, while realising the value of the Brahmin in their offices, had been struck by his general failure in an executive capacity."*

In the State forces and higher police posts, the Mohammedans, with their traditions of rule and authority were generally prominent and the Rajas were in reality collecting their own companies to fight on the side of the British.

The hostility of the other castes to Brahmins, and especially Mahratta Brahmins, is well brought out in the following summary, quoted in the Times, of the evidence given before the Reforms Committee in Simla in 1924, by Mr A. N. Sarvi, a Mahratta lawyer representing the Mahratta and other non-Brahmin cases in the Bombay legislature. He maintained that existence of separate representation for the backward classes was essential, as without it, Brahmin ascendancy would be reasserted, but the Brahmins, having obtained privileges in the name of the masses in the past, had not allowed the masses to share in them. Had the Brahmins dealt fairly with the masses, the illiteracy and backwardness, now so prevalent, would have disappeared generations ago. When Sir S. Aiyar (a Madras Brahmin) suggested that it was the government and not the Brahmins who were to blame, the witness refused to accept the suggestion. He pointed out that local boards have long been in existence and that the Brahmin majorities in those bodies had built schools in Brahmin areas and none in the non-Brahmins areas. Moreover, the Brahmins had dominated the public services to the exclusion of the other castes.

He considered that the time was far distant when it would be reasonable to talk of India as a 'nation', for neither the Hindus nor the Mohammedans had sufficient cohesion to form one. The present attempts to adopt a meaningless phrase like 'one nation' would hamper the efforts of the backward classes to improve themselves, because the advanced classes were entirely self-interested and obstructed the efforts of the backward classes to advance. On the other hand, Mr Sarvi declared that the British Government usually has identical interests with the masses.

The Times Simla correspondent added that – as might be expected – Mr Sarvi was severely heckled by the Brahmin members of the committee, of whom there were three (this in itself shows how even the Government unduly favours this privileged class), but on the whole he maintained his position.

Mr. Servi was only stating notorious facts, apparent to every honest observer in India, although apparently hidden from the Government of India and the India Office. (Reference to the India Office here implies the Secretary of State, by this time the Labour Peer, Lord Olivier). One wonders how Mr Sarvi got on after his speech was reported.

Gandhi's treatment of the 'untouchables' whom Dr Ambedkar had gathered in a vocal minority, was a classic example of mendacity. He wrote and spoke so much that it is almost impossible to credit any one man with so much contradiction in terms. He was in two words, an inveterate liar.

When the British left India, in a population of 500,000,000, despite self-interest, there were still only 500,000 members of the Party of Congress.

By the time of Montagu's visit in 1917, Gandhi was wearing the clothes most Indians wore in their own homes, although in public they adopted a more formal dress. To Montagu, who had been meeting people who showed their respect by dressing with formality, it was suggested that Gandhi *"dresses like a coolie, forswears all advancement, lives practically on air and is a pure visionary"*. Montagu appears not to have known that Gandhi could draw on the enormous funds of the millionaire, J. D. Birla, nor had he ever had to pay for Gandhi's repasts of the most delicate and costly nuts and fruit in great quantities. Montagu also imagined that Gandhi had solved the indigo trade problems. This again was delusional and accounts for Montagu excusing Gandhi after the 1919 rebellion and accepting his claim of apology. However, we know that Bolshevik funds had come from Stockholm, which, together with funds from the wealthy mill-owners in Bombay – Gandhi's friends – had helped to fund the rebellion. The funds for the support of the families of those killed or convicted for crimes during the disturbances in Amritsar, which were administered by Swami Shraddanand, came chiefly from outside the Punjab, notably Bombay, which was Gandhi's base. Gandhi was, himself, very wealthy and his dress as a pious mendicant was purely a disguise.

The most obvious of Gandhi's activities, which was accepted by those who were not on the spot, was the grand fiction about Dyer having massacred hundreds of people and of the iniquities of Martial Law. To have set off a rebellion which failed, even after the acceptance of help from the enemies of the country, needed explaining and Dyer became the explanation.

As soon as the discussions in Parliament were over and he knew that he was safe, Gandhi followed up this justification of riot, by initiating his non-violent, non-co-operation campaign, in which his followers perpetrated the most ghastly cruelties of any in recent years.

In Malabar, with the help of the Ali brothers (for whose release from imprisonment during the war for campaigning for the Pan Islamic movement, he had threatened to go on hunger strike while Montagu was still in the country), Gandhi roused the Moplahs to take over the courts and murder and massacre thousands of people. Sir Sankaran Nair commented in his book 'Gandhi and Anarchy': *"The results were disastrous both to the Mohammedans and the Hindus. More than two thousand Mohammedans killed by troops according to official estimates, thousands more in other ways, larger numbers wounded: the number of Hindus butchered in circumstances of barbarity, skinned alive, made to dig their own graves before slaughter, running into thousands. Women and purdah (veiled) women too, raped, not in a fit of passion, but systematically and with calculating revolting and horrible cruelty for which I have not been able to find a parallel in history. Thousands of Hindus were forcibly converted (by circumcision). All this directly due to the visit of Gandhi and Shaukat Ali and to the establishment of Khilafat organisations. They carried on their activities openly, without obstruction from the authorities, the Government of Madras prevented from interfering with Khilafat agitators by the Government of India, who are therefore as responsible as if they had directly ordered all this frightfulness."* He refers to the Viceroy, Lord Reading.

The apparent reason for the Government of India (by then under the Viceroy, Lord Reading, Montagu's friend) doing nothing, was that the claims against Dyer and the British, which Gandhi and his co-agitators had propounded, had been accepted by Montagu, with his trust in Gandhi, so his nominee as Viceroy had been instructed to do nothing.

In the event, the women of Malabar wrote to the wife of the Viceroy and begged for Martial Law to be imposed. Only then, far too late in view of the atrocities committed, were Martial Law and the necessary troops brought in. The number of arrests was ten times those of the Punjab rebellion. Nair was himself, one of the ruling castes of Madras. Letters from Lord Willingdon, then Governor of Madras, make clear his anguish at not being able to stop the movements for which Gandhi had, on various visits, been responsible. No only the Moplahs of Malabar were involved, but also the workers at the British factories, whose houses were burned down and who lost their jobs when the factories were also burnt, due to Gandhian agitation. Gandhi and the Ali brothers had received Bolshevik funds and promised the Moplahs that Afghan soldiers were coming to help them.

Sankaran Nair collected and correlated not only the activities of Gandhi's 'non violent, non-co-operators', but added the minutes of the Provincial Legislatures, showing the vacillating weakness of the Indians who were in a position to impose penalties. It was the beginning of virtually the whole of India becoming terrorised into submission by Gandhi's dictates. Since Gandhi intended setting up Courts and colleges, many children were taken from the existing educational establishments, falling out of the established educational stream, and thus they did not qualify for the jobs which required evidence of aptitude from the existing examination system. Barristers, (Gandhi's main supporters), probably saved some of the mayhem because they found that if they abandoned their existing jobs, others took their places, so they did not leave the existing Courts and the Gandhi courts were not successful, but the whole miserable agitation was allowed to run on and on, while Lord Reading continued to do what Montagu had told him to, treating Gandhi as a visionary saint.

Finally, as Gandhi collected still more volunteers, Montagu in England had to step in. Unable to move Reading on his own authority, he went into a Cabinet Meeting and told of his determination that Gandhi should be arrested. Reluctantly and only after one more discussion with Gandhi, Reading instructed the Governor of Bombay to make the arrest.

Gandhi was tried in the bungalow of the local Magistrate, instead of in the Court, because there was fear of crowds and trouble. There was none. In the small room,

Gandhi stood peaceably and said that if he had the opportunity, he would do it again. Of course he did do it again, - again and again - but with later Viceroys, the actions was rather more quickly over.

The lies did not end there. To Montagu, Gandhi claimed he wanted *"the millions of India to leap to the help of the British throne."* Montagu added at that time, a year before the Rebellion, that none of the Indians showed any sign of wanting the British to leave. Gandhi claimed that he would rouse more men to join the army. The Indian army was a volunteer force and at the time (beginning of 1918) Britain was being seriously weakened by the fighting in France. A couple of years later in 1921, after his involvement with the Rebellion had been condoned, Gandhi wrote in 'Young India' *"The National Congress began to tamper with the loyalty of Indian Army in September last year (1920), the central Khilafat Committee* [of which Gandhi and the Ali brothers were central members] *began it earlier still. We must spread disaffection openly and systematically until it pleases the Government to arrest us."*

Of course the Government did finally arrest them, but looking back on this time in history, it is extremely amusing to read, hear or see on Television, the claims of a repressive and cruel Government (in the shape of the handful of Britons working among the Indians), ruling India.) The Marxist instruction to alter history has been well implemented. From this interference with the Army, [and a Colonel in the Jats has told me that the troops respected Gandhi very highly, which to the Indian mind would mean a tendency to follow the person respected] came the later weakness of the Indian Army, when soldiers went over to the Japanese, at a time when India was in the most grave danger and their own people would have suffered severely if the Japanese invasion had been successful.

One of the Ali brothers of Khilafat fame and closely involved in the Moplah uprising, Mohammed Ali, only realised Gandhi's perfidy in 1930, when he resigned from an unappetising Congress: *"We refuse to join Mr Gandhi,"* said his old ally, *"because his movement is not a movement for the complete independence of India but for making the seventy millions of Indian Mussulmans dependent on the Hindu Mahasabha"*. It was a pity he had not realised this before.

We see him making a continual claim of guilt and obeisance to the attitudes, whether Hindu or not, which he feels to be important. One of these is Ahimsa, the practice of harmlessness. To reconcile this with his claims of guilt, makes the complexity of his character and behaviour almost psychopathic. No self restraint governed his thinking, so that we go from the 1919 rebellion about which he and Nehru lied constantly and the Malabar Rebellion, with his comment that he would do it again, to the ludicrously named non-violent, non-co-operation campaign, with its effects. During the Salt March, when the press lined up to witness the 'terrible' behaviour of the police, it provoked one eye witness (Webb Miller writing in 'I Found No Peace') to write: *"I have seen men who have not been within yards of a lathi* [police brutality was repeatedly described in terms of their baton or lathi usage] *fall on the ground and cry out that they have been hurt. I have seen them plastered indiscriminately with iodine, rushed on to a stretcher and driven away accompanied by roars of sympathetic cheers. I have actually seen a harmless spectator of a lathi charge seized by over zealous volunteer ambulance workers and held down on a stretcher, kicking and struggling and protesting his innocence of hurt, while an eminent Parsi doctor bound up his head and arm".*

We see the same in the descriptions of the carrying of people on stretchers at Gandhi's hometown of Ahmedabad in 1919. The agitators used the two pronged attack of behaviour and claim, both false. At Amritsar, the claims made in the Congress Report are brazen. The people coming over the bridge to loot and rape in the Civil Lines have to be in mourning, barefooted, bareheaded and unarmed, longing for their beloved leaders, without the lathis, which the same crowd would later use to beat out the brains of their victims in the City.

Gandhi could 'apologise for a Himalayan blunder' over the 1919 Rebellion, when he saw the effects of his so called passive resistance or satyagraha, and the manifest depravities of the non-violent non-co-operation movement. Nevertheless, when Bhagat Singh was arrested for the murder of a British police officer ( J. P. Saunders) in mistake for someone else, together with his Head Constable, Chanan Singh who came to his help and for throwing a bomb into the Legislative Assembly in 1929 and was ordered by the judge to be hanged, Gandhi started a worldwide appeal for the man's release. Whatever the wish to sympathise, the ordering of hartals throughout India was bound to lead to trouble, which might have been expected after 1919. In Cawnpore, the Muslim population refused to join the hartal. The Hindu population, including many of the upper and middle classes, acted with all the certainty of righteousness to obey the dictates of Gandhi, and paid the usual casteless and untouchable members of Cawnpore society to break up the Muslim shops, rape the women, slit them open when pregnant and destroy and burn everything to an extent of such nightmare horror that it became, in the 1930s, a name for obscene cruelty. Gandhi's usual apology and threatened fast were accepted as if valid.

These accounts could be repeated, for they went on all through the Quit India Movement, when the Commonwealth, including India, was fighting for the safety of India. Again, the horror continued in 1947, when Nehru, with Gandhi's knowledge, took the next step of subdividing the Punjab, while the communal killing was already going on, leading to further tragedies and ruthless murders amounting, some say, to ten million people. So much for Ahimsa.

As for lies, one of the most obvious and best recorded was the Gandhi treatment of the joy at the Prince of Wales' arrival in India in 1921. Gandhi, despite pages of Press reports and photographs of the millions pouring into the city of Bombay and swirling around the Prince, claimed that such a festival of joy had never happened, although many of his Congress acolytes went to watch, saying that they would gain garlands of glory for looking at the face of the son of their King. Gandhi had been burning cloth that did not have his approval and his followers stripping women of their saris if they did not wear Khaddar, (which as anyone knows who has tied a sari, cannot be so used). So he claimed that the welcome had never taken place.

We do not know if Gandhi used cannabis or bhang or other drugs, but we know that he spent some forty or so years endeavouring to resist the sexual compulsion, yet never achieving its conquest. We know that he believed he was divinely inspired. We know that those who were not, or are not capable of impartial observation, or perhaps do not recognise the difference between good and evil, believe him to have been a saint. The facts make up a picture of self-aggrandisement, an apparent incapacity to say the same thing twice or keep to his word, ruthlessness in terms of the claims that he made and for which he was prepared to claim that he was fasting to the death. We know that none of this was reality. His behaviour certainly raises some doubt, either as to his sanity in terms of serious psychosis, or what we might call something akin to pure evil, such evil as that of the thugs [referred to in the introduction] which might not appear in the same light to the Indian mind. The thugs dedicated their activities to Kali, the Goddess of Destruction. To Gandhi, the age was the age of Kali, 'Kali Yuga' as he called it. The words used as a code sign by the thugs were 'Ali Brothers'. Was it merely a coincidence that the two Ali Brothers were involved with Gandhi, first in the Khilafat Movement and later when they worked together during the Malabar Rebellion which was Bolshevik funded? Was it coincidence that Gandhi dismissed the Rowlatt Report as insignificant and not worth reading and later stirred up rebellion on the ensuing Rowlatt Acts? Was it coincidence that the widespread conspiracy running throughout India, was largely based on the methods of Kali, with the young dedicated to the murder of anyone who reported the conspirators, or gave evidence? The coincidences are too many to allow that his intention was to work for what he believed to be a Divine Age, to which he owed allegiance.

Buchan also wrote of 'the fanatic' and it is certainly applicable to Gandhi. *"He is always in the technical sense mad – that is, his mind is tilted from its balance, and since we live by balance he is a wrecker, a crowbar in the machinery. His power comes from the appeal he makes to the imperfectly balanced, and as these are never the majority his appeal is limited. But there is one kind of fanatic whose strength comes from balance, a lunatic balance. You cannot say that there is any one thing abnormal about him for he is all abnormal. He is as balanced as you or me, but, so to speak, in a fourth dimensional world. That kind of man has no logical gaps in his creed. Within his insane postulates he is brilliantly sane. Take Lenin for instance. That's the kind of fanatic I'm afraid of."*

What he did achieve was the accolade of the ruthless dictator – fear. His Congress minions followed in his footsteps, lying about virtually everything that affected the rebellion. Nehru's best lie having been published in his autobiography, about Dyer's behaviour on a train, has been repeatedly quoted. It takes time to assimilate the constancy of fabrications on which Dyer and British rule was later judged.

But what of the claims that Gandhi must have done something good? What of the claim that he helped the Untouchables - 'harijans' as he called them. Harijan means greenhorn. Yes, he did take a token two into his ashram, thus, according to Hindu concepts, making all those in the ashram Untouchable themselves and embarrassing Nehru. As Beverly Nichols has pointed out, he could have helped more fundamentally by demanding that Untouchables might enter the Temples or schools, but he did not. When, after the 1935 India Act (giving so much independence that it meant only agreement in the Viceroy's Council for India to be given full Independence in 1947) the decisions were made about voting powers, Dr. Ambedkar, the leader of the Untouchables, asked for an Independent vote for his people. It was a sensible move, since there are Untouchables all over India in almost every village and without an independent mandate their voice could not be heard, particularly with the Hindu vote being under the control of the Brahmins. Gandhi, on Ambedkar's claim, went into a fast (as he said, to the death), unless the Untouchable vote was to be included in that of the Hindus. Ambedkar stood out for it alone, but in the end he gave in. Few people knew that Gandhi's fasts to the death were merely a bright wheeze and this was not confirmed until Woodrow Wyatt noted it in 1946 in his interview with Gandhi in his 'Diary of an Opinion'. It is interesting to note that Penderel Moon, the I.C.S. Indian historian, did not understand why it mattered so much. Not only would it have given a voice to these tragically treated people themselves, but without the amalgamation, the Hindu vote would not have overtaken the mass votes of all other divisions – Muslims, Parsis, Christians and so forth. The result can be seen in the continuing Hindu/Brahmin oligarchy of the present day.

One other matter needs to be touched upon - the funding of the Gandhi rebellion. It was known at the time through Sir Charles Cleveland (Head of Indian Intelligence) that large sums of money were coming to India from Sweden. These were traced to Bombay, from whence Gandhi came when he set out for Delhi and where he had close connections – and still the Hunter Committee said there was no evidence of conspiracy. Black knew of the sums coming into India from Tashkent, where the Communist controller, who has previously been Consul in Calcutta, could send it down by mule over the Pamirs into India. Funds had been brought in through the German agencies at the beginning of the war and undoubtedly continued. Hitchcock, in his secret report on the Malabar Rebellion, mentioned Bolshevik funds coming in. With the links of the Khilafat movement, the pro-Caliph or Turkish movement of Gandhi and the Ali brothers, funding from Parvus and the Committee of Union and Progress, would undoubtedly have been available. Sir Mark Sykes, whose assessment of the C.U.P. was available to Montagu, mentions the involvement of Congress with the funding from the United States, which also helped the German High Command with Lenin's activities.

# Chapter II
# THE FUSE

Just as Churchill's description of Lenin's entry into Russia as a 'virus' arrived just in time to prevent Russian democracy taking root, so also the virus of rebellion in India. Annie Besant and Gandhi claimed they were inculcating in India a sense of self-respect. The more ponderous movements of Government were working towards the same ends. *"The expediency of broadening the basis of government and the demand of Indians to play a greater part in the conduct of affairs in this country, are not matters which have escaped our attention."* Thus the Viceroy, Lord Chelmsford, speaking in relation to the announcement of August 20th 1917. Sir Michael O'Dwyer, speaking a little later: *"Government, while opposed to any sudden or catastrophic constitutional change, recognises that among a large section of the community there is a growing desire and a natural desire, for an increased measure of self government"*. In the same speech he warned of too precipitate a movement, comparing it to Ireland and Home Rule there, seeking an Ireland aimed at the restoration of a legislature and a separate executive, though with limited powers, which Ireland had enjoyed for centuries down to the Union of 1800. *"The great majority of the Irish people supported the movement .... unhappily, the nearer it came to realisation, the greater became the practical difficulties. The old feuds and factions were revived with increasing bitterness and threatened civil war. A year ago one section of the supporters of Irish swaraj (the Sinn Fein or Swadeshists) following in the footsteps of our Punjabi Swarajists, allied themselves with the king's enemies and brought about an abortive rebellion. That was speedily suppressed but it has left a fatal legacy of distrust and ill feeling which all good Irishmen whatever their creed or politics, deplore. In the matter of Home rule, I fear the case of Ireland in so far as it is analogous at all, conveys to us a lesson and a warning."*

At the same period, Mrs Besant, speaking publicly against the War Loan, said *"India will realise why I have striven for Home Rule after the War. Only by that can she be saved from ruin, from becoming a nation of coolies for the enrichment of others"*.

In the background, frequently forgotten by simplistic historians, India had been subject to the mutually repellent components of the body politic, only checked by a strong central government, as noted by Vincent Smith in his 'Early History of India'.

Beyond that, there is a tendency, which has been recognised among some Indians, for India to erupt every fifty years or so, as if by some sub-conscious, sub-continental force. There was thus some predisposition shown in 1857, again in 1919, in the 1940s and in the 1980s and 1990s, with the Sikhs, and again at Ayodhya, when the ancient Moslem mosque was pulled down stone by stone to be rebuilt as a Hindu temple.

In 1919, the Rowlatt Bills going through the Legislature marked the first move to indicate that 'the enemies of the King' were involved. The Amir of Afghanistan, our great support against the German invasion from Afghanistan, was murdered and with that action in February, the German faction under his son Amanullah, made their move. By the end of March, the tribes were moving up behind the Frontier, hidden by the hills.

With the passing of the Rowlatt Act, Gandhi initiated hartals, in which no one could trade or hire. It was not an original form of boycott. Har Dayal of the Cambridge Mission, Delhi, together with Lajpat Rai and others, had formulated it in Lahore in 1908 - boycott and passive resistance - but Gandhi, never original, was heard to say that the British were now full of pride in their victory and considered themselves masters of the world - a significant indication of that inclination to attribute to others, one's own attitudes. It was certainly not that of the British in 1918. He then went on to say that he was master of a weapon, which would bring them to their knees. Sir Michael O'Dwyer, the recipient of this information, was then warned by his Hindu informant to 'look out for his next move'.

In September 1918, the Sedition Committee (Rowlatt Committee) findings were published. The findings were that *"in all the main provinces of India within recent years, bands of conspirators, energetic and ingenious, although few in number, had caused discord or committed crime with the object of preparing the way for the overthrow by force of British rule. In Bombay, the conspirators had been purely Brahmin. The Bengal conspirators, although a small fraction of the enormous population of that province, spared no pains to attract educated youths to their ranks from schools and colleges. Gradually they established a terrorism, which made evidence of their doings exceedingly hard to obtain. In the Punjab, returned emigrants and others had attempted to bring about a bloody revolution in the critical month of February 1915. The fact was that that the ordinary statute law was unable to cope with conspiracies rich in ramifications, extending over enormous tracts of country largely devoid of roads and railways, among people crowded, ignorant and credulous. Their propaganda had produced a number of murders and robberies in their own province and had penetrated to Bihar and Orissa, the United Provinces and Madras, where it failed to take root, but led to sporadic crime or disorder. All the individual cases stand so closely interconnected as parts of one whole that they form, both as to the personnel and acts of crime, one continuous movement of revolution, which must be regarded as living and prolonged in all its parts until the movement is completely extinguished."*

The British, as in the 'Hind Swaraj' of Gandhi, were to be expelled from the country. *"...in the meantime a fanatical organisation must be created which would develop its inspiration by murder of officials and ... would refinance and arm itself by the plunder of peaceable Indian folk justified by the most cynical reasoning"* – thus the detailed report of the Rowlatt Committee, to which Gandhi gave no respect and the reason why the ensuing act was needed. Barindra was joined by his brother Arabinda Ghosh and with their followers, they formed the Anushilan Samiti (Society for the Promotion of Culture and Training) which very quickly gathered five hundred branches aimed at publishing journals including the 'Jugantur' which promoted racial hatred. 'Since the soldiers in India were recruited from the people, they should be alerted; for since the rulers were foreigners (feringhi), it was not murder for conspirator to kill them; the arms of the soldiers would become theirs and by causing alarm in the minds of the rulers, they would be destroyed'. A yogi, writing to the Jugantur, spoke of loot and plunder driving him mad.

Howls erupted from the Extremists when the report was published, but their preparations did not flag. In January 1919, the Government of India announced their intention of proceeding with the legislation recommended by the Committee on the opening of the February sessions of the Imperial Legislative Council. Two progressive judges, Mr Justice Beachcroft of the Calcutta High Court and Mr Narain Chandarvarka of the High Court of Bombay, as a committee, wrote their report on their findings, which had been invited by the Government of Bengal *"Our study and examination of the cases have impressed us with the correctness of the conclusion arrived at in their Report by the Sedition Committee 1918."*

Extract from the Bombay Chronicle of March 1st, 1919: *"The Satyagraha Vow being conscientiously of the opinion that Bills known as the Indian Criminal Law (Amendment) Bill No. I of 1919 and the Criminal Law (Emergency Powers) Bill No. II of 1919, are unjust, subversive of the principles of justice and destructive of the elementary rights of individuals on which the safety of the community, as a whole, and the State itself is based. We solemnly declare that in the event of these Bills becoming law and until they are withdrawn, we shall refuse civilly to obey these laws and such other laws as a Committee to be hereafter appointed may think fit, and we further affirm that in this struggle we will faithfully follow truth and refrain from violence to life, person or property."*

From the Bombay Chronicle of March 3rd, Satyagraha Sabha. *"At a meeting of the signatories of the Satyagraha pledge held on Saturday, the following Executive Committee was appointed:*

*President :- Mahatma Gandhi*
*Vice-President- Mr. B.G. Horniman (Editor of the Bombay Chronicle)*
*Members of the Committee (With power to add):*

*1   Mr Jamnadas Dwarkadas*
*2.  Mrs Sarojini Naidu*
*3   Dr Erulker*
*4.  Mr Subedar*
*5.  Mr. L.R. Tairsey*
*6.  Mr Azad*
*7.  Dr. Walker*
*8.  Mr. Jamnadas M. Mehta*
*9.  Mr. L.J. Khare*
*10. Mr. V.A. Desai*
*11. Mrs. Awantikabai Gokhale*
*12. Mr. Chanilal Ujamsi*
*13. Mr. R.N. Mandlik*
*14. Mr. Jemal Narandas*
*15. Mr. Harsang P. Thakerses*
*16. Mr. Vithaldas V. Jerajani*

*Secretaries: -*
*Dr. Sathya*
*Mr. Shraikerlal Baher*
*Mr. Umar Sobhani.*

At that time, Gandhi was imagined to be a saintly man and Sir Michael O'Dwyer's information would have seemed to many to be unpleasant and extraordinary. In the debates that followed, starting on the 12th March, two amendments were proposed .and passed by the Indian Members of the Legislative Council. Malaviya expressed himself strongly on the fact that Gandhi had sent telegrams to the Viceroy who had done nothing to stop the legislation. There were threats of rebellion if the Bills were to go through.

The British official members, including the Home Member Sir William Vincent, spoke most patiently, saying that 'the conscience of the Government in the matter of this legislation is quite clear. He blamed himself only for some fault or deficiency in his presentation of the case.

In the meanwhile, Gandhi, in Ahmedabad, was publishing prohibited literature which the Committee had selected for dissemination:

Hind Swaraj by M.K. Gandhi, Sarvondaya, or Universal Dawn by M.K. Gandhi. (This was in reality a paraphrase of 'Unto this Last' by Ruskin).

'The story of a Satyagrahi' by M.K. Gandhi (being a paraphrase of the 'Defence and Death of Socrates' by Plato).

'The Life and Address of Mustafa Kemal Pasha' (printed at the International Printing Press). Mustapha Kemal was of course a member of the Young Turks.

There followed a long rationalisation of the breaking of the law about these books, claiming that they had been chosen in order to cause as little disturbance as possible between the governors and the governed.

A good deal of other literature was handed out for cyclostyling by the purchaser, who would need only to spend an Anna or so for the first sheet. Among these were Thoreau, Mazzini, and various leaflets pointing out how little money and what appalling poverty there was in Britain.

On the 18th March, the Bills were passed. Information was given that there would be hartals. The first took place in Delhi on March 30th, together with hartals in various other places. There was another extensive action on the 6th April and then on April 10th there was a widespread signal. Gandhi, in the meanwhile had been giving speeches, as had his friends, virtually daily to the crowds. An example is one made by Mrs Naidu (a wealthy woman) *"We are all poor people earning a few annas a day. We do not understand politics. We understand what we mean by our honour. In fighting the Rowlatt Bills, we are fighting for our honour (izzat)"*. Speeches in much the same timbre were being made on the 4th, 5th and 6th in Bombay. Gandhi's theme after the Delhi rising was that the people who had been killed or wounded were martyrs. For those who imagine that British rule was repressive, it is interesting to see that in talking to Francis Griffith, then the Acting Commissioner of Police in Bombay, he spoke limpidly of his intention not to bring out the mill-hands *"probably for many a long day"* and yet on the 4th, he had given a speech in which on one hand, he told the mill-hands he did not wish them to come out on the 6th, and yet that he desired them to stop work on the Sunday, which was, in fact, the 6th.

Having promised Francis Griffith that he would not try and draw in the mill hands for whom he had helped to negotiate an increase in pay (he had also helped the mill owners by reducing the claim of the workers), it was the mill-workers who formed the crowd that attacked public buildings and people in Ahmedabad. The hartal on the 6th was called by him 'Black Sunday'. On the 5th of April, he was in Bombay and planning to leave for Delhi. The Government of India and the Punjab Government had ordered that, after the eruption in his name at Delhi, he should not be allowed into the Punjab.

Gandhi later gave as his reason for wishing to visit the Punjab, his wish to meet Kitchlew and Satyapal, whom he had not previously met. Perhaps that was to cover the fact that any claim to wish to address the ordinary people would have sounded rather hollow, since he spoke only English and Gujerati. Few ordinary people in the Punjab spoke English and he knew no Punjabi. It is here that the timing was most precise. It was believed that the Rebellion was timed for May 11th, the date of the eruption at Meerut in 1857, which started the Mutiny. This is quite likely, since astrologically and climate wise, similar factors would have applied as had applied in 1857. By May, the British troops would find the climate too severe and be of little use, as worked out in the Afghan War, where the heat was so intolerable that British troops were passing out and having to be taken away by ambulance. It was at the beginning of May that Dyer left for Thal. He was at Thal, already under siege by the Afghans, on May 23rd.

The likelihood is that the date of the Rebellion had to be moved forward and the timing went awry.

The hartals were believed to be practising discipline for the outbreak ahead. They were the opportunity for the underground movement to get the population into order. Like bindweed, the root structure was already in place, merely strengthening, extending and making new growth until the final eruption.

The release of Annie Besant had given fresh impetus to political activity in the Punjab. Amongst the political activity, more and more speeches and newspaper articles carried anti-Government excitement and more and more newspapers were being started.

At Delhi, the Muslim League and the Congress held joint sittings. Mrs Besant's popularity increased as she had given large sums to various Hindu projects. At Delhi, the speech of Dr Ansari, calling on ancient hatreds and fears, like 'ancestral voices prophesying war' was a direct incitement to rebellion. That was in December 1918. Sir Michael O'Dwyer had banned the speech from his Province and other provinces did the same. Throughout that winter, Sir Michael was on tour, holding durbars in the main, rewarding the rural population for war services. The durbars gave support to Government and in later months, helped to keep peace. Nonetheless, Gandhi's announcement of March 1st defying the Rowlatt Acts was having its effect, as extremists, using his words and the speeches in the Legislative Council, made more of both..

On March 23rd, Gandhi, marshalling his forces, announced hartal for the whole of India for March 30th. Delhi, with her links with Afghanistan, using the preceding razzmatazz of joint Congress and Muslim League meetings, went straight into hartal, followed, as would be the action everywhere, by violence.

Underneath all this, Amritsar, salient for the Afghan entry into India, had become a focal point for Bolshevik as well as Indian political movements. Germany and Russia were gradually formulating the International Socialism that has blossomed and flowered against the peace and stability of the Commonwealth and the Empire ever since. This was the strategic point both for troop movements to the Frontier and for population movements throughout the Punjab, on the direct route to Jullundur, the site of the area command.

In PART 3 Chapter VI is recorded the letter from Miles Irving, Deputy Commissioner of Amritsar, sent to the Commissioner of the Punjab, expressing his anxiety about the security situation. It was delivered by hand on the 8th of April and was probably dictated to his chief clerk on the 7th. Was the letter made known to Gandhi, justifying his claim to have the servants of the government 'under his hand' and did that account for the timing of his attempt to go to the Punjab on the 8th? Did the reply authorising the removal of the local leaders of the Nationalist movement, suggest the need for immediate action? We cannot know, but the timing is suggestive.

# Chapter III
# TIMING

In accordance with the general Principles laid down by the conspirators and the Rowlatt Report, everything was in place for Rebellion.

The First Principle was 'The organisation of a nucleus - including many educated people'. In Gandhi's conversations with Moti Lal Nehru and Abdul Bari, Gandhi explained that he had centres everywhere - even the servants of the Europeans and the government office clerks were in his net, as reported by the Intelligence Services.

The second Principle, 'Spreading ideas among the masses through the nucleus' had also gone on apace. It was clear in the Rowlatt Report, it was even clearer in the propaganda about the legislation. It had been spread throughout the country 'from the Himalayas to Cape Cormorin', as was said later in the Lords' debate.

The third Principle, 'Organisation of terrorist means, military and terrorist' had already been fulfilled in the Ghadr movement and with the collection of lathis at Amritsar. There was further evidence with the bomb making apparatus and the collection of instruments for wire cutting and disabling all communications.

Fourth Principle was 'Agitation'. Thoreau, Mazzini, plagiarism of any literature likely to stir up anger, speeches encouraging law-breaking and violence, together with the ludicrous claims about the Rowlatt legislation were all used to excite the hostility of the uneducated and the acquisitiveness of the criminal.

The final Principle, 'Rebellion', would appear at the right time. Subsequent historians have been bamboozled by the claims that Rowlatt really was the cause of the Rebellion, because it fits with the invented tales of British repression and appeals to those who feel guilty about the British Empire.

Those who knew India, realised that it was anger by the conspirators at the threat of suppression of their activities, which motivated their hatred of the legislation.

Durga Das is near the point when he says that the Act was 'Gandhi's opportunity.' Indeed this is clear from his autobiography. But again, why?

It seems probable that with the Germans still fighting in the Caspian and with the effective take over of Russia: with continuing German funding of the Bolsheviks; with Lenin having declared his intention of 'setting the East ablaze' and ready to join in, with an Armistice signed, but Peace not yet agreed, the conjunction of all these factors with the intention of the Illuminati to move towards world government, suggested to Gandhi that the time was ripe.

However, what was an opportunity for Gandhi was also a warning. Though he would use the Rowlatt legislation to claim that the British were intent on repression, he was aware that once the legislation was put into effect, the options for action by the rebels would be severely curtailed. The legislation was published in India on the 9th of January 1919, but not effective until ratified by the assent of the Governor-General on the 21st March.

Gandhi's 'window of opportunity' was short, if he was to take advantage of international events, before local circumstances and the new legislation put a stopper on action. It may be that this caused the date of rebellion to be advanced.

The members of the Oriental Desk had in fact moved to Petrograd and to Moscow so reliance could be placed on the Russian involvement. As we know from the descriptions of the depots at Jullundur, there were very few troops in India. In the main, the troops there were raw recruits or war weary soldiers about to be sent home. There was one further spur to the activation of the conspiracy at that point. Annie Besant's fulmination about the repression of Indians by the British was all the more persuasive because she was herself British. Yet those very same repressive British were about to give India 'democracy'. We know that a million people hardly constituted a widespread democracy, but we also know that already, Indians were on every Council - and elected at that - yet the propaganda of hate did not mention these facts nor (naturally enough) bring them to the public notice. The hatred was based on the British presence, the claimed British repression. The clear implication was that if Indians had power, the young men coming straight from college would get the jobs which the British presently held[30]. The fact that what the conspirators wanted was Brahmin rule would not be mentioned. Any mention of reforms made rebellion essential, for otherwise, the whole image of the British oppressors would be blown, and with it, all chance of the take over of India.

The evidence is clear. The Congress scheme which tied the British District Officer to Indian supervision, the power of the purse in Indian hands, these points were important for the politicians, the men who stood to gain the power, but they were not significant material in the face of democratic elections and the Legislative Assembly which would follow.

---

30   The members were few, in the I.C.S. - rather under 1000 jobs were British held

# TIMING

The propaganda about the Rowlatt Acts was to be the trigger for the first shots in a rebellion with its centres, its 'nuclei', already in place, including many educated people. Because of the Acts, those first shots went off too soon.

Actions essential for the rebellion quickly followed the publication. The speeches against Rowlatt in the Legislative Council, which included many Indians put forward by various organisations, or by the Governors chosen representatives of various bodies from which they had been elected, representatives of the Bar Associations of the Muslims, the Hindus and so forth, as Sir Umar Hayat Khan remarked, they influenced the people through their newspapers and by word of mouth and through the cyclostyled or printed handouts produced by such people as Gandhi. They more than influenced, they enraged, they incited to fury, the educated people who knew about them, and made clear that the British could and did over-rule these prestigious men, representatives of many groups, speaking, so the people imagined, for them.

If Gandhi had the image and trappings of a saint, Malaviya, as an ascetic Brahmin, had, for the intellectual population, a similar significance, possibly even stronger, since his veganism, his careful refusal to eat anything which the 'melecha' had prepared, or cast their shadow over, showed the highest principles and power of Brahmanism and wielded enormous power and prestige among Indians of every class. Gandhi's work in South Africa had brought acclaim, in the same strain as that of Bipin Chandra Pal, who wished the Indians to take over the Empire because, being so many, they had the right [even if they had missed the point, that the British by their impartiality and Christian kindliness had a standard far above the Indians and one which the Indians themselves preferred]. Gandhi already had in his mind the incitements that he had used in South Africa. There, he had described the 'Black Act' in terms which stirred thousands of people to believe him. He had marched the people, prepared in their trusting way, to oppose what they believed to be injustice, across the boundaries of the Orange Free State, caused his followers to be imprisoned, as he was to do later in India and landed up with nothing except the ability of Indians to use their own non-Christian marriage rights. The thumbprints and the £3 registration fee remained, as it was reasonable that they should. It was Gokhale who asked him to return to India and advised him to do nothing for the first year except travel round India and begin to understand the situation. It was due to his South African movement that he had gained his reputation. Today, those Western people who believe him to have been a saint, must avoid reflecting on his actions and using their own reasoning powers, while innocently accepting the carefully prepared but mendacious biography broadcast to the world,

M.M. Kaye tells a story of an Indian friend of the family, Khan Sahib (this name indicates that the man was a Muslim) a man of the book, as are Christians and Jews, therefore more in touch with the concept of objective truth, more so, than the Hindus (of whom Gandhi was one). Nevertheless, Khan Sahib spoke for all Indians when he told Cecil Kaye, her father: *"When the British are asked a question"*, he said, *"they will instantly reply with the truth, and perhaps consider later if it might not have been wiser to lie. Whereas we of this land will always answer first with a lie; and only afterwards consider if it might have served us better to speak the truth."* All of us who worked and lived amongst Indians and meted out justice in accordance with the laws of Islam and Hinduism, and in the case of criminal law, in the mode of British law which rests on the concept of truth, knew this. Truth was alien to many, but those who today, lie about us in India and believe Gandhi's interpretations, are landed with the corollary that the British must have been telling lies, since the Saint was speaking his much declaimed 'truth'. None of these worthy acolytes spoke to the Khan Sahib or lived amongst Indians or understood their point of view. This lack of understanding has caused much of the present acceptance of the Gandhi story about South Africa, the Rowlatt Acts and the Amritsar incident.

If he had not claimed so vociferously that he was going to fight for the Harijans (the Untouchables), his later treatment of Dr. Ambedkar over the vote for the caste-less ones might not have shown him to be a two faced rogue, claiming concern for these ill-treated people, putting Brahmins at the head of the Congress and in positions of power by the amalgamation of the Untouchable vote with the Hindu vote, while sticking firmly to the stratification of caste which debased those beneath caste.

Caste is Hinduism; caste, with its stratified social mores meant Brahmins were the great stumbling block to a more even distribution of power amongst Indians themselves. Part of the acceptance of Gandhi was that, though he was not a Brahmin, to him, Hinduism was paramount and that entailed Brahminism. Among the political parties, there was a specifically non-Brahmin party, but the bulk of the higher posts in the Judiciary and in other areas almost automatically went to Brahmins, the intellectual force in India. Every endeavour was made to appoint members of other castes, but Hinduism being what it is, like a Roman Catholic priesthood in olden times, this priesthood rules. Lord Roberts, himself the grandson of an Indian woman, believed that the Mutiny was started because this priesthood believed that Christianity was a threat to their power. Durga Das makes clear the racist feelings which caste supports, for the untouchable or caste-less claims could not be approached with anything but distaste by Brahmins.

This then was the man who, through Sir Charles Cleveland's careful Intelligence work, was shown to be discussing the plans for rebellion with Moti Lal Nehru in 1918.

The background up to that time has been well described by M.M. Kaye, who was a child in that earlier India. Her description of the relationship of her parents with Indians, and of herself and her brother and sister, makes the feelings clear. As a girl in the 1940s, I met more Indians than Britons on terms of close friendship in my parents' house. My own friends were more likely to be Indians than British, and as M.M. Kaye remarks, in the Empire, there was no consideration of colour, only whether people were good or bad. She makes one error. Her claims that the 'heaven-born', the members of the I.C.S., were far better off than the Army were not correct. Mollie Stainton, herself the widow of an Indian Civil Servant, had a sister married to a Major in the Army who thought the same. Together they worked out what they were paid, how much they had to pay into their respective pensions and so forth. The Army sister to her surprise, found that her Indian Civil Servant sister was considerably the poorer in salary and, as Mollie Stainton adds, the Army did not have to entertain every odd body that came through the District, as did the Indian Civil Service District Officer, with no diplomatic allowance to help. M.M. Kaye's descriptions of India are redolent of the life we lived and although I had an English Nanny and not an ayah, so did not learn the language as a toddler, much of what she describes was the same as I remember from my own slightly later experiences.

So when the Briton/Indian division began to show in 1918-1919, it naturally made a most unpleasant atmosphere. Gandhi told Moti Lal Nehru that he had the servants of the British on his side. Fortunately, for my parents' sakes, this was not so, as will be seen in my mother's descriptions of the life in the Fort at Amritsar, so carefully omitted from the Attenborough propaganda story. Gandhi also claimed that he had all the clerks at his disposal and although this was certainly an exaggeration, the matter relates to the timing of the outbreak - the final rebellion. Rash Behari, a clerk in the Forestry Department, was involved in the earlier conspiracy that included Amir Chand, a teacher in the Cambridge Mission School in Delhi, where Gandhi's acolyte, C.F. Andrews was also employed. That conspiracy was unveiled, as was the Silk Letter Conspiracy, by Sir Charles Cleveland. The forestry clerk was concerned with training students in anti-British activities that included the attempted murder of the Viceroy, but Rash Behari was not by any means the only clerk involved in the sedition.

Sir Charles Cleveland was a good friend of Mohammed Ali of the Khilafat movement. Sir Charles, a good friend to British and Indians alike, was a man of spiritual and physical strength; who had battled with a panther, resulting in near death and the furious mauling of his large frame together with the near loss of an arm. He was advised by doctors to have it amputated, but he then spent some years getting rid of the poison that threatened to kill him, by his extraordinary will power. There can have been very few men of such courage and strength.

Not only did he love women, he overpowered criminals and was, whether directly or indirectly, responsible for much of the secret information in these pages. As to his initiative in gaining information about Gandhi and Moti Lal Nehru, this included Gandhi's conversations with the Mullah, Abdul Bari, offering him the headship of the Muslims of India. Gandhi certainly aimed high! The offer was dependent on Abdul Bari changing the Muslim belief in the *dictat* of Abraham in the killing of a calf, to the killing of a goat. What is interesting is that Gandhi never seems to have contemplated for a moment the altering of caste, as had Ramakrishna and his follower Vivekananda, or the earlier founder of the Indian Mirror who advocated inter-caste marriage. If Gandhi had wished to help the Untouchables and the lower or casteless men, this could have been of greater benefit than the continuation of racism implicit in the mere concept of Untouchability. These outcastes, in many ways similar to lepers in the Britain of an earlier time, were not allowed to go into schools, nor temples, and when in desperation, some of them became Christians, they were still treated a-socially, to the extent of being allowed the communion cup only in a subordinate rotation, when others were at the altar with them.

We see only in the Secret Evidence of the Hunter Committee, that Gandhi and Moti Lal Nehru were talking of the position of the people who would obey the leaders of the rebellion.

Nehru gives one clue to the action, when he describes the feelings of Indians towards the Germans and the war. It was, he says, the desire to see the British humiliated by being beaten that gave them a common concern with the Germans. The core of the understanding with which, in our tolerant way, we ruled the Empire and formed the present Commonwealth and its principles, was basically Christian. Christianity guided us, from the first steps in the Charter of the East India Company in the early 17th Century, to the end. It was this religion that persuaded General Dyer to take the step he did to preserve the lives of four hundred women and children; to protect the law-abiding population of Amritsar and the lives of his small force - and gave him the courage to do what was necessary. Today, the miasma which seems to govern our media, has inculcated into our schools, not the religion that was our backbone, that led to the smashing of the rebellion which was in place to run like fire throughout the whole of India, but instead of that Christian belief, the anthropological concept of relativism. Our backbone, our sense of right and wrong, has been eroded, just as Parvus by his development of pragmatic Marxism, eroded the morality and strength of Christian Russia.

One of the characteristics of the Parvus method was to abandon responsibility, substituting passion for ideas, which gave free rein to any sort of devilment of which man is capable and which is purely evil. This overrode all thought of loyalty, history, concern for one's country, and replaced it with a type of internationalism in which, personal responsibility had become irrelevant. These poisonous concepts of Parvus, of his adjutant, Lenin, of Marx, Lenin's mentor, had weakened the natural beliefs in the servants of Government which India held, to a large extent, up to that time, weakened the moral fibre of the world and made it possible for the words of Gandhi to corrode it, replacing the beneficence of trust, with Gandhi's particular breed of anarchy. After all, there was only one central concept, the unwise political pacifism, which he himself was quite happy to deny in the rebellions of 1919, 1922 and again later. Malabar was an example, as was Bolshevism in Russia. It should be clearly remembered that the protagonists of the Muslim/Hindu entente, gloried in their sedition, their incitements to rebellion and their capacity to rouse it, however bestial the methods or results. Those mischievous cruelties might have been prevented if the British Government had not claimed that the officials on the spot wrongly handled the first step in 1919 and had not given credit to the untruthful accounts of the rebels.

An Indian woman recently asked me why Indians are so arrogant. Sir Michael O'Dwyer referred to them as *"the most aristocratic nation on earth"*. We do not know the answer, but it could have to do with caste. The British, of whom 'The White Man's Burden' was written, had a caste in India, although not of their naming. They were called 'sahib-logh' or, when in the Indian Civil Service, 'Heaven Born' - a term which amused us, but did not convince us.

Today, we get so used to the anti-British attitudes of the media that some of us (or those of us who were not in India) believe the mendacious nonsense put out on our screens about 'Divide and Rule' or 'British Brutality', invented by those who wish to justify their role as 'freedom fighters' by making up exciting tales. The matter of 'Divide and Rule' has already been dealt with – for anyone of even limited intelligence, it would be silly to imagine that a man, let us say a Deputy Commissioner in charge of a district of a million souls, whose job it would be to keep the peace, would be likely to stir up trouble which might end with the loss of his own life. It was the job of these men (and their wives) to help the different castes and creeds to sort out differences and, as far as lay in the power of one man in such a position, to keep the peace and encourage co-operation and friendship between members of different religions and caste affiliations.

The discipline was not unique; for years the British had learnt to live in a difficult situation. Today, someone living among Indians of various creeds and castes in Britain, may find himself the only man who speaks to all his Indian and Pakistani neighbours - his position is much the same as was ours.

But the experience was not learnt in a haphazard way. As far back as de Warren at the beginning of the 19th Century, for an outsider, the standard of behaviour of the British in India was reckoned exceptional. *"The perfect English gentleman never demeans himself or does anything derogatory; he displays his rectitude and self-respect in all the little details of his life. The inner man will never betray him, because it is of the same calibre as the outer man; he could live in a glass house, all his actions will bear the light and defy criticism."* De Warren's description does not only apply to the civilians but to the men who became soldiers. Fontannier, writing at the same time remarked on the simplicity of Government and its accessibility and it should be remembered that until quite recently, the highest aim for men from other countries, including India, was to become like an 'English Gentleman.' Sadly, most of the integrity shown in the quote from de Warren, has been lost, but in the beginning of the 20th Century, it was still the mark of the English gentleman and (a part of the effect of the pressures of life in India), those in the Indian Civil Service. While the so called 'freedom fighters' were opposing the attempts of the British to hand over India intact to a democratic government, they thought that they were fighting for Indian rule, when they were really trying to implement the clever plans of their leaders for the Hindu Raj, rather than democracy. Indians themselves were already involved in ruling India, with only seven hundred Britons out in the districts in the latter years, subordinate to the Government of India.

From earliest times the British have had a mobile society. Hardy, the servant's son knew it, Robin Hood was thought to have been the last of the Bohuns, Cardinal

Wolsey, a richer man than the King, knew it as he stepped up to the highest levels from a childhood as the son of a butcher. We knew this within our own families and those of our friends. we could see the rise and fall, and we had no Untouchables as a threshold to keep our position always in the superior realms. Untouchability was not to us a sin, as it is to Indians, nor are we in the same way, racist.

The claims of Marxism, of Bolshevism, of Socialism, were different. In the case of this un-mobile religion, workers and the working-class were always set, like flies in amber, as the only worthwhile class, those at the top being similarly fixed as worthless. The Indians may not have seen the inverted similarities to their own stratified society, but it is probable that they did and they certainly used it in making out that the people whom Dyer had killed were the disciples of Marx in an unfair society. That impression hid a society, which was never ever again treated as fairly, but the Untouchables had to remain to keep the parrots on their perches. Despite a Constitution that specifically denies caste, for it claims to be a secular society, untouchability still survives. The Minority Rights Group found evidence of the children still sitting outside schools, endeavouring to hear and learn through the aperture which was the window, but not too close so as to sully the children inside by their shadows: their parents (and presumably themselves) were being burnt to death in the villages, with the police looking on. They were a substantial part of the British white man's burden. It was they who most desperately wished the British to stay and prayed the Prince of Wales on his visit in 1921 to ask his father to let us stay, but to increase the confusion in the foreign mind, the propaganda film 'Gandhi' had to claim that the crowd fired on by Dyer was made up of women in their wedding clothes. That there were women present is a part of the imagery that has no relation to fact. Just as Gandhi's clothes were not merely in tune with his sainthood in the Indian view, they accorded with the Western view of poverty. The socialist smokescreen could not possibly have allowed the wealth of a Gandhi, or indeed of any Indian, to disturb the false image being made of the brutality of the British. The fact that we had a hard time making ends meet: that we had no homes in Britain to go to when we left; that under us India had prospered phenomenally and that many Indians were far wealthier than even the most senior officials, has been concealed – nor, more importantly, our rather kindly and lax dispensation of the law.

Dr Ambedkar rose to his senior position in the Untouchables Party not through any help from Gandhi, who was claiming great concern for the Untouchables, but because his father, working in the Indian Army, managed to save enough to send his son to be educated in the States. On our leaving, the Constitution of India stated there were no castes. In a recent directive to all Government workers; Untouchables could no longer be called by that name, people working in Government service were instructed to call them 'harijans'. As the Khan Sahib said, in India, truth came to be meaningful only after some thought.

The same concept describes the propaganda that must have been formulated and spread even before the Rowlatt Legislation was enunciated by the Committee in 1918.

The speeches in the Legislative Council fulminating against the Legislation gave credence to the inventions and strengthened the belief of the credulous and innocent population in the leaders who appeared to be protecting them. So persuasive was the behaviour of those leaders that subsequent historians have imagined that their intention was for a democracy that would overturn a repressive Government. If there had been repression, then the Bills would have been described accurately. It was the lack of any link between Government practice and the legislation that makes the falsity of those tales clear. Democracy was never the issue. To stir the anger of the mass of the people in the most decisive way was the intention. There is no mention whatsoever in any of the propaganda of the basis of the Rowlatt Bills or their intention. One historian (Percival Spear in the Oxford History of Modern India, 1740-1947. O.U.P., 1965) described the Bills accurately: *"The two Bills allowed judges to try political cases without juries and gave provincial governments power of internment"*.

The agitation was intended to rouse the people, simple and trusting folk, to a necessary rebellion. By 1919, everything was ripe for widespread insurrection, which, if the descriptions of the legislation had been remotely correct, would have been reasonable.

Nehru writes with an appearance of simple sincerity and if he had not invented the silly story of Dyer in the train, he might be trusted. Prior to the Montagu visit in 1916, leading members of the Muslim league and of Congress had met in the Nehru home to discuss the formulation of the Lucknow Pact. The Pact agreed the sharing of ministries between Muslims and Hindus in the event of democratic elections. The Pact was to survive until, with Nehru's plans before them and after the Round Table Conference in 1930, the subsequent India Act of 1935 and the election in 1937, Muslim ministries were not forthcoming and Jinnah, as the leader of a proud people, was driven to stand out for Pakistan. That Pact, at the time it was agreed, had already made a bridge between the two great religions of India.

With Montagu's visit, there was a certain degree of 'wait and see'. Mrs Besant, whose atheistic socialism had been to a certain extent replaced by Theosophical Hinduism,[31] still gave no encouragement to democracy, since ancient Hindu rule had been an autocracy, which agreed with the theme of her belief in the perfection of India with out the British. She was interned and the Nehrus were furious at her internment. After all, Nehru had become a theosophist after hearing her speak at Allahabad when he was thirteen, although his theosophy, by 1919, had been submerged in the underlying socialism. He refused to go into the I.C.S., the vocation of so many of the friends he knew at Cambridge. Dr Kitchlew, one of the leaders of the Amritsar centre of the Rebellion, had known Har Dayal and after leaving Cambridge in 1910, travelled across Europe and met the men of the Oriental Desk at Berlin, as did Jawaharlal and his father, Moti Lal Nehru. The latter was President of Congress in 1918, suc-

---

31  Theosophy includes Illuminism, the origin of socialism. Bepin Chandar Pal, Lajputrani, who with Bhai Parma Nand had been endeavouring to acquire propaganda from Krishnavarma.

ceeding Annie Besant as the President of 1917, having changed his feeling for the British with the changing mood. In London, they met the other Indian politicians who knew in 1917 of the funds pouring in from international sources, which Mark Sykes had pinpointed and, together with Gandhi, these two men created the propaganda story on which Attenborough's film is based. That travesty of a story persuaded A.J.P. Taylor to write in the Oxford History of England that Gandhi changed his mind about the British after the 1919 Rebellion. For the editors to accept such a claim is still as extraordinary an example of the effectiveness of really good lies in propaganda as can be found.

Kipling's 'white man's burden' aptly looked into the future:
*"And when your goal is nearest,*
*The end of others sought,*
*Watch sloth and heathen folly,*
*Bring all your hopes to nought."*

Since Gandhi is, to a degree, central to the 1919 rebellion, it is necessary to grasp his position clearly, if this book is to be recognised in its historical context.

Sankaran Nair, in his 'Gandhi and Anarchy', dissects the Gandhi claims of the behaviour of Gandhi after the Reform Bill of 1919 was published. He writes:

*"The methods advocated by Mr. Gandhi and the Congress are directed against Western civilisation, against the class that fought for and won the reforms and the Montagu reforms schemes of constitutional progress. They have failed miserably and, as was natural, more violent methods leading to direct conflict with the forces of Government have followed. In South Africa, he is responsible for creating a situation which makes a peaceful and satisfactory solution practically impossible. His factious policy in India stands in the way of further reforms ..."*

That is a sentiment which my father much later subscribed to, when he said *"India would have got independence five years earlier if it had not been for Gandhi"*.

Of the Malabar rebellion inspired by Gandhi and of which he said that he would do it again, Nair wrote: *"For sheer brutality to women, I do not remember anything in history to match the Malabar rebellion ... atrocities committed more particularly on women, are too horrible and unmentionable that I do not propose to refer to them in this book"*.

'Gandhi and Anarchy' is probably the most explicit of the publications on the rebellion. Interestingly, it has disappeared from all the library shelves except one.

Gandhi, in explaining his behaviour, claimed that it was due to the behaviour of the officials in the Punjab. To this Nair wrote:

*"The real truth of course is that the Punjab grievances are only pretext for this agitation (Malabar rebellion) by the violent section headed by Mr Gandhi ..."* and then *"Perhaps I should add that considering the undisciplined fanaticism of the non co-operator, and historical ignorance of the development of political organisation, it is probably just as well that the councils were in their inception, preserved from such a calamitous invasion."*

He is referring to the councils elected after the Reform Bill in 1919, which Gandhi ordered his followers not to join. This, as Nair pointed out, was later reversed, as so often with Gandhi, of whom it might be said that anything he said at one moment, unless it was vicious (as with his untrue claims about the Punjab) could, and often would be, reversed at any time that it suited him so to do.

As to the Rowlatt Report, Gandhi, who was staying in Madras at the time of its publication, being one of the people involved in the general conspiracy, wrote *"Its recommendations startled me. They seemed to me to be totally unwarranted by the evidence published in its report."* He was referring to the report of those incidents earlier summarised and from 1919 onwards, Gandhi used the Punjab disturbances as an excuse for everything else and on that basis, claimed British brutality and Indian justification, regardless of fact.

With Dyer on the North West Frontier and the Rebellion under control in the Plains, there followed apologies from Gandhi, relief from the population at last allowed to live in peace with their government, and a growing masquerade for the benefit of the leaders and Western opinion. This last was possible because of Montagu's suppression of information in the Press.

Even before Dyer had left for the Frontier on April 14th, with the perception of the Ahmedabad riots fresh before him, these were Gandhi's words: *"In the name of Satyagraha we burned down buildings, forcibly captured weapons, extorted money, stopped trade, cut off telegraph wires, killed innocent people and plundered shops and private houses…It is open to anybody to say that but for the Satyagraha campaign there would have been none of this violence."* It is most noticeable that not a word is said of this admission in Chapter IV of the Hunter Report that describes Satyagraha. That chapter calls it an innocuous doctrine and says that it has nothing to do with the excesses of the mob.

A further indication of the inaccuracy of this Report comes in paragraph 48. *"The Amritsar crowd was a crowd of mourners - bareheaded, many unshod and all without sticks. It was on its way to the Deputy Commissioner's house to plead for the release of its loved ones."* These, of course, were the two doctors, the leaders of the Amritsar part of the rebellion. In opposition to this quote, Hose refers to p.42, vol. 1 para. 11 of the Hunter Evidence. Mr Beckett: *"I heard a noise like the noise of the sea ... the crowd were all shouting and behaving in the most irrational manner, making faces, waving their hands ... they were hitting our horses ... when they got nearly to the foot of the bridge, there was a pile of half-bricks and stones lying, and they started throwing these."*

The piles of stones in baskets under cloths at Ahmedabad, by the entrance to the Queen's gardens at Delhi, at Anarkali, at Lahore, and these at Amritsar, as well as others, placed at strategic points, are a further indication of the subtle way in which the movement was managed.

Hose again *"Report paragraph 12. The firing did not take place until after this."* Bearing in mind that Gandhi based his claims for the validity of the Moplah Rebellion on the behaviour of the officials in the Punjab and continued to claim a massacre to the time of his death, his claims at the period, or immediately after the rebellion, need to be quoted. He said:

*"Almost immediately after the Ahmedabad meeting I went to Nadiad. It was here that I used the expression 'Himalayan miscalculation' which obtained such wide currency afterwards. Even at Ahmedabad I had begun to have a dim perception of my mistake, but when I reached Nadiad and saw the actual state of things there and heard reports about a large number of people from Kheda district having been arrested, it suddenly dawned upon me that I had committed a grave error in calling upon the people in Kheda district and elsewhere to launch upon civil disobedience prematurely, as it now seems to me."*

In the speech from which Sir John Hose quoted, Gandhi said *"The buildings burnt down were public property and they will naturally be rebuilt at our expense. The loss due to the shops remaining closed is also our loss"* and a little later, *"Each group can collect its own contributions and send them to me through its collectors."* When the Government applied a levy to the city for exactly these depredations, Gandhi achieved a further rising against anything so unjust. It is difficult to imagine Gandhi building new Government buildings with the money collected and given to him.

One of the main concerns of Gandhi, in secret discussions with the Mullah Abdul Bari in 1918/19 was that the Muslim religion should be altered so that Abraham's (to Muslims, Ibrahim's) sacrifice of a calf should be altered for that of a goat. If the Mullah were to take that step of persuading his congregation, then he would be put in charge of Islam in India. This is Gandhi at his tortuous best, trying to reconcile the irreconcilable in order to further his plan for power. It was as much of a confidence trick as the Salt March,[32] and as the pretence of peacefulness by fasting in the face of the murderous violence which he was himself encouraging.

---

32    The Salt Tax had been abolished when the new Assembly was voted in 1921; but in 1923 the same Imperial Legislature had restored it as a necessary facet of the budget

# PART 3
# MOBS

## Chapter I
## DELHI

The Mutiny of 1857 was so much in the forefront of the minds of the British in India in 1919, that its differences from, as well as its similarities to, contemporary events, need to be appreciated. Much of the confusion rests in the claim that 1857 was a 'War of Independence' a term coined as a propaganda ploy. The soldiers who, from playing with the white children under the veranda one day, were so aroused by incitement and hashish that they were bayoneting them to death after murdering their parents the next, were trained sepoys, armed and knowing how to use those arms to defeat the small resistance they met, with the same strategies and expertise as their officers. It was a Mutiny not a war, just as the 1919 rebellion was a widespread conspiracy of ordinary people, not of trained soldiers.

The similarities of approach lay in the need for a background conspiracy to encourage the soldiers, in one case to rise against their officers, in the other to function concurrently with other places in India. The leaders of the 1919 rebellion were always in sight, rousing, encouraging forward, giving directions, as with the orders to the people who made up the mob at Amritsar to gather in the Jallianwalla Bagh, or as my father describes, when he was endeavouring to hold up the mob on the bridge trying to get to the Civil Lines, or at Ahmedabad, seen in the crowd handing round trays of sweets to the people who were destroying buildings or firing at the police and soldiers.

Where the main mistake has been made is in this claim of racism against the British. Many of these claims come from Americans, for instance Freyn and Sayer (although Sayer is Canadian), for the American nation has been deeply racist in a way the British never were. Even during the Second World War, America would not allow Jews into Country Clubs or to bathe in the ordinary swimming pools, let alone people of coloured skin. There were also problems in this country over the acceptance of negro soldiers by ordinary people. Their sensitivity to racism is vivid in their minds as a result of its proximity, historically speaking, to their attitudes to slavery and the colour bar. It is almost impossible for them to imagine that we did not think as they did.

Where the Mutiny does relate to the events of 1919, or indeed with any other rising or excitement in India, is in the way that every eruption spreads. The difficulty for the British and Indian forces in preventing the Mutiny taking over all India, was that it spread largely by copycat methods (supported of course by the Brahmin conspiracy). It did not disturb the centre of Government, then in Calcutta, although steps had to be taken to disarm the regiments which might have risen, but the trouble lay in the almost viral spread, which led to one regiment after another rising and joining in. The Sikhs, so recently freed from 'Sikh misrule', fighting with the British at the small house at Arrah in Bihar, show that racial proximity where there was no Brahmin interference, had no negative effect. The 50 Rattray Sikhs and 15 European and Eurasian men fought to defend their position against thousands of mutineers, laughing and joking, surviving every difficulty even when their water ran out and they had to dig a well, until they were relieved.

The viral spread was exactly the concern of Dyer and its halt, the main expression of his success.

The other similarity, to be expected in a nation that worships Kali and destruction as well as Vishnu and construction, was the exciting effect of violence on the minds of the rebels. Colonel Malleson, writing about the Mutiny, describes the Rani of Jhansi as 'intoxicated' prior to the massacre of women and children. This intoxication can be seen on the face of Udham Singh after his killing of Sir Michael O'Dwyer, and his wounding. of the Marquis of Zetland, the Secretary of State for India, in 1940 and this 'intoxication' went with the yells for 'white blood' heard by the women and children in the Fort at Amritsar on the 10th April and later.

The foolish treatment by Lord Dalhousie, the Viceroy prior to 'Clemency Canning', at the time of the Mutiny, in interfering with traditional methods of inheritance, (although it could have given more legitimacy to inheritance and reduced infighting), together with the Brahmin conspiracy and their fear of the power of Christianity, could not be said to have any correlation with the Rebellion of 1919. That was simply the desire for power and humiliation, with German, and later, Bolshevik help. If the Germans had won, the leaders would not have regretted the loss of the democratic spread, given by the British.

However one more thing came out of the rebellion. This was Gandhi's spiritual image. Throughout the evidence that gives background to this book and to the rebellion, there is mention of magic. When Gandhi was finally arrested after the terrible disgrace of the Malabar Rebellion, Harcourt Butler told of how this punctured Gandhi's saintly image, because it was shown that this magical person was not able to fly out of prison. It had been imagined that no prison bars could be his cage, that just as he had flouted the great Sirkar, he would be able to fly out of any prison. The more educated people saw him slightly differently, in more material terms, but he had given enough of an image of sainthood to persuade most people including the Muslims. What he was propounding, he claimed, was the spirit of India - just as Hitler (and the Kaiser before him) propounded the spirit of Germany, just as Stalin following Lenin, the great image of Russia. The error in Stalin's case was to have proclaimed atheism; in Hitler's case, to put too much emphasis on his own person. Gandhi, initiating much the same pretensions as Hitler in his 'Heil Hitler', claimed his leadership to a religious nation directly from the Divinity through himself by the expression 'Mahatma'. In 1941, the German radio station at Zeesen, in a special broadcast to India proclaimed *"The German people respect Mahatma Gandhi as much as Adolf Hitler. Herr Hitler has the same principles as Mahatma Gandhi."* Wherever one walked in the Bazaar, the German nation could be heard.

The German infiltration of the tribes was, as in 1915/16, still carried on in 1941/42, while in the plains, Subhas Chandra Bose tried to take over Congress, started the Indian National Army and then fled to Berlin. Gandhi, Nehru and the others, held tight to their Congress while writing to Hitler and starting the Quit India movement, so that Japan and the Axis powers very nearly took over India.

Tom Roger's Qashqai, who attacked the oil refinery at Abadan in the Second World War, as they had attacked British interests in this earlier time, were in the same position as the Mahsuds, the Afridis and the Waziris, in their subjection to German propaganda. The ongoing pro-German behaviour of Nasir Khan, the chief of the Qashqai tribe, in the Second World War illustrated the same pan-Germanism mentioned by Raeder Bollard, which affected the rousing of the tribes in Afghanistan. Brigadier Fitzroy Maclean wrote, in his 'Eastern Approaches', of his arrest of the Persian General Zahedi, also working with Nasir Khan to facilitate the entry of German troops into Persia.

M. N. Roy, the Bengal writer, summed up the attitude of political India in 1942, an attitude which was intrinsic to the pro-German attitudes of 1919: *"Germany, not the Germany of Goethe, Lessing and Beethoven, nor of the rebels of 1848, nor of Haeckel, Helmholtz, Koch, Virchow, Planck etc., but the Germany of the Kaisers and of Hitler, has always been the beloved of the Indian nationalist. In contrast to this curious sympathy, Indian nationalism has never felt any sympathy for France, the land of great revolutionary traditions."* And then, almost mimicking the incitements and concepts recorded in the 'Sedition Report', which Gandhi dismissed as not giving sufficient reason for the Rowlatt Act, *"The cult of the omnipotent State, which prevailed among the Prussians, found full and explicit warrant in the teaching of Hegel. The logic of tyranny was gilded by the ethical beauty of sacrifice. The state was God. In the name of that abstraction, millions must be prepared to work, to suffer and to perish. That is exactly the ideal that Mr Rajagopalachari placed before the youth of our country. The rise of the modern German nation represented the realization of that ideal. Why then should we despair?"*

One has only to know the Hegelian metaphysical doctrine of State in order to visualise 'the power of the spirit' which, according to an accredited leader of Indian Nationalism, saved Germany and will save India also. That mystic power is not a moral force, but brute force in the most highly organised form. That is the Gandhian creed of non-violence. We must thank Mr Rajagopalachari for having practised the other part of the creed, namely truth.

German infiltration still existed, but the internal Indian conspiracy did also. The exception in the Second World War was that, despite Italian and German propaganda emanating largely from the German and Italian Missions at Kabul, the Afridis asked to join the Indian Army, much as the Rekis or the Hazaras, mentioned in Dyer's 'Raiders of the Sarhad'. The Amir in the first war was able to hold back the incursion of German troops, while in the second, the Italian and German Missions inside Afghanistan were told to leave. In these remote areas of Persia, where the tribes were effectively little kingdoms of their own, the link with Kabul was simply an overlordship, not total control. The propaganda coming up from the plains of India in the Third Afghan War was a joint activity with the German and Bolshevik agents, which suggested a successful and integrated rising. As with Gandhi in India, religion also took its part in the 1930s and 1940s when the Faqir of Ipi, pro-German, continued with propaganda through the tribes much as Pingle during the first war had done among the regiments in the Punjab.

The misunderstanding about Gandhi and his spiritual intentions was as persuasive to Muslims as to the British. What came out of the 1919 Rebellion was nothing very much except a belief which Lord Samuel, visiting India in the 1930s, blew away in his description of Gandhi doing darshan to a crowd in Delhi. He remarked that he felt nothing; indeed the darshan of Gandhi gave none of the spiritual impact which he claimed, along with his followers. The pity in 1919 was that the Muslims, frequently subject to caste and therefore in the power of the Brahmins, believed, as they do today, in a spirituality that had a political bias quite contrary to Gandhi's own claims. Jinnah gave speeches in Bombay alongside Mrs Naidu. If even this brilliant farsighted man was convinced by the image, how could those other ordinary people see through Gandhi? Only in the North West Punjab, where people such as Sir Umar Hayat Khan had a keen sense of values, an instinct, and the historical knowledge of an earlier time in the Great Mutiny, did the Gandhi myth not hold water. If India had been less religious, the confidence trick could not have been sustained for so long. How could ordinary people disbelieve someone who claimed *"I am the Hindu mind?"* If the remark had not been totalitarian, it could have been said to be one of the few truths the great man uttered.

Only the Sikhs with their beliefs based on the Granth Sahib and the words of Guru Nanak, could hold fast to their own beliefs, but then Guru Nanak held all the wisdom of reason and beliefs that run nearer than any other religion to those of Christianity.

For a country with so many Gods, a man who said the right things (even if they changed from time to time) and was in tune with the Brahmin leadership, would be accepted as a master of high intellectual discrimination and great strength of mind and able to ask questions.

At Delhi, as later in Amritsar, as in Lahore and Ahmedabad, the first step in the uprising was the fuss about the confectionery contractor on the Delhi station. Asked to shut up shop he said that he could not do so, because he had a contract to supply sweets that he could not break.

A gradually growing crowd assaulted the man and dragged him across the platform to another room. The Railway Police, not surprisingly, went in to protect the contractor and arrested the men who had assaulted him. A growing crowd collected, as commonly occurred in India and attacked the police, refusing to disperse until the Police had released the men they had arrested.

The police did release the men, but the crowd, bent on mischief, presumably incited by the leaders of the hartal, continued their demonstration, breaking windows, pulling down the gates across the station, and refusing to disperse. Their behaviour became so rowdy that the police outside were called. The crowd continued to gather and expand, further stone throwing crowds arrived, collecting in the Queen's Gardens and picking up brickbats from various repair works being done there. The stone throwing became such, that the police, and the soldiers who had been called in to support the police, were seriously harmed, some having to be taken to hospital and the troops had to fire. These provocations were such that it is difficult to imagine that they were not orchestrated, as they were later at Amritsar.

The casualties that resulted were 8 killed and 12 wounded among the Indians, 24 wounded among the British troops and police.

One of the incidents that took place is of particular relevance when claims are made about an unarmed crowd in the Jallianwalla Bagh in Amritsar. One of the crowd coming up close to a British soldier used his lathi to lever away the man's rifle, leaving him unarmed.

Dyer's fear that the crowd was going to surround him at the Bagh was well founded.

The determination shown by the Delhi rioters at that earlier time could have led to man after man attempting to disarm the soldiers in the Bagh, regardless that they were firing and the thousands in the Bagh would have found the overpowering of 50 men within their power. It was because this was a real possibility, that Dyer, at that later confrontation, placed 25 Ghurkhas armed only with kukris in front of the men who were firing.

In Delhi, the patience of the British soldiers brought in from a depot outside the city, showed in the way in which they put up with the stones, brickbats, lathis and other missiles hurled against them by the mob, trying to push them back into the station. The mob believed itself to be justifiably aroused by the arrest of the people who had dragged the sweet contractor across the station; although the men had already been released. Incitement and justification were typical of the Indian mind.

## Decay

In the middle of all this, strangely enough as in Amritsar later, some Ghurkhas arrived

on Delhi station on 30th March. A party of Manipuris were taken off the train going through Delhi and helped in clearing the station. 200 of them were armed and lined the Queen's Road outside the station.

The mob meanwhile attacked the Telegraph Office, and joined in threatening anyone who wished to work, turning people out of tongas, threatening shopkeepers and generally taking over the town from the Red Fort to the Clock Tower. Delhi was gradually taken into the hands of the rioters and mob rule. As in all the towns, the attempt to take over was supported by the establishment of a policing force of leaders and men, mainly educated men, who were in sympathy with the conspiracy.

The Manipuris were moved up to the Clock Tower and told that if anyone came too near them that they should present bayonets. It was the moment for magic. 'Soul-force', Gandhi's phrase was the vogue, and Swami Shraddanand, going up to speak to these hill men who did not speak Punjabi, approached them and spoke to them. Their presentation of bayonets confirmed him in the belief that his soul force had worked, since they did not proceed to fire, which to him meant that they had been stopped by spiritual force rather than orders.

Hakim Ajmal Khan, in correspondence and sympathy with the Afghans, also attempted to disperse the mob in the station - he had arrived from staying with friends (or could it have been from a visit to the Frontier?). His efforts were not successful and he admitted to the Superintendent of Police and the Deputy Commissioner that the leaders were no longer the same as those who had led before - much as Miles Irving told the Punjab Government in his letter.

Travelling through Delhi on the 30th, on his way back from leave, which had given him an opportunity to visit the beautiful old buildings of India, the Kutub Minar, Fatepur Sikri, the Taj, General Dyer was with his wife and niece in their car, when one of the crowd leapt onto the open folded roof, and although he apparently did not react, he undoubtedly saw it as part of the seriousness of the situation, as did the sight of Hindus and Muslims sharing the same drinking vessels, which led him to remark that they had done this at the time of the Mutiny.

Delhi was different from the other towns in one important respect: It was there that Moti Lal Nehru started writing down a Report of all incidents, by people who came in at the time or immediately after - an indication that the report was planned as part of the movement. If Satyapal and Kitchlew had not been deported, they would possibly have done the same at Amritsar. The reports gave fuel to the spread of the rebellion, being published immediately in the press and when the Hunter Inquiry went to Delhi, the reports were available to be consulted. The rest of the Congress Report was written long after - six months after - the events that they claim to portray and on which Furneaux, Draper, Sayer and so many others have based their reading of the Rebellion. It may be claimed that the intervening six months was the same for the British and the Indians. Indeed, but during those six months, the propaganda invention and agitation had made a significant difference to the minds of those who were there and to the whole climate of opinion. The Indian mind, always interested in popular opinion, would be unlikely to retain the first image in the face of the last. The British would have had to write their official reports in April immediately after the various risings. This has never been made clear in the history.

Thus we have a situation in which there had been violence. The city, as later at Lahore and at Amritsar and to an extent at Ahmedabad, had been taken over and held by the mob for a night. Barron, the Commissioner of Delhi, the Police and the Army, were in agreement not to fire unless absolutely necessary, and the hartal went on until the 5$^{th}$ April. Moreover, its success in achieving the disruption of the seat of winter Government for India and the length of time that it went on had an enormous impact. The administrators in India believed that they were helping things to settle by behaving passively. An extra guard had had to be put on the Juma Masjid on the 3$^{rd}$, but by the 5$^{th}$, except for a guard on the station, all troops had been removed.

Correspondence arrived for the Delhi authorities suggesting a visit from Gandhi to calm the feelings in Delhi. Lord Willingdon had left a little earlier, with contumely from the Home Rulers, but much praise from India merchants and citizens. Pressure was put on the Bombay Government, under the Governor, George Lloyd, to stop Gandhi leaving Bombay on the 8$^{th}$, as he threatened to do. On the 9$^{th}$, with Gandhi already on his way, the Government of India which ruled Delhi, and the Punjab Government, issued the orders to stop him crossing the border into the Punjab, which would also prevent his entry into Delhi. (Delhi, formerly in the Punjab, being changed to the centre of Government, had become a province in its own right.) Once again people swarmed round the station, but this time Gandhi did not arrive and there was a sporadic outburst of violent rioting by about 50 people when the news of his being turned back was understood.

Among the papers Gandhi later put in with his written statement were several about his removal:

*"From our own correspondent:*
*Mr Gandhi arrested. Order not to enter the Punjab or Delhi.*
*Taken to unknown destination.*
*His message to his countrymen (Muttra April 10$^{th}$)*
*Mahatma Gandhi on way to Delhi was arrested at Palwal and brought back at night to Muttra where he was detained till morning. A special train took him away by Bombay, Baroda, and Central India Railway route. The destination is not known. Mahatma Gandhi is in a very weak state of health and is reported to be suffering from pain in the chest".*

(Later)

"We have received the following message from the Private Secretary to Mahatma Gandhi (Delhi April 10$^{th}$) Mahatma Gandhi on his way to Delhi at Kosi was served with an order not to enter the Punjab, not to enter Delhi and restrict himself to Bombay. The officer serving the order treated him most politely and assuring him it *would be his painful duty to arrest him if he elected to disobey, but that there would still be no ill-will between them.*

*Mr Gandhi smilingly said he must disobey, as it was his duty and that the officer ought also to do what was his duty. In fact the few minutes that were left to him he dictated the following message, laying special emphasis in his oral message to me, as in the written message, that none shall resent his arrest or do anything tainted with untruth or violence which were sure to damn the sacred cause."*

The message already recorded followed, but with this opening paragraph:

*"It is of the highest concern to me, as I hope to you, that I have received an order from the Punjab Government not to enter the province and another from the Delhi Government not to enter Delhi, while an order of the Government of India which was served on me immediately after, restricts me to Bombay. I had no hesitation in saying to the officer who served the order on me that I was bound in virtue of the pledge to disregard it, which I have done and I shall presently find myself a free man, my body being taken by them in their custody. It was galling me to remain free whilst the Rowlatt legislation disfigured the Statute Book. My arrest makes me free. It now remains for you to do your duty, which is clearly stated in the Satyagraha pledge. Follow it and you will find your Kamadhenu. I hope there will be no resentment about my arrest ..."*

Since the Rowlatt Legislation had not yet been brought into use, no one could flout it and be arrested. Gandhi had been arrested under the Defence of India Act. Any pretence of innocence by Gandhi, in encouraging people to be arrested, and if not, to make some sort of trouble, was intentional. His hope of arrest, his hope that his arrest would be broadcast, was cleverly upstaged by the manner in which Superintendent Bowring handled the matter.

On April 22nd, the Telegraph service was still being interfered with. Day-by-day there were instances of *"wire cut near distant signal"*, *"All wires cut..."*, *"wire cut maliciously ..."* and on the 22nd, *"a piece of wire wound maliciously round insulator and stalk..."*. Apart from the upheaval that ran through the town on the news of Gandhi's arrest, there was quiet until the 10th, when the whole thing flared up again. By that time shopkeepers were heartily sick of the whole business.

# Chapter II
# AHMEDABAD

*"Early in the morning of April 10$^{th}$, a rumour reached Ahmedabad that Mr. Gandhi had been arrested - an exaggeration of the fact that he had been stopped at Delhi and had to return to Bombay instead of proceeding to the Punjab"* wrote G.E. Chatfield, Deputy Commissioner of Ahmedabad in his written statement on the events of April 1919. *"The rumour caused great excitement. I heard of it at about 9.00 a.m. when the Police Sub Inspector, Khas Bazar, informed me on the telephone. I saw the District Superintendent of Police and arranged with him to have the forces of police at the main stations in the city strengthened from his armed guard."* Sub Inspector of Police, D.D. Khotawala gave evidence that on the 9$^{th}$ there had been a meeting of several thousands held in Manilal's Mansions to protest against the Rowlatt Act. He was questioned by Hunter.

*"Q. How far was the Rowlatt Act known by the Public?*
*A. The public had a very vague idea about the Rowlatt Act.*
*Q. .Did they give it a particular name?*
*A. Yes, Kala Kaida - Black laws.*
*Q. Were they in a state of considerable excitement and discontent over the Rowlatt Act?*
*A. They were.*
*Q. On the 10th April as we know, did news reach Ahmedabad that Mr Gandhi had been arrested on his way to Delhi and turned back?*
*A. Yes Sir.*
*Q. What effect had that?*

> *A. Soon after this information was received shops were being closed and work came to a standstill. Sugar was distributed in the bazaars and business was at a standstill. There was a sort of general hartal.*
> *Q. I think various circulars were issued?*
> *A. Yes.*
> *Q. Did these circulars intimate that Mr Gandhi had been arrested for breaking a law of Government?*
> *A. Yes Sir.*
> *Q. That the news should be received by the Ashram people with great rejoicing and that the day should be observed as a holiday?*
> *A. Yes Sir.*
> *Q. Were the people also urged to carry on their work with redoubled zeal and agitation?*
> *A. They were Sir.*
> *Q. When you were speaking to Mr. Boyd, did you get a telephone message to the effect that a gentleman had been assaulted on the Richey Road?* [Mr. Boyd was the District Superintendent of Police.]
> *A. Yes, Mr. Arisu Dalal.".*

The Sub Inspector went on to describe the massing of crowds and the three armed parties of police sent to three different parts of the City - Khas Bazar, Richey Road and Kalupur. He himself had gone to Richey Road where he had seen huge crowds of people quite boisterous and riotous, molesting people driving in shigrams or tongas. He said that the crowd consisted mainly of Hindus although Mohammedans of the Mill locality joined and the mill employees came later. The crowd had made a set on the Gaiety Cinema, because the proprietor had not observed 'Black Sunday' and they broke the electric light bulbs and pulled down and burnt posters. He had tried to get the crowd back but had been unable to because they were so unruly. They were shouting 'Gandhi ki jai' and 'Bande Mataram' and were giving out books, in this case Gandhi's 'Hind Swaraj', which was proscribed.

Finally he went to the dispensary of Dr. Kanuga where he also found Mr. Patel. These two prominent members of the Satyagraha movement then tried to disperse the crowd, which they were unable to do. Together they went on to where they met a so called Satyagraha, Bhogia Bhagat, a gambler. He was leading another mob and shouting about the injustices of the British. Leaflets were meanwhile being distributed by Desai Indulal Yajnik and Vallabhai Patel about Gandhi's arrest.

Bhagat was still with him and demanding, not asking, that the police be withdrawn, while the mob wanted to set the cinema on fire. Stones were thrown at the police when they refused to withdraw, aimed with intent, one hitting the sub Inspector on the head. They later took to throwing bricks at him as well.

A meeting was announced on the riverbed for that evening. At about 3.00 p.m. he got information about two Englishmen who had been taken off their vehicle and were hiding in the flourmill, Messrs. Steeple and Sega. News came through that a policeman had been killed and that there had had to be some firing. On the sight of a wounded man being taken to the hospital, the mob behaviour became frenzied. Although the leaders endeavoured to restrain the mob, they took no notice of them. However some sort of orderliness was achieved at the meeting on the riverbed where about 30,000 people attended.

That was the first day as far as the Sub Inspector was concerned, but on the 11th, the announcement that Anasuya had also been arrested was spread through the City and the situation became even worse. It was far more virulently against the British. A young Sergeant Fraser was hacked to death and his body left lying in the road whence it was taken to the hospital. Lieutenant Larkin was struck with a sword in his chest and although rushed to hospital died shortly after his arrival. The mob set fire to Government buildings with great care to avoid any Indian property but when the fire brigade arrived it was stopped and the hoses were cut to pieces by educated men. When Larkin was lifted to be taken to hospital the policeman asked him who had struck him and was told a man who was a school teacher. Another attack was made by a Jain (that group of people who believe that not even an insect should be killed). Asked the extent to which the educated people had helped with the rioting, Khotawala said that he knew they were feeding the rioters and helping them with funds.

Of Sergeant Fraser found lying in the road he said *"The face was badly cut up and there were some blows and cuts on the hands and foot and the wrist was torn asunder from the body"*.

Buckshot was replaced by ball ammunition as it arrived from Headquarters. The Telegraph Office was set on fire; military pickets were put at the important centres. A further European had been murdered in a shop in the Richey Road.

*"It was all hatred towards the British rule; it was written that the British Raj was gone, the King of England is defeated, Swaraj is established, kill all Europeans, murder them wherever they are found."*

He had photographs which were not reproduced. No Indians were harmed, except a police constable, Imran Khan, who was murdered trying to defend two Europeans at the Prem gate. Unarmed police were stripped of their uniforms and let go free. There were two Indians who were robbed and threatened, apparently because they were both magistrates, but they managed to get away. He went back to the killing of Sergeant Fraser, which distressed him as it did everyone else. A mob had come and attacked Fraser but it was the second mob led by the Jain that killed him; the first mob had been made up of Hindus.

By the morning of the 12th, things were beginning to come into order and on the 13th, although the policemen did not see people taking notice of Colonel Frazer or his handouts which amounted to a form of Martial Law, the rioting had died away in time for Gandhi's arrival later. The attitude of virulent and frenzied hatred which had been incited against the British and anyone in the government, was reversed in the case of Gandhi, who had inspired this hatred in so many and such subtle ways. They worshipped him as God, Khotawala said.

Mr Desai, speaking for the Gujerat Sabha told Hunter:

*"I just want to show your Lordship that the educated people had nothing whatever to do with this affair".*

In fact, Lieutenant Larkin had not died, he had been ordered to block a road and recovered from the wound.

Lieutenant Macdonald, Assistant Controller of Contracts, left his camp for the depot in the city on the 11th. He had been driven by a mill owner to the Delhi Gate where a Parsi, a Mr Lahar asked him to go back. He said that a mob was coming up the street, destroying Government property and that they would kill him if they found him, so he went to a police telephone to ring the Collector [sometimes known as the Deputy Commissioner - this varied according to the Province]. The mob did indeed arrive and before he got through on the telephone. They proceeded to wreck the police shelter just within the Delhi gate and set fire to a Sub Post Office. For good measure they assaulted the Parsi, then riding a bicycle.

They assaulted a Tonga wallah and the police fired at them. The shots had absolutely no effect but the Tonga got through. He then gave Lahar a message, which he thought he would be able to get through wearing a black coat and hat. He did in fact get through with the message.

Asked about the mob, Macdonald said they were mainly mill-hands. There were various respectable educated people. They pointed out to the mob that Larkin was standing in the police chowki, they were actually inciting the mob to attack the chowki and the police, two sergeants and a constable who were unarmed as he was himself. The policemen and he were up some stairs. The mob tried to come up to get him and threw a soda water bottle at him which hurt him and led to his very nearly losing a finger. *"I was told in English and also in Urdu that they intended to kill me they had already killed one European and that there would not be any Europeans left alive by morning."*

This went on for two hours, when some troops arrived which saved him, just as the mob said that they were going to burn him. In his cross-examination by Setalvad he was asked again about the leader. *"And you observed him talking to them? Yes, this man kept haranguing them".* Although this man was in the forefront of leadership, there were others with him. Lieutenant Fitzpatrick, with others, remarked on the black coated men who incited the mobs. It was he who had given the orders to take up the body of Sergeant Fraser and he had been badly stoned under circumstances in which it was clear that there had been a careful arrangement of stones and bricks for the purpose. *"Very elaborate preparations had been made to stone the police and the military. There were bricks and in every store of the fruit vendors market just outside the gate where I was stationed, pebbles, bricks, stones and all sorts of things were put in there."* On the matter of the type of people present: *"It is only a question of identification of uniforms and clothes. There was one Satyagrahi again there. There were a number of black-coated people who were supposed to be wearing black coats for mourning. There were about 6 or 8 sanyassis, mendicants or so-called priests, they were exciting the mob the livelong day. I saw 60 or 80 trays of sweets being taken out by very respectably dressed Hindus and thrown into the mob, they were cheered by those people. Every time they shouted the 'Jai' there was a roar of 'Jai' going up. I have not mentioned another point. There were so called stretcher-bearers who made their stretchers the means of communicating from mob to mob. Evidently they used to slip down the streets and get in amongst the crowd and they would raise their hands and then went the 'chalo', 'maro' and all these sort of things."* This man really knew what he was talking about and when Setalvad tried to shake him on his description of what had been going on he answered well and clearly:

> Rankin: *"Q. Who was the man arrested on the 2$^{nd}$ when he was following a charpoy?*
> *A. A little Mohammedan mill boy. The other had a goatee beard.*
> *Q. You never got a chance to identify your other friend?*
> *A. I never did unfortunately.*
> Setalvad: *Q. This Little fellow you spoke of and whom you describe as having a goatee beard, had he no cap but a pagri?*
> *A. He had no cap but a pagri.*
> *Q. You say he was a Satyagrahi?*
> *A. I say he was pointed out to me as a Satyagrahi wearing the Satyagrahi uniform.*
> *Q. Were you told that the pagri was a distinctive feature of the Satyagrahi uniform?*
> *A. Yes.*
> *Q. Are you sure?*
> *A. Yes.*
> *Q. Are you sure?*
> *A. Yes.*
> *Q. A pagri is a common head-dress for Hindus?*
> *A. And also for Mohammedans.*
> *Q. Why do you say that the pagri was a distinctive mark?*
> *A. Because of the way it was tied - it was a roundabout thing.*
> *Q. What is called a Pheta?*
> *A. That would be almost like a Marwari."*

Lieutenant Fitzpatrick survived through a fairly heavy cross-examination which, after dealing with the men wearing black coats which he said was for mourning for Gandhi's arrest (nor was this contradicted by Setalvad), the latter then turned to the food being brought to the rioters.

> *"Q. About the food of rioters, you said you saw people bringing trays of laddoos?*
> *A. Yes, jalabies too and gulab jamans also.*
> *Q. Where did you see this?*

> *A. I saw them coming out of an alley at Pankar Noka. There is a gateway there. From the gateway I could see long streaks of people coming out with trays to feed the mob.*
> *Q. Who were these people?*
> *A. Men who were dressed in white with gold pagris and they were perfectly jubilant at the idea. They were respectably dressed people of the Ahmedabad society according to what I saw from their apparel.*
> *Q. Now, where were they bringing the sweetmeats from?*
> *A. From a lane on the left which is supposed to contain all the sweetmeat shops in Ahmedabad.*
> *Q. The rioters themselves were buying the sweets?*
> *A. No, they were being brought by respectably dressed men, not by the rioters themselves".*

Then to the stones in the fruit stalls. *"They were covered with cloths"* said Fitzpatrick

He was asked whether he had lifted the cloths, - he had. Where were the shop keepers? - He did not know, the shops were deserted. Then Jagat Narayan started asking about the crowd that had been burning down buildings. They were drunk, Fitzpatrick had said so in his statement. Having said he had sent in a report to his superior officer he was then told that he had not.

*"You said you never made a report at all?*
*I did say I made a report and on the matter of the crowd being drunk*
*To the effect they were drunk?*
*I never said the whole crowd was drunk*

*I was mistaken then"* Astonishingly, Fitzpatrick or the stenographer then has him saying *"I beg your pardon then."* This type of cross-examination went on for five pages of two columns in 6pt.

When these people examined Percy Marsden and my father, they both described the experience as being cross-examined as though they were criminals. This hectoring when the evidence displeased the Indians, was quite outside the techniques required in an investigative inquiry. The involvement of the members of the Committee clearly showed extreme partiality, although this was not mentioned later, since the volumes of evidence were not widely available,. Fitzpatrick's evidence, which cannot all be fitted in here, is a classic example. He had identified a Sadhu at the subsequent tribunal. It has to be born in mind that the tribunals trying the people involved in the rebellion took place prior to the Inquiry in October 1919 or in January 1920, when the Ahmedabad Session took place. Already by then, most of those involved had been released under the King's amnesty (in reality Montagu's) and so had this Sadhu. He had been interfering with the troops whom he had tried to persuade to let the mob continue rather than stopping them.

Interesting as these details of the evidence are, they can be lengthy. I therefore mention simply in passing that the doctor's wife, the doctor being extremely popular, had her home surrounded by a mob about to burn it down. She stood on the verandah with a revolver in her hand and threatened to shoot anyone coming any closer and gradually the mob was dispersed.

The electric power station, the railway station and other important buildings including the Telegraph Station were attacked. When it was over, J.A. Guider, the Deputy Inspector General of Police C.I.D. was sent down to Ahmedabad to carry out an investigation. His job was a difficult one he said. That he found it difficult to get witnesses, but then, in India it was always difficult to get witnesses.

At the subsequent Enquiry, he was asked if he finally overcame the difficulties and on what principles had he made arrests - on prima facie evidence, replied Guider.

*"Q. The first arrests produced a startling effect on the people?*
*A. They did. The mill hands absconded."*

He finally had to get onto the mill owners and explain that there would be no wholesale arrests and only those against whom evidence was forthcoming would be arrested.

Here we come to the main issue - the grounds on which the propaganda story rests, which claims that action at Amritsar led to the destruction of the British Raj. The excusing of people who had done wrong, where there was not sufficient evidence to convict was one thing, but the full scale amnesty for those who had been tried and found guilty was another. That action, which was instituted by Montagu, the castigation of the Fitzpatricks, my father, Percy Marsden and so forth, combined with the continued adulation of Gandhi, re-emphasized the weakness of Government resolve. In the months and years that followed, law and order became doubtful, as the top conspirators, when imprisoned, lived in observable luxury, like Gandhi, for instance, in the Palace of the Aga Khan. By the treatment of the rebels and the rebel leaders, people who had incited to rob, burn, loot and murder, the whole frail fabric of the structure of law and order in India was weakened.

We would never again be in a position to stop this wholesale evil, nor to restrain the leaders from committing more and grosser cruelties.

Effectively, with the Rebellion and the ensuing treatment of the criminals, we so weakened the stability of India that we would in time, by degrees, be unable to hold the reins firmly enough to hand over power without 'the leaders' longed for and planned for chaos, which, as I believe, no one in power realised was their aim. That weakness was inherent with Montagu and to a lesser extent, Chelmsford, the Viceroy. The latter did his best by inserting into the Government Reports his gratitude for the work of Sir Michael O'Dwyer, even if he could not add to that the gratitude previously expressed for General Dyer.

Enough has been written about Ahmedabad to give the flavour of the situations from April 10th to the 13th, when Colonel Frazer and the many other people who risked their lives or who died for India's peace and prosperity won out against the well planned strategy of the forces of anarchy.

Gandhi gave pages and pages of giggling and self contradictory evidence; the Indian members of the Commission dealt with him with kid gloves apart from Setalvad, who seems to have been intrigued by the satyagraha theory, finding it inexplicable in terms of logic and reason. Gandhi claimed that there was an organisation behind the whole thing - as if we did not know. The various leaders, who had been amnestied by then, were also given free rein.

Since rebellion in Delhi and, Ahmedabad had by then been reduced, with the utmost suffering by the British and the greatest possible brutality by Indians, in Bombay, (where, thanks to the cavalry which rode straight at the mob so that they moved speedily to the sidewalks), rebellion hardly took place. Gandhi's message to his people had so far worked in reverse. His prophecy of British brutality and the implicit gentleness of the Indians had been disproved.

In case people are still concerned about Gandhi's health and his pains in the chest, or his soul leaving his body when he was arrested and when he did not know where they would take his body, The Policeman, Griffiths, at Bombay, made a point,. Griffiths observed that when the cavalry charged down the main thoroughfare in Bombay, Gandhi leapt nimbly to one side. One man at least was convinced that Gandhi was not sick, at least in body. But he also took the opportunity of telling Gandhi how things were going in Lahore and telling him in strong words what he thought of his behaviour in inciting such a rebellion. For those who imagine that Gandhi was innocent and did not know what was going on, it should be remembered that the Malabar rebellion was still to come.

# Chapter III
# VIRAMGAM

The Bombay Presidency cannot be left without mention of Mr. Caldecott, Assistant Collector of Salt and Excise from Kharaghoda, who wrote of a chit (note) from Mr. Prescott saying that a light engine had come in from Viramgam on the 12th April and had brought in the Railway Traffic Inspector, who had been badly hit about the head by rioters at Viramgam, asking him to send the doctor to his bungalow to attend the Traffic Inspector.

*"This I of course did at once. I also rode down to Mr. Prescott's bungalow and saw the Traffic Inspector, from whom I gathered facts of what was going on at Viramgam with as little delay as possible. Having done this, I rode across to the engine driver's bungalow and arranged with the driver who had just brought in the Traffic Inspector to take us back to Viramgam with three ordinary wagons attached to the engine. From here I rode back to the sepoy lines and gave instructions to the Khan Bahadur and Subedar to get as many of their men ready as soon as possible.*

*We all eventually got off after the regular train had left Kharaghoda for Viramgam. With Mr Prescott and myself were the Subedar and 56 rank and file.*

*When we reached Patri, I got the Station Master to wire the Station Master Jhund, to detain the passenger train there so as to let us pass and get into Viramgam before it. These instructions were carried out. When we got one and a half miles outside Viramgam we were informed by the permanent way gangsmen that the lines had been pulled up, so we had to finish the remainder of the journey on foot, reaching Viramgam a little after sunset. Considerable looting was taking place in the station yard from wagons on our arrival. Our sepoys however cleared the whole yard within five minutes after firing a volley or two into the air. I then went to the Station Master's bungalow to see what had happened to that official whom I found in rather a perturbed state of mind. I gave him a guard to look after his bungalow and then went across to Mr. Thornley at the mill to see what had happened to him, but I found that he had left for Karaghoda by bullock cart across country taking with him his engineer and family. I then went across to the missionary's bungalow where I luckily found all correct. I left a couple of sepoys here also to guard the bungalow. From there I proceeded straight to the Government Treasury where I found considerable damage had been done and looting was going on in the Treasury room. To save what remained of the Treasury and to rescue the police armed guards I had to take some stern steps. After order had been restored, one man was found dead near the Treasury after we had entered the office and two were found badly wounded, (one of whom died next day). Another man was found dead outside the office compound. Three looters were arrested and put under custody. I found the police guard had had a very rough time of it and were in a very demoralised state. I collected (after some time) ten armed policemen who were hidden away in different places and gave them a Jamadar and ten of my sepoys, thus leaving a guard of twenty armed men over what remained of the Treasury. Before leaving the Treasury, I had pulled down a corrugated iron barricade which the mob had erected in front of the treasury compound and from behind which some of them had been firing at the police and also patrolled the surrounding area and being satisfied that everything was quiet I marched the men back to the station, where I found a special had just arrived with 100 men of the 97th Infantry under Major Cochrane and Lieutenant Eales. I reported myself to the Major, who then went off to the Treasury with some of his sepoys to see things for himself. I was left behind with Lieutenant Eales to choose suitable spots for posting guards on roads leading to the town of Viramgam. After this I again returned to the station, where I placed guards of our own men in the station yard, especially on the broad gauge transhipment platform and metre gauge goods yard. It now being midnight and everything quiet I went off with Mr. Prescott to Mr. Thornley's bungalow for the night. Next morning, at the request of Major Cochrane, I got up the leading Sethias of the place whom Major Cochrane interviewed and who were told to go off and advise the people that if the shops were not opened by the afternoon he would issue a proclamation to the effect that if any groups of ten and above were seen loitering about in the day time they would be shot at by the military without warning and single persons would be liable to the same thing if seen out in the streets of the town between sunset and sunrise. It is needless to report that this threat had the desired effect and everything was normal by 5.00 p.m. All shops had been opened and life was going on as usual.*

*Rioting had lasted from 11.00 a.m. of the 12th to, say, about 10.00 p.m. of the same date, after which, nothing happened. During this time the Station, Post Office and Municipal Office had been burnt down and part of the Treasury had been damaged by fire. The Third Class Magistrate, who gave the order to armed police guard at the Treasury to fire at the mob was eventually captured by the rioters, who poured kerosene oil over him and burnt him alive* [on top of the Government papers]. *The sepoys on leaving Karaghoda, I must say, were in rather a shaky condition, many of them being only recruits and not knowing what was in front of them. I gave every man who did not wish to accompany me, the chance of falling out and I am glad to say they all refused to do so. After we had once started operation at Viramgam, the sepoys and amaldars settled down and did their work like men and I felt proud of them. Mr. Prescott gave me most valuable assistance and thoroughly helped to keep up the prestige of the department. The acting Subedar, - an old soldier - also accompanied me and his presence helped to put confidence into our men. I sent the sepoys back the next day by the midday train after finding their services were no longer required. The Major asked me to convey a message from him to them to the effect that they had done 'damn well' which message was duly conveyed to them. This message bucked the men up immensely and I saw that they knew that their services had been appreciated."*

From Nadiad came the news of the effects of Gandhi's arrest and of the incitement there. Rai Sahib Trivedi wrote: *"On the 11th, the news spread throughout the district and hartals and meetings protesting against the action of the Government were the order of the day. In the morning, Janardhan Sharma went with a mob to the Government High School and forced the Headmaster to close the school early. In the afternoon, he went to Anand and there he delivered an exciting harangue and sang inflammatory songs. At night, he again lectured at Maulvi Sheikh Imam's lecture to an audience of about 10,000 persons. By this time, the news about the murders and riots at Ahmedabad on the 10th and 11th, due to news of Mr Gandhi's arrest, had been received in the district and at Nadiad, the nerve centre of the district, the people were in a highly excited state of mind. No doubt Mr. Maulvi requested his audience to be quiet and peaceful but the highly exciting news of the happenings in Ahmedabad, which reached the district in a highly exaggerated form, were not conducive to peace and order. A sort of mad frenzy seized the people and the feelings of resentment against the Government were uppermost in the minds of everyone. Reports about firing on the people at Ahmedabad made the resentment stronger and everyone feeling a sort of sympathy with the rioters began to think how he might best serve them against the Government. The station staff at Nadiad, being no exception to the frenzy reigning all round, divulged the news about the passing of the troops special to Ahmedabad. The question of the moment was how to stop the troops from reaching Ahmedabad. Some young men carried away by frenzy made a conspiracy to derail the troops special and eventually with the assistance of the information about the timing of the expected arrival of the train, gleaned from the station staff did remove a rail, causing the derailment of the troop train special. Providentially however, no one in the train was injured though a delay of several hours occurred to the troops in reaching Ahmedabad. The next morning, i.e., on the 12th, the news of the derailment spread through the district and the act was generally looked upon as a meritorious act. Janardhan Sharma even made a speech to that effect at Chaklashi. News of the happenings in the Punjab also reached the district through newspapers by this time and the Punjab and Ahmedabad events, coupled with the serious local offences against the State, brought the Government prestige to its lowest and the frenzy of the people increased in an inverse ratio. In Anand, the mob enforcing the hartal on those who were unwilling, even committed violence and set fire to the house of a sweetmeat seller named Rogilal who refused to observe the hartal. But for the tact and personality of the local Sub Inspector, the mob would have attacked the Government and European dairies at Anand. The attitude of the mob was so dangerous that special measures had to be adopted to protect Government buildings, dairies and houses of Europeans. After the mob had attacked the licensed vendors on the station platform, the European station master at Anand believed the atmosphere so very hostile to Europeans that he left for Baroda with his family. By the afternoon of the 12th, the news of the destruction of the telegraph office at Ahmedabad and the cutting of the telegraph wires between Barejdi and Kamj were quite known in large towns and villages on the railway line and by midnight, telegraph wires were cut by the villagers of the large villages of Naranda, Anand and Vadod, where sub-branches of the Home Rule League existed and where Home Rule passive resistance and anti-Rowlatt agitation had previously been carried on very vigorously. At Uttarsanda, a very active Home Rule village, a culvert on the railway near the station was set on fire but the police arriving on the scene in time, no damage was done. On the morning of the 13th, Mr. Gandhi, while passing to Ahmedabad, advised the people on the platform of the Nadiad station to welcome him, to observe peace and order and in the evening his message was read out in a big public meeting where it was resolved the hartal should be opened the next day. The public feeling was however very sullen and resentful and the exaggerated news of the happenings in Ahmedabad and the Punjab calculated to excite the feelings against the Government were circulating all round. In consequence, for some time the efforts of the local authorities were directed chiefly towards the prevention of disorders like those in the Punjab and in Ahmedabad as there was a great deal of likelihood of such disorders breaking out in the district at any moment."*

Rai Sahib Trivedi was the Deputy-Superintendent of Police at Kaira District.

## Chapter IV
## LAHORE

Everything had been reasonably normal until April 6$^{th}$, when an all-India hartal and demonstrations against the Rowlatt Acts had been directed. Troops were moved into the Fort and the Cavalry was brought up for the support of the Police. No shots were fired.

On the 10$^{th}$, the news of the deportation of the two doctors, Satyapal and Kitchlew at Amritsar reached Lahore at about 3.00 in the afternoon and orders reached the troops in the Cantonment at about 5.15 p.m.

The first men available, 150 men of the 2/6 Royal Sussex, were immediately sent to Amritsar. Other detachments as fast as they could be collected, were sent by Royal Air Force Lorries to the Lahore (Civil) Area. The central Telegraph Office, the Gymkhana Club, European Hotels and the Government House were all either occupied by detachments of troops or under troop protection by 7.30 p.m. and the 17$^{th}$ Cavalry reached the Mall at about 7.15 p.m. The result of this prompt action was that as the crowd which had apparently heard of the deportations at four o'clock, poured out of the City through Anarkali and made for the Central Telegraph Office, they were met by forty troops, waiting with fixed bayonets. There was a speedy change of plan. After a little hesitation, the crowd moved to take over Government House down the Mall. The small detachment of police barring the way was pressed back and at this moment the Deputy Commissioner, Mr. Fyson and the Deputy Inspector-General, Mr. Cocks, came on the scene. Realising that about 100 ladies and children would be at the Gymkhana Club about half a mile down the road, they ordered the police to open fire.

One man was killed and five were wounded. The mob was checked and the reinforcements arriving, the police were enabled to drive the mob back to the City.

Colonel Johnson's comment on this was that *"I think there can be no two opinions that the action of Messrs Fyson and Cocks saved Lahore that night from scenes of outrage and murder compared to which those at Amritsar would almost have paled into insignificance."*

At 10.00 p.m., the police in Anarkali, having been heavily stoned, finally fired - once again, one man was killed and five were wounded. During the night, the excitement and hostility of the crowd was such that it was decided to remove all police from the City and leave their numerous posts unoccupied, and in the hands of uncontrolled mobs. Johnson felt that this was justified by the situation. In the meanwhile, strong detachments were being posted at the Pumping Station, Reservoir, Power Station, Central Jail, Ravi Railway Bridge, while the Headquarters of 43rd Brigade was moved into Lahore. The detachments were made up of Indian troops.

In the City itself, meetings were held; prayer meetings of Hindus and Muslims were held at the Badshahi Mosque and meetings at which sedition and rebellion were openly encouraged.

On the 12th, the decision was made to go into the City and regain control. At 9.30 a.m., Johnson arrived at the Delhi Gate with Cavalry, British and Indian troops and police, in all about 800 men. It astonished him to look back, when he wrote his report, that they succeeded in making their way through excitable (what Trivedi would have called frenzied) crowds with so little bloodshed and he put it down to the Air Force. He had arranged with the Air Force to bomb on a given signal. As he entered the bazaar, he told the leaders of the crowd that should a shot be fired or a bomb thrown at the troops, the aeroplane would clear the road for the troops with bombs. Having given his warning he then waited until the leaders had been able to inform the crowd.

He subsequently reported, *"During the march through the city, an excited crowd emerging from the Badshahi Mosque, managed to surround the rear guard which was attacked by sticks and stones whilst bricks were thrown from the roofs of houses. To reduce the pressure and clear the mob I had to order the police to fire a few rounds, less than 20, which resulted in the death of one and the wounding of three or four men among the crowd which at once fell back. Posts were established at three points in the City, garrisoned by detachments of British and Indian troops and armed police."*

Johnson then commented that a large meeting was held at Amritsar on the 13th in defiance of orders, at which a small detachment of Indian troops fired, causing considerable casualties. He said, *"It is only fair to record my opinion that this incident had a far reaching effect on the seditionists and agitators in Lahore and was probably no small factor in enabling me to re-establish and maintain order in the area under my command without further bloodshed."* He was however, then faced with the concentration of destructive and paralysing hartals to which the seditionists turned in order to extend their activities.

Among the leaders who in some way evaded arrest, was one who later told him that the object of the crowd that went down the Mall was only to insult, not to murder Europeans. Johnson's comment on this was *"For such a mob of Indians to insult a*

*Briton is but the equivalent of his murder, as such action must obviously lead to forcible resentment, which in turn would mean the beating to death of the European."*

This claim that mobs armed with lathis and stones were not intending murder has been reiterated later. Johnson follows the assertion through to its logical conclusion. My father was so covered with bruises after holding the mob up at Amritsar that he could not lie down properly. The fact that the intention was humiliation, is central to so much that was done throughout the rebellion, the Hunter Inquiry and altogether to us later on.

This idea is urgently important if motive is to be understood. Gandhi's message that no reforms falling on their heads were wanted, - those earlier claims which were central to most of the later speeches, which have continued to be accepted among the less knowledgeable, indicate that the Indian leaders did not want an orderly and well administered India, they actually wanted the chaos which their actions brought about in India, so that they could humiliate, decry, despise and dismiss the work of so many Britons which had unified and transformed a country in savage disarray. Gandhi, Bipin Chandra Pal and others did not want to take on a unified and contented India, they wanted the chaos to be returned so that they could say 'Look at the way the British left India!' Johnson's management of the hartals and the Martial Law was superb. Under his excellent management the City came slowly to its feet and when he finally left he was also besieged with thanks. Martial Law under which he had functioned, (it was agreed by the Government of India on April 14th) was so successful that the people regretted the time when it stopped.

But the two great mill wheels, - the concepts of British law and order, running sun wise and the Indian Nationalist determination to wreck it, running widdershins, against the sun, continued to turn until, with Mountbatten and a Britain ruled by the very men who had supported the Indian Nationalists throughout, the possibility of continuing was gone. It meant that the concern for an integrated India of all races creeds and castes could no longer be sustained with the necessary force to keep the wheel turning with the sun.

# Chapter V
# KASUR

Mr. R.F. Mitter, Extra Assistant Commissioner, Kasur, was Sub-Divisional Officer, Kasur from 5th April until the 15th, just 11 days. He believed that the people of Kasur would never have had any hartal or demonstration if left alone, but business relations with Amritsar enabled those from Amritsar to coerce the Kasur traders into line. There was a hartal on 11th April, but that passed off quietly.

From Ahmedabad and the cotton mills, through Ghandi's influence on the piece-goods traders, where withholding deeds of credit could break a man's business, the rebellion was pushed forward.

In Mitter's words: *"On the night of 11th April, it was told me (subsequently) that some men from Amritsar came into Kasur and took charge of the hartal on the 12th. They began by getting the schools closed and induced the boys to follow an improvised bier. The shouts of the boys, 'Rowlatt Bill hai-hai' attracted protestors, and grown up men also of the hooligan class gradually joined the procession as it made its way through the various streets. When the procession had become quite large, the leaders suddenly directed it towards the Railway Station. Here it seems the leaders began the work of destruction and the others followed suit in earnest, youth class probably in the spirit of pure mischief.*

*From the station the mob moved towards the Ferozepore side along the Railway line and as a train coming from that side was coming in, they held it up, started to loot and attacked the European passengers. The Indian passengers were not molested. After a few minutes the train moved onto the station and 3 Military non-commissioned men got out of the train. The mob stoned them and 2 of them who had revolvers fired at the mob but hit only one man on the foot. Two of them were severely injured and died the same day, one escaped.*

*It was after all this had been done that I received information at my house that the mob had become violent and after sending word to the Deputy Superintendent of Police, I started for the Railway Station with the Tahsildar and 2 or 3 other gentlemen who had just then come to my house with news. While nearing the Railway Station I saw that men with nippers were cutting the Telegraph line and that some men were carrying away packages from the station. At this stage the Deputy Superintendent of Police joined me with two rifles. We dispersed the mob at the Railway Station, attended to the two military men lying at the Station - one dead and one seriously wounded, - sent word to the Assistant Surgeon to come at once and moved on to the rescue of Mr. and Mrs. Sherbourne who were reported to be at Kot Hakim Khan (Hakim Khan's house). From there I returned to my house to send a message by a messenger (the wire being cut) to Lahore for military aid and the Deputy Superintendent of Police took the Sherbournes to his house.*

*After despatching the messenger to Lahore, I went to the Deputy Superintendent of Police's house and as just then the Naib-Tahaildar and others brought word that the mob was bent on plundering the Treasury and would not disperse, the Deputy Superintendent of Police and I went with a few armed constables to the spot and finding that the situation was as reported by the Naib-Tahsildar and quite desperate, I sanctioned firing on the mob. The firing dispersed the mob and everything was quiet after that. My order was quite justified, for, in my opinion, there was no alternative if further arson and murders were to be prevented. I was relieved on the afternoon of the 15th April and had practically nothing to do with the investigation."*

## Chapter VI
## AMRITSAR

When news of the trouble in Delhi at the end of March reached Amritsar, the Deputy-Commissioner, aware that Amritsar was the Bolshevik centre in the Punjab and also aware of the activities locally of two of Gandhi's lieutenants, set his mind to the precautions which might be needed to maintain law and order, if the Delhi trouble spread. As a result, he wrote a letter to Arthur Kitchin, Commissioner of the area, to express his concerns. The letter, dated 8 April 1919, was received by the Chief Secretary to the Punjab Government, before being passed to the Governor.

The letter was read out to the Hunter Committee by the chief Secretary in camera and was recorded in the Secret Evidence. In it, Miles Irving expressed his concern about the security situation in Amritsar. His concern had been roused by events on the 5th and 6th of April. At a meeting of Honorary Magistrates at his house at 5.00.p.m. on the 5th, the general view had been that the hartal called by Gandhi for the 6th would fail.

However, at about the same time, Drs. Kitchlew and Satyapal, the Congress agitators, announced that the hartal would take place, despite having earlier agreed to cancel it. It appeared that they wished to show that the authorities were helpless. The shops were all closed on the 6th, a group of boys disrupted a cricket match by pulling up the wickets and mats and the match did not continue, while a crowd marched round the city in a defiant manner. Irving suggested that there were others behind Kitchlew, that he could not control Amritsar in the face of widespread rioting and needed troop reinforcements. He also suggested that definite strong action was required, since standing back only increased the crowds' confidence.

The Punjab Government, in a reply to his letter, authorised the deporting of the two agitators. On the evening of the 9th of April, with the reply to Miles Irving's letter, the officials in charge of Amritsar gathered at the Deputy Commissioner's house.

They went through the plans for the following day, for they were expecting trouble when, under the Defence of India Act, Kitchlew and Satyapal were to be deported to Dharamsala. The various picketing duties were worked out and allocated and on the following morning, they rode round before most people were awake to see where they would all go if their expectations of trouble were fulfilled. At each bridge over the railway, there were to be posted three soldiers from the garrison artillery. If trouble arrived, a Magistrate would go to each post. The expectation was that the crowds would come over the bridges to loot the Civil Lines, the suburbs where the officials lived. The police were also warned about their duties: Mr. Plomer, Deputy Superintendent, said in his evidence to Hunter that *"the instructions I got were to have an Armed Reserve under Inspector Marshall, to hold the Police Lines Level Crossing and the mounted police to remain in the Lines. In the city, there were to be three Armed Reserves of 25 men, each under Deputy-Superintendents of Police, Khan Sahib, Ahmed Jan and the City Inspector, Ashraf Khan. I had to take my orders from the Deputy Commissioner (Miles Irving) and also to have information conveyed to the Officer Commanding the Station as regards the movements of any mobs in the city."* He had given these instructions at about 7 or 8 in the morning. Secrecy was to be the main safeguard of the process for removing the two doctors, Kitchlew and Satyapal, the main leaders of the Amritsar agitators, who had both taken the Satyagraha oath. They were to arrive at the Deputy Commissioner's bungalow at 10.00 a.m., which they did, and leave with Police Superintendent Rehill by car, with a party of military in plain clothes. This was carried out and the car left at 10.30.a.m.

Mr Plomer saw Rehill and the other car going past and rode into the Deputy Commissioner's compound to tell him that he was going to telephone the city police and the line police to stand to. He received a message from the City Inspector at about 11.00 to 11.30 a.m. to say that there were mobs on the move and that they were going to the Aitchison Park under the leadership of Bugga and Ratto with the idea of asking for the release of the two deportees. Bugga and Ratto were Kitchlew's lieutenants and were afterwards convicted for the murder of the two bank managers. Bugga was an unsavoury person with brokerage of some sort in the city and was the head of a gang of goondas and had a lot of riffraff under him. They were both men of influence over the mob. Plomer immediately informed the Deputy Commissioner of the situation and then galloped to the Ram Bagh to inform the Officer Commanding, who was unfortunately out posting mounted pickets at the points he was to hold. Eventually Plomer found the officer at the Railway Station.

The idea had been that the Magistrates should be warned by the Deputy Commissioner of the whereabouts of the mob and the need for them to take their place with the garrison pickets. The effect of the removal of the two doctors was not envisaged as being severe, although safety plans had to be made and my father went to court in riding breeches in case he was needed.

Mr. Beckett said: *"I might have been working for half and hour or an hour, ready in my riding kit for anything that might happen, with my mare waiting ready saddled outside and only needing the girths to be tightened, when Miles Irving, the Deputy Commissioner came into my Court. There seemed to be trouble in the City, but all the telephone lines had been cut. Would I please go down to the Hall Bridge and take up my place, if the Report was true?*

*It did not take me long to get on my horse, but there did not seem to be any immediate urgency. I was smoking my pipe and trotting along the road on Mary, who had a good fast trot. I was about half a mile away from the Hall Bridge when I heard a sound that I had never heard before and which I am not particularly anxious to hear again. It was for all the world like breakers booming along a stormy shore. I quickly clapped my pipe into my pocket and dug my heels into Mary to gallop the rest of the way as fast as I could.*

*On the bridge which runs up and down again rather steeply giving one a wide view, I found my lance-corporal and two bombardiers* [he meant lance-bombadier and two gunners] *facing the largest crowd I have ever seen. It is impossible for an untrained eye to count such numbers, even approximately. I have since heard it estimated that there were thirty thousand in the crowd and it may be correct. Fortunately, so far as we were concerned, they were concentrated on a narrow front, about wide enough for two vehicles to pass."*

His crowd estimate may have been correct, because there were an estimated 70,000 people in the Aitchison Park, ready to start on their frenzied racist attack on any and every Englishman whom they met.

The claim is that the crowd was peaceful until fired on and it was safe in the city until. after that. Indeed, near the Kotwali, where the crowd had left for Aitchison Park, it was quiet, but Miss Sherwood later recorded that she saw men sawing down poles from shop awnings and seizing hold of anything likely to serve as a weapon and rushing out of the city. She also mentioned the large number of lathis that had poured into the town. Amongst the Hunter evidence there is only one man who claimed that the crowd was peaceful and that my father (apparently) wearing a white coat, fired at them. How that statement got into the Hunter Inquiry when there were many people such as Gerard Wathen, who were sitting and waiting to give evidence and were never called, cannot be imagined. In keeping with the omission of Peshawar from the investigation, there must have been some manipulation of witnesses, for the crowd that met my father was evidenced by everyone who saw it as being in a state of frenzy, shouting epithets, threatening to kill the Deputy Commissioner by tearing him to pieces, using every expression of fury and hatred and behaving in a wild and completely unreasonable way. My father and his little picket tried to hold them back while being stoned, brickbats being hurled at him and them (more him than them, because their horses would not stand, while his, being a polo pony and used to pucks hitting her, was not so uncertain), their horses hit with lathis and in an extremely dangerous position.

Behind the scenes, boys, (probably the ones that had pulled up the wickets at the cricket match) had gone round the town telling the shopkeepers that if they did not shut their shops they would be looted. The claims made by Gandhi and the Congress Report are not only untrue but also silly. No one stands in front of an hysterical and out of control mob of some thousands for pleasure and the claims about the crowd being peaceful and asking the whereabouts of their leaders without threats, is not in keeping with any Indian mob of which I have ever heard. Since my father was unarmed and the picket of garrison gunners, probably unused to horses, could not hold their mounts, no firing took place until the reinforcements arrived and my father and his companions left. It was then a matter of deciding whether to let the crowd through or be dangerously stoned, as at Delhi, as at Ahmedabad, fairly obviously part of the plan. They did hold on, knowing that if they allowed even a suspicion of relaxation, the mob would come below the level of the bridge, fan out, and be able to function on a front wider than they could possibly hold. The foot bridge that runs parallel to the main bridge became the pathway for a man dressed in the usual black, as at Ahmedabad, encouraging the stone throwers and lathi users to greater and greater activity. My father, without the experience of Lieutenant Fitzpatrick, did not realise that the bricks and stones had been put there ready for the attack, but thought they were there coincidentally.

As he arrived, he replied to the hysterical, almost frenzied demands to know where Kitchlew and Satyapal had gone, with something placatory, such as 'you will be informed later' but that his orders were to see that they did not cross the bridge. The shouting and yelling probably made it difficult to hear him, but undoubtedly the main body of the crowd had little interest in what he was saying anyway.

His words were: *"I do not know how long all this went on. I thought at the time it was for twenty minutes, but someone who was watching from the Ram Bagh has told me that it was only five minutes and he is probably right, for one loses all sense of time on these occasions and I was wondering all through it how long it would be before we were relieved. Gradually we were forced back, losing valuable and irrecoverable ground every time there was a bolt to the rear* [by the horses of the garrison gunners] *and losing it more rapidly as we were driven back to the descent and the crowd gained more confidence. At last we were at the foot of the bridge where there was a stack of bricks lying and the real trouble began. The bricks came in a steady hail, luckily not very well aimed. I don't know what happened to the other beasts; I think they must have galloped straight back to their stables. Mary"* [his horse] *"still stood up to it, but was getting a little restive; you may get a polo ball or two hit quite hard up against your flanks but not a whole succession of them.*

*When I had to give evidence before the Hunter Commission, there was an Indian lawyer on the dais who seemed to be taking the part of cross examining counsel for the rioters. I had referred to a hostile crowd when I gave my evidence and he asked me why I had called it hostile. Agreeing with Mary, I said that whenever anyone threw bricks at me I usually took them to be hostile, after which I was asked no further questions."*

Here is a good moment to point out that this interchange is not in the Hunter evidence. My father never, as far as I know, saw that evidence, which until recently, has been difficult of access. His evidence adds one more to the list of Michael O'Dwyer, Dyer himself and Umar Hayat Khan, who are known to have been wrongly reported.

*"It seemed a miracle when I looked round over my shoulder at this moment and saw an orderly line of men in khaki, with the Deputy Commissioner among them, for I did not really think I could hold out by myself much longer, when once the crowd had got among the bricks. Here I am afraid my account is liable to become confused. My own impression was that the men I saw were a small body of civil-police. What I know to have happened afterwards is this. Our descent from the Hall Bridge had been observed from the Ram Bagh and a platoon of the Royal Sussex was sent to protect Civil Lines, but for some unknown reason they were ordered to go to the District Courts, which lay a mile or two behind. The officer in charge of the platoon found everything quiet there. Having seen for himself where the trouble was, he put his men into tongas and galloped them down to the Hall Bridge where they arrived in the nick of time. There was some firing and an agitator who was urging the rioters on from the footbridge beside the Hall Bridge was shot through the head. The crowd then fell back at once behind the bridges which were henceforward held by men who were in a position to fire if necessary; but I believe there was no more firing here, or very little. The crowd then swirled back to safer areas, splitting itself up into three or four groups that swept through the city howling and screaming for 'white blood.' Once the crowd reached the foot of the bridge and could fan out, it seemed to me impossible that a small body of police could hold them back. I asked Miles Irving whether he would like me to warn the people along the route, which the rioters were likely to take and then ride out to the Khalsa College, and he said 'yes'.*

*Then I went from bungalow to bungalow jumping compound walls where I could, to save time. Mary thought that the game was over and that she was due for home; as soon as her head was turned she nearly pulled my hands off my wrists, but I knew by now that I might have to be in the saddle for the rest of the day and my only other pony, Julia, was a nervy beast that I was trying to bring back from racing to polo and she would have been no use for this sort of work, so Mary and I had a bit of an argument, as I did not wish her to exhaust herself."*

In the Congress story, this had been a peaceful crowd. No one involved in the Inquiry seems to have looked into the detail. Anyone who has done so, has been told that they are lying because the Congress Report says otherwise, or in my case, that I am trying to exonerate my father for firing! In these circumstances, I turn to the written statement of Miles Irving.

*"Between 11.00 a.m. and noon, crowds began to collect in the City and Aitchison Park. Information was received by telephone at noon* [he does not say which telephone or which lines were working and indeed by the time he wrote this he may have forgotten] *that the crowd intended going to the Deputy Commissioner's house and the Military were warned. The Deputy Commissioner, proceeding to the Hall*

*Bridge about 12.30, found that an angry crowd had poured over it, driving back a small mounted picket accompanied by Mr Beckett, Assistant Commissioner. The picket was stoned and could not hold the crowd back but the opportune arrival of mounted supports held them temporarily. The Deputy Commissioner rode to the Officer Commanding Troops to explain the situation and while he was absent, the mounted troops were again attacked and pressed back and on being called back by Mr Connor, 1st Class Magistrate, opened fire wounding and killing a few rioters. This was at about 1.00 p.m. This, and the arrival of a body of police under Mr. Plomer, Deputy Superintendent of Police, held the mob. A British Infantry picket further augmented the forces. Finally the crowd was driven back over the railway line but not before the infantry had been obliged to fire. Up to this point the casualties among the rioters were small. The military then took charge of the Hall Gate Bridge and the footbridge."*

Mr. Plomer, Deputy Superintendent of Police, Amritsar, having found the Officer Commanding Troops, went to the Police Lines, where he had a spare armed Reserve of 25 men and a few mounted police. As he said: *"with whom I hurried to the Railway Foot Bridge and intercepted the mob, which at this point consisted of' several thousands and was in possession of the Footbridge, the Railway Lines and the road near Madan's shop. The mounted picket of the column was stoned by the mob and had fallen back to the crossroads further down and had already fired on the mob when I arrived. The mob fell back to the Foot Bridge with the Police facing them with bayonets fixed and at the ready position, when some members of the local Bar rushed forward and asked me not to fire and that they would take the mob back to the city. I agreed to this. The mob was induced to retire by these gentlemen and by the time the Infantry arrived, the Footbridge and the Railway Line were practically clear of it. The Foot and Over Bridge were immediately taken over by the military and the Hospital Crossing by the police picket. In the meanwhile a mob had entered the Railway goods yard and assaulted Mr. Bennett, the Station Superintendent who-had a very narrow escape. Guard Robinson, who was in the yard, was less fortunate and was overtaken and beaten to death with lathis."* His body was described later as a bundle of bloody rags with no resemblance to a human being.

Before leaving the mob coming over the Hall Bridge I turn to Mr Connor, the extra Assistant Commissioner, earlier described as 1st Class Magistrate. By the time of the Inquiry, a lot of the troops were up on the Frontier and the man who first fired, Lieutenant Dickie, was not available as a witness.

Connor had come straight from Court, sometime about 10 00 a.m., to the scene just this side of Madan's shop on Queen's Road. He had been told to go to the Kotwali, but he could not get beyond Queen's Road, where he came across a military picket trotting back at a very fast pace, being stoned by a large and very dense crowd. They were real stones, stone ballast for road making which were on the other side of the railway line. The picket consisted of about three men of the ammunition column and three Indian mounted sowars. Two of the British soldiers were armed, one with a pistol and the other with a carbine, but not the sowars. Their officer was Lieutenant Dickie who said 'Oh for God's sake send reinforcements.' He was being stoned at the time and was in very serious peril. Connor, asked if he had given instructions to fire, said that effectively he had done so, by saying it was up to Lieutenant Dickie. The question was touching on the legal requirements for troops to fire on civilian mobs, since for Dickie to fire legally, he had to have permission from a Magistrate. Later in the day, Miles Irving handed over the responsibility for restoring order in the City to the military This was ad hoc Martial Law since proper Government Martial Law did not come in due to the broken communications. Finally, the wireless had to be used to send the request for notification of Martial Law to Sir Michael O'Dwyer and they were afraid that they would be too late, as there was a storm at the time and they doubted that a message would get through. This became very much a part of the propaganda about Dyer's firing, claiming that Dyer had no right to fire at all. This was not correct, for by the end of the 10th, Irving had handed over to the military and the first of the orders not to gather or the people would be fired on had been posted throughout Amritsar.

Dickie was very glad to have even an order of that kind and two men dismounted and took cover behind culverts near the bridge and fired three or four shots. They had been finding it hard, as had my father, not to bolt into the Civil Lines and all this time the women and children were in very great danger, although luckily, they did not realise how serious it was. The effect on the crowd was to bring them to a dead stop.

The crowd had been making a murderous yell, not the usual cry of the previous days. Connor was asked whether he spoke to the crowd in English and, like my father of course, said he was speaking to the crowd in the vernacular. While he was standing there speaking to the wounded, bricks were thrown at him from the roof of Madan's shop. Narayan claimed that girls were doing this, but Connor did not know whether this was true, saying that since the door was open, people could have gone inside.

At last the crowd, excluding the wounded that were taken to the hospital, went back either over the line or the bridge to the other side. But in the meanwhile, the mob in the city had set fire to several buildings and Connor later heard that at that very time, Mr Stewart was dying.

A further witness wrote his memories some years later; a young man recently having joined the Ghurkhas, was travelling with them to the Frontier for training. He was talking to his superior officer, Lt. Crampton as they came under the bridge to the railway station and hearing a lot of noise, looked out of the window, being missed only by inches, by a lathi which was thrown in. One of the claims of the propagandists, as if the death of Guard Robinson was not enough, was that this peaceful crowd was carrying no lathis.

My father described this incident from his viewpoint. *"At this moment a train appeared. As it slowed down we saw to our great relief the faces of Ghurkha troops looking out of the windows, but the relief was only momentary. Though the train slowed down it did not stop but began to pick up speed and passed on. Something must have been done to stop it lower down the line, for it came to a halt a few minutes later before the first carriages had left the platform. An officer stepped out and I went over to speak to him. I was still under the impression that he and his men had been sent to help us but he looked completely bewildered and I discovered that he had not even heard that there was trouble in Amritsar. He was merely conducting a party of troops en route for somewhere else. When I suggested that even so his men would be better employed at Amritsar, he replied - and no doubt quite correctly - that he could not divert his men without orders from some superior military authority.*

*I don't know what happened after that, but I know that in the end, the Ghurkhas were detrained and took over the railway line for the night. They were very useful indeed and their arrival at this moment was an extremely lucky accident for it meant that the great danger, to avert which we had been on the strain all day, was over for the moment.*

*Some week's later, Miles Irving received an angry letter from a lady in England. It appeared that her son, a young officer who had just come out from England, was with this party. The letter was full of abuse for the brutal cruelty of the civil authorities, whom she held responsible for the fact that her boy had been forced to sleep out of doors all night on the hard ground with his boots on (which was what most of us had to do that night). It was an atrocity, which evidently ranked in her mind above all the other atrocities committed in Amritsar. I suppose that the boy had tried to brighten up his letter home with a few vivid touches about the hardships he had undergone; but I hope that he never knew about his mother's letter. I have a feeling that it would have made him very, very unhappy."*

That boy, who later became a Justice of the Peace in England, remarked on the incident -of sleeping with his boots on in his note in the Imperial War Museum. The night that he did this was the night of the 13th, when he was on duty in case there was a further outbreak in the city and slept in the environs of the Kotwali.

While the mobs were pouring through the town, Miss Sherwood was bicycling through the narrow streets, overseeing the schools and calling on the parents of the children in her care. She encountered a mob which raised cries of 'She is English'. She wheeled round and tried to escape but she took a wrong turning and had to retrace her steps. She reached a lane where she was well known and thought she would be safe, but the mob overtook her and she was also attacked from the front. Being hit on the head with sticks, she fell on the ground but got up and ran a little way, where she was again felled, being struck with sticks even when she was on the ground Again she got up and tried to enter a house, but the door was slammed in her face. Falling from exhaustion she again struggled to get up, but everything became dark and she thought she had become blind.

Towards the end of the chase, she was seized by Abur Din who seized her dress and threw her down. His brother Jilla pulled off her hat, Mangta alias Gidder and Lal Chand struck her with their fists. She got up and staggered on till Wilyate took her by her hair and having knocked her down, took off his shoes and gave her five or six blows on her head. She got up and struggled a little further, until Sunder Singh hit her on the head with his lathi, finally knocking her down. All the time the mob was shouting 'Victory to Gandhi', 'Victory to Kitchlew' and finally as they left, 'She's dead.'

She later wrote *"It should be remembered that had a European man treated an Indian woman so, there would have been a gigantic row, and rightly so, and if a particular street of Europeans had looked on and shut a door against her, we should say it deserved almost any punishment. Personally, I should prefer no such order had been carried out"* [a reference to the so-called 'crawling order' see Part 5 ch. iv]. *"I hear not the cries of 'Kill', 'Kill' in that street, but the shouts in another of 'Leave her alone, she is a woman.' It was an Indian who rescued me, an Indian house that gave me shelter, and Indian hands that first dressed my wounds, and that is full compensation, and I would not have it otherwise."*

The missionaries themselves in the schools wrote later of the terror to which they refused to succumb, going into a back room and praying to God while they listened to the mob tearing down the building and setting fire to it.

The events were summarised by Miles Irving as follows: *"Part of the crowd repulsed from the crossing, attacked the Telegraph Office and destroyed the Telephone Exchange and were beaten off just in time to prevent further damage, by a detachment of the Railway picket, which had been sent forward by the Officer Commanding as soon as the first sign of trouble began. This must have happened about 1.00 p.m., as a conversation was taking place over the telephone at that time between the Municipal Engineer and the Agent, Alliance Bank, about the crowds coming back into the city. Another part of the crowd turned to the goods yard where they did considerable damage by fire and killed Mr Robinson a guard. They also chased the Station Superintendent but were turned back by the railway picket. The arrival by chance of a detachment of Ghurkhas about 200 strong finally secured the railway station.*

*Within the city all European and all Government property was attacked. The National Bank of India was sacked and burnt and Mr. Stewart, the Agent, and Mr. Scott, his assistant, were murdered. The Alliance Bank was attacked and the Agent, Mr J.M. Thompson was murdered. The Chartered Bank was attacked but the Agent, Mr J.W. Thomson and his assistant Mr. Ross, were rescued by the police from the Kotwali.* [the policeman in charge, with a small number of police were able to do this by the simple method of entering the Bank and shouting 'pukharo', 'pukharo'.] *The Religious Book Society's Depot and Hall were burnt down, but the inmates, who were Indian Christians, escaped. The Town Hall and the Sub-Post Office attached to it were fired and the Sub-Post Offices to the Golden Temple, Majith Mundi and Dhab Basti Ram were looted. The Zenana Hospital was entered and every effort made to find and kill Mrs. Easdon, the lady doctor in charge, who however escaped. Miss Sherwood, a Mission lady, was caught cycling in the city and brutally attacked, being rescued with difficulty. The mob burnt the Indian Christian Church and attempted to fire the C.M.S. Girls' Normal School but was driven off by police from the Police*

*Lines. The electrician to the Military Works, Sergeant Rowlands, was caught by the rioters near the Aitchison Park and murdered*

*There was further and organised attempt to cut communications. Telegraph wires were cut and Bhagtanwala Railway Station on the Tarn Taran line was burnt and looted. An attempt was also made on the main line of rail towards Lahore but was defeated by fire from the Railway Police Guard on the Down Calcutta Mail.*

*The mob also made another attempt to burst into the Civil Lines and after repeated warnings was fired on by order of the Deputy Commissioner at the Hall Gate Bridge. There were probably twenty to thirty casualties caused at the time. This was at about 2.00 p.m.*

*In the meantime, civilians had been collected at the collecting stations, the Alexandra School and one of the canal bungalows. Lieutenant Colonel Smith had, according to the plan, promptly evacuated the ladies of St. Catherine's Hospital and the Missionaries in the city, as it turned out, at considerable risk. As soon as the road to the Fort was picketed, civilians were removed thither. Appeals for help had been sent to Lahore by an officer on a light engine and also by phone. As soon as communication was established at about 10.00 p.m., 400 reinforcements arrived from Jullundur and Lahore. The City was entered and the Kotwali occupied at midnight.*

*The Commissioner, Mr. A J W Kitchin C.I.E., and the Deputy Inspector General of Police, Mr. D. Donald, C.I.E., arrived by motorcar from Lahore at about 5.00 p.m.*

*The same night, an attack was made by a mob of villagers on Cheharta Railway Station. The mob only broke the windows of the station itself, and proceeded to loot a goods train that was standing in the yard."*

Meanwhile, Lieutenant MacCallum was sitting at the crossroads with some of the Ghurkhas, in case any more attempts would be made on the Civil Lines. *"We sat in the ditches at the cross roads* [the ditches called culverts by Connor] *for many weary hours. The only excitement was the occasional individual coming from the city with his bit of loot. The loot was confiscated without much protest and the individual went on his way. Thus the night continued until a mounted policeman arrived to tell us to go back to the railway station. We arrived with our loot, mainly cloth bales. The civilian disappeared and I went to report to O.C. Amritsar who had established his office in the railway station waiting-room. I reported and handed over the loot. While so doing, two ladies in Indian dress with stained faces arrived. Indian friends had helped them out of the city. All very interesting and I retired for a bit of food and bed."* These ladies, Dr. Easdon being one of them, were then, according to my mother, taken to the Fort.

At Delhi, Ahmedabad and Lahore, it is clear that the suppression of the main impetus of the rebellion was due to the availability of a weight of troops and police. At Amritsar, as Miles Irving had warned, the number of troops was so small that it could not hold onto the city, let alone reclaim it. There was a tendency to think that Miles Irving, like many Indian Civil Servants, was too nice a man to take the situation firmly enough in hand and there was certainly a tendency to not recognise the seriousness of the situation. Nonetheless, during the days that followed, when the Congress Report and the Indian element on the Committee were to claim that the city was quiet, it was Miles Irving who stated without hesitation, that within the city, it was Hindu-Mussulman nationalist rule and the Sirkar, outside.

If it is understood that the method used to rouse active revolt, of meetings leading to hartal, followed by more meetings and instructions, then with the continued cutting of communications (with metal clippers specially made for the job) and the destruction of railway lines and stations, the situation was not simply quiet, but merely the necessary preparation for more of the same.

In the background was Kasur and other troubles in the towns and villages in the Punjab. In Amritsar, there were regular meetings: to hear the telegrams sent by the doctors to say they were well and to indicate that the way to alter the Rowlatt Bill was by Soul Force; messages that Jat Sikh villagers were gathering round the Chatiwind Gate, claiming that they were coming in to loot; to hear from Chauk Mundai that there were some Sikhs and a Muslim who were telling the people that there was a: union among the villagers who were coming into the city by various ways, who would unite at one place to loot. These pieces of information were relayed on the 11th and the townspeople were becoming nervous and wondering how they could protect themselves. It is relevant to note that Nehru wrote that there were many ways into the city, which were known to them and not to Government.

On the 12th, a big meeting was to be held at 8.30 a.m. at Dhab Katikan, to discuss the following actions:-

'To carry the dead body of a Sikh of Peshawar in procession, who was shot on 10th April, 1919 and died last night in Katra Ahluwalian.

To depute volunteers to check, and if possible, to stop food stuffs taken from the City to the Fort for Europeans.

To arrange to have a hartal in horse and cattle fair.

To collect subscriptions in order to feed the poor Indians.

To open the shops from 7.00 p.m. to 9.00 p.m. today to sell food stuffs.

To make private arrangements to guard the city from villagers who intend to plunder the city.'

In the oral evidence, witnesses described the prevention of food being brought into the city and one of the first orders made after the 13th was to stop this and see that fresh food was brought in. Irving does not make clear how serious this was, since it was effectively a form of siege of the forces of government. Smith has pointed out that his orderly could not buy food in the bazaar unless he was out of uniform. Even more serious was the determination of the leaders to starve out the British, both the women and children in the Fort and the solders in the Ram Bagh. There had been no incident in which it had been considered necessary to put women and children into a Fort since the Mutiny sixty years before. In this case, the one hundred or so women of British birth were joined by the Eurasians from the Railway houses and the one hundred or so Indian women and children from the Mission School, so nearly burnt down before they were saved, first by Colonel Smith and then by the Indian Police. All milk, fresh vegetables, fruit and meat were stopped being taken into the Fort by the rebels, or into Amritsar for the troops; no fresh or indeed any produce was sold to the police or the troops unless they were out of uniform. The women and particularly, the young children, suffered in the heat without fans and with the lack of latrines and water, and at least one child, the baby of Miles Irving's family, died of dysentery. The only food available was bully beef and biscuits from the soldiers' rations, and even those were running out.

Various policemen were threatened, both in Lahore and Amritsar. Irving claims that attempts were made to stop the spread of disorder in the villages, citing Tarn Taran, where there was incipient trouble throughout. This was the most worrying aspect. Villagers, he says, were pouring into the city, not only for the Baisakhi Fair. This indicates some lack of communication, since Fazl Dad Khan, Khan Bahadur, stated specifically in his evidence that he left Amritsar on the 11th because the Fair was over. He was going by train to Lahore. Mrs Wathen describes the Baisakhi people trotting away down the Lahore road on the same day. In view of the fact that the Baisakhi people had valuable horses and cattle with them, it seems virtually impossible that they should have stayed to be subjected to a hartal, even if they had not left the previous day anyway. The threat may simply have been a form of sabre rattling, used to show the power of the organisers at the meeting on the 12th.

By the 12th, it was said in evidence from Lala Tek Chand Jaini of Jandala, people in the villages were sharpening their axes ready to come into Amritsar for the 13th. They left before he could stop them. Bearing in mind the thousands of people involved in the rebellion in Amritsar alone and the ill treatment of people who were in favour of the Government, evidence given supportive of government was courageous and risky. Lala Tek Chand was a brave, brave man to speak by the time the Hunter Commission came to hear his evidence.

By the 13th, therefore, we have villagers pouring into the city for loot or murderous mayhem, determination to claim the actual rule of the city by the insurgents, together with some concern that a very strong element of Jats might be joining in, which would imply that the news was spreading that Amritsar was up for grabs. More seriously, it was being claimed that the Sirkar was over and that British soldiers did not dare fire. If my father had gone to the Hall Bridge armed, with a larger group of soldiers and had fired firmly, one wonders whether the rebellion might have been snuffed out on the 10th. As it was, the kid glove method of defence rather than attack gave the wrong signal. I believe that, as India is ruled today, there would have been none of this patience and restraint, but then they, like Dyer, know their own people.

# PART 4
# THE MAN

## Chapter I
## LIFE & CAREER

It has been said that all the history of a man is present when he steps on the stage. Reginald Edward Harry Dyer's step onto the stage of history held within it a man of compassion who, as a child, had gone shooting in the forest near Simla and, missing a bird, had hit a monkey. The sight of the little creature with tears streaming down her cheeks, trying to wipe the blood off her coat, led him to give up shooting except for the pot, or for necessity. Living in the Himalayas, exploring and walking and camping in those Rhododendron-clad hills, he saw all the wild life – mahseer, hyena, bear, leopard and he spoke the local language of Hindustan. Although Colvin doesn't mention it, it is unlikely that he did not learn at least a smattering of Pahari. Even as a boy, he had that quickness of thought and reaction combined with courage, that living a lot of the time in wilderness gives. Coming round a corner on a hill path one day, he met a hyena barring his way. Remembering that wild animals are frightened of the human eye he stared it down and slowly the hyena backed and walked away. According to Colvin, Dyer was still a small boy and was escorting his little sisters home from school at the time. His role was not only a courageous one but one of protectiveness to his sisters, who, remembering the event, recounted it to Dyer's biographer years later. In much the same way, he dealt with snakes. On one occasion pulling a snake's tail as it tried to escape into its hole, the snake suddenly came out and little Rex was left rolling down the khud-side, still holding onto the snake's tail.

His early education was at Bishop Cotton's school in Simla. Then he and his elder brother, Walter, were sent off the Middleton College in Cork, Ireland, wearing solar topis and kukris stashed in their cummerbunds! Rex and Walter learned early to be laughed at by their peers. At this juncture, the children had learned independence of mind, courage and the capacity to manage on their own. From the hills of India, he had gained easy acquaintance with the hill men as well as with the people who worked at his parents' brewery. Rex at the age of eleven, (thirteen in the case of Walter), had travelled from India on their own, with their own cheque-books and bank accounts, to survive in a country they did not know.

Middleton College was a Protestant foundation from the time of William II and the headmaster, the Revd. Dr. Thomas Moore, with his daughters, were entertained by these two boys who were laughed at as 'wild Indians' and had to fight their way through the bullying nature of the times. But the adjective most repeated about Rex was that he was 'gentle and good natured' with everyone and of an open easy sunny disposition. The school had running fights with the Town boys and a contemporary remembered the prowess of the tough little 'Hector' in the forefront of the fights. Determined not to forget his native language of Hindustani, he used to read pages in the language in a book he brought with him from India. Latin and Greek he could not learn, but he began then to show the aptitude for mathematics, which he used later to develop a rangefinder lens.

One of the most extraordinary things is, that these two boys were left to their own devices during the holidays from school. In time, Rex decided to go into the Army, Walter, his brother, to study Medicine. The school itself had an interest in the Army and Rex studied Military History and Strategy. He enjoyed boxing, swimming to the Black Rock, chess tournaments (at which he showed great aptitude) and for a brief time, he went to the Rotunda with his brother, but the dissecting sickened him and so he went to a London crammer to prepare for Sandhurst, which he entered in the 1884 year, being then just twenty.

From Sandhurst, he was Commissioned in the Queen's Royal West Surrey Regiment; the Second Battalion then being in India. Dyer joined the First Battalion. It was traditional for people going into the Indian Army to have to go into a British Regiment for a year first, which was frequently a difficult experience for Officers from India, but at this time Dyer was intending to remain in the British Army. Among his fellow officers was Charles Monro, later the Commander-in-Chief in India at the time of Amritsar. It is said that Rex used to teach Monro boxing, but their relationship was friendly enough. Monro was six years older than Rex Dyer.

Also within the experience of the young Dyer was his Regiment's involvement with the Civil Arm in Ireland in 1886, picketing the streets of Belfast to prevent disturbances between Orangemen and the Irish Nationalists.

After Belfast, the next step in his career was to Burma, which gave him the experience and insight into the volatile situation that can so easily erupt in the East, so prone to the sorts of disorder that were a part of India when the British first went there. During the Burmese War, he encountered the chaos where the Boh, similar to the Viet Cong in a later time, were running through villages, elusive, murderous, lying in wait behind stockades, shooting and vanishing, crucifying stragglers and friendly villagers. Dyer was there for nine months. He gained a medal with two clasps and a great deal of hard won experience. He must have learned the necessity of bringing order out of the chaotic misery of Burma. When he asked the local barristers and men of standing to take over various jobs to restore order in Amritsar, the men he used were the men who had been encouraging dissension and later on, in one of the many twists that have been used in the imagery against him, he was heavily criticised for asking these men to help in the restoration of law and order to their own town.

His return from the Burma front gave him another experience. While going down river one day, dozing in the cabin of a steamer, he heard shouts and cries for help. The sounds he had heard of running footsteps, were of the crew, setting upon his bearer, whom they were obviously intending to kill – the usual trouble of a difference over religion, so common in the East. Dyer, standing over his servant, knocked the assailants down as they came up. His boxing skills floored them and they were left either flat out on the deck, or fleeing. With peace negotiated with the ship's crew, he left for India. A further taste of the future followed – having left without any concern about ongoing troubles, he then found when he got home, that the Master and crew of the steamer on the Irrawaddy took him to a civil court. With his father's help, he wrote a reply adequate enough to stop proceedings and to make his Colonel, who might have considered his action serious enough to cause repercussions, roar with laughter and shout 'Shabash'.

Dyer's parents at this time began to further prosper. Dyer *père* was a chemist and he took his brewery to Lucknow in the face of disbelief that beer could be made in the plains. At that time refrigeration was becoming more and more efficient and where, in previous times, the dak runners would have come down from the Hills with sacks of ice from the mountains on their backs, to be stored in ice houses and cellars, Dyer was now able to keep a regulated temperature and expand his business.

Strength, gentleness, chivalry, compassion, quick responses, a fine mathematical mind and the capacity for loyalty and affection. In later years the romantic streak in his nature led him to give up his position in the British Army to go into the Indian Army, because his mother refused to continue to give him an allowance if he married little Ann Ommaney, the love of his life.

The first thing he had done when he found that Ann was prepared to marry him was to go down to the Bazaar and buy a lump of gold which he then hammered into her engagement ring.

General Dyer's mother was a tough and in some ways, hard woman. She had nine children, having come out to India on an East Indiaman before the Mutiny, and Mutiny stories must have been recounted to the children. Colvin suggests that the women who managed to escape the mutineers, took shelter in the Hills, some in Simla, possibly in the Dyer household.

On the 4th April 1888, Dyer married Ann Ommaney in the Jhansi camp. Mrs Dyer, Senior, had undertaken to help them to the extent of £100 for the first year, but after that it was a matter of 'As you have made your bed, so you lie on it'. He had taken a Commission in the 39th Bengal Infantry, where Colonel Ommaney was in command, endeavouring to pull it together and Dyer was stationed at Cawnpore and then Jhansi, in the Central Provinces. On the move to Jhansi, the ladies marched with the regiment because there were no trains. When the Regiment was finally shown to be beyond redemption, it was disbanded and Dyer was appointed Wing Officer on probation, 29th Punjab Infantry. Later, its title was altered twice and it became the 10th Battalion, 15th Punjab Regiment, but Dyer, whose knowledge of Indian languages was intrinsic to his life, undoubtedly would have learnt a good deal of Bengali to add to the other languages he already knew.

His next move was to Peshawar where, on operations with his regiment to respond to the murders of two officers and five Ghurkhas, seeing someone jump over the wall of a fort and out the other side, he leapt over both walls, but was reprimanded for surmounting an obstacle without knowing what was on the other side. His friend at the time got the D.S.O. for this little junket. The stories that are told of regiments on the frontier are fascinating. One such is of an annual tug of war which went on for an hour and nine minutes, led to those Sikhs who were dragged across the line by Dyer's group having the skin stripped from their feet and having to be taken to hospital, where one man died. The experience in this regiment, composed of Sikhs, Mohammedans and Dogras, must have extended the young officer's experience and knowledge of men. (In the matter of tugs-of-war, the Government, after that, discouraged such games and ordered that if the men were going to go in for such exercise, they must wear boots.)

One aspect of army life was mobility. While being moved to Nowshera by train, he stacked his luggage on the only tikka gharri available and returned from his last visit to the train, to see his tikka gharri setting off with another traveller, so he told the man that it was his. The new traveller in the gharri was the local Tahsildar, who told Dyer that since he was an important official, Dyer's claim did not count. Dyer insisted - the Tahsildar pushed him away, Dyer retaliated and by this time a crowd began to collect which, urged on by the little official, began to go for Dyer with lathis and stones. His boxing skills were used for a while but he was gradually being overwhelmed, when running feet brought in sight his Sikh men who were coming to rescue him. It is remarkable that Dyer, being hit with a lathi (used to crack a man's skull), survived. It is probable that he was wearing a topi that protected his head. The crowd tactfully disappeared before the Sikhs could deal with them according to their merits; and Dyer himself ordered his men not to take retribution. However when he got back to camp, he found himself covered with bruises from the waist up. Of course, the Tahsildar did not let the matter rest, but instituted a Court case. The Judge was a friend of his and the Tahsildar came into court veiled. Withdrawing the veil he showed a discoloured face. *"And now"* said the judge *"we are to deal with this disgraceful assault"*. Dyer's lawyer had warned him that the case would probably go against him, so he had undertaken his own defence. He said *"I protest against the pre-judgment of the case. I ask it to be noted that the court has spoken of a disgraceful assault before hearing the evidence. In these circumstances, I refuse to submit to its jurisdiction and give notice of appeal."*

The judge recognised his error and the case was dismissed.

Another tale of Dyer's behaviour with his troops is told by Colvin, how, when visiting Amritsar with some of his Sikhs, the men put up small tents beside the train for their wives. Later, hearing a racket, Dyer thought it to be his soldiers, found it was, and that they were beating up a man. He got his troops to leave the man alone, at which the onlookers began to look threatening, so he told them clearly that he would find out the true events and treat his men with firmness if they had done wrong. His men then told him that the man they had attacked was a Peeping Tom, who had been peering round the tent flaps at their womenfolk. On this, Dyer accepted that their behaviour was understandable and the matter was left, but this sort of control and concern made him an object of respect to his men.

There are many stories about Dyer. A Sikh Honorary Captain wrote of Dyer's loss of teeth (and damage to his palate) from a hockey stick wielded in a game by 'Kean Sahib Bahadur'. A report from the Official Historian of the War, mentions Dyer in his second time at Camberley (Staff College), when he was in a group of greats, including Allenby and gives the comment on Dyer, 'This officer has shown great force of character', but for Dyer himself, it was a difficult time. He was extremely shy and most of the other officers had relations of some standing, were living in big houses and educated at the same schools. It is interesting to note that later, when Dyer was speaking to my father, he gave him the impression that he felt that after the Hunter Committee, he might be ostracised in Britain, where he intended going to live on retirement. The tales brought into the various books on Amritsar, seek to make him out as a pushy braggadocio, arrogant and self-righteous. There seems to be a simplicity and recognition of the eternal verities in his make up, that belies these claims.

Dyer went to the School of Musketry at Chungla Gully, being awarded an extra first class certificate. Before leaving for Europe, he and his wife had climbed in the snow covered Himalayas. Then the friendship of a young Raja of Poonch led to a tiger shoot on elephants, with Mrs. Dyer on a very unsafe howdah crossing the river in spate; then with the Raja's help, going to Jhelum by boat. The boat capsized on rocks, but mercifully, Dyer was able to rescue his wife, since the boat had been tied to the team on the shore. His energy seems to have been limitless. He did a course in Field Works at Chatham, which he passed with distinction and went to Paris to learn French. He studied Military History and Military Law, which was useful when he came to write his answer to the Army Council in 1920. He stayed with the Ommaneys at West Malling in Kent. There then came the attack on Chitral in 1895 and he left Europe in order to be with his Regiment to help, but arrived almost too late. This was the incident when Umra Khan, with help from Afghanistan, cut off a British Mission. Townsend of Kut was one of those who were under siege at Chitral and it is said that seven future generals were involved.

Dyer was next at Delhi and then Peshawar. At Peshawar, the family lived in a house known as 'the last house in Asia.' During that time, he suffered the cracked jaw, which put him out of action for a while. Then the Hindus set fire to the wooden houses of Peshawar where the Muslims lived and turned off the water supply so that there was no means of help. The Muslims, attempting to protect their women folk from being seen, stood at the doors of their houses, preferring their families to be burnt to death, rather than be seen by other eyes. Once again, Dyer was in the forefront of helping these poor people, coming back home with his face blackened, red eyes and heat stroke, severe enough to send him to bed packed in ice, under a system which gradually restored him to health.

The endeavour to help Indians in need displayed by General Dyer was not displayed by him alone. Again and again in the various problems that arose, the British in India helped through the tragedies of famine, earthquakes and other disasters. The Quetta earthquake in the 1930s, in which hundreds of British helped at the same extent of exhaustion as Dyer, has been graphically described by Raleigh Trevelyan. By then, the Indian politicians were becoming envious of the British and tried to spread a different picture to the world; but at the time of the Peshawar fire, political envy and enmity was only present in small patches. By the 1930s, the whole feeling in India had begun to change.

Where he would have been outstanding was in his intimate knowledge of the Indians and their religious attitudes and languages. His brother officers would have known he was 'country bred' but since he was as courageous, as quick or quicker and as friendly with them as they with him, this would have caused no division whatsoever among the ordinary Indian Army officers.

Even in those days, unjust law sometimes came from above – from the people whom Field Marshal Sir Henry Wilson was later to refer to as 'the frocks'. Edward VII was introduced to India at the Delhi Durbar in January 1903. In 1902, an Indian cook had been brutally assaulted and died outside the barracks of the 9th Lancers at Sialkot. Although the Regiment offered a reward for the finding of the assailants, no culprits were brought forward. The military authorities punished the whole Regiment, although Sir Bindon Blood gave information to show that it was not the solders, but an outsider who had committed the crime. The Government of India publicly censured the Regiment for lying ('under the stigma of concealing a criminal assault leading to the death of a defenceless native'), although the Regiment denied any such concealment. Everyone knew that they were innocent and when Curzon arrived at the Durbar, he was met with a resounding silence. On the arrival of the 9th Lancers, they were met with resounding cheers. Dyer would have been present and joined in with this display of annoyance at injustice, cheering the 9th with the rest.

Another dangerous exploit was with his stepbrother in a coracle of Dyer's making. They went down the River Tonse, following its course from Chakarta in the Hills to Kalsi and the Jumna in the Plains. They were, for much of their time, in rapids and over waterfalls, white-water, and finally had to abandon the little boat. A voyage expected to take three days took seventeen and nearly led to the loss of both men's lives. They met a bear which they had to shoot, nearly starved, lost themselves and had to struggle back to where Mrs. Dyer was awaiting them at Chakarta.

The family went back to England and General Walter Kitchener offered Dyer, by this time a major, the command of the 19th Punjabis, but news came that his little son Ivan was very ill and not expected to live. Dyer saw no alternative other than to apply for long leave and also go to England. Ivan had pneumonia followed by congestion of the lungs, but while Dyer was sailing back to Britain, his son recovered. His leave lost him the regiment and the offer was not repeated, despite having been made on the grounds of the excellence of Dyer's staff work. To Dyer, the recovery of his much loved son seems to have compensated and here I think he showed a rare quality. At a time when men were not so involved with their children, it seems to me probable that in returning to England for his wife and his other son's sake, he showed something of the concern for others, despite the risk of loss of personal interest which was later to lead him to act unselfishly to stop the making of the 1919 rebellion.

It was on his return that, having been appointed Musketry Instructor at Rawalpindi and Chungla Gully, he began to see the vital importance of a better range finder. As an instructor he was outstanding – again his sympathy for others led to instruction of a simplicity and calibre that helped each and every student that came before him.

In the South African War, the failures and shortcomings of the human eye in new lights and environments had cost the British Army so dear that many minds were set at work to find an aid or an alternative. Mr. Conrad Beck, the well known optical instrument maker, who carried out his specifications, told Colvin that Major Dyer's first range-finder was an extraordinarily good instrument, light, handy and serviceable for distances up to about 3000 yards. From then on much of his spare time and spare cash was spent on improving the range and accuracy of this instrument. His stereoscopic inventions were running on different lines, but on the same intention as Professor Forbes of Edinburgh and in the event, at that time he was discouraged by the Engineers at Woolwich, who thought the stereoscopic principle was impracticable. His efforts continued into his retirement. He could not have got to the position that he did in stereoscopic sighting, if he had not had a highly mathematical mind.

Rex was not the only one from his family who was intellectually bright. His father, the manager of the Murree Brewery and later the owner of the Solon Brewery in Simla, was a brilliant physicist who had applied his mind successfully to the making of beer in the hot climate of India. The Murree Brewery continued to supply the beer drinkers of India until the time that the British left. It made Solon Whisky as well. [Today, it continues to flourish, based not in the Hills but at Rawalpindi, despite the prohibitions of supplying liquor in Pakistan.]

Dyer returned to India as second in command of the 25th Punjabis at Rawalpindi. Although he had been unsuccessful with his range finder, Mr. Conrad Beck had described him as a 'high-minded public-spirited man' and he further added what by now we should know – 'it was a great pleasure to work with him.' It was a great pleasure for the Indian soldiers, for the other officers and for his children. A letter from him to his son Ivan, written at about the time he was at Rawalpindi runs *"If mother comes out you must remember the promise you made me and look after Geoff like a man. You must keep to the right road as far as you can, and remember that it is only by trying hard we can manage this. Have your fun but never be a sneak."* It is typical that after this he adds *"I don't so much care if you do not happen to be very learned when I meet you next, but I shall be very disappointed if you are not of the right sort."* How many fathers of that period must have considered these as the best aims possible and how many of them would have also written with the humour and affection that Dyer shows, demonstrating his own simple, direct nature. He was promoted to command the Regiment in 1910.

In the 25th Punjabis, there were not only Dogras, Sikhs and Punjabi Muslims, but also Pathan Kattaks. These were remarkable people. They were Sunnis as opposed to the bulk of their compatriots, who are Shias. They were the only trustworthy and loyal Pathans and later, in 1919, when the Pathans rose and killed their officers, the Khattaks made a shield round them and protected them at the risk of their own lives. The Dyers knew and appreciated these men very well – they had their own traditions and dances and had something of the Tartar race in their way of life. There were dances and Khattak music round great log fires and a man's name called by the Subedar Major would bring forward a man who was an acrobat to perform after the dancers. Dyer encouraged the wrestling and other sports. In 1911 the Regiment furnished the guard of honour for the Royal family and Dyer became friendly with the King (George V).

The following year, with the voyage to Hong Kong on duty, the men were told that if they were sick, they should be sent home. Piru, Colonel Dyer's Dogra orderly, on the prow of the ship and looking at the far horizons of the Indian Ocean said *"How shall I ever find my way back?"* Always interested in Indian traditions and fables, Dyer noted that a Dogra, Nantu, had been bitten by a snake and was in grave danger. After the voyage to Hong Kong, Nantu was bitten again and again near to death. By then Nantu had been, as was foretold, bitten seven times, seven years running, and Dyer had had Nantu's baggage searched to see that he had neither snake nor snake poison in his belongings. Each time it was touch and go that the man would die. On the last occasion, seven years from the first, Nantu pulled the snake away from his foot but did not kill it. An old priest had warned him that if he killed the snake he himself would die and thus he was freed from the spell. Dyer consulted Colonel Rennick, an expert on the Dogras, who told him that 'there were such men'. The priest in fact was a Pandit, a Brahmin. In the earlier pages of this book I have made clear the influence that the Brahmins held over Hindus and indeed some Mohammedans, and the magic which they and others could perform. Dyer knew these things well, not only from his childhood, but from his interest in the men with whom he worked.

In Hong Kong, one of his soldiers, one Harman Singh, was a great wrestler and fought the ju-jitsu Chinese wrestlers and won. So well did he do, that Dyer took him to Japan to see how he did there. With the death of an Emperor, the meetings never came off but as to the Chinese methods, Harman Singh said, *"Sahib, in India wrestling is a very ancient science. We know all these tricks but we do not use them. If they try to gouge out my eyes, I shall be ready for them and I shall twist their heads off."*

Although Dyer accepted the claims of his Sikh sepoy, since he could observe from beginning to end the methods of ju-jitsu, he remained sceptical about Nantu, the man who was bitten by snakes. Though he had examined Nantu's baggage, Nantu had been bitten even in hospital. Where there were those of us who saw and believed in the magic of India, Dyer, with his analytical mind, doubted after the end of seven years (after the war) if the tale was true. The Pandit and the sankhia snake must both have followed Nantu from India to China.

In recent years there has been a film ("The Jewel in the Crown") written by a man who was in India in the army during the war and is incorrect about India on almost every point, except that the determined following of the policeman by a Pandit on a bicycle rings true. Generally, the writer was indulging in a series of images that were as ludicrous as they were untrue. For those of us in India at the time, the story is unpleasantly inaccurate.

In the meanwhile, Ann Dyer was being undermined by ill health. Gradually, the illness became worse and once again Dyer applied for leave on the grounds of family sickness. He took her home via the Pacific and Canada, unwittingly following in reverse the route of the Ghadr Sikhs when they came into India. During 1913, they spent most of the year in a house at Woking and then at Hampton. He himself went on with his prism work and when he went back to Hong Kong, Mrs. Dyer went into a nursing home in Bournemouth.

On his way back, he was on privilege leave in Japan when War broke out on August 4th 1914. Dyer himself knew how serious it was and wired home for his children to join up. Ivan by that time had left Uppingham and had already volunteered, but Geoffrey, still at Uppingham, did not join then, at Ann Dyer's insistence, as she thought he should wait until he had completed his schooling.

Dyer returned to India, once again to Rawalpindi. He became a member of General Gerald Kitson's Staff. The large numbers of recruits, which we have seen being collected by Sir Michael O'Dwyer, had to be turned into fighting soldiers and in this work Dyer became thoroughly involved. Colvin, writing round to anyone who knew Dyer, received from Kitson the following reply: *"an excellent staff officer, having been through the Staff College, he was thoroughly trained. He was a very genial, pleasant companion, full of fun and humour, and I was very fond of him."* The interesting thing about such letters is that they were written after the political diatribes. The writers wrote in the teeth of these bitter criticisms; and must surely have felt particularly strongly to do so.

Being at the headquarters of the Rawalpindi Division and in the position of the chief Staff Officer, Dyer was in a position to know exactly what was going on. He knew of the existence of the Bhawani Mundir, founded in 1905 to glorify Nationalism under the shadow of the Goddess of Destruction, Kali; of the Abbinav Bharut Nasik, founded on the principle of the Russian Anarchist Secret Society, with its closed cells almost impossible to run to earth; he knew of the Shining Light at Amritsar, the chief members of which were Ajit Singh and Ratto or Rattan Chand, whose involvement in the rebellion is mentioned in the chapter dealing with Amritsar - all part of the nation-wide conspiracies.

In later years, when General Dyer had left India and people from all over the world subscribed through the channel of the 'Morning Post' in gratitude to him for what he had done, including the many small sums sent in by individual Indian soldiers, he first doubted whether he should accept the money. Then, on being told that it was being given by people who respected him and were grateful and it would be wrong to refuse their kindness, the money was given to Geoff to buy and stock a farm, Ashton Fields, in Gloucestershire. Dyer himself, hoped to get some sort of a job, but after the weight of hatred aimed at him, he not only found this difficult, but all his problems of ill-health, the arterio-sclerosis, thrombosis and related ills took this opportunity to reduce his naturally buoyant nature to one of deep depression.

We, who so many years later have suffered the Attenborough film, with its imagery of Dyer as a stupid arrogant man, may be surprised that in the late 1920s and early 1930s, anyone who knew him would have cared to stand and be counted as one of Dyer's admirers. I have quoted my father on his opinion of General Dyer and I have used other quotations. Nowhere have I found any criticism of him except from those, like Nehru, who never met him (and merely invented an image in keeping with the propaganda story he wished to perpetuate.) The Attenborough film even invented questions from the members of the Hunter Committee which were never asked (unless they were asked and then not recorded), which would infer a personal knowledge of the Hunter members which Attenborough is unlikely to have had. No-one who knew Dyer and has written about him, considered him to be other than a man full of humour, intelligence and courage and a good friend.

It is, therefore, no surprise that, towards the end of February 1916, General Kirkpatrick, Chief-of-Staff at Delhi, sent for Colonel Dyer and gave him orders to take charge of the military operations in South East Persia. A small force consisting of one regiment of Indian cavalry, four pack guns and a battalion of Indian infantry had been based on Seistan, out on the Persian Afghan frontier, in 1915. This little force, strung out over some hundreds of miles of frontier between Robat and Birjand, had as its main business, to keep the southern half of the Persian/Afghan frontier intact (the Russians keeping the northern half) and to stop German ammunition, machine guns and wireless from entering Afghanistan. Their adventures would make a story in itself as, for example, the capture of Winckelmann, a German staff officer with a caravan of donkeys laden with gold, by Colonel Claridge and his Rajputs and a cavalry march of 94 miles in 24 hours in weather so cold that when they halted they built a fire between each pair of horses. Sufficient to say that, at the beginning of 1916, the Germans, having occupied Kirman and got the Sarhadis on their side, were becoming altogether too formidable to be dealt with by the lines of scattered posts.

# Chapter II
# THE SARHAD CAMPAIGN

The adventure to stop ingress into India by the Germans through Baluchistan, referred to in the extract from Colonel James' story, told in Part I of this book, was written about by General Dyer after his retirement in 1920, when he was living at Long Ashton, near Bristol. A man who was then a boy, with the vivid admiration of that boy, remembers seeing him as a 'great man', though he was by then an invalid leaning on his wife as he went for walks. The story is important because it indicates, as does James, the true character of Dyer the soldier. In a situation of great danger, his courage, his ability to take the steps necessary for the safety of his men and his instinctive regard and understanding of the tribesmen of the Sarhad, shine out.

Sarhad means 'border' and this was an area that lay between Persia (Iran), Baluchistan and Afghanistan.

In 1916, on his own, Dyer, then a Colonel, set out with an armoured car, a driver and his bearer, to stop the ingress of German propaganda, arms and funds into Baluchistan through the Sarhad, with the help and connivance of the tribes.

For driver, he had managed to exchange the allotted driver named Allan for his brother, General Kitson's car driver, who was the better mechanic. He was also a great trencherman and consumed such vast quantities of food that rations were frequently short.

His adventures were described later by Colonel Landon; by Colonel James; in an article in Blackwoods Magazine by Major E B Yeates, as well as by Colvin in his 'Life of General Dyer', who used information from all of these above and by Colonel Claridge.

Dyer stopped for an hour at Pindi to collect his kit, took the train to Quetta and thence to Nushki.[33]

At Nushki, he received a telegram report that the Baluch raiders had cut the lines of communication along his intended route. The telegram was couched in terms that warned of the danger, almost to the extent of ordering him not to proceed. Knowing that to get to the Sarhad was of the utmost importance, Dyer went on, expecting further instructions at Robat.

A note in pencil to his wife from Seistan, told her that she might not hear of him for 'many a long day', giving his address and saying how glad he was to be doing something at last. 'Best love to you, dearest, and to the boys', but that was not all. It is clear that he expected trouble, since he gave a list of share holdings, property, details of his life insurance and, since she was in England, told her that the furs and a jewel he had bought for her were on their way. That was on 25th February 1916. On the 27th, he left. The journey from Nushki to Robat was 375 miles and the time he expected to take was five days.

The road was barely even a track, with sand drifts, out of which they had to dig the car, or deep pools of water into which the car sank above its axles. Then Allan discovered he had left the petrol tap open and they had lost almost all the petrol, so the precious supply for the journey had to be used at once, leaving them without any reserve for the rest of the way.

Miraculously, they found a supply in large cans at a dak bungalow where they stopped for the night. The Kansammah (cook) who looked after the bungalow was away, and they had been searching for water when they found the petrol at this place. When he returned, they were told that it had been left by a previous traveller, who had found the road so impossible that he had decided to go no further. *"Petrol in the desert, petrol where one could as soon have expected to find a Bond Street Jeweller."*

On the third night, they found the road blocked at the post of Mushki-Chah by camel caravans loaded with food for the scattered British outposts. The camel-men were afraid to advance because of reports that the country ahead was in the hands of the Raiders. There was an alternative route, even less used than the one that was blocked by the camel caravan, so Dyer, determined not to delay, took the Webb-Ware route to Saindak. Rocky ravines and small nullahs were their lot, to such an extent that, where the road disappeared, Dyer got out of the car to see whether or where it had gone. He took with him a hurricane lamp and then, overhearing voices, realised that there were men ahead. At first he was afraid the voices were those of the Raiders, but then he was challenged and found that they were the voices of the men of the Chagai Levies. Their leader, Idu, called out *"I am Idu of the Chagai Levies, friendly to the British Government"*. The men had seen the headlights and thought they were German airships. One of the men had levelled his rifle at Dyer, but had

---

33   Many of us in India had relations and ancestors there also. The author's uncle had helped to build this railway at the end of the 19th century.

been restrained by Idu who had spotted that the lamp was in the hands of one man. *"Let us wait and see who he is."*

Idu was not only one of the Chagai Levies, but a Reki, one of the tribes who had remained friendly to the British and he became Dyer's right hand man. *"Never once, in all the months to come did I find his wit and humour fail."* Humour was one of the bonds between Indians and British and particularly between the British and the tribes.

Idu piloted the car into the fort at Saindak. Next day, they went on to Robat where the officer, Major Landon, whom Dyer was to relieve, was seriously ill. Major Landon was an officer in the 35th Scinde Horse and, with two others, was employed as an Intelligence Officer in Persia by the Indian Government. Major Landon later wrote *"I have read through the General's 'Raiders of the Sarhad' again and of course he minimises his own action. For instance the journey across the desert to Robat was an amazing feat, through the most difficult country and with no guide. At that time, the road was practically non-existent and obliterated by very big sand hills."*

The posts that had initially been set up years before, to protect India from the Russian threat to India, had been used in a counter strategy, turning the corner of Afghanistan. The chain went as far as Robat, Nasratabad and Birjand. The Raiders had managed to isolate them and, by holding up the caravans, almost starve them out. Effectively they were under siege, interest of course, being loot. Colonel Dyer's own kit, his charger, Galahad, and spare tyres had been looted, and an indication of the terrifying behaviour of the Tribesmen was shown by the treatment of Dyer's syce, stripped and tortured to the extent that he was a broken man and could never work again. The tribes, like the Afghans, mutilated the bodies of dead and wounded when their owners were beyond defending themselves, under the belief that mutilated, they would remain dead in the afterlife. Kipling knew about this, for it is touched on in his poem about the soldiers in Afghanistan.

> *'When you're wounded and lie on Afghanistan's plains*
> *And the women come out to cut up what remains*
> *Just roll to your rifle and blow out your brains,*
> *And go to your Gawd like a soldier,*
> *(Refrain) Go to your Gawd like a soldier.*

From Jalk in the East to Galugah in the West, the Sarhad was inhabited by the tribes of the Raiders, the Gamshadzais, the Yarmohammedzais in the centre, while in the West were Ismailzais. The leaders were respectively, Halil Khan, Jiand Khan and Juma Khan. Jiand was acknowledged overlord and was the oldest. It was his fort at Khwash (which means sweet water) that was the capital and the centre of the Sarhad.

Each tribe held about a thousand families and could muster about 2,000 fighting men. Armed by the Germans with Mauser rifles, they were nomads, living in camel hair tents with camels, herds of goats and slaves. They were of the Sunni sect, which was useful when the dissension between the Sunnis and Shias led to help being forthcoming.

Tom Rogers, visiting Nasir Khan, head of the Qashqai tribe in the 1940s, described the way of life. *"At the time I met Nasir, his tribe was on the annual migration from winter quarters around Firuzabad in the lower lying areas of the Fars province in the high mountain valleys lying North-West and now free of winter snow. To the outsider, this ancient twice yearly mass migration up and down the mountains was a stirring spectacle. Attended by drovers on foot or horseback, great flocks of sheep and goats moved slowly along traditional tracks away from roads. Not far away trailed a long line of camels, mules and donkeys carrying the tribe's belongings, tents, household equipment of every kind (the 'house' of course being a tent), food and personal possessions. In nests of rugs on camels lolled women and children in bright tribal dress alongside lambs or kids too young to walk, or lame. On horseback along the lines of animals moved tribesmen with their rifles, their shining bandoliers as much a token of virility as armament. It was a marvellous experience to see so old a way of life pass by.*

*With a companion, I was a hundred miles or so North of Bushire when a mounted Qashqai tribesman approached. He informed me that Nasir Khan had made a halt nearby and expressed readiness to see us. I knew three things about the Qashqai. They supported the Germans in the 1914-18 war, they continued to be well disposed towards them between the wars; and now they were thought to be in touch again. I thought this a good reason for not shunning Nasir. Nasir's home for the night was an oblong tent of dark goat-hair cloth with vertical sidewalls, one open to the air. There were one or two bright tribal rugs of the Turkish pattern that came with the tribe from central Asia some 700 years ago. Nasir was shown to be ready to receive German forces in the event of a breakthrough in the Caucasus. He had even prepared some landing grounds and planned others. We also had evidence that some senior Persian officers were plotting with him. In the 1914-18 war, the alterations of the roads by our troops were decided less by sound road engineering than immediate tactical needs. The troops were the South Persia Rifles formed to move against the Qashkai* and other tribal elements working with some first class German agents such as *Wasmuss, Zugmayer and Niedermayer."*

The men were fine-looking, slim and graceful with fine intelligent faces and aquiline features; their women were often good looking and unveiled. The name 'Raiders' came from their means of livelihood, raiding villages and towns as far away as Meshed. 'They know no fear and seldom show mercy' and they were the terror of the country. Their own country was sparsely cultivated, crossed by range after range of bare volcanic hills with rugged peaks and precipitous sides of which the Koh-I-Taftan stood out at over thirteen thousand feet.

In order to force the hands of the tribes, Colonel Dyer ordered a Durbar, to be held at Kacha. Only the pro-British Rekis arrived. Dyer, as always ingenious, decided that the only way to make an impression was to become a General. He wired to Simla with this request and in the meantime, cut up bits of red cloth to put on his shoulders in as near as possible the conventional form. Landon became his Brigade Major, although stipulating that this must be on Dyer's own head.

Having his tabs in place, he asked Idu to spread the news that a famous British General had arrived with a large force of 5,000 fully armed troops. It was to be made clear that the General was angered at the disobedience of the tribes, and he was going to attack them, marching first against Halil Khan and in the direction of Jalk. The telegram went from Persia by devious ways, the wires not being cut, as later in India, because the tribesmen believed that the wires were inhabited by devils which if let loose, might attack them.

His vast troop was made up of forces from the garrisons of Nasratabad, Robat and Kacha. They consisted of two mountain guns, seventeen sowars of the 28th Light Cavalry, nine trained soldiers, sixty five raw recruits and two maxim guns of the 12th Pioneers, about fifteen of Idu's Chagai Levies, and around fifty unarmed Rekis. With this tiny force were six hundred camels, carrying supplies for the troops and fodder for the horses and camels. With all these, Brigadier General Dyer, having received his promotion, marched towards Khwash, having set out from Ladis on 8th April 1916.

Eighteen miles further and on the following day, scouts reported Jiand Khan, the leader of the Yarmuhammedzais and overlord of the Sarhad, on the spurs of Koh-I-Taftan, encamped with about 2,000 men. In a strong position, Jiand put Dyer in a situation of some danger.

General Dyer's first step was to put the 65 untrained infantry in charge of the camels. The mountain guns were brought up on low hills to the left; the two machine guns in the centre; and the cavalry moved forward under cover on the right. Deployed, they saw a man coming towards them with a white flag. Jiand had sent one of his greatest chiefs, Shah Sawar, a relative, to ask Dyer to a conference. If the General, accompanied by only one man, would advance towards Jiand's army, Jiand would meet him to confer.

The belief spread by Idu's men, that Dyer had 5,000 men behind him (the camel train had become an imaginary army) had been accepted by Jiand. If he had allowed any delay, the truth about his forces would have been bound to become known, so Dyer refused to agree to a conference. He sent back the message that he would give the messenger time to return to Jiand but then he would fire a shot into the air and hostilities would begin. By no means would he spend time on a conference with a scoundrel like Jiand.

The bluff began to work immediately. Shah Sawar asked to remain with Dyer, since it seemed safer than to be among the Yarmuhammedzais and Jiand. The man with him was sent back to Jiand with the message.

Colonel Landon later described the position among the low hills taken up by Dyer. *"The shallow and wide nullahs descending from Koh-I-Taftan crossed our line of march like huge ocean waves, very good objectives for advancing by leaps and bounds and equally good for retirement."*

The continued need for the deception of the size of his force led to positioning the little army so that Lieutenant Hirst with his 17 cavalrymen could be shown on the top of the hill, the hidden ground behind them covering the scarcity of numbers. These men were to feint to the left flank and rear of Jiand's force. The big horses held a brave appearance as they topped the hills. As soon as the shot had been fired, the cavalry moved rapidly to the right, the machine guns opened fire, the infantry (consisting of nine trained men and a handful of Chagai levies) rushed forward in the centre. Dyer's entire army was involved in the attack – about 50 men with guns and, of course, the 17 horses.

Jiand's fire was rapid but inaccurate. The machine guns and the mountain guns got the enemy's range and the cavalry turned Jiand's left flank. Panic ensued. Jiand, persuaded that this vast army was upon him, mounted his camel and told his men to scatter and run. Dyer and his officers following as they were, mounted and firing revolvers into the press, soon found themselves with no one to chase and an almost bloodless victory.

The victory resounded throughout the Sarhad. Jiand and his forces had been beaten and the re-assembly of those forces took time. Jiand had been taken in; the speed of the attack and the bluffs had won, but only for as long as the tribes did not know the bluff itself.

Dyer, pressing on behind the fugitives, was unable to catch Jiand, who fled into the Morpeish Hills. Knowing that any slackening of pressure would give time for his bluff to be called, he advanced to the cultivated land of the Yarmuhammedzais where their barley and wheat were growing, still green, before sending a message that if Jiand and his men did not surrender, 500 camels would be let loose on the crop, the food for their flocks and their families for the winter. Dyer saw to it that their women and children, who had been abandoned by their men folk and were found hiding nearby; were given assurance and food and water. He assured Jiand that he and his men would be treated honourably as prisoners.

Colonel Landon again: *"He had a great ability for understanding the point of view of the tribesmen he was fighting, and in general he had a great sympathy with them. His humanity was very marked and caused wonderment in the tribes. For example, his refusal to bombard (with two guns) the remnant of the Yarmuhammedzais who had taken refuge in a bolt hole in the Morpeish Hills after their first defeat, and whose women and children could not climb out."*

The message about the crops being eaten by the camels was bracketed with an order to Jiand to surrender before the time limit ran out. Jiand sent a message of surrender and shortly after, arrived on a camel with a few attendants. He was a striking man, with the same hawk-like features as the others of his kind. Both Dyer and Landon described him as 'a very striking figure, very like a nasty unclean vulture.' At this time he was broken with humiliation and loss, for among the 11 men killed in the fight was his son. Typically, Dyer treated him with courtesy and sympathy, but pointed out the folly of his betrayal of his ancient friendship with the British and his new links with the Germans, whose stories, Dyer made plain, were lies. He demanded the return of the Government camels and stores as well as his own kit that had been captured between Nushki and Robat. The meeting took some time and while it went on, Jiand was looking about him for the vast army of 5,000. Said Dyer, it was not the army that the man saw, but merely the advance guard, arrived to take Jiand prisoner.

The plan that continued to affect the minds of the Sarhadis was the claim of Idu's men that they had been defeated by the General and his vast force; they now claimed that there was going to be an attack on Halil Khan and his people. As a result, Khwash was open to Dyer with a much smaller force than would otherwise have collected to defend it, so the next step would be Khwash.

Jiand, allowed to keep his arms, was kept on parole; he swore on behalf of himself and his tribe on the Koran that he would never raise a hand against the British Raj again.

The next step became urgent as news came in that Halil Khan and his Gamshadzais were on their way to help Jiand. Dyer sent a message to Muhammad Hassan, the commander of Khwash, to say he would be arriving shortly, that Jiand and Shah Sawar were prisoners in his hands and unless he surrendered the town by noon, Dyer would blow it to the skies. The story that had reached Muhammad Hassan was exaggerated by the tribesmen themselves, in order to excuse Jiand's surrender, so a further 16 miles' march saw Dyer at the new camp at Khwash, with Muhammad Hassan's herald and envoy waving white flags.

Muhammad Hassan had heard all about the defeat of his chief, saw the stupidity of attempting resistance and willingly surrendered himself and his fort.

The Yarmuhammedzais garrison marched out as Dyer marched in. The 70 yards square fort, with loop-holed thick mud outer walls 30-foot high, had two strong gates. It would have been almost impossible to breach the walls by assault and the quiet surrender was something of a miracle.

That evening, Halil Khan arrived with 50 of his men, armed with the inevitable Mauser rifles, and also surrendered. Resolute and intelligent, Halil was particularly interested to know how Jiand had been defeated and the whereabouts of the 'vast British forces'. He was left guessing. Dyer then took the next step in his dangerous game. he called a durbar of the leaders and harangued them, asking them where were the Germans, their allies, and as for the claim that the Germans had become Mussulman, he would give them a lakh of rupees for each German they found who had converted. The truth was that the Turks had become Germans, taking orders from their new masters, drinking wines and doing other things against the Koran. The Sheriff of Mecca was their true spiritual leader and he was on the British side. Could they not see that the Sirkar was their true friend; that their interests lay on the side of the British?

But for Idu, the General might have believed that the tribesmen had turned away from their previous misdeeds, but Idu with his spies moving about among the tribesmen, warned Dyer that they were resentful and vindictive and would turn as soon as they had an opportunity. They were already suspicious and if they discovered the truth of the trick worked on them, he might be certain of their hostility.

With Shah Sawar and his men as advance guards, Halil and his Gamshadzais on the left and Jiand with his Yarmuhammedzais on his right, all as far apart as possible, with the Rekis left in charge of Khwash, Dyer set out to attack Juma Khan at Galugan. The placing of these men was due to his attempts to disguise the paucity of his own forces, and to keep those men on parole as far away from each other as possible. The infantry went with the baggage and the cavalry and a few infantrymen with the General as his personal escort.

One other chief remained, the Raja of Bampur. To him went Idu's spies, telling him of the power and intention of the British, the spies themselves once again appearing as fugitives, terrified by what they had seen. The Raja was so frightened that he fled from the imaginary British Army approaching his stronghold, to the British Political Officer at Makran on the shores of the Persian Gulf and threw himself at his feet. The force with Dyer made a forced march of five days to Galugan on short rations, only to find that Juma Khan had fled to the hills surrounding the place. The same message as had been sent to Jiand was sent to Juma, and the chief came in to make a submission. The General liked the look of Juma, whom he described as a man with a very pleasing well-cut, high-bred face, always full of smiles and laughter, as though life were one huge joke. Idu also liked him, saying: *"If Juma Khan gives you his oath on the Koran he will keep it."*

The Sarhardar, who had also helped Dyer continually; now warned him that returning to his base at Kacha with all the tribesmen on parole, was by no means safe or secure. The weather was hot; food supplies were running short and there were 80 miles between him and Kacha. The chiefs were afraid of being driven into a trap at Kacha and every night mutiny was expected from them. With shortage of water, brackish when available, they nonetheless won through and found in the fort an ample supply of food and fresh water at last. Dyer felt that the only hope for a permanent solution was to cement friendship with the tribes, and he ordered another durbar with the heads of the tribes and their associates. Again he pointed out the folly of putting their trust in the Germans and he put before them a document, beautifully drawn up by the Sarhardar, pledging loyalty, promising to hand over information about the Germans and handing over their overlordship to the Sirkar. Thumbprints were put on the documents; oaths taken on the Koran, large presents of money were handed over and the tribesmen were given permission to return to their homes.

Dyer then sat down to write his report to Simla. With a handful of men, he had subdued the Sarhad and secured a treaty which should clear up the problems for the future. Raiding did not only affect the British, for it also encompassed massive raids on Persian towns and villages with the removal of women and children as slaves. One such raid had just been carried out by the Yarmuhammadzais, and it seemed possible that this aspect of the activities might now be cleaned up to the benefit of all.

## THE SARHAD CAMPAIGN

As he was ending his report, Idu burst into the room to say that, hardly had Jiand left Kacha than he had called a meeting of the Raider chiefs and their men and ordered an immediate attack on Khwash, where they would attack the General's force which they had realised was contemptibly small.

All had agreed except Juma Khan, who said that the British General had treated them well, had spared their lives and their crops and had given them gifts, so he rode off with his followers into his own country.

Landon and the Sarhardar agreed to Dyer's next plan: Since Jiand would take some time to collect his forces, there was just time to begin the march back to Khwash on the following day. To get their forces in order and defend Khwash, Landon would lead the army to Khwash in seven days while Dyer and Idu, taking the armoured car, which Jiand and his men would believe to be some emanation of the devil and which Dyer considered would be more useful then seven guns, would proceed by a more circuitous route to Khwash.

Allan met them nine miles out of Kacha, having been at Robat until then with the car. Another difficulty arose, when Idu, believing that the car was up to anything, led them into a ravine in which the car could neither go forward nor turn, and they had to dig a hole through the wall of the ravine. With endless pushing and heaving, and a long hairpin loop in the route, they managed to get to the rendezvous with Landon on time.

Parting in the morning, they continued their different and extremely difficult ways. Dyer spent a night with Idu's Rekis, before meeting another group of Rekis on camels and persuading them to join forces. This group told them that Jiand was advancing with a big army and was probably already at Khwash.

Idu's eyes picked out a distant band of 18 Yarmuhammedzais under Izzat, one of the raider leaders, recently returned from a raid in Persia, who had been sent to reconnoitre by Jiand. Idu, wily as ever, showed himself a true diplomat. After concealing his own party in a ravine, he himself wriggled out and told Izzat much the same story that had been told before with the addition of the Overlander armoured car whose radiator holes, he claimed, would fire bullets at the press of a button. *"I have come to save your lives. If I return and tell him you are going to fight, you are all dead."*

By these and other stories Idu reduced Izzat to such fear that he made abject surrender. Izzat said Jiand would be at Khwash the following day

It was typical of General Dyer that he did not wait any longer but, although the sun was setting, he decided to set out and push on overnight. A terrible march ensued. With the help of the Rekis and Izzat's men, the car was dragged with a rope, pushed through hills and nullahs, then through terrain of up-ended blocks of quartz which ripped the tyres and tubes and they had to keep stopping for Allan to renew these, muttering the while that he was of the bulldog breed and would not give up. In the sweltering heat they dragged the car even on its rims, until Allan, nodding off as the sun rose, the car went over the hillside into a nullah. But in the plain below, five miles away, Khwash could be seen. The car had to be abandoned; they rode into Khwash on camels, Izzat being made to ride beside Dyer for fear of treachery. A sentry (one of the five infantrymen), standing on top of one of the towers, received the General's wave with much joy. He came rushing out and told them to hurry, as Shah Sawar was camping nearby with a large force. With Izzat beside him and his followers in the square, Dyer occupied the highest tower. Idu was sent again on his efforts at subversion, this time to Shah Sawar. Meanwhile, a message was sent to Major Landon to push his cavalry forward at the fastest pace.

Again Idu practiced his gentle persuasions, this time on Jiand, telling him that Shah Sawar and Izzat had surrendered; tales of the devil-filled cars and that their treachery had enraged the General - enough of the same to delay Jiand from attacking that night, with the result that he just lost the golden moment. The little garrison at Khwash, looking out anxiously for the cavalry under Landon as the morning broke, saw a figure riding fast towards them. It was the Sarhadar, Khan Bahadur, full of energy and character, a marvellous man, riding ahead of the army at risk to his life.

Then the dust of the approaching cavalry, infantry, guns and camels, approached and they entered the fort with a sigh of relief - the fort was safe.

There was nothing left for Jiand but once again to make submission. Then came Halil Khan, submission from them all, protestations of loyalty, everything – to an extent where Dyer thought it worthwhile asking them if they would like to provide a corps of levies with the chiefs as officers, the pay would be good. They pretended to agree. Halil begged to be allowed to return to his family. The General agreed but before he left warned him, looking straight in the man's eyes, *"Halil Khan, if you play me false, or even raise your hand against me again, I will blow off your head."* Halil Khan pulled the Koran from under his robe and swore upon it that he would never fight the General Sahib again.

Jiand Khan, again asked to return the booty he had captured; miscellaneous loot including Government camels, the General's own kit and four (very much needed) tyres, together with four hundred Afghan camels finally produced them.

In the quiet weeks that followed, Dyer blew up the outer walls and the three smaller towers of Khwash, substituting trenches as outer defences, reinforced the tall tower and mounted a machine-gun on top, created an extensive vegetable garden to supplement the rations and obtained reinforcements of a squadron of the 28th Light Cavalry. However, this increased the shortage of animal feed and urgent action was required if the garrison was not to be starved out. An appeal to Jiand to share the crops which had earlier been spared was turned down flat.

Dyer then thought of Murad, a chief who had been ousted by Jiand and who was at Kursimabad, another fertile valley. From him, he was offered as much bhusa as he liked for nothing. With this offer came the warning not to trust Jiand with his plots and evil intentions.

News came in of letters from Shah Sawar to the Germans, begging them to come to the aid of the tribes and telling them that the British had only tiny forces. Shah Sawar's letters to the Germans had just been intercepted; his submission was protested yet again. For Jiand, he had to watch and wait, but Shah Sawar was tried by a drumhead court martial and sentenced to death. His wife came to Dyer and begged for his life, saying she would see to it that he did not play false again. This was the Gul-Bibi, the most beautiful woman in the Sarhad, or possibly in the world. Idu as usual played his part. He had seen that Dyer had observed that Shah Sawar was sweating and, although resigned to his fate, carried himself with dignity. Idu went and told the Gul-Bibi that her husband had been tried and was due to die, but remarked that, of course, Dyer did not really wish to have the man killed. She ran to Dyer and threw herself at his feet and begged him to save her husband saying she would go bail for him. *"I swear to you that if ever my fool husband raises his hand against you again or breaks his word to you, I will shoot him with my own hands. I the Gul-Bibi swear it."* This was the woman who was so beautiful that Shah Sawar had given up Khwash for her.

In this war of troubles, the next step by Jiand and his men was to burn down the stacks of Murad's bhusa. Dyer had to go to Kursimabad to get this desperately important matter cleared up. Although by this time, Landon had returned to his position as Intelligence Officer in Persia, having been replaced by Major Sanders of the 36th Sikhs, some of Landon's Intelligence men had discovered that Jiand intended to attack and capture the General when he went to Kursimabad.

Murad knew that Jiand's men had been responsible for the burning of the bhusa. Dyer set out with a small escort with as many guns as could be safely taken from the fort. Five miles from Kursimabad they came across Jiand with a large force. Surprised at the size and strength of Dyer's escort, he sent a messenger to ask if he could come in and pay Dyer his respects and having arrived on his camel, he claimed he had nothing to do with the burning of the bhusa. Dyer held to his intention and said he was riding to Kursimabad to enquire into the matter and that Jiand should come there for his case to be heard. At the entrance to Kursimabad, surrounded by standing crops, was a large tree with a mud platform over its roots which seemed the most suitable place for the court hearing, so he sat with Major Sanders on one side of him, the Sarhadar on the other.

Murad came first saying that the bhusa had been burnt, and producing a Yarmuhammedzai, whom he had captured and whom he knew had done it. As Murad brought the man forward, the crops suddenly erupted with armed men from every quarter. More than 200 men sat with their rifles on their knees, surrounding Dyer, who realised that he had made a tactical error in leaving his small troops three-quarters of a mile away. His 12 infantrymen were on his right; his cavalry were dismounted behind the tree with their rifles in buckets on their horses, but with their lances in their hands.

General Dyer had fallen into a trap. He knew it - they all knew it, though not one man showed it by the quiver of an eyelid. Proceeding with the inquiry, he asked Murad's prisoner why and by whose orders he had burnt the bhusa. Nur Mohammed sprang up and shouted defiance, saying that the country being theirs, they had the right to burn bhusa or anything else. Dyer told him to sit down, but Nur-Mohammed replied with a sneer and a threat. Dyer ordered his arrest, but as the sepoy stepped forward, every Yarmuhammedzai sprang to his feet with his rifle at the present. The General, in a fury and calling them dogs, reached out a hand caught hold of Jiand Khan and forced him to the ground at his side. The Yarmuhammadzais looked at their chief, now old and who had lost his nerve and sat cowering. Hesitation and doubt spread among the threatening crowd and most of them sat down. On a swift order from Dyer, Major Sanders and the escort sprang forward and disarmed the men who remained standing and those sitting down were told to pile their rifles against a nearby wall. Like sheep they obeyed and all was over. He then told the Yarmuhammadzais that he had had enough of them, and to his escort, he gave the order for their arrest. Many of them ran away, but 60 were taken and bound in threes with their own turbans and marched off to camp. Dyer later said that his action had been almost unconscious – it had not been planned. The fact of the matter was that it saved his life and that of his men.

Dyer then sent to Quetta for orders for dealing with the prisoners. While waiting for a reply, he set about freeing the Persians who were slaves with the tribesmen. By offering to buy the slaves on fixed terms he freed a large number. They had little in the way of clothing and material was commandeered from Kacha for this purpose; he carefully restored the health of those who were sick or starving and organised a caravan to take them back to their homes. He made a list of them to which each appended his thumb print and sent them off with Izzat on the understanding that if they were not safely returned to their homes, Izzat and his family would be punished in their place. It was ordered that the prisoners should be sent back to Saindak where the Hazara Pioneers would guard them until taken to Quetta. The prisoners, 47 in number, including Jiand and his son and some of the most dangerous chiefs of the Sarhad were sent off for the nine days march from Khwash to Saindak. They were accompanied by the maximum guard he could spare - three troops of cavalry, 75 infantry and two maxims under two British officers. This was three-quarters of his entire force.

On a morning in July 1916 they started off, pitching their camp on a hillside with a rough zareba of barbed wire round the prisoners, all except Jiand and his son, placed inside with sentries over them. In the middle of the night, the sentries, hearing stealthy sounds from the enclosure, fired into the darkness. The whole camp was roused, lamps were brought, the officers rushed to the zareba and to their horror, found it empty. The prisoners had flung their clothes over the barbed wire, borne down and broken it with their weight and escaped naked into the hills.

At two o'clock the next morning, a weary sowar rode into Khwash and gave the General the disastrous news. Disastrous indeed; for Quetta had sent 300 Hazara Pioneers to Saindak to escort the prisoners and a wireless troop was at that moment coming to Khwash and would now be in danger. Dyer himself would have to suffer the sarcasm of the people at headquarters, but worst of all, the whole campaign had rested on prestige and that had virtually been destroyed.

The next fear was that Halil Khan and his Gamshadzais would join with the escaped prisoners to rescue Jiand Khan, so Dyer had to take immediate action. With Idu, the Sarhadar and Major Sanders, he set out with the very few men he could spare from the garrison. That evening, they had a rendezvous with the escort and re-arranged the forces. He took 25 of the cavalry, 50 of the infantry, and two machine guns, ordering the officer in command of the escort to intercept the wireless troop, take them along to Saindak and there hand over Jiand Khan and his son to the Hazaras. He himself, with his fighting force, made a night march of 12 miles to Kamalabad to intercept Halil Khan who he felt certain would attempt a rescue of Jiand and his son.

He was so nearly successful. Halil Khan, who had been born at Kamalabad, left the place to flee into the hills and Dyer comforted himself that at least Jiand Khan would be safe at Saindak in a short time, but another messenger then arrived, saying that Jiand Khan and his son had actually been snatched.

Only later did he discover what had happened. 19 of the escaped Yarmuhammadzais had run, naked as they were, to Kamalabad, where they clothed and armed themselves, returning to the rescue of their chief. They had attacked the weakened escort and after a long fight, in which many on the British side were killed and the two British officers wounded, they went off carrying Jiand Khan and his son, many of the rifles and much ammunition with them.

What remained of the escort would certainly have been massacred if they had not met up with the wireless troop and its escort, which were thought to be the advance guard of reinforcements. It turned out that the escort, entering a defile where the cavalry who had been the flanking party in the plain could no longer operate, the infantry, being dead beat, had neglected to throw out adequate flanking parties.

He returned to Khwash and sent out all the men he could spare (a small detachment of cavalry and infantry) to bring in the wireless troop and the remainder of the prisoners' escort, dispatching a camel messenger to the officer commanding the Hazaras asking him to join, if possible, with Colonel Claridge and bring his force to Khwash.

Jiand Khan, with a large force took up his station three miles to the North-East of Khwash and Shah Sawar, the man whose life had been spared, worried the garrison from the hills to the South-West. They attacked at night.

In order to keep up the appearance of the garrison being well manned, Dyer had kept them on the outer defences during the day but at night, they were withdrawn into a small fortified area, with the two maxim guns trained on the empty camp, one from the fortified sector and one from the remaining tower. When the enemy attacked, they swarmed into the empty camp expecting to find the garrison, but were instead met with emptiness and heavy rifle and Maxim–gun fire. In the darkness, they managed to withdraw with their dead and wounded, but did not repeat the attempt.

Colonel Claridge in the meantime, pushing out warily and swiftly, overtook the escort, joined up with the officers commanding the Hazaras and took command of the column now escorting the wireless troop. Some days later, he came with the whole column safely into Khwash.

General Dyer now felt himself able to take the field. Jiand Khan meanwhile had withdrawn to beyond Kamalabad, to the Sar-i-Droken valley on the farther side of the Morpeish Hills.

On 28th July, with the 300 Hazaras, two mountain guns and two machine guns, together with a squadron of cavalry and some Rekis, General Dyer set out. Colonel Claridge was left at Khwash and with his force, Dyer took the British officers, Major Sanders (Brigade Major), Major Lang, Captain Moor-Lane, Lieutenant Bream of the Hazaras, Lieutenant English with the guns, and Captain Brownlow in command of the cavalry. At Khwash, Colonel Claridge's careful deployment of his remnant of the original force and his two machine guns, prevented any further attack; but he did manage to discover the man who had been giving the Raiders information and by making him a prisoner, stopped further leaks.

Jiand had placed his flocks in a valley some 75 miles long, guarded on one side by the precipitous Morpeish Hills and by the Sar-i-Droken range on the other. The valley could only be entered through a narrow gorge called Dast Kird in the North-West, or equally almost impossible of access and easy to defend, on the South-East end at a place called Gusht. Idu pointed out that if Dyer attacked one end the valley, the herds could be sent out of the other, when the way would lie open to Khwash. Since Gusht lay on the border of Gamshadzai country, Halil would probably join in Jiand's fray and an independent chief at Gusht would undoubtedly join in if he thought there was a chance of the Hazaras being defeated.

General Dyer made his camp at Kamalabad, with the Morpeish Hills between him and the Sar-i-Droken valley. He knew that from the hills he was being watched by hundreds of pairs of eyes; being a man of ingenuity, this gave him an idea. Just before nightfall, he ordered Captain Brownlow to advance in the direction of Dast Kird, making as big a show as possible, before returning after nightfall as quietly and quickly as possible. Brownlow, working with his General's intentions, at the farthest corner of his march collected and lit piles of brushwood that flamed into the night. The impression given to Halil Khan was that the whole force was camping there on its way to the Dast Kird.

Jiand Khan fell into the trap and sending his flocks in the direction of Gusht, he marched all night to Dast Kird. In the meanwhile, together with the returned cavalry, General Dyer set out for Gusht.

*"I think"* said Major Yeates, *"one of General Dyer's most noticeable characteristics was his friendliness and accessibility to everyone in his force. He was always ready to listen to anyone's suggestions, whether he was a commanding officer or a lousy Baluchi tribesman. I remember when he was contemplating forcing the defile beyond Gusht and committing his force to a march of some forty miles through extremely difficult and almost unknown country, he called up the senior officer of the Hazara Pioneers and discussed it thoroughly with him. The result was that the*

*Hazaras felt it a matter of personal honour that the column should go through. Not that he was liable to be unduly swayed by his advisers. Once he had made up his mind, no man could be more unshakeable in carrying out his plans. He always seemed to have a complete grip of the situation and be ready for any emergency. If a messenger came to his tent at 3 a.m. with unexpected information, he would issue the necessary orders without hesitation or waste of time - he never was at a loss for some expedient."*

All soldiers must admire the beauty and simplicity of the particular piece of strategy which evoked this encomium. General Dyer set the two forces, his own and the enemy's, marching in opposite directions. While Jiand was pressing along the 15-mile road to Dast Kird, the British column was getting well on its way over the much greater distance that separated Kamalabad from Gusht. By the time Jiand had discovered his mistake, the General (on the other side of the range) had gained two marches.

Says Lieutenant Colonel Landon, *"By that ruse, General Dyer, after marching three days (somewhere between forty and sixty miles), reached the Gusht defile ahead, but not very far ahead of Jiand Khan. He would have found it difficult to force the passage had he been opposed since the opening into these precipitous and rocky hills was very narrow with an isolated pimple crowned by a mud fort in the middle. The spurs rose steeply from the nullah bed, and were 2000 odd feet above it – stiff climbing on an August day..."* As it was, he received a cordial welcome from the local chief and made an unopposed passage through the defile. The Yarmuhammadzais, making a desperate effort to recover their lost advantage, arrived the same night at a point only five miles down the valley.

They were from 1,000 to 1,500 strong and there were besides, as the chief of Gusht told the General, Halil Khan with his Gamshadzais only two marches away to the North.

That night the column encamped by a fine kareze or water channel, three miles along the valley, and next morning marched three miles farther, in the face of sniping which grew hotter as it advanced, and encamped again in a strong position near a spring. Halil, as the General knew, intended to join Jiand, which would give Jiand at least another 1,000 men, and the General decided to attack the Gamshadzai position before they came together.

Next morning at five o'clock, this attack was begun – up the hillside towards a defile called Saragan; but the defence was so strong and the ground so difficult that by eleven o'clock the main body had advanced only half a mile, and the General, seeing the attack must fail, withdrew his forces – not without some loss – under a covering fire from the Maxim and mountain guns. In the meantime, a body of the enemy descending from the hills had attacked the picket post guarding the spring where the column had camped and captured the position. The General himself with Brownlow and a dozen cavalrymen, rode forward to gain this vital point, were met by a heavy fire, but dismounted without loss, attacked and retook the picket post.

'Then Dyer, realising how difficult it was to reach the enemy in the hills, decided to remain in the open and await developments. He had brought food for a month; the enemy had only sufficient food for four or five days and were, besides, prodigal with their ammunition at long range. Reckoning that the disparity in strength would tempt them to attack, he chose the strong position where he had first encamped within the valley, and there resolved to wait. As he made his short retreat to this position the enemy pressed in upon the sides, showing him that he was surrounded, and promising to spare his life if he would surrender. They had occupied a little mud fort on a hillock near the gorge and commanding the camping ground, but were driven out of it by Lieutenant English with his mountain guns.

Under the lee of this hillock and owing to the convex shape of the neighbouring hills, the encampment could not well be sniped. There were however some low hills running out from the sides of the gorge in which an enemy might collect and from which he might attempt a night assault. From that quarter the General expected the attack, and accordingly under cover of darkness, he placed two strong pickets, each of 50 men, on either side of a little valley which led towards his position.

While Dyer was making these arrangements Halil had arrived at Jiand's camp with his men and had harangued the Yarmuhammadzais on their lack of enterprise against such an inferior force. *"If Jiand Khan had lost his nerve, then Halil would lead them to victory."* To this Jiand agreed; for being old and weary, he did not want to carry on. Halil was so convinced that he would succeed that he wrote to the Khan of Bampor saying Dyer was already a prisoner in his hands and inviting the Khan to come and share in the loot. Leading only the Yarmuhammadzais into the hollow below where Dyer had secretly posted his pickets, he then prepared to rush the camp at dawn.

The Yarmuhammadzais moved as silently as cats in the darkness. They were not aware of the pickets, nor the pickets aware of them until just before daybreak when, an enemy rifle going off by accident, the pickets fired into the hollow. Dyer rushed out of his tent knowing that what he had provided for had come about. Instantly he gave orders that every man in the camp should reinforce the pickets.

As the shadows of night lifted from the valley, Halil Khan and his men were completely exposed to the concentrated fire from above. They fought desperately, but by eleven o'clock the fight was over and such of the enemy as remained alive were in full flight.

*"Halil Khan"* wrote Lieutenant Colonel Langdon, *"poked his head over a stone of his sangar and a bullet hit the stone, mushroomed and took the top of his head off."* The body was found below in the hollow. One of the Rekis remembered Dyer's words at the Durbar in Khwash and the story was told that the General Sahib was a prophet and had kept his word.

But that was not the end of Halil Khan; an Indian Officer of the Hazaras came to Dyer and told him that since the Yarmuhammadzais had dug up the bodies of the Hazara and hideously mutilated them, it was fitting that they should do the same to the body of Halil Khan. Dyer asked the officer who had killed the man - the answer came that it was the Sahib. *"Then,"* said Dyer, *"to whom does the body belong, to you or to me?"* The Hazara replied: *"To you, Sahib."*

In accordance with the courtesy of his behaviour throughout his life, he then gave Halil Khan a full soldier's burial, calling in mullahs to carry out the rituals. The Hazara Officer was sent to Gusht for a new winding sheet.

Dyer was a dedicated Christian, much as many people were at that time and there is the story of his insistence on the Officers of his Regiment going to church parade since he considered it should not be merely the Other Ranks who were required to attend. He also knew and respected the religions of others.

The battle of Dast Kird was not the end of the fight. The Gamshadzais were still not defeated even though their leader had been killed. Firstly, the tradition of the Sarhad that the victor in a fight had to take the flocks of his defeated enemy had to be fulfilled. The column had to make three days march to find and collect the flocks and herds - three days with almost no water, before marching back to Khwash.

To defeat the Gamshadzais finally, General Dyer set out again with an additional small force of a few Chaghai levies under Major Hutchinson.

Again there was a dreadful march in the blazing heat; this time after two days they arrived at a small valley surrounded by hills, in the bottom a small water hole and a few stunted trees. Exhausted with their march and the setting up of their camp, the men threw themselves on the ground to rest. Even the General, taking advantage of a small bush, dropped down and slept till well into the afternoon. Never quite off duty, on seeing two flashes of lightning, he recognised the signs of rain. The area where they were had been marched over by Alexander the Great in ancient times and a large part of his army had been swept away by a sudden flood. Dyer may not have known about that event, but, though overhead there was a blue sky and his men were sure there would be no rain, Dyer insisted on the bulk of them removing their tents from the valley and erecting them higher on the side of the hill. They grumbled bitterly, fatigued and complaining that it was not necessary, but Dyer insisted, saying that the valley would be turned upside down, so sulky they might have been, but they had to obey. Hutchinson, dozing in his tent at the bottom of the valley, was also recalcitrant, murmuring sleepily that it never rained in Baluchistan in August and again, Dyer had to insist. All, save a handful of men including some Chagai levies unnoticed behind some bushes, moved.

Quite suddenly with a roar, a flood swept down the valley, filling it from side to side. The levies and the Sarhadar, who had remained below, climbed into the branches of some stunted trees out of the flood; their kit left behind. The Sarhadar was rescued by a Reki, who, mounting his horse, forced it into the flood and reached the tree where he was hanging. In the morning the General awoke to find the Hazaras crowding round his tent waiting to thank him for saving their lives and hailing him as a prophet. The evidence was clear – upside down trees proved that he had spoke truly when he said *"The valley will be turned upside down."*

The column went by way of Gusht to Zaiti, climbing uphill from 5 a.m. until midnight. The Gamshadzais occupied two strong forts at Jalk; 11 miles ahead, when a message arrived asking for terms and suggesting withdrawal on both sides. Always keen to avoid unnecessary bloodshed, Dyer agreed, but the hotheads among the enemy refused to agree his terms.

A short withdrawal by Dyer was interpreted to mean that there would be no immediate attack, but he divided his force into two parts; one encampment was the transport with a sufficient guard, the other a striking force, which was quietly roused at midnight and marched off without anyone knowing what it was about. Before dawn, the force was outside the town of Jalk, and as the cavalry charged through the town, the enemy taken completely by surprise ran out the other side, leaving behind many of their rifles with the women and children.

Thus was peace restored to the Sarhad. Again and again Dyer had been forced to take the action that he disliked in order to bring the tribes to their senses and make the Sarhad safe against German infiltration. Only the Rekis and Juma Khan had realised that he wished for peace and had shown themselves capable of reliable agreement. Dyer said *"No race, white or coloured, ever held in respect man or government showing weakness or indecision, and it was a little use attempting to make friends with these tribesmen without first inspiring them with a wholesome respect for British arms."*

Having received the submission of the two tribes, Dyer applied for leave and left Khwash. *"I had had eight months of continual work in the hot weather of the Sarhad and was very near the end of my tether. As a fact, I was suffering badly in health and in many ways, and our medical officer insisted upon an immediate return to India for a long rest; a diet of sand and salt water must in the end affect one."*

Major Yeates described in Blackwoods Magazine the journey back across Baluchistan; as he was also invalided back to India in the General's car. The Overlander had to be driven along camel tracks from well to well for 400 miles. Heavy sand drifts had blown up from nowhere at one point 20 miles from the nearest well and the General and Yeates had to get out of the car and push it, 'the blazing sun beating down on us all the time.' The car finally broke its axle shaft, but Allan, having a spare, replaced it and they had to retreat to an earlier water hole and start off again next morning. *"I had an unforgettable demonstration of Dyer's bulldog tenacity once he had undertaken a course of action,"* wrote Major Yeates. It should be remembered that both these men were being invalided back to India!

Ann Dyer, in a rented house at Finningham, Suffolk, cheap because it was in the flight path of enemy planes, received a telegram, the first communication since February 1916: It said *"Arrived Simla after exciting time, Dyer"*.

The Government of India recommended General Dyer for the C.B., the highest award possible for such an action. They did not confirm the annexation of a corner of Persia and were disturbed by the protest of the Persian Government about the alterations to the fortress of Khwash which they had been told was of unprecedented height. The rumour obviously arose from Dyer's joking suggestion to the Raiders that their demolished walls were going to be sky-high.

Dyer was given command of the Jullunder Brigade. Instead of the four regiments that normally made a brigade, he had nine infantry regimental depots, wholly occupied with recruiting and training fighting men for the armies in the field.

Galahad, Dyer's magnificent chestnut Arab stallion, had been killed in the Sarhad. He was riding an artillery horse while giving a demonstration of the result of modern artillery fire on trenches, when the horse, slipping or baulking on the edge of a trench, reared up and fell backwards onto his rider. Dyer managed to hold the horse up so that it did not crush him, but the hard cantles of his artillery saddle came down on him as far as his chest.

There was a long hospitalization at Abbotabad, where at first he lay in agony, not being expected to live by the doctors, unable even to write. Then on 19th April, 1917, he dictated a letter to his wife, necessarily fairly formal in those days:

*"My horse fell on top of me at Akora and squashed the life out of me, but no bones are broken and I am making a quick recovery. I do hope you are improving and are taking an interest in life as far as the awful state of things will allow you to do. It is possible I will come home shortly but it depends on the Chief of the General Staff. I got Ivan's letter yesterday, and it was very good and thrilling and I am replying to it. Much love your affectionate husband – Rex"*

On 4th May Dyer cabled from hospital that he was making recovery fast and that he had been recommended six months' leave in England, but pleurisy developed in the injured lungs and not until the July did he sail for England, reaching Finningham in the autumn.

By then he was still a wreck, only able to crawl a few steps with the aid of sticks, but with his usual patient determination, he practiced and practiced until he became capable of walking in the normal way although still suffering pain. He tried fitting himself to a saddle, unable at the beginning to open his legs and nearly fainting with the excruciating pain, but at last he succeeded and then came a medical board. His prowess at bluff must have helped, concealing the agony from which he was suffering, for he persuaded the doctors he was completely fit. Ann commented later, *"He was determined not to be out of it."*

Ann Dyer, with a son in the war as well as a husband, distressed by the war and the news of it, had had a nervous collapse, from which she did gradually recover, but the tales told about Dyer tend to overlook his normal loving family life and the anxiety of his dear wife. It can be seen that he did his best to protect her from the worst anxieties in relation to himself, as was typical of the chivalry of men of stature and standards of that generation. Throughout the ensuing years, her sufferings form a part of his story. When he died, she moved to a smaller house opposite their previous one, with the Buddha statues that filled the garden of the first. She continued living in Long Ashton, in which she had the solace of the respect and affection of the people who had also been a support to her husband.

Dyer's deep affection for his family and the interest and care in which he held his two sons was typical of his nature, a character shown in the respect and affection for his troops; and above all his will to survive through every trouble.

In mid-winter, 1917, Dyer, passed as fit, travelled back to Bombay on the *Ormonde* with a contingent of unfit Australians, who were determinedly expressing themselves in making a rough house, regardless of the effect on the ship's company. He showed that extraordinary gift of encouraging, calming, bringing into sensible order these wild young men by talking directly to the ringleaders. By April 1918, he was back at Jullundur.

We know about Dyer working hard, of his strange ability to forecast events and cheer and control rowdies; we know about his courage, his patience in bearing pain; we know of his freeing of the Persian slaves, his compassion (possibly not sufficiently recorded in this book) for the women slaves in rags for whom he commandeered bright cloth for their clothing to help them to restore their dignity. We know that he loved and suffered from loving with anxiety for his wife and family; and then, with the tale supported by Colonel Stead, we know of his humour and capacity for enjoyment.

On his return to Jullundur he took pity on the Cyclists and the other war-weary soldiers waiting at Jullundur for their release. We know of the celebrations for the Armistice; including Dyer in fancy dress, on a camel, pretending to be a Chief from the Sarhad, even taking in Douglas Donald, the policeman of Jullundur, the brother of the Warden of Fisheries in the Punjab, with his ability to speak Persian. It was a time of laughter and happiness, of paper-chases (many organised by Dyer), of parties and dances and of his wife and son being restored to him a few brief months before Amritsar, the Third Afghan War and the tragedy of the hatred and insult, the loss of reputation and retirement and death at the age of 63. Unexpectedly being given a full military funeral was an indication that the Army, at least, knew him.

# GENERAL R.E.H. DYER C.B.

**A BRISTOL F2B OF 20 SQUADRON R.A.F. AT AMBALA, INDIA IN 1921. A MACHINE OF THIS TYPE WAS USED TO MONITOR THE CROWDS AT AMRITSAR ON 10 APRIL 1919 (PHOTO. BY COURTESY OF THE FAMILY OF CPL. H. SIMPSON.)**

**ARMOURED CARS IN RAMBAGH GARDENS AMRITSAR 19 APRIL 1919. THESE 2 VEHICLES WERE TOO WIDE TO ENTER THE JALLIANWALLA BAGH ON 13 APRIL. (PHOTO. BY COURTESY OF AMANDA STACEY)**

**SOLDIERS CHECKING LUGGAGE AT AMRITSAR STATION AFTER 13 APRIL 1919. WITH LARGE NUMBERS OF LATHIS AWAITING COLLECTION, THE CONCERN WAS FOR CONCEALED SWORDS, AXES, OR FIREARMS.**
**(COURTESY OF AMANDA STACEY.)**

**THE ALEXANDRA HIGH SCHOOL FOR NATIVE GIRLS EVACUATED ON THE ARRIVAL OF THE RIOTERS, WHO SACKED IT. USED AS H.Q. 1/25 LONDONS 27.4.1919**
**(COURTESY OF AMANDA STACEY)**

**PUNJAB RIFLES (I.D.F.) ARMOURED TRAIN SECTION, LAHORE, 1919. THIS TRAIN RE-OPENED THE LINE OUTSIDE AMRITSAR FOR GHURKHAS ON 10 APRIL 1919. (COURTESY OF NORTH WESTERN RAILWAY WEBSITE)**

**BULLET STRIKES ON PRESERVED WALL AT JALLIANWALLA BAGH, AMRITSAR, 25 JANUARY 2007. ALL ARE ABOVE HEAD HEIGHT, THOUGH SOLDIERS WERE FIRING FROM A MOUND. (WIKIMEDIA.COMMONS)**

# Chapter III
# GRIP

It was clear by the time that Dyer arrived in Amritsar on the evening of the 11th April 1919, that with the tiny number of available troops, things were still very dangerous indeed. In conditions of riot, the 'liberal' approach, which made the Indian Civil Service so loved throughout the countryside, had to be put aside, because of the risks to the law-keepers of being attacked and as a force, destroyed, with more serious disturbances to follow. To change suddenly from what another well-known Indian historian has called the 'walking ombudsmen' into people called to act against the common mood, was difficult and probably troubled Miles Irving. Later members of I.C.S. understood this very well.

On the morning of the 11th, when the leaders came to demand rights of burial for their dead, in the first instance in the Jallianwalla Bagh, Miles Irving had stood firm and told them there could not be a procession and issued each one of them with a notice.

*"The troops have orders to restore order in Amritsar and to use all force necessary. No gatherings of persons or processions of any sort will be allowed. All gatherings will be fired on. Any persons, leaving the city in groups of more than four, will be fired on. Responsible persons should keep indoors."*

Wathen, at the Khalsa College, was asked to tell his students that a state of war had broken out and they must settle down. All third class railway passengers to Amritsar were stopped, so as to avoid any more people coming in for the Fair to replace those who had already left. Village headmen had been told to carry out watch and ward along the railway lines that ran near their villages. Major Macdonald marched troops as far as the Kotwali, leaving pickets on side streets - this was the only area of the city that was under military control and the Kotwali was the only police station in military hands in the town. The people themselves knew how serious and dangerous the situation was for Europeans remaining outside the Fort.

Melisent Wathen noted the threat of aeroplanes being used to bomb the city, averted, so she said, by the pleas of her husband, as can be seen in the extract from her diary in Appendix III.

There had already been communication with Jullundur Area on April 5th, when a code message was received from Divisional H.Q., Lahore, warning of expected trouble over the Rowlatt Act, with the added note 'special precautions Amritsar'. Briggs, Dyer's Brigade Major, was not certain whether the message meant that Division had given the warning, or that it came from Amritsar, in reply to a code message asking whether Division had sent special instructions to Amritsar. The message was received that there had been no special instructions, but that they were in touch with the civil authorities and that they were expecting trouble.

On the same day a message was sent from Division, asking Jullundur to send one Indian officer with 20 men to Amritsar. Dyer was away, so Briggs dealt with this on his own. The picket for the railway station was therefore sent, to be under command of Captain Massey, Officer Commanding at Amritsar. Massey was from the 1st Battalion, Somerset Light Infantry.

On the 6th, Briggs was in touch with Colonel Burlton, the Deputy Commissioner at Jullundur and at his request, posted a squadron of cavalry in the vicinity of Jullundur City and a company of infantry on standby in the cantonment, but nothing happened, either at Amritsar or Jullundur, apart from the various hartals.

On the 10th, first a wire from Amritsar asking for British infantry, gunners and an aeroplane, urgently, then while decoding this, a wire from Division arrived - and from Division, the same but as to troops, 100 Mohammedans and 100 British were needed at Amritsar. Briggs sent to the General, who gave the necessary order for the movement of troops and when he got back to his bungalow, Briggs found a further coded wire from Amritsar about the murders and a request to expedite the troops. Together, they went to the station in order to commandeer a train: Dyer decided that there should be 200 Indian troops sent, rather than the original 100. The first train that could be commandeered was the 3.00 a.m., which the stationmaster accepted. This was at about 5.30 p.m. Having informed the regiments and with Dyer saying: *"If the situation is really serious the mob will have cut the telegraph wire"*, they went to the telegraph office and found just that. The lines had been cut at about 4.00 p.m. The only way to get the message through to Amritsar was to send it via Ludhiana and Lahore.

At 1.00 a.m., the troops were sent off and Briggs gave Major Clarke of the London Regiment a letter to say that he must get to Amritsar at any cost, if necessary commandeering vehicles to get there. The troops sent were 100 25th Londons, 100 59th Frontier Force Rifles and 100 2/51st Infantry. Officers travelling on the Bombay train said that they had seen mobs hanging round the line and shaking their fists as the train went by. The next deduction was that the line would be cut and in fact this was found to be so near Manawala, but it had been repaired by the time the troop train arrived. They arrived in Amritsar at 5.15 a.m., 11th April.

Dyer, hearing from Lahore that he should go and take charge at Amritsar, checked with the Commissioner of Jullundur that this would be alright and set off. He left Jullundur at 6.00 p.m. by car and reached Amritsar at 9.00 p.m., where they found Irving, Plomer and the troops on picket duty at the station.

Because later on it was claimed that he took too much on himself, it is important to put down from his own words, his own understanding at the time that he reached Amritsar. *"As Commander of the whole Jullundur District, of which Amritsar is but one point, I was in touch with the general situation there and during the events that followed, I was kept in touch also with the general situation in the Punjab. I had been struck with the general unrest and inflammable nature of many elements of the population. I was particularly well acquainted with the Sikh population of the countryside. The threatening nature of the Afghan situation was also present to me, also the weakness of the internal military situation and the threat to communications. On my arrival at Amritsar on the evening of 11th April, as is generally conceded, I was confronted with a crisis of the gravest kind. On the 10th, the mob had risen, killed everyone of European nationality in the city upon which it could lay its hands, burned banks and Government buildings and been held off the European settlement outside the city, only with the greatest difficulty. The situation had already been handed over to the local commander by the civil authorities, as being a military one and beyond their control. I found a clear conviction upon the part of local officials, and abundant signs that a determined and organised movement was in progress, to submerge and destroy all Europeans on the spot in the district and carry the movement throughout the Punjab and that the mob in the city and the excitable population of the villages, were being organised for this purpose. In the end, general looting and mob violence against the whole law abiding Indian population, as well as against the troops and authorities would have resulted.*

*For two days the city had been in the hands of the mob and no Government official or European could enter it, without an escort of troops. That in law and in fact, I was confronted not with a riot, but with open rebellion.*

*I had only a small force of troops at my disposal, consisting of 407 British and 739 Indian, many of them only partially trained. Amritsar is a city of 150,000 people, and the countryside is densely populated, with a people of an inflammable character. The arrangement of the city and the civil lines did little to facilitate the problems of control and defence.*

*The signs that met me and the reports which I received, left no doubt as to the existence of an organised mob with leaders and a definite purpose of outrage and destruction."*

That was the background. Captain Briggs noted the actions that followed their arrival at Amritsar in his Report, which was not included in the Hunter Report, because by the time it was written, he was dead.

> *"The General, the Deputy Commissioner, Superintendent of Police (Plomer) and myself with an escort of 50 British soldiers went to the Kotwali in the city to fetch the City Superintendent back to the station. As we passed along, buildings which had been fired were still smouldering."*

Dyer had a long discussion with the City Inspector, Mohammed Ashraf Khan and Briggs took down the names of the leading agitators as the Inspector gave them and arrangements were made for their arrest.

> *"From this interview it was apparent that the situation was very serious indeed. The mobs were treating the troops when they marched through the city with contempt, spitting on the ground. It appeared also that the villages were gradually being drawn into the rebellion by malicious lies.*
>
> *By the time we had arrived, all women and children in Amritsar had been placed in the fort, which was a great weight off one's mind, and which must have been a very serious problem to the Officer Commanding Amritsar on 10th April, with the few troops at his disposal."*

At 2.00 a.m. they retired to bed and the following morning, plans having been made the night before, they were already altering troop placements, reducing fixed pickets to the minimum and moving their headquarters to the Ram Bagh, the shady garden surrounding the Club.

At 10 a.m. on the 12th, all available troops marched to the Sultan Wind Gate, where an aeroplane flying overhead had informed them there was a large mob. Only with the greatest trouble, with the men in the mob spitting and shouting 'Mussulman ki Jai', was the mob dispersed. Dyer, faced with this situation continuing, despite the presence of the troops, knowing that at any moment trouble would break out yet again in this climate, decided to make his intention more seriously clear, by marching through the city with a proclamation, intending to follow it up by taking strong measures. It is here relevant to point out that the crowd was determined to stand on its lawlessness, intent on such behaviour as would humiliate the British troops. In books about Amritsar, the signs that are a language that needs to be read and understood, are left out of the narrative, for they have not been grasped. For an Indian mob-in the Punjab, to spit at the soldiers was indicative of an attitude that no soft words could overcome. Retreat, in the hope that it would all blow over and die away, was not an option and of course, Dyer (and Briggs) knew this. Nothing was to deflect Dyer from taking the steps that were urgently needed, so he planned to march through the city, while parties were detached from the main troop at the Kotwali, in order to effect the most important arrests.

When they got back to the Ram Bagh, it was to find a message from the Commissioner that 200 Sikhs from the Manjha were intending to raid the City. This was a report that had to be taken seriously in military terms, although the Commissioner himself did not place much reliance on it. Thus at that moment, there had already been the notice given to the leaders who were in charge of the burials and the proclamation that made even clearer that the town had been handed over to effective Martial Law.

The notice issued on the night of the 11th and sent round the town on the 12th ran thus-

*"Handed over to G.O.C., 45th Brigade, and signed by the Deputy Commissioner. Midnight 11th – 12th April 1919.*

*The troops have orders to restore order in Amritsar and to use all force necessary. No gathering of persons, nor processions of any sort will be allowed. All gatherings will be fired on. Any persons leaving the city in groups of more than four will be fired on. Respectable persons should keep indoors.*

*True Copy*

*Amritsar*
*11th April 1919*
*Deputy Commissioner*
*Sd. Miles Irving"*

In the light of that order, it is not surprising that Briggs felt that the behaviour of the crowd on the 12th was unreasonable and that Dyer was concerned at its behaviour. Briggs stated *"When we arrived back from the city the General dictated his proclamation to me and I wrote and gave it to the Deputy Commissioner to have translated and proclaimed round the city. This Proclamation is known as No. 1 Proclamation. All day long, messages were coming in of turbulence, confirming the seriousness of the situation. At 10.00 p.m., British soldiers in lorries proceeded to the Ashrapore Mission Hospital to rescue two English ladies who were calling for help. In fact the situation had become a military one. We were cut off from Headquarters by all means of communication except by airplane. Supplies from the city were practically impossible to obtain."*

On the 13th April, a further notice was sent out.

PROCLAMATION No 2 NOTICE

*The inhabitants of Amritsar are hereby warned that if they will cause damage to any property or will commit any acts of violence in the environs of Amritsar it will be taken for granted that such acts are due to the incident in Amritsar City and offenders will be punished according to Military Law.*

*All meetings and gatherings are hereby prohibited and will be dispersed at once under Military Law.*

*Certified True Copy*
*F C Briggs, Captain, Brigade Major*
*13th April 1919*
*For Brigadier General Commanding 45th Brigade*

It seems that the dating of this Proclamation as 13th refers to its implementation, since it was written on 12th.

It is one of the interesting angles on the Amritsar incident, that neither Hunter, nor seemingly anyone else, recognised this succinct description of the position for the troops. They were under siege and if the existing position with the agitators in charge of all communications and all food supplies were to have continued, then, effectively the insurgents would have won. It may be replied that there were troops available at Lahore, but with the villagers beginning to move, it was also likely that the railway lines would have been destroyed. The Afghan business which started very shortly afterwards (technically May 4th) could well have come in earlier. If Johnson at Lahore had not got things under control (and he had not at that time) and the surrounding district, towns and villages had continued to rise unabated, at the least, the situation would have become extremely grim. At its worst, Government could have gone under.

Though there were troops in Southern India, this was a time when troops had to march to railway stations, frequently as much as twenty or more miles, because there were so few lorries. To move soldiers, in an army already decimated due to the war and with its soldiers, either not yet fully trained recruits, or officers and British and Indian soldiers wishing to go home, would have been difficult. The difficulty has all too often been completely underestimated.

By the 13th, Dyer was determined to make sure, if he could, that the mob should be absolutely sure that he meant business. *"At 9.00 a.m. next day (13th), all available troops marched through the city again and No.2 Proclamation was read at all important streets and corners. The rebels sent a counter proclamation after us, saying that we dare not fire and that we had no shoes or some such nonsense."* wrote the Brigade Major, Captain Briggs and they gave it out despite the message given out by the Town Crier, 'Malik Fateh Khan, reading the Proclamation clearly in Urdu and Punjabi. To the Hunter Committee, Fateh Khan said clearly *"I read it out in Urdu twice and thrice I repeated every word of it and afterwards I explained it in Punjabi, again twice and thrice."* Not only did he explain to crowds of five hundred to a thousand, permitted to collect to hear him, he also gave out leaflets printed in Urdu. The list of places at which he stopped was:

| Ram Bagh Gate | Hall Gate | Dhab Khatikan | Namak Mandi |
| Majith Mundi Kitwali | Hathi Gate | Katra Safed | Killa Bhanglan |
| Loha Mandi | Queen's Statue | Lohgarh Gate | Bazaar Dhab. |
| Bazaar Chillianwallah | Tanda Talaab | Hall Bazaar Chowk | Katra of Dulab |
| Chowk Karam Singh | Bagh Jhanda Singh | | |

Interestingly, in his evidence, he referred to Ram Bagh as 'Company Gardens', [from the old 'John Company', the name by which the East India Company was known for so many years.]

For British soldiers, the length of time this march took in the blazing heat, was distressing – they were actually marching from 11.00 a.m. to 3.30 p.m. By that time, Dyer, always careful for his troops, decided that this was enough and returned to the Ram Bagh. Anyone old enough to remember the old Amritsar city will realise how comprehensive such a tour would be, in days when people were wandering through the streets with nothing to do and the shops closed. Behind the march, people were talking of meeting and Obaidullah, a policeman, told one group that they were not to meet in the Jallianwalla Bagh. Yet even Dr. Fauq, a close friend of Drs. Kitchlew and Satyapal, knew that everyone was talking of the meeting to be held in the Jallianwalla Bagh at 4.00 p.m. The people, many of whom had relations in the countryside outside Amritsar, were being told that they would no longer have to pay land tax if they went and 'what can the military do? They can't fire on us'. The poor people, their heads full of the claims that the British Raj was over, despite the evidence of their own eyes having seen the troops march through the town, believed the lies. There were to be reforms in which the British would no longer rule, 'self-government' was the buzzword, even amongst the lowest and most ignorant of the mob. The mere fact that they had spat at the soldiers with immunity would have supported them in this belief that the soldiers would not fire, even with the episodes on the 10th.

Already the disturbances had got as far as Lyallpur. With no spare troops, an airplane was sent to bomb the mob in Gujranwala, which was setting fire to the town and threatening the Europeans. Women and children, who had taken shelter in the Treasury buildings, were in grave danger. The bombing was a matter of eight very small bombs, four of which exploded, killing 16 people and wounding a few in the fields, but without troops, nothing else could be done other than this desperate attempt to restore some sort of order. The rioting stopped at once. The railway line was also pulled up and the station burnt. In later days, Havelock Hudson's remarks about the judgement of the man on the spot, was to be overlooked by the hysterical claims of a later generation that knows nothing of India.

In Lahore, Major Morgan was told to send Major Macdonald, his second in command, with a Company of his Regiment and 40 men of the Royal Sussex. Kitchin, the Lahore Commissioner, had then sent a letter to Beynon, the General of the Division, saying that nothing was being done - Morgan must go himself. On Dyer's arrival, Morgan offered to return to his Regiment at Lahore; but Dyer's reply had been *"I would like you to remain with me for the present."* By the Railway came a message from Beynon, 'Remain with General Dyer for the present.' Morgan was in the Ram Bagh when Dyer and his troops set off through the city with their proclamation, together with Irving and the policemen in a car. The bulk of the troops were on guard duty, so Dyer took half of what remained. He left a message.

*"If we are not back by 2.00 p.m. you must come into the city and look for us."*

Kitchin, later asked whether he had agreed with Dyer's actions, said he had not known at the time, but if he had disagreed he would have said so.

Kitchin had learnt, all along the road over which he drove to or from Lahore, that people were preparing to loot. Loot goes with murder and arson, for they seem to be, as they were in the time of the Mutiny, inextricable. From Jandiala, came a report of 80-90 men sharpening axes and shouting, the village constable unable to stop them from going on their way to Amritsar on the 13th. The way of one village was probably much the same as the way of hundreds of villages.

Dyer says he got back at to the Ram Bagh at 1.30 p.m. but that conflicts with the return of the troops at 3.30. Briggs says that they got back at 4.00. Perhaps Dyer returned before the main body of troops to which Briggs referred. The fact of the matter was, that hearing from Rehill that people were beginning to collect in the Jallianwalla Bagh, through the medium of a letter from the local Cinema Manager who, disguised as an Indian, had been in the Bagh, Dyer realised that something must be done. We know that Dyer was a man of great perception. He realised that if about a thousand men had already gathered, there would be many more on the way. Lala Jolwanhar Lal, the police Inspector, went to the Bagh shortly before the soldiers arrived and at that time, estimated the crowd as numbering something in the region of 20,000. He said he had already seen men walking towards the Bagh with lathis in their hands. Lathis, the strong-bamboo canes, iron shod, were at that time classed as a lethal weapon in the criminal code. When Dyer noted the points that had determined him to fulfil his proclaimed intention, his first mention was that of the 'Danda Fauj'. This was indeed the 'Danda Fauj' – the Bludgeon Army.

*"I personally had ample time to consider the painful duty I might be faced with. I had heard a great deal about the Danda Fauj, I was aware of the dastardly acts of cruelty which had been committed on the 10th. Messages, written and verbal, were momentarily coming in to me on the 12th and 13th April, telling me of fresh acts of violence and of the growing seriousness of the situation. Amritsar, from a military point of view, would soon be completely isolated, if matters were allowed to continue as they were doing. Communications by rail, telephone and telegraph had already been once severed.*

*The 'hartal' continued in Gujranwala, Lahore, Lyallpur and other large cities.*

*My work that morning in personally conducting the proclamation <u>must be looked upon as one transaction with what had now come to pass</u>. There was no reason to further parley with the mob; evidently they were there to defy the arm of the law.*

*The responsibility was very great. If I fired, I must fire with good effect. A small amount of firing would be a criminal act of folly.*

*I had the choice of carrying out a very distasteful and horrible duty or of neglecting to do my duty, - of suppressing disorder or of becoming responsible for all future bloodshed.*

*We cannot be very brave unless we be possessed of a greater fear. I had considered the matter from every point of view. My duty and my military instincts told me to fire. My conscience was also clear on that point. What faced me was what, on the following morning, would be the Danda Fauj."*

In his later Report to the Army Council in England, he made the point that Amritsar was the storm centre of a rebellion. *"The whole Punjab had its eyes on Amritsar and the assembly of the crowd that afternoon was, for all practical purposes, a declaration of war by leaders, whose hope and belief was that I should fail to take up the challenge. If Amritsar had been merely an isolated incident and not the storm centre of the Punjab, or if the danger from the countryside; our constant preoccupation, could have been ignored, ...I should have acted precisely as I did. I looked at the realities of the case as a whole, as a soldier is bound to do"*

And in another part of the same report (p.12) *"The following may be taken as a summary of the motives and grounds of my action:-*

*I had before me the general situation summarised in the dispatch of the Secretary of State. Starting in Amritsar itself, violence, murder and arson of the most savage description had occurred three days previously. In addition, I knew of the cloud from Afghanistan, that broke three days later.*

*I had before me in the Jallianwalla Bagh, not a fortuitous gathering which at worst, had assembled negligently or even recklessly contrary to a proclamation, but a mob that was there with express intent to challenge Government authority and defy me to take any effective action against it and in particular to defy me to fire upon it.*

*I knew that it was, in substance, the same mob that had been in course of organisation for some days and had committed the hideous crimes of 10th April and was the power and authority, which for two days, had ruled the city in defiance of the Government. I had in fact, the rebel army in front of me.*

*I knew, as far as human foresight could go, that if I shirked its challenge and did not then and there crush it, it would have succeeded in the design of its leaders, contempt and derision of Government power would have been complete, and that there would infallibly follow, that night or next morning, a general mob movement both from inside and outside Amritsar which would have destroyed all the European population, including women and children and all my troops and involved in its ruin the law abiding Indian population as well.*

*Leaving a reserve, I marched with the picketing parties and a special party consisting of 25 rifles 1/9th Ghurkhas (these men had been given rifles from the Fort but there were not enough for the other 40 Ghurkhas who had only Kukris), 25 rifles, 54th Sikhs F.F. and 59th Sikhs F.F. and 2 armoured cars. These were all the troops available, after providing for the pickets, reserves and duties. I proceeded through the city towards the Jallianwalla Bagh at the usual pace, dropping my picketing parties as I marched. The gathering in the Jallianwalla Bagh must have received ample warning of my coming and I personally, had ample time to consider the painful duty I might be faced with. I passed with my infantry through a narrow lane into the Jallianwalla Bagh and at once deployed them to the right and left of the entrance in the square."*

Jamadar Jitbahadur told 2nd Lieutenant MacCallum that the General Sahib told us to double through the narrow road leading to an open square and then said 'Ghurkhas right, 59th left, fire'.

Dyer then mentions that the armoured cars could not get through the lane.

*"I was faced by a dense mass of men evidently holding a seditious meeting. In the centre of the square was a raised platform and a man on it was gesticulating to the crowd. The crowd appeared to be a mixed one consisting of city people and outsiders.*

*I did not see a single woman or child in the assembly. Many villagers were, I understand, induced to come to the Bagh by a promise that their taxes and land revenues would be abolished as the British 'Raj' was at an end. Evidently, those who came believing the British "Raj" was at an end, were themselves not very innocent."*

The Government of India referred to it as an excited and defiant mob. Continuing the earlier series of reasons, Dyer wrote:

*"(e)      I knew that this result would lead to a similar result in numerous places throughout the Punjab.*

*(f) I knew that ineffective action against the mob would gravely endanger my small force on the actual spot and make its safe withdrawal difficult and that its destruction would infallibly produce the results indicated in the last two paragraphs.*

*(g) I knew that on the four occasions when firing took place on the 10th in Amritsar, its effects in preventing disorder and restoring security had been quite ineffective and that with the small body of troops at my disposal and the large determined and defiant assembly before me, I could produce no sufficient effect except by continuous firing.*

*But if any one dominant motive can be extracted, it was the determination to avert from the European woman and children and those of the law-abiding Indian community, the fate which I was convinced would be theirs if I did not meet the challenge and produce the required effect to restore order and security. I am conscious that it was this motive which gave me the strength of will to carry out my duty."*

This was no vain claim. He had already seen the miserable group of women and children in the Fort; he had seen Miss Sherwood with her head almost battered in and on the point of death; he must also have spoken to Dr. Easden, whose compounder had opened the great wooden doors to the mob to search the hospital building for her, leaving only when Mrs Benjamin had gone on her knees, in front of the very cupboard where Dr Easden was hiding, saying that her mistress had gone, while the mob with lathis were determined to find her and give her the Sherwood treatment. He knew of the ladies at the religious book shop, who were in danger of being killed, but for Colonel Smith; he knew about the missionary ladies and children, over whose terrified heads, the mob was determined to burn down the mission school; he knew of Fazl Dad and the ladders to enter the Fort. He knew that women were in no way sacrosanct, rather seemingly a target for brutality: he knew of Mrs Sherbourne and her three children, who had been chased by a mob, frenzied with the battering to death already of the warrant officers. He must have had in his mind something of MacCallum's reaction, *"greatly shocked to see, by chance, a barrack room of women and children who had been brought to the Fort from the Civil Lines for safety. There was a terrible quietness in the barrack room. The ladies seemed so bemused and sad. Imagine leaving your own comfortable bungalow or quarters to be put in a room with a long line of beds, cots, camp beds or floor, with no privacy."*

At the back of all this was the consciousness from the knowledge gained from his parents, who had helped woman, men and children escaping from the Mutiny only 60 years before; of Cawnpore and the bibi-garh, of Neill's terrible finding of the women in 'safety' who had been hacked to death by butchers, their bodies and those of little praying terrified children, put into the well. He knew what would happen if he did not take the immediate and essential action, that, if left, would be too late. He was right. Those seditious leaders who cared nothing for the pain and suffering they were causing, were to put the triumphal statue of the leader of the mutineers over the well where the bodies of the ladies and the little ones lay, when we left 25 years later. Their ideals in 1919 could hardly be expected to be any different. Dyer knew his Indians when in such a mood.

*"I fired and continued to fire until the crowd dispersed and I consider this is the least amount of firing which would produce the necessary moral and widespread effect it was my duty to produce, if I was to justify my action. If more troops had been at hand the casualties would have been bigger in proportion. It was no longer a matter of merely dispersing the crowd, but one of producing a sufficient moral effect from a military point of view, not only on those who were present but more especially throughout the Punjab. There could be no question of undue severity."*

This was a report written for the Commander-in-Chief, a military report, but for those who do not grasp the seriousness of the situation nor the military position, it may seem ruthless. It is a record of one of those points in history, like the taking of Delhi during the Mutiny, which needs an effort of understanding to grasp the need of the occasion and recognise it in context. It has naturally given rise to a mass of what can only be called ignorant criticism; each phrase used without reality or context and largely linked with an interpretation of Dyer's motives, that were completely opposite to those he, in reality, held and which the previous extracts from his report have shown.

His brief summary of the firing leaves out his fear that the mob might come round behind him. Briggs describes the incident thus; *"... we saw an immense crowd. I believe it has been estimated at more like 25,000. The crowd was composed of men; no women or children were seen during the whole time we were there* [the absence of women and children is evidence of the nature and intentions of the crowd]. *After firing a few rounds, the mob split up and two large subsidiary mobs gathered together in two opposite corners of the Bagh. It looked for a minute as if they were meaning to rush us. The General Officer commanding therefore gave orders to direct fire on these two crowds. The mob gradually disappeared. The party then marched back to the Ram Bagh. On arrival at the Ram Bagh, the men's pouches were examined. 1,650 rounds had been fired. Fire was directed on the crowds, not on individuals."*

This incident of the crowd appearing to be about to rush the little group of soldiers, was repeated by Colonel Morgan to my father, and Lt. Sexton, (now Major Sexton), was told it by people in the bazaar a few days later and by many others. Bearing in mind that the little force was at most 0.5% of the mob, which may indeed have been anything up to 70,000, the entire action was an extremely courageous one. The men in the crowd were the same as those who had taken over the city and held the city. Many of them may have been paid to join in, as Colonel Smith pointed out when he asked what loot could the crowd have got from the church [or the Mission School] and that they must have been paid to bum it, for otherwise what gain could they have got? It is clear that many of these men were riffraff, goondas, hooligans, the scum of the towns and villages, led by the middle class. Had they been sepoys, as were the mutineers in 1857, trained by the British, then there is no doubt that they would have taken their chance and attacked Dyer's small force. If he had not seized this opportunity, the Jat Sikhs from the villages around, the Ghadr Sikhs; the men who had fought in the war and the men from the Manjha, would have poured in a day or two later, to join the throng. A few days of that would have been a clear sign that all administration had gone and it is likely that the army and the police, so sorely tempted themselves over the last months, would have joined in.

As Shakespeare so aptly wrote, *"There is a tide in the affairs of men, which, taken at the flood, leads on to fortune"*. Since the Afghans and Bolsheviks outside would undoubtedly have entered India then, as they did a few days later when they besieged Thal, the rampages and chaos of Bolshevism would have taken over and destroyed India and the Indians.

Many people have claimed that the troops fired high deliberately, supposing that they were disaffected. These people forget that, in 1919, firing over the heads of a crowd was a standard tactic in riot situations. Mr. Caldecott mentions it in his report of events at Viramgam (PART 3 Ch. III). A photograph taken in the 21$^{st}$ Century, of bullet marks in a section of the original wall, show that the marks are all above head height, though the soldiers were firing from raised ground. Lord Lamington noted later that over 1,000 bullet holes were made in the walls. It was the possibility that civilians outside the Bagh, but in surrounding buildings, might have been struck in this way, which led to the practice of firing over the heads of a crowd being discontinued by the British Army after 1919.

Following the firing, everything went quiet. The next day, the people who had been asked to open the shops and had refused, themselves came and asked for permission for them to be opened.

There are so many conflicting stories about the firing that it seems wise to add a few more details from Colonel Morgan's reminiscences.

Morgan does not say, as did Draper, that there were two exits available, but more like eight, which explains how, despite the locked gate, the crowd got away in so short a time. It is claimed that they did not fire at particular persons. He mentions the exception of a man with a red beard [a sign that he had been on pilgrimage to Mecca, a Muslim]. *"We opened fire immediately and as soon as the rebels turned their backs on us we ceased fire. Some two minutes after this cease-fire the rebels surged towards us again, so fire was reopened and was continued until all were turned away and were making a definite attempt to get away. Fire was opened once more on one man, a fellow with a red beard who was trying to rally the remnants against us. I regret to say he was not hit, but our little force was not one of marksmen."* These breaks in the firing may help to explain why Hunter's complaint-of firing too long was unjustified

Morgan explains the availability of only 25 rifles: *"...ever since the mutiny in 1857, a certain number of rifles were kept in every station for civilians to defend themselves in case of another mutiny. There were 25 in Amritsar and these were issued to 25 of the Ghurkha recruits. What of the new battalions in India? They might have thought the British Raj is finished, we had better join up with the rebels who we knew were trying to get at the Indian soldiers. My own Subedar Major brought me a letter from the rebels telling him now was the time to murder all the British officers. Fortunately he did not agree so I am still here to tell the tale."*

He complains that in the book by Furneaux, [pub. Allen & Unwin 1963] the list of troops is incorrect: *"This is pure fiction, these troops were not there at all on the 13th.*

*I should remark that these young battalions in India were very short of regular officers. I had one. All other British officers were I.A.R.O. (Indian Army Reserve Officers), youngsters anxious to do their bit but with little or no military training and some could not speak the language.*

*After 8 p.m. we started out again and visited all the sentry posts and the City gates, the curfew was 100 per cent, there was not a soul in the streets.*

*The next day, General Dyer brought in some troops from Jullundur and I returned with my men to Lahore."*

On the evening of the 13th, a detailed account of all that had happened that day was sent to Simla and no exception was taken to any part of it, either by Army Headquarters, or the Government of India.

Dyer's report continues: *"Prior to the firing on the 12th and 13th, the City Inspector had done all he could to get the shopkeepers to open their shops. Their reply was that they would do nothing until Kitchlew and Satyapal had been released and the Rowlatt Act repealed, yet subsequently to the 13th, these same shopkeepers came to the City Inspector and asked that they might open their shops. I convened a meeting of these men and all shops were opened on the morning of the 14th. Soon after the 13th, Honorary Magistrates, leading citizens, Municipal Commissioners, Raises and Chowdhris expressed an admiration for my firm action and said that it had saved Amritsar and other cities in the Punjab from complete plunder and bloodshed.*

*On the morning of the 14th April, Mr. D. Donald, Inspector-General of Police, Lahore, informed me that it was intended to hold another meeting around the Golden Temple. It was not hard to gauge the significance of this. It was evidently thought that I should again open fire on the meeting and some of the bullets would hit the Golden Temple, whereupon the whole Sikh community would have been up in arms as one man. This would also mean that the Sikh Sepoy would, in all probability, be up in arms and a most serious situation be the result.* [This did happen after the terrible firing on the pilgrims at the Golden Temple in 1984, when, although it was kept a secret, troops did rise, but in another account, they are said to have been fired on and killed in numbers with their hands tied behind them. The attitude to Sikhs in India has since been shown to reduce the opportunities to rise to higher positions in the Army].

*I accordingly at once despatched a message to Sardar Arur Singh C.I.E., the Manager of the Golden Temple, to say that if his Temple was defiled in any way, all the troops at my disposal would protect it. I asked Sardar Arur Singh to come and see me at once with Sardar Sunder Singh Majithia, the head Sikh of the Amritsar district.*

*Persistent malicious rumours of the bombing of the Golden Temple and raping of Sikh girls at Amritsar were afloat and one realised then, that the great object of the mutineers was to get the Sikhs on their side."*

Dyer wrote *"I was born in India and have served in Punjab Regiments all my service. I know the language very well and I consider I am an authority on what was going on in and around Amritsar. I know many good and trustworthy retired Sikh officers. I called these men to come and see me.*

*After April 13th, the situation was clearer and one saw that the Sikhs were not in the rebellion to any extent and that it was my duty to keep them out of it."* The two leading Sikhs came to see him and agreed to stop the rumours and it was due to them that the meeting did not take place near the Golden Temple.

Dyer's next move was to go and see Michael O'Dwyer and tour the district with a mobile column, to show that the Sirkar was still strong, that all those nasty rumours about the bombing of the Golden Temple and the Sikh girls were untrue, to talk straight and to the point to the population and to be certain of having the Muslim population on our side, in view of the possible trouble over the Turkish Peace Terms.

*"Daily, many old Sikhs came to see me and assured me that all would be well. Accordingly, on the 21st April, I proceeded with a moveable column of 100 British, 100 Indian, 20 Indian Cavalry, and 2 armoured cars to Gurdaspur."*

At Gurdaspur, Harcourt, the Deputy Commissioner and Glascock, the Superintendent of Police, met him. There, he was told that things had been much better since the 13th April, but prior to that they had been very threatening - also at Dhariwal and Batala. He then marched through the three towns and spoke very seriously to the people. The effect had seemed good. On the 24th, he marched through Cina and Bugga Atari in Amritsar district; then to hold Durbars with Miles Irving at Raja Sansi and Atari, which were exceptionally large. On the last, Mahant Shri Kripa Singh. of Guru Sat Sultani also accompanied him. This influential and powerful Sikh priest gave him *"invaluable service in keeping the Sikhs straight and denying the many malicious rumours which had been systematically disseminated amongst the villages in the whole district".*

The next step was on the 28th, when he went with the Assistant Commissioner, Puckle, to Sur Singh where the Ferozepore moveable column had arrived. Here, he found particularly serious disaffection and spoke to the heads of the village and the lambardars of the neighbouring villages - he believed to good effect.

This very heavy work, bearing in mind that by this time, it was the hot weather in good earnest, had the effect of allaying fears and settling the people down in relation to the Rowlatt Act as well as all the trouble. He had no doubt that these villages were on the brink of joining in the rebellion prior to the 13th.

For anyone who was in the Punjab in later times, for instance, Steven Robinson, Superintendent of Police at Amritsar from 1945-1947, who recorded the subsequent quiet of the Punjab in the years that followed this determined removal of doubt, this encouragement and the rebuttal of rumours, this steadying process of concern for the welfare of a people racked by false rumours and untruth, has to be recognised as part of the cause. Through the non-violent non-co-operation movement, through the years of propaganda and incitement, through the Quit India movement, the Punjab was remarkably quiet. There were the Akali riots in the early 20s and later the Khaksars, but while the rest of India was kept in a state of agitation, the Punjab was surprisingly calm. It was due, at least in part, to the outstanding service given by Fazli Hussain, who set up the principles of government in those early years after the Montagu/Chelmsford Reforms had altered the way that India was governed, also to Sikander Hayat and then Khizzar, who would have liked the British to stay and did not wish to move over to Pakistan. These men and the various members of the Government worked in a sound way, in removing the doubts about the Rowlatt agitation, Dyer played a hand that showed the dangers of believing in the propaganda of the time. There is no doubt that the officers and priests whom they knew and who were such admirers of Dyer, brought much of the Sikhs trust back to the British Government - back from a situation in which many of them came from villages on the brink of being brought into the rebellion.

As Dyer wrote in his report: *"The effect of the events of April 13th and those moveable columns, snatched the villages from the hands of the agitators and thus the latter were left alone. On these columns, I simply talked plainly and to the point. No whippings were administered."* So well remembered were these talks, that they are mentioned in the 1923/4 depositions for the O'Dwyer v. Nair case. Again, in the matter of the Indian Army, he spent much time in sorting out the needs of the troops and when it is remembered what proud service the Punjabi men gave in the Army in the 1939-45 war, his determination to keep the Army out of the trouble deserves much credit.

On the 30th April, he organised a meeting of Brigadiers at Jullundur to discuss the matter. Then the great honour was paid him and Briggs of being made Honorary Sikhs at the Golden Temple, at the shrine of Guru Sat Sultani.

On the 4th May, the trouble from Afghanistan that was anticipated became public and on the 6th, war was declared. On the 8th, he proceeded to Jullundur, leaving in his place, Lt. Col. Hynes of the 1/25th Londons. When he went to the Frontier on May 23rd, Col. The Honourable W. F. North in turn relieved him.

At the end of his letter, Dyer made clear his position about whipping. He called it whipping, not flogging, as was correct, although the propagandists referred to it by the term that in those days meant the cat or the lash. In India, people were not flogged, but the claims of latter day authors, in their usual way of melding anachronism with inaccuracy when they have a point to make, makes this difficult to understand.

Dyer says that he had six people whipped in the street where Miss Sherwood was felled, but since the street was closed at both ends, this was private. Three were whipped in the Ram Bagh, four in the Kotwali. In all, 25 people were whipped in Amritsar, but this was after 14th April and Martial Law had been declared. They had all been tried. In his usual honest and direct way, he said that he believed that whipping, like the lash had been in the Army, was best done in public in order to dissuade others. He had begun to put up a platform between the fort and the city, but he had been ordered to take it down.

Local opinion among the Indian population did not seem to be at all against Dyer at the time. If anyone was shocked, it was among the Europeans. Gerard Wathen asked one of the parents of his students what he thought of the Brigadier's action; he received the reply that it was a little harsh, but that it had done much good. 'A little harsh' about sums up the feeling, along with the opinion that a little harshness had been called for. It seems to have been assumed by many people as a matter of course, that General Dyer had intended to kill as many people as possible in order to stamp out the trouble by means of a vigorous effort of repression, but as I have tried to explain, this was not so. The authorities at the Golden Temple made him an Honorary Sikh at a public ceremony before he left Amritsar and I do not see how they could possibly have done that, if public opinion had been at all strongly against him.

My father said: *"I met Dyer two or three nights later, at a dinner at the Miles Irving's house. He was looking worn out and haggard, particularly about the eyes. We asked him what was the matter. He replied that he had not slept a wink since the shooting. Of all the people to whom the firing had come as a shock, it came as most of a shock to Dyer himself He told me that every time he tried to close his eyes, he saw the scene as vividly as he had done at the time, and had to open them again. That was why he had not been able to sleep since it occurred. He had often had to kill people in battle, he said, but he had never had to order firing upon a civilian crowd before."*

My mother's memory, as well as relief and gratitude when the Army sent the women and children to the hills, was clear about the time immediately after the firing. She said much later, in the BBC Time/Life film: *"He came into the Fort, looking very unhappy. We found the only bottle we had and gave him a drink. He said 'I've saved you women and children, but I'm for the high jump.'"*

# Chapter IV
# DYER AT THAL

On May 28th, Sir Arthur Barrett, commanding the North West Frontier force, told Dyer *"I want you to relieve Thal. I know that you will do all that a man can do."* It was presumably at that interview that Dyer, worried about Amritsar, told Barrett that the influences which had inspired the rebellion were starting an agitation against those who suppressed it. Sir Arthur Barrett's reply was *"That's alright, you would have heard about it long before this if your action had not been approved."* Of course, the Army had approved it. This was a sound response, which would have applied to an army officer in doubt about having gone beyond his remit, who might have had to face a Court Martial. No-one could have foreseen the behaviour of the Secretary of State for India, which would lead him to over-rule any question of Court Martial, insisting instead on an extraordinary investigation by a Committee, largely manned by the disaffected or inexperienced. Acting as judge and jury, their findings were accepted despite their obvious partisan nature. There had been a Mesopotamian Commission, but this had looked into the errors of administration and certainly the German officers and the Turks who besieged and attacked Kut were not put onto the investigating panel! The words of Havelock Hudson, the Adjutant General, at the Indemnity Debate which took place in September, make clear that he believed that what Dyer had done was not only right, but in keeping with Army Regulations.

As to the instruction to relieve Thal, Barrett's knowledge that Dyer would do all he could do and his decision to use Dyer, indicates his appreciation of a man capable of dealing with difficult situations. Obviously, Thal was a matter of urgency. If Eustace gave way, the tribes would have been jubilant and would have arrived from far and wide to help Nadir Khan. Dyer had been told to take what he wanted and for transport, he took 62 lorries from Peshawar as far as Chat. At Kohat, he took four of the six 15-pounders from the Frontier Garrison Artillery at the Kohat Fort.

For their transport, he had to use seven of his motor lorries to drag the guns and carry the necessary ammunition since there were no horses or anything else to carry them. The Sarhad had taught him the use and necessity of military bluff, so he tied tree trunks to the backs of some of the other lorries to look like guns and attached to them, tree branches, to make a dust cloud. So speedily did he work that it was only the 29th (his orders having been given by Barrett on the 28th), when his artillery train set out.

A mobile column was being formed at Hangu, twenty-six miles along the road. Dyer left instructions-that the units of his Brigade should be sent on to Togh by train as soon as they arrived at Hangu, while Dyer set off by car to Togh, eight miles further on.

The troops involved were:

HQ 44 Infantry Brigade,
1 Squadron, 37th Lancers
89 Battery, Royal Field Artillery
Four 15 pounders, Frontier Garrison Artillery
1 section, 23 Mountain Battery
1/2 Section, 57 Coy., 1st Sappers and Miners
1 Section, Pack Wireless
1 Armoured Motorcar Battery
1/25th London Regiment
2/41st Dogras
1/69th Punjabis
3/150th Infantry
250 Rifles, Frontier Force
1 Company, 2/4th Border Regiment
The strength of the infantry together was 2,000 men.

With his men round him at Togh, Dyer spoke to them, asking them to use their greatest efforts to rescue their comrades at Thal. The treatment by Afghans of wounded was widely known to be merciless and no one would have wanted to think of any of their friends being subjected to such torture. Colvin, writing of this incident wrote: *"His words touched the hearts of that strangely assorted force of veterans and war levies, Punjabi peasants and men of business, so that they marched to the last of their strength and some of them dropped in their tracks."* That summer was exceptionally hot, the temperature in the shade being 120°. At four o'clock in the morning of May 31st, they were marching along an open valley between steep hills. There was no wind and little water and as the day went on, the rocky hillside reflected back the sun from its boulders making it a furnace which became almost intolerable. Men wrote that of those who went through this heat, one man collapsed at every halt and was left to be picked up by the ambulance. Dyer marched much of the way beside them, which drew great admiration from his men. Allahdad Khan, his bearer, helped Dyer as much as he could, by pressing wet towels round Dyer's head, when opportunity offered. Between marches on foot, the General drove ahead with the advance guard, reconnoitring the position before the rest of the column arrived, The troops reached camp by four o'clock in the afternoon.

When they arrived, Dyer was lying under the staff car, the only visible shade. One of his staff officers went up to one of the London's and asked if he had any water to spare but there was almost none. To quote Colvin again *"most of the men by that time could hardly speak, so swollen were their tongues and lips."* From the diary of Captain Briggs comes the comment that the troops marched excellently. and then to Colvin again: *"if it is not invidious to particularise, we might pause here to admire the spirit of the London's, which had had no real rest since it entrained at Peshawar at 2 a.m. on the 28th. It was a battalion of 1st Line Territorials in far off pre-war days, 'Cyclists' composed of London clerks and businessmen. They had arrived in India in 1916, had gone through Waziristan in 1917, had suffered so much from dysentery and malaria, that they had come down with one man fit and been sent to Murree to recuperate. They had hoped to get home when Armistice came, but were found too useful in India. When they were mobilised on the 6-7th of May, their strength for field service was 21 officers and 300 other ranks. Such was the battalion that swung into Darsamand in excellent marching order on that roasting afternoon of the 31st May"*.

In their ranks was Herbert Swinnerton, later my parents' lawyer, who, as a private, took part in that march and told me of it - one of the many people who have given me information for this book.

The new arrivals in camp were first rested, before the camp was entrenched and picketed. Communication was established with the signallers at Thal from a visual station at Fort Lockhart on the Samana Ridge. On 1st June, at 5 a.m., the column set out for Thal, pickets being placed on the low hills South of the Ishka Lai nullah. In the meanwhile, Dyer had collected any information that was available and reconnoitred the hills to the West of the area. Arrangements were made for him to meet with Major Wylly, General Eustace's staff officer, at a landing place two miles from Thal, through the agency of one of the airplanes belonging to the Thal garrison.

From this source, he got a most valuable picture of the positions of the Afghan troops and the tribesmen. The former, together with the howitzers, were on the far side of Thal, on the farther bank of the river Khurram. On the right of Dyer's approach, on the spurs of the Kaddimakh were 2,000 tribesmen with a few regulars and four guns and to the south, on the Wazir hills, below the Ishka Lai nullah, was a strong force of 4,000 Khostwals and Wazirs under the command of Babrak Zadran. He decided that the force under Babrak Zadran should be attacked first, but in order to make his design less obvious, he fired on the other heights as well.

Yet once again, he could not have decided on his plan without an immense and detailed knowledge of the terrain and of the tribes and their relations with one another. Just as at Amritsar, he could not possibly have taken the steps he took, without realising the full seriousness of the position. He knew firstly that Babrak's position was weak; the man had no guns, his force was a mixture of Wazirs and Khostwals who did not get on with one another and thirdly, (but for Babrak most seriously), he had no line of retreat except across the Khurram river. Typically, Dyer gave his orders verbally and in sufficient detail, that his assembled officers were all made aware what each unit of the force had to do.

The Punjabis, supported by the 3/150th, attacked the hill, while the Londons and the Dogras, the Sappers and Miners and mountain guns made a movement to cover the advance. The attack was made so suddenly and the artillery fire so well directed, that Babrak's men, who had gathered the impression that the whole British Army was moving up the valley, were seized with panic and scattered in headlong flight.

By four o'clock, the Punjabis had taken the heights, with the loss of only four men wounded. 200 men of the 3/150th were left to occupy the position, the remainder of the troops being withdrawn to a camp on the road, while a section of the Field Battery trotted forward to Thal and silenced the enemy guns at Khapianga. Colvin's report, quoted so freely in this chapter, was partly derived from the narratives of such people as Colonel Hynes, commanding the 1/25th Londons and from the war diaries of the 16th Division, the 45th Brigade and the 1/25th London Regiment at the Historical Section of the War Office (by courtesy of General Sir J. E. Edmonds). What follows is largely from the Official Account of the Third Afghan War, 1919, compiled in the General Staff Branch, Army Headquarters, India (Calcutta) in 1926. There is also a despatch by Sir Charles Monro, Commander-in-Chief, India.

Eustace's plight had been dreadful. Of his garrison, he had lost 90 casualties among the troops and 100 among the animals. Shortage of food and lack of water made things worse, but over and beyond this, since the perimeter of the fort was five miles in length, he was vulnerable on all sides. Dyer was not only concerned with the relief of Thal; he also wanted to defeat the enemy. His experience in the Sarhad would have given him sound basis for knowing that, if he did not, the enemy forces would collect again, cause the same sort of trouble and the tribes would be likely to join in. The danger for India was always the possibility of more of the same if the wrong was not put right quickly. This was something we were to learn again later, with Gandhi's continual agitation.

Dyer took over the command of all the troops, General Eustace returning to Kohat. The next morning, the troops launched a further attack on the enemy position on the lower slopes of the Khadimakh, North-West of Thal. For this, Dyer used two battalions of the Thal troops as well as his own force. As he began his advance, information came in that Nadir Khan had been reinforced - four battalions of regulars and a battery of artillery, thus raising his numbers of regular troops to 19,000 infantry and thirteen guns.

Nevertheless, the effect of Babrak's reports had weighed so heavily on the other side of the argument, that General Dyer received a letter from Nadir Khan saying that he had been ordered by the Amir to suspend hostilities and asking for an acknowledgement of this communication. Dyer, whose knowledge of the Oriental was profound, gave him a characteristic answer: *"My guns will give an immediate reply and a further reply will be sent by the Divisional Commander, to whom the letter has been forwarded."* (Official account of the Third Afghan War P 61. The story is taken from the Diary of the 45th Brigade, kept by Captain Briggs.) Nadir Khan waited for neither the one nor the other. One of Dyer's spies reported that Nadir, as he watched through his binoculars, the advance of the columns along the valley from his position on the hills, observed *"My God, we have the whole artillery of India coming against us!"* He retreated with all speed, being bombed by the Royal Air Force, which dispersed a number of Zamukhis who had joined Nadir's forces. The armoured cars and the squadron of Lancers went up the left bank of the Khurram to harass his retreat and the guns of the 89th Battery moved forward to shell his camp at Yusuf Khel. Thinking of the welfare of his men in the appalling heat as usual, Dyer withdrew his infantry to camp, but the following morning early, he advanced at the head of his column to Yusuf Khel, fording the river Pirkasta and finding the Afghan camp empty and in a state of wild disorder.

Two guns, cordite dumps, German ammunition and Nadir's tent with the carpet, stool and standard still in it, had been abandoned. The booty had to be left because they did not have the wherewithal to carry it away and on their return the following day, they found that the tribes had stripped the camp bare, like vultures on a carcass.

Dyer, despite having felt the heat very badly like his troops, and having fainted with the heat and a dreadful headache when he was giving those original orders, wished to overtake the Afghans, since he knew that due to their elephant transport they would inevitably be very slow, but this he was ordered not to do. Nonetheless, despite the extreme heat and the sufferings of his entire column, he had relieved Thal, saving General Eustace, Sir Arthur Barrett and the Commander in Chief from an awkward predicament which might have ended in disaster if he had taken longer, or failed in his methods of relieving the siege.

The Commander in Chief's dispatch ran as follows: *"During the advance of General Dyer's column on Thal, the extreme heat made the long marches exceedingly arduous and exhausting; but march discipline and spirit of the men were excellent, and the commander and troops deserve great credit for the manner in which the operation was carried out. General Nadir Khan's enterprise was a move that, had it met with a greater measure of success, might have compromised our plan of campaign. The salient of Afghan territory, which reaches out between the Tochi and Khurram valleys, enabled him to concentrate on the flank of our main communications through tribal country. An attack on the Khurram undoubtedly promised more important results, for had Nadir Khan succeeded in raising the Oraksai and Afridi tribes against us, the effect would have been felt in our operations in the Khaibar."*

The Amir's request for a cease-fire was granted; an armistice was signed on 3rd June and this put an end to the pursuit of Nadir Khan, but not to the dangers and hardships of the troops. Sir Charles called their next position a period of inaction; but to the troops it was a great hardship, since their efforts had been expected to relieve them from their spell of duty, so that they could now go home. Sir Charles' attitude was undoubtedly thoughtless and inhumane. He was a man who followed, almost mindlessly, instructions from Government in Britain, as was shown later by his treatment of Dyer, but he, the man on the spot, did not point out the serious problems of following flawed policy, when his own men were to be badly affected by it.

And Dyer? By October, he would have known of the Indemnity Debate, in which the elected Indian members of the Legislative Assembly had spoken in various degrees of viciousness and virulence about all those who had suppressed their rebellion - Dyer in particular - but he was already undermined by that fearful campaign in the ghastly heat and his personal worry about Amritsar. He had returned to Peshawar and received the congratulations and thanks of General Barrett and was given ten days leave to Dalhousie. On 2nd August, he was ordered to Simla, to be congratulated by his old comrade, the Commander in Chief. He then returned to Dalhousie to write the report on the Amritsar incident, which was included in the Hunter file of evidence and on which I have relied to a great extent, but his witnesses were already dispersed throughout the world - Europe, the Frontier and so forth. His Brigade Major, Captain Briggs was still in the Khurram Valley and his information and papers were sadly missed by Dyer, but by the 25th he had completed the task. This report, written in poor health and in haste and without the help he obviously needed, was to be the ground for attack on him, mainly on his motives rather than his action.

Malcolm Hailey, later a member of the Government of India and the Governor of the United Provinces, was shown his report. Hailey was an unexceptionable man, very popular with everyone; but a man who seems not to have recognised the pitfalls in the statement which I have taken straight because it is relevant. The out-of-context quotes that are used from it are used by men of little sympathy or understanding and probably without a grasp of the actual situation with which Dyer was faced. Everything cannot be quoted in full, but to quote out of context and with an almost illiterate grasp of the situation about which Dyer was writing, let alone failing to account for his writing it in the circumstances that he did, is to be arbitrary and partisan. In the event, these people have fed the propaganda story and lost sight of the true events. Hailey's only comment, that it would be 'tactless' to describe the mass of people as rebels, in itself shows that Hailey had no grasp of the situation. In 1924, Malcolm Hailey became Governor of the Punjab and was a very good Governor, one of those who benefited from the suppression of that same rebellion. As children, my sister and I went to Government House parties, my sister being a member of the 'Bluebirds', the Indian version of 'Brownies'.

The 45th Brigade was ordered to Chaklala as part of the concentration of troops on the frontier for the Mahsud campaign, one of the results of the Afghan War. The Brigade spent a wretched time in tents though Dyer, able to have his wife with him for a short while, was given an office building. His niece also joined them in this basic residence, a sort of stone hut, six miles from Rawalpindi. One month later the 45th was ordered to leave for Bannu, while Dyer was to go elsewhere to another command. Parting from his brigade was a bitter blow to such a man, but the greatest grief was at the parting from his Brigade Major who had been such a stalwart through the Amritsar affair and the Afghan campaign, even dosing Dyer with brandy and aspirin as ordered by the doctor when he went down with heat stroke.

That sadness was in fact the last farewell. Just prior to the Hunter hearing in October, Briggs was taken ill. It was thought to be appendicitis, but Dyer's niece, who had become engaged to Briggs, dancing with one of the doctors who had been present when he went into hospital, told her later that Briggs had been murdered by consuming powdered glass. This is a very common way of getting rid of people in India. It is virtually untraceable and extremely effective though an unpleasant and painful way of dying. It should not have been surprising, if Dyer was to be the Aunt Sally, that Briggs, his one support, should be put out of the way. Until he went into the Courtroom where the Hunter hearing was held, he expected to see Briggs. It was only at the hearing that he received the heartbreaking news that this man, almost a son to him, was dead.

# PART 5
# THE MINISTER

## Chapter I
## AMBITION

Edwin Montagu; almost straight from University and President of the Cambridge Union, was swept into Parliament with the flow of the Liberal majority in 1906. By a little pushiness, he was taken on by Asquith as his Private Secretary and through the years that followed, he was supported through depressions and anxieties to the point at which he fulfilled his ambition to become linked with India. That ambition, his driving force, gave him little peace when using the powers which his intellect claimed was right and he became the charming ebullient, sympathetic man that he could be, as long as his powers moved in support of his ambition.

It was under Asquith, with Lord Morley as Secretary of State, that he first went to India as Under Secretary in 1912. Liberalism holds, as its deep ideal, the destruction of existing traditions. For Montagu, the existing traditions in India were the position and power of the Viceroy atop the hierarchical structure of government, down to the District Officer, with the tahsildar and his village responsibilities, and in between the two, a growing system of elected and nominated bodies of Indians, both in the Provincial Governments and Municipal Councils. The lynch-pin was the District Officer, whose powers, although quite clearly defined, were also flexible and gave to India a remarkably stable form of government – India having been, since time immemorial, based on autocratic rather than democratic systems, except where, in times of settled peace, the natural evolution of village life led to the choice of head-men and officials for village patwaris. Even these powers were subject to the Deputy Commissioners (called Collectors in some areas), so although his powers were formal – the inspection and collection of taxes, the job of magistrate, in charge of the police and the judiciary, the care and control of the people in his District - he could use these powers with what wisdom he could muster, and was known in the villages as the father and mother of his people. It was, incidentally, uncommon for him to have many more than ten people in his office, to do the necessary paperwork. His area would cover certainly a million souls and in some cases where the population was less dense, many square miles. In the case of Kangra District in the Punjab, the area under the District Officer's control was the size of the whole of Wales.

It was at this official the agitators aimed their shafts; it was this man whom Montagu spurned, refusing to go out into the Districts to see how India was ruled. It was his power the nationalist politicians avidly sought. They wished to transfer the trust in an extraordinarily outstanding group of rulers, the District Officers, to nationalist politicians who would stop at nothing, So anxious were these men for power, that they gladly worked with Germans or with Bolsheviks, who intended taking the power which the nationalists believed they could retain. With the failure of the rebellion, the people who cared for the peace and welfare of the people of India continued to be the District Officers, through to 1947 and after, a growing number of whom were Indian themselves, but with the standards of training of the Indian Civil Service.

As a Liberal, Montagu concentrated on the charming, highly educated top echelon of Indian politicians, with whom he came to believe his Jewish blood, with its oriental origins, brought him close. The District Officer, who was criticised by these people, was not really within his ambit, unless in a town. At that time, 99% of India was rural.

Liberalism had become by then, not the liberalism of the Whigs of an earlier time, but something well tinged with the attitudes of socialism and equality, together with a strong antipathy to hierarchical structures.

With all his concern for fairness, it was surprising that Montagu did not see the inequalities of Brahminism when he went out to India,, or the inequality implicit in the ideas of caste. He only saw that these people wanted to rule their own country and that it was unjust that they did not. At Cambridge, he had read Humanities and not History, let alone Indian history. When he became Secretary of State for India, did he know that the politicians were closely linked with the German hegemony of the time and that their friends were working against Britain on the Oriental Desk in Berlin? It seems unlikely that he did not know through the Intelligence reports, but when one has made friendships, one tends to put loyalty to them before doubts of a patriotic nature.

It was a time of great change in Britain. After the landslide victory of the liberal party in the 1906 General Election, Herbert Asquith became Prime Minister in 1908, following Henry Campbell-Bannerman. Under Asquith, Churchill and Lloyd George brought forward a change in taxation and gave the unemployed dole money in 1910. In 1911, in order to overcome resistance in the Lords to the Government's policy on Ireland, Asquith pushed through The Parliament Act, stripping the Lords of any powers over financial bills and slipping in a clause which deprived the Monarch of the power to reject legislation [his Irish Bill had been refused by Edward VII]. We still suffer from the after-effects of that folly, which allows large majorities in the Commons to pass bad laws for lack of proper checks and balances.

The beginning of the war in 1914, against an enemy who had been in long term preparation, was bound to be difficult. Asquith, while helping Montagu through to his precious Under-Secretary-ship, had presided over the problems of Agadir, the steps to prevent war by agreeing to parity with Germany over the fleet and the alteration to the power of the House of Lords. Then with the war, the problems had come thick and fast; difficulties on the Western Front, the Dardanelles, Kut and the need to hold a Cabinet together, which led to parting with Winston Churchill, whom the Conservatives could not stomach as a member of the Coalition team.

Throughout, Asquith had had a confidante and adviser, a cousin of Clementine Churchill, Venetia Stanley. In 1915, his acolyte, Montagu, married her at a time when the Press was hounding Asquith and on several fronts, the War was going very badly. He was indeed to be pitied, seemingly betrayed, and under such pressure from many directions that it is hard to see how he survived. He wrote to Venetia Stanley, *"Never since the war began had I such an accumulation (no longer shared) of anxieties. One of the most hellish bits of these most hellish days was that you alone of all the world - to whom I have always gone in every moment of trial and trouble, and from whom I have always come back, solaced, healed and inspired -were the one person who could do nothing, and from whom I could ask nothing. To my dying day that will be the most bitter memory of my life... I am on the eve of the most astonishing and world-shaking decisions - such as I would never have taken without your counsel and consent."*

In the teeth of Press campaigns claiming that Asquith was pro-German, that he was losing the War, on December 5$^{th}$, 1916, Bonar Law, Curzon, and Lloyd George resigned, forcing Asquith's hand and his retirement from his position as Prime Minister.

For a while, Edwin Montagu, having Asquith to thank for his repeated Ministerial appointments - Financial Secretary to the Treasury, Chancellor of the Duchy of Lancaster, Minister of Munitions - would not leave his benefactor to join Lloyd George, but in June 1917, on Churchill's re-entering the Cabinet of his friend Lloyd George, Austin Chamberlain, the Secretary of State for India, , resigned and Lloyd George asked Winston's friend, Edwin Montagu, to take the post. It was Montagu's dream and ambition; he had fallen in love with India and had worked indefatigably, if one-sidedly, for the Indian politicians ever since he had first become involved with the sub-continent. He joined the Cabinet as Secretary of State and due to the unbalanced nature of his approach and his lack of understanding of India, the India so graphically described by Nirad Chaudhuri, and quite outside the capacity of his vision and interpretation, there followed what was to happen later.

Any Briton going to India, like the young men who went out to work there, initially felt the same inability to grasp the completely different traditions and standards of the Indian civilisation which had gone on for so many years. Only the length of the I.C.S. training which the young men went through made it possible for them to act in the remarkably even-handed way in which they did. Montagu had no such training. His experience had been mixing with charming intellectuals, educated at Oxford or Cambridge or London, with much the same concepts as the rest of England's young intellectual elite. What he had not understood was that the verbal claims and expressed interests of the educated Indian made no difference to their underlying traditions and beliefs, which had nothing to do with equality, democracy, or loyalty to the Raj and the Empire. Charm is like a thick coating that obscures the feelings underneath. It was with a certainty that these people were the same as him and sincerely in agreement with his ideas that Montagu set out, leaving his bride of two years behind, to visit India in 1917 and change the way she was ruled. Like St. George setting out to slay the dragon, not understanding that the dragon was already being slain by the processes already well in hand, through which, the British were giving India the same democratic institutions that they themselves had evolved over centuries. These could not simply be applied on top of the existing system, without careful and deep consideration. At that time, our interest, as it had been since the Mutiny and the Queen's promise to give Indians more say in their own government, was to bring Indians into the seats of power, but always thinking of this power as being handed to men of integrity who would support rather than undermine the slow building of a democracy.

Montagu suffered from the same tunnel-vision which affects so many of a Liberal persuasion – the conviction that they alone have the answer to the inequalities of life and take little notice of the opinions of those who do not agree with them. In consequence, he disregarded the constraints on improvident actions supplied by the Committees and consultations used by the British in India to maintain some sort of control. He imagined himself to be in a position of total power, much as some of his contemporaries believed in the power of Bolshevism.

He took no notice of the Lords who, in their debate, warned against letting out of her detention in Ootacamund the seditionist President of the Theosophical Society, Annie Besant, who was endlessly critical and destructive about the British Government and who, with Tilak, started the Society for Home Rule. He agreed to the ending of her detention in the teeth of opposition from the Madras Government, who had seen the trouble she was causing. When looking later at the information available through the processes of the Hunter Commission, he took no notice of the evidence, nor of Dyer's appeal to the Army Council, but almost as if he were one of the seditionists, took the view derived from the nationalist propaganda. Unhappily, Churchill supported his friend with the sort of language which helped us so much during the Second War.

In the Commons, Montagu's attacking speech was based on only two or three incidents, gravely distorted and in the main from the Congress Committee Report, not from Hunter. Sir John Hose at the India Office, with the benefit of his experience gained during a long career in India, warned Montagu that the Congress Report was thoroughly unreliable (after all Gandhi had to a large extent collected it) but of course Hose was not in a position to go public. Montagu would also have seen Mark Sykes' report before he went to India in 1917. That report had important things to say about the growing 'peace movement' which was being encouraged by the Bolsheviks, aided by the Germans and beginning to raise its voice in the Labour Party in England.

Sykes was well aware of the wider implications. He wrote: *"The whole of these various forces were in sympathy with the C.U.P* [The Committee of Union and Progress, the pro-German rulers of Turkey] *long before the war. The Morel pacifists worked up Italian atrocities in Tripoli. The international financiers have always come to the rescue of Turkey since time was, by bringing pressure to bear in the right direction in order to improve or increase the value and scope of their concessions. The Indian and Egyptian seditionists have been on the side of the C.U.P. ever since the Turkish revolution (1908) which so happily coincided with revolutionary modernism, with reactionary Islamic fanaticism. The Lucien Wolf and Jackie Schiff*[34] *anti-Zionists are Russophobes, pro-Turks, who have become pro-German and are now definitely fixed in that camp.*

*When these forces work for peace individually and collectively as they are doing now, and their operations are accompanied by tentative feelers, first by Morgenthau's expedition from the U.S.A., but of which the Indian Seditionists had early knowledge in London and then by movements in Switzerland, we may assume that the C.U.P desires a peace.*

*When the Dardanelles campaign was still in the balance and Bulgaria had not yet come in, these movements were strong. When Brusiloff's great offensive synchronised with a chance of Bulgaria's withdrawal and Rumanian participation, the movement is once more repeated.*

*Before closing this paragraph, it is well to emphasise the fact that each of these forces is evil, corrupt, and hostile, either to this country or the welfare of mankind, and that not one of them desires our future security."*

To quote again from his report: *"I now come to the reason why the C.U.P. desires peace. The Turks have probably come to the conclusion that the war will be one of exhaustion, and that both sides will be almost equally exhausted, that war-weariness is growing in Europe, that the weariness will result in a conference at which there will be a good deal of give and take, and that it will be useful to get Turkey's situation fixed and settled as advantageously as possible before the conference begins. The C.U.P. desires to come out of this war with an assured political and strategic position from which it can henceforth pursue its world policy, the main lines of which are:*

1. *Pan-Turanianism [Turkic super-state] reinforced by*
2. *Political control over the Moslem world*
3. *A firm grip on the control levers of international finance*
4. *Close co-operation with the various revolutionary movements in Europe and the U.S.A., such as Syndicalism* [government by labour unions], *Larkinism* [followers of Marxist Jim Larkin], *the workers of the world, Leninism.*

*The question therefore is on what terms can we negotiate with the C.U.P.? I put it thus, for if we negotiate at all, we should realise that we are negotiating with the*

---

34   Joseph Schiff was an influential Jewish-American banker who seems to have controlled or advised Woodrow Wilson and other international bankers and financed Lenin when he was forced to withdraw from Russia and go to Finland, after his initial Spring entry into Russia.

*C.U.P. Itilaf parties, Liberals, Old Turks, etc. are merely cloaks under which the C.U.P. might act. It is vital, strong, well organised, and can cast its net very wide indeed. There are two axioms which should govern our negotiation.*

*1. We must not try to be clever.*

*We shall be negotiating with past masters in all the arts of chicane, suggestion and atmosphere influence, bounded by no moral scruple of any kind. We must in our negotiation be absolutely straight and frank. Sir L Mallet suggests that we should let our terms be known discreetly in C.U.P. quarters.*

*I submit that it is impossible to be discreet when dealing with an occult organisation which has agents in Allied and Enemy camps. Whatever go-between we use; and no matter how vague and hedging are the messages our go-betweens convey, the C.U.P. will be able to show whomsoever they wish what we are doing and will, moreover, divine exactly what our motives are. We must therefore say exactly what we mean, when we send a message to the Turks, and tell all principals what we are doing, otherwise our Allies will get the information from enemy sources.*

*2. We must steel ourselves to observe a strictly moral course*

*We are dealing, as Sir L Mallet shows, with people who know no difference between right and wrong. If we depart for one instant from the path of right, we are endeavouring to compete on an impossible handicap. The men of the C.U.P., like the Jacobites of the French Revolution or the Prussian militarists, know of no moral barriers; assassination, subornation, bribery, massacre, and terror are the ordinary workaday terms of political thought.*

*Sir L Mallett has suggested that "it might be worth attempting to 'suborn' a Turkish general. Such a course would, I submit, be wrong and expose at least to a harvest of the same sort of ridicule and discredit we reaped when we tried to buy Rahini Bey, the Governor-General at Smyrna and Khalil, the besieging General at Kut. Subornation is not the business of the British Government any more than assassination; justice and policy dictate our assuming an attitude that she be above suspicion.*

*If it is admitted that we must be straightforward, and must not allow ourselves to become privy to doubtful actions, it must at first appear that our hands were tied, and that no negotiations of a useful kind could be undertaken, since secrecy and rascality are the foundations of Turkish diplomacy.*

*The C.U.P. desires to get an advantageous peace out of the present war, and probably considers that a secret and discreditable pact is the only way in which it can be obtained.*

*Then the C.U.P. will probably endeavour to split the Entente by secret, separate, and simultaneous negotiations with Great Britain and France, in order to reproduce on a greater scale the Anglo-French suspicion in regard to Syria and Egypt which existed before the war. If the Turks could, secretly and separately, offer Palestine to Great Britain, while offering Syria to France as a monopoly for the Levantine French financiers, with French political advisers under Turkish suzerainty, both nations would be in a state of permanent enmity, while the Turks could not only continually play us off one against the other, but also take every opportunity of promoting native hatred of the French in Syria and of the British in Egypt.*

*Another object of the C.U.P. will be to break off our alliance with the Arabs. The Arab movement menaces one of the most valuable assets of the fundamentals of the Sultan's claim to the Caliphate, weakening the C.U.P.'s hold on the Moslem world and taking the great Pan Islamic gathering, the annual Pilgrimage, beyond the reach of its direct influences. At the Pilgrimage, the Turks, if they hold Mecca, have an opportunity of dispensing propaganda not only to Asia but also in Moslem Africa. Sir L Mallett says: 'Amongst other questions, our engagements with the Arabs will require careful investigation, with a view to ascertaining how far we are committed to the King of the Hejaz.'*

*I admit that this is the wrong way of looking at the question. It is not a matter of finding out how little we can do for the Arabs, as of understanding what the C.U.P. will do to us if they regain their position in Arabia. If we leave the Arabs in the lurch by abandoning the cause of the principle, Arab nationality in Iraq and Syria, while standing out for a small independent kingdom in Hejaz, the C.U.P. will be able to inflame the Syrians and Baghdadis with a rancorous hatred of us, and it will be but a short time before the King of Hejaz will be pushed out of Mecca by a Moslem army from the North, or overthrown by a C.U.P. organised revolution; and Pan Islamic C.U.P. propaganda will assume a virulent form at the very moment when we are coping with domestic political problems in Egypt, the Sudan, and India ... ".*[35]

The remaining few lines of the Report are about Armenia and the C.U.P.'s intention to cause more trouble there. It seems possible, from its influential position with Islam; with the Ruler of Turkey, the Caliph at its head, that the C.U.P. was another mantle for the Muslim variety of the Illuminati, Roshaniya.

One thing Sykes did not mention was the occult background to the German intention in this. One of their moves was the removal of the historically significant altar from Pergamon to be placed in an equally significant position in Germany

Throughout this book, as the facts have come to light with the influences behind the scenes, the threads disclose an ongoing logic which Sykes in those earlier times had grasped and grasped well. Buchan's novels were an endeavour to put the situation before ordinary people, so that they could see something of what was going on under their noses. 1917 showed the outcome of those sinister influences uncovering themselves in the Bolshevik Revolution and in the extreme polarisation of the intellectual and Labour followers in Britain. Pacifism was one outcome, Bolshevism was

---

[35] Mr King MP was fined £100 for writing a letter in which among other things, he acted as a go-between, between the Sinn Fein Rafolovitch and Mr Pichton. King was a member of the 1917 Club, the club which was pacifist and revolutionary – much as Gandhi in India. Mark Sykes the author of this paper was the son of a Yorkshire landowner; he travelled widely in the Middle East as a young man. His wide knowledge led to his helping the refugees in Aleppo where he was probably poisoned; on his return to Europe he attended the Peace Conference to help with the Arab question, being supportive of Feisal and the new lands.

another. James on the East Persian Cordon found that people thought Bolshevism a part of the German activity – which of course it was – and in Britain there were meetings in praise of the Revolution, which people claimed they hoped would now come to Britain.

Montagu evidently disregarded the Sykes report, for on the same day in 1922 that Gandhi was arrested for his implication in the Moplah rebellion (voicing his intention to repeat his offence), the Secretary of State was forced to resign from the Cabinet, because he wished to support Turkey in the Peace treaties, contrary to Government policy, believing that the Khilafat movement was important for the Muslims of India. His political fall was as meteoric as the rise had been. Having destroyed Dyer in his support for Gandhi, with his vicious speech in the Commons Debate, he now faced the arrest of his idol and his own sacking as illustrations of his wrong-headedness.

Montagu died at the age of forty-five, on November 15th, 1924. He died from angina and syncope and one wonders if this sentimental, tender, nature loving man, was affected by the news of the O'Dwyer/Nair court case, which must by then have shown him that, despite his popularity in India, he had made a drastic mistake. He had already seen something of it when he had insisted to Reading that Gandhi must be arrested in 1922, when he commented disparagingly on the Indian political scene. He may have realised then, but the damage had been done and India would be handed over to the Hindu Raj, with dreadful suffering for the ordinary people and more especially, for the Untouchables.

His first visit to charming India was at the age of 33, in 1912; he had learnt neither humility nor judgement; his partisanship was supported by an arrogance that could encourage the then Secretary of State, Lord Morley, to believe that the Secretary of State, not the Viceroy, ruled India. It was inherent in this view, that of a young man without experience or understanding, to under-estimate the essential position of the Viceroy's Council, on which there was already an Indian Member, and the Imperial and Provincial Legislative Councils with their elected and appointed Indian Members, sitting beside a handful of official members; the Provincial Councils, the same with only a few 'official Members', the Municipal Councils with only one District Officer in the Chair, and even then he might be Indian. It was the attitude of an ebullient, arrogant and foolish young man. There followed the actions in keeping, backed by the power of the big Liberal majority with little experience, swept into Parliament in 1906. Montagu had come straight from Cambridge and the irresponsibility of student life, to the Secretary-ship to the Prime Minister and the flurry of success had undoubtedly gone to his head. He was never to win a seat again, but his humbling experience in 1924 had been too late for the lesson he had not learned, which lifted the hand off the reins of India, to her ongoing loss.

In Parliament, he had been asked by Mr Gwynne why he had not arrested Gandhi after the rebellion of 1919 and his reply was that Gandhi had apologised. Far from it! Gandhi had put the blame on his own 'Himalayan Miscalculation' - that the people had not had sufficient training in civil disobedience – hardly an apology.

As for the mere deportation of Horniman, the editor of the 'Bombay Chronicle', one of the early signatories of his Satyagraha and a steady reporter of anything that could help Gandhi's movement (including invented letters from British soldiers and reports of non-existent mutinies), Gandhi commented *"The act of the Government seemed to me to be surrounded by foulness which still stinks in my nostrils. I know that Mr. Horniman never desired lawlessness. He had not liked my breaking the prohibitory order of the Punjab Government without the permission of the Satyagraha Committee..."*

Thus his reference to the action which Attenborough shows as Gandhi behind bars! – and Gandhi then excuses himself on not having received Horniman's letter. These little taradiddles indicate such a degree of twisting and turning that Montagu's behaviour could not have been balanced if it were to fit in with it. That, of course, was Montagu's intention - to fit in with the Nationalists, not realising for one moment that the plan for India to become a Dominion, democratically ruled, was outside those politicians parameters. Or did he realise it? Was he aware that his Indian friends were seeking the 'Hindu Raj' and in a preview of later ideas on multiculturalism, did he approve? As Venetia Montagu recorded in her extracts from Montagu's notes on his journeys round India in 1917 and 18, *"Hinduism is caste."* Clearly, he understood that there was a difference between Hindu rule and British rule, for democracy and caste are incompatible, but those were exciting times, with politics and religions in a state of flux. Dialectic Materialism, Theosophy, Anthroposophy, and Spiritualism were all contending for followers and who could know where the truth lay? His own Jewishness, unlike his father's, was cultural rather than religious.

Perhaps that explains his attitude to Annie Besant, who was, as Lord Sydenham remarked 'an Englishwoman, bearing with her the prestige earned by others', but who was combining the religious tokens for an enhancement of her position and her words. What she said, since we English put some emphasis on truth, would have been accepted, not because she said it, but because so many had been heard before her. Having released her from detention, he effectively joined his own name and position to her vehicle. His own prestige arose from endless Secretaries of State or Presidents of the Council of India who had served before him and the rebellion was thus empowered in Indian eyes.

With the Russian Revolution going on apace, Montagu came to India, on the crest of the wave. As Dyer, with his deep knowledge and insight said, *"Mr Montagu is a very clever man, but he does not understand India."*

# Chapter II
# IGNORANCE & SUPERSTITION

When Edwin Montagu died in November 1924, the 'Times' published a sort of encomium on him, which shows him in a more clear and understandable light: *"In his loveable and complicated character, great subtlety of intellect was curiously mingled with great simplicity of mind. He had the trustfulness of a child It was often betrayed and he suffered agonies of disappointment and surprise, but his confidence always returned, ready for the next encounter. He never got tired of being sorry for people ..."*

This man, ambitious and idealistic, went to India with the plan to alter the entire way in which India was governed, in his sights.

His innocence did not appreciate the attitudes of the Indians, a matter which had exercised the British over the years as they endeavoured to give these loveable people, in the words of the Reforms Report, *"a system which has won the admiration of critical observers from many lands, and to which other nations that found themselves called upon to undertake a similar task of restoring order and good government in disturbed countries have always turned for inspiration and guidance."* The next phrase was *"England should be proud of her record in India."* The point that is so often forgotten today, remembered only in books, like those by John Masters on the Thugs for example, is that: *"Our rule gave them security from the violence of robbers and the exaction of landlords."* - from cruelty and despotism. The India to which we came as the great Moghul Empire was decaying was one of banditry and frequent terror. The process that brought to India the 'placid, pathetic contentment of the masses' was not, as Parvus and the revolutionaries claimed, exploitation, but trade, which led to the growing prosperity of India, evidenced by recent Indian writers, in detailed analysis. The tables of economic growth show the same.

No mention has been made of Nadir Shah's sacking of Delhi in 1739, or of those such as Sir John Malcolm and his efforts to contain and destroy the Pindaris, the ruthless gangs which ravaged India at the end of the 18th Century. Though they are mentioned by Gandhi in his 'Hind Swaraj' as being unexceptionable and easily reduced to civil behaviour by him showing them his chest, they are forgotten. The emphasis now is on exploitation, anachronistically applied, without any recognition for the concern of the early British traders to protect their own settlements and the people around them. It is like Attenborough portraying Dyer as a savage, or Montagu accusing him of shooting at women and children in Amritsar, while ignoring the mob's desire to climb into the fort for loot and outrage, as was shown in the evidence.

It is unlikely that Montagu knew about the Pindaris, whom Sir John Malcolm described as arising *"like masses of putrefaction in animal matter, out of the corruption of weak and expiring states."* The effect of these ravages was to extend their lawless outcome, because the landless men were recruited to the armies of the Chiefs.

In his 'Memoirs of Central India', Sir John Malcolm described the Pindaris as being unencumbered by tents or baggage, travelling simply with horses and a few handfuls of cake for them. *"The party, which usually consisted of two or three thousand good horses with a proportion of mounted followers, advanced at the rapid rate of forty or fifty miles a day, neither turning to the right or left, till they arrived at their place of destination. They then divided, and made a sweep of all cattle and property they could find; committing at the same time, the most horrid atrocities, and destroying what they could not carry away. They trusted to the secrecy and suddenness of the eruption for avoiding those who guarded the frontiers of the countries they invaded; and before a force could be brought against them, they were on their return. Their chief strength lay in their being intangible. If pursued, they made marches of extraordinary length (sometimes upwards of sixty miles), by roads almost impracticable to travel for regular troops. If overtaken they dispersed, and reassembled at an appointed rendezvous; if followed to the country from which they issued they broke into small parties. Their wealth, their booty and their families, were scattered over a wide region, in which they found protection amid the mountains, and in the fastness belonging to themselves and to those to whom they were either openly or secretly connected, but nowhere did they present any point of attack; and the defeat of a party, the destruction of one of their cantonments, or the temporary occupation of some of their strongholds, produced no effect beyond the ruin of an individual freebooter, whose place was instantly supplied by another, generally of more desperate fortune and therefore more eager for enterprise."*

They came from all communities, and latterly, were matched by Pathan freebooters. There were more, with the 'criminal tribes', of Bhils, and the Thugs, whose secret depredations, as Sleeman discovered, were frequently supported by the local Rajahs acting as fences, so that no innocent traveller was safe. All this is neatly forgotten – a situation where extremely brave people, without self-interest or desire for gain, helped a population that was in parlous straits.

There were also the Maharajas, whose armies, supported by the French and their officers, were a further peril. In the spin off from their defeat, the Indian trait of unforgiveness shows clearly. Sir John Malcolm settled the Peshwa of the Mahrattas, (to the regret of Warren Hastings), on the banks of the Ganges with a pension of eight lakhs of rupees a year. His successor, the Nana Sahib, in the time of the Mutiny, shot down the British prisoners he had captured at Cawnpore as they, under a promise of safety, got into boats to go down the river. That was not enough; again on promises of safety, the Nana Sahib was responsible, despite the pleas of his ladies, for the deaths of the women and children who had been left behind in the women's house. This same resentment was shown by Mrs Indira Gandhi's generation, when the well, into which their corpses had been crammed, was topped by a celebratory statue of the leader of the mutineers, Tantia Topi.

It is unlikely that Montagu, who read General Studies at Cambridge, knew of India's history; he might have felt sorry for the people who lived in uncomfortable circumstances and in an unhealthy climate, but who were necessary to keep the peace of India. If he had grasped the seriousness of his undertaking, if he had had less enthusiasm and more wisdom, he might have come across Malcolm's description of the India of his time, and if he had, he might have had doubts about the Indian Nationalists and been more able to tell the good from the bad and the timeserving. Malcolm had written to the East India Company Directors in 1824, to put the Indian situation clearly. Of Hindus, he wrote that they are the unchanged people. *"They are to my knowledge, adepts in the spreading of discontent and in exciting sedition and rebellion. My attention has been, during the last twenty five years, particularly directed to this dangerous species of secret war against our authority that is always carrying on by numerous though unseen hands. Letters keep up the spirit by exaggerated reports, and by pretended prophecies. When the time appears favourable from the occurrence of misfortune to our arms, from rebellion in our provinces, or mutiny in our troops, circular letters and proclamations are dispersed over the country with a celerity that is incredible. Such documents are read with avidity. The contents in most cases are the same. The English are depicted as usurpers of low caste, and as tyrants, who have sought India with no view but of degrading the inhabitants and robbing them of their wealth, while they seek to subvert their usage and religion. The native soldiery are always appealed to and the advice given to them in all instances I have met, is the same – Your European tyrants are few in number – murder them!"*

This was not written just before the Mutiny of 1857, nor before the carefully planned rebellion in 1919, but in 1824.

Even so, he had noticed on his journey through India in 1817–18 that: *"one has here, as elsewhere, among the educated Indians a desire for more power. Not, I think, for democracy; for horrible as it may be for an Englishman of my way of thinking to learn, the clever Indian wants executive power and executive opportunity, but he is not a democrat. He believes in caste, he believes in wealth."*

Sir Harcourt Butler put it differently, as the Lieutenant-Governor of the United Provinces [now Uttar Pradesh], when speaking about the Reforms Scheme in 1918: *"I want to impress upon you the enormous difficulties which beset this question of reforms. It is enormously difficult to graft the ideas of Western democracy onto an ancient social system, of which a prominent feature is the institution of caste. It is enormously difficult to harmonise the aspirations of a modern industrial Empire with the aspirations of an essentially spiritual and conservative land like India. May I quote to you the saying of an able Chinese statesman? 'To speak in a parable; a new form of government is like an infant, whose food must be regulated with circumspection if one desires it to thrive'. If in our zeal for the infant's growth we give it several days' nourishment at once, there is small hope of its ever attaining manhood."*

In India, superstition is endemic: in the 1930s, it was still possible for a man to levitate by magic; in the 1970s, the author watched an elephant given the personality of Ganesh, the household God, walking slowly through a bazaar in Madurai in Madras, taking an orange here and a banana there, from the open stalls, and thus blessing the proprietor's business; in the 1980s a woman, whose son had to go to court on a charge of theft, sat on the grave of Sir William Wedderburn [a friend of Montagu, who resigned as a High Court Judge and joined Annie Besant and was a one time President of Congress]. The son was let off and her conclusion was that Sir William was a pir, a saint; from that day forward, every year on the date of her son's release, she placed a bottle of whisky on his grave, in her belief that this was what Sir William, as an Englishman, would most have liked. Another Wedderburn, a Scottish lawyer of an earlier time, had helped Clive when he was being attacked in Parliament, but no-one had called him a saint.

Behind all this was the overarching sinister superstition; the control of the Hindu masses by the caste system, confirming their subordinate position to the Brahmin hierarchy. There are school children to this day who sit outside the schools, not allowed in for fear they may pollute the children of the men of caste; there are the anti-prayers, which in such a system could affect those whom the controllers wish to be destroyed. Can it have been pure coincidence that, when Dyer was about to be sent back to England, all his possessions being in the bank at Rawalpindi, the bank was burnt down – or that Captain Briggs died on the operating table at Bannu and could not give evidence to Hunter?

Could this powerful magic affect the people in power – Montagu, the Viceroy, Lord Chelmsford, the members of the Hunter Committee? Even Dyer himself remarked when at last he saw the record after three months and his voyage back to England, that it was not what he had said? Just as the evidence recorded as given by Sir Michael O'Dwyer and that of Sir Umar Hayat Khan were denied by both men? Sir Umar Hayat Khan, having tried to correct his, finally tore it up in disgust.

The magic of the sort of conspiracy, to which Sir John Malcolm referred in 1824, continued through the Mutiny in 1857 and through the cow-killing riots at Patna. Sir Harcourt Butler also wrote in the same vein; *"Such notices were circulated freely at the time of the Mutiny. They were inculcated in the revolutionary movements of the Mahrattas on the West and the Bengalees on the East of India in the first decade of this century. These two revolutionary movements were at first independent of one another but preached the same doctrines, followed in each case by assassinations. There have been other movements to encourage the idea that the British were leaving India. The cow-protection movement of 1893 in the Eastern districts of the United Provinces, which ended in extensive rioting, was conducted with great secrecy and took a form explosive to government. British rule was in abeyance for some days. The Hindus appointed their own officers, imposed fines, established pounds for cattle and stopped altogether the reporting of crime. The marching of a British regiment through the affected area at once restored order and confidence.*

*With the tree smearing movement; in the early morning, villagers would find one or more groves in which every tree had a circle of mud with hair admixed. The government analyst reported that the specimens of hair sent to him were the bristles of a pig or pubic hair of a fakir. About this time I had a fakir in my camp for about a fortnight. I learnt a lot from him round a camp fire and he was well cared for. One evening I referred to the tree smearing and that night he disappeared. In 1893 and on this occasion the tenants refused to pay their rent because a kshatrya raj was coming".*

As well as the assassinations, there were the mysterious and successive 'fading away' of various Britons. Curzon's wife faded away and died after he had divided Bengal; Lord Sydenham's wife and daughter both died in much the same way after he had upheld the decision of the judgement to imprison Tilak; Lord Sydenham was the Governor of Bombay at the time. Wavell and Linlithgow were worn out and broken in health. None of these remarks do anything more than show a sinister background, which could easily influence the minds of men less strong than those Montagu was later to castigate – even his own death in 1924 might be ascribed to some sort of link with the fears of which Lord Ampthill spoke in the Lords.

But Montagu's reputation had reached India earlier, in 1910, through Sir James Dunlop Smith, Secretary to the Viceroy, Lord Minto, a man of character and much respected by Indians. His knowledge of India and Indians was such that it was believed that much of what Kipling wrote derived from Dunlop Smith's experiences, and certainly he was a man who had many Indian friends. In 1910, Montagu had just become Under Secretary of State for India and so was of interest to those who would have to do with him. Sir James said *"I have seen Montagu, a cleverish young Jew with a certain amount of University air about him and hopelessly ignorant of India and of people in India of whatever race or colour. I don't fancy he will ever have much to say to India, but in the present chaos, the work of every department is at a standstill."*

Supported by Montagu, Lord Morley, the Secretary of State himself, was being irritating; *"Your Excellency asks if no one can moderate the Secretary of State's perpetual interference. I don't think anyone can. I have tried to do what I could, but any attempt in that direction hitherto has resulted in further interference."* Sir Edward Penderel Moon, describing this behaviour, says: *"unused to practical affairs his [Morley's] vanity was tickled by the idea that he could now control the fate of millions and, strongly abetted by his Under Secretary, Edwin Montagu, he interfered constantly in the details of administration and also insisted on his sole right to appoint members of the Viceroy's Council, regardless of the Viceroy's own wishes. Minto never allowed himself to be ruffled, endured one or two Councillors sent to him 'who were not only useless but mischievous', humoured Morley whenever he could, and by quiet and courteous insistence, generally got what he wanted on important matters."*

There is a tradition amongst many people, that those who have been brought up with livestock learn calmness and balance, unlike those who live in urban surroundings. Minto had previously been Governor-General of Canada, fought under Lord Roberts in the Afghan War of 1879, had ridden four times in the Grand National and had won the French Grand National at Auteuil.

Dunlop Smith wrote to Lord Minto from England about some speech given by Montagu: *"Montagu's speech is nothing but the lecturing of a set of schoolboys by a pedagogue of the most priggish type. Even his reference to Your Excellency is offensive. But His Majesty's Government and the India Office are delighted with the speech, which they describe as a 'Triumph'! Then throughout the whole speech, there is not one word about the late or the present King and no allusion to the effect produced in India by the late King's death ...*

*A despatch has just gone, saying that the time has come to take away from local government, the power they have of taking direct action in sedition cases. The sole reason for this is to furnish His Majesty's Government with a sop to fling to the Socialists in the next General Election."* It should be remembers that the Socialists and the Indian Politicians were very close, although Moon says that Congress purported to be a Liberal party.

Dunlop-Smith's letter had been written on 29th July, 1910; Montagu's speech had been given on July 26th. 'The Pioneer' at Allahabad commented that *"Mr Montagu, when citing in his elaborate Budget speech a portion of the Act of 1833, for the purposes of showing the Secretary of State's great powers and responsibilities, was very careful to make no reference to section 39 of the same Act, which provides that the superintendence, direction and control of the whole civil and military government of all the said territories and revenues in India shall be and is hereby vested in a Governor-General and Councillors to be styled The Governor-General in Council."* The article went on to point out that the Act under which, in that time, the Secretary of State actually derived his powers was the Act of 1858 (just after the Mutiny) in which he would, in effect, take over the duties of the Board of Control which in turn took its powers from Pitt's India Act of 1784. The matter was a serious one, for the Under Secretary had made a spurious and unconstitutional claim that the Viceroy was the 'agent' of the Secretary of State. In one step, Montagu had relegated India's position in the Empire, to which further reform would give or lead to Dominion status, to that of a Colony, ruled by the politicians in England. He had done worse. He had pointed out that Lord Minto would shortly be leaving and Lord Morley would be staying on. Of such is the idiocy of unlearned idealism. At that moment, Montagu, aged 31, had been in the saddle for five months. The Indians he would have known were such people as Jawarharlal Nehru and his near contemporaries, who would have been at Cambridge with him. These would probably have been men who knew and used India House, the centre started by Krishna Varma, which influenced the anarchists of Indian politics. Nehru remembered Edwin Montagu coming to the debating society of Trinity College, 'The Magpie and Stump', although by then, Montagu was a Member of Parliament. The students Montagu met at the time of Nehru were probably much the same as the students of his own day; Nehru describes the Indian students as using the most extreme language when speaking of Indian politics. They were excited by the violence taking place in Bengal, and although people such as Diwan Ram Lal, a High Court Judge in the Punjab many years later, settled down into the existing institutions, there is little doubt that Montagu's experience of Indians before he went there was that of the most nationalistic and left wing of the sub-continent; the people who would later be involved with the 1919 Rebellion.

Dr Kitchlew, who went on to a German University, was one of Nehru's contemporaries. Lajpat Rai, Gokhale and Bepin Chander Pal, were visitors, speechmakers to the young Indian students. Montagu would have been among these, so that when he took on the position of Under Secretary of State for India and began to throw his weight about, his main knowledge was of the anger of Indian students about their British rulers, just as is mentioned in the speeches from the Lords' Debate on his later visit, which would typically have had all the foam of political rhetoric, nothing of the way India was actually ruled, or the peasants lived and worked.

The result was that when a note came from Lajpat Rai via Ramsay Macdonald, Montagu was enthused by a complaint that the judge at Midnapore had been rude about the murderers of the two Kennedy ladies, and said that he believed that the entire system of judgements in India should be altered to have a further tier of supervisors above the judges. He suggested the new plan to the Chief Justice in England, Sir Lawrence Jenkins, who considered it unworkable. It was the sort of idea that might come to any ebullient young man who thought he had power to use for good, without knowing anything about the existing situation. It also affected Montagu's attitude to the Indian Civil Servants when he later went to India and resulted in his refusal to go into the Districts and meet the men who ruled India on the ground, or see how they carried on their work.

Ramsay Macdonald had been to India and met the most avant-garde politicians, as would Montagu himself when he went out; Macdonald was very much in favour of the Bolshevik Revolution, as were large numbers of British intellectuals. Communist propaganda was believed and the movement supported by the political Left, especially in the Labour Party. In 1917, Lloyd George would not at first interfere with the Stockholm Conference or with the attendance by one of his Ministers, Arthur Henderson, together with Ramsey Macdonald and delegates from the workers and soldiers Committees. The intention of the Conference was that all the proletariats of the World should unite to stop the War. Lord Robert Cecil, then the Foreign Minister, considered that if anyone should go, it should be Macdonald and in the meantime Henderson resigned as a Minister. By May1920, a Russian Trade Delegation had been permitted to come to England and Krassin and Kameneff and Miliutin were given passage on one of the journeys to and from Moscow in a destroyer. They brought with them jewels that they sold in Hatton Garden with which to pay the 'Daily Herald', the Labour Party organ, to which the Congress had also sent £10,000; where the delegates were hobnobbing with Councils of Action. Tom Quelch and William McLaine of the British Socialist Party left for the Third International in Moscow. Three other Russians of the Delegation - Klishko, Nogin and Rosowsky had arrived on May 16th. Quelch at this time was there and but for Russian money his Party would have been practically non-existent. Henderson was to say much the same to Lord Davidson in 1929. Churchill spoke in March about the proposed Bolshevik delegation and its treachery.

The gradual infiltration of Bolshevik influence in various forms was therefore affecting the British Government, even before Dyer arrived home on 8th May 1920, having been invalided out of the army.

Macdonald it was, who advised King George V not to invite his Russian cousins to safe life in England, as he said, because Britain herself might be led into revolution. Ramsay Macdonald was to become the Prime Minister of the Labour Government in 1924; the Government that made such a noise about the MacCardie decision on the O'Dwyer/Nair case, that there were threats of removing him from the Bench. It was also the Government that was subsidised by the Bolsheviks and Macdonald himself became a friend and correspondent of Gandhi. The influences which would later have a strong effect on the British Government's attitude to the suppression of the information on a nationwide rebellion and the Third Afghan War were already in place when Montagu took up his position. Without knowledge or experience of India, he was extremely pliable.

His overwhelming conceit in relation to Indian affairs was to disgust Lady Minto and, as she wrote, also the Indian newspapers, when Montagu persuaded Lord Morley, his Superior, to claim that it was the Secretary of State and not the Viceroy who ruled India. His liberalism seems to have veered towards republicanism at that date, when he showed no respect over the death of Edward VII, nor showed it to the new King George V. Since the King Emperor was, at that time, the lynch pin that held the different creeds and races of India together, this omission was serious enough to appear to flout the monarchy.

The position of the King also affected the Indian Princes, many of whom had a direct relationship with the King, some with the Viceroy, and some with the Viceroy's Agent. In the case of very small princedoms, they were subject to the District Officers. India, being essentially autocratic and having traditions that applied to the Princely powers, was given a shock by the neglect of the necessary respect which supported the rulers and gave cohesion to the ruled.

In 1908/09 the Morley/Minto Reforms had been passed. The reforms were known as the Indian Councils Act and widened the franchise to include Indians in various government bodies, both in the Provinces and in the central Legislative Council. Minto also appointed onto the Viceroy's Executive Committee, the Viceroy's Council, Lord Sinha Sachendra Singha, an eminent barrister who lost a large portion of his income in taking up this post.

In 1912 Montagu went out to India. He experienced that art of the confidence trickster, which assured him that he understood them while they were really understanding him. Relations were cemented which could not be easily set aside and which led him, when he later went out to India again, to dismiss as trivial or irrelevant anything which suggested a conspiracy behind the hatred of the British and anger at their bureaucratic rule by Councillors and civil servants and every form of Government work. It was as though he was encouraging the people without any national sense into the open, to build their Nationalist Politics. He opened the door to seditionist power.

Between the 1912 visit and 1914, he had two more years at the India Office and then became Financial Secretary to the Treasury, where he learned the relevance of financial arrangements and then in 1915, at the age of 36, he was in the Cabinet as Chancellor of the Duchy of Lancaster. In 1916, he was Minister of Munitions. Lloyd-George's offer of Secretary of State for India followed. As in the present day, those encouraging moves towards world rule, the people with the covert power, saw him obviously in the hands of the seditionist Indians who, in their turn, were in relations with the C.U.P, so they knew that he would be offered the job and would get it.

Hard evidence is not there, but circumstantial evidence is. In terms of influence and behaviour, it seems this exceedingly unwise man was about to betray India and years of peaceful rule.

Montagu's own reforms were to have a strong effect at the time they were worked out - time when the underlying tensions, strains and conspiracies were coming together, as Harcourt Butler said, and when India had already gone through the infiltration and incitement of the Germans. In 1919, with the unsound methods of distribution of seats for the Legislative Councils, they put paid to any sound progression towards the freeing of the British from the responsibility for India until it came, almost by force, in 1947.

From the period of his Secretary-ship and the undermining of the men on the spot, Hindu Raj became an immediate possibility and communal violence increased throughout India for the last 27 years of our time. The determination with which the British and many outstanding Indians had worked for nearly a century - such people as Bahadur Sapru, Maulana Azad, Khizzar and even Jinnah, whose action in demanding Pakistan, was only the result of the Hindu Raj faction and the refusal to grant Muslim ministries after the 1937 elections – those people believed that an integrated India was possible, until the power which had seeped into the hands of the conspirators of an earlier time, determined to take over India themselves without concern for the vast minorities, forced a different route.

**Chapter III**

**VISITING**

Given that Montagu was passionately in love with India and, like so many people in love, did not understand the nature of the beloved, and given that Lloyd George needed everyone he could get on his side, the offer of the position of Secretary of State was inevitable.

The idea that India should be given a further step towards Self-Government had already been bruited. The loyal behaviour of the Indian troops had shown Britain the courage and quality of the solders who had fought in France and bravely helped to defend Kut. John Buchan later put the matter in focus when he said: *"But it was the performance of India that took the world by surprise and thrilled every British heart. India, whose alleged disloyalty was the main factor in German calculations. The British Commonwealth had revealed itself at last as that wonderful thing for which its makers had striven and prayed – a union based not on statute or officialdom, but on the eternal simplicities of the human heart."*

Already in 1916, Austin Chamberlain, then Secretary of State for India, had agreed to further steps; Lord Chelmsford, Hardinge's successor as Viceroy, a Liberal Peer who had been governor of two of the Australian states and was then a captain in the Territorials in India, put forward constitutional plans for advancement[36]. The War Cabinet was doubtful, but Lord Meston, Lord Willingdon and others persuaded the Cabinet that some statement of policy was necessary. Once again we have an instance of the vulnerability of the British nation at war, being pressed into unwise decisions.

---

36   Lord Chelmsford agreed with Montagu throughout most of this time. Montagu bullied him unmercifully, but the first step, the release of Annie Besant was agreed rather in terms of the blind leading the blind.

Chamberlain wrote to Lord Chelmsford saying: *"What would have seemed a great advance a little time ago would now satisfy no one and we must, I think, be prepared for bold and radical measures."*

The British public at large regarded this momentous step as a grateful response to the valuable help of India. However Lord Curzon, as a retired Viceroy, wrote that *"the classes to whom it is proposed to offer additional concessions have no right to claim them on the ground of war service, for they have rendered no such service. On the other hand, those who have helped us most in the war neither ask for nor want the particular reforms now under discussion."*

This is the point made throughout this book, but the urban people, while making enormous profits through the clothing and armament factories moved to India and the increase of sales of their own products, had also been generous with purchases of war loan. If at that moment, the politicians had given a firm undertaking to see that those who had worked for the war were rewarded, the ensuing reforms might have given India a more balanced step forward.

By August 1917, Curzon and others had formulated the announcement which Montagu was to make on the 20th, having replaced Austin Chamberlain.

*"The policy of His Majesty's Government, with which the Government of India are in complete accord, is that of associating Indians in every branch of the administration and the gradual development of self governing institutions with a view to the progressive realisation of responsible government in India as an integral part of the British Empire. They have decided that substantial steps in this direction should be taken as soon as possible."*

As Mrs Nesta Webster, the wife of an Indian policeman remarked, *"Why responsible? Had the Government of India then proved irresponsible hitherto?"*

In the teeth of Indian and British concern in Madras (the Governor being Lord Pentland), Montagu, together with Lord Chelmsford, released Annie Besant from her internment at Ootacamund where, under the Defence of India Act, she had been placed, due to her activities as a dangerous agitator.

Montagu claimed that this was to secure a 'tranquil atmosphere' for the proposed visit by the Secretary of State and his travels to look into the proposed reforms.

In English literature there is a character called Molesworth, who, if involved, would probably have voiced the doubts that were widespread. He might have said that 'As any fule kno', to free a lady who had been causing so much trouble, having been convicted by three judges, two of them, Indians, would be unlikely to cause anything more than wild excitement and a further expectation of licence in the matter of agitation.

In the House of Lords, retired Governors, Secretaries and Under-Secretaries of State and even Viceroys, pointed this out. Montagu, knowing it all, refused to compromise.

The message went out to Nationalist activists, that Montagu was expected to submit in the course of Indian bargaining and his later reforms were turned down by the

National Congress in their meeting in 1919 at Amritsar, while the Hunter Committee was still sitting in Lahore on the 'Disturbances'.

Annie Besant, by this time the President of The Theosophical Society, deserves a word on her own. She was born in 1847 and at the age of 20 married a clergyman, Frank Besant. She had two children, whom she left with him, going off to do various things, but mainly involved with Socialism, Unions and the leaders of early Socialism, such as Charles Bradlaugh. She was a firm atheist (and wrote the Gospel of Atheism) until she met Madame Blavatsky and became a Theosophist. She started the Hindu University of Benares (later taken over by Hindus, jealous of her eminence), and a girls' school in the same town. It was, interestingly, from Benares that so much of the Bengalis propaganda flowed to the rest of India. Her influence was great. Nehru, for instance, was tutored by one of her protégés[37]; she was President of Congress in 1917. Her achievements were widespread. She learnt Hindi and translated the Baghavad Gita; she spoke so beautifully that even Montagu mentions her voice. She died in 1933.

Madame Blavatsky, Russian born in 1831, founded Theosophy and the Theosophical Society in New York in 1875, with a Major Olcott. It had a principle based on Buddhism and was intended to create a 'universal brotherhood of man'.[38] At that time, Socialism and Theosophy were closely linked, although Theosophy claims no political connections. Annie Besant, in India in 1917, was preaching the golden age of Hinduism to which the many Hindu societies aspired. The British Bureaucracy, of course, was an antithesis of such a concept and her attacks on it led to agitation and rioting. The illogicality of her claims did not seem to dawn on her – the golden age of Hinduism, when everything was perfect, denies the reasoning of Gautama Buddha, who found the sufferings of mankind so great that he went into the forest to meditate the matter of withdrawing from this miserable, ongoing cyclical situation. Her interest in Home Rule and getting the British out arose from the idea that this would lead to a return to a Golden Age. Her accusations in describing the awful behaviour of the British were hazy and when she was removed to Ootacamund where she could walk about and see her friends, she considered it reasonable to describe her detention as 'being dropped into an oubliette'. On the other hand, she was one of the few who supported the firing at Amritsar, saying that when wives and children were in danger, it should be expected that soldiers would fire.

Just as Annie Besant indirectly influenced Nehru, Blavatsky, (thought by General Sir Bindon Blood to be a Russian spy) had Krishnavarma as a disciple. With the University of Girls' School at Benares, it is unlikely that they did not inspire many more people. Rudolf Steiner, the Austrian philosopher, was a member of the Theosophical Society before leaving it and setting up the Anthroposophical Society, due to some

---

37   Ferdinand Brooks as an Illuminati Theosophist tutored Nehru for three years.
38   This was of course the Illuminist prescription which was the yeast for the French Revolution with its Illuminist concepts, so favoured by the Jacobins.

of the clear errors in the theosophical leaders' thoughts. He warned Annie Besant in 1923 or thereabouts that the time had not yet come for the British to leave India.

Lord Sydenham, who had been Governor of Bombay, had supported Tilak's arrest because of his incitement to murder subtly linked with magic in his paper, 'Kesari' in 1908. In 1916, when Lord Sydenham had retired, Annie Besant, Bal Gangadhur Tilak and Bepin Chander Pal, (the latter being overtly in favour of Hindu Rule) were pushing Home Rule. Tilak and Bepin Chander Pal were both refused entry into the Punjab in the middle of the War by Sir Michael O'Dwyer.

Thus Lord Sydenham was fully aware of the seriousness of the situation in India, as was Sir Michael O'Dwyer, still at his post in the Punjab and Sir Harcourt Butler, similarly in the United Provinces.

Lord Sydenham had put forward to the Lords, the following notice on the Situation in India:

To draw attention to the present situation in India, with special regard to the internment and release of Mrs Besant: and to move for papers.

*"My Lords, it is always an exceedingly difficult thing to say when a line ought to be drawn in checking of freedom of speech or of writing, but I think it would be agreed to by everybody that such freedom must be curtailed if it is used to threaten public order or to sow the seeds of murder and of outrage.*

*In India it is absolutely necessary that restrictions of this kind should be enforced. The mass of the people is ignorant and perfectly ready to believe any false statement that may be made to them; they are credulous to a degree that can hardly be conceived here. I should like to give your Lordships an instance of that of which your Lordships may not have heard. When we first started plague inoculation in India, a story was widely circulated in the Bombay Presidency that a holy man had said that an Indian with white blood would drive the English into the sea; and that we were pricking the arms of Indians in order to find the Indian with white blood and kill him off in good time. Besides that, the people of India are very easily excited and serious disturbances often occur through the passing around of some obvious fiction which in Western countries would not attract a moment's attention. Everyone who has lived in India must know many cases of that kind, and when disorders thus promoted occur, then the most hateful duty of Government comes into play, and you have to put them down by force.*

*But we have more direct evidence than this of the necessity of these restrictions in India. All political agitation in India from the first, has been accompanied by assassination, and in many cases, the assassins themselves have named the newspapers and the speakers from whom they drew the inspiration of murder* [he then went on to quote the case of the murder of Mr Jackson which has been described earlier]. *Could a more tragic confession ever have been made? And was that young decadent Brahmin the real criminal? Other murderers have told the same story in different words and surely all such cases as that, show we cannot allow speech and writing that is proved effective in leading young Indians into crime.*

*Mrs Besant, who was formerly a student of Theosophy, joined the ranks of the extremists, and started a home rule movement of her own. She wrote a book that contains more reckless defiance of facts than I have ever seen compressed into the same small space and in her paper 'New India' she appeared anxious to imitate the most dangerous language in which the Indian press has indulged. She told excitable young Indians that India was a 'perfect paradise' for 5,000 years before our advent; and that it had become a 'perfect hell' owing to the 'brutal British bureaucracy'. Those are her expressions, not mine. She said that India had been 'converted into a land of permanent famine and pestilence, and its children, a race of effeminate weaklings.' She accused the British Government of depriving a weaker People of their liberty and retaining them under her rule in perpetual slavery, under the plea of civilising them and bettering their lot. There are no freer people in the world than Indians under our rule, and such oppression that exists, is that of Indians by Indians, and it would be increased a hundred-fold if we handed over the reins to the small body of Brahmins and lawyers whom Mrs. Besant is trying to lead. Surely, language of that kind is exactly calculated to arouse an excitable people to rebellion. And would not rebellion be fully justified and even become a public duty if the British Government were really inflicting permanent famine and pestilence on India and holding India in perpetual slavery?*

*To those of us who have been called upon to play a part in governing India, and whose only thought has been to do the best we could for the people of India, such expressions, of course, seem the wildest possible nonsense, but there are millions of people who are perfectly ready to believe them. In olden days, pestilence and famine were attributed to the wrath of the gods. It is an English woman who tells Indians that they are due to a Government, which had done its utmost, with great success to combat both pestilence and famine.*

*But Mrs. Besant's libels on our countrymen do not end with false assertions of that kind. In a book which is now about to be published in India, to gain the advantage of her fresh access of notoriety, she states that for every wrong done to a white woman in Africa, 'tens of thousands of Kaffir women are outraged.' I think the noble Earl and the noble Viscount who filled, with great distinction, the office of High Commissioner in South Africa would repudiate that statement.*

*Mrs. Besant then goes on to generalise, she says 'It is there that lies one of our greatest sins, the utter disregard for morality where coloured women are concerned, the shameful disregard of womanhood in every country whereunto Britain has entered and where Britain rules'.*

*That is a specimen of the mental food which Mrs. Besant provides for excitable young Indian students in a country where the treatment of women is one of the great bars to progress. In her purely theosophical days, Mrs. Besant distinguished herself by violent attacks on the missionary bodies in India and by strong opposition to the teaching of the Christian religion in India. I cannot speak too highly of the British and American missions who are doing, to my knowledge, a wonderful work in uplifting the depressed classes of India.*

*Since Mrs. Besant has combined theosophy with politics, her language and activities and writings have taken a peculiarly dangerous form. A very distinguished Mohammedan, who wrote to me that he could not understand why the Government permitted a propaganda that was having a disastrous effect upon Indian minds, firstly brought these activities to my mind. At length, the government of Madras decided to enforce the provisions of the Press Act, and Mrs. Besant was ordered to give security for the good conduct of her paper. As the violence of that paper, 'New India' continued quite unabated, the security was sequestrated. That gave her a right of appeal to the High Court of Madras. Three judges, of whom two were Indians, heard the case and the action of the Madras Government was confirmed. I will quote some fragmentary passages adduced at the trial that may have had an effect in influencing the decision of the High Court.*

*'When crimes are committed legally, when innocence is no protection; when we live in a state of anarchy, we should be better off in a state of savagery, for then we should carry arms and protect ourselves. We are helpless. We pay taxes to be wronged.'*

*There has been no more tranquil province in India than Madras until Mrs Besant took up residence there. Here is another passage:-*

*'News of Prussian aggression and German atrocity are communicated to India to bewilder the Indian imagination. They are committed under pressure, under passion. They are common. But what does this mean, this perpetration of atrocity in civic life in peaceful times, in a peaceful Province? The German crimes are excused and compared most favourably with the mild and quite ineffective action of the Government of Madras.*

*One passage in 'New India' quoted at the trial, was written by a notorious extremist who commented on the assassination of a very valuable Indian officer in Calcutta. He said:*

*'No reasonable Indian has ever publicly encouraged these crimes. There was quiet and even courageous determination in the conduct of the assassins. They are idealists, though heroism may, according to some people, be too noble a word to apply to them. In consequence, people are not even moved by a spirit of retributive justice towards them. We must recognise them as political offenders.'*

*Well might one of the Judges point out that this was 'pernicious writing which must tend to encourage assassination by removing public detestation of such crime.'*

*The decision of the High Court and the sequestration of the security given, produced no effect whatever on the editor of 'New India' and after further considerable delay the Government of Madras resorted to the Defence of India Act, which gives power of Internment. Lord Pentland explained his action in a speech, which was calculated to allay any kind of public misunderstanding. It was a most excellent speech and I am informed that it had the full approval of all real Indian opinion in Madras. it has been suggested that Mrs. Besant was doomed to languish in prison, and in a very mischievous manifesto addressed to her 'Brothers and Sisters in India,' she announced that she was about to be 'dropped into the modern equivalent of the Middle Age oubliette.'* There is a very considerable difference between an oubliette and a comfortable residence in Ootacamund, which Mrs. Besant selected for her internment. At Ootacamund, she was free to walk about, see her friends, and help in working up a violent agitation for her release, but she was prevented by the 'brutal British bureaucracy' from continuing to fly the Home Rule flag over her residence.

The Viceroy approved the internment of Mrs. Besant, and the late Secretary of State, in another place on June 26th, also approved the action of the Government of Madras, and stated his opinion that Mrs. Besant's propaganda was dangerous to the peace of India. An eminent Hindu wrote to me these words:

'Ever since her internment, a virulent agitation has been going on for her release. The Home Rulers met in conference and decided to carry on passive resistance unless she was forthwith released.'

He added – 'If she is released unconditionally, without giving any assurances as to the future, the position of the Government of Madras would be extremely difficult. I do not think they could maintain peace and order after such a blow to their prestige.'

That is the view of a very able Indian who is alarmed at the violence of the present agitation, and who understands perfectly what Home Rule of Mrs Besant's type means at the present moment. On July 30th, a Joint Conference of the Congress and the Muslim League sent to the Viceroy and to the Secretary of State a long resolution, most discourteous and menacing in tone, demanding the immediate sanction of their political proposals and the 'immediate release' of Mrs. Besant and her two disciples. These people were released unconditionally, and Mrs. Besant has been making a triumphal progress throughout India: and as an act of open defiance to the Government, she has been elected the President of the coming Congress that is to be held at Calcutta. But further than that, there is a fresh agitation naturally started for the release of other interned persons who also are a danger to the peace of India. The Government of Madras is responsible for law and order among 42,000,000 of very excitable peoples. It had shown the most wonderful forbearance; and its mild action had been fully approved both by the Secretary of State and the Viceroy. At Simla, it is quite impossible always to form an accurate view of a difficult situation in a far distant Province. In 1857, it was a very small group of strong men on the spot who saved the Punjab and enabled its resource to be brought to bear for the Great Mutiny. And during this war, one fearless Irishman has not only dealt most successfully with the most dangerous conspiracy since the Mutiny, but has so far won and kept the confidence of the people of the Punjab that they have furnished recruits in unprecedented numbers. There is nobody in India to whom the country owes more than to Sir Michael O'Dwyer. I ought to say that while the Madras Government was overruled with regard to the internment, the Bombay Government, that had wisely declined to allow Mrs. Besant to enter the Province, must also have been overruled by some separate order. These proceedings have been explained, and I cannot think *that the explanation was satisfactory. I hope that my noble friend will be able to make out a better case than was made in another place.*

*The main points in the apologies, so far as I can make out, were two. It was declared that the release was decided upon in order to tranquillise the present situation. My Lords, does concession made to flagrant breakers of the law ever tranquillise any situation? What has been the effect of that policy in Ireland? The second point was that Mrs. Besant had telegraphed the Viceroy that she was 'ready to co-operate in obtaining a calm atmosphere' during the visit of the Secretary of State to India. Surely no more remarkable reason could be given for releasing a person who had persistently and grievously offended against the law and who had refused to make any promise of amendment. The effect is to take the offender into a kind of partnership. As a natural and perfectly certain result of all this, there is widespread indignation and alarm among European residents throughout India, and also among loyal Indians who have not the same means of expressing their views. Never, since the time of the Ilbert Bill, has there been anything approaching the strength of the present feeling aroused by these proceedings, and the justification is, in my opinion, far stronger than it was in the eighties of the last century.*

*The British community in India is a very small body scattered over vast areas. The services which maintain order and conduct the administration are a mere handful of men among 315,000,000 of people. Their authority and even personal safety depend upon the visible strength of the Government in India. I know very well that the word 'prestige' is hateful to every true democrat, but in Eastern countries, the prestige of the Government, or the respect which it commands, which is just the same thing, is the only possible guarantee of the authority which is required every day for the preservation of public order. What would be the position of the two or three British officers in a far remote country district if they had not behind them the full support of a Government known to be strong? If the masses in India ever come to believe that the Government can be coerced by the threat of a noisy minority, then India will be launched well on the road to anarchy. The paramount authority which alone holds, and alone can hold together, the vast medley of races, languages, castes and creeds that constitute India must be maintained. Peace and order are the very greatest interests of the masses of the people of India. At the great meeting of Europeans held at Bombay, there was no sign of bitterness between West and East, or of any colour distinction. Mr. Wardlaw Milne, the President of the European Association appealed to –*

*'All moderate men, whether English or Indian, to use their joint influence to secure that the realisation of Indian aspirations should be steady and sure.'*

*At the same time, a strong and just resentment was expressed against concessions to threats of the small body of Brahmins and lawyers which Mrs Besant was trying to lead.*

*Behind the present issue there is a far greater question. India is extraordinarily prosperous just now, as is Ireland. There have been three good monsoons and huge sums have flowed into India for the purchase of materials required for the war. No strain is felt, except by the fighting classes, which mourn the loss of some of their best and bravest men. This is the time selected by the extremists to make proposals accompanied by threats – proposals which, if accepted, would make all Government impossible in India, and that is what they desire. A small section of adult Indians and a large proportion of ignorant and excitable students have been artificially worked up into what I can only describe as a state of political intoxication and unfortunately extravagant expectations have been raised by incautious utterances which have been treasured up and which will certainly bear fruit in due season. The extremists have captured the Congress and the Moslem league, which I assure your Lordships, do not represent the truth of Indian opinion. Such conditions very closely resemble those in Ireland, where the late Viceroy has told us that laxity of government led straight to a serious rising and where Sinn Feinism, which a few years ago was regarded as the creed of a few irresponsibles, has quickly grown into a dangerous revolutionary movement.*

*But there is another and even more striking analogy. All free peoples welcome the Russian Revolution, because they believed that autocracy would at once be replaced by liberal rule based on free institutions. But what happened? A small body of irresponsible persons at Petrograd, some honest idealists and dreamers, some anarchic Socialists with an eye to plunder and some others bought with German money, instantly attempted to seize upon power and very largely succeeded. Almost their first action was to issue in the name of democracy a manifesto, which instantly crippled the fighting power of the great armies of Russia, which had won our admiration before for their gallantry and devotion. There never was such a tragic scrap of paper as that and never since the war began have the Allies had to face greater disaster.*

*Government throughout Russia has for the present, lapsed and anarchy prevails. The masses of uneducated Russians are the helpless prey of the agitators, and true liberty has for the time vanished. The Russian Government, as we know, is most earnestly striving to restore discipline in the armies and order behind the front, but the task is one of appalling difficulty and it may take some years to accomplish. No graver warning of what revolution may mean has ever been given, and the conditions in India very closely resemble those in Russia, except that the Indian peoples are far less homogeneous and there are far more racial and religious antagonisms among them than anything which exists in Russia. The India of today is the creation of British rule, and I believe it is the finest achievement of the British Race. I am sure that the noble Earl, who devoted seven most strenuous years to the advancement of the people of India, would agree with that statement. If we ever permit our rule to be weakened, we shall quickly alienate all that is best in India and court a disaster deeper and darker than that which has befallen the hapless Russian people. The sane and moderate party in India is strong in numbers; it is earnest and it includes a large non-Brahmin element, the landed interests and a large number of Mohammedans. It is only beginning to be organised. At present, it wields no influence here, where the Indian Soviet has very many friends and it suffers from intimidation. Here again is an analogy to the case of Ireland; but the social caste and religious pressure that can be brought to bear in India far exceeds anything of the kind that exists in Ireland.*

*My Lords I move for papers, because there is ignorance of the present situation in India. The Censorship is very active and our Press here is so much occupied with other matters that it cannot find space to deal with Indian affairs. Papers were asked for in another place, and the Secretary of State said that, with a view to laying them, he wishes that they should be complete. The Papers, which I would specially ask for, are three in number. First, the admirable reply of the Viceroy, to the so-called Press-Deputation, which waited upon him in March last, in which he specifically dealt with the case of Mrs. Besant. This would enable Parliament and the public to understand the kind of language, which the Indian papers, controlled by the Indian Bolsheviks, have used and also the necessity of the maintenance of the Press Act. Circumstances alter cases, and only six years ago, Mrs. Besant gave strong testimony to the necessity of the Press Act. Writing in the Christian Chronicle she said:-*

*'The Press edited by Indians, with one or two honourable exceptions, is curiously irresponsible, printing any amount of anonymous personal abuse without making the slightest attempt to distinguish truth from falsehood. It is this lack of the sense of responsibility which has rendered the Press Laws necessary; but while they protect the Government, they leave the Press free to pour out any amount of filth on private individuals.'*

*The second of the Papers that I would ask for, would contain the speech of Lord Pentland and the note of the Government of Madras giving reasons for the internment of Mrs. Besant. These papers would show the tender consideration of the Government of Madras towards Indian opinion, and they would refute any charge of arbitrary action on their part. The third Paper, which I think should be given, is the manifesto of the Joint Conference of Congress and the Moslem League, which was sent to the Secretary of State and the Viceroy on July 30th. That Manifesto is couched in language which might have been used by the German Foreign Office to Venezuela. It is the kind of language, which is hateful to all loyal and sober Indians, and it is necessary that Parliament and the Public should be placed in possession of it.*

*My Lords, I am not in the least a reactionary. I am most anxious for many reforms in India – reforms that would give greater responsibility to the Indian people, and give them more training in the handling of great affairs. This is not the time to discuss these reforms, but I do hope that any proposal that may be made by the Government will receive the most careful consideration in your Lordship's House. I also hope most earnestly, that these proposals will not take the form of concessions to a very noisy party which is wishing to set up a little oligarchy in India, and to take advantage of these times of stress which are falling so heavily on the British people at home and overseas. Our only object should be, now and always in the future, to secure the gradual and orderly advance of India towards nationhood, and with the advance to nationhood, self-government would of course, come automatically. I hope I have not detained your Lordships too long. I have raised these matters very reluctantly, and only because I believe we are in danger of drifting into a false paradise as regards the situation in India, and the true interests of the Indian peoples, for whom, as long as I live, I shall cherish affection. I beg to move."*

Moved. That a Humble Address be presented to His Majesty for Papers relating to the present situation in India, with special regard to the internment and release of Mrs Besant - Lord Sydenham.

Lord Lansdowne came next. He had been a Viceroy for five years until 1893; he had inaugurated a Council Act while in India, but he was a man of distinction also - he had been Governor General of Canada and had filled various Government posts including that of Foreign Secretary. He had been one of those to whom Von Bernstorff refers, who wished to negotiate peace with Germany in 1915. He was not therefore, (nor indeed do any of the Lords seem to have been) a hard and dogmatic man; a man of some influence and great position would describe him more accurately.

He was clear that the suggestion of the release of Annie Besant must have come from 'the Secretary of State's side' and that there could be no doubt about that. The release was suggested by him in connection with the announcement of policy which he was about to make, and the suggestion was repeated a few days afterwards with a request that the Government of India would come to a decision as soon as possible. Lansdowne agreed that it was almost impossible to resist the pressure being put on him by Whitehall.

He noted that the internment of Mrs. Besant was a precautionary, not a punitive measure, not that the common mass of the people of India would be able to differentiate, but they would know that the Indian authorities had released her after she had committed an offence.

Knowing, as he did, the ways in which Governments work, he suggested that the assurances which were needed for Mrs. Besant's release had been given by an 'influential source'. He did not know who these influential sources were and we should be glad to hear something of them; he presumed that the trump card was the Besant telegraph to the Viceroy in which she promised that she would co-operate in securing a calm atmosphere during the Secretary of State's visit. That seemed to him a most extraordinary bargain.

*"It is not an undertaking on Mrs. Besant's part to stop from writing seditious matter, it is that she will co-operate, I suppose with him, in obtaining a favourable atmosphere for him during his visit. I must say that, in the political jargon to which we are accustomed in these days, there is no expression to my mind that is more detestable than that phrase of obtaining a favourable atmosphere by means of this kind. We are familiar with it in other connections, and you will find, if you examine its meaning carefully, that what it generally means that in order to obtain a fairly quiet time you are going to run away from someone or something. You are going to do that in order that you may get a calm surface, regardless of the undercurrents which may be flowing below and of the storm which may be muttering in the distance.*

*I wish to add that it seems to me, that the need of dealing cautiously with the situation which now exists in India, has been very greatly increased by the fact that the new Secretary of State is believed to be, and has announced himself as being, in favour of what is called a very strong policy of Home Rule for India. In the month of July, in the debate on Mesopotamia, he made a very violent attack upon the system of Indian Government. He described it as 'too wooden, too iron, too inelastic, and too antediluvian', to be of any use for the modern purpose we have in view. 'It is an indefensible system of government', he said, and he goes on to qualify that, by saying that he does not see any demand for complete Home Rule for India."*

Lord Lansdowne went on to expostulate about the 'intemperate' criticism of the Indian Government and that Montagu was proposing a federation of Provinces and Principalities.

He noted that Lord Islington had previously pointed out the development of legislation through the years which had led to the Council Acts, concerning the representation by Indians on the Councils of 1861, 1892 and 1908, which showed how progressive our rule had been in India.

Historians today do not seem to realise that such developments, the logical effect of a rule by people who had themselves evolved such systems, could not have arisen in a country where the rule had always been authoritarian and princely. The nationalists never used their knowledge of government or history to appreciate that, without British rule, they would not at that point, have had any say in their own rule if the British had not ruled the Dominion of India. Princely States were sometimes exceedingly well run; Mysore was one, Hyderabad another. By the time we left, Princely rule, on the whole, had achieved the standard or beyond of British rule, but there were others, still of a sort that India had had, when the British beat the Pindaris. Decadent rulers were preponderant then, as can be seen by anyone who had read Sleeman's report 'Diary of a Journey through Oudh'. There seems to have been no recognition that it takes strong Government to do the work of protection from invasion from outside and from crime inside and that, to a degree, the British had achieved. Sleeman's other work on the Thugs shows that Indian States had not the strength of morality to maintain control. (In this present time, the Prime Minister of India has commented on the internal corruption, and much the same could be said of Pakistan, and now, both nations are nuclear powers.)

After he had spoken of the greater association of British with Indians in every branch of the Administration, with which everyone agreed, Lord Lansdowne went on to say that Montagu was a different man as far as his speeches were concerned, before he got into the Government. *"The fact remains that there are two Mr. Montagus. There is the official Mr. Montagu and the unofficial Mr. Montagu. I am afraid that the Mr. Montagu whom the malcontents in India are prepared to welcome with open arms, is the unofficial Mr. Montagu, and that he will be received there by a great many people as the apostle of a Home Rule movement, a sort of emissary of Government, who has come to overhaul the Government of India, root and branch, from a Home rule point of view. That therefore, Montagu must take great care what he said, for it would be scrutinised carefully. I feel quite sure that a man of Mr. Montagu's great ability will recognise thoroughly, the need of proceeding very warily and of avoiding carefully all appearances of paltering with in any way, the kind of disaffection which we know is rampant in many parts of India ... the treatment of Mrs. Besant ... I cannot help regarding as a serious blunder and one which had undoubtedly greatly alarmed the whole of the loyal classes of India."*

Lord Islington, Under Secretary of State, gave a lengthy speech defending, rationalising and excusing Montagu's action and quoting the Viceroy as having taken the action to release Mrs. Besant on his own authority. He ended by commenting on the request for Papers. He claimed that they had either already been published or that they should not be published. Of the Congress and Moslem League letter to the Viceroy, he said it had already been published in India; of the note from Lord Pentland to the Viceroy, he said it would not be in the public interest to publish it – a most unsatisfactory and possibly time-serving speech. He endeavoured to allay the fears of the noble Lords on the question of the Secretary of State's intentions; he used as encouragement the fact that Montagu had been an Under Secretary of State and was therefore fully familiar with the intricacies of the problem and he gave flattering descriptions of the other members of the Mission – Sir William Duke of the India Office, Lord Donoughmore, Mr Charles Roberts (another previous Under Secretary), Mr Seton (later Sir Michael Seton) also of the India office.

Lord Middleton followed. He was a former Secretary of State for India. *"My Lords, I think my noble friend, Lord Sydenham, needed no justification, besides his own speech for introducing this Motion, beyond the speech of the Noble Lord who has just sat down. We are of course, familiar in this House with the manner in which he discharges his duty and with his power of convincing himself and others, but I confess the speech he has just made did not leave an aroma of conviction. I do not think you could have had a more unfortunate sequence of events than those which the noble Lord (Islington) has had to record. He made at the close of his speech an announcement which I am sure your Lordships will have been glad to hear – that whatever occurs in the Mission undertaken by the Secretary of State for India, whatever high authorities are consulted, no decision will be taken without the previous agreement of the Cabinet, and without Parliament having an opportunity of discussing it."*

He said that no such step as that of August 20th in relation to any of our Dominions had ever been made before; the speech of Montagu on the Mesopotamian Commission was unwise – incurably unwise – and he then quoted Montagu's remarks in his attack on the House of Commons and its control over the Secretary of State for India and his attack on the India Office. He attacked the powers of the Viceroy, which he had said should be greater and he attacked the way the powers of the Secretary of State were interfered with by the cumbrous machinery of the India Office, which were such that he could not properly control the Viceroy. Montagu said that the House of Commons should bring pressure on the Secretary of State, so that he could control the Viceroy much more effectively and interfere on other matters on which he had not up till then been able to touch. Lord Middleton pointed out that for the people of India to realise that the purpose of the India Office is to control a Secretary of State who might be too advanced was lamentable and a travesty of the true reasons for the India Office, which was made up of people who had been in India and knew it and could advise a Secretary of State who had not been in India. He went on to encourage the other Peers who had also been Secretary of State for India to support him in this opinion.

He pointed out that the previous Viceroy, Lord Hardinge, had asked that no steps should be taken during the war and Lord Islington had not made out a good case to go against this advice. He spoke with admiration of the enormous assistance India had been able to give to our armies in France and elsewhere and of the debts of gratitude…: *"But I do feel that we have a right to enter a protest on three points. First, on the vacillating policy as adopted between the India Office and the Government of India in regard to the particular case which has been cited; and secondly, because a man in so high a position and with so high a record as the present Secretary of State, should first have made the speech, which he did as a private individual, and then have been allowed, when he became a Minister, to make announcements which practically seemed to follow on his previous speech, at a time when it was impossible for us to challenge them in Parliament or to ask for an explanation; that it is in pursuance, not only of the traditional policy of Parliament, but also of the only system under which Parliament can possibly keep any control, that we have made, as we do make, a protest against the methods which the Government have adopted in dealing with the most important question in the Indian Empire."*

The Marquis of Crewe followed. Although we may think of Lord Morley as being the Secretary of State with whom Montagu worked, in fact for most of Montagu's time as Under Secretary, Lord Crewe was the Secretary of State for India. It is not surprising therefore, that Crewe should have taken a defensive position, both in terms of Montagu and of Lord Chelmsford, who, though not Viceroy during Crewe's time, (having been appointed a year after Crewe left the India Office), would have been recognised as being in a difficult position, over which, there must have been some concern not to make it worse.

The gist of the speech was to praise Islington for making it plain that Lord Chelmsford had not been pushed around, but acted in his own understanding; that it was wrong to blame Montagu for making a speech before he could possibly have known he would become Secretary of State - but much of the time was spent comparing the Indian situation with that of Ireland and pointing out his own feelings about the India Office systems, which on the one hand, had helped him, on the other had irked him when there were delays in getting matters through for Acts and so forth. He did not know that he should go as far as Mr. Montagu apparently did in speaking of the cumbersomeness of the India Office (at which point Lord Middleton shouted out 'hear, hear') but as he looked back, he remarked at the needless delays. He doubted whether detention helped. He thought that Lord Islington had made his point that

Lord Sydenham should not have the Papers. Both Islington and Crewe had worked with Montagu and probably met the many Soviet Indians in London who were also speaking to Montagu; they would have seen the whole matter with rather less experience of India, or impartial oversight, then did the other peers.

Lord Carmichael followed - it was his maiden speech in the House of Lords. He had been Governor of Madras and of Bengal – the latter at the time when the Ghadr incursion happened and when the India Act had to be brought into law. He knew about the problems and about Sir Michael O'Dwyer's position and actions in dealing with a dangerous situation. One of the clearest indications of Montagu's partiality is that when Sir Michael himself retired, he was not made a peer which, on his record, he should have been. Lord Carmichael spoke of the Defence of India Act which Sir Michael had pressed through to the Viceroy and into law, to protect India from the infiltration of returning propagandised Sikhs and others for mutinous purposes and the use of funds and business for the same purposes. The point had been touched on more than once in the debate, that the removal and detention of Annie Besant had not been punitive but rather a precaution; Lord Carmichael supported this and quoted Sir Michael's detentions as being in the same sense. He said that he knew the Defence of India Act almost by heart; he knew what he was talking about. He had kept people in detention for as short a time as possible. He continued: *"If Sir Michael and I had any difference, it was because I thought he did not keep his people in for long enough and took steps when he was not able to keep them."* He himself had kept his people longer and did not have to take further steps. He was concerned that this debate would be reported in India and his successor should not be put in an uncomfortable position.

His precise words on Sir Michael's detentions were *"I am perfectly certain Sir Michael acted purely from a precautionary point of view. We have only to look at the number of those against whom the Punjab Government took steps – steps which did not result in those being proceeded against, being continued for any length of time."*

Lord Curzon, then Lord President of the Council, stood up to speak with all the confidence he bore as an aura around himself. He congratulated Lord Carmichael, he had a go at Lord Middleton, he asked whether it was fair to quote Montagu prior to his appointment as Secretary of State, he would come to Montagu later.

On the matter of Annie Besant, he agreed with Sydenham's speech. Besant had been opposing Indians in a Moderate line, but what he did wonder (and Lord Lansdowne had put this), why had this lady not been deported from the country? On this he believed that the only Act which could cover such a move was one that was a hundred years old. His next point was about the announcement of August 20th and here he spoke of the delay; 'for months' the Government of India had been appealing for something to be done – this was nothing new. All over the world there was unrest; Russia, Ireland and many little countries. Amongst them all was India - it was the feeling of the time.

It had seemed to him that the Viceroy's request that the Secretary of State should go to India, to discus the Viceroy's concerns and listen to the representations of important persons, would be the best and most speedy way of resolving the difficulty. On the matter of Mrs. Besant, the intention was not to criticise the action of Lord Pentland, but the Viceroy had accepted Mrs. Besant's undertaking. He did not make the point made by an earlier speaker that the agitation had died down, that calm had been restored, and for those of us who have taken in the significance of the whole of India reacting, then going quiet, this act of appeasement merely indicated the hold of the agitators on the country at large at that time. Nor did he make the point, as an earlier speaker, that the fact that she was an Englishwoman, working against her own people, was a salient feature in the agitation, because she would have been, as were we, trusted and believed. On the matter of Lord Sydenham's Papers, he thought they should not be given.

As an *'eminence grise'* in the policies on India, with Montagu claiming that he was his mentor, Sydenham then accepted that the powers that be were not going to carry out his request. Curzon had not recognised the serious effects of his action in dividing Bengal and did not recognise, twelve years after he had left India (and as Lord Carmichael had said, things change very quickly in India) the implications of Montagu's attitude. The probable effects of such an attitude were not to be expected of a man who had been used to directing, rather than understanding.

Lord Sydenham, with no alternative, agreed to forgo his Papers.

The situation in England at that time provides the background against which Government attitudes may be seen. Morel, the pacifist Labour MP, like Sir Edgar Speyer, was a naturalised Briton, originally French (his name was Georges Eduard Pierre Achille Morel de Ville) and was also pro-German. The 'Evening Standard' in those days more courageous, or more secure in the patriotism of Britain, than is the Press in the present day (when the extraordinary behaviour of M.P.s, who vote to give away British sovereignty and Habeas Corpus with no apparent thought of their responsibilities to their voters, barely mentions that what is going on is treason), printed an extremely accurate description of Morel's activities.

The 'Evening Standard' of 31st July 1917 wrote as follows:

*"The Committee of the Workers' and Soldiers Council is also an outcome of the 'Morel' movement, which is responsible directly or indirectly, through the parent body, the U.D.C.* [the Union of Democratic Control] *for the whole of the Pacifist organisations and propaganda through which 'Morel' is attempting, by a variety of insidious appeals, to weaken the war resolutions of the people and foment industrial troubles in order to cripple our military efforts. The same master hand has woven this network of organisations. Messrs. Philip Snowdon, Ramsay MacDonald, Ponsonby, Trevelyan are, consciously or unconsciously, all creatures of 'Morel' and quite insignificant without him. This pro-German exploits their follies and their prejudices in the same way that he uses the cowards and the shirkers and the Quakers and the Syndicalists and the elements of anarchy wherever they are to be found. He has been working cunningly and assiduously for many months to save Prussia from defeat, and he has used any instrument that came to his hand. I shall continue, therefore, to call the 'Workers*

*and Soldiers' Council, a product of the 'Morel' movement whose founder should long ago have been deprived of his naturalisation, by Act of Parliament if necessary, and expelled the country as an undesirable alien."*

Everything must have been in place ready; the Peace Conferences in Paris and Stockholm, to which the Labour M.P. and member of Cabinet Arthur Henderson wished to go with Ramsay Macdonald; the move to go to Russia by Ramsay Macdonald, to consult with the Workmen's and Soldiers' Soviets, to which he was given a passport, though the National Union of Seamen and Firemen's Union under Havelock Hudson, refused to carry him - it was as if Britain was ready on tiptoe for the start.

Not only in Britain were things in place. In Russia, bearing in mind that Brest-Litovsk was not signed until the beginning of 1918 and Russia still in chaos, it is extraordinary that in the year following, the Russians were selling Tsarist jewellery, taking out funds, and subsidising the Suffragettes and the 'Daily Herald', which in 1919 the Indian seditionists were also funding to the extent of £10,000 – more like £100,000 today.

It is the British intellectual and Socialist blindness to the horrors of Russia and Bolshevik rule, the refusal to recognise events which allowed the panegyrics free rein, which are the most interesting attitudes of the time. It is as if, when faced with horror, people prefer to imagine that it is good rather than evil. Visitors to Russia actually believed the tales of an earthly paradise with which they were regaled almost as if they had been hypnotised. James on the East Persian Cordon, Blacker up in Tashkent, both knew, as did the whole of India and much of China, of the brutalities which had driven people from their homes in squalor and misery. Refugees including Princes came to the West also, and worked as waiters or in any way that it was possible to save themselves from starvation. Why, one must ask, did the left wingers, in Britain and the States and generally, claim for one moment that such a catastrophe was a success and that the people of Russia, shot down if they did not co-operate, turned out of their homes, taken from their children, were in reality living in the first heaven of peace and justice the world had ever known?

The immoralities of theft, murder, arson and rape were not seemingly known, but James and Blacker knew that the Soviets on the border lived in endless orgies, just as the inspirer of this appalling regime, Parvus, had done in Switzerland or the Jacobins in the French revolution or the Illuminati in America. The left-wing intellectuals in this country must have known something – yet the theory they spread and supported was entirely different. Moreover, it seems that this demoralisation was of the essence of this cult; which gave rise to Armenian genocide; in India, the depredations of the 1919 Rebellion with its attacks on women and Indian schoolchildren, the later depredations in Malabar, all a symptom of the corruption and immorality which should not have been accepted for one moment by civilised persons, or perpetrated by the same. The claims of the seditious enclave in India could have been accepted only with the recognition that people of such moral decrepitude would be bound to make use of any excuse to hide their own evil. It is a human weakness that when people forego long-tested moral principles, they have no way in which they can control their basest instincts. We should recognise this in many people today, as Sykes saw it and knew.

It was in this climate that Edwin Montagu left for India. Much as the rest of his left-wing generation, he would take little notice of the opinions of anyone who did not agree with him and his fellow politicians. The constraints lay in the methods of Committees and Missions which the British used as some sort of control. He believed himself in a position of total power and, much as those of his contemporaries who believed in the wonder of Bolshevism, he believed that he was about to build the Kingdom of Heaven on Earth. He took no notice of the Lords who, in their debate, warned against letting out of her detention in Ootacamund, the seditionist President of the Theosophical Society, Annie Besant, who was endlessly critical and destructive about the British Government and who, with Tilak, started the Society for Home Rule. He agreed to the cessation of her detention in the teeth of the Madras Government, who had seen the trouble she was causing.

The Mission set off on 18th October 1917, six days before the Debate in the Lords. It was a pity that Montagu probably never heard what the Lords had said. They travelled in the way of the very rich at an earlier time, across Europe to Taranto (in the old days it might have been Brindisi) where they boarded the ship Bristol, arriving at Port Said two days later. Montagu then had discussions with Sir Reginald Wingate, who had been previously put in charge of the British Military side of the Arab adventure, being already a Sirdar of the Egyptian Army. At the time of the Battle of Omdurman, he had tried to help Churchill to telegraph an article to the 'Times', which Kitchener blocked.

He was a man who had dreamed of the Arab revolt for years; he had replaced Sir Henry MacMahon, who had been placed in charge of the political side, while Wingate was moved to the military side of the Arab Revolt. He was absolutely delighted at the success of the Revolt; he had put his own reputation on the line to support it, and at the time of Montagu's visit, was High Commissioner in Egypt. He is known, from the mention in 'Seven Pillars of Wisdom', for replacing Auda Abu Tayi's teeth, when the Chief of the Taia smashed them, because they would not chew the meat he loved so much!

There is absolutely no doubt that Reginald Wingate would have known Mark Sykes. He knew Lawrence well and he would have known of Lawrence's opinion of the German menace in the East and of the Indian relationship, but Montagu appears to have written nothing about him in the Diary, apart from the note that he and Wingate had discussions on Egyptian and Indian affairs.

From Cairo, where in the old days, the travellers would have taken camels through the desert to Suez and then boat to Bombay, the Mission voyaged in the Kaiser-I-Hind from Port Said to Bombay, having stopped at Aden on the way, for lunch with the Resident.

Their arrival was the cause of great excitement. Since Indians are frequently responsive to opinions of others, that Montagu had been quoted as being in favour of Home Rule would mean that there would be a greater influx into the movement of people who wished to attract his attention, in order to 'fit in' with what they thought was his mood.

His words, his attitudes and his actions throughout this visit are something of a mystery. He appears to have believed that the Indian politicians were sincerely interested in democratic government, mistaking their charm for evidence of integrity. He enjoyed dining with them, singing 'Bande Materam', the Nationalist song, with them, but he refused to visit the Districts, to view the work done by British and Indian members of the Indian Civil Service – the men who were running the country. He disregarded the warnings of Indians who could see the likely outcome, as he had ignored the information on German involvement, supplied through official papers. Was he ignorant of the Defence of India Act, more stringent than the Rowlatt Acts of 1919, which he admitted was necessary?

Before he left for India in October, a secret report to Cabinet about Turkey must have passed across his desk, for it dealt with attempts to get Turkey out of the War, a subject of great moment for Muslims in India. (See also PART 5 Chapter I)

The report was written by Sir Mark Sykes. He was appointed to the Foreign Office after completing his education at Jesus College, Cambridge and became the Government adviser on areas of influence in the Middle East, culminating in the Sykes-Picot Agreement, which gave Syria to France in 1916 on the break up of the Turkish Empire and after the Arab Revolt. Coming back to Britain to his family of six children in 1919, he was already exhausted after his work with the Armenian refugees, the sufferers from the German-Turkish massacres, followed by his appearance at the Versailles Peace discussions. Thus debilitated, he caught influenza and died at the age of 39. He was a man of great insight, goodness and intelligence, an upholder of both Zionism and the Arab Revolt, a protector of the Armenian refugees at Aleppo, a man of outstanding gifts. The Sykes-Picot agreement was negotiated when he was a mere 37 years old. His biographer, Roger Adelson ('Portrait of an Amateur' Cape 1975) thought he could have competed with Churchill for the commanding position of the Tory party, although he called himself a 'Tory Democrat'.

His report used the Admiralty's intelligence and two advisers, Dr. Weizmann and M. Sokolov. He identified those wishing to bring Turkey out of the War as 'pacifists of the Morel type, international financiers wishing to maintain a corrupt military regime in Turkey, Indian and Egyptian Muslim seditionists and their sympathisers (Pickthall, Rosher, Field and Mrs. Zeynab Charlton) and fourthly, Semitic Anti-Zionists, who were undisguised pro-Turco/Germans - Wolf in London and Schiff in New York. The whole of these various forces were in sympathy with C.U.P. long before the war.

John Buchan's 'Mr Standfast' and other novels show the danger of the pacifist movement. Morel was one of the seniors in the Parvus command.

Montagu met an enormous number of people, including some of those that have already been mentioned; not Sir Umar Hayat Khan, but then he would not have put himself forward and was probably in France. Although he did not meet the Ali brothers, he spoke to Sir Charles Cleveland about them. Cleveland was the head of the C.I.D. and Montagu got on with him very well. About the Ali brothers: Sir Charles Cleveland had been a friend of theirs in the old days and he recalled how Mohammed Ali had come to see him just before the Turks entered the war. It was the last day of Ramadan and Mohammed Ali was very hungry. Cleveland gave him a roaring meal, at the end of which Mohammed Ali wished success to the British arms and sent a telegram to Talaat Bey begging the Turks not to come in against us. He has frequently said that he wished he had never sent the telegram, but he did send it, Cleveland keeping it overnight and getting his approval in the morning. At the end of this note, Montagu's comment: *"What a pity it is that he has gone wrong!"*

The first person of importance he met, since she was central to the visit, was Annie Besant. She had been to see the Viceroy about the release of the Ali brothers. She had told the Viceroy that she quite understood that she could not have Home Rule at that point - she wanted the Congress Scheme then, and Home Rule when the war was over.

On 26th November the Congress and Home Rule League came to Montagu bearing a casket, which the Government had strictly ordered should not be done. As the casket left the place where Montagu was sitting, it was dropped and broken. A terrifically big casket, bought by people from all the ends of India, made and engraved for him personally. Despite it being broken, Montagu kept it. Montagu noted *"We were now face to face with the real giants of the Indian political world. We had not the dupes and adherents from the Provinces, but we had here a collection of the first class politicians of the various Provinces. Old Surendranath Banerjee the veteran from Bengal read the address, which was beautifully written and beautifully read. There was Mudholkar from the Central Provinces, Jinnah from Bombay, Mazhar-ul-Haq and Hasan Imam from Bihar and Orissa, Gandhi, Mrs. Besant, Kesava Pillai, and so on.*

*All the brains of the movement were there. But the difficulty is, as I have often said, that owing to the thinness with which we have spread education, they have run generations away from the rest of India, and whatever may be done in theory, in practice this would be only another and indigenous autocracy.*

*The Congress and Moslem League were followed by the Punjab Provincial Congress with a shorter but good address and then Mrs. Besant and the great Tilak came with their Home Rule League, and read us a more extreme and a bitter address, but one which was undoubtedly interesting and good. Of course the Home Rule League's demands are the same as the Congress, the Home Rule League having been started to do the propaganda of the rather old-fashioned Congress. Mrs Besant said she found that Congress held its meetings near by Christmas each year and between whiles went into sleep. It is her activity and her League that has really stirred the country up into a condition in which it is no longer true to say that political interest is confined to the educated classes. Mrs. Besant in her white and gold embroidered Indian clothes, with her short white hair, and the most beautiful voice I have ever heard, was very impressive and read magnificently. Bannerjee was loquacity itself, garrulous, sedulous, but there was no sign of moderation or compromise in him. The Congress scheme was the least he would accept. This scheme, really in its essence excludes naval and military matters, but on all matters of internal administration, makes the irremovable Executive responsible to an elected majority on the Councils, and gives them the power of the purse, so that it is practically responsible government at one fell swoop. They would hear of no alternative.*

*They were followed by Jinnah, young, perfectly mannered, impressive looking, armed to the teeth with dialectics, and insistent on the whole of his scheme. All its shortcomings, all its drawbacks, the elected members of the Executive Council, the power of the minority to hold up legislation, the complete control of the Executive in all matters of finance, all these were defended as the best makeshifts they could devise short of responsible government. Nothing else would satisfy them. They would rather have nothing if they could not have the whole lot. I was rather tired and I funked him. Chelmsford tried to argue with him, and was tied up into knots. Jinnah is a very clever man, and it is, of course, an outrage, that such a man should have no chance of running the affairs of his own country*[39].

*Afterwards we saw the renowned Gandhi. He is a social reformer, he has a real desire to find grievances and to cure them, not for any reasons of self-advertisement, but to improve the conditions of his fellow men. He is the real hero of the Indian question in South Africa where he suffered imprisonment*[40]. *He has just been helping the Government to find a solution for the indigo workers of Bihar. He dresses like a coolie, forswears all personal advancement, lives practically on the air and is a pure visionary*[41]. *He does not understand details of schemes; all he wants is that we should get India on our side. He wants the millions of India to leap to the assistance of the British throne. In fact, I may say here that, revolutionary or not, loathing or not, as they may do, the Indian Civil Service, none of these Indians show any sign of wanting to be removed from connection with the British throne.*

*Then at six we saw Mrs. Besant herself. That was an interesting interview if ever I had one. She gave me the history of the Home Rule League, how she felt it necessary to get hold of young boys, how if the Home Rule League policy could be carried*

---

39   This is not quite true; he could not have been Viceroy, but at that period, he could have been on the Viceroy's Legislative council where laws were passed and altered when put forward in principle. He could have joined the I.C.S. Instead, he had become a barrister and was later on the advocacy team to the Privy Council. Beverley Nichols later exactly matched this remark in his book 'Verdict on India'. What he did do was to see the need of Pakistan and as Moon was to say later, Pakistan owed its existence to Jinnah.

40   As later in India, Gandhi was given special treatment in prison and since imprisonment was his aim, it can hardly justifiably be called 'suffering'.

41   From Nirad Chaudhuri to E. J. Thompson, there is an ongoing mass of evidence that, far from living on air, Gandhi lived on the most costly nuts and fruits and was a great expense to hosts. Naidu later said that it was extremely costly to keep him in poverty.

*out, she was certain they would forswear anarchy and come to the side of the constitutional movement. She solemnly assured us that India would have, and insist upon having, the power of the purse and the control of the Executive. She fought shy of any of all the financial problems. She said she was not a financial expert. She got over it in that way. She kept her silvery, quiet voice, and really impressed me enormously.*

*If only the Government had kept this old woman on our side*[42]*. If only her vanity had been appealed to! She is an amusing old thing, in that, knowing perfectly well that the interview was to be in Chelmsford's room (because they take good care that I should never see anybody important without him), she turned up and sat in my tent, and coming in from dressing I found her waiting there*[43]*. I told her the interview was in Chelmsford's room and she drove me in her motorcar, and explained to me the fact that I had not received a welcome from the Indian people was simply due to their recognition that the Government would not allow it. She implored me to come to the Congress. Oh, if only Lloyd George was here to take charge of things! He would, of course, dash down to the Congress and make them a great oration. I am prevented from doing this. It might save the whole situation. But the Government of India have carefully arranged our plan so that we will be in Bombay when the Congress, the real Indian political movement, is in Calcutta, and they now plead plans as an excuse for not accepting the invitation that it showered on us.*

*I forgot to chronicle an amusing incident of the morning. After the Home Rule League deputation, Mrs. Besant and Tilak came forward to present to Chelmsford and myself copies of their memorial. Mrs. Besant asked the Viceroy if she might put a garland round his neck. He told her 'no' and took it into his hands. Tilak did not ask me but placed the garland round my neck, so that, if it gets out, it will be found that I have been garlanded by the renowned Tilak, who is only a few years out of seven years penal servitude for being, at any rate, indirectly, connected with his newspaper writings, with the murder of an Indian official.*

*Another amusing incident happened at the close of the interview with Mrs. Besant at which she demanded our presence at the Congress. She said 'You know that I am President of the Theosophical Society, and I want to ask you two whether, if I do what*

---

42      Montagu's general attitude is epitomized in this belief; that Besant could somehow have been manipulated into acting differently. Although she did not appreciate the significance of the Brahmin hierarchical system as a socialist, she could not have been moved, at that period when Socialism had not shown its true colours in Russia, to accept the Anglo-Indian method of government under any circumstances and it indicates Montagu's own way of trying to get what he wanted and its effect in the Dyer debate. His belief was in manipulation rather than in the functioning of free will. As with the Congress meeting, he thought of persuasion rather than, as the British approached the matter, with respect for Indian ways.

43      In the Theosophical directions, there are a number of magical ways of influencing people. It is probable, almost certain, that Besant will have been using this magic when she was in Montagu's tent and when she drove him to the Viceroy's room. The success is shown by her attitude to Jinnah as opposed to his attitude to her and to Gandhi. Magic of that nature works mainly through the emotions and feeling.

*they want me to do and go home, I should be allowed to come back to India.' This was not a matter connected with reforms and I was not allowed, therefore, to express an opinion, but I am bound to say, I admired Chelmsford's handling of this awkward question more than anything I have seen Chelmsford do. His face broke into a sweet smile, and he said: 'Well really Mrs. Besant, you know that my desire is to get you safely out of India. Do you think it is likely, if I ever achieved this great end, I should let you come back?' 'Oh' she said, 'then I shall not go.' Chelmsford, still laughing said 'Is it human to expect the Government would allow you to come back and make more trouble for us, if we once got rid of you?' She laughed too. Then he said 'But as a matter of fact, it is against the rules for a woman to travel now.' 'Oh' she said 'but they will not mind my being drowned.' 'Well, the only thing that would make them let you go' he said, 'was if I said I wanted to get rid of you from India.' It was all in good nature and mostly chaff, and I think she went away quite satisfied."*

Of the people who were on the Rowlatt Committee, Montagu spoke to Sir Sidney Rowlatt himself. When he first came out as a High Court Judge of the King's Bench, Sir Sidney had found the journey, with the permits and so forth during the war, extremely difficult, and when he had finally arrived at Bombay, no one was there to meet him, no rooms booked and he had no money. Montagu had been *"really, very, very angry"*, but he had met him before and thought him a very nice fellow. Referring to the Defence of India Act presumably, he explained to him that government by means of internment and police was naturally a delightful method which built up only trouble probably for our successors, and *"I hoped that he would remember what was Parliamentarily defensible in listening to the plan which had been prepared for him by the Government out here."* Sir Sidney travelled home with Montagu in April 1918 after the Rowlatt Report and the proposed Legislation had been completed. It is still interesting to know whether Montagu actually understood – or even if he was told - the seriousness of the situation in India. His ebullience may have led him to believe that his Scheme, which was disliked by all the Provincial governors, would alone solve Indian unrest.

Otherwise, he only seems to have met Sir Verney Lovett, the Honorary Secretary; Mr. P. C. Mitter, of the Calcutta High Court and a Member of the Bengal Legislative Council, Sir Basil Scott, Chief Justice of Bombay, and Mr. Justice Kumaraswami Shasti of the Madras High Court. None of those men had ever met each other before, so the Rowlatt Report, on which so much of the information about the Germano-Indian situation is based, was written by those who had deliberated and agreed and were all men of experience.

Montagu had worked out a scheme which later was found unworkable, but at that time, he was thrilled by it and the bulk of his discussions and comments are on whether or not the people agreed with 'my Scheme'. In fact, it had been invented by one of Milner's young men, a man called Curtis, who did not know India and had no experience of the intricacies of caste and varying religions – this is to excuse him, but it does not excuse Montagu's trust in the soundness of the Curtis scheme, described as 'a spider's web spun out of the brain of a doctrinaire pedant'. This scheme known as 'diarchy' was effectively the test applied to anyone to whom Montagu spoke; thus to Mitter, we get little of the Indian's character from the conversation. This was followed by an interview with the Curtis deputation. Montagu again: *"As these people have got really the only workable scheme yet evolved, they were very interesting and I wish I could have had longer with them. What interested me was that both Colonel Pugh and P. C. Mitter, who spoke on their behalf, repudiated the sub-division of Provinces and wished the State Council area to be equal to that of the Provincial area, so that the Curtis scheme has now become my scheme. Hurrah! This is progress and I am not in the least alarmed that, despite the independent and spontaneous development of my scheme before I had seen Curtis or any of them, it will lose me the pride of authorship."*

Of Lovett he wrote: *"Sir Verney Lovett who came first, and who is Revenue Commissioner, is a wise old thing, who backs on the whole rather reluctantly, not Meston's scheme, but the scheme of the U.P. Committee. He wants the Division as the unit of the State Council*[44]. *He thinks it is ridiculous ever to look forward to the Provinces as a disappearing unit, and he says that communal representation must be now continued in India. I told him that a Division was, in most provinces, a quite unnatural division of territory, and I gave him my scheme as an alternative. He asked me what I would do if my Ministry were quite unsatisfactory. I said you could dissolve the elected Chamber. He then said: But what if you get the same lot back again? I said, what would you do under your scheme in a similar situation with a Divisional Council? Oh he said, then you would have a row in the Division; I would have a row in the whole of the Province (presumably he meant 'you'). That is true, but I do feel very strongly that you must trust these people."* Montagu went on to expound his own personal attitude: *"Everybody is looking for statutory safeguards which make them all think that we view them with suspicion. Surely a better way is to do what we have done in every other country, and give them a sense of responsibility by imposing confidence in them."*

About a year after the Mission left India (May 1918), there would be the rebellion and in October of that following year (1919) there would be the Hunter Committee. Of the people who sat on that Committee there were two in the Diary; the Vice Chancellor of Bombay University, Chimanlal Setalvad, who received a knighthood before that time; *"an extremely clever lawyer and a very nice fellow, who argued extraordinarily well. We put before him our scheme and he has gone away to think about it."* Setalvad came back to say that he approved the modified scheme.

He dined with Sultan Sahibzada, Ahmed Khan, who was to be the Muslim Member of the Hunter Committee. Two brothers had married two English sisters - with this

---

[44] A Division was an administrative area of a Province being a group of districts – about 5 districts to a Division, about 5 Divisions (give or take) in a Province; for example 29 Districts in the Punjab.

man he got on well. We have the comment of Edwin Montagu on one other member of the Hunter Committee, Pandit Jagat Narayan, though not in the Diary. It was felt unsuitable, since the main seat of the trouble in 1919 had been in the Punjab, that Narayan, who had recently in a public speech denigrated Sir Michael O'Dwyer, the head of that Province, should be a member of the Committee. Montagu's comment was the *"nothing would do the Government of India more harm than the allegation that we fear Indian opinion and make safe appointments that command no confidence among those they were supposed to represent."* Narayan was a close friend of Gandhi. Montagu also met Sir Charles Carmichael Munro, C.-in-C. India.

The entries in Montagu's Diary lead, in the main, to mention of the Commander-in-Chief voting against his plans in the Council; but one entry on January 16th, mentions having dinner with him. *"In the evening I dined with the Commander-in-Chief and got him to admit that his ambitions were to get rid of local armies. I said this involved an army for Indian defence. He is coming to lunch on Friday for a business talk."*

It hardly shows any depth of understanding or friendship and Monro later remarked that Mr. Montagu made him feel as though he were being pushed towards a precipice.

The other people mentioned, who are relevant to this aspect of history are Sir Michael O'Dwyer and Mrs Naidu. Of Mrs Naidu one of the first signatories in the Satyagraha Committee; *"We had an interesting deputation from the women, being led by Mrs. Naidu the poetess, a very attractive and clever woman, but, I believe, a revolutionary at heart. She is connected with Chattopadya of India House fame. The woman who had drafted the address was a Mrs. Cousins, a well-known suffragette from London. Cousins himself is a theosophist, one of Mrs Besant's crowd."*

For Sir Michael there are a number of entries. Montagu claims that O'Dwyer went away delighted from the last conference with Governors – surprising, since Sir Michael is criticised as being out of date and for his involvement in the Punjab disturbances.

Throughout, Montagu played tennis, evening after evening, and at weekends went to stay with the various Princes, shooting tigers and other game. His particular associate was the very clever, but cruel and manipulative Maharajah of Alwar, who had to be removed from his State in the 30s, when his son inherited.

As has already been said, Montagu refused to go into the Districts, far and away the most important point of Indian rule closest to the people, probably the most interesting aspect of India which those who have left India look back on with warmth.

He also did little to placate or interest the officials that he did not meet and their irritation, they put into rhyme.

*We pray for Edwin Montagu*
*Give him O lord his utmost due*
*What that may be we cannot tell*
*But chance it Lord and make it hell.*

## Chapter IV
## THE HUNTER INQUIRY

The growing hysteria was well in place when the Hunter Committee came to sit in Delhi at the end of October 1919, having been appointed on the 14th, for already, the inversion of the truth about rebellion had been achieved by the speeches given in the Legislative Council meeting. The power of leadership and status, a matter of great importance in India, ensured that the speeches would be accepted. The loyalty that was so much a part of Indian sentiment was to be reversed. The admiration and respect due to courage and bravery in war, against the rebels and against an invading enemy, were lost as bravery was made into brutality. It took six months from April to October for the political leaders to change the story, from the gratitude of the people of Amritsar, queuing in their thousands to thank General Dyer, to the allegations of massacre.

The claims that the crowd in the Bagh had been listening to letters written by their beloved leaders when fired on, changed respect and admiration into furious anger and hatred just as Gandhi had claimed, and which Besant had been reiterating from her haven of internment at Ootacamund – 'British brutality'. The mob, the 'vast and hostile' crowd of Miles Irving's account given to his daughter[45], were listening to a diatribe and poems on murder, which they had two days earlier committed on innocent men, nearly on an innocent lady missionary and on the Indian women and children in the Mission School (about 200 of them), not forgetting the Eurasian families in the railway complex, let alone the women and children in the Civil Lines. Evil had become good, good had become evil - the same inversion which had turned Russian

---

45   This description of the crowd in the Jallianwalla Bagh was told by Miles Irving's wife to her daughter Margaret in the early 30s, when she was talking to her in bed, and recounted to the author by Hilary Irving, in recent times before Margaret died, and while they were still in touch and able to talk to each other and check that the story was actually true.

patriotism into Bolshevism and anarchy, convincing a country that to stop fighting against a ruthless enemy was good.

From the Indian nationalists' hatred of the British, linked with Hindu religious beliefs and inspirations, the public perceptions were altered to accept an image which would be used from that time on. A few people were grateful for the repulse of the Afghan invasion, but the image of General Dyer as a cold-blooded murderer was too persuasive to be forgotten. Nehru travelled by train to Delhi after the Hunter Committee interview of Dyer, during which the hall was packed with laughing, jeering, heckling students and people completely under the influence of the lies reaching them from all sides. Nehru claimed that he had travelled on the same train as Dyer and that he had heard Dyer, wearing the caricature (of that time) 'Striped Pyjamas' claiming that he had Amritsar at his feet and could have killed everyone. Nehru (and those who believed him), overlooked the matter of the direction in which the train was going. Dyer was going to Jullundur - travelling in the opposite direction from Nehru - and could not have been on the same train.

Truth, facts, understanding, horror at the way the women and children and the missionaries had suffered, or the European civilians had been murdered; all was forgotten.

The incorrect claims about numbers provided by Munshi Ram and his nationalist helpers were accepted by Hunter, despite the doubts of the later Deputy Commissioner of Amritsar, Francis Hely Burton, and were later shown to have been entirely wrong, when the Langley Committee sat in 1921. Among the claims made, was that of the bodies in the well, which was later made into a sort of shrine. Divers were sent down and found that the claim was entirely spurious; all they could find was some rags and an old cooking vessel.

Only one thing mattered - hatred of General Dyer, who had risked his life and the lives of his handful of Indian soldiers, to stop the mob going on the rampage again.

In this matter of propaganda we have the same again today. We are battered by the claim that the European Union will solve all our problems; that we can no longer take care of ourselves. For this euphemistic concept, we have surrendered our control of our borders, though the call to surrender our currency and hand our gold reserves to the European Bank has, so far, been resisted. That our borders were used to keep out drug traffickers and criminals and control the influx of economic migrants is not mentioned. More serious is the claim that we will no longer have European wars since the E.U. has brought peace to Europe. That is a lie. N.A.T.O. brought the peace, but now sovereignty has been given away to an organisation whose most powerful component is a serial aggressor.

So in the Debate in 1919, black became white. It was only a question of providing sufficient supportive evidence, even untrue evidence, to convince everyone that in fact it was true; black IS white.

By the time that General Dyer gave his evidence at Lahore on November 19th, having just been told that Captain Briggs was dead (he did not know then that he had been killed by being given powdered glass in his food), he gave it in the face of a heckling crowd (for the room was not cleared or quieted), to a Committee without Briggs' statement (which had been written and sent to the Hunter Committee but not included in the evidence because Briggs was dead). His evidence was recorded by clerks, who, either because they were politically indoctrinated, or through subversion and weakness, had written down their version of Dyer's evidence, while Pandit Jagat Narayan and Setalvad and Ahmed Khan had been persuaded, or persuaded themselves, that Dyer was a monster. Neither they, nor the English Members, had insisted on the room being cleared before they asked their questions; by the time he had been cross-examined, as the author's father and Percy Marsden from Kasur remarked, as though they were criminals (and they both knew, as Magistrates, what that meant), Dyer's evidence was available to be used against him. On his evidence, news was at last sent back to England and to the English papers and the Reverend Andrew Gibbon, then a schoolboy, remembered in conversation with the author, the horror of the school at what they had read in the 'Times'.

In India, Nirad Chaudhuri also remembers his own horror on the date of writing. Already the Allahabad Sewa Samiti had 'collected' the 'necessary' figures of casualties, both deaths and wounded. Already, Pandit Malaviya's speech claimed that this was a peaceful crowd up for the Baisakhi fair, although the Fair people, together with the holiday-makers, had left on the 11$^{th}$, since no one stays in, or comes to, a city which is in flames and controlled by a murderous mob. His words were shown to have been untruthful by evidence put forward firmly in the Indemnity Debate, showing that the illegal crowd was listening to a poem on murder, not the letters from their 'beloved leaders'. Already the claims about the well had been clearly and specifically refuted. Now, the new type of propaganda was being used. No longer was it the old magic of Tilak and his 'Kesari', the various calls to magic or submissions to the Gods of that earlier period; now it was the more direct methods of Parvus, Marx, Lenin and Bolshevism, which depended on the actual reversal of truth – lies replacing truth, leading to the proliferation of actual lies which threw, still throw, a shadow and make truth itself obscure.

In the Hunter hearing, there was much questioning about the 'crawling order'. A group of the members who were either ignorant, as in the case of the British, or subversive in the case of the Indians, cross-examined Dyer in detail about this order and its effect. It was a useful lie to make out that Dyer had been humiliating Indians, because accusations of racism was beginning to flourish at that time, thanks to the propaganda which was intent on dividing rather than healing divisions. No one of good intention on that Committee grasped what Miss Sherwood later wrote in 'The Globe', that this was a 'genuflecting order' not a 'crawling order'. She had been in the Fort and though grievously ill, had heard all that was going on; she knew that when the author's mother was asked to type out the order, it was meant, as Dyer said in his evidence, to show respect. The Indians, certainly the two Hindus, Setalvad and Narayan, would have known – and if Malaviya had been there he would have known, that it was a mark of respect, when men would actually bend (or genuflect) as they passed the house of a respected Indian.

This had been confirmed and described to him as well by Nirad Chaudhuri. Dyer, knowing India far better than the British Members, more indeed than most of the Indian members, had put forward an idea that was entirely suitable for a city where a woman had been beaten so severely by men that she was left for dead. Of course it was orchestrated for the West. O'Dwyer did realise and see its political potential and told Dyer to stop it, but Dyer's knowledge of India did not take account of political expediency, but stemmed from a lifetime knowledge of India, a knowledge which could lead him to say *"I am Indian"*, much as the author of this book used to say *"I am Punjabi."*

The truth about the 'crawling order' had been completely obscured; nonetheless, the new Governor of the Province, Sir Edward Maclagan, congratulated Dyer on his evidence and wished that all Europeans would stand up for women as General Dyer had done. Dyer, under that lethal cross-examination on the 'crawling order', in a flush of indignation, described the beating of Miss Sherwood and spoke of the honour and sanctity in which all good men held women, whatever their race and people. *"If men want to fight, let them fight, but let women be left out of it."* There was silence in the room for a moment, and then a burst of applause. This passage is not reported in the evidence.

The lies about this order have, in Richard Attenborough's film anyway, obscured the fundamental gentleness and chivalry of General Dyer, the man who had saved so many slaves from hardship in the Sarhad. In doing so, Attenborough made a film in the Parvus mould, without truth or history.

Who then were these people, The Hunter Committee?

Hunter himself was a Liberal Scottish Judge whom, Draper claims, fought with Pandit Jagat Narayan, so that they were not on speaking terms. The result was a Majority Report and a Minority Report, written by Narayan. It would be almost impossible for a Scot (the Scots in those days had a fundamental love of truth) to have got on with a man who was determined to present a story in complete conflict with the evidence of the witnesses and who used all his skills as a criminal lawyer to make a dispassionate inquiry impossible. In the House of Lords' Debate, Lord Justice Sumner of the Appeal Court added a further insight. *"I do not desire to say one word about the Hunter Committee. I do not desire to say one word about the Minority Members of it, except that, having read the cross examination to which they subjected General Dyer, I think (and they themselves would admit this I believe) that they came to that Inquiry with information which was not derived simply from the evidence that had been laid before the Committee. They came to that Inquiry with a point of view which, to say the least of it, they were determined to present, and present vigorously – they went beyond the point of view of what Dyer had really intended."*

General Sir George Barrow was a close friend of the Commander-in-Chief, Sir Charles Carmichael Monro. Of Thomas Smith little is known, except that he was a member of the Legislative Council of the United Provinces, nor of Mr. W. F. Rice, Additional Secretary to the Government of India Home Department, except that he would have known from the Fortnightly Reports, what had been happening in the Districts and what can be found in the Service Manual. Walter Francis Rice had been educated at Balliol College, Oxford and appointed after the exam of 1890 – so he would have been about 50. He had been sent to Burma and very quickly, after his appointment starting in 1892, become an Officiating Secretary to Government (1900). From then onwards, he had been creeping up in his Burma Government and from there had moved to the Government of India in April 1919, was on special duty from March to May 1920 and retired in 1922. He was therefore inexperienced in the work of a District Officer and would not have any particular knowledge of India.

Rankin – the Honourable Mr. Justice Rankin of the Calcutta High Court - we do know about. He was brought up in Scotland, the son of a Minister. After a brilliant school career he went to Trinity College, Cambridge. He read Moral Science and became the President of the Cambridge Union, following Edwin Montagu in that position. He was called to the Bar in 1904, practising mainly in bankruptcy and commercial cases and in 1916 gained a commission in the Royal Garrison Artillery. On returning to the Bar in 1918, he found his practice dispersed and, having met the Chief Justice of the Bengal High Court earlier in his career, and at his, Sanderson's, suggestion, he took up an appointment as Judge on the Calcutta High Court. When he was appointed to the Hunter Commission, he knew effectively nothing at all about India. His knowledge, such as it was at that time, included not even Rice's limited knowledge of Burman affairs and district life. Brilliant and able as he was, he was probably a Montagu plant, not sufficiently informed to grasp the salient points of the evidence put before him. Rice and Smith rarely asked questions. Hunter and Rankin among the Britons and the two Hindu lawyers, Setalvad and Narayan (at great length and with much repetition), asked the most, apart from the Chairman.

With Setalvad, we have dealt. Narayan was a Member of the Legislative Council of the U.P. and would therefore have already known Mr Thomas Smith. Sardar Sahibzada Sultan Ahmed Khan, Montazim-ud-Doula, married to an English woman, had a Cambridge degree and was a Barrister and Member for Appeals for Gwalior State. Among them all, there was not one man who knew the District life of India, where we lived and worked among Indians and therefore knew their customs and might have had experience of the risings which were a part of Indian life and could have given some indication of the difference between a riot and a rebellion. In his Minority report, written as though to persuade a judge as Barrister for the prosecution, he produced the most pungent of the obscurantist remarks written about General Dyer: *"It is pleaded that General Dyer honestly believed that what he was doing was right. This cannot avail him if he was clearly wrong in his notions of what was right and what was wrong; the plea of military necessity is the plea that has always been advanced in justification of the Prussian atrocities. General Dyer thought he had crushed the rebellion, and Sir Michael O'Dwyer was of the same view. There was no rebellion which required to be crushed."*

In the matter of the 'the point of view they intended to present', Narayan had been going around Amritsar with Gandhi, a mere 20 or so miles away from the Hunter meetings at Lahore, working out the political viewpoint for the way to handle the failed rebellion and asking people angled questions, as were the questions asked to Dyer and, as Melisent Wathen remarked, stirring up feelings which had by then died down. It was these questions and the information collated for the Congress Committee report that showed that Narayan had had previous knowledge.

## DHARMSALA ST. JOHN AMBULANCE DIVISION IN MARCH 1944.

**NAWABZADA SIR MALIK KHIZZAR HAYAT TIWANA, K.C.S.I., O.B.E., PRIME MINISTER OF THE PUNJAB 1942-47. HIS FATHER GAVE EVIDENCE TO THE HUNTER COMMITTEE**

**TURNHAM'S GILL, HENFIELD, SUSSEX. BN5 9HX**
HENFIELD 2051

0273, 492051 January 2ⁿᵈ 1982

Dear Mr Chapman,

I was very glad to get your letter of December 16th telling me of your experiences at the time of Amritsar, which I found most interesting. I had expected that quite a few letters would have come in, but yours was the only one. The fact is, I suppose, that the great majority of those with any personal memories of 1919 are now dead, + in a few years there will be no one left to tell of what happened to them. Do you know anyone who served with you then who is still alive? I should dearly like to collect reminiscences of people who knew what it was really like at the time.

I don't think myself that there was any risk then of another mutiny because that could only have been started by the Indian Army, as the first one was, + my experience was that the Indian officers + sepoys were in no mood for an uprising; in fact both in my regiment + in others. I knew the British officers were on very friendly + happy terms with their men.

But there was a risk of bombings + riots of the kind we hear so much about now in Northern Ireland; nearly always started by a few "activists". In dealing with this risk I think that Gen. Dyer was unwise to use so much force, + the casualties which resulted have been used as propaganda ever since. But I also think he has been unfairly treated, as both at the time + later on, he has been used as a scapegoat, when the real responsibility was the Government's.

If you feel inclined to write again with any further reminiscences I should be delighted, + also I should be glad to hear of any other men still alive who were at or near Amritsar

Meanwhile my best wishes to

Jan/Feb 1982.

Yours sincerely
Eric Whittome

**LETTER FROM J.E. WHITTOME, DEPUTY LIEUTENANT OF SUSSEX IN 1982, TO S.P. CHAPMAN EXPRESSING HIS DOUBTS ABOUT THE TRUTH OF THE GENERALLY ACCEPTED ACCOUNT OF THE AMRITSAR INCIDENT. HE WAS AN OFFICER IN 2/34 SIKH PIONEERS IN 1919 AND HELD UP IN AMRITSAR RAILWAY STATION BECAUSE OF THE RIOT. MR. CHAPMAN SERVED IN 1/25 LONDON REGIMENT IN 1919. (COURTESY OF SIMON PARKER-GALBREATH.)**

## Chapter V
## HUNTER EVIDENCE

So we have been given the impression of a peaceful mob, provoked, according to Congress, by my father firing on it. He was not armed nor indeed could he have been without having signed the necessary forms and being given a weapon.

What still continues to surprise and shock me, is the disparity between fabrication and fact, together with apologies from Labour peers and the Duke of Connaught, which gave enormous mileage in propaganda terms to Gandhi in the following years. More will be seen in the firing called the 'Massacre', a few days later.

In my father's evidence to the Hunter Committee comes the question about the telephone wires. They had been cut between Amritsar and Lahore and close to Colonel Smith's residence. Col. Smith was the Civil Surgeon, the Indian Medical Service man who ran the Hospital. In India, we had a free hospital service long before such a thing in Britain. When he heard about the mobs he was operating on a cataract case. Why, one wonders, were the Hospital and the District Courts effectively cut off? It is interesting that the later claim that the wounded were not taken to the Hospital was added to the rest of the propaganda story. Col Smith's reply was that the Hospital was open and ready and ambulances also, if anyone asked for them. No-one did.

Colonel Johnson at Lahore, remarking on the firing at Amritsar, assumed that Dyer's firing had been carried out under the Defence of India Act, where Dyer knew the law.

Colonel Harry Smith knew the poor people as well as he knew the rich. To a civil surgeon in India came all groups and classes of people and the poor who, in the usual way, having no opportunity of expressing their opinions, felt he was the man to tell. So when he gave his opinions, they were well-founded. As a matter of interest, his observations exactly coincide with my father's about the municipal elections. He said:

"The unrest appeared to commence in earnest when the Rowlatt Bill was being dealt with in the Viceroy's Legislative Council. The politicians so grossly misrepresented that Bill, that they led the people to believe that-there were almost only three functions in life which did not put everyone completely under the supervision of the police - to be begotten, to be born and to die. This did not merely apply to the male population, but the Zenana was invaded by the same wholesale propaganda. In my opinion high prices of foodstuffs had nothing really to do with the affair. The people whom high prices of foodstuffs affect most seriously are not 'politically minded'. The politicians, to serve the political purpose, of course used high prices. I doubt if even Turkish affairs influenced the city Moslem as much as on the surface would appear. What influenced both Hindu and Moslem was more allied to a wave of Bolshevism, if some of the parties were not even in the pay of the Russo-German Bolshevist organisation. What facilitated the operations of the 10th of April was the fact that the present system adopted in Municipal elections, necessitates that aspirants for seats in the Municipal Council shall canvass for votes. Formerly, the 'classes' and the 'masses' were not in intimate touch with each other. The present system implies organisation. The organisation has no scruples about employing the headmen of the hooligans, of which there are many, for purposes of intimidation. Hence for April 10th, there was experience of organising the poorer elements of the city and the hooligans, so that it was a comparatively easy matter with the funds at the disposal of the politicians to organise revolutionary mobs. If the Indian gentlemen who give evidence were examined on this issue, I have no doubt they will support my views.

I observed the development of the change in the temper of the people from being reasonable to being revolutionary [this was also recognised by my mother and Mrs Melisent Wathen]. After the hartal on the 6th of April, their mental attitude was to be able only to see different shades of red, so to speak. This does not apply to all. There are many men in Amritsar who disapproved of the whole propaganda, but who, I am convinced, were so terrorised that they were afraid to be seen visiting an officer's bungalow, Those who command the chiefs of the hooligans of Amritsar - this requires money - can terrorise almost any resident.

The hartals here on the 30th March and on the 6th April were a masterpiece of organisation. I observed that the Hindus and the Moslems on the 8th and 9th of April were drinking out of the same cup and that the Moslem reciprocated by having the Hindu tikka painted on his forehead. On the 9th, in my opinion these hartals had nothing to do with religion, but they were designed and organised by Mr. Gandhi, or by a revolutionary organisation behind him, for the purpose of developing a little discipline and a revolutionary spirit. I had no doubt, from the great success of the hartal on 6th April 1919, that they intended to have another hartal at no distant date, on which the red flag would be heaved up everywhere at the same time, but that the saving of the situation would be in the fact that they had developed the revolutionary spirit to such an extent, that it was certain to get out of hand somewhere at any moment, in which case the whole organisation would go astray. Once it went out of *hand, I was confident that reasoning with these people would be of no avail - that prompt force would be necessary.*

*As to the affairs of 10th April 1919, they indicated a detailed organisation of people who had 'wind in the head.' The details were local but the affairs elsewhere in the Punjab and in the Bombay Presidency taken together with the hartal, indicated a Central organisation. I expressed at the above-mentioned interview that apart from the Arya Samaj element in the villages, that the village communities were not in the movement and that it was essentially Arya Samaj and Municipal Moslem. When Law and Order was thought to be 'out of time', the zamindar was, as he would be at all times, ready to go looting and from such information as I possess, if Martial Law had not been proclaimed and force used on the 13th April 1919, Amritsar City would have been looted by the martial Sikh villagers next day and would probably have suffered a much heavier mortality than Martial law caused.*

*That Sikh villagers did not act earlier, I explain by the fact that, in my opinion, the city people did not take them into their confidence and that they were then not in the organisation, as the city people were afraid that they would at once go looting and display all the vices associated with looting under such circumstances. I was present at Amritsar throughout this period and can give details if required."*

On this statement, Smith's cross-examination would be lengthy, if embarked on at all. In the event, it took ten pages of double column tiny print format. He was probably speaking in this way to Sir Michael O'Dwyer on the 9th, when he was at Government House and equally, he probably had a good deal of influence over the decision to deport Kitchlew and Satyapal. His analysis seems as accurate any I have read and he was also one of the very few who had the insight to see Gandhi's position in the Rebellion. Gandhi himself said in the Ahmedabad Inquiry that there was an organisation behind the rebellion. He merely omitted to say that he was behind the organisation.

Lord Hunter went into some detail with Smith about the feelings in Amritsar going back to January. Smith said that he thought the people believed the claims being made by the politicians and that the attitude to himself was that he happened to be, as you might say, a Government philanthropist in the medical line. It was only when the second hartal came on that the peoples' attitude towards him changed and, since they believed the rumours to be true, they would be in a very angry state of mind. He had asked some of the men with advanced political views whether they had read the Rowlatt Bills and they had not. He agreed with the fact that there was some effect among the educated Muslims about Turkey and there was the matter of platform tickets on the Railway, but his remarks made most clear the effects of the Municipal elections in the previous winter when the forces of hooligans were such that one man was not allowed to leave his house the entire time. He mentioned the hooligans as leading to a form of protection racket and blackmail - that the man who paid them no longer needed a night watchman [a situation, which in our day, was filled by the same sort of people, retired burglars and so forth]. On the matter of the combined use of drinking vessels, he said that it was an indication of joint organisation, political but not fraternal. He dismissed the idea that it was the firing at the bridge - the point that was central to the politico's imagery; of the peaceful crowd being shot at by my father causing a riot - saying *"My opinion is that the whole violence went off practically at once in the different parts. I got on the ambulance immediately and went off into the city across the police lines to bring out the three European Missionary Ladies and Indian Christians. I got back with them and returned for the middle school, which is across the Police Lines crossing and close to it, but sheltered by a garden. I walked into the walled enclosure and saw a party there smashing everything and the under storey of the main building on fire. The moment they saw me they made a dash for myself. I was armed with a walking stick. I got on the ambulance and got off. The driver happened to go by a circuitous route and came round to the police lines and by the time I got there the police had gone to their relief."* The time? *"One or two.*

*When I was going for the missionaries, I could see smoke in the city. When I got the length of the Missionary Hospital, I could see from there that flames were coming out of the buildings, so that the whole business seemed to me to have been one. They were stopped coming across the Railway and they proceeded, shots or no shots, to violence. That this plan was organised is to me clear.*

- Q. *Why do you say that?*
- A. *The class of men whom I saw at work on that building was not the middle class of the city. They were hooligans. They were the class of men whom I would expect to be looting shops in the neighbourhood of the National Bank and so on, under normal circumstances, as distinct from burning schools."*

There were some more questions and then he was asked if he considered the lives of Europeans were safe in the city that day? His reply: *"When I saw the Church on fire, considering that it is as much a sacrilege to a Hindu or a Mussulman to interfere with a Church as to interfere with a Mosque or a Temple, I came to the conclusion that this show meant the white man, root and branch."*

He was asked whether it was essential in the interests of safety to put the women and children into the Fort and he replied that for the missionaries, it was essential, but for the women and children in the civil lines, it was not quite so urgent as long as the railway line was held - he gave them a latitude of an hour or an hour and a half.

He was then asked about the attitude of the people and he said it was supremely sulky. As to whether it was safe for a European to go into the city during the next few days, he thought not without a guard - that he himself had been asked to attend a patient in the city, but not wishing to use a guard, he had asked for the patient to be brought to him.

To Rankin's questions, he said that the mobs had been organised previously and from an eminent Indian he had learnt that these gangs were organised on the 9th *"and that there was a butcher attached to each gang."*

He was asked *"If the gangs were prepared to loot anywhere, why did they not loot Indians?"* His reply *"Effectively because they were organised; they were acting under orders."* Did he know the organisers? He did not know the heads of the organisation.

Rankin wanted to believe that the outbreak had been a spontaneous ebullition without organisation. Smith made clear that if this were the case then the Indian shops would have been looted. He pointed out that the class of hooligans had burglars among them and loot would have been their intention. He pointed out that the villagers had got the message that there was no longer law and that the Sikh villagers were coming in for loot. For evidence, he gave the instance of stalwart Sikh villagers coming to persuade him to give one of their friends who was a soldier a medical certificate and that the attitude of these gentlemen was respectful, *"but they looked like a lot of gentlemen who were ready to go anywhere."* He knew the villages well and he was told that the villagers of the Central Punjab were ready to loot Amritsar. As might be expected, the Indian lawyers pressed him on his concern about agitation. Was he against political agitation in the Punjab? *"By no means. I am a democrat - not so long as they did not interfere with the rights of the citizens."* Had he studied the Rowlatt Act critically? He had, and after a number of questions about the attitude of the Indians in the Legislative Assembly of every shade of political opinion who opposed the Bill, slowly through more questions came his point *"I do not consider they are misguided people; I consider that a system of irresponsibility implies opposition and nothing but opposition and that is history."*

I give these examples of his opinions to indicate the man himself and the attitudes of Indians who trusted him and that this was the attitude of the times. Smith left the service in 1921; he probably felt, as did many others, that the India that he had worked for was irrevocably changed. He gave details of the situation, which Setalvad endeavoured to discount by suggesting that the quiet state of the city during the days after the 10th meant that Martial Law was unnecessary. That was another of all the peculiarly irresponsible questions and statements which could have elicited real information if the Indians had been interested in the truth about the suppression of a dreadful outbreak of murderous violence. They were clearly interested in nothing but pushing him into a corner where his valuable evidence could be invalidated. Narayan, reiterating the peaceful state of the city after the 10th, was met with the fact that Smith's own police guard could get no food in the city if he wore his uniform. The plan in each town was the take-over by rebellious mobs and the forming of mini-soviets in the hands of the rebels. The endeavour to take over everything led to the setting up of food co-operatives, so that the entire supply of food coming into the town would be in the hands of the rebels, something that had not even happened in the Mutiny, when in the Fort at Agra, markets were set up, selling food. The Bolshevik method had not been worked out then, but in 1919, in Amritsar, no food was to be brought to the town except for the rebels and those who gave in to them. People wishing to sell milk, vegetables and fresh meat to the women and children and the soldiers were attacked and beaten and did not try twice; all Government servants, the women and children, the police and the Army, were under siege.

The food coming in to the town was for rebels only, people who could be taken as part of the new system. From Narayan came the questions that were directly related to the Congress Report that he had helped to collect. Smith, who worked for a salary and did not charge, was asked if he had charged for various operations.

Q, About Bodh Singh, did he know him?
A. Possibly, but then he knew many people.
Q. Did he tell him he should charge him Rs.1,500 for the amputation of an arm or a leg?
A. It is untrue.
Q. Had he told people who came to him to go to Gandhi or Kitchlew?
A. It is an absolute falsehood.

He knew Kitchlew and Satyapal very well and said later that they were not organisers; they were much smaller men than organisers. On the matter of whether the Hospital had been open and ready on the 13th and 14th, Smith said not only that it had been ready and open but also as soon as the telegraph wires were cut he had ordered in ample supplies. In all these questions and cross examinations, Setalvad and Narayan questioned the men who, with enormous bravery, had saved the city, as if they were disparaging them. Even when overwhelming evidence showed exactly what the men said was true, these lawyers continued in the same vein, with no appreciation of the immense bravery and steadfastness that had been shown. With all the indications of lack of compassion, lack of shock at the cruelties of the mob, these lawyers showed most clearly what we were up against from the politicians in India from that date on.

The statements about the quiet state of the city after the 10th of April, so forcefully pressed by the Indian lawyers at the hearing, need to be examined with care.

Those so-called quiet days were the beginning of the women's time in the Fort. Worse fears came later and accumulated, with news coming in of the woman and three children threatened with death when the warrant officers had been attacked at Kasur; when Miss Sherwood was brought in later and other women, including Dr. Easden, who had had to hide in the Zenana hospital while the mob searched for her. It was claimed by Congress that this searching for a woman doctor who had looked after wives and families was reasonable, because she had stood on the roof of the Hospital and said that it was a good thing that the members of the mob who had been wounded had been hurt. It was, as with the evidence invented about Colonel Smith, untrue - and even if it had been true, it was hardly a good reason to seek to murder her. Narayan came to the Hunter Committee ready armed with such tales from the streets where he had walked with Gandhi and been given excuses for the depredations of the mob. Sir John Hose, reading the Congress screed on which our media relies with such gusto today, observed that it could hardly be given as the reason for the death of one of the bank managers, that he produced a revolver from his desk when the mob broke into his office in a frenzy carrying lathis. They did attack him, they did finally kill him, although it was not certain whether it was after or before he had been thrown out of the window onto the bank furniture and papers and doused with kerosene oil and set on fire.

The reason given for such a ludicrous claim was that the mob was still, by Gandhi's standards, being provoked from its peaceful mien into violence, which it would not have displayed on its own.

Thus Miles Irving's brief report about what had happened. He managed to get information through to Lahore during the afternoon, asking for help. Kitchin and Donald were sent over and the position of the civil administration being what it was, control was handed over to the military. On the following day notices would be given to the leaders that the military were in control and would fire on unlawful gatherings.

Miles Irving was a gentle man and was prepared to make statements that were not evidence in the strictest sense. The Congress used every one of these. An example was the statement that the crowd going up to the Hall Bridge was peaceful, to the extent that it did no harm to the civilians it passed. If he had seen the evidence of Mohammed Ashraf Khan, the City Inspector, he would have known how Jarman had had to be rescued and taken to the Kotwali. Again, Ashraf Khan, under heavy cross-examination because of his relationship with Dyer on the latter's arrival, said that the crowd might have been peaceful up to the time of the shooting. He had heard about the shooting and then there was a lot of excitement, but he was too far away to know about the firing at the Hall Gate. Since he knew that there were between 75-80,000 men on the move, burning, murdering and looting, in this matter I would rather rely on Smith, who as soon as he heard that the mobs were on the move, went to rescue the ladies from the religious books shop and the missionaries and found the crowd very violent indeed.

It is necessary when looking at Hunter to grasp that there were inaccuracies, that people under cross-examination say things which they would not say on their own, that the audience of students and politically astute men was shouting and moving chairs, jeering and heckling. We have to pick out what holds together and make the most of it. It has to be our main and most reliable source of information where we do not have personal records, but the clerks got the papers into such a mess that they handed them to the 'Pioneer' newspaper to sort out.

In addition to the evidence given to the Hunter Inquiry, however, we do have the information provided by individuals who were involved.

The people in the Fort went to their uncomfortable sleep, hearing in the bazaar the screams for 'white blood' and seeing the electric light blazing and lighting up the sky. My father, going to bed on the roof, found that not only was he bruised all over, but he had a burn on his thigh where, when he dropped his pipe into his pocket as he was riding towards the Hall Bridge, the dottle had burnt a hole in his pocket.

The Risaldar Major, Khan Bahadur, having heard that the mob were going to fetch ladders and climb into the Fort to get the women, offered his services and that of a handful of his friends (leaving the necessary guard to protect the men who were supplying him and his stock with feed, from the attentions of the goondas). He first offered help to my father who, when he was later transferred to the Salt Range, met him again and remembered that awful night. My father told him that as a civilian, he could authorise nothing, but he then went to one of the officers who most gratefully accepted the help of a guard on the Fort during the night. In fact he had wished to help all day but had been unable to get across the lines from their tents to speak to anyone. He had came to Amritsar for the Baisakhi Fair to sell horses, but left the next day because of the danger to his stock.

Kitchin and Donald arrived with 175 Baluchis and Sikhs from the Frontier Force. With them was Major Macdonald who then took over the responsibility for the town. It was then that Kitchin said: *"We wondered whether we were the only white men alive in India."*

With the arrival of the soldiers, a party went into the city and rescued the four men in the Kotwali and recovered the body of Thompson and the two bodies of Stewart and Scott from the National Bank. These were taken to the mortuary in the civil lines.

*"We came via the station to the fort, arriving about 1.30 a.m. and wearing pagris"*, said Jarman later.

There had been one more fear for the ladies in the Fort. When an officer came in asking for the use of their only lantern; a body had been found on the glacis of the Fort and it was thought to be that of Thompson, whose young newly-married bride was in the Fort. Very quietly therefore, they took the body in, only to find that it was the body of the electrician Sergeant Rowlands who, armed only with an umbrella, had been set upon by the mob carrying lathis and beaten to a bloody pulp with no resemblance to a human being.

As soon as my father left the bridge he went from bungalow to bungalow rousing people to go to the rallying post, which was in fact the same bungalow in which he and my mother lived, although it was actually rented by a Mr. and Mrs. Jeffries. In India we were not allowed to own our own houses; we were not able to have houses in England either, since if we did we had to pay double income tax. My mother was resting after lunch, the heat was almost unbearable for it was the beginning of the Hot Weather and shortly before the parsimonious rules of the Government would permit the use of fans in offices on April 22nd. Her bearer came in and told her that a lady had arrived and after a few moments when she went into the drawing room she found it packed with people, some of whom had babies and small children with them. She had forgotten that the house was the rallying post. My father had roused them from their chores, some very reluctant to get their babies up from sleep and join with the others.

Not till just after five did Fazl Khan Bahadur, Risaldar Major of the Indian Army, see all the European boys and girls and women in the civil lines beginning to go to the Fort in motors, tongas, and carriages. They were accompanied by two or three officers on horseback. Melisent Wathen described them as huddled and miserable like men just out of the trenches. My father wrote *"I should like to say something about the people at the Rallying Post, in view of the impression given about Europeans in such circumstances by novelists who have never been in anything more dangerous than a party in their own honour. There was a little hysteria, I believe, though I saw nothing of it till the following day when a woman fell at my feet and implored me to prevent her husband going back to his work in the city. At one time when I was not there, a rumour came in that the crowd had broken through and was rapidly approaching..."* His reference was of course to E. M. Forster, who made the Rallying Post scene and the Fort into his Club scene in a 'Passage to India'. Since no Club ever behaved in any way that resembled what was suggested in the novel, Oliver Calder, in the Garwhalis in 1919, was astounded when he saw the scene in a play produced by Frank Hauser many years later at the Playhouse at Oxford. His astonishment was made up of anger and disgust that such a rotten caricature of women in clubs in India could have been invented. Years later the Comtesse de Brievelet, the daughter of Malcolm Darling, told me on the phone from Paris, just before she died, that the story was based on the Amritsar image of the women who were in such fear and misery, not knowing whether their husbands were alive or dead. My father tried to make it clear that the scene was wrong as Oliver Calder also knew.

# Chapter VI
# INDEMNITY DEBATE

It has been imagined that the British governed India with no control from the Indians. This is not correct. On the Legislative Council, the number of elected or appointed members was far greater than the number of those who were a part of Government, representing the different Government Departments and who were known as the official members.

Among the Indians were several of whom we have already heard. The most prominent in the Indemnity Debate was Pandit Mohan Madan Malaviya. It was he who was to press the case against indemnification for the officers and officials who had done what they could to stop the Rebellion. Foremost amongst the claims for indemnification was General Dyer.

Sir William Vincent, the Home Member, was the first to speak. It could be said that in his first words, he showed that Government was on the run, yet he had been forewarned and forearmed with the knowledge of the fortnightly reports, which had arrived regularly on his desk.

"*My Lord*, [this being to the Viceroy, Lord Chelmsford] *it may be said that Martial Law was not necessary in the Punjab and that the Government made a mistake in proclaiming it. I do not seek to argue that point now. I believe that any such course would be unfair to those concerned, primarily or indirectly concerned, until the Committee of Inquiry has recorded the evidence of the facts. The decision on that matter must rest with the Committee in a great measure and after their report has been received, with other authorities, but, irrespective of this question, the position of our officers must be protected. I do not know if I make myself clear on that point. What I wish to say is this, whether Martial Law was necessary or not, our officers, our subordinate officers were bound to carry out their duties, and to give effect to the orders given them and they cannot be penalised on that account.*

*My Lord, I will now, if I may, proceed to explain the Bill, clause by clause. I will not deal with clause I, which is of no great importance, but proceed at once to clause II. That clause indemnifies any officer of Government, whether civil or military, from any action, civil or criminal, in respect of any matter or thing done for the purpose of maintaining or restoring order, but I want Honourable Members to read and fully consider the effect of the proviso to that clause: 'provided that such officer or person has acted in good faith and in a reasonable belief that his action was necessary for the said purpose'. Those are really the governing words of the clause. I think I have already said, or at any rate I say now, that this bill will in no way forestall the inquiry by the Committee, and I will proceed to justify that statement."*

He continued on these lines, repeating that the officers would not be protected if they had not acted reasonably and in good faith, that they would not be protected if they had been guilty of excesses which could not be justified, and that the Inquiry would assess blame for the disturbances and recommend: *"any form of punishment for any officer of Government who has not acted <u>bona fide</u> and in a reasonable belief that what he did was necessary. Further, in any case, this Bill does not affect the report of the Committee. This Bill protects officers against proceedings in the Courts of Justice. The report of this Committee will, whatever be its value, in no sense be evidence for the purpose of any such case. That is a matter which can only be decided on evidence in the Courts."* And then again. *"the report of that Committee will not be limited or barred by this Act in any way. The Government of India has decided, for the satisfaction of their own conscience and to meet the public demand, to appoint a Committee to inquire into the disturbances ...*

*If this Council says that in a time of this character, when the country was in great disorder, and I put it very mildly, officers who, acting on the understanding that Martial Law has been proclaimed by an authority which is superior to them, over whose actions they have no control, if officers acting on that assumption and acting <u>bona fide</u> and perfectly reasonably are not to be protected by Government, then the future prospects of Government officers is very serious. How can any member of this Council expect an officer to act confidently, firmly and decisively if he knows that this Legislative Council and the Government will repudiate his action at the first opportunity. Is he not entitled to come down here and say, 'I have done what I am told, I have acted perfectly reasonably, I have acted fairly, I have acted <u>bona fide,</u> now give me that protection which I am entitled to by all constitutional practice.' My Lord, in a Resolution published by this Government some time ago, I think during the period of the disturbances, we solemnly promised that we would afford all those charged with the onerous duty of restoring order, our full countenance and support, and it is in fulfilment of that promise that I now come to this Council and ask Honourable Members to ratify what we then promised, believing that this is a just and honourable course which must commend itself to all Members here...Whether any particular action was reprehensible, whether it was right or whether it was wrong, is not a matter that comes within the scope of this Bill."*

Sardar Sunder Singh Majithia spoke next. He was the chief Sikh in the Punjab.

" ...*I wish to be assured fully that Government has no intention to afford protection to those who have acted against the strictest sense of justice and against good faith. Though personally I have no doubt on that point and I am sanguine that Government have no intention of that sort, but an assurance of this nature will satisfy public opinion in this country. One thing more before I give my assent to the measure before the Council. I would like Government to agree and to concede that all cases tried under Martial Law will further be examined and that wherever injustice is found to have been done, those who are detained in jails will be given their liberty. I am glad that the point has been conceded and that two High Court Judges will revise these judgements and I thank the Government for this. I have no wish to ask any clemency for those who committed atrocities, but on the report of the Committee of Inquiry, I would suggest that amnesty be granted, as I think that many of those unfortunate persons have, in the heat of the roused feelings, been led astray from paths of righteousness and of law-abiding citizens of the Empire. With this assurance that the Act does not whitewash all actions done in bad faith as against good faith and with a promise of a further reconsideration of the cases tried by the Martial Law courts, I would give my assent to the order before the Council. I have avoided making any mention of the unfortunate happenings in my province, as this Council Chamber is not now the right place for them to be ventilated. They are in a way sub-judice and until the report of the Committee of Inquiry is published, we must suspend our judgements. The other day I asked for an assurance for the protection of persons who come to tender evidence before the Committee of Inquiry. I understand that the Home Member is willing to give that assurance and that steps will be taken to duly proclaim this to the people. I would, therefore, beg my Honourable friends and colleagues to refrain from bringing in matters which are now in the province of the Committee of Inquiry to inquire into and sift."*

The next speaker was Pandit Malaviya, highly respected in the Indian community, a clever lawyer who began by following the pattern laid down by Pandit Narayan, calling the Rebellion 'disturbances', before starting his lengthy speech, in the convoluted way in which the lawyers tended to do, with the 1715 Rebellion in Britain. Going through the Lords-Lieutenant, Deputy-Lieutenants, Justices of the Peace and so on for some length, he agreed that in 1715 there had been a rebellion. He went on:

*"The Honourable the Home Member has said that where there has been disorder and it has been found necessary to proclaim Martial Law, certain acts have had to be done which may not be strictly defensible and that an Indemnity Act, almost as a natural consequence, followed. Now my Lord, your Lordship will see and the Council will see that the essential part of this enactment is that there was a rebellion which had to be suppressed and put an end to ...* [or again] *These enactments* [from which he quoted large extracts] *clearly lay down that the legislative body which is to give its sanction to the acts which were performed during a time of trouble were necessary for the suppression of a rebellion or riot which amounted to rebellion and that they*

*were so very necessary that the legislative body ought to justify them and indemnify those who had taken part in them. It is not every ordinary riot, which would come in the category of the riots mentioned there. It must be a riot which, as Lord Halsbury points out in his article on the Laws of England, must be a riot or rebellion amounting to war."*

He then quoted from Vol. VI of Halsbury at some length. His next step was to turn to the law in India, and to Regulation X of the Act of 1804 under which Martial Law was declared in the Punjab on 14th April 1919.

*"Now my Lord, it is clear that this Regulation can only be justly put into force when there is either a war or open rebellion against the authority of the Government. Your Lordship, in establishing Martial Law by the notification dated Simla, the 14th April, 1919, consequently said "Whereas the Governor General is satisfied that a state of open rebellion against the authority of Government exists in certain parts of the province of the Punjab; now, therefore, in exercise of the power conferred on him, he is pleased to make and promulgate the following Ordinance. Now, my Lord, the public have not been told what were the circumstances which constituted a state of open rebellion in Lahore. I gave notice of certain questions and I wanted to find out what it was that constituted a state of open rebellion. The Government told me that the questions could not be answered in view of the fact that an inquiry had been ordered and it would not be in the interests of the public that these questions should be answered"*

The proof of rebellion was dismissed as being lamentable violence against people and property, which had been caused through the repression by the Government of India shown in the enactment of the Rowlatt legislation. Having cleared the way, Malaviya could then quote the *"strong condemnation of the All-India Congress Committee at the passing of orders under the Defence of India Act by the Punjab Government and the Government of India, against a person of such well known noble character and antecedents as Mr. M. K. Gandhi ...."* and then again, this subtle way of reversing the facts by adding: *"The Committee cannot help feeling that if these orders had not been passed, some of the regrettable events that followed them may not have happened."*

We now know why Gandhi's alleged arrest was so important and was so frequently reiterated. It was to be used as the justification for the violence which occurred.

The All-India Congress Committee had also sent a long cablegram to His Majesty's Secretary of State and to the Premier in which they had drawn attention to the seriousness of the situation. Though he gave no date at first, it was sent on 28th April as follows:

*"All-India Committee desire most earnestly to represent to His 'Majesty's Government intense gravity of present situation in India, real causes and need for change of policy pursued at present. While deploring and condemning popular excesses which have occurred in some parts of the country and which popular leaders have everywhere used their influence not unsuccessfully to restrain, Committee urge*

*impartial consideration of circumstances which have so aggravated and embittered feelings of people throughout country as to make such outbreaks possible. Resolution of Government of India dated 14th Instant, describing present situation as arising out of Rowlatt Act agitation makes only partial statement of case. Undoubtedly intense universal bitterness of opposition to Rowlatt Act forced through legislation by official votes against unanimous protest of all nonofficial Indian members and in face of unparalleled opposition throughout country was immediate cause of recent popular peaceful demonstrations, but subsequent excesses were provoked by needless and unjustifiable action of Government of India and Punjab and Delhi Governments against so revered a personality as that of Mr. Gandhi and against other popular leaders. For complete understanding however of present discontent and its causes other important factors must be considered."*

After dealing with the factors, which included India's services during the war (omitting to mention that these services were rendered by an army officered by the same people who put down the Rebellion and ignoring the fact that the Congress leaders and their friends on the Oriental Desk in Berlin were not a part of the services India rendered to the Empire during the War), the attitude of European and Anglo-Indian officials towards the Reforms and the fate of Turkey and the Rowlatt Bills, he went on: *"In such circumstances, the two Rowlatt Bills were introduced and the principal one forced through Council in spite of unanimous opposition of non-official Indian Members, appeal for postponement and reconsideration and warnings of agitation that would inevitably follow throughout country which was stirred by this measure and uncompromising attitude of Government in degree unparalleled in history of country, Committee here cannot enter in detail as to justifiable apprehensions caused by passing into law of this Act.*

*They are content to represent that it is total distortion of facts that an agitation against a measure placed on Statute book in time of peace depriving subjects under any circumstances of sacred right of free and open trial and otherwise restricting fundamental liberties and depriving accused persons of normal and essential safeguards designed for protection of innocent persons, should be regarded as an unreal agitation engineered by political agitators for their own ends. Committee have no authority to discuss merits of passive resistance movement led by Mr. Gandhi, but would emphasis that nothing but feeling of high-souled patriotism and intense realisation of injustice involved in passing of this measure could have actuated man of his saintly character and noble record. Committee submit that so far as facts are publicly known, no violence had anywhere been committed by the people until the arbitrary restrictions placed on Gandhi's movements leading to his arrest and forcible deportation without any announcement of his destination while he was on his way to Delhi with object of pacifying people after unfortunate episode there on March 3rd. Grave allegations were made that authorities in Delhi unjustifiably fired on crowds killing and wounding several. Government of India has ignored demands for inquiry into this and has published ex parte statement of Local Government, exonerating local authorities on unconvincing statements. Had Gandhi been allowed to proceed Delhi, Committee believe he would have restored normal conditions. Government, by his arrest and deportation, provoked outbreaks in Ahmedabad and Viramgam. Outbreak had become imminent in Bombay also, but it was averted by wise action of authority in restraining Police and Military and efforts of Gandhi and other leaders pacified people and restored quiet.*

*Committee invite attention to the contrast between rapidity with which tranquillity was restored in Ahmedabad by presence of Gandhi, his co-operation along with that of other leaders with authorities and continuance of disorders in Punjab where reckless and horrible methods of repression under Martial Law such as public flogging of citizens in streets, dropping of bombs from aeroplanes, wholesale firing on people assembled in streets, have been resorted to. These methods of repression have created horror and resentment throughout country.*

*Committee recognises need for strong measures to deal with popular violence where occurring and popular leaders and bodies and all public men are ready to co-operate with Government in putting down popular excessively violent movements against authority, but use of such methods as have been in force in Punjab antagonise feeling of people towards Government and sow seeds of bitterness and distrust.*

*Committee most earnestly urge His Majesty's Government to intervene and put an end to these methods and to order the appointment of commission of officials and non-officials to investigate causes of discontent and allegations of excesses by authorities in repressing public outbreaks.*

*Committee strongly urges His Majesty's Government to consider that popular discontent has been provoked by causes set forth above. At Amritsar, disturbances followed immediately on Sir Michael O'Dwyer's action in arresting and deporting Dr. Kitchlew and Dr. Satyapal. Committee most earnestly represent that situation cannot be dealt with by repression and attitude of sternness towards people displayed in Resolution of Indian Government of 14th instant which gave free hand to Local Governments to employ every weapon in armoury of repression and is sadly lacking in spirit of conciliation. Situation calls for highest statesmanship which will deal with it in spirit which animated British people and Indian people in their recent struggle for maintenance of liberty and freedom of peoples from despotic domination and not in mood of ruthless repression.*

*All-India Congress Committee feel that they can appeal with confidence to His Majesty's Ministers to consider this representation with sympathy and to take definite steps forthwith to reverse the policy of repression and to satisfy Indian feeling with regard to the Mohammedan question, the reforms and repeal of Rowlatt Act. Committee respectfully submit this action alone will secure real peace and contentment in land."*

(At this stage the Council adjourned for Lunch.)

That telegram was sent on April 28th, at a time when India was quiet and by no means in favour of the leaders of the Rebellion. Bearing in mind Montagu's character, which these clever men knew well, it was a masterly stroke to send such a subtly undermining missive. If Montagu had gone into the Districts on his visits, if he had got to know the men who kept India quiet and prosperous and in peaceful contentment, he might have been sufficiently conscious of the motives to have resisted the effects on his mind. Dyer's remark quoted by Colvin was *"Mr Montagu is a clever man but he does not understand India, nor Indians."*

For those of us who worked and lived in India, the subtleties of this telegram and the description of events from the All-India Congress Committee viewpoint were typical of everyday behaviour in the courts and committees. For us, such expositions were normal, and part of what was available to deduce the truth of any matter. We were not right all the time, but we did our best and the honesty and upright dealing which had made our reputation in the world and the relationship we had with India and Indians gave us the ability to avoid being duped by chicanery. It is the heart of this book, based on actual incidents, that by the twisting of facts, by lies about them, by malevolent interpretation, a case was made for an invented story which had no basis in truth, and which has given the British, as well as Dyer, a completely false image still being quoted today.

The incidents at Ahmedabad were put down by Colonel Fraser, not by Gandhi - far from it. It is in the unpalatable story of the Moplah Rebellion that we see that Gandhi had no ability to put down anything, nor did he do so in 1947, when millions were killed. His unsaintly character made it impossible, nor did his friends claim his capacity then. His appearance in Bengal had no such effect in 1946 - rather it stirred more trouble. But it was on these claims that a Secretary of State convinced the Government, of which he was a member, to act in a most disgraceful way to Dyer. As this book shows, to refute lies takes many more pages and words than it does to tell them. The Christian precepts in the education of the men who were involved in ruling India at that time would have precluded lying, twisting and inventing in the manner of the Pandit, and it was exactly that upright behaviour that made them trusted and capable of administering justice to a country riven by caste and religion, and with ideas that relied on dissembling and convincing by any means.

Pandit Malaviya irrepressibly continued his dissertation through that day and the day that followed. He was in a strong position, for the declaration of Martial Law had been made by the Viceroy's Council, and the Government of India was in the hands of the Legislative Council which Malaviya was endeavouring to control. His argument was that there had been no rebellion, in which case there was, in law, no right to indemnification. His further point was that this had been a disturbance by the people because of repression. That later historians have accepted this, is an indication of the success of the propaganda which largely relied on the exceptional regulations implicit in the Rowlatt Act, yet which, by excluding any of the factual accounts of the people themselves, has persuaded successive generations to accept a ploy in keeping with that of Lenin or Marx or Goebbels, Only the facts themselves, gathered by observation or involvement, can disprove such propaganda.

Malaviya's argument rested on questioning the basis for the Martial Law order which had been promulgated. At the beginning of the debate, Sir William Vincent had said clearly that this question was not allowed. Malaviya had been reprimanded previously for insisting on a question that had been disallowed. He had then stated, *"I do not know of a reprimand and I do not recognise any such reprimand. I am entitled on a Bill before the Council to draw attention to every fact. I was perfectly right, I submit, to do what I did. The facts of 'rebellion' could be delayed as long as they were put before the Committee of Inquiry. Your Lordship will kindly remember that since this unfortunate declaration of open rebellion in the Punjab, which among other evils contributed to the Afghan War, by the declaration of this open rebellion and the establishment of Martial Law in the Punjab, the Punjab Government shut the rest of India and the world out from the knowledge of what was happening in the Punjab."*

He gave, as example, the exclusion of C. F. Andrews, who was representing a newspaper; the man who had worked at the Cambridge Mission School, source of so many of the anti-British bomb throwers and conspirators, who had met Montagu in India, when more relevant contacts were omitted. Malaviya then cited the newspapers and journalists which were not allowed to enter the Punjab. The fact that Andrews had applied to the Viceroy for entry to the Punjab, after being told he could not have a permit and had then gone there anyway, was not mentioned. No legal proviso was considered to be reasonable.

After lunch Malaviya started on his disquisition about the events, many of which I have already noted in previous pages. This was the All-India National Congress tale which would, almost word for word, be reiterated by the Minority Report of the Hunter Committee. It was the story to which Lord Sumner referred when he said that the Indians had come to the Hunter Committee with knowledge that they had not gained from the hearing itself.

The fact that it had not been capable of being compared with the evidence of the men who had put down the rebellion, since their evidence was not then available, made little difference to the Minority men of the Hunter hearing. Where the evidence of those who had dealt with the rising did not fit, the Minority attacked, bullied and, as my father and Philip Marsden commented, treated the officials as criminals.

Here are the spurious claims that it was Gandhi who had quieted the riots at Viramgam and Ahmedabad, rather than the Salt Official with the handful of men who came with him, rather than Colonel Fraser at Ahmedabad. No, it was Gandhi, who had arrived after the risings had been stopped, with great danger in the case of Viramgam. So it was in this climate, that every claim invented prior to the Indemnity Debate would be supported and promulgated as if true. The crowd at the Jallianwalla Bagh was a spontaneous gathering, largely made up of the people from the Baisakhi Fair. To give it the ring of truth, he did allow that Lala Kan Haya Lal, "a very old and esteemed pleader of Amritsar" had been claimed to be the speaker, but said that Lala Kan Haya Lal told him personally that he never was approached and that he never gave his consent to preside, that this was falsely given out.

That rare admission, designed to demonstrate that nothing else claimed was false, was used to disprove the claim of rebellion and the need for Martial Law or the firing, which was on innocent and unarmed people from the Baisakhi Fair. There is no mention of the removal of Land Tax, of the poems to murder, or to the city-wide warning. This last was not heard because the Baisakhi Fair people knew nothing of what was going on, had seen nothing of the smoking buildings nor heard of the proclamations as the soldiers marched through the city of Amritsar on the day before.

In England, Montagu had stated on 18th April *"At Amritsar on 13th April, the mob defied the proclamation forbidding meetings. Firing ensued and 200 casualties occurred."* Malaviya was saying that there had been 500 deaths.

On the 22nd May, Montagu spoke of rebellion and revolution, but he was by then maintaining silence on the matter of the firing at Jallianwalla Bagh. *"Evidence accumulates every day that there is in India a body of men who are the enemies of the Government, men whom any Government, bureaucratic or democratic, alien or indigenous, if it was worth the name of Government, must deal with."* He mentioned the unprovoked attack by the Amir of Afghanistan, prompted by Bolshevik agents. *"Let us talk of an inquiry, when we put the fire out. The only message that we send from the House today to India is a message of confidence in and sympathy with those upon whom the great responsibility has fallen to restore the situation. Then will come the time to hold an inquiry, not only to help us to remove the causes, but in order to dispose, once and for all, of some of the libellous charges which have been made against British troops and those upon whom the unpleasant duties in connection with these riots have fallen."* He was still praising Gandhi as *"a man of the highest motives and the finest character, a man who his worse enemy, if he has any enemies, would agree is of the most disinterested ambitions that it is possible to conceive, a man who has deserved well of his country by the service he has rendered both in India and outside it, and yet a man who his friends – and I would count myself one of them – would wish he would exercise his powers with a greater sense of responsibility and would realise in time that there are forces beyond his control and outside his influence who use the opportunities offered by his name and reputation."*

Montagu, just like the people of Ahmedebad, Bombay and the Punjab, had seen the matter differently in April; by September, the climate of opinion had changed and was to be fixed in that change for all years to come, until Colvin and O'Dwyer published the facts.

On the 19th September, the Honourable Mr. J. P. Thompson stood up to speak. *"With your Excellency's permission I should like to make a few remarks on the amazing speech, to the last quarter of which we have been privileged to listen. I do not propose to touch on the legal question, or questions of constitutional law that have been raised by the Pandit. They will no doubt be dealt with by the Legal Member, if he thinks there is anything in them that merits a reply..."* He then took up some points from the speech given prior to the Pandit's by Mr. Chanda, that on the 11th April orders were issued by the Punjab Government prohibiting the publication of any accounts in the newspapers. He pointed out that the order that was passed applied to both Indian and English newspapers, requiring that all accounts should be submitted for pre-censorship prior to publication to make sure that they were accurate. The necessity of accuracy in a state of such unrest had already been indicated in the speech of the Pandit - not surprising, while extravagant rumours abounded causing further trouble. The next point with which Thompson disagreed was the claim that Sir Michael had made the order against Gandhi coming into the Punjab out of revenge for the fraternisation between Muslims and Hindus at the Ram Naumi festival. *"I have the greatest admiration for Sir Michael O'Dwyer, but I do not think that anyone here would claim for him that he was a prophet. The fraternisation at the Ram Naumi took place on the 9th of April; the order for the exclusion of Mr. Gandhi was passed, as far as I can remember, some 48 hours before fraternisation took place.*

*I think in all the cases with which I shall deal, I shall be able to show the Council that the story which has been given by the Pandit is a distortion or an exaggeration, or a misunderstanding of the facts. The first case he mentioned was that of the exclusion of a gentleman from the Punjab who was so well known that the Pandit could not even give his correct name; he called him Mr. Hume ... [Here the Pandit said C. Andrews]. His real name was C. F. Andrews. On the 5th of May, the Punjab Government received a telegram from the editor of the 'Independent' newspaper of Allahabad* [This newspaper was owned by Pandit Malaviya], *saying he, along with the editor of the 'Bengalee', 'New India', the 'Amritsar Bazaar Patrika', the 'Hindu' and the 'Leader' proposed to depute Mr. Andrews to the Punjab with a view to report to the Indian press on the condition of affairs in the Province with special reference to the administration of Martial Law. At the time when that request was made, two of the papers on whose behalf it was made had been excluded from the Province - one more of them has been excluded since - and almost all of them have distinguished themselves by the bitterness of their attacks on the Punjab Administration. Now, my Lord, I put it to the Council, if these papers wished to obtain the good office of the Punjab Government with the military authorities, in order to enable Mr. Andrews to enter the Martial Law area, was this quite the most tactful way of doing it? I do not think there is a single Member here My Lord who will answer that question in the affirmative."*

Then on the Jallianwalla Bagh: *"I do not wish to dwell on this extremely painful incident, but I merely wish to offer one or two remarks in regard to the number of casualties. The Honourable Member has hinted that more than a thousand people were killed there. He told us yesterday that 530 had been traced, but what the Punjab Government has done is this. We made a proclamation in Amritsar and in the surrounding villages inviting all persons who have any information in regard to the names of those who had met their deaths there, to come forward and give that information to Government. We knew that private organisations were at work collecting information on the same subject. I make no doubt, my Lord that that proclamation also came to the notice of the Pandit. Our enquiries show that the total was 291, and*

*I claim that any information, which asks us to accept figures beyond this, must be received with the gravest suspicion."*

The next speaker was General Sir Havelock Hudson, Adjutant General to the Army, the man in charge of army discipline. Extracts from his speech were quoted suitably in the Dyer report to the Army Council, and indeed most of his speech was suitable in the context in which he gave it. The difficulty in much of this book is to give an impression that will also extend the understanding of the reader so that something of the essence of India will stir his or her imagination. Henry Havelock Hudson had experienced much of what he spoke about. If he had not, his words and his sympathy, with the men who stood to be tossed aside at the whim of the conspirators in order to prove their case, would not sound so clearly even to-day. *"My Lord, my only reason for intervening in this debate is to clear up one or two remarks, which have been made by my Honourable friend the Pandit as regards the action of certain officers, and others connected with the suppression of rebellion in Amritsar. I do not think the Honourable Member has given these events in-their clear perspective. The first event to which I shall refer is the Jallianwalla Bagh, and in order to give the situation as it would appear to the Officer Commanding at Amritsar, I must ask your Lordship's permission briefly to state the situation at Amritsar on the 10th of April. We have the attempts of the crowd on the Civil Lines, the troops stoned and ordered after due warning to fire; the attack on the Telegraph Office; the Telegraph Master rescued by an Indian officer when in the hands of the mob; the murder of a European guard at the goods station; the murder of the Manager and Assistant Manager of the National bank; the. murder of the Manager of the Alliance Bank; the attack on the Chartered Bank; firing of the Town Hall and its sub-post office; looting of the other post offices; attack on the Zenana Hospital; and attack on Miss Sherwood; the burning of the Indian Christian Church, and attempt to fire the C. M. S. 'Girls' Formal School'; the murder of a sergeant of the Military Works Department; a second attempt of the mob to break into the Civil Lines; troops again stoned and ordered to fire, later on towards nightfall systematic destruction of all lines of communication; and finally, the destruction of two small railway stations and the looting of a goods train.*

*My Lord, does not this read rather like the preamble of the Indemnity Act on the Gordon riots of which the Honourable Pandit kindly made us a present? The above would be the situation as it would appear to an officer who found himself in such a position as confronted the General when he assumed command at Amritsar on 11th April last. It will be realised, I think that the situation was one of unexampled gravity. The Commissioner of the Division has definitely stated that the situation had passed out of his control, that he must rely on the military authorities to restore order by the exercise of military force.*

*The city was in the hands of an unruly mob; organised attacks had been made on Government property; Banks had been burned and looted; railway and telegraph communications had been interrupted; inflammatory posters inciting to 'die and kill' had previously been posted on the clock tower in the heart of the city, and the lives of Europeans had been taken in circumstances which I shall not describe in detail. It would be clear to the officer in command that the rebellion was not confined to Amritsar alone. He would be aware of the riots at Delhi and Lahore. And he would have had an opportunity of gauging the temper of the people by his personal observation. He would have been aware of the danger of the spread of the rebellion into the surrounding districts. As an officer in a highly responsible position, he would know that it was his duty to take all measures necessary to restore order and that his actions would be judged by the measure of his success in so doing. He would also know that he would be held personally responsible for any action of his which might be considered to be in excess of the reasonable requirements of the situation. You cannot conceive that any officer on whom such a responsibility had been thrown would enter on his task with any spirit of light-heartedness; nor would an officer of his seniority and experience (he had 34 years' service) set about his task with a disregard of the sanctity of human life or with a desire to exact reprisals for the acts of rebellion which had already been committed. His first act would be to dispose his troops with a view to the protection of life and property. His second would be to warn the populace as to the result, if it became necessary, to use military force in the suppression of further disorder. These are the steps, which were in fact taken by the officer in command at Amritsar.*

*On the 11th and 12th, he re-organised his troops and on the 12th, he marched a column round and through the city in order that a display of force might have its effect on the minds of the populace. We have it on record that the bearing of the inhabitants was insolent and that many spat on the ground as the troops passed. From the shouts of the mob it was clear that they were in an entirely unrepentant spirit. No military force was used on this occasion as the officer in command decided to issue proclamations as to his future intentions before employing such force. From a military point of view he would have been quite justified, I hold, in using force on that day, but the General Officer Commanding decided to pursue his policy of patience and conciliation. A proclamation was issued on the evening of the 12th and on the morning of the 13th April, the Officer Commanding marched with a body of troops through all the main streets of the city, and announced by beat of drum his intentions of using force should occasion arise. The people were permitted to collect in order to hear the proclamations.*

*The announcement that unlawful assemblies would be dispersed by fire was received with jeers and cries indicating that the mob had no belief in the sincerity of the warning given. While the troops were still in the city, information reached the Officer Commanding at about 12 o'clock that, in spite of his proclamation, a big meeting of rebels would be held at the Jallianwalla Bagh at 4.30 that afternoon. As this place had been used before for meetings and as large assemblies had been addressed by the heads of the agitation on the 29th and 30th March and the 2nd April, and as a dense mass meeting had assembled here on the 6th during the hartal and had listened to speeches intended to bring government into hatred and contempt, it would have been clear to the officer in command that he might expect deliberate defiance of his orders. Now, he was well aware of the events of the 10th of April when the murders of Europeans and the attacks on property had been made and when the firing, which had been employed to suppress these disorders, had been totally inadequate. The officer commanding at Amritsar had to decide at about midday on the 13th of April how he would act if the projected meeting took place in direct defiance of his authority. After making dispositions for the safety of his command, he found that he had but a small striking force at his disposal. I believe that the number was 25 men of one regiment and 25 men of two other regiments, belonging to the Indian Army and in addition, 40 Ghurkhas armed with Kukris only, and two armoured cars. Realising the gravity of the situation, the officer commanding did not send, as he might have, a subaltern in charge of this small force. He realised that it was an occasion on which he, and he alone, must exercise the full responsibility. He marched this force straight to the Jallianwalla Bagh, leaving the armoured cars, which he had also taken with him behind, because they could not get into the Bagh. On reaching the Bagh his force was confronted by a vast assembly, some thousands strong, who were being hartalled by a man standing on a raised platform. The Honourable Pandit would give us to believe that this was a fortuitous meeting of villagers and that they were listening to a lecture. That was not so in accordance with the facts as far as I have been able to gather. It was clearly the duty of the Officer in Command to disperse this unlawful assembly. Realising the danger to his small force, unless he took immediate action, and being well aware of the inadequacy of the measures taken to restore order on the 10th of April, he ordered fire to be opened. The crowd was dispersed and the force was withdrawn. I have given the Council this narrative to show how the situation would be viewed by the soldier and will content myself with saying that from the military point of view, the sequence of events justified the exercise of military force, and that the object of his exercise was fully attained. Also from a purely military point of view, the Officer in Command would have been gravely at fault had he permitted the elements of disorder to continue unchecked for one minute longer.*

*"The next point, which I wish to turn to, is another one to which reference has been made. It is the issue by the Officer in Command of Amritsar, of orders that any person who wished to pass the scene of the assault on Miss Sherwood should be made to crawl on their hands and knees. As this incident has been described at a meeting of the Bombay Provincial-Congress Committee and All-India Home Rule League as a 'paltry assault on a woman', I think it only right to remind this Council of what actually had occurred. In the first place, I would say that this is not merely an isolated instance to assault European ladies. We have it on record that on the 10th of April, the mob entered the Zenana Hospital in their endeavours to find the lady doctor in charge, who however escaped. After leaving the building the crowd again returned, on information given by a disloyal servant, to search for her again, breaking open the rooms and cupboards in their march which was fortunately fruitless. On the same day the mob attempted to set fire to the Church Missionary Society's Girls' Normal*

*School, in which were four lady missionaries who remained hidden. I am sorry to have to refer in some detail to the assault on Miss Sherwood, but it is necessary, because I wish this Council to view the situation as the Officer Commanding on the spot must have viewed it. This lady had for many years been working in the city, she was greatly respected and the assault on her was characterised by extreme brutality. The following abridged account is taken from the judgement of the Commission which tried her assailants.*

> *When she was bicycling from one of her schools to another, she encountered a mob which raised cries of 'kill her she is English'. She wheeled round and tried to escape but took a wrong turning and had-to retrace her steps. She reached a lane where she was well known and thought she would be safe, but the mob overtook her and she was also attacked from the front, being hit on the head with sticks. She fell down but got up and ran a little way where she was again felled, being hit and struck with sticks even when she was on the ground. Again she got up and tried to enter a house but the door was slammed in her face. Falling from exhaustion she again struggled to get up, but everything seemed to get dark and she thought she had become blind.*
>
> *Her dress was seized, her hat was pulled off, she was struck with fists, she was caught by the hair and beaten on the head with shoes and was finally knocked down and struck on the head by a lathi. She suffered grave injuries to the scalp and was in a critical condition when she left for England.*

*I feel sure that the Council will agree that it is not surprising that the Officer in Command took the view that some unusual measures were needed to bring home to the mob that such acts of violence directed against defenceless women could not be tolerated. Something was required to strike the imagination and impress on all the determination of the military authorities to protect European women. This Council can easily understand how easily the feelings of soldiers would be outraged by acts of this nature and that they might be led to uncontrolled reprisals. Incidentally it is worthy of note in this connection that we have no charge against any of our soldiers during this rebellion. It is easy, My Lord, to criticise the orders issued by the Officer in Command at Amritsar, but the circumstances were altogether exceptional and the punishment, though humiliating, was not such as to cause danger to life or physical hurt.*[46] *Except on one occasion, when a body of prisoners were brought down the street in which Miss Sherwood had been assaulted, no compulsion was brought to bear on any individual to submit to the order. The order remained in force for a*

---

46   The clear inference from Hudson's words is that he did not understand the significance of the crawling order. Only a man who knew India as well as did Dyer knew that the 'crawling order' was not a matter of crawling as of genuflection, something that an Indian such as Malaviya would have known. My mother typed the 'crawling order' and knew what a degree of thought Dyer had used in order to stop further harm to white women or any violent expression of anger from the British troops.

*period of five days and there is good reason for the belief that, except for the party of prisoners already mentioned, those who were subjected to the order came voluntarily to submit to it for the sake of notoriety of martyrdom. One man after going down the street on his hands and knees three times had to be stopped from giving further exhibitions.*

*My Lord, the order was of course an unusual one and not one which might have been considered necessary by other officers in like circumstances. The Officer in Command at Amritsar will doubtless be prepared to justify his action should he be called upon to do so.*

*My Lord, my object in recounting to this Council in some detail the measures taken by the military authorities to reconstitute civil order out of the chaos produced by the state of rebellion, is to show that there is another side of the picture which is perhaps more apparent to the soldier than to the civilian critic. No more distasteful or responsible duty falls to the lot of the soldier than that which he is sometimes required to discharge in aid of the civil power. If his measures are too mild he fails in his duty. If they are deemed to be excessive he is liable to be attacked as a cold-blooded murderer. His position is one demanding the highest degree of sympathy from all reasonable and right-minded citizens. He is frequently called upon to act on the spur of the moment in grave situations in which he intervenes, because all the other resources of civilisation have failed. His actions are liable to be judged by <u>ex post facto</u> standards and by people who are in complete ignorance of the realities that he had to face. His good faith is liable to be impugned by the very persons connected with the organisation of the disorders, which his action has foiled. There are those who will admit that a measure of force may have been necessary, but who cannot agree with the extent of the force employed. How can they be in a better position to judge of that than the officer on the spot? It must be remembered that when a rebellion has been started against the Government, it is tantamount to a declaration of war. War cannot be conducted in accordance with standards of humanity to which we are accustomed in peace. Should not officers and men who, through no choice of their own, are called upon to discharge these distasteful duties, be in all fairness accorded that support which has been promised to them? My Lord, I feel before I conclude, that I must make a reference to the amendment which the Honourable Mr. Chanda has proposed. I must confess that I heard this with some amazement. I suppose that there is no class that really suffered more by the disturbances in the Punjab than the forces of the Crown. Here they were at the close of four years of war; most of them were looking forward to demobilisation and their hard-earned leave and many of them to a return home. They were suddenly called on to perform what is the most distasteful duty as I have said before, which soldiers are ever required to carry out. They had nothing to do with the outbreak of the disturbances or with the imposition of Martial Law. They only did their duty and as recognition, the Honourable Member suggests that Government should defer till some indefinite date, the fulfilment of their promises of support. My Lord, it may be within the recollection of Members of* *this Council that Honourable Members both inside and outside this Chamber have repeatedly referred, and that with legitimate pride, to the services rendered by India and more especially the Indian Army. It was only last week that this Council listened to the Honourable Mr. Sarma's eloquent tribute to the services of that Army and yet it is that very Army that the Honourable Mr. Chanda, by his callous amendment to this Bill, would leave in the lurch. For what effect would the amendment have if accepted? Officers and men would be liable to prosecution for any illegal act committed under Martial Law, and as Martial Law is in itself no law, all their acts under that law would be illegal. Actions for damages, for illegal arrest and a host of other charges could be preferred against them and the question whether they acted in good faith would have no force with the courts which try their cases. My Lord, I think all soldiers would view with suspicion, if not horror, the airy suggestion that Mr. Chanda made that the actions would not come up at once, that they would be postponed for a month, then perhaps for two, and then again for three months and so on indefinitely. The Manual of Military Law which is the soldier's only guide, is silent as regards Martial Law; there is only one chapter in the whole of that book relating to Martial Law, but that chapter is written by Lord Thring, and there is one sentence in it, which is the soldier's sole guarantee, which I quote below: it runs as follows:-*

*'It is only necessary to add that, when a proclamation of Martial Law has been issued, any soldier who takes, in accordance with the official instructions laid down for guidance of those administering Martial Law, such measures as he honestly thinks to be necessary for carrying to a successful issue the operation of restoring peace and preserving authority, may rely on any question as to the legality of his conduct being subsequently met by an Act of Indemnity.'*

*The Government, My Lord, has taken the only honourable course and that is to introduce an Indemnity Bill at the earliest possible occasion. To have done otherwise would have been the negation of Government and repudiation of its obligations."*

Sir George Lowndes, Law Member, spoke as follows:

"Whatever we may like to call it, a rebellion or an insurrection, whatever politicians in this country may like to call it, we have to deal with the facts, not with the words we use to describe them. The question we have to consider here is, whether at the time when Martial Law was put in force in India, the situation was such that the civil authorities were unable to cope with it. Therefore, let us not quarrel over words or discuss the difference between rebellion, insurrection and revolution. The practical question before the Council is whether there had arisen in the Punjab at this time a state of things with which the civil authorities were unable to deal. We have been told in this Council that no such state of things existed. I would much rather have left the question where my Honourable friend, Sir William Vincent left it in his opening speech, not discussing whether it was necessary to proclaim Martial Law, but leaving that to be discussed by the Commission. I would rather merely assume that Martial Law was *declared, for as my Honourable Colleague put it, it follows essentially from that, that there must be an act of indemnification and validation. Some Honourable Members, led by that redoubtable champion of the liberties of the people, who is still sitting here after his temporary disappearance, thought fit to go into all the happening for what purpose, I frankly cannot say, I cannot conceive. What this Bill proposes is that only acts which were done <u>bona fide</u> and which were believed to be reasonably necessary for the restoration of maintenance of order are to be the subject of indemnification, or validated in part, nothing else. The Honourable Pandit spent some hours telling us of a number of acts that would not be covered by the Act. He went through the whole history of what has happened in his own <u>bona fide</u>, which could not have been necessary, and which therefore, if I may say so, would not have been touched by this Act.*

*The only argument I have heard against it is that of the Honourable Members who said there were no serious disturbances in the Punjab, and of those who said, 'by all means let us have an Indemnity Bill, but not today.' Well, that it is necessary to have some Indemnity Act is beyond question. I will tell the Council in a moment what a length of precedent there is for it. But apart from its being strictly constitutional, I should like to put the question very plainly indeed to some of my Honourable friends in this Council, and I would appeal especially to my Honourable friend, the Maharajah of Kazimbazar, whose speech indicated a somewhat hesitating acceptance of the proposals before this Council. Do you or do you not want to be protected in your lives and property, whatever may happen in India? Do you wish the Government to do what I have spoken of as the first duty of Government, namely to protect your life and property? And that if they cannot do it through the police, do you wish them to do it by the use of the Military? Let us have a plain answer to that question from anyone who is not prepared to agree to a Validating Bill. If you do not want it, tell the Government you do not want it and the Government will not do it. Let me tell you this, that if this Council will not indemnify the solders who have had to enforce Martial Law in order to preserve the public peace, they will not willingly do it again. You cannot place these unpleasant duties on your officers and at the same time leave them, as Mr. Chanda suggests, at the mercy of the Courts. That is not the way to treat officers whom you have asked to protect your lives and property. You have got to indemnify them at the earliest opportunity, and unless, I say, you do that; they cannot be asked to take any risks in protecting you. Why should they? Why should a man, in order to protect your life and property or to protect my life and property or anyone else's, do that which he knows may subject him to the direct penalties of the law? Remember when we talk of indemnifying officers, it is not the high officers of Government that you are asked to indemnify.*

*The second aspect of the question was whether the Act would in any way affect the position. I have not the least hesitation in answering that question. The only thing that we by the Bill seek to validate are acts done <u>bona fide</u> for the maintenance of law and order, and the Council may take it from me that this Bill will not in any way prejudice the Commission of Inquiry."*

Sir William Vincent's speech in reply (19th September):

"*My Lord, when I closed my opening speech on this Bill, I said that I had avoided, as far as possible, prejudicing any question that would come before the Committee or saying anything that might provoke racial feelings. I believe it has generally been accepted by this Council that that was my attitude. But I was a little surprised by the honourable Mr. Malaviya of all people in this Council, suggesting that I was attempting to prejudice the work of the Committee and that, because I had ventured to put it to the Council - and I think Sir George Lowndes also said the same thing - that if the Committee of Inquiry appointed to inquire into this matter found that a man had acted reasonable and <u>bona fide</u>, I was quite sure they would not hold him in any way to blame. Well, after I spoke, the Council heard the various statements made by the Honourable Member himself, attempts to create prejudice, to minimise various facts and to place before Council <u>ex parte</u> statements as to particular incidents on which it was suggested that this Council should condemn particular officers of particular actions.*

*My Lord, the Honourable Member has received such severe castigation from the Honourable Law Member that it really would be an act of cruelty to say anything more of his speech. I can only say, even if I had in any way been guilty of attempting to prejudice the decision on any point by the Committee or of creating an atmosphere of bias in respect of any matter, it would have been a case of Satan reproving the sin, for no man has been more guilty in that respect than the Honourable Member himself. But I leave it to Council to judge if I said anything which would prejudice the inquiry. My Lord, I regret very much, however, that an attempt has been made by the Honourable Member and by others, to place particular incidents before the Council to make <u>ex parte</u> statements as to what happened on particular occasions, because I think that statements on the one side necessarily evoke from others contradiction, and that this Council was therefore placed in a very unfortunate position in regard to such incidents – incidents of which, as the Honourable Mr. Sinha said, the Council do not know much, of which they now have had stories from one side and stories from the other, and I feel that it would have been much better if both sides had left all these incidents alone. Such a course would not have affected this Bill and Council would have left the whole of the facts to the Committee of Inquiry to decide.*

*I must, however, disclaim any intention to justify any particular action. It was for instance suggested that I was attempting to indemnify officers who were concerned in the Jallianwalla Bagh incident. My Lord, I had no such intention, nor can any such intention be deduced from the Bill. The question whether these officers will be indemnified or not will depend on the findings of the Courts as to whether their actions were <u>bona fide</u> and reasonable or not. I do not seek in any way to prejudge the point.*

*In the course of the debate the Honourable Sir Dinshaw Wacha inquired whether the passing of this Bill would in any way affect the Committee of Inquiry. The answer has been given. The Committee of Inquiry is an administrative Committee. Its report will have no legal effect. The result will be, when it reports, that the opinions and* *recommendations will have to be decided by the authorities in order to see whether any person is to be punished or censured or commended administratively, but that has nothing to do with the Courts. That report will not be evidence in the Court. The legal liability of those concerned is a separate matter and can only be settled by either the common law or a Bill of this character. As to pending suits, is it fair that we should leave officers who, <u>ex hypothesis</u>, as I said before, have done their duty, with a possibility of being sued – or that we should say to them "Well, you may be indemnified for doing what was right, or you may not, we will tell you that six months later, when the Committee of Inquiry, which has nothing really whatever to do with your legal liabilities, has decided some other point. I submit that is not a right position for Government to take."*

Sir William Vincent's 2nd Speech on the motion 'that the Bill as amended be passed' – 25th September

*"Turning to other speakers, My Lord, may I say that in my opinion the whole debate on this motion to pass the Bill has resolved itself into an occasion for a discussion of totally irrelevant matters? All kinds of details have been brought up which really are not before the Council at this stage at all. Many members have indeed taken the opportunity of the motion to answer criticisms that are made of their speeches on previous occasions, and a part of the day at least was spent on recriminations. Statements of fact made on one side were almost inevitably answered by others, and the result has been, however, that the Council has been invited indirectly by some Members, like the Honourable Mr. Malaviya, and almost directly by others, such as the Honourable Mr. Thompson, to come to definite conclusions on inadequate information and <u>ex parte</u> statements, as to particular incidents during these risings. You have one Member saying one thing, another saying something quite different; on many occasions neither of them speaking from first hand knowledge; and on their statements this Council is asked to condemn or justify the conduct of individual officers. I used the word 'condemn' deliberately – I took down one statement used by the Honourable Mr. Madan Mohan Malaviya when he said that a particular officer was guilty of criminal dereliction of duty – I put it fairly to the Council that such a statement is neither fair nor reasonable. These are matters for the Committee. I will take one incident, which has been repeatedly referred to, this unfortunate Jallianwalla Bagh affair. My Lord, no one deplores the loss of life on that day more than the Government. It has been, and must be to all of us, a source of great distress, and it does not really make so much difference from this point of view whether the number killed was 300 or 500. In either case the loss of life is serious enough in all conscience and greatly to be regretted. But we have no right in this Council either to justify or condemn that action. It is not part of our duty; it does not come within the scope of the Bill. General Hudson has, it is true, put before the Council certain considerations relating to this occurrence, but as I understood him – he was merely attempting to put the matter as it might have appeared to a military officer at the time and was not in any way putting his personal views before the Council. That is*

*the way I understood his remarks. I mention this because his statements have been made the ground for attacks on him; and it was suggested he sought to justify what was done. I do not think that the Council, when they have considered the position, will for one moment accept that as a fair presentment of his intention. What I ask the Council to do now is, not to prejudice this matter in any way, neither to condemn nor to justify any action, neither to say a man is innocent not to say he is guilty until the proper time for such a decision shall arrive. Does this question come within the scope of this debate? Is there anything in the Bill that justifies a man or condemns a man? I maintain there is nothing. All that the bill enunciates is a principle. It does not say that a man is justified or blameworthy for his conduct on any particular occasion. It leaves that to the Court to decide from a legal point of view. In so far as administrative action is concerned, that is also a question outside the Bill altogether, which can be decided as I have repeatedly explained to this Council, only after the Report of the Committee is received. What could be fairer? The question whether an officer acted bona fide or not is left to be decided from the legal point of view by the Courts save for this provision, that there is a presumption that he has acted bona fide and reasonably. Let me take the case again of Jallianwalla Bagh. What is the position? If the action of any particular officer is found to be unjustifiable, if all the allegations made today are true, what will be the result? It will be a matter for the Court. Either the Court will find it justifiable and reasonable or unjustifiable and unreasonable, in which latter case the normal legal results will follow. Similarly, so far as administrative action is concerned, if the action was unjustifiable, then undoubtedly the Committee will condemn it. But is it fair to any officer to condemn him behind his back, unheard and without his having an opportunity of making a statement and offering his explanation? Is it fair to him to come here and make statements, which affect his character, his honour, his sense of justice, and his sense of humanity? But, My Lord, we are not now deciding whether Martial Law was necessary or not, but whether in any case to protect our officers when they have acted bona fide? It was for this reason that I deprecated the discussion of the necessity for Martial Law in this Council altogether. I asked the Council then to forbear from discussing that question, because it necessarily must come before this Committee of Inquiry. The position I have always taken up is, that we believed that Martial Law was necessary, but whether it was necessary or not, we must protect our officers who have acted bona fide and I have never yet heard any argument which has satisfied me that I was wrong on that point. We do not seek to indemnify our officers for specific acts; we are not doing so either administratively or in respect of legal liability; we are only laying down principles on which indemnity should be granted I am told, however, that officers need no such protection, and that they must depend on their protection under the common law. This point has also been dealt with by the Honourable the Law Member, and I will only say to Council that these references to legal dogmas leave me cold. The real question is a simple one on which any man of sense can judge for himself. Each Member of this Council must judge whether a* *soldier or any officer of Government who carried out the orders of his superior or did his duty in suppressing these disorders <u>bona fide</u> and honestly is or is not entitled to be indemnified against legal liability for his action. There is no good citing legal dogmas and constitutional theories in such circumstances. The question is, are you going to afford the men reasonable protection or not?"*

By the time that the Indemnity Debate took place, the hysterical mood throughout India had been aroused by the Congress 'information'. The mass of comment and justification for acts of astounding brutality had been spread by the Press, just as had the propaganda about the Rowlatt legislation, together with the word-of-mouth claims. In the Rowlatt debate, in the Legislative Council, Pandit Malaviya had given what Nirad Chaudhuri describes as 'a measured speech'. One British newspaper, 'The Statesman of Calcutta', had written that he talked the hind leg off a donkey. By doing so, the British attitude, in Indian terms, had been fixed as unsympathetic and in keeping with what followed, but whereas in the Rowlatt speech, Malaviya had used all the polemics of an Indian lawyer in claiming the injustice of the Act and its deprivation of personal respect and liberty, neither strictly true, but polemically capable of exaggeration (untruth by inference, incitement and misinterpretation). By the time of the Indemnity Debate, the Pandit's speech was not merely a fine example of casuistry, but jam-packed full of any information that could stir the mind of a nation, already touchy following the reporting of events in Congress, including those by the leaders of the rebellion.

Havelock Hudson's speech, or the pleas of the official members, would not have reached the populace to the same extent, as Malaviya would have known well. The Debate could quite easily be presented to the public as the Indian speakers claimed. The British viewpoint would not have been considered to minds already stirred up by the well publicised claims of pity and "injustice" of Martial Law for which the cases going before the Privy Council were gathering money for appeals.

Throughout his speech, Malaviya produced the examples that would later be forced on the ears of the Hunter Commission before the packed halls of the hearing, to the excitement of the auditors, to the inevitable subversion of any possibility of justice or truth. Inquiries are presumed to be dispassionate, calm and intellectually honest. This one was the antithesis and ended up as a propaganda rostrum against the British despite the endeavours of the Chairman to keep the hearings calm.

Picking an example of the Malaviya rhetoric from the Indemnity Debate speech out of the pages at random, I give an example of the difference between what he said and what happened to the man whose experience he gave as an example of the peacefulness of the crowd streaming through Amritsar to the Hall Gate to loot the Civil Lines. The point that Malaviya was making, was that this man was perfectly safe walking along in the middle of the crowd.

I quote Lala Jiwan Lal, Inspector, Criminal Investigation Department on the 'peaceful crowd'. *"On the 10th April, while I was at Amritsar, at about 11.30 a.m., the news of Kitchlew and Satyapal's deportation were received in the city and spread like wildfire. All the shops were closed in no time. I was in the Hall Bazaar at about 12 noon, where a large mob collected and moved towards the civil station. The mob went over the footbridge and the road bridge to cross the railway line. The appearance of the crowd was extremely hostile ... The crowd was threatening to tear the Deputy Commissioner to pieces. People were openly abusing the Government and the Europeans. Municipal pipes, telephone wires, electric wires were also smashed ... A Sikh and a Mohammedan openly preached murder of Europeans and told the people that British Raj had almost ended ..."* [one wonders why Kitchlew and Satyapal were 'deported', while Gandhi, under slightly similar action was 'arrested'?]

Ashraf Khan, Inspector of Police, Amritsar, said in his evidence to the inquiry, 'the first thing done was to murder the Europeans at the National Bank.

- Q. Why did they (the Police) threaten to fire on the crowd?
- A. Mr. Jarman, the Municipal Engineer was there; with some men we wanted to bring him and so we did.
- Q. Why did you threaten to fire upon the crowd at that time?

Ashraf Khan: Only to save Mr. Jarman, and we did bring him into the Kotwali.'

The position was that Mr. Jarman was crying out and the police rescued him, although the evidence claims the crowd of 60 or 70 people were not at that moment doing anything. At that time, the Town Hall was already on fire, and in the Kotwali, Jarman remained until General Dyer went into the City and brought him out wearing Indian costume, so as not to draw attention to himself.

The description of the mobs is not irrelevant, they were the people later collected in the Jallianwalla Bagh.

As in this snippet of evidence, where there was a doubt that might affect the Congress story, the evidence is not altogether clear. The stenographers, it should be remembered got into such a muddle that the papers had to be collected and correlated by the 'Pioneer'. It is probable that this was, at least in part, contrived.

Malaviya's story was simply that Jarman walked along with a perfectly orderly crowd.

The points that the Congress leaders had bent their evidence to prove, were:

1. That there would have been no rioting if the British officials had not provoked it.
2. That consequently there was no rebellion.
3. The people who were arrested were consequently inspired by British actions not rebelling.
4. To support these claims, the crowd going over the Hall Bridge had to be fired on before they did anything, and then it was natural, if misplaced anger, that led them to murder and mayhem.

5. The City, as in other areas, was quiet when Dyer came to Amritsar on the 11$^{th}$. The crowd, being people in for the Baisakhi Fair, did not know about the warning. Consequently, with no sign of rebellion, Dyer fired on innocent people.

At that time there were few films and no facility by which people can be filmed and then put onto a computer-generated background (or even the people themselves manipulated by computer) - but that is how the Congress Committee Report and story were made. The incidents are cut outs, with people behaving differently according to the intention of the image-makers in circumstances and backgrounds which do not fit in the real sequential events of those terrible times.

Having invented the story, it was not actually put on film until Mrs. Indira Gandhi, the daughter of Pandit Nehru, one of the image makers, paid Richard Attenborough out of Indian Government funds to do the technical work in 1983. It was then cast in concrete. To see the same (invented) incidents appearing as though they were historically accurate, time after time, in books, in extracts on film, in newspapers, on the radio, is to see and hear one of the most complete examples of propaganda invention and falsification that has ever been made. In most examples of propaganda, one finds little difference according to the exponent of the time, but in this one, the one expounded by Pandit Malaviya at the Indemnity Debate in 1919, the story, even the phrases, are always the same. When the people who were involved say something different, as in the Hunter Evidence, we find them hectored and bullied into saying something from which the false story can be extracted in the same image as had earlier been invented.

My father, Miles Irving, Connor, Massey, and others knew that the firing that had taken place on the Hall Bridge did not occur until some while after the crowd had been stoning the military for some time. Connor gave the order to fire because he and his small detachment were in danger, but this can never be allowed, since it does not fit in with the claim that my father fired (with a non-existent weapon), on a peaceful (not a murderous) crowd. Lala Jiwan Lal, the C.I.D. man is always dismissed, for one reason or another. Percy Marsden - and any one else - is always out to humiliate Indians, however simple the action, however commonsensical and relevant to the issues of the time, and this pretty picture of British brutality is now on film, the subject of history lessons in India and throughout the world.

Unfortunately, neither the conspirator's involvement in the Afghan War, nor the treatment of Indian women and children by the mobs and their leaders, nor Havelock Hudson's speech, nor the plight of the women and children in the Fort, are allowed to disturb a completely false but very carefully worked out image for all time.

The point that comes out of this debate is that the Indians, led by the conspirators and the earlier pressure to stop the Rowlatt legislation, were no longer capable of recognising or agreeing the necessity of supporting the systems of law and order.

Interestingly, through the 1984 firing on the Sikhs at Amritsar, through Ayodhya and other upsets in India since we left, there has not, so far, been any such Indemnity Debate or any claim that under exceptional circumstances, Martial Law should be declared as a visible expression of Government admission that civil authority was no longer able to administer law and order. Incidents have been permitted without public discussion and actions covered, far beyond those alleged in the 1919 rebellion.

For the discerning observer, intentions, actions, claims and propaganda, as demonstrated by the principals involved in the government of the Indian sub-continent since 1919, have provided prime examples of how truth can be distorted or hidden, to further a political agenda. Let us not suspend our sense of impartiality and accuracy in that same way, as we observe contemporary events.

## Chapter VII
## THE INDIA ACT

At the Congress Conference immediately after Montagu's visit in 1917, Tilak and two others walked out, on the grounds that they were not able to put forward their political views at the behest of the Viceroy, since the Conference was about how India could help the war, which at that time, just prior to the Americans coming in, was causing grievous concern. Tilak had not been included in the invitation to the Viceroy's Conference, and he thought that he should have been. Congress sent Gandhi and another, Gandhi having written to the Viceroy saying he was prepared to go to prison for the release of the Ali brothers.

Montagu wrote: *"With regard to Tilak, if I were the Viceroy, I would have him at Delhi at all costs. He is, at the moment, probably the most powerful man in India and he has it in his power, if he chooses, to help materially in War effort. If, on the other hand, he attached conditions of a political nature, as indeed he would at such a conference, things would be said to him which would forever destroy his influence in India, at least so I think. If he is not there, it will also be said that we refused to select the most powerful people. To think in terms of personal power was to play into the negative ball game. When people act under the rule of law it is not. Tilak is already saying that in his speeches and it would have completely taken the wind out of his sails if he had been invited as one of the leaders of Indian opinion. Of course, one can always say 'No help from such a source', but still there it is. I read a speech of Tilak's on board ship and it is quite obvious that he will not accept our report proposals. This seems to me all to the good, he is the leader of the opposition."*

After four months in India, talking to all the groups who chose to send delegations to see him, admittedly nearly all of them putting forward the Congress proposals, he had grasped nothing of the seriousness of a situation in which, because of the exercise of threat and terror, there was no one capable of opposing nationalist views except the

British and the Indians in the Indian Civil Service and they were constrained by the need of impartiality in the executive.

Montagu had in no way grasped what a cousin of B. G. Tilak, N. Tilak, wrote in 'The Times of India': *"It is indeed, an extremely difficult hour for those high-souled Brahmins, who, abhorring the course proposed by the Extremists in politics, are genuinely loyal to their country and their King. As for the non Brahmins, they have only one idea, one goal, and that is the safety, permanence and continuity of British rule in India."*

With this concern for the people of India in mind, the government needed legislation to carry on peacefully during the gradual transfer of power. The hysterical attitudes of the nationalist politicians and their incitements may have looked to the outside world as if this were legitimate politicking, but their activities ignored the way in which the British were moving towards something on the lines of self-government in a federation which could have protected the Princely provinces as well as those of British India. Corelli Barnet, in his delineation of the break up of British power, shows clearly the forces involved. Without lifting a finger themselves, the leaders of a tiny and polarised minority attempted to take over power by violence and mayhem.

The Report arising out of Montagu's visit was published in July 1918, containing the Government proposals for altering the existing method of governing India. The words of the Reforms Report ran thus:

*"Our rule gave them security from the violence of robbers and the exaction of landlords, regulated the amount of revenue or rent they had to pay, and assured to both proprietor and cultivator – in the latter case, by the device of occupancy right – a safe title in their lands ... Hitherto they have regarded the official as their representative in the councils of government; and now we have to tear up that faith by the roots, to teach them that in future they must bring their troubles to the notice of an elected representative – further that they must compel his attention."*

And then later: *"We are not setting out to stir 95% of the people out of their peaceful conservatism and setting their feet upon a new and difficult path merely at the bidding of the other 5% ...our reason is the faith that is in us, but as things have developed, that representation is, in the main, Brahmin."*

This halcyon image was supported by the descriptions of the Indian people in the pages of the Report on the proposed reforms, which reforms were brought in while Hunter was still sitting. The group of men with Edwin Montagu who wrote the Report had travelled all over India and even into the Districts. Edwin Montagu himself refused, despite pressure, to go into the Districts and see how the vast landmass of India was governed in the areas where the bulk of the population lived. Himself a townsman, he stayed in the towns with Governors or Maharajahs, tiger shooting, but into the hub of British rule, the Districts and their Headquarters themselves, he did not stray. His friends were the urban nationalists. As Under Secretary of State in 1910, he had supported them and denigrated the District Officers. He was, as so many, delighted and charmed by those educated politicians who knew so little of the countryside themselves and had less interest, working, propagandising, agitating only for their own power.

In April the Seditions Committee [Rowlatt] had submitted to the Government of India their joint unanimous report.

As had been expected, the Seditions Report was met with a shower of abuse by the extremists; the Moderates made little comment (the Moderates being Montagu's expected supporters of his scheme). Bearing in mind that India was, at that time, 95% agricultural, the country as a whole just got on with its work, concerned by the fact that the monsoon was delayed. The District Officers were occupied with heavy routine duties and extra war work and for each one of the people who might have understood the Reforms proposals, there were thousands concerned with how to buy food if the rains failed, depending on the Government for help. Montagu's plan had overlooked the fact that in India, politics were largely unknown.

Since the bulk of the Moderate movements were lawyers, one wonders whether any of them asked himself how he would have formulated a Bill to stop the deep-seated, cruel and widespread sedition, linked with giving help to a nation's enemies, other than the Rowlatt legislation.

Thus the lawyers' attitude to the Rowlatt Acts – merely to be used to excite and make hysterical a nation of people who, whether labourers or urban politically incited youth, had neither the framework nor the experience necessary to say, as did Tek Chand Jaini, *"The babu-log have seized their opportunity ... in their lust for power."* At the moment that Montagu left India, the road that lay ahead was unavoidable, for he was still unaware of the true nature of the situation to which he was about to apply legislative change. He was imbued with a fundamentally flawed concept that democracy was a shared goal - as today, in this country, so many accept the concepts that they are given and go, like sheep to the slaughter, not knowing how to resist.

The point of comparison is that the take-over of a nation was being attempted by a tiny number of politicians, who were in place to usurp the power of the existing Government. The comparison with the Bilderberger today is that again, a tiny number of people are trying to take over the power of the nations, regardless of the wishes of the people. In India, the Moderates were vocal, (although in relation to the Rowlatt Report, they reserved comment) but they differed from the Extremists in that they trusted the British, whereas the Extremists claimed they did not. The British, with better manners, did not say publicly that they did not trust the Indians.

What happened in 1919 was simply an example of a Secretary of State who did not dare stand against Congress opinion. In his treatment of Dyer, despite a good knowledge by that time of the seditious conspiracy that included the Congress leaders, he did not want to flout what he was accepting as Indian, rather than Congress Opinion.

For India, the era of control by ruthless and uncaring men went on to the end of our tenure. One man saw to it that at least some of the Muslims would be saved in Pakistan, for Jinnah was to become one of those who dared to stand and be counted.

The idea of people like Bepin Chandar Pal and Gandhi was to reduce India to the chaos that she was in when the British arrived. That blood would be spilt was irrelevant – more, it would be the effective purification from the foreigners. So great had the hatred become, so indivisible from the superiority of the Hindus over the British, since the stirring of religious fervour had put blood into the froth of the incendiary articles in the Press, that Montagu's ideas of 'trust' would no longer seem relevant. How can 'trust' order the thoughts of men who believed they were above moral sanction?

The pity was that Montagu, like Attenborough, believed that Gandhi's sainthood was something akin to Christian sainthood. It was not, nor were the demands for independent rule the same as the democratic concepts of Montagu. They wanted Hindu Rule, the restoration of the dignity of Hinduism in the face of the control, justice and protection of the British. Hinduism, with its emphasis on destructive as well as constructive Gods, was not something Montagu had understood, nor had he understood the traditional hatred by the Mahrattas of the Muslims, ignited with the worship of Shivaji by Tilak.

Least of all did those Europeans building up industry and prosperity escape the pantheon of hate. Thus, the Council of the European Association on the Reforms – *"The Council had been struck in perusing the report, by the failure of Mr. Montagu and Lord Chelmsford to realise the importance of the European non-official community in India ... and when the report does expressly refer to the European non-official community ... it is mainly to offer some respectable platitudes. The hostility of the report towards communal representation for Indians, other than Mohammedans and in the Punjab, Sikhs, is without justification. Nationhood can never be achieved by placing minorities or a backward majority under the heel of a clique, excessively intolerant in social relation and avid of political power."*

After those months of planning, the Rebellion began. It spread, until it was put down by probably one of the most courageous acts of our era. The reports in Britain gave little idea of what had happened. The India Office issued a statement on 18th April 1919, mentioning the events and 'at Amritsar on 13th April, the mob defied the proclamation forbidding public meetings. Firing ensued, and two hundred casualties occurred.' Questioned on the subject in the House of Commons on 16th April, Montagu mentioned the riots in Bombay, but said nothing about the Punjab. In his speech to the Committee on 22nd May, Montagu spoke of the events as *"rebellion and revolution."* He added, *"The danger is not past; it exists. It is not something that is finished; it threatens."* A week later, all reports on the 'the disturbance' were stopped – as also reports of the Afghan war.

He deplored the fact that Englishmen *"in no way connected with the Government and in no way responsible for the deeds – misdeeds or good deeds, of the Government – had lost their lives and had been foully murdered"*. He regretted that *"official Indians and non-official Indians had been done to death ... even many of the rioters deserve our sympathy, for when these things occur, the man who loses his life as a result of a soldier's bullet is as much the victim of those who prompted the riots as those who were killed by the rioters themselves".* Questioned about Gandhi, he described him as *"a man of the highest motives and the finest character, a man whom his worst enemy, if he has any enemies, would agree is of the most disinterested ambitions that it is possible to conceive, a man who has deserved well of his country by the services rendered both in India and outside it, and yet a man, who his friends – and I would count myself as one of them – would wish would exercise his powers with a greater sense of responsibility, and would realise in time that there are forces beyond his control and outside his influence who use the opportunities offered by his name and reputation."*

Montagu must have known that the Satyagraha vow, which Gandhi made his followers sign, was an oath of 'civil disobedience' to such laws as he and his Committee might veto and was an effective part of the illegal conspiracy that had fomented the rebellion. Those hartals that preceded that rebellion itself were held to bring Government into contempt and make Government impossible – as was the incitement to his followers to achieve imprisonment. He had, by the time that Montagu spoke, been shut out of Delhi and the Punjab as 'dangerous to the peace of India.' As he was later to trumpet in 'Young India', *"The National Congress began to tamper with the loyalty of the Indian Army in September last year (1920), the Central Khilafat Committee began earlier, and I began it earlier still. Every non-co-operator is pledged to create disaffection towards the Government."* It is probable that the tampering with the army was going on while he was claiming as his wish to Montagu that *"he wants the millions of India to leap to the assistance of the British throne."*

A year later, in his analysis of the Congress Committee Report for Montagu, just prior to his speech in Parliament, Sir John Hose of the India Office wrote 13 points that encapsulated the position.

His most emphatic point was: *"The second point upon which I lay as much stress as I can is this. The report published by the Congress Committee is based on untested evidence: It does not confine itself even to that evidence but relates gossip, contains manufactured illustrations and misrepresents facts. I will give a few instances of its nature so that there may he no doubt of the value to be attached to it."* Writing nearly 80 years later, it is clear that the Congress Report has been relied on in all the books written against General Dyer, to a far greater extent than the Hunter Evidence, (which, despite its omissions and its prejudiced cross examination and summary by the Minority Committee, is of far greater standing. Even so, the Secret Evidence has barely been used in subsequent reviews of the events.) The claims even by Hunter are questioned, where they make allegations which the Government of India was in a position to deny, such as the treatment of prisoners, which was put forward as a criticism of the Committee.

Montagu went on to give his view that there was a conspiracy behind the rebellion: *"Evidence accumulates every day that there is in India a small body of men who are the enemies of the Government, men whom any Government, bureaucratic or democratic, alien or indigenous, if it is worth the name of Government, must deal with."* He went on to speak of the unprovoked attack on India by the Amir of Afghanistan, prompted, he said, by Bolshevik agents, and promised to exact stern and just punishment for the raids and invasion perpetrated by unscrupulous forces on the people under our protection. He justified the Rowlatt Act on grounds that it was directed against a secret and formidable conspiracy. There must, he said, be an inquiry, but *"let us talk of an inquiry when we have put the fire out. The only message that we send from the House today to India is a message of confidence in and sympathy with those upon whom the great responsibility has fallen to restore the situation. Then will come the time to hold an inquiry, not only to help us to remove the causes, but in order to dispose once and for all of some of the libellous charges that have been made against British troops and those upon whom the unpleasant duties in connection with those riots have fallen."*

On 29th May, Sir Michael O'Dwyer, having stayed on till the worst of the Rebellion was over, left the Punjab for England. He spent a great deal of time informing the India Office and endeavouring to inform the Prime Minister about what had actually happened. Nothing appeared in the 'Times'. Miss Sherwood, coming back to England, also endeavoured to inform the Secretary of State, which was agreed in questions he answered. Nothing was said about the Punjab.

Throughout the long summer, fortnightly reports show the gradual increase in propaganda; these reports were written regularly to the head of each Division, who would correlate them, and then forward them to the Provincial Government, which would forward them in turn to the Home Member of the Government. At first, those coming from Bombay and Poona gave information that Gandhi had been stoned and shouted at for leading the rebellion, by the people who had suffered. Gradually the propaganda increased and claims were taken seriously. For instance, the claim that there were dead bodies in the well in Jallianwalla Bagh was accepted, but divers were sent down to check and found that no such bodies existed, though it is to this day part of the propaganda, and was shown in the Attenborough film. Today, a small shelter has been built over it to give emphasis to the mendacious tale.

In September, the Indemnity Bill was debated in the Legislative Council. It should, in a normally impartial assembly, have gone through on the nod, for when Government orders soldiers to use their power to stop a rebellion and orders Martial Law, it does not expect its servants to be charged with the killing done at Government's request. The Indian contingent on the Council, anxious to increase the anti-British tale, clamoured for Dyer's hanging, and imprisonment for the other officials who had helped to restore order. There was little doubt that the Members of the Legislative Council, such as Pandit Madan Malaviya, who were deeply involved with the conspiracy and the rebellion, would not wish the suffering public to realise that they were guilty and the officials innocent.

The position was still that there was an official majority and the Indemnity Bill was pushed through with the full support of the Army Member, Sir Havelock Hudson, whose speech graphically described the difficulties for soldiers called to the support of the Civil Arm, having had no opportunity to put things into order before this became necessary.

If it had not been for the Official Majority, there is little doubt that the men who had acted at the command of Government would have been punished for their help. The arguments went backwards and forwards to England and it might have been then that Montagu lost his head.

On 10th December 1919, in Cabinet, Montagu was congratulated on the way he had got the India Act through Parliament, as a Bill on the Table waiting for the draft Rules. The Prime Minister stated that, in view of the fact that the Government of India Bill would probably become law before the prorogation of Parliament, it was proposed that the King should be asked to send a message to the people of India in regard to the character of the Bill. The question had been raised as to the desirability of the Indian Legislature being opened by the Prince of Wales in person. The King had expressed his approval of the proposal, and the Prince of Wales was willing to undertake the mission. If the Cabinet agreed, it had been proposed that the King should be asked to mention in His Majesty's message: 'The Prince of Wales to visit India for the purpose of opening the Legislature during the winter of 1920-21.'

The Cabinet agreed:-

a) That the opening of the Indian Legislature by the Prince of Wales in person was eminently desirable, and should have an admirable effect in India.

b) That the Secretary of State for India, in presenting to His Majesty the draft of a statement by the King to the people of India, should refer to this proposal.

c) That the Secretary of State for India should also include in the draft of the King's message, some expression of confidence that the people of India would await the measures for giving effect to the Government of India Act in tranquillity and without any disturbance of the peace.

On 16th December 1919, there was a Debate in the House of Lords in relation to the need for the House to resolve itself into Committee for the India Act.

The man who opened the Debate was Lord Ampthill. After the usual appreciation of the way in which Lord Sinha, the Under-Secretary had spoken and a comment on the unusually light-hearted way in which Lord Curzon had spoken about the Bill – a tone of light optimism, almost of gay nonchalance – he took up his deep concern about the Bill itself. In the organ of the Moderates - who would throw off their mask as soon as the Bill was passed in India – their comments on the Joint Committee were headed 'Betrayal'!

Lord Ampthill said: *"The public has been kept in the dark with regard to the state of affairs in India, which I can assure the noble Lords, is very serious indeed. Within the last two days we have been allowed to hear something of the appalling peril from which we barely escaped. The storm which is brewing is one which cannot be weathered by pouring oil on troubled waters – murderous revolt is ready to break out at any moment and even in the municipal elections in different parts of India, intimidation has reached a pitch which would be beyond belief in this country. It is an ungrateful task to oppose myself to the opinion of the large majority of members of both Houses and to express complete disapproval of a measure, which is receiving such complete benediction in this country. Such, however is the duty that I owe to my conscience and, as it seems to me, to the people of India. I shall feel some measure of my former responsibility towards those people to the end of my existence. In these circumstances, I should be false to them, false to my own countrymen, and untrue to myself if I did not express my real conviction in regard to this measure and the manner in which it has been promoted. I am profoundly convinced that those of you who live will bitterly regret your share in this work. I pray God that I may be mistaken, but such at present is my conviction. I have always been strongly in favour of political reform in India. The records of debates in this House bear me out in this and entitle me to say that the views as to reform which I held while I was still in India were much in advance of those held by your Lordships when the Morley/Minto reforms were debated in this House. Sympathy with Indian aspirations and more particularly, with their claims to be treated as British subjects throughout the Empire, were frequently expressed in your Lordships' House and on those occasions it is not too much to say that my voice was as of one crying in the wilderness. I am still in favour of progress and reform and if the passage of this calamitous measure could be arrested I should be the first to advocate a fresh attempt on different lines.*

*Nothing short of the transformation of the soil and climate of India to a character similar to that of our own will make the people of India adaptable to social and political institutions like those of this country. I purposely couple the words social and political, for social reform and political reform must go hand in hand. They always have been inseparable and always will be inseparable. That is a truth that is entirely ignored by the Bill. Indeed, the measure which you are about to pass in haste will be to set back and hopelessly to impede such movements for social reform as already exist in India. So far from it being a movement to promote progress, in the opinion of a very large number of people in India, one which will bring about reaction, since it places power in the hands of those whose real object is reactionary. ...Caste. That institution is more ancient and more firmly established than any religion in the world, and it is, in fact, an essential part of the Hindu religion. Caste baffles definition. The essential thing is to bear in mind is that Caste and Hinduism are not two things but one thing and indivisible. It has been said that the Caste idea is the soil, as well as the body of Hinduism ... regarded as being of Divine origin. That system starts from an axiom, held to be divinely revealed, that men are unequal and must remain unequal; separated accordingly into groups and that whatever happens, the Brahmin must remain at the top of the social structure while all others must serve and worship him. The institution of Caste is 3,000 years old; it affects 250,000,000 people. No Hindu can escape from the dominance of the Caste idea, which also affects a large part of the Moslem and Christian community in India. Since Hinduism and Caste is one and the same thing, no modification of the system is likely to take place for generations to come. The supremacy of the Brahmin will continue to be acknowledged by the masses of the people so long as Hinduism endures; and the Hindu religion – this is the point to which I am bringing your Lordships – is absolutely opposed to the democratic doctrine of the equality of all men before the law.*

*Such, then, is the soil in which it is fondly hoped that democratic institutions will take root. Nothing in the world is so bitter and so enduring as Caste animosities are and that is why it is necessary to have a strong and impartial Executive for the preservation of peace and order in India. That is why we are there in India. That is our justification for remaining. This Bill, however, will fatally weaken the Executive, and impair its impartiality for remaining. That is a defect which runs all through the measure. The eminent authors of the Report were under the delusion – an incredible and perilous delusion – that the acceptance of their ideas would 'soften the rigidity of the Caste system'. In the use of that and similar phrases for the justification of their policy, they showed themselves as ignorant of Indian life as they must be of social conditions on the planet Mars. Elections and ballot boxes will no more alter the relations between the Brahmin and the low caste man than the bestowal of votes on women will alter the physical differences between the two sexes. The actual fact is – I beg your Lordships to take note of this – that the Home Rule movement in India has been attended by a Hindu revival which is closely connected with it.*

*The Varnashrama Dharma movement, as the name implies, has no other object than that of reviving the rigidity of the Caste system, and it is a movement promoted solely and entirely by the Brahmin politicians. But there are none so blind as those who will not see. If our ultimate object is to make India self governing so that she may eventually take her place among the independent sovereignties of the world and at any rate, be able to do so in case we should be unable to maintain our present protection, then we must first of all make her self reliant, in the sense that she will be able to protect herself against foreign foes and to prevent internal strife and disorder. The first duty of every State is to provide for security, but for a century past, India has relied on us for the armed force and particularly for economic strength, without which, no state can be secure or independent. It seems to me, therefore, that there is no statesmanship or even foresight, in a scheme which so completely ignores this prime necessity."*

He went on to develop his theme of national Security and then continued: *"Again, if our ideal is to make India democratic so that she may be fit for future self government, we must make it possible for all classes of the people to acquire a democratic spirit. But this Bill makes any such thing impossible in that under the system of election which is contemplated, the Brahmin minority will have the power, as they certainly have the intention, to suppress all democratic inclination.*

*Such an ideal of future independence, not wrested from us by revolt but freely conceded after due education and training as from parent to child or from teacher to pupil, is a fine ideal and one to which I gladly subscribe. For my opinion is that it is impossible to justify an intention of keeping one race in perpetual subjection to another[47], nor can we feel sure that we shall always be strong enough ourselves to maintain our present protection of India. But the only means of approaching such an ideal is deliberately precluded by the scheme in this Bill. I am thinking mainly of the Madras Presidency when I say that it is only by a much wider system of communal representation through communal electorates that you can give any chance to the vast majority, who are not 'politically minded' of so becoming. They need special protection until they can organise and prepare and equip themselves to take their proper place in the new order of things. They need power to promote that social reform, without which political reform is useless and even dangerous to them; but they cannot hope to get that power if the Brahmin is placed in a position to dominate over all, as he is by this Bill.*

*Take the case of the Madras Presidency, that part of India which I know best and of which I have the best right to speak. The Brahmins there, who are only 3 per cent of the population, occupy 80 per cent of the places in the public services and the Councils of the country. The Non-Brahmins who form 70 per cent, excluding the depressed classes of Hindus, pay almost the whole cost of the administration – for the Brahmins, although they own property, hold lands that are free from taxation, both from the land revenue and the Irrigation Tax. But these Non-Brahmins who form 70 per cent, have no powers at present, and they feel strongly that this Bill will put them in an even worse position. I cannot do better, my Lords than give it in their own words by quoting one of the repeated Resolutions which were passed unanimously by the South Indian Non-Brahmin Confederation. Here is one of them."*

'This Confederation is emphatically of the opinion that any scheme of constitutional reforms which does not provide for the separate representation through communal electorates of Non-Brahmin classes, will arrest the progress and irretrievably impair the interests of these classes which form the bulk of the population, besides effectively undermining British rule, which is so essential to India's welfare.'

*"But the case of the other Provinces is similar, in very varied circumstances. So long as we have to govern India – and we must govern India until we have made her fit to govern herself, to defend herself and to maintain law and order within her borders – so long, of course, we must have a strong Government. The dual system of government in the Provinces which is contemplated will unquestionably divide and weaken authority and the Bill in its present form will weaken and impair the authority of the Governor-General both in the Executive and in the Legislature.*

*The incredible fact is that, but for the chance visit to India of a globe trotting doctrinaire, with a positive mania for constitution-mongering, nobody in the world would ever have thought of so peculiar a notion as 'Diarchy.' And yet the Joint Committee tells us in an airy manner that no better plan can be conceived. My Lords, it is indeed sad to think that British statesmanship has become so sterile and bankrupt that it is*

---

47    Lord Ampthill's concern for our position was not at this point in history accepted by Brahmins, for Caste is also race and the Harijans are another race for the Brahmin, Aryan invaders.

*obliged to adopt a scheme which is almost universally condemned. The strength of British Rule in India has depended more than anything else, upon our prestige and upon our known desire and power to administer impartial justice. When we have no longer the power to hold the balance, even between the rival claims of castes, classes, races and religions, that prestige will be gone. Indeed it has already suffered irreparable damage in the eyes of those classes who have hitherto looked to us for justice and protection against oppression – the classes from which we have had loyal assistance and support in all circumstances.*

*What they have seen all along and what they see now, is that which never entered into their wildest dreams – namely, the Great British Sirkar yielding to intimidation at the hands of political agitators, some of whom have been branded by the State as dangerous criminals. We have been committed to this disastrous measure, step by step, by furtive intrigue, without previous deliberation in Parliament, and without the agreement of the people of India. In fulfilment of pledges given on our behalf, and cunningly misinterpreted, we have got to do that which places the whole future of India in serious jeopardy. That is the position to which we have been brought, while we were engaged in a life and death struggle with Germany, by the adroit collusion of schemers in this country with schemers in India, in a movement which is as obscure in its origin as it is disquieting in its outward manifestations.*

"Here is another, my Lords, which was passed on June 22 last" -

'That this Conference regards the equal distribution of political power among the different classes of the people as the first necessary substantial step towards responsible government in this country and while expressing gratification at the special representation of Mohammedans, Sikhs, Indian Christians, Europeans, Anglo-Indians, and the depressed classes, urges the creation of a Non Brahmin Hindu electorate as the indispensable foundation for popular government, in the absence of which any constitution reform will be unreal, dangerous, unworkable and sure to give rise to great discontent.'[48]

"There I have given you, in their own words, the opinion of the vast majority of the people of the Madras Presidency. I am saying nothing which is not in accordance with those views. That view is shared by all the experienced British Officials of the Madras Government, and the Government of India themselves declared that, unless something was done to secure to the Non-Brahmins a fair share in the Legislature, they would be unable to meet the charge that they were acquiescing in the establishment of an oligarchy in Madras. But there is nothing in the Bill. We have only a pious hope expressed by the Joint Committee, that Brahmin and Non-Brahmin will meet

---

48   It has already been mentioned that Gandhi went on a fast to the death when Ambedkar requested in 1935 that the Depressed Classes should have separate constituencies. The backward step on which Gandhi then insisted to bring these people into the Hindu vote is made clear by Ampthill's exposition. Not only would they lose their voting rights, but also in Madras as an example, nearly 30% more votes would become part of the Hindu constituency.

*and settle their difference in discussion. It is not too much to say that this is a wholly fatuous suggestion.*

*There is a similar and equally grave objection to the Bill in the Province of the Punjab. In that Province, the bulk of the population consists of a sturdy, independent peasantry, from which half the Indian army is recruited. Under this scheme, these men who are intensely jealous of their rights will be grossly under represented as compared with the urban majority of the population. To place the welfare of these warlike peasants at the mercy of the politically-minded dwellers in the towns is simply to ask for trouble, and the prospect of friction and disorder in the Province is very serious indeed.*

*My Lords, I have spoken from the point of view of a former Governor of Madras, and referred chiefly to the main objection to the Bill, which is felt by the people of that Province. So far as Madras is concerned, the Bill fails to pass the 'crucial test' which is imposed by the Secretary of State himself – namely, 'whether the proposal will or will not carry India towards responsible Government' – in that it creates an Indian oligarchy in place of a British bureaucracy."*

For those who are able to appreciate the subtleties and near-anguish of Lord Ampthill's speech, the historical nub of the whole of the intention of this book should become clear.

India at that time had reached and emerged into a state of Nationhood, which could have further evolved into full democratic unity. The Hindu Raj, the aim of the politicians, meant 'Brahmin Rule'. He says it plainly. Brahmin rule had one stumbling block; the massive respect and trust for the British Bureaucracy. The clear aim, evidenced by the closing of the main gate of the Jallianwalla Bagh, by Gandhi's claims to have been arrested, by the emphasis on the brutal British bureaucracy by Besant, by the use of every possible incitement to rise and provoke, which epitomised the Rebellion, was to break that trust. The beating of British bank managers to death - indeed the beating of any Briton to death - by incited, provoked and probably paid mobs, was to show that we could be destroyed, we could be frightened. As Colonel Smith, the Civil Surgeon pointed out, the destruction of a church was completely contrary to normal behaviour and was designed to destroy the respect for our God and our people. Never did such a terrible compound of evil thought concentrate on one place as at Amritsar, incorporating the desire that the British would not dare put it down and it would spread – for the leaders in each town were already in place – throughout the Punjab and then throughout India.

Colonel Smith also referred to the Soviet in the city of Amritsar.

The point that Ampthill did not make specific, for it is inherent in everything he said, is that lower castes and untouchability are symptoms of racism. Today we have Draper, Sayer, Perkins and many others claiming that the British in India were racist – too often, people fasten onto others their own unappetising traits. What the British did have was prestige; not necessarily from the then present individuals, but from those who had gone before – the Malcolms, the Lawrences, Nicholson,

Edwardes, Taylor; so many others, who had given us a tradition to live up to and a format within which to work.

Just so today in this country, this curious and sinister scheme of domination by the European Union and the loss of our democracy, are destroying the traditions and supports which, through the centuries, we have evolved for better government, justice and good social mores, so in India then, the German influence had worked to support and encourage a destructive domination by a handful of people, the Brahmins, whose oligarchy continues to rule India to this day. So it was in Russia, where the removal of a good man, the Tsar and the development of democratic and popular rule in the Duma under Prince Lvov and Karensky, was to be replaced by the Parvus interpretation of Marx – domination by a group of dictators, called working class, but nonetheless dictators, which continued almost to this day and has been succeeded by the exact lack of grasp of the true meaning of democratic institutions of which Ampthill warned. Democracy does not function without democrats. In Germany at that time there were only the beginnings of the concept of democracy; in Britain the need for democracy is a soul feeling struggled for by people like Cromwell, who had no idea of it as being represented by universal franchise. Today, our traditions, the supports of our civilisation, are being abolished and with them, our democracy. Such laws as Habeas Corpus and Jury Trial, for which men fought, are being removed; our intrinsic belief in freedom and tolerance, in the supremacy of law over rulers and ruled alike, made possible by our institutions, are being, not merely eroded, but actually removed by those pressing Germano/French ideas that are not ours and do not hold high our ideals. Our safety is at risk from those, like the British and Indian schemers, or the fools who had no idea of the seriousness of Ampthill's speech, who allowed the safety and repose of India to be taken over.

The passion felt by Montagu for the Congress, for these men, deeply involved in the rebellion, made them the apparently suitable successors for the impartial and upright British officials whom he hated so strongly. His idea was that Congress, like prefects in a school, should be trusted and given power because they agreed with his idea. Their leaders were Brahmins, or Hindus and Muslims who were part of the code. They had helped to persuade him that the British were bad and wrong; they declared that we had always tried to Divide and Rule; that the Great Mutiny was not a mutiny but 'The First War of Independence'. Montagu, flattered and with a popularity he would never know again, was too intent upon his dream to question their view.

The most important of their words was their claim that they wanted democracy, when they really wanted their own totalitarian rule. They wanted power. The desire for power leads people to use any intrigues; to pledge any future action, to misrepresent any word or phrase. If Ampthill had been alive in 1942, he would have seen again the unappetising spectacle of Britain defending India, while the Congress and Gandhi raised every spurious argument to make the Quit India Movement gain strength and get the British out of India. Never were there people of such a traitorous disposition, but by then, as Lord Linlithgow and then Lord Wavell found, the Governor-General did not have sufficient power in his own hands to control or suppress the upheaval, even though it led to the Front being cut off. By then, the 1935 Act - based on the Simon Commission proposals, that in turn were based on the proposals of the Congress Brahmin, Jawarharlal Nehru - had eroded still further the powers of the Viceroy, enhancing (thanks to Gandhi's insistence) the Hindu voting power and by the blind folly of this same Hindu majority, leading the Muslims out of India, through Jinnah, into Pakistan.

For those many who imagine that the Hindus would have treated the Muslims well, or even now are, presumably, so doing, it should be borne in mind that, as on every other issue, through charm, influence, and possibly more serious activities, the Viceroy agreed to Menon and Nehru's request for the alteration of boundaries, so that a road to Kashmir and the headworks of the river Ravi would be transferred to India, resulting in complete drought and starvation in the Canal Lands in Pakistan, fed by the headworks.

How was this done? The Radcliffe Boundary Commission worked on the principle of contiguous majority tahsils. To hand over the road to Kashmir and the headworks, the actual parameters of the Boundary Legislation had to be set aside. The tahsils, through Gurdaspur for one, were Muslim majority. But then, apart from the Tarn Taran, so was the district of Amritsar, which was also handed over to India. The Mountbattens however, for the various reasons which are well known, were closely linked with the Hindus and did not show the impartiality by which we had maintained our rule.

The areas involved in the alteration of boundaries were the worse affected in the ensuing appalling deaths of Muslims, although throughout India in 1947, in Delhi, in Kangra, in the United Provinces and many other places, the wholesale murders of Muslims and, to a much lesser extent, of Hindus, were the sacrifice made by the oligarchy that cared more for power than for the people. That sacrifice, that cruelty and murder of men, women and children, over such a wide area of villages and homesteads on which people had lived and earned their living, man and boy for centuries, compares with the ravages of Stalin, of Pol Pot and with the terrible intentional deaths of the millions whom Hitler murdered in the concentration camps. I do not believe it possible to accept the leaders as normal people who, offered the help of British troops in peacekeeping, refused them because of the hatred and racism which had built on the insidious propaganda of the Germans prior to and during the First World War. As the author's mother wrote in her description of life in the Fort at Amritsar, it was impossible to believe that the mobs would murder their own people, when they burnt down the mission school over the children's heads; so it seems impossible that the protection of their own people at the time of Partition appeared irrelevant and so secondary to the quick take-over of power. It is natural that the ongoing anti-British propaganda has had to be invented to excuse them from their complicity in wilful murder. Gandhi, talking to Lord Wavell, said that India could have her bloodbath if she wanted it, rather than let British soldiers provide protection, not torn, as were Indian troops, by their own personal involvement.

Montagu's attitude had become increasingly polarised. Arriving late at a Cabinet meeting just prior to the India Act going through Parliament, he wanted there to be no question of Lord Sydenham being included on the Committee. In fact by then, Lord Sydenham had already been appointed, so Montagu had to put up with it. Lord Willingdon, then Freeman Thomas, on his arrival in India as Governor of Bombay (which Sydenham had been some time before), told Montagu that Lord Sydenham was out of date, but the 'Manchester Guardian' man, Walker, was amused to find that Lord Sydenham was a great figure in India and that 'they actually attached importance to what he said, and feared him.' Truth is always disconcerting to those whose ideas are based on political aims rather than realities. So in the Committee, we find Lord Sydenham with firm and detailed concern, challenging some of the rules. He was questioning the position of a Governor who, on coming out to India for the first time, would no longer have two men to advise him, but one. Further that he was no longer to be a member of the Legislative Council. *"I think that it is desirable that there should still remain, at all events for the first period of transition, two European advisers to the Governor?"* Or, *"I think it is very unsatisfactory that everything in this Bill has to be referred to rules and that if you try to introduce a definite principle you are told, 'It is no use; this will be provided in the Rules by and by, and you will have an opportunity of seeing the Rules.' If you held it out that the principle of communal representation would be recorded as part of the Bill, then I am certain it would bring contentment and prevent serious unrest among the non-Brahmin population of Southern India."*

It was to be expected that the 'Guardian' man, fresh out from England, should chafe against the detailed analysis of situations about which he knew nothing, in the rebellion-loving demeanour of Britain at the time. Any one attempting to prevent total freedom would seem out of date, but Freeman Thomas was to think quite differently when he was transferred to Madras. As Governor, he began to see something of the attack by Gandhi on the British mills, followed by the Malabar Rebellion which took place in his province and for which he could not bring in Martial Law, nor persuade the Viceroy to do so. It was left to the women of Malabar to write to Lady Reading to beg for it and for the Viceroy to give it by certification; after the loss of thousands of lives. Reading after all, was a close friend of Edwin Montagu and had accepted the Montagu frame of thought and direction.

But the most interesting question came from Lord Ampthill. *"It is a most extraordinary thing, that the joint Committee go out of their way to provide, that a man who has been convicted of a criminal offence, entailing sentence of imprisonment of more than six months, shall be qualified to sit on the Legislative Councils after five years. This provision is so singular, so unlike anything in our own laws, or in any laws that we have yet heard of, that one must ask for some explanation. It looks as if it were intended for the benefit of some particular individuals. If that is the case, we ought to know who they are and why this leniency towards convicted criminals is to be shown. In view of the Report of the Joint Committee, which is a positive invitation to elect or appoint to these Legislative Councils, men who have been convicted of criminal offences and undergone long sentences, it is absolutely necessary to call attention to this and to ascertain what is at the bottom of this very singular provision. I hope your Lordships will put in this proviso and prevent any misunderstanding of the law when it comes into being."*

'Provided that a person dismissed from Government service on conviction for a criminal offence shall be disqualified from membership of the Councils of State or the Legislative Assembly.'

Lord Sydenham gave his support: *"In the best interests of these Legislative Councils to be formed now, it is desirable that those people who have been convicted of a criminal offence should be excluded from their body."*

Our constitution is strong and flexible; in theory, it safeguards our rights and the powers of Government to an extent unparalleled in the world, but it depends on those we elect being honest and reasonable men. They are not the Constitution, nor are they given power outside the rights given to us under Magna Carta and the Bill of Rights (and its precursor, the Declaration of Rights) of 1689, but it relies on the integrity of the people elected. The Sovereign is the embodiment of the Constitution and in fact, cannot alter it. By her Coronation Oath and the successive Oaths of Allegiance, she holds her Ministers, to whom she has given power, to the laws that bind her. In Montagu's case, he discussed what would be done in Cabinet, put a Draft bill on the table and published it, and probably wrote the Kings Proclamation himself, which he might or might not have discussed in a Privy Council Meeting. The reason for his determination to get the Bill through without discussion was because he knew that the Congress of India had refused to give evidence to Hunter unless the imprisoned rebels were released. The Proclamation released prisoners and members of Congress could therefore give evidence; this meant that Gandhi at Ahmedabad could give his evidence – pages and pages of it – while the Committee sat and listened. The only useful information that he produced was that there were 'evil men behind it'. The Proclamation had to be appended to the India Act, a cause for rejoicing therefore, for the Proclamation.

Without the Queen as Sovereign, we would, in the present day, have no protection from any dictator who chose to take over, not because it is a matter of election but because she embodies our Constitution, which would fall to the ground without her.

However, we have not kept our representation in order, for we have allowed a representation to grow up based on the Party Whip. Every now and again, we are in most grievous danger from Ministers who act without authority. In theory this can be put right, but the selling of our sovereignty by Edward Heath to the European Union and the unwise payment of the Charlemagne Prize to him for help to Europe has not been rectified and should have been. With the Blair Government, we have lost the protection of Habeas Corpus, won by our ancestors from the Monarch at the time of Magna Carta and are now, under the Animal Welfare Amendment Bill and the Terrorism Bill, liable to be removed to prison without that safeguard. The rights to our own property, including stock and chattels have also been taken from us by the Blair Government, under the Animal Welfare Bill, by which the Minister (which also means Government employees) may come onto our land and kill our stock and pets and we can be imprisoned or fined if we try to stop them.

Under the Right to Roam Act, we have lost all rights to the privacy of our own property, even our gardens. The European Arrest Warrant requires our police to arrest a citizen on the request of any other member nation, without providing any evidence to support a charge, even for acts which are not offences here. So bewildering are these Bills that we have to ask: 'But why?'

The India Act similarly handed over power, without considering the loss inherent in the process.

In the case of Montagu, his intention in rushing through the India Act rather than having the prolonged representative discussions prior to the Bill being enacted, was clearly to help his friends to put across the evidence that he hoped to use in his speech.

A few days later, the Government of India Act was passed (23$^{rd}$ December 1919), and Section 6, sub section (2), states that provisions may be made by rules under the principal Act as to qualifications to be required in respect of members of the Executive Council of the Governor of a Province, in any case where such provision is not made by section 47 of the principal Act, as amended by this section.

Under section 47, there are no qualifications, except that persons who have not been elected cannot sit for more than six months. This meant that those loyal to the Government effectively could not be appointed to positions in the Councils. The number of the electorate was 1,000,000, out of a population of 350,000,000 in British India.

One week later the India Act would be published in India with a Proclamation from the King. The additions made to the proposed Proclamation gave a good indication of the intention behind the clause questioned by Lord Ampthill.

There had been a number of remarks about the way in which the Bill had been pushed through Parliament without sufficient time for full debate, clarification and qualification, with such an extremely important measure. Something of the effect on the Hunter Committee, still sitting, was added by Lord Hunter, with the presentation to the Home Department of the Report, dated 8$^{th}$ March 1920, Agra, which stated: *"The Committee held their first meeting at Delhi on 29$^{th}$ October, when the procedure to be adopted by them was discussed. It was resolved that persons or bodies desirous of offering evidence should be invited to lodge with the Secretary, a statement in writing (to be signed by a barrister, advocate, pleader or yakil) of the facts which they desired to prove and an outline of the points or contentions which they were prepared to substantiate. The statements were to be accompanied by a list of witnesses whom it was desired to have examined and a short synopsis of the evidence of each such witness. The Committee were prepared to hear applications from the persons or bodies who lodged statements, for leave to attend the sittings by a barrister, advocate, pleader or yakil. Intimation as to the proposed procedure was duly made in the press.*

*The Committee heard the evidence of witnesses on 8 days at Delhi, on 29 days at Lahore, on 6 days at Ahmedabad, and on 3 days at Bombay. All the witnesses with the exception of Sir Michael O'Dwyer, General Hudson, Mr. Thomson and Sir Umar Hayat Khan, who gave their evidence in Camera, were examined in public.*[49]

*At Delhi, the All-India Congress Committee appeared by counsel, cross-examined witnesses put forward by the authorities and called witnesses of their own. At Ahmedabad there was a similar appearance by the Gujarat Sabha.*

*In connection with the inquiry at Lahore on 12th November 1919, I received a communication from the President of the All-India Congress committee, that a resolution had been come to by that body that, 'in view of the situation created by the refusal of the Government to accede to the request for the temporary release on adequate security of the principal Punjab leaders at present undergoing imprisonment, the committee regrets that it finds it impossible to co-operate with the Disorders Inquiry Committee by appearing before it and tendering evidence on behalf of the people.' It was suggested in the letter that it was still possible to remove the impasse, if the Committee could see its way to recommend the release for the period of the inquiry, of the principal leaders under such security as might appear adequate to the Government.*

*The suggestion made in this letter was considered by the Committee, who were unanimously of the opinion that it was not within our province to review the discretion of the local Government as regards the release of prisoners. A reply to this effect was sent by the Secretary to the above communication. In this letter there is the following message:*

'If, in the course of their enquiry it should appear that the evidence of any persons now in custody is necessary to throw light on the causes of the disturbances or the measures taken to deal therewith, such persons will be called before the Committee, and, in that event, the Committee do not doubt that the Government of the Punjab will place no obstacles in the way of their appearance. The Committee observe, indeed, from the communication of the Private Secretary to the Lieutenant-Governor, of which a copy is annexed to your letter, that an assurance has been conveyed to you on this point, and also an undertaking that proper facilities will be allowed for consultation between persons in custody and counsel engaged in the enquiry which has been entrusted to the Committee, and Lord Hunter's Committee would expect

---

49　It is noticeable that the three most important witnesses who had the most detailed knowledge of the rebellion and the background causes, were examined in <u>camera.</u> None of them was concerned about the possibility of their evidence being made public. The fact that it was not heard in public meant that the Bolshevik links within the knowledge of Sir Umar Hayat Khan, the Secretary to the Punjabi Government and of the Adjutant to the army, all of extreme importance, were not available to the public, indicating a further attempt at cover-up.

that in this matter, the Government would afford the fullest reasonable facilities. Lord Hunter has independently suggested to the Punjab Government that this should be done. Beyond this, Lord Hunter's Committee feel that they cannot properly make any further suggestions.[50]'

*I may add that the Punjab Government agreed all the suggestions made by me on the above lines. In my opinion, no further concession was necessary to give the Congress Committee the fullest opportunity for placing before us any evidence relevant to the material of the Inquiry.*

*The All-India Congress committee did not appear before us at any of the sittings in Lahore. We, however, gave ample opportunity for the presentation of non-official evidence in terms of the notice we had issued as to procedure. In fact, a number of witnesses sent statements to us and were examined as to complaints about the action taken by the officials during the period of the disturbances.[51]*

*On 30th December, after the conclusion of our sittings in Lahore, I received a telegram from Pandit Malaviya in the following terms; 'As principal leaders have been released in pursuance of royal proclamation, my committee is now in a position to lay non-official evidence relating to Punjab before Disorders Committee. In the event acceptance of my committee's suggestion, it is assumed that official witnesses will be recalled for cross-examination when necessary. Wire reply.'[52]*

*I also had a communication to a similar effect from some of the imprisoned leaders who had been released. It appeared to me that the request to re-open the inquiry was not, in the circumstances, quite reasonable and the Secretary at my request, sent a reply in the following terms: 'In view of the fact that the Committee has sat at Lahore for over six weeks and has now completed the hearing of evidence there, that full opportunity was given for the presentation of non-official evidence and that it was open to your committee to cross examine witnesses during that period, Lord Hunter regrets that he is unable to accept the suggestion of your committee.' The course which I then took was subsequently approved by the Committee. I may say that I had the less reason to regret that this was the only course open, as the evidence which had been given, appeared to me to contain material for our reaching a decision upon the different points coming within scope of our enquiry, it being no part of our duty to re-try individual cases.*

*In conclusion etc. William Hunter President."*

---

50  The claim was frequently made that the Congress (the main leaders and instigators of the Rebellion) were not allowed to give evidence because the leaders were in prison. This is a fairly common misunderstanding, put about by the leaders and mendacious in the extreme.

51  The emphasis on the behaviour of officials is interesting, since those complaining had just led a rebellion against the Government. If anyone still imagines the British to have been ruthless…!

52  In terms of Indian courtesy, the telegram shows clearly that Malavaya thought he had the British on the run. The attitude is significant in terms of Montagu's behaviour later.

One point is not made clear in all this. The release of prisoners had come in time for the Ahmedabad sitting, at which, if Congress had kept up their boycott, Gandhi could not have given evidence without the King's Proclamation.

There was one important date left. On 28th December 1919 the Congress met at Amritsar. The meeting had been planned for Amritsar at the 1918 Congress at Delhi, where already the plans for rebellion had been clearly seething below the surface. Amritsar, the Bolshevik centre, was to be the centre of triumph.

Moti Lal Nehru was freshly involved in going round Amritsar, Lahore and Kasur with Gandhi to collect information, going with Pandit Jagat Narayan to the Khalsa College at Amritsar; to Kasur, where Gandhi turned on his charm to Percy Marsden, and blessed the head of little Edmund Marsden in his pram. As a logical consequence of the boycott of the Hunter Committee, it was decided to appoint a non-official Inquiry Committee to hold almost a parallel inquiry on behalf of the Congress. The fact that the Indian section of the Hunter Committee did not disagree with the proposals made by Lord Hunter was because they knew that the Congress was evolving a far more effective story. It was published untested, full of mocked-up photographs – as in one case, Sir John Hose pointed out, the arm of a soldier supposedly watching some gruesome spectacle was 'at the present' - but it was in keeping and to be expected. It was, after all, the product of the leaders of the rebellion.

Some examples of the inaccuracies have been mentioned. There are other contradictions to the whole event under review. So, on Page 150 of the Congress Report: 'Kundan Lal age 10, sentenced to transportation for life for 'waging war'. In fact, 'This boy who is 14 years old, was not sentenced at all but was acquitted. He was caught by a subordinate judge running out of a mob that was attacking a railway station, when the police began firing on the mob. His own evidence (page 906) is that he went with the mob.'

As an example of the perversions which have persuaded so many people to this day: Congress Report, page 156 –

*"The Satyagraha movement restrained the violent tendencies and passions of the people. The Satyagraha movement was conceived and conducted in a spirit entirely free from ill will and violence."* [That is what Mr Gandhi signed on 20th February 1920.]

[This is what he said on the 14th April 1919, while the perception of the Ahmedabad riots was fresh before him]. *"In the name of Satyagraha we burnt down buildings, forcibly captured weapons, extorted money, stopped trade, cut off telegraph wires, killed innocent people and plundered shops and private houses. It is open to anyone to say that, but for the Satyagraha campaign, there would not have been this violence."* It is most noticeable that there is not a word of this in Chapter IV of the Congress report, which described Satyagraha. That chapter calls it 'an innocuous doctrine' and says it had nothing to do with the excesses of the mob.

It was on this Congress Report that Montagu based his speech and on which countless 'historians' of the Amritsar event have based their beliefs, but Montagu had before him Sir John Hose's expert and contemporary analysis, based on all the papers to his hand.

Montagu had put his shirt on the Congress; he expected that, if he got the Act and the Proclamation through Parliament in time, it would be discussed by Congress. It was, and it was utterly rejected by a vast majority, expertly orchestrated by Moti Lal Nehru. Only one man voted in favour of the reforms – Gandhi – the man who was to order his extremist followers not to stand for election in the ensuing years.

# Chapter VIII
# MONTAGU'S SPEECHES

The House of Commons debate on the 'Amritsar Incident' took place in April 1920. Edwin Montagu, as Secretary of State for India, got to his feet to speak on the motion that the salary of the Secretary of State should be reduced. The House was full, Mrs. Dyer was sitting beside Lady Carson in the Gallery and for much of the time, she was weeping. It was Sir Edward Carson who spoke for Dyer.

Mr. Montagu: "*The Motion that you have just read from the Chair is historic. For the first time in its history, the Committee have an opportunity of voting or of paying the salary of the Secretary of State for India, and I notice it is signalized by a very large desire for reduction. I gather that the intention is to confine the debate to the disturbances that took place in India last year. That being so, after most careful consideration, not only of the circumstances in this House, but of the situation in India, I have come to the conclusion that I shall best discharge my Imperial duty by saying very little indeed. The situation in India is very serious, owing to the events of last year, and owing to the controversy that has arisen upon them. I am in the position of having stated my views and the views of His Majesty's Government, of which I am the spokesman. The dispatch which has been published and criticised, was drawn up by a Cabinet Committee and approved by the whole Cabinet. I have no desire to withdraw from, or to add to, that dispatch. Every single body, civil and military, which has been charged with the discussion of this lamentable affair has, generally speaking, come to the same conclusion. The question before the Committee this afternoon is whether they will desire to censure them. I hope the debate will not take the shape of a criticism of any of them. It is so easy to quarrel with the judge when you do not agree with his judgement*".

Sir Edward Carson: "*And with an officer too*".

Mr. Montagu: *"The Hunter Committee, which was chosen after the most careful consideration, with one single desire and motive, to get an impartial tribunal to discharge the most thankless duty to the best of their ability was, I maintain, such a body. I resent very much the insolent criticisms that have been passed, either on the European Members, Civil and Military, or upon the distinguished Indian members, each of whom has a record of loyal and patriotic public service. The real issue can be stated in one sentence, and I will content myself by asking the House one question. If an officer justifies his conduct, no matter how gallant his record is – and everyone knows how gallant General Dyer's record is – by saying that there was no question of undue severity, that if his means had been greater the casualties would have been greater and that the motive was to teach a moral lesson to the whole of the Punjab, I say without hesitation, and I would ask the Committee to contradict me if I am wrong, because the whole matter turns upon this, that is the doctrine of terrorism."*

Lieutenant Commander Kenworthy: *"Prussianism."*

Mr. Montagu: *"If you agree to that, you justify everything that General Dyer did. Once you are entitled to have regard neither to the intentions nor the conduct of a particular gathering and to shoot and to go on shooting, with all the horrors that were here involved, in order to teach somebody a lesson, you are embarking on terrorism, to which there is no end. I say further, that when you pass an order that all Indians, whoever they may be, must forcibly or voluntarily salaam an officer of His Majesty the King, you are enforcing racial humiliation. I say thirdly, that when you take selected schoolboys from a school, guilty or innocent, and whip them publicly, when you put up a triangle, where an outrage which we all deplore and which all India deplores has taken place and whip people who have not been convicted, when you flog a wedding party, you are indulging in frightfulness, and there is no other adequate word which could describe it.*[53] *If the Committee follows me on these three assertions, this is the choice and this is the question which the Committee has put to it today before coming to an answer. Dismiss from your mind, I beg of you, all personal questions. I have been pursued for the last three weeks - I have been pursued throughout my association by some people and some journals with personal attack. I do not propose to answer them today. Are you going to keep your hold upon India with terrorism, racial humiliation and subordination and frightfulness, or are you going to rest it upon the goodwill, the growing goodwill, of the people of your Indian Empire?*

*I believe that to be the whole question at issue. If you decide in favour of the latter course, well then, you have to enforce it. It is no use one day passing a great Act*

---

53    One of the incidents chosen by Montagu for his 'terrible speech' was that of school boys at Kasur who had been caned at the request of their headmaster, by the Assistant Commissioner Percy Marsden, just back from fighting on the Persian Cordon - the boys responsible for attacking and nearly killing an English woman and her three children. Asked to put forward the culprits, the headmaster put forward the six most puny of the boys. Marsden picked out the six strongest on the basis of common sense. Later on leave, he went to see Montagu, who told him he should have caned them all.

*of Parliament, which, whatever its merits or demerits, proceeds on the principle of partnership for India in the British Commonwealth, and then allowing your administration to depend upon terrorism. We have got to act in every department, civil and military, un-intermittently with a desire to recognize India as a partner in your Commonwealth. You have got to safeguard your administration on principles of that Order passed by the British Parliament. You have got to remove any obsolete ordinance or law which infringes the principles of liberty which you have inculcated into the educated classes in India. That is your one chance – to adhere to the decision that you put into your legislation when you are criticizing administration. There is the other choice – to hold India by the sword, to recognize terrorism as part of your weapon, as part of your armoury to guard British honour and life with callousness about Indian honour and Indian life. India is on your side in enforcing order. Are you on India's side in ensuring that order is enforced in accordance with the canons of modernization and love of liberty in the British democratic way? There has been no criticism of any officer, however drastic his action was, in any province outside the Punjab. There were thirty seven instances of firing during the terribly dangerous disturbances of last year. The Government of India and His Majesty's Government have approved thirty six cases and have censured one. They censured one because however good the motive, they believed it infringed the principle that has always animated the British Army and infringed the principles upon which the British Empire has been built."*

Mr. Palmer: *"It saved a mutiny."*

Captain W. Benn: *"Do not answer him."*

Mr Montagu: *"The great objection to terrorism, to the use of force, is that you pursue it with no regard for the people who suffer from it and that having once tried you must go on. Every time an incident happens you are confronted with increasing animosity of the people who suffer, and there is no end to it until the people in whose name we are governing India, the people of this country and the national pride and sentiment of the Indian people act together in protest and terminate our rule in India as being impossible on modern ideas of what Empire means. There is an alternative policy: I assumed office to commend to this House and which this House has supported until today. It is to put the coping stone on the glorious work which England has accomplished in India by leading India to a complete free partnership in the British Empire, to say to India, we hold British lives sacred, but we hold Indian lives sacred too. We want to safeguard British honour by protecting and safeguarding Indian honour, too. Your institutions shall be gradually perfected while protection is accorded to you by ourselves against revolution and anarchy, in order that they may commend themselves to you.*

*There is a theory abroad on the part of those who have criticized His Majesty's Government upon this issue, that an Indian is a person who is tolerable so long as he will obey your orders, but if once he joins the educated classes, if once he thinks for himself, if once he take advantage of his educational facilities which you have provided for him, if once he imbibes the idea of individual liberty which is dear to the British people, why then you class him as an educated Indian and an agitator. What a terrible and cynical verdict on the whole."*

Mr. Palmer: *"What a terrible speech."*

Mr. Montagu: *"As you grind your machinery and turn your graduates out of the University you are going to dub him as belonging at any rate as the class from which your opponents come."*

Hon. Members: *"No."*

Colonel Ashby: *"That is not a point of Order. We are here to hear different points of view and all points of view."*

Brigadier-General Cockerill: *"On that point of Order, Mr. Chairman: Are we not here to discuss the case of General Dyer, and what is the relevancy of these remarks to that?"*

The Chairman: *"Mr. Montagu".*

Mr. Montagu: *"If any of my arguments strike anybody as irrelevant"*

Mr. Palmer: *"You are making an incendiary speech."*

Mr. Montagu: *"The whole point of my observations is directed to this one question: that there is one theory upon which I think General Dyer acted, the theory of terrorism, and the theory of subordination. There is another theory, that of partnership, and I am trying to justify the theory endorsed by this House last year. I am suggesting to this Committee that the Act of Parliament is useless unless you enforce it both in the keeping of order and in the administration. I am trying to avoid any discussion of details which do not, in my mind, affect that broad issue. I am going to submit to this House this question, on which I would suggest with all respect they should vote: Is your theory of domination or rule in India the ascendancy of one race over another, of domination and subordination..."*

Hon. Members: *"No!"*

*"... or is your theory that of partnership? If you are applying domination as your theory, then it follows that you must use the sword with increasing severity..."*

Hon. Members: *"No".*

*"... until you are driven out of the country by the united opinion of the civilized world."*

Interruption – an Hon. Member: *"Bolshevism!"*

*"If your theory is justice and partnership, then you will condemn a soldier however gallant..."*

Mr. Palmer: *"Without trial?"*

Mr. Montagu: *"...who says that there was no question of undue severity and that he was teaching a moral lesson to the whole Punjab. That condemnation, as I said at the beginning, has been meted out by everybody, Civil and Military, who has considered this question. Nobody ever suggested, no Indian has suggested, as far as I know, no reputable Indian has suggested, any punishment, any vindictiveness, or anything more than the repudiation of the principles upon which General Dyer acted. I invite this House to choose, and I believe that the choice that they make is fundamental to a continuance of the British Empire and vital to the continuation, permanent as I believe it to be, to the connection between this country and India."* [54]

Sir William Sutherland, writing to Lloyd George at Spa about the Debate, commented *"Under interruption, Montagu got excited when making his speech and became more and more racial and Yiddish in screaming tone and gesture. Carson followed Montagu, and his cleverest thing was his quiet tone, so apparently traditional and British, which made Montagu's excitement look all the worse... Winston made an excellent speech ... Asquith backed Montagu and served oil – salary oil all round."*

The Government might have been defeated but for Churchill's speech. The speech was one of such decisive cruelty about Dyer that it is surprising to know that, a matter of a year or so later, Churchill was working with Sir Michael O'Dwyer to try and save India from the gradual erosion of all that had helped to bring her to the point at which the incidents in these pages took place. What moved Churchill to speak as he did? Was it fear of a Government defeat, loyalty to a friend? Had he not read Dyer's submission? We do not know, but his eloquence carried the argument.

From the time of that speech onwards, the claim has been made that Dyer's action in the Jallianwalla Bagh was the cause of the break up of the Empire. It was not, of course. It was Montagu's speech, following the conspiracies backed by German funds and propaganda and then the addition of the same from the Bolsheviks, which showed up the weakness of a Government. The disease spread and today we have heard such people as Peter Jay supporting the infamy against the Commonwealth and the Empire.

On 23rd March 1922, at odds with the Prime Minister over Turkey, Edwin Montagu made his speech of resignation.

He referred to his expectations that, as a member of the Nations involved in the Peace Treaty, India should have had a voice in the Treaty of Sevres. He said that he thought with Lord Reading, that the people of India were entitled to know and the people of Great Britain were entitled to know, what were the views that were being put forward by the Government of India on behalf of the people and had therefore

---

54　The examples that Montagu gave of cruelty: the wedding party took place at Lahore where a deputy assistant magistrate (Indian), appointed for the Martial Law emergency, followed the rules too closely about processions and was dismissed as a result.

The flogging of the boys has already been mentioned in an earlier note. It was not done in public. Flogging, as he called it, was in fact 'caning' – the cat was not used in India, and the cane was a common punishment, usually carried out in the extremely public venue of the courtyard outside the Courts – it was regarded in India as better for poor families than imprisonment which deprived the family of the breadwinner. People of education or class were not caned, in the usual way.

Montagu must have had his doubts about the Congress story because he asked Hose whether the author's father (Beckett), who had to hold up a violent crowd coming to loot the Civil Lines, had actually said as much. The Congress story was that the crowd had been peaceful and that Beckett had fired on them and thus started the rioting. He was not armed, he would have had to sign for any armament and he did not.

published the message from the Government of India to him. He then went on to claim that they were not dictating to the people of this country that their views had to be harmonised, before continuing on Cabinet responsibility.

He mentioned the likely disastrous effects on the Muslims of India and upon the Muslim world. On the Treaty, he continued: *"I have used, I hope with moderation and with a recognition of the difficulties, the right of freedom of expression on the affairs of the Middle East as they affected India"*. He had thought that, if he resigned, it would have meant that he despaired of getting justice and just terms in conformity 'with our pledges' and hence the potential disastrous effect.

*"The third reason why I have never thought it necessary to resign until now was that until quite recently I had every right to think that I had the loyalty and confidence, not of some of my colleagues, but of all of them. Lastly, as I leave my work, may I say that the fascination of India's problems has obsessed me all my life – the Princes and the native states, each with their individual characteristics, the people of India awakened and growing, often with ill defined ideas; their races, theories, history, views. A glorious conception in thought, it was, and I think it is, of the British Commonwealth of nations: bound together with the ties of freedom and mutual respect and all the parts acknowledging no difference of race or creed or constitution or institutions; a country owing allegiance, unswerving and devoted to one King Emperor, the grave dangers of becoming rushed on the one hand to chaos, and on the other hand being frightened into reaction, a record unparalleled in the history of the world for unselfishness and personal sacrifice of the British effort in India. I longed for nothing better than to devote myself as long as I could to these all absorbing problems and not to leave undone or half done, at a most critical moment, the work in which I gloried. I have parted this week from colleagues in the India Office and in India with whom I have worked for a term of years with uninterrupted accord and I have laid down the proudest title that in my belief an Englishman can hold, the title of Secretary of State for India which means the right in particular to serve the King, this Parliament, India, and this is the unhappiest moment of my life."*

This was the man whose almost luciferic approach to his position in India led to the request for him to become Viceroy, both from the Theosophist Annie Besant and from a number of Indians.

The part of the speech already quoted, made by Montagu in the House of Commons on 23rd March 1922, started with a diatribe against the Government for having asked for his resignation. He blamed Lloyd George, he blamed Lord Curzon who, he said, knew about the telegram which he had been sent, but gave him no warning about publishing. The telegram was from Reading saying that there was feeling among the Indian Muslims about the Treaty of Sèvres. Montagu claimed about Cabinet Government, on which presumption Lloyd George had acted *"I have said and I say it again, that in my view, rightly or wrongly, the publication of this telegram was not a matter that I need bring before the Cabinet"* and later in his speech he mentioned that he had referred to 'private correspondence' and that he had misquoted it; there he did accept that he had made a mistake. Resignation, with which he disagreed, was by no means a new precept in terms of Cabinet decisions; Palmerston, at the time of Napoleon III's *coup d'etat*, when he divulged his opinion to the French Ambassador, had had to resign in 1851, but behind Reading's telegram and Montagu's action in allowing its publication, was a hint of ongoing collusion with the circle that had been involved in the Turkish Ottoman Caliphate movement. Sèvres had been signed in the previous years but not ratified; it gave the Hejaz independence from Turkey, gave a number of Independencies and Mandates with other parts of the Ottoman Empire and waived the war payments, since Turkey was in no fit state to pay indemnity, although carrying the burden of war guilt.

More seriously, since we know of the involvement of international banking, both in Lenin's ingress into Russia; in the Congress Party in India, indeed in many other areas, a group of bankers, known as the Council of Ottoman Public Debt, took over Turkey's finances and her administration. Kemal Ataturk took over as President in the following year. The Treaty of Sèvres was altered and called the Treaty of Lausanne, which was signed in July 1923, after discussion having started in November of the previous year. The areas of Eastern Turkey that had been taken in the Sèvres Treaty were restored under Lausanne, including Erzerum, which had been suggested by the Conference at Sivas in 1919. The Turkish war with Greece was successful and ongoing at the time of Montagu's resignation; Lloyd George being very much on the side of the Greeks, it is likely that his involvement arose on this issue.

Montagu had appointed Reading over the head of Lord Willingdon, to whom he had promised the position of Viceroy, under his own 'superintendence and control'. It therefore seems probably that Reading sent the telegram with the interests of Montagu in mind. This has to go further, since Reading, who had been Chief Justice, had, with Lloyd George, been involved in 'insider dealing' over the extension of the Marconi telegraph lines across the Middle East just prior to the War. Reading was really not a suitable appointment and he did not have, any more than Montagu, the insight to get Gandhi's measure or indeed, recognise the effect of his long discussions with Gandhi on Indian attitudes and interpretations.

Montagu had told J. E. Woolacott, 'Times' India Correspondent, (a great man in those days prior to national radio broadcasting) that he was fed up with the Indians.

*"We have granted these people a brand new Constitution and now, before the ink is dry, they are demanding another. I will be no party to any change unless it can be shown either than the machinery of the Constitution has proved unworkable, or that those who are working it have given proof of their fitness for further responsibility. Neither of these conditions exist, and I may tell you that my position in the matter represents the considered decision of His Majesty's Government."* That was in 1921.

In 1920, after the Punjab Disturbances Debate, immediately after Gandhi was cleared by Montagu in Parliament of all liability for the 1919 rising, , he had embarked on his non-violent non-co-operation movement with his ever growing numbers of 'volunteers' armed with lathis and, in similar vein to Hitler's Brownshirts, set out on violence and cruelty of every description. Montagu had made no excuse for any British or any Indian District Officer who used Martial Law to contain the 1919 rising, but he made excuse for the 'volunteers' by simply not noticing them. Even Annie Besant had remarked on the 1919 incident: *"The cutting of telegraph wires, the derailment of troop trains, the burning of railway stations, the setting free of jail birds, are not the actions of Satyagrahis, nor even of casual rioters, but of revolutionaries."*

Mrs. Besant was against the Rowlatt Act and not expected to see the matter in such terms.

It is not entirely surprising that when she saw the tragedy of the Moplah Rebellion, Mrs. Besant, who knew Madras well, was horrified at what she saw and spoke up where Montagu did not. She said: *"Mr. Gandhi may talk as he pleases about non co-operation accepting no responsibility. It is not what they accept, it is what they demonstrate – the slaughter of Malabar cries out his responsibility. Mr. Gandhi asks the Moderates to compel the Government to suspend hostilities, that it let loose the wolves to destroy what lives are left. The sympathy of the Moderates is not, I make bold to say, with the murderers, the looters, the ravishers, who have put into practice the teaching of paralysing the Government, of the non-co-operators, who have made war on the Government in their own way. Could not Mr. Gandhi feel a little sympathy for thousands of women left only with rags, driven from home, for little children born of refugee mothers on the road or in the refugee camps? This misery in description, girls, wives, with eyes half-blind with weeping, distraught with terror, women who have seen their husbands hacked to pieces before their eyes, in the way Moplahs consider as religion*[55]*, men who have lost everything, hopelessly crushed, desperate."*

Into the maelstrom, Gandhi ordered that all young men over 18 should become 'volunteers' claiming that he had aroused the 'spirit of rebellion'. In this Moplah Rebellion, with Bolshevik funds, Gandhi and the Ali brothers claimed that the Afghans would come in to help get rid of the British who had just given Indians a Parliamentary Constitution. This was the Gandhi way and relevant only because it gives some picture of the background to the need for Montagu to resign.

Montagu had accepted as an apology, Gandhi's claim that he had made a 'Himalayan blunder' in 1919. There had followed the India Act (after the Rebellion), but Montagu had never been into the Districts, never spoken to the District Officers and thus knew nothing of the Government of India on the ground floor or the way in which it had been kept at peace over the years.

Due to his handling of the 1919 Rebellion, he had given the impression that the Punjabi Martial Law was wicked and on this claim Malabar – Moplah - was inspired. That the only grumble was that middle-class men, not used to prison, had been imprisoned in crowded and unsuitable prisons was hardly the point, since that had always been the intention of Gandhi's eruptions. But what was serious was that

---

[55] Quote from Gandhi's speech in which he said the Moplahs' bravery must command admiration … they are fighting for what they consider is religion in a manner which they consider is religious…

neither Montagu nor Reading did anything to cool communal tensions. The Reforms put forward by Montagu had left out the necessary controls to help the democratic systems, which he and Curtis had intended to flourish – controls which were in the Governors' reforms, but were omitted from his. Communalism ran rife; the tendency, picked out by the Ali brothers, for Gandhi and his followers to work for 'Hindu Raj' rather than for India, continued apace. We may have noticed in recent times (1992) the police standing by and watching while Muslims were beaten, and something like 2,000 people were killed as a result, as attempts were made to demolish the ancient mosque at Ayodhya, built on an even more ancient Hindu site to the God Rama. At the time of writing, there is permission to rebuild a Hindu Temple on the site, as long as both Muslims and Hindus agree – an impossibility in this nation that cannot forgive – in view of the earlier actions. So, instead of Montagu going into the villages and Districts and learning first hand that communalism is an incipient problem, he apparently backed Gandhi, that architect of Hindu Raj – if not overtly, in many, many actions - and left the new Assemblies without the necessary controls fought for by successive Britons, to bring India into a state where they and their impartial and patient rule would not be needed.

But, the most serious action on his part was to abandon the careful directives of the India Act, taken through Parliament as the Mutiny was going on apace in India. At the keen advice of John Stuart Mill, writing the Report for the East India Company, ten or more, probably 15, advisers were to be on an 'Indian Council', to agree the actions of the Minister for India and advise. These men, who were to have spent at least ten years in India, were not to hold power, except that the Minister was not to send instructions to India without their agreement – which he could override, but in that case he had to give reasons. Only in great urgency might he act without their say-so.

Among the Montagu papers in Trinity College Cambridge, there are the details of the advice of Colonel Sir John Hose, already quoted. He warned Montagu that the Congress Report was inaccurate, untested evidence and clearly unsound. Montagu had given his speech in Parliament exactly on the Congress Report about which Sir John had warned.

As Sir Michael O'Dwyer returned to England and various officers, together with Miss Sherwood (miraculously recovered from near death), wrote to newspapers or dropped information at 10 Downing Street, more and more light was shed on the unrest in India. Montagu, giving permission to Reading to publish his dispatch, gave Lloyd George the opportunity, as Moon writes,[56] to 'take advantage' and to demand Montagu's resignation.

If Colonel Sir Mark Sykes had gone to India in the place of Montagu, with his clarity of insight and his knowledge of the difference between right and wrong, there

---

56    Moon says that the bulk of the people who took part in the Rebellion of 1919 were Muslim. I do not find this to be correct in view of the list of the claimants for compensation and the depositions for Sir Sankaran Nair and Sir Michael O'Dwyer.

is little doubt that the possibility of the rebellion coming to a head; might have been avoided.

His biographer, Roger Adelson ('Portrait of an Amateur', Cape 1975) thought Montagu could have competed with Churchill for the commanding position of the Tory party, although he called himself a 'Tory Democrat'.

When later, it came to looking at the information available through the processes of the Hunter Committee, he took no notice of the evidence, nor of Dyer's appeal to the Army Council, but almost as if he were one of the seditionists, took the view derived from propaganda. Churchill followed his friend with the purple phrases which helped us so much during the Second War.

Dyer would of course have known about Pan-Islam and its German links; he would have met many of those tragic Russian refugees and, being experienced with Indian methods of thought and talk, he would have known the quality of the rebels and recognised the tip of an iceberg which was in place to destroy the people of India in order to give power to a tiny few. The most extraordinary thing about the speeches of Montagu, speaking for the Government and for the Indian Nationalists, is that he did not mention the women and children having to be put in the Fort; he did not mention the hundred and more Indian women and children who had to join the British women, nor the Eurasians from the Railway houses, where the rioters, in their strategy to destroy the railway had killed, but only the action of General Dyer in firing on the mob when it collected again for further attack, taken completely out of context.

Lord Ampthill, a one time Viceroy, in the Lords Debate on the rebellion taking place in 1920, commented on the Hunter Committee which sat in 1919, *"But the most deplorable results of this delegation of the ordinary duties of the Indian Government* [to look into the matter of such a Rebellion] *was that the Hunter Committee failed to accomplish the ostensible object of their mission – namely the causes of the widespread disturbances. They were unable to discover, what was apparent to European and Indian alike, that there was a widespread and carefully organised conspiracy to overthrow the British Government in India by force. A conspiracy that was connected with the scheme for an Afghan invasion and which was within the cognisance of the enemies of England in other parts of the world. I beg your Lordships to take careful note of the facts that the Committee were very careful to refrain from saying that there was no evidence of such a conspiracy. What they said was that in the evidence before them there was nothing to show that the outbreak in the Punjab was part of a pre-arranged conspiracy. The evidence, however, was available, and available in abundance."*

So extraordinary was Montagu's attitude in the debate of 1920, that we have to accept that in some way either, his mind was taken over prior to 1917, or he was himself joined with those 'enemies of England in other parts of the world.' The application of the 250-year rule to information at the National Archives about Indian political infiltrators and the Third Afghan War must have been at his *dictat* and on his shoulders, rests the ensuing behaviour of Indian politicians, leading finally to the barbarous treatment of the people suffering from the division of India and Pakistan, (which the politicians insisted should not be policed by the British Army) and the present day threats of atomic warfare.

The reason for Montagu's attitude throughout, aggressive rather than impartial, as were the opinions of the Indian nationalists, has to be questioned, if the behaviour of the British Government over Dyer and the *laissez faire* treatment of Gandhi is to be seen in context. The epitome of his actions throughout was attack rather than observation and assessment. His attitude was as uncaring, as lacking in human concern as those of the Germans, the Turks in Armenia and the Bolsheviks in Russia. It was a time when mankind could have taken a giant step out of barbarism and did not. Sykes had warned of the corruption and evil and the background activities of the German/Turkish C.U.P. and still the powers that be in England did nothing. Dyer was treated appallingly for having saved India from that 'widespread and carefully organised conspiracy which was within the cognisance of the enemies of England in other parts of the world'. Though those words are Lord Ampthill's, they were implicit in the knowledge of 'Europeans and Indians alike'. With his attitude, Montagu damned the integrated development of India, which had been the role of the British for close on 300 years.

To Montagu's lack of comment on the dangers and sufferings of the women and children, or any mention of the background conspiracy, was added the usual propaganda clip; the ascribing of motives, in this case entirely untrue, as he would have known if he had glanced at Dyer's appeal to the Army Council.

In this context, it seems possible that his speech was written for him by one of the seditionist Indians then in London. As regards this possibility, Lord Ampthill's later words seem relevant: *"The persons who had organised the rebellion, had been baffled in their treasonable plot, got to work again. They brought pressure to bear on someone – perhaps upon the Secretary of State – and they either intimidated him or obtained his sympathy. It was then that the Hunter Committee was appointed* [with the inclusion, at Montagu's insistence, of the friend of Gandhi, Pandit Jagat Narayan] *nominally to investigate the nature of the causes of the disorders in Bombay, Delhi and the Punjab, but really to find some means of shielding the Government of India and the Secretary of State from the public blame which was being engineered against them – blame of which they were in unreasoning dread."*

The matter was put in a nutshell by Dyer, after listening to the speech by the Secretary of State, Edwin Montagu, a speech as treacherous to those Indians who had proved their support of law and order, as also to the men involved in putting the rebellion down, such as my father and the man at Kasur, Percy Marsden; *"Mr. Montagu is a very clever man, but he does not know India."* If he had and if he had read the Government reports on Dyer's action in the Sarhad, and later in Afghanistan, Montagu might have come out of the disastrous 'Looking Glass Land' into which he had run, and this must have helped India then and until we left. As it was, he set going disaster after disaster.

The only way in which he could have decapitated Brahmin power was to give to the Brahmins a Brahmin electorate, separated from the rest of the Hindu electorates: powerful men without power. It would not have worked for some time, but it would have given the Indian people the possibility of learning about democratic rule. I doubt whether he could have done it, and if he had, he would have been faced with the loss of his new found friends and almost undoubtedly, ignited a further rebellion.

Yet he did know something of the Indian mind and as far as he was able, he spoke out in 1921 to A. E. Woolacott, the 'Times' Correspondent. It was at the time of the dreadful Gandhi-organized rebellion in Malabar. He said with emphasis: *"We have granted these people a brand new Constitution and now, before the ink is dry, they are demanding another. I will be no part to any change unless it can be shown either, that the machinery of the Constitution has proved unworkable, or that those who are working it have given proof of fitness for further responsibility. Neither of these conditions exist and I may tell you that my position in this matter represents the considered position of His Majesty's Government."*

Woolacott goes on: *"In the latter days of his life, Montagu had no illusions about India. If he had lived longer, he would have seen further proof of the irresponsibility of the Legislative Assembly which, with the best of intentions, he had helped to create. The years immediately following the inauguration of the Reforms were years of strife and bloodshed in India and, unhappily, the Members of the Assembly have too often adopted implacable hostility towards measures designed to enable Government and its officers to suppress revolutionary conspiracies and to protect law abiding citizens"* ('India on Trial, A Study of Present Conditions'. 1927, Macmillan).

On 23rd March 1923, on the same day that Gandhi was arrested, Montagu gave his speech of resignation in the House. When he had power, he had regarded only the powerful, not those without power. His eyes were clouded, so that he could not see the difference between right and wrong, and could not appreciate the way that, almost like umpires, we had given India her chance of peace and happiness. He could not see what we had done, nor the intentions of the nationalist politicians, which he must have known about, but though the miasma had begun to clear, it was too late to go back to the advice of the men of experience, such as Sir Michael O'Dwyer or Lord Ampthill. We do not know whether he was motivated by pride or Liberal theory, or just did not see through the evil men who seem to have used him. Dyer, at the end, described him accurately: *"he did not know India"*. Those who suffered, continued to suffer, thanks to the men of power and ambition who considered the lower castes and casteless as merely pawns in the game.

It may be that it was the Divine Will that this man would be tempted by those who had no feelings except for themselves; that India should be merely incapable of continuing with an element of British rule.

It is significant that, in the 1950 Indian Constitution, discrimination was strictly forbidden between races, castes and religions. What then of the Untouchables? In the 1955 Act, renewed in the 1976 Act, 'Protection of Civil Rights', it has become illegal to call people 'Untouchable'. Is it an advance? Though the name has changed and they are now called Harijans, a rose by any other name, will smell as sweet.

# Chapter IX
# FINAL DEBATE

In February 1921, with Lord Chelmsford still Viceroy, the Montagu/Chelmsford Reforms were in place and the Legislative Council was now the Legislative Assembly. The Duke of Connaught, Queen Victoria's last surviving son, opened the Assembly with the words applied earlier by the Civil and Military Gazette to the Rebellion – 'A blot on the fair face of India' - but now, referring to General Dyer's action in the Jallianwalla Bagh.

Montagu's attempt to persuade Indian opinion that Britain had recognised Dyer's infamy had succeeded only among those who, for one reason or another, did not know the true nature of events. In India, the attitude had been taken that, due to the result of the debate in the House of Lords and the gift collected for General Dyer by the 'Morning Post', the whole British people stood behind the inhumanity of Dyer and no fair treatment of India could be expected from them. Nirad Chaudhuri had accepted Nehru's spurious description of General Dyer on the train, as being factual.

With Chelmsford leaving in April 1921, Indian leaders and politicians had written to Montagu to take on the Viceroyalty: Annie Besant for instance, writing *"You can make of your Reform Bill what none other can - using it for all it is worth - and it is worth a great deal as you described it. If it succeeds in winning Indian confidence, you will have saved India to the Empire, as well as have saved her from a state like Russia ...."*.

It was in a climate of admiration for Gandhi that the Debate took place, despite his order that people should not stand for the elections to the new Legislative Assembly. Jamnadas Dwarkadas, the first member of Gandhi's Satyagraha Committee in Bombay, stood and led the Debate.

The Debate on the Martial Law Administration took place in Delhi on 15th February 1921. The Resolution, having been somewhat modified, was accepted by Government and carried unanimously.

The Resolution as originally drafted ran as follows:

*"This Assembly recommends to the Governor General in Council* [the Viceroy's Cabinet, effectively]*:*

*1. To declare the firm resolve of the Government of India to maintain that the connection of India with the British Empire is based on the principle of equal partnership and perfect racial equality, Indian lives and Indian honour being held as sacred as British lives and honour;*

*2. to record his opinion and express regret that the Martial Law administration in the Punjab in 1919 departed from these principles and was calculated to deeply wound the self-respect of the Indian population by subjecting them to unnecessary hardship and humiliation.*

*3. to mete out deterrent punishments to officers who were found guilty of improper exercise of their powers and to take steps to relieve the Indian revenue of all payments towards the pensions gratuities or compassionate allowances to such officers; and*

*4. to satisfy himself that adequate compensation is awarded to the families of those killed or injured at the Jallianwalla Bagh or other places on the same scale as the compensation awarded in the cases of Europeans who suffered or were killed during the Punjab disturbances."*

The few words introducing the Final Debate by the Secretariat of the Punjab Government, ran thus: 'An important Resolution was moved by Mr. Jamnadas Dwarkadas at the meeting of the Legislative Assembly, held at Delhi on the 15th February 1921 on the administration of Martial Law in the Punjab in 1919. An interesting discussion took place and the non-official members of the Assembly argued the popular point of view with force and vigour; while the representatives of Government made frank speeches in explaining the sympathetic attitude of Government. Eventually the Resolution having been somewhat modified was accepted by Government and carried unanimously. It will not be devoid of interest to give a summary of the whole discussion.'

It is here that we come to Jamnadas Dwarkadas' Resolutions.

Jamnadas Dwarkadas, presumably in the Legislative Assembly at Gandhi's request or with his permission, opened the new approach. Reasonable punishment or prevention of rebellion, according to him, were humiliation - what he wanted, as Montagu also claimed in the House of Commons, was equality with white people.

Jamnadas Dwarkadas expatiated on the Resolutions in a lengthy speech: *"I would earnestly ask the Government of India and this Assembly to believe me when I say that in bringing forward this Resolution at the very opening of our first Session, I am animated by a desire not to open old wounds which are closed but to heal wounds which are festering in the very heart of India, wounds which can never be closed until this matter is faced with a real attempt on the side of each to appreciate the standpoint of the other by a frank exchange of views to lay the foundation of right and cordial co-operation in the new era which has opened for us all: that I am not moved by any wish to retaliate for the past but to give confidence to my people for the future. In an atmosphere of mutual distrust no good thing can grow. A fear exists that similar troubles may cause similar severity in the future and while we are prepared to support the Government in the preservation of order and the guarding of public security, we ask that no measures shall be taken which humiliate the loyal and estrange the patriotic, or in the words of the Secretary of State's despatch, are more like the actions of man in an enemy country than the treatment of fellow subjects, by those to whom they look for protection.*

*If this Resolution is met, as I venture to believe it will be, in the sincere desire for co-operation in which I offer it, then the past can be thrown behind us and we can go forward together and fulfil His Royal Highness' desire to forgive where we have to forgive and join hands and work together to realise the hopes that arise from today.*

*I am one of those who believe that the connection between Great Britain and India is essential. That it is conducive to the growth, prosperity and happiness of India and to the establishment of Great Britain as a mighty empire among the nations of the world. I believe that the connection between Great Britain and India is essential for the progress of both and for the welfare peace and progress of the world. I am emphatically of the opinion that the separation of India from Great Britain is not only detrimental to the interests of this country, but fatal, I venture to submit to its future importance."*

Coming to Clause II, the mover said: "The second clause of my resolution expresses India's feeling on the administration of Martial Law. It demands an expression of regret from the Government of India, holding that the principle enunciated in the first clause of my Resolution was departed from during the administration of Martial Law in the Punjab. I need hardly remind the House, that Indian opinion with one voice regrets the excesses committed by the mob and have time and again expressed severest condemnation of these excesses. It condemns equally Indians and English who exceeded the legitimate use of the great powers placed in their hands. With confidence I appeal to the Government to declare what I am sure they feel, that such excesses are condemned by them as strongly as they are by the public opinions of Indians."

The mover then proceeded to clause III and as discussion centred largely on this clause a lengthy quotation is justified:

"The third clause demands deterrent punishments to officers who were found guilty of improper exercise of their powers. In this connection I may be permitted to point out that the answer given to the question put by Mr. Sachchidananda Sinha in last September has failed to satisfy Indian opinion. Uncompromising critics of the Government apprehended that the latter would spare those who were responsible for the policy and allow their wrath to fall on Indian subordinates. We were loath to *believe it. But as hard fate would have it, Government, which unfortunately went on committing blunder after blunder, let off the real culprits with light penalties and two Indian subordinates whose guilt was proven but who, under no stretch of the imagination, could have had any hand in guiding the policy, were selected for a heavy punishment.*

*Both expediency and legal difficulties lie in the way of revising these punishments with the result that we start with a handicap when we make this demand.*

*I approach the whole of the third clause with some diffidence. Difficulties arise in its application that do not exist in others. I recognise that there is an apparent injustice in penalising guilty persons, as it were, a second time. An ordinary criminal once acquitted or lightly punished cannot be arraigned a second time even on new evidence. But, Sir, we do not know that all the officers concerned have been penalised and if they have been, it should be known for the future protection of our people. No Government need be ashamed of having done justice to the people whom it rules.*

*We do not know that justice has been done but we know that our people were wronged. At least let us know that those who have caused the bitterness in the Indian mind which has been played upon and enhanced by men who avowedly desire to break the connection between Great Britain and India so that it has become a menace to internal peace and an encouragement to external foes may at least be removed from immediate contact with people they have wronged."*

Mr. Jamnadas Dwarkadas' remarks on clause IV were as below:

*"The fourth clause is the putting into practice of the principle enunciated in the first. It demands that in awarding compensation, the status of persons killed or injured will be taken into equal consideration both in the case of the British and Indians. It is the proof that the Government regards Indian and British life and honour as equally sacred. Money in either case is a poor compensation for loss of life or for humiliation inflicted on the weak by the so-called strong. That is true in both cases; but it is equally true that such poor amends as can be made in money should be made equally in both cases."*

Mr. Chaudhri, in seconding the Resolution, adverted to the passage in His Royal Highness' speech on the administration of Martial Law in which he said: *"The employment of such measures is subject to clear and definite limitations and His Majesty's Government have always insisted and always insist on the observance of these limitations as jealously in the case of India as in that of England herself"*

Mr. Chaudhri welcomed this as an earnest for the future and then proceeded to outline the limitations to which Martial Law is subject in England.

Sir Jamset Jeejeebhoy confined himself mainly to clause III of the Resolution. He said: *"All Indian political parties demand the adequate punishment, on the lines indicated by the Mover, of those who have made improper use of their powers. Is it a wise policy on the' part of Government to withhold punishment where punishment is justly due? Let me not be misunderstood. I am not supporting Mr. Jamnadas' Resolution on the ground of mere political expediency only, but I attach greater importance to the consideration of bare justice. I hope therefore the Honourable the Home Member will see his way to withdraw his objection, if he has any, to clause III of the proposition before the House, and will recognise the imperative necessity of making a whole hearted response to the demand for justice which the Resolution contains."*

The next speaker was Mr. Harchand Rai Vishin Das. He was of the opinion that his Royal Highness had not been placed in possession of all the facts and he felt constrained to speak with some freedom on admittedly painful subjects. He contended that General Dyer's action was wholly unjustified. While condemning emphatically the brutal behaviour of the mob at Amritsar on the 11th April, he considered that General Dyer fired on an entirely peaceful meeting. The introduction of Martial Law was unnecessary and a blunder. The indignities inflicted on Indians demanded redress, and he pressed for further punishment of officials in certain cases. He considered that reparation should precede any appeal for forgiveness.

His Excellency the Commander in Chief in a brief speech said, *"Having only recently returned to India, and not being in any way officially connected with the Amritsar disturbances of 1919, I think I can claim to be in a position to view this deplorable affair dispassionately and without bias. In doing so I must support my predecessor in so far as punishments that were awarded to the military officers are concerned, and, though I am fully alive to the mistakes and the errors that were committed and though I fully appreciate and weigh the remarks that have been made by the Proposer and Seconder of this motion, I must adhere to the attitude that has been adopted by my predecessor Sir Charles Monro. The case has already been adjudicated on by the highest military authority. I am strongly averse to reopening the question of those punishments, especially after what has been said in this Chamber by His Royal Highness the Duke of Connaught in opening it. Such a course, notwithstanding the arguments that have been put forward by Members who have already taken part in this debate, would, in my opinion, do no good and might conceivably do an infinity of harm."*

In concluding he added with emphasis: *"I desire to repudiate any idea that the repressive measures which may be necessary should be intended directly to influence other situations at a distance from the immediate seat of the disturbance itself. In other words, it is no part of the duty of an officer, in such circumstances, to attempt to produce a moral effect upon the country at large."*

There followed the anxiously awaited speech of the Home Member, the Honourable Sir William Vincent. He referred to the extreme importance of the debate. Indian and European opinion alike was waiting the result of the debate and feelings were excited on both sides. He dwelt on the imperative need of moderation in discussing the Resolution before the House. He complimented the Mover on the manner in which he had brought forward his case. He was glad of the opportunity of doing what he could to allay the deep feeling of resentment which prevailed even among men of a reasonable frame of mind and of explaining the attitude of Government, which he believed, quite honestly, to have been grievously misunderstood by many. He realised that Indians felt very bitterly in this matter, the iron had entered deeply into their souls. But he thought it was necessary that both sides should be careful on certain points, namely that there were many things on both sides which were in every way reprehensible, which every honest man must condemn and bitterly regret.

On the one hand we have wanton murders, crimes of violence unparalleled at any rate for many years in the history of this country, dacoity, arson, looting, attacks on communications and other crimes of a very grave nature which at one time threatened the very structure of the administration. On the other hand, we have over-drastic and severe punishment, the excessive use of force and acts which have been interpreted and, I am afraid, reasonably interpreted, as calculated to humiliate the Indian people in a manner which cannot but be regarded as unpardonable, morally indefensible at any time but more so than ever at a time when the Government is about to enter upon a system of responsible Government.

Beginning with the most noteworthy case of such action, that of General Dyer, the Government of India stood entirely by their despatch of May and the despatch of His Majesty's Government. Quoting from these papers, the Government of India considered that General Dyer 'had exceeded the reasonable requirements of the case, beyond what any reasonable man would have thought to be necessary, and he did not act with as much humanity as the case permitted'. The Home Government had laid down for such cases the principle of 'using the minimum force necessary' and the Government of India endorsed this.

The Government of India dissociated itself from the attitude taken by certain persons both in this country and in England - even in Parliament, on this question.

The Government of India repudiated the idea that the lives of Indians are valued more lightly than the lives of any other of His Majesty's subjects, or that Martial Law may be enforced more rigorously in India than elsewhere. Honourable Members would see that drastic measures being taken in Ireland were in many ways more severe than those taken in India. The Government of India desired emphatically to repudiate the idea that an officer is entitled to treat the honour of Indians lightly or to take any measure, which tends to humiliate them. With these remarks the Honourable Home Member said that he trusted that he had met the first part of the Honourable Mover's Resolution.

Proceeding to Part II of the Resolution, Sir William Vincent said that the great majority of the officers of Government behaved with all propriety and consideration. *"But there were many cases of improper conduct by individuals - conduct which might indeed be described by a worse adjective - for which we can only express deep regret. I may say at once, however, that this expression of regret for the acts of individual officers, while general in character extends in particular to those actions which were calculated, or believed to be calculated, to humiliate Indians, and which caused such resentment among the people of this country."*

The Home Member expressed the regret of the Government of India to Mr. Manohar Lal and Mr. Gurdial Singh for their detention under arrest for an unreasonably long period.

The Home Member believed that many of the mistakes made were due to inexperience and to want of proper instructions as to the duties of both of Military and Civil officers; for the future, Government had caused to be prepared a Manual of Instructions for the use of officers, if unhappily they should be called upon to face a similar situation. In these instructions it was made clear that the use of force was to be strictly limited to the real necessity, that the issue of Martial Law orders was to be strictly limited, that the ordinary Courts of Law were to continue, as far as possible, to deal with ordinary crime, that improper punishments were not to be awarded, and, above all, anything likely to cause racial humiliation to any class of His Majesty's subjects must be avoided. Proceeding to Part III of the Resolution, the Honourable Sir William Vincent first cited the following passage from the speech of Lord Sinha in the House of Lords: *"I desire to make it dear that what my fellow countrymen in India desire is the vindication of principles and not the punishment of individuals. That is of secondary importance. Indeed it is of importance only so far as it tends to give effect - adequate or otherwise - to your vindication."*

The Home Member asserted that the authors of the Congress Report took much the same view.

He went on to say: *"And on this question of punishment and the wisdom of opening various matters which have been fully investigated and adjudicated on by His Majesty's Government, I would ask Honourable Members to bear in mind certain general principles. I do not speak of provocation, to which I understood the Honourable Member to refer, but I feel strongly that Members of this Assembly should attempt to realise the very difficult, dangerous and unprecedented situation with which our officers were faced. It is easy now, in the calm atmosphere of this council to criticise the conduct of these officers, to find fault with this act and that act, to say that an officer behaved wrongly here and wrongly there. But I should-like individual members of this Assembly to put themselves for one moment In the place of these officers and say honestly, if they were in such a difficult land terrible situation, whether they would not have been guilty of some indiscretion, some errors or worse. There are those Sir, who do not realise the serious nature of these disorders and who even now, say they were of a minor character, and there was no attempt to subvert the Government. This is a matter on which Government have no doubt, and I would ask any Member who really has misgivings on this matter to read for himself once again, not the opinion of those who investigated the doings and disorders but the history of events, to read the speeches delivered, to examine again the posters published at Lahore and elsewhere, to study the maps annexed to the reports, recall the murders and various outrages committed and the widespread and deliberate attacks on communications; and I think he will be satisfied himself, that these officers were faced with a very grave and very difficult situation, and it was essential - I do not defend the improper acts I wish to be carefully understood on this point - but I do seek to say that it was essential that these disorders should be quelled very speedily. The men who had to deal with the situation had to come to decisions of the utmost moment, promptly and without a second thought. Can anyone of us say that in such a crisis, when faced with responsibility for the lives of others, his conduct would have been such that it would not have been open to criticism, if judged in the calm atmosphere of this Assembly, at a great distance of time and place? Would not any Member of this Assembly, if he were on trial for errors, for culpable conduct, for improper actions, demand consideration for the circumstances - would he not say, 'I am entitled to be blamed for what I have done, I am liable to be punished, but I am entitled to receive consideration for the very difficult position in which I was placed, and I am entitled to ask that those in authority over me shall consider what my previous record of service has been and what my conduct in the past has been towards Indians and towards the Government. I believe that every Member of this Assembly, I believe that the Honourable Mover himself, if he had really any subordinate under his control, would give the fullest consideration to these factors in assessing punishments. Our officers are not perfect instruments and they never will be. They are liable to err, to yield to evil, like anyone else. In such circumstances, I submit to this Assembly that it is perfectly right that Government should express in unmistakable language their disapproval of improper acts, that they should take every step to prevent their recurrence and that they should express their deep regret to those who have suffered, even that they should make reparation - and I will explain what I mean by this later - so far as it is in their power. But the punishment must not be vindictive and must bear relation to all the circumstances of the case. And it is in this view, the Government have approached these cases, It would have been perfectly easy for us to sacrifice an individual, to dismiss an officer and so satisfy public opinion. But Government has to be just to its officers as well as to the public, and it is in that spirit that they have approached the question, which is now under discussion. There is no question of maintaining prestige or anything of that kind. The Government have only done what they believe to be just and I ask the Assembly to believe that we have attempted to act honestly and that we have done what its right to the best of our judgement, what we believe to be right, without regard to prestige of any kind. I may add that we have been criticised with some severity for the action that we have already taken, I hope also that this Assembly will consider in their minds, what the effect of excessive severity must be, whether any Government, any Administration, can expect its officers to do their duty if they are treated with undue harshness. Members of this Assembly will remember that our officers may at any moment be called upon to face similar situations - I hope not of such gravity - but there are forces of disorder abroad. Our men must be called on from time to-time to decide as to what immediate action ought to be taken to suppress disorder and riots, when force is to be used, when they are not to use it and I firmly believe that if, in the cases under discussion, undue severity, not reasonable severity, but undue severity, is used, it will be most disastrous to the administration of this country. And I ask this Assembly, now taking a large part in the administration and as influencing this Government, to remember that, as a cardinal factor in dealing with the merits of this case."*

At a later stage in the Debate, the Honourable the Home Member took the opportunity of explaining the actual effect of a censure on an officer in the Service of the Crown, as he believed that Honourable Members had perhaps not appreciated this sufficiently. He said: *"not only does it have a material effect on a man's promotion, but, apart from that, it attaches a stigma to him which it takes many years to efface."* He was able to quote from a letter received by Government from one of the officers censured, in which that officer, in asking for long leave to England, expressed his firm intention to seek a new career, seeing that he had been blackmarked and that using his own words, 'my career in this country is blasted'.

The Home Member was discussing some individual cases of punishment when his time limit expired. He was however permitted to add the following remarks on clause IV of the Resolution: *"The Government do not admit any legal liability on this account. Even if the loss of life is due to the misconduct on the part of an individual officer, I do not think that Government ought to accept liability on that account. Nor do they think that the position of these men is on the same footing as those of persons murdered at Amritsar and Lahore who have a statutory right of compensation. At the same time, we feel that the message of His Royal Highness is addressed as much to us as to the Indians, that it applied to Europeans officials, non-official Indians, all alike. We are very anxious to go as far as possible to meet the Honourable Mover. We are also very anxious to do what we can to obliterate ill feeling over this matter. Therefore, though we cannot admit liability, yet we are prepared to make an admission that the grants of money to those who suffered at Jallianwalla Bagh and those injured by aeroplanes at Gujranwala have not been generous, or possibly adequate, and we are prepared to ask the Punjab Government to increase the amounts and deal with those men or their dependants, in the case of those who are unfortunately dead, in a much more generous manner than has been done in the past."*

Mr. A. B. Latthe then moved an amendment to Clause II, to confine the expression of regret to some of those adopted in the course of Martial Law administration. He pointed out that it was more reasonable to do this than to condemn the entire Martial Law administration.

Sir William Vincent cited the Congress Report to show that the number of officers held blameworthy was very small compared with the large number of officers employed.

Bhai Man Singh supported the original Resolution.

Mr. Saniarth argued that the original Resolution cast no reflection on individual officers who may have administered the Martial Law in a humane spirit.

The amendment was put and negatived.

Clauses I and II were then put to the House and carried.

The debate continued on Clause III.

Mr. Darcy Lindsay on behalf of the elected European Members identified himself with the views and sentiments expressed by the Home Member. He had hoped that the Mover of the Resolution would have seen his way to withdraw Clause III, in view of what had fallen from the Home Member.

Mr. Jatkar then moved an amendment to Clause III in which he proposed the appointment of a Committee to determine in the light of information afforded by the Hunter and Congress Reports, the officers who, in their opinion, were guilty of improper exercise of their powers, and report them to His Excellency the Governor-General with a view to deterrent punishment being meted out to them.

Dr. Sir Deva Prasad Sarbadhikari opposed the reopening of the whole enquiry contemplated by Mr. Jatkar. He was however of the opinion that more severe punishment should be imposed on certain officers. By 'deterrent' punishment he did not necessarily mean drastic, revengeful punishment or severe in the ordinary sense of the term, but punishment that shall deter in the future improper exercise of powers. He realised the difficulties in the way of Government.

Mr. Jatkar's amendment was negatived.

Sir Godfrey Fell, Secretary Military Department, addressed himself to the conduct of these military officers whose conduct had been impugned in connection with the disturbances of 1919. He pointed out that in the case of the military officer primarily concerned, the only action which the Government of India was competent to take, was to call upon him to retire. Any further action lay with the Army Council. Sir Godfrey Fell emphasised the severity of the punishment for a military officer of being called upon to retire in the circumstance in which this officer left the Army.

As regards the General Officer who despatched airmen to Gujranwala, Sir Godfrey Fell dwelt on the difficulty of his position seeing that Gujranwala was isolated and immediate action had to be taken. Any excessive action taken by the six officers was not so much due to errors of judgement on their part, as to the fact that orders issued to them were not sufficiently explicit.

Government had strongly condemned the use of 'fantastic" penalties'. Every officer whose conduct had been impugned had received various degrees of censure. But, he said, *"on the whole question of the administration of Martial Law, the Government of India have pointed out that the officers charged with the administration of Martial Law cannot be expected to act, in abnormal conditions with that care and circumspection which are possible in normal times, nor can such a standard be rigorously applied for the examination of their actions as might be applied in the calm atmosphere of safety after order has been restored."*

Sir Godfrey Fell proceeded to assure the assembly that the disciplinary action taken was precisely the same as would have been taken if the officers concerned had conducted themselves in exactly the same way against a riotous and dangerous crowd of Englishmen, Irishmen, Scotsmen, or Welshmen. He mentioned this as he had heard it suggested that officers were leniently treated because they were dealing with Indians.

Finally Sir Godfrey Fell dwelt on the repugnance of the Army to being called in to deal with civil disturbances and he asked for sympathy with them in this extremely distasteful duty. He maintained that, on the whole, the Army acquitted itself very well in 1919 in exceptionally trying circumstances, their relations with the civil community being marked by tact, conciliation and restraint.

The Honourable Dr. Sapru accepted the view that a deterrent punishment was one which would deter officers in the future from repeating conduct which was the subject of controversy. The issue was therefore narrowed to this: Are the punishments which have been inflicted such that we may, as reasonable persons believe that on a similar occasions which may arise in the future, with the additional circumstance that fresh instructions on the subject are being issued, our officers are likely to repeat the same course of conduct which has exposed them to attack?

Dr. Sapru was prepared to believe that the punishments inflicted, which involved officers in obloquy, would have a restraining effect. He however, ventured to think that the substantial portion of Resolution was that which sought to vindicate the honour and self-respect of India: Government had, it would be admitted, shown a proper sense of courage and propriety in admitting and expressing in unequivocal language their regret for the excesses of certain officers. In Dr. Sapru's opinion, the question of punishment was of minor importance.

Mr. Eardley Norton, as one who laboured for and with Indians for 43 years, identified himself with them in their feelings as regards Amritsar and other incidents. The Mover had, in a sense, justly asked for the further punishment of certain officials. But he appealed to the generosity of Indians. He asked them to forget and forgive on this point. He felt certain that this would bring them all the nearer and closer to the Englishmen, and would lead up to the great accomplishment of the political end which was their ambition.

Mr. Cotellingarn and Mr. Kamat supported Mr. Eardley Norton's appeal and endorsed the view of the Honourable the Law Member that the most important portions of the Resolution were Clauses I and II. Mr. Kamat considered that the Mover had obtained practically all that he wanted. He said: *"We have had from the Government of India an assurance about the equality of status between Indians and Europeans. We have also had a condemnation of the officers concerned with the Punjab affairs. We have also had an assurance that a manual of instructions for the prevention of indiscriminate use of Martial Law will be prepared for the guidance of officers. We have also had an assurance that adequate compensation, even generous compensation should be awarded to people who have not been granted compensation. I believe these are all gains we have secured. I believe that, if we do not press for punishments, we shall close the chapter in a spirit of goodwill. If we press for Clause III firstly, there are certain objections from the point of view of the Army Regulations, secondly there are objections from the legal point of view in enhancing punishments, and, thirdly, as I have explained, on general political grounds, in view of the spirit in which we are entering upon our task, it would be highly impolitic, unstatesmanlike, and it would be violating the spirit of fellowship in which we have entered our new life."*

Mr. Janinadas Dwarkadas, rising to reply said that, after listening to the statements made by the Home Member, the Military Secretary and the Law Member, he felt convinced that it was not advisable for him and for his colleagues to press Clause III to a division. Opinions might differ as regards the suitability of the punishments awarded, but he was now convinced that Government, in dealing with the case, had not been influenced by considerations of race. This was the point that had struck him most in the Honourable the Home Member's statement. He asked the Assembly to support him in withdrawing Clause III.

The motion to withdraw Clause III. was affirmed by the House.

Clause IV was put and carried.

Before the Resolution was put as a whole, Dr. Sir D P Sarbadhikari made the following remarks:'

*"Sir, the other day, amidst pomp, splendour and grandeur this Assembly was inaugurated. Today in our own inner circle, we have decided to perform a ritual, which to my mind has a very high significance. In all temples, consecrated to the uplifting of humanity, purification is necessary. The atmosphere has to be cleared up and we are attempting it to the best of our powers. As Mr. Eardley Norton has said, one of the great difficulties, in the way of public men outside this Assembly, has been this Punjab question. It was necessary that the united mind of the representatives of the people, whose representative character may be lightly challenged by irresponsible people, it was necessary that the united mind of India, such as it is, should be expressed here in the most unequivocal terms. That has been done today. We can never hope to reconcile the irreconcilable; but so far as in us lies; it will be our duty to go forward on the path of moderation and sanity. Of that we have the earnest today. I congratulate the Honourable Mover on the way he has brought forward this motion, and the representatives of the Government who have met us more than halfway. We hope, Sir, that this augury will be always helpful and the affairs of the Assembly will be conducted in the way they have begun today."*

Mr Jamnadas Dwarkadas said: *"I endorse the views expressed by my friend, Mr. Norton, and by my friend, Sir Deva Prasad Sarbadhikari. I would remind this Assembly of the fact that today we close the chapter of the Punjab, that there should be no more Punjab in this Assembly, and if we can help it, anywhere in the country.*

*Let bygones be bygones. We have a good deal of work to do in the future. There are many problems awaiting very tactful handling and the highest and best in us will be called upon to bring about the solution of these problems. Let us then put our heads together, non-officials and officials, with one aim of leading India as soon as possible to the goal of responsible government, work together like men, and I can assure this House that the end is certain, a complete triumph."*

The Resolution as amended was then put and carried.

Lord Chelmsford, who had come to India as a Captain in a Territorial Regiment, for reasons not understood by us, was appointed Viceroy in 1916 by the India Office, whose avowed aim was to get the British out of India. Hence we see the Montagu/Chelmsford reforms as a beginning of the unwise surrender to unrepresentative Indian politicians. So Dyer, who was such a fine fellow in May, became a scapegoat in October, simply and solely to appease the Indian politicians. Dyer asked for a Court of Enquiry or a Court Martial, first in India and again at home, but it was refused in both countries.

# PART 6
# THE AFTERMATH

## Chapter I
## THE OUTCOME

Though Sir Michael O'Dwyer's book "India as I Knew It" was not published until 1925, it refers to the trials of offenders, largely because in the case O'Dwyer v. Nair (1924), the behaviour of officers in the Martial Law period was laid at O'Dwyer's door. He firstly gives chapter and verse for the placing of Martial Law adjudication in the hands of the military. He had suggested to the Government that it should be subject to the advice of the far more experienced officers in the civil administration. Government had overruled his request. Nonetheless, the officers, many of them in the Indian Army, were men of experience in India. He quotes Colonel Johnson (in charge of Martial Law in Lahore) in his instructions to law officers; *"Officers will not allow resentment to obscure their judgment in the proper administration of justice. In the measures undertaken under Martial Law, there should never be any suspicion of resentful retaliation."*

Having made plain his own opinion of the various orders, criticising only the crawling order [it is necessary here to bear in mind that although he knew India well, he had not, like General Dyer, been brought up in India and would not have known what Miss Sherwood knew, about the actual genuflecting concept that underlay it] he went on: *"A little knowledge of Punjab customs would have given the Committee a clearer insight; but it did not, unfortunately contain a single member who had ever exercised administrative authority anywhere in India, and five out of the eight members were lawyers."* One explanation of the whipping sentences (258 were so punished out of 1,800 people convicted) is that nearly half of these whippings were inflicted in out of the way places - Kasur, Chukharna, etc., far from a jail, and in the absence of railway facilities, where it was deemed expedient to inflict the punishment on the spot rather than send the prisoner to a distant jail to be imprisoned. There were even cases in which the prisoner asked to be whipped rather than fined.

In 'The District Officer in India', there is a case where the culprit was delighted to be whipped; and for poor people who needed their men folk earning rather than imprisoned, caning was a very real preference. Whipping with a cane is a recognised punishment in the Indian Criminal Law, and is a very mild affair as compared with the English flogging with the cat.

The Government of India's opinion on the matter of Martial Law administration was that it accepted the view of the Hunter Committee that the administration of Martial Law in the Punjab was marred in particular instances by a misuse of power, by irregularities, and by injudicious and irresponsible acts.

They went on to say: *"It is to inexperience, to ignorance of local conditions, and lack of guidance when confronted with an abnormal situation, rather than to deliberate misuse of power, that most of the mistakes committed must be ascribed."*

O'Dwyer continued: *"They then, very sagely, lay down the principles, that any area in which in future it may be necessary to enforce Martial Law, senior officers should be appointed to act as advisers to the various military authorities, but they unfortunately omitted to state that this was the very system that I had proposed to them on the 16th April, viz., general civil supervision of Martial Law administration, but which they had decisively vetoed on 18th April when they directed me to abdicate in favour of the General Officer Commanding* [General Beynon].

*In his despatch of 26th May, 1920, Mr. Montagu criticised the Hunter Committee for inadequate condemnation of these 'improper punishments and orders'.*

*He added that these things would not have occurred 'had the civil authority been able to retain a larger measure of contact with the administration of Martial Law,' and pointed out what the Government of India had overlooked. 'That as regards the administration of Martial Law generally, Sir Michael O'Dwyer had evidently contemplated an arrangement by which civil officers would be accorded a recognised position to advise on military administration.'*

*In this matter I personally had no reason to complain of the dispatch, but the result of the orders was the censure or other punishment of many officers, civil and military, who had done splendid service in repressing the rebellion and who were sacrificed by an ungrateful Government to the clamour of the very men who had engineered that rebellion. What makes the action of the Coalition Government, of whom Mr. Montagu professed to be only the mouthpiece the more deplorable, is that neither the Government of India nor the Secretary of State expressed any detestation or condemnation of the acts of the rebels and murderers. Indeed, six months before they decided to punish their own officers, they had by a premature amnesty or commutation of sentences, liberated all but 5 per cent of the eighteen hundred persons convicted of waging war, murder, arson, robbery, wrecking railways and telegraphs, and other such offences. Their thunder was reserved for their own loyal but unfortunate servants. No wonder! a loyal Sikh magistrate exclaimed, 'How long can a Government last from which its friends have nothing to hope, its enemies have nothing to fear?'*

*The only result of this sacrifice of their principles, their servants and their friends to placate their enemies has been to excite the contempt of, and encourage further defiance by, the latter. They doubtless reason like my Irish Republican friends; 'And who could have any respect for a Government that lets down its own people?'*

Sir Michael went on to write about the comparison between the Punjab and Malabar Rebellions; *"The lesson was not lost on the enemies of British rule or on the servants of Government in India ... the consequence would appear when the Government of India had again to handle a rebellion."*

Sir Michael meets the extracts from the fortnightly reports thus: *"Much has been said and written of the Martial Law atrocities. The unscrupulous propaganda, so sedulously pursued by the extremists to discredit the weapon which had foiled their designs and to vilify those who had made use of it, created a widespread impression both in England and in India that the authorities, military and civil, went out of their way to inflict racial humiliation on Indians. The Government of India at that time were 'on the run' and left the field open to the Indian extremists, while Mr. Montagu's unfortunate speech in the Dyer Debate lent some support to that grossly unjust view."*

One matter does not appear in the Fortnightly Reports or in the details of allegations against the Government servants in the Congress Reports - the links of the conspirators with the Afghan War. Sir Michael's exceptionally able review of the events under the last days of his administration (he left the Punjab on 26th May and came to Bombay on 29th May 1919) deals with the Afghan rising as well as the events under Martial Law.

*"It was and is, common knowledge, that the Afghan invasion and tribal risings were encouraged, if not instigated, by emissaries from Delhi and Amritsar and that early in April, on receiving news of the outbreak of 30th March at Delhi, the Amir had begun moving troops towards our border. Meantime, Afghan intrigue had been busy throughout India, and, as in April, the Afghan Foreign Minister had written to the Afghan envoy at Simla asking him to obtain allegiance from Hindus and Mohammedans. 'Afghanistan shares the feelings of the Indians and is determined to support them. If you get the chance please get exciting articles* [a similar ruse to that being carried out by the German Press against the British from 1870 on] *inserted in newspapers. It is essential that Ghulam Hasan and other agents should win over the hearts of Hindus and Mussulmans, win favour with the Hindus, remove the ill-feeling of Mussulmans against Hindus, induce the Hindus to unite with the Mussulmans'* [against the British]. *The result of these nefarious plots was that the Chief Commissioner at Peshawar warned us to be on the look out for outbreaks on 15th May, the date originally fixed for the Afghan attack and simultaneous risings in India.'* This was the time when the Government of India were pressing us in the Punjab to abolish Martial Law!

*The above information tallied with what I had heard about 20th April, that the Punjab risings of 10th to 15th April were premature, precipitated probably by the rumours of Gandhi's arrest and the removal of Satyapal and Kitchlew from Amritsar* *on 10th April. It was fortunate for us that the rebellion went off at 'half-cock' before the Afghan and Frontier tribes were ready. Peshawar was really the key position in the larger movement contemplated. But Mr. Montagu, when questioned in Parliament, said there had been <u>no disturbance in Peshawar,</u>* [Author's underline] *and he distinctly excluded Peshawar from the ambit of the Hunter Committee which was only authorised to 'investigate the recent disturbances in Bombay, Delhi, and the Punjab, their causes and the measures taken to cope with them.' Hence the Committee refused to take any evidence showing the connection between the Punjab rebels and Afghanistan and the Frontier tribes. Had they done so they would have hesitated to put on record the extraordinary view that <u>on the evidence before us there is nothing to show that the outbreak in the Punjab was part of a pre-arranged conspiracy to overthrow the British Government-in India by force.</u>"* [Author's underline]

How opposed that extraordinary view was, even to Afghan admissions, is shown by the statement of Ali Ahmed Khan, the principal Afghan member of the delegation sent to sue for peace after the Afghan defeat. He said publicly in the mosque at Rawalpindi on 1st August 1919, that 'the recent action of Afghanistan (i.e. the Invasion of British India) had been the result of her sympathy with the Indian Mussulmans.' That statement was made eight months <u>before</u> [Author's underline] the Hunter Committee Report was submitted. Even so, the evidence of the doings in Peshawar was put in front of the Committee in the secret sessions.

In the hearing of the case O'Dwyer v Nair, the bearing of the Afghan menace on the situation in the Punjab and on the measures we had to take there, was clearly realised by the Judge and duly impressed on the Jury.

At Ahmedabad, the bulk of the cases against those arrested were dismissed as there was not sufficient *prima facie* evidence against them, so the accused were set free.

There were no fatal casualties in the Bombay Presidency among the rioters. The two fatalities on the side of those attacked by them were Sergeant Frazer of the police, who was hacked to death, and the Mamlatdar at Viramgam, who was thrown off a balcony where he was hiding and burnt to death under a drenching of kerosene oil.

Six months after the incident in Amritsar and the massive gatherings to thank him, there was a determined attempt to persuade the people of India that what Dyer had done was in keeping with the claim made by Gandhi and the claims of Mrs. Besant that the British were brutal. The Hunter Committee was appointed, but this took some months to get up a head of steam and by the time the Hunter Committee sat and questioned Dyer, three months had passed, including the hot weather and General Dyer's exhausting campaign on the Frontier, where he had relieved the British troops under siege at Thal. In the same way as after his Sarhad Campaign, the Army congratulated him for his actions.

With the Indian members of the Committee having disagreed with the Majority (the British members with the Chairman), they gave their opinion on the firing. First, that he started firing without giving the people who had assembled a chance to disperse; second, that he continued firing for a substantial period of time after the crowd had commenced to disperse. Their opinion illustrates their lack of knowledge or their deliberate ignoring of the then current army practice of dispersing hostile crowds by firing over the heads of the people. An example appears in the report of the clearing of the station yard at Viramgam by police in PART 3 Chapter III.

On the second point, the dispersal was hindered by the deliberately locked gate, part of the crowd turning back on itself and posing a threat to the soldiers and Dyer's concern that this murderous crowd should have no opportunity to re-form.

The supportive evidence was that it was not known to what the crowd were listening. In the Punjab Government Report, evidence was given that they were listening to poems on murder. We do not have any record of the poems being read in the Jallianwalla Bagh on 13th April, but if they were similar to the example recorded in APPENDIX IV of the kind of verse being written at the time, in the rhythm of war songs, it was not surprising that Dyer on arrival had met a 'vast and hostile crowd' as he told Miles Irving later. It is ridiculous that Gandhi should have claimed that the Indians were gentle people and the British violent.

Hunter, as with the conspiracy cases, did not use the Punjab Government Report. Dyer and Briggs knew it to be 'a vast and hostile crowd'. Miles Irvine knew this well enough for his wife to tell their daughter, Margaret, this when she was twelve. To claim that the crowd was peaceful is really very silly, taken in context. The reason for this interpolation is that it was on the Hunter comment and on the hysterical attack on his name that the Commander in Chief, Sir Michael Carmichael Monro, ordered Dyer home on retirement, on grounds of ill-health. Monro had been a friend of Dyer previously and he knew of his record; when one reads the lengthy correspondence between him and Montagu in 1920, it is possible to credit that he did this in order to save Dyer from worse. Once Dyer had been invalided out and retired, which at 55 was not exceptional, he was safe. Certainly, if the disgusting attacks on him are left on one side, he had retired, had not lost his pension and was able to live in England in peace. Monro is one of the people whom Montagu met and spoke to frequently in India and is also one of the few people who are on record with his own opinion of Montagu's behaviour.

The constant denigration of anything done by Government continued. Gandhi, editing 'Young India', denounced the Military Tribunals. Looking at this today, we can but remark on the openness of a Government that, after an outrageous rebellion, with the main leaders deeply involved with our enemies, we gave those same leaders so much leeway to criticise the cases in which their own comrades took part.

On the matter of alterations in India, 'The Hindustan' an extremist paper, declared that the abolition of the Secretary of State's Council was a triumph for the Congress which had been demanding its removal for years. The Secretary of State's Council was made up of eminent retired Indian administrators and Army officers. Without it, a Secretary of State who, like Edwin Montagu, probably knew little if anything about India, having been to India only on brief visits, would be unable to turn to men of experience for advice. The ensuing years were to show that Secretaries of State would, like Montagu, be almost subservient to the Indian politicians whom, they could not realise, were out of touch with their own people.

Nothing was beyond the constant criticism by the Press in general and by the constitution of the Joint Committee of Parliament to discuss the reforms. 'The Jugantur', a newspaper for the backward classes, found that the Committee contained few who favoured the demands of the non-Brahmins. The extremist papers as well as the moderate ones, looked askance at the Joint Committee, on the ground that it contained reactionary elements, particularly from the House of Lords [this probably meant Lord Sydenham amongst others] and it was expected that the Committee would not go beyond the Southwold recommendations.

The attitude of disagreement with any man who was in favour of the stability of British rule was shown in the criticism of the appointment of Mr. Shafi in the place of Sankaran Nair on the Viceroy's Executive Council. While 'The Muslim Herald' expressed gratification, the other newspapers called him a slavish adherent of Government and 'damaging criticism' emanating from one of the Punjab cases was quoted against him. In fact, this man was one of the most outstanding men from the Punjab, a friend of the first Prime Minister, Fazli Hussein, and one of the men whose presence in the Viceroy's Council was to help India to overcome the effects of the rebellion.

So we come to the end. We see British amelioration triumphing over a merciless Rebellion - one that brooked fair to becoming a second Great Indian Mutiny, except that while Indian soldiers mutinied in 1857, by 1919 were loyal to the Crown and defended Britain and the standards and civilisation for which we stood. They would do so in the main again in the next war. They did not, like the sepoys in 1857, turn from playing with the white children on the officers' verandas to murdering them and their parents. With the characteristically euphemistic terminology of a later age, the Mutiny, on which so many of the steps of this next rising were based, had become 'The First War of Independence'. The Indian population appears not to have looked closely at the facts, but just accepted what it was told.

Penderel Moon said that the mutineers had been inspired by loot; Lord Roberts, that the Brahmin oligarchy had become afraid of the power of Christianity.

In 1919, it was certainly Brahmin-led to a large extent and loot was the main incentive of the mobs. They may have been paid and organised, but the loot that could be carried away from a bank was far more important then the shouts of 'kill all English, Gandhi ki Jai'.

In the final count it was, as I hope I have made clear, not Dyer, but the nationalist leaders who made Jallianwalla Bagh inevitable, by their claims that the peaceable English would not fire, that the Raj was dead, that if men went to the Bagh, Land Tax would be stopped - that they would be rewarded. The little boy with a drum supported it all; and then, once the crowd was in the Bagh, the locking of the gates so that as many as possible out of the 20,000 or more would be killed.

## THE OUTCOME

Dyer did not make the situation in the Bagh, he merely had to deal with it, to prevent the wild-fire spread of a Rebellion that would become inextinguishable. 'Rawly', General Rawlinson, who had threatened to refuse to go to India if Dyer and the officers were penalised, did finally go. Sir Godfrey Fell picked out one innocuous phrase with which he could have agreed, but omitted to point out that Dyer, the officer in command of the Jullundur area, could properly refer to the area outside Amritsar with concern because it was within his responsibility. Rawly went on to lift the censures from the officers, but some of them had already left when he arrived.

Black is white and white is black; fair is foul and foul is fair. The officer involved had gone quietly into retirement. Apart from writing of his concerns about India in 'The Globe' and writing about his adventures in the Sarhad, Dyer claimed no more attention. We would know nothing of him afterward, but for a boy of eight who saw him walking out with his wife, leaning on her arm, and knowing that he was a 'great man'.

The activities of the Indian political leaders were those of men and women who did not care for the people, who had none of the humane sense they claimed Dyer lacked. Behind the scenes, they stirred up feelings against Dyer that Amritsar at the beginning did not feel, for Amritsar knew from what she had been saved. In the spiritual terms of Dr. Sir D. P. Sarbardhikari, it was Dyer, by his sacrifice of himself in his acceptance of the orders to retire on grounds of sickness and through his suppression of an evil Rebellion, who made the Reforms possible and the ameliorative atmosphere in the Assembly. Without Dyer's action, the horrors which would have followed would not have been forgotten, the Indians could not have been forgiven, the rift would have been immutable and India would have fallen then into the hands of the evil men referred to in the Debate and lost that Christian civilisation that we had brought to her through long hard years of work. India and her sort of democracy would not exist today, for the totalitarian aspect of her rule would have been extended to the whole country in a sort of repressive and corrupt dictatorship, had not her elders of the time of the Rebellion decided to move towards a more responsible form of government. It might be said that if Dyer and the other officers had not put the Rebellion down, Montagu's Reforms could never have taken place.

When I started thinking about Amritsar in 1919, I knew only what my parents and their friends had said about the incident. I knew from them that they would almost undoubtedly have been murdered and the women and children raped and killed, that Dyer's courage was their saving and that without him, they would probably not have lived. I also knew that he had hated the action that he considered (as did they) to be absolutely unavoidable if they were to live.

For my mother, the sound of the mobs in the bazaar always rang in her ears, the shouting for 'white blood', the lights in the city, while they had one lamp, [as we would have said, 'one butti' and no electricity for fans]; the lack of fresh food or indeed of anything but the soldiers' rations of bully beef and biscuits, the many cases of dysentery with only three latrines, and the resultant death of Miles Irving's little boy.

All her life she disliked India and if it had not been for our dear bearer, Mohammed Ashraf Khan, I believe she would have found it impossible to stay. My father did attempt to find work elsewhere, even writing to an American friend to get a job in the States, but before anything came to light, my mother became pregnant and he realised that he would have to stay in a secure post. My sister was born on 1st December 1920. My mother must have become pregnant at about the time she was writing [with my father's help] the article she wrote on life in the Fort, for 'Blackwoods Magazine', published in the March 1920 edition. She felt sick throughout the period before she went Home for her confinement. In a country where we had no flush toilets [in her case until almost the time that they were leaving India for good, when she had one put into her bathroom in Gupcar Road] she always had to light a cigarette before going to the gusselkhana, for she never got over the shock which her olfactory nerves suffered when in the Gobindgarh Fort. In fact, she did spend a great deal of her time in England, coming home in the Spring and only returning in the Autumn. Up in the Salt Range, [their next move], they were for a while extremely happy, but she never forgot her initiation into Indian life in 1919.

So I knew that Dyer was a Good Thing, I knew several of the people who knew him, I heard from Herbert Swinnerton, our family lawyer, of the Cyclists march to Thal and of Dyer's fine leadership there and in Amritsar; I knew the Miles Irvings and Miss Martin, who had been their governess at the time. Advancing age persuaded me that I should write down what I knew.

All my research served to increase my admiration for Dyer, his strategic ability, his grasp of the Indian temperament and of the situation in general (as one would have expected with a senior army officer), and the picture revealed has shown up the quicksand on which the public actions were based; a conspiracy of such powerful ramifications, that once the anti-Rowlatt propaganda had been started, rebellion became the unavoidable next step. I would hazard a guess that the hierarchy of the India-wide conspiracy would, if successful, have taken over India then and Indian leaders would not then have had the civilising experience in Government which they did have during the ensuing 27 years before we left. Since the propaganda incitement was so clear and repetitive, the British would have been massacred as at the time of the Mutiny but for one thing, - the Army. The Indian Army, largely Punjabi, would not, I believe, have joined in. It was for this reason that Gandhi, the Ali brothers and others already mentioned, worked on the Army. It was probably to undermine the mass of Muslims in the Army that Gandhi was so keen to work with the (Muslim) Khilafat movement, but not until the Japanese were at the gates of India did he gain any success, in the form of the I.N.L.A. (Indian National Liberation Army), which he and Nehru, having squeezed out like a sucked orange, then abandoned.

The important aspect which is omitted from the image given elsewhere of India, is that there were two layers present. One was 'loyal' in the way that Umar Hayat Khan was loyal, loyal to his country and recognising that India needed the British, as Jamnadas Dwarkadas claims also to have recognised. The other layer was blatantly disloyal to India. Although the Government represented the King and loyalty to the Crown, underlying this loyalty to the Crown was loyalty to country. What moved Gandhi and his friends (for want of any other defined leadership) was their hope of replacing the British in the hierarchical structure. Their grasping disloyalty to their country is shown in working on the Oriental Desk in Berlin and in Moscow, their encouragement, possibly even incitement, of the Amir to make war on their country, their relationship with the Germans on the East and West frontiers of India and with all that, the underlying creeping poison which was left intact, ready for more, after Dyer had lanced the first abscess. There is no doubt that they were, in the devious ways of men wanting power, extremely clever. Dyer, meeting one of his Indian friends, commented on an anti-British speech the man had just made, and asked him about it. The man replied that he had a family and had to earn his living and that he would get no position unless he spoke like that. The change brought about in the Rebellion was that people who wished to get on joined with the others who wished to take over at all costs. The result was a lot of double speak which made life less comfortable after 1919.

My father barely mentioned Amritsar, although I heard him talking to people like Blacker, Swinnerton and others on very rare occasions. He was a man with far too many interests to mention it to any extent and anyway, the memory was an extremely unpleasant one. I knew he had held up a lot of shouting people throwing stones at him and some others, coming over a bridge. He helped to draft the 1935 India Bill on which Mountbatten, some years later, was able to hand India over to the Indians. This seems clear if one looks at the history of India, after Gandhi, leading the 1919 Rebellion, did his best to stop all advance.

Only in his seventies after retiring, [he had been offered the Principalship of the School of Oriental Studies] when he was an eminent Art Historian, , a specialist on Lely, Hogarth, Blake and then to a greater extent, Constable, did he read 'Massacre at Amritsar', one of the books which started my interest.

An Indian Civil Servant remarked to me *"he was the best civil judge that we had"* and added, *"anyone can be a good criminal judge, but he was the best civil judge."*

My own reaction to the book was the reaction of a child, and interestingly, the opinion of one adviser in the Montagu papers. *"Why didn't he fire on the mob?"* was the question of those of us who thought that if he had fired, he could have stopped the whole Rebellion, but of course then, I did not know what I have since discovered, that he could not fire because he did not have a firearm or permission to carry one. I did not know that it was an India-wide Rebellion, based on an India-wide conspiracy. The Congress Committee invention, that his firing on the mob of 30,000 had set the mob off going for loot and rapine in the Civil Lines, remains. My childish belief was based on a more effective approach, as I thought.

The fact of a well-knit India-wide conspiracy was dismissed as unproven by the Hunter Committee. Peshawar, where the evidence was clear, was dismissed when put before the Hunter Committee sitting in secret, further evidence being refused quite brusquely by Pandit Narayan when Thompson offered it, saying he did not wish to hear any more.

Even Miles Irving's suspicions had been aroused, as General Dyer had quoted in his affidavit to the Army Council. Irving said: *"They were working up some kind of mischief which I could not foresee. It struck me that the leaders of the movement were disciplining the mob with a view to some concerted form of passive disobedience to authority which would paralyse government. My idea was that they intended to avoid any collision with authority that would justify armed intervention and to train the mob to do what they were told."* That observation from an experienced District Officer (he had entered the I.C.S. in 1898) would not have been lightly made. Of course it fitted in with Gandhi's claim of passive behaviour.

As Dyer remarked, the assembly was primarily of the same mobs which had murdered and looted and burned three days previously, and showed by their truculence and contempt for the troops during the intervening days, that it was a deliberate challenge to Government forces, and that if they were not dispersed and dispersed effectively, with sufficient impression upon the designs and arrogance of the rebels and their followers, we should be overwhelmed during the night or the next day by a combination of the city gangs and of still more rural bands.

# Chapter II
# THE IMPLICATIONS

Curzon was one member of the Cabinet who had claimed that his Divisional Commanders had approved Dyer's action in 1919. Montagu, of the same Cabinet, believed only Gandhi. In 1940, at a time when the Indian Army was of vital importance, Udham Singh shot and killed Sir Michael O'Dwyer, the retired Lieutenant-Governor of the Punjab and wounded Lord Zetland (previously Lord Ronaldshay, Lord Curzon's Private Secretary) at a meeting in Caxton Hall. Also on the platform with Sir Michael was Sir Percy Sykes, an Indian Army man, who had fought in the Boer War and was the first British consul at Kerman and in Persian Baluchistan. He had actually founded, in 1898, the Consulate on which Dyer had to rely to get his message back to India from Seistan. He raised and commanded those equally helpful South Persian Rifles that aided Colonel James in 1917 and commanded them until 1918. Udham Singh was described by Indians as a martyr from the days of the Amritsar firing in 1919, but his visits to Germany suggest a more likely role was as a German spy, and a very useful placement, in view of the continuing use of the propaganda about the firing. Altogether, he was an unsavoury character, claimed as a martyr by Indira Gandhi.

In 1974, under a Socialist government, the body of the murderer was exhumed and sent to India for a martyr's burial. As with the making of the 'Gandhi' film, the Indian hierarchy was still intent on exhibiting the acrimony that led to the placing of the celebratory statue of Tantia Topi, the leader of the mutineers, over the well at Cawnpore, into which the chopped-up bodies of women and children, promised safety, had been put during the Mutiny.

Could this strand of rancorous spite ever be eradicated from the Indian political scene? The killing of Sir Michael O'Dwyer, the wounding of Lord Zetland, at a time when the feelings of Indian soldiers were paramount, if we were to have them fighting with us for the protection of India, were certainly a part of the German plan, but the statue of Tantia Topi and the treating of Udham Singh as a martyr in 1974 were purely Indian.

Once again at that time, General Umar Hayat Khan Tiwana was giving advice, this time as the adviser to Zetland (Secretary of State for India) on the Indian Army. His son, Khizzar Hayat Khan was the Prime Minister of the most martial of the Provinces from 1942 and Udham Singh's action did not, as far as I have been told, have any adverse effect.

Another influence added to that from Montagu's treatment of India, of General Dyer, of Gandhi and of the District Officers under his aegis as Secretary of State, beside the rule of the Viceroy, Lord Reading and his treatment of the people caught up in the Malabar Rebellion, was that of Lord Halifax, whose long metaphysical chats with Gandhi led him to near-pacifism and might have lost us the last war, since it was he who was suggested as the Prime Minister to follow Chamberlain. Percy Culp of the 'Sunday Pictorial' thought that Halifax should be hanged. Out of 2,400 letters to the Pictorial only 73 were against Churchill's return to power, the sign of a nation that was at last roused to action.

Later on, Nirad Chaudhuri, the man who had to leave India and was helped to do so by among others, Laurens van der Post, brought into public light the true need of India for the British rule.

One earlier stand had been made. In 1923/4, that brave and loyal man, Sir Michael O'Dwyer, libelled by Sir Sankaran Nair in his book 'Gandhi and Anarchy', put forward the truth, which the Labour Government then and in 1947 refused to credit. Before Mr Justice MacCardie, O'Dwyer disproved the claims about Amritsar and the 1919 Rebellion. In the case in the Queen's Bench Division of the High Court in London, his evidence was retained in transcript form until Lord Denning had it shredded in the 1980s, when he was Master of the Rolls.[57] The only remains of this case were the depositions. The previous story of Dyer's irresponsibility in firing as he had was retrieved, though Mr. Justice MacCardie, at the request of the Applicant, had looked at the Amritsar incident in detail. MacCardie's judgement was clear: *"I am glad to observe that whatever criticism may have been made upon the conduct of the plaintiff and other officials in India, throughout the whole case no-one has challenged in the slightest way the un-corruptibility, ability, absolute honesty, and efficiency of the civil officers who have been called before us."*

Speaking to the Jury, he said *"Subject to your Judgement, speaking with full deliberation and knowing the whole of the evidence given in this case, I express my view, that General Dyer, in the grave and exceptional circumstances, acted rightly, and in my opinion, upon the evidence, he was wrongly punished by the Secretary of State for India. That is my view, and I need scarcely say that I have weighed every circumstance, every new detail that was not before the Hunter Committee; but that*

---

[57] The author wrote to Lord Denning to ask for his reason for doing this, and received no reply.

*opinion which I now express is an opinion which you as a Jury may say you disagree with, and may take up another position in regard to the matter."*

The result of this costly case was that Nair lost his fortune fighting it. O'Dwyer gained nothing; but the Liberal/Labour faction (by this time, 1924, in power) were so outraged that they tried to get MacCardie removed from the Bench. Even the pro-Gandhi extremist newspaper, 'The Servant' was not so violently angry: *"Sir Michael O'Dwyer,"* it wrote, *"thus stands vindicated before the bar of public opinion in England. He has had justice at last at the hands of a British Jury. Sir Sankaran Nair has paid the penalty of writing a book in haste. He is today a sadder, if a wiser man."*

The damages were put by a majority Jury at £500[58] and costs, but then there was a left-wing member of the jury, Harold Laski, who had worked on the 'Daily Herald' and lectured in Political Science at the London School of Economics and who had been to India and met Gandhi. *"His dissent"* wrote Sir Michael later, *"doubtless deprived me of the heavy damages which the remaining eleven would have awarded and the charities to which I would have allocated anything over and above my actual costs, suffered accordingly."* Three years later, Arthur Henderson, he of the Peace Movement, who wished to go to Paris and Stockholm with Mr. Ramsay Macdonald, looked in on Lord Davidson and told him that the Bolsheviks were still subsidising the Labour Party in 1928.

O'Dwyer, typically, having won his case, sent at once to tell Dyer, by then too ill at his home at Long Ashton near Bristol to come to London himself. All that remains of the case now are the 'Times' Law Reports and the depositions of the Defendant's witnesses in India; these are useful, in that they also give evidence of the Langley Committee, which had sat on the question of the compensation to be paid to victims and families of those who suffered at Jallianwalla Bagh. The Committee sat at the order of the new Legislative Assembly in 1922. Alexander Langley, a highly popular man, had himself been a one-time Deputy-Commissioner of Amritsar. In India, such an offer of compensation would, in the normal way, have brought in thousands of claims, which would not necessarily have been sound. Despite some of the claimants saying that they had small babies with them, which was not within Briggs' or Dyer's or any other witness' observation, and quite outside what would have been possible with such a crowd, the numbers were reduced from close on 1,500 casualties to rather less than 200. Compensation was claimed for these unlikely babies, who, of course, had been killed. The figures are unlikely to have reached 150, of whom many were crushed attempting to leave by the main gate, locked by the rebel leaders themselves.

The figures accepted by the Hunter Committee, which have since been reiterated on every possible occasion – where India in her generosity has not added a nought or two – had been collected by the Sewa Samiti. This was an association run by a man

---

58    This was exactly the sum given to Lady O'Dwyer after her husband was shot in Caxton Hall, as her compensation.

called Swami Shraddanand, who was a friend of Gandhi. It was a typical example of the British friendliness and trust in Indian sincerity, that they had left the counting of bodies to a friend of the man whom they knew had ignited the Rebellion. It was also extremely stupid of them, but at that time, they were fully occupied in sorting out the aftermath of the troubles and as they and their Secretary of State believed, in bringing Anglo-Indian relations to harmony again. Even in Hunter, we find in the evidence of Francis Burton, by then replacing Miles Irving as Deputy-Commissioner of Amritsar, stating that he did not know the numbers, since many of the names had not been recognised by the headmen in the villages to which the names were ascribed.

Despite the brave action by Sir Michael, none of this information has persuaded subsequent writers on the subject to mention the discrepancies between the Hunter claim and that of Langley, nor of the evidence given in the O'Dwyer v. Nair hearing. That case was one of the actions marking the ongoing endeavour to put the Indian story into its true framework.

Needless to say, the results of the Langley Committee findings have never been widely published. The Legislative Assembly may have ordered the investigation, but the results did not fit in with the propaganda and the ill-founded allegations of the number of casualties which still only amount to a tiny proportion of a vast and hostile crowd.

By contrast, the firing at a peaceful crowd of pilgrims by Mrs Gandhi's army in 1984, where the White Paper produced by the Government claimed 493 people killed, 86 injured and a further 1,600 unaccounted for, are, we might hazard, casualties of something like 2,200, if the Sikhs themselves did not claim far more. For them, the deaths in the armed forces, with Sikhs found killed with their hands tied behind them, come to a further 10,000. The numbers allegedly present in the Golden Temple precinct were 3,680. If this were so, then those killed (close on five hundred), are a formidable percentage of 3,680, compared with the Jallianwalla Bagh in 1919.

It is not the intention of this book to make out that deaths are irrelevant. In the case of the 1919 Rebellion, people had been warned and it was typical of Indian legalistic reasoning that much emphasis (with no tested evidence) was put on the peacefulness of the crowd, in itself unlikely in view of defiance of the warnings. The next legalistic ploy was to claim they had not all heard, despite the list of places where the Town Crier, the Military, the Deputy Commissioner, the General and the Police went. It is my intention to show up the baseless claims of the propagandists that have inexplicably been accepted throughout the ensuing years. It took a brave Prince, the Queen's consort, to question the numbers in 1997. A Canadian Scientist, having been round the town with a friend whose parents were among the missionaries in the Fort, took up with the Guide the matter of the alleged unprovoked attack by Dyer, for he had seen the memorials in the churches to the bank managers who had been beaten to death with lathis by that same Jallianwalla Bagh mob, and yet the *canard* goes on.

# THE IMPLICATIONS

Mrs. Indira Gandhi was known as Durga, the Hindu Goddess of Destruction, but Dyer was acclaimed by the people of Amritsar. Made an honorary Sikh, he was offered by the priests of the Golden Temple a further 10,000 troops to defend India under him on the Frontier and thanked by the people of the City itself for saving them. It is in the peculiar acceptance of propaganda and lack of interest in facts or reality that the story lies. Sir Michael's case versus Sankaran Nair was a step, but the perversion of history that Marx believed to be essential for the success of his policies, has still not been stopped.

For this we have to blame Edwin Montagu, for we all knew that the Indian politicians were rather less interested in truth than in propaganda. Montagu had put his whole weight behind the invented story, rather than the reports and evidence of the people in the field – or even that of the Hunter Commission, unsoundly chosen to support his own partisan approach.

In 1939 the same plan was intended; but still the enormity of the idea of 'Hindu Raj' had not been grasped by the rulers and Viceroy after Viceroy had bent over backwards to fit in with their own ideal that democratic rule with care for minorities was intended, never being corrected by the politicians themselves. The great loss was that Hinduism put hierarchy before anything else.

In 1940, on the platform at the Caxton Hall as well as Sykes and O'Dwyer, was the Marquis of Zetland, the man who, as Lord Ronaldshay, had written Curzon's biography, and knew India. The man who had been advising the Marquis on the Indian Army was a man, now Sir Umar Hayat Khan Tiwana, whom we have met before. There would have been ample time to disillusion Zetland, but then an ideal that had so successfully built up an Empire could not have been dismantled overnight.

In India, we had Lord Linlithgow, who genuinely believed he could have achieved Federation by July 1941, still struggling with all his soul to achieve the basis for the hand over of power to India. Gandhi, sitting in the Lodge on 4th September 1939, almost weeping as he spoke to the Viceroy of 'the possibility of the bombing of Westminster Abbey or Westminster Hall', said that he contemplated the war with an English heart. All too soon, the Working Committee of the Congress meeting at Ramgarh adopted a resolution passed by the mass of the meeting on 20th March 1940, that Congress refused to participate in the war, undertaken for imperialist ends and for the strengthening of the Empire which was based on the exploitation of India and other Asiatic and African countries. It strongly disapproved of Indian troops being made to fight for Britain (in fact, without conscription, they were all volunteers), wholly rejected Dominion status within the imperial structure and repeated the demand for a constituent assembly based on adult suffrage. Withdrawal of the Congress Ministries must 'naturally' be followed by civil disobedience, to which Congress would resort as soon as it was ready or as soon as circumstances permitted it. The responsibility for launching it was left explicitly to Gandhi.

The dictator had stopped weeping over the bombing of London and had moved to further disruption.

Throughout the 1930s, Gandhi had continued his insidious endeavours, as did his nationalist friends. Now, in 1940, with Nehru, he tried to stop India coming into the War. The Indian Army stayed firm; it fought with the Commonwealth in Africa and on other fronts, to the everlasting gratitude of any man of reason who did not want Germany and Japan to take over the world. It was a great power in the saving of civilisation.

However, Gandhi's intentions were to see that India was taken over by the Axis Powers. He encouraged Indian soldiers to come and see him secretly at night. He started the wicked Quit India Movement, when the Japanese were actually in India, in an attempt to let them take over India by getting the Commonwealth and Indian Divisions of the 14th Army left unsupported, by violent and hysterical mob action on the lines of communication. He and Subhas Chandra Bose, the latter broadcasting to India from Berlin, made some headway with the army, in encouraging those men who had believed them, to join the so-called Indian National Army, which mostly consisted of Indian prisoners held by the Japanese, who tortured those fellow prisoners of war refusing to join. Nehru and his cronies, speaking against any punishment of these traitors, encouraged riots in support of their views, but the Indian Army in general, fought gallantly against the Japanese invader, as their share of Victoria Crosses testifies. In his book 'The Turn of the Tide', based on the War Diaries of Field-Marshal Viscount Alanbrooke, Arthur Bryant wrote: *"Throughout March* [1942] *the succession of disasters in the Far East continued. On the 7th the invasion of New Guinea began and Rangoon was evacuated; the last resistance in Java ceased next day. Within three weeks all Lower Burma was lost. At sea, with Singapore and the Sumatra Straits in their possession, the Japanese were ranging far into the Indian Ocean, sinking and bombing as far as the Cingalese and Indian coasts, and on land, in full cry after Alexander's army, were bearing down on the gates of the Raj. 'It is not easy' Churchill wrote to Roosevelt, 'to assign limits to the Japanese aggression'. With the failure that month of Cripps' mission to India and ever-mounting tidings of British disaster, the vast, restless subcontinent seemed on the verge of revolution, with many of its nationalist leaders preaching co-operation with the enemy, and Britain's allies, America, Russia, and China, adding fuel to the fire by ill-timed ideological propaganda about the doom of an outworn imperialism and the inevitability of immediate 'liberation'. Only the firmness of the Viceroy and the loyalty of the Indian Army stood between the land and anarchy."*[59] The fact that Nehru was being asked to form an interim government at the time and that India was virtually a Dominion, meant that the "National" could have been left out of the name of the traitors' army after the final handover of power, but these poor deluded men were not served with the loyalty they might have thought they deserved; they were never employed in the Indian Army again.

Throughout all this, the real Indian Army did all it could, up to and including the handover period, to help to protect the people of India.

---

59    Arthur Bryant, 'The Turn of the Tide', Reprint Society 1958, p. 285.

Throughout the years between 1919 and 1947, the dictator achieved, through fear and lies, his power and world-wide support, particularly from the U.S. and he went on to cause the horrors of Cawnpore, of the Indian States, of Quit India, culminating in the final horror of the Partition, made by him and an English Labour Government. Rumour has it that Mountbatten was blackmailed into a speedy handover. When in early 1947, the then Viceroy, Field-Marshal Lord Wavell, offered the use of British troops to assist in policing the deeply divisive partition of India, including the Punjab and Kashmir, Gandhi refused, saying *"if India wants her bloodbath, let her have it."*.

Parvus was no longer alive, but he would have felt his clever disruption to have been well-imitated by his successors and that Nehru's 'doctrinaire' attitudes would well support his cause.

The attitude of Congress looked like blackmail or delaying tactics. To many of us, it looked like the behaviour of recalcitrants, determined to make as much trouble as possible. Jinnah and the Muslim League hardened their attitude, but that was a symptom of the pressure for Muslim equality of representation. Jinnah's position was to become a straitjacket, trying to protect Muslim interests against the pressure for a 'Hindu Raj', of which Mohammed Ali and Umar Hayat Khan had warned at an earlier time and which Montagu had been too innocent to recognise. At his time, the British, carrying out the actual work in India, were still sufficiently in command to be capable of holding the runaway horse on the road ahead before it had broken the traces. By Linlithgow's time, so much in the direction of power in India had been ceded, that an alternative stance could no longer be taken - we were holding on by the skin of our teeth.

In later years and at the request of Lord Mountbatten, Nehru might write for Sukarno in Indonesia: *"Tell Sukarno that nobody could have wished for the British to leave us alone in India more ardently than I did. But even now I hope they are not leaving too soon. However, they have given me three things of lasting value: a non-political and incorruptible civil service; a non-political and incorruptible judiciary; and a non-political army. Without the minimum of these three things a modern democratic government would be totally impossible. Tell Sukarno he has not even got one of these things and he had therefore better pipe down."*[60] Yet in 1939 and onwards, this man, who was to scream hysterically at the mobs in Delhi murdering Muslims, himself led similar mobs to scream at the officers of the British Raj. An Indian officer of great prestige, a Sandhurst man, described to me the hysterical advance of Nehru, at the head of a mob to do some dreadful damage. He was so out of control that this man, a cavalry officer, saw no means of stopping him except by unsheathing his sabre, something totally forbidden in army regulations. However, it worked. Nehru might, in various memoirs, have recalled his imprisonment on unfair grounds,

---

60   Lawrence van der Post quoted this letter in his book 'Walk with a White Bushman'. The author gave permission for its use before he died.

with the attitudes of a revolutionary, but when he was not imprisoned and wished to be, he approached Raymond Vernede and asked him for the gift of imprisonment. The endless streams of young men and women whom the BBC manages to find to claim false imprisonment should understand that this form of punishment was *de rigueur* as a member of the Gandhi dictatorship.

I illustrate how some Indians viewed imprisonment with another such wish, written by another District Officer, this time on the North West Frontier; the name of the willing prisoner, 'the Red Shirt', Ghaffar Khan.

The tale was told by the late Edward Lydall. *"Most of the inhabitants of the North West Frontier province were stoutly supporting the war, but a minority, distinguished by the wearing of red shirts, had decided to denounce it. The shouting of anti-war slogans became a popular pastime and the red shirts of Nowshera followed their leader, who held the local rank of 'General' in marches through the bazaar, so I wrote a poem, mildly mock-heroic, perhaps – on the subject of his Mission - and circulated it in the bazaar. The General felt strongly resentful and called at my house to protest. As to that, I replied, I would make him a proposal. If he and his followers would cease their anti-war activities I would write no more lampoons. The General was delighted. Nothing, he assured me, could be fairer. A solemn treaty was immediately drawn up and signed by the General and myself. We were now fast friends and peace reigned in Nowshera.*

*It was however, some three months before I saw the General again and then he came creeping into my house privily by night. This surprised me, for I had supposed that all was well between us. I was sending him periodical douceurs to console him for his inactivity. What could be the trouble now?*

*'Sahib,' said the General, 'You have got to put me in jail'.*

*This I considered a most unreasonable request. 'Why on earth should I put you in jail?' I asked.*

*'Because,' said the General, with a melancholy expression, 'I am losing face with followers. Everyone is saying that I am in your pay.'*

*'Well so you are.'*

*'That,' said the General, 'is not the point.'*

*The General was of course right. I should have to see what I could do to help him. In return perhaps, he would help me.*

*'What would you be prepared to do,' I enquired, 'to persuade me to put you in jail?'*

*'Well,' he said, 'what do you suggest?'*

*'If I put you in jail,' I replied, 'would you consider starting a pro-war movement – with shirts of a different colour of course?'*

*'Certainly, Sahib' said he, 'readily, provided, that is, that you pay for the shirts. How much jail would that earn me?'*

*'Well, I thought about a week.'"*

*'No, no,' the General emphatically objected, 'six months.'*

*'Now General,' I wheedled, 'don't be unreasonable. Remember that I have to consider the jail budget. Let us compromise on two months.'*

*'OK' said the General, who after all was a reasonable man.*

*The scene in my court the following morning was truly impressive. All the General's followers were in attendance as their handcuffed leader was led to the dock.*

*'Up the rebels!' shouted the General.*

*'Up the rebels!' yelled his followers. Dense crowds were gathering and the excitement was intense.*

*Finally, when the evidence was complete I delivered judgement. The case against the prisoner had been proved up to the hilt. The crime that he had been conspiring to commit was desperate and dangerous and I saw no alternative but to sentence him to two months.*

*The General's eyes flashed. 'Never,' he shouted, 'had he been so unjustly treated' and with a final cry of 'Up the Rebels!' and a broad wink at me, the General was led away through the shouting crowd and deposited in the jail, from which he sent me a happy visit letter."*

This was at the time of the Quit India Movement, when India was in turmoil. Whatever may be claimed today by the less knowledgeable producers in the B.B.C. and other media, the fashion, indeed the behaviour that was obligatory, as with the Red Shirt General, was imprisonment. Claims by the Indian today, that imprisonment was carried out as a matter of dreadful repression is merely a continuation of the propaganda of the time – Gandhi's image-making for the West and the United States. In the United Provinces, Raymond Vernede was asked by Nehru to imprison him and complied as had Edward Lydall for Ghaffar Khan. Gandhi, on his Quit India Movement, was imprisoned - in the Aga Khan's palace.

Montagu never even achieved the grasp that Nehru had, when he wrote the message to Sukarno, in terms of how the British had achieved the pacification, integration and prosperity of India, which Montagu came inadvertently to destroy.

# Chapter III
# THE LESSONS

That British writers in more recent times have filled books with support for the Rebellion and the rebels, and against the Rowlatt provisions, indicates the way in which history is now taught. Pupils are asked to imagine they are members of the peasants' revolt, Indian extremists, Irish rebels, but never asked to imagine the difficulties of Government – never to think of the reasons and alternatives in the management of states and the differences that applied to those thoughts in earlier times. The teaching is, as was Gandhi's anarchy (though not in so many words), like the insidious teaching of Parvus and his agents, which underlay the Bolshevik Revolution, the acts of the Young Turks and the C.U.P., the seditious movements that have erupted all over the Middle East and much of the world. That the teaching affected Britain and France is clear. Ramsay Macdonald, the Labour politician, was in the forefront of British politics, while Churchill, who had grasped the true German intention, was kept out in the cold, effectively muffled by Reith's refusal to let him use the broadcasting medium, just as the B.B.C. muffles the truth about the Bilderberger and the loss of our sovereignty and our laws in the European Union today. The menacing, hidden, sedition that is creeping upon us today, keeping a hold on the minds of people in power, or influencing them, is merely a continuation of the same thing that moved through the minds of the politicians in India at the time of this book. It is supplemented by the baleful influence on children, which continues, a mixture of attempts at social engineering through education; at multiculturalism by the teaching about comparative religions, when many children have had no means of knowing what religion is, since they have grown with no knowledge of it – so how can they compare? The effects of such propaganda, which destroys or distorts the meaning of words and actions, causes and effects, is that it leaves people weak and open to any appeal of wickedness or superficiality or, as in this country today, sensuousness, for without truth, feeling and sensual excitement are all that is left.

The people of India have been unable, for one reason or another, to take part in their democracy, just as we, weakened by poor education and teaching systems, are brought up to believe that stimulation instead of experience and understanding of truth, are the way to a happy life. We have not understood Jesus' teaching that the Kingdom of Heaven begins within us.

Today in this country, we face another perilous time. The German idea of World Rule, proposed in 1888, but finding its roots in Anacharsis Clootz' speech to the French Assembly in 1792, is taking over the laws of this country. The fight for freedom from Rome, begun under Henry VIII and consolidated by the Reformation and the Protestant Succession, has been overtaken by a different totalitarianism, in the behaviour of the British Parliament towards the European Union. With the Treaty of Lisbon and the finalising of the structures of European integration, have gone those precious rights that we as a nation fought for through the centuries – the right to claim innocence until guilt had been established, the protection of Habeas Corpus and the flexibility and possibility of change inherent in the democratic system. Instead, we have laws made by unelected bureaucrats behind closed doors, politicians and police immune from prosecution and a system of justice based on Corpus Juris, rather than the Common Law of England.

Those anxious to suborn Britain, with the collusion of treasonous Ministers; degenerate and un-knowledgeable Parliaments, without a thought for our history and traditions, or the protection of our people whom they were elected to serve and with media subservient to global financial interests, have apparently succeeded in destroying our sovereignty and distorting our national identity. We face the same systems which led to the 2.00 a.m. knock on the door by the Gestapo and the arbitrary removal of people from their homes without a charge. The ideas behind these moves are not new. The plan for world rule, from Clootz and his claim that 'The Universe will form one State, the State of United Individuals, the immutable Empire of the Great Germany, the Universal Republic,' has continued through many people. There have been idealists like Mirabeau and Victor Hugo, conspirators like Parvus and Lenin, to Sir Max Waechter, a friend of the Kaiser, who, at the London Institute in 1909, suggested a scheme for a Federal Europe in the interests of world peace. In 1913, 'The European Unity League' started, with 20,000 supporters and many names of important persons, including Ramsay Macdonald, only to be destroyed by the war.

In the 'Morning Post' of 28th April 1924, Sir Max Waechter returned to the attack, publishing a manifesto headed 'The United States of Europe'. He wrote: *"The German Emperor showed that in every way he approved of my plan, but I could not induce him to take action. He was by nature a pacifist, but unfortunately he was constantly surrounded and influenced by the War Party"*.

In this country, as in Hitler's Germany, the dissidents, the people who stand for what is best for their country, are called 'trouble-makers' and when they stand for seats in Europe or Britain, their selection Committees are leant on by the inevitable powers behind the scene and they are not selected. In Hitler's Germany, a student, Sophie Schlock was arrested for sending round leaflets against the War in her college and her brother was hanged; we have not yet come to that in this country, although Bernard Connolly, having worked for the E.U., was hounded after his book 'The Rotten Heart of Europe' was published a few years ago.

But I am tired of propaganda. In working on this book I have learnt of the sliding quicksand on which the 1919 Rebellion was based. In a similar way, the European Union of the present time has quietly and softly removed all our bastions of civilised democracy, and we can now, now that we have complicit Ministers, appease the I.R.A., let the murderers out of prison, as did the Lloyd George Government, and punish those who stand for free speech and our civilised and well tried democracy. [61]

'All that is necessary for evil to triumph is for the good man to do nothing', is a saying attributed to Edmund Burke. It applied at that moment in India, where the evil was in the acceptance of the lies broadcast by the people who were intent on ruling India and were massed in the Legislative Council, on the Provincial Councils and were clerks in the government offices throughout.

It appears that there are no Sir Michael O'Dwyers in our halls of power today, no Churchills, able and prepared to start a 'Diehard Conservative Party', as in the 1920s, in response to the infiltration of the Bolshevik Labour Party and the appeasing Liberals. We have no Edward Carsons, prepared to protect the Protestant element in Ulster, few of the anti-Parvus Europe element and few enough who can stand up and be heard in a country where the B.B.C. is one of the worst of the propagandists of our time.

The components of the conspiracy are strands in a web that can be recognised, step-by-step, but are still so fine that the whole cannot be grasped except in actions and new sorts of behaviour and attitude. We can see the 'good' people either coming up against a storm of denigration or quite simply dying, to be replaced by people of an altogether different calibre. Hugh Gaitskell's death made the void that was to be filled by Harold Wilson, the man who worked hand in glove with Russia and under whom, inflation rose to 25 per cent and Britain became so weakened by the costs of the nationalised industries and the unions. Then Margaret Thatcher, whom we now learn was removed at the agreement of The Bilderberger Group, the group behind the plans for Europe and with Edward Heath as a core member, Geoffrey Howe as a member, and the meeting taking place on the Island of Toja, protected by armed forces. The move was made, knowing that the Iron Lady would not go into a Federal Europe, so the web of poison concentrated on her.

---

61    In July 1999 a 78 year old man in Liverpool was arrested for putting in his window a sticker saying 'Vote UKIP [United Kingdom Independence Party] and keep free speech'. He was arrested under the Xenophobia Clause in the Amsterdam Treaty, in force from 1 May 1999. His sentence would be 14 years, but has not, to date, been carried out.

John Smith was another good man, but the void caused by his death was filled by a man determined to take Britain further and further into the European Union - this organisation of International Socialism. We see the attitude being worked out in the extraordinary rudeness to the Queen on her Indian visit in 1997, the gloating of Indians at the rudeness and lack of respect of their leading politicians. Having invented the stories that give them the so-called right to bitterness, demanding apologies from the present generation, ignoring what the British did for India.

Knowing what we now do of Count Von Bernstorff's intentions for Turkey, the friend and ally of the Germans, there is no doubt that if France and Britain had lost the War, similar sanctions would have applied. The plans for the Second World War written out by Ribbentrop were similar, and the movements towards economic and political union are similar today. The Scots, as an example, having been stirred by insidious weasel words against the so-called injustice of being part of Great Britain, to press for independence, quite largely on the spurious claim that they would then benefit from their own oil, are now finding that the production is a common supply, common to the European Union, under the auspices of the Bilderberger and Germany. They are a loss to Great Britain, and their oil revenues are lost to them. Whereas by World War II, the people of Europe could still refer to the betrayers of their own countries as Quislings, today, with the insidious undermining of all feelings of patriotism, we are pushed gently by propaganda into believing that we gain by betrayal.

The secret society behind all of this, the Bilderberg Group, has an influential membership amongst the great and the good, not confined to politicians. Though Howe and Heath featured as the first betrayers and were even prepared to rid us of our democratically elected Prime Minister, because of her opposition to a Federal Europe, they have been followed by many others from the major political parties, all in their turn, breaking their promises to the electorate and giving away more and more of the heritage which is not theirs to give. So lethargic; so divided and unknowledgeable are we, that we do not even recognise the spider's web that Buchan spoke of when writing about 'Ivery'. Anyone who questions the slide towards dictatorship is labelled a 'conspiracy theorist'. Those men who write frankly, like Bernard Connolly, who, from being in the position of head of the Exchange Rate Mechanism, wrote the book 'The Rotten Heart of Europe', which showed the B.B.C. position as a propagandist organisation, the loss of independence for the Netherlands to Germany, France being almost lost to any independent action, who was then sacked, against all the laws of Europe or Britain, by a man who had never read the book. Connolly has been warned never to go into the Brussels building again and his life has been threatened. When his case for wrongful dismissal was heard in the E.U. Court, it was dismissed, not on the grounds that what he had written was untrue, but because it was critical of the E.U. When Marta Andreassen, appointed Chief Accountant of the E.U. in 2002, refused to sign off the accounts because of flaws in the system, she was sacked. Eight years later, nothing has changed, the accounts are still not cleared – a situation which would prevent a British company from continuing in business.

The clever idea of getting rid of boundaries means that we cannot defend ourselves, for we have no country to defend - patriotism negated. In any case, we cannot control our borders and uncontrolled immigration is changing our society and putting our services under stress.

Even Ulster has been subjected to the pressure to give up her boundaries by the Gauleiter Governments of our time.

The claim of a Common Market was mere window-dressing; the first treaties were already victories imagined by a defeated nation and should not have been agreed by the nations who won the war. De Gaulle, in agreeing them, took on the role of a Petain. Britain joined because Heath showed a degree of perfidy in relation to the democracy which he led, which seemed and still seems, after all this time, beyond the belief of sane people. Subsequent leaders of this country have followed in the same way, disregarding the democratic responsibilities inherent in the British Constitution.[62] Never before did Britain fall prey to such perfidy, to such men determined to remove the fundamental rights that this nation has developed throughout the centuries. Those of us, by whose work these men are paid, knew nothing of what was being done in our name. They were paid to protect us and instead they have handed us over to a slavery which is extinguishing our primary productions, our industries, our laws, our independence and our rights under the existing Constitution, and they have added to these actions, permission to the public-funded broadcasting medium to propagandise us far more constantly and subtly than ever was the case with William Joyce and the propaganda of the Second World War.

When the truth about the events in Amritsar on the 13th of April 1919 is recognised, it is possible to draw out the real lessons which can be learnt from that unhappy occasion. They are as important in the New Millennium as they have always been.

The first lesson to be learned is that the outcome of dangerous occasions rest on the quality of the individuals involved. Crises are not averted by laws or government diktats, but by upright and courageous individuals applying themselves to solve problems unselfishly. It has always been so. If we look back over the centuries, we can see a number of men and women whose lives, either by their actions or their influence, have changed our lives for the better. Too frequently, they have done so in the face of entrenched or official opposition. Lawrence, because of his support for Feisal and the King of the Hejaz, stands out in this story, but the man who took his whole life in his hands and dared to risk his career out of humanity for those for whom he was responsible, Rex Dyer, is probably one of the greatest. That his sacrifice has been recognised and appreciated by everyone who knew or suffered from the rebellion, is one thing, but, as with Lawrence, his action resulted in personal suffering, in Dyer's

---

62   A Deputy First Minister, apparently bent on destroying our Constitution, has declared that there is no such race as the English.

case to an extraordinary degree. Not the least of that suffering was the burden of unjust opprobrium borne by him and his family through the years following 1919.

As is so often the case in this world, ruled by 'the Father of Lies', those guilty men and women, whose actions and words led to that suffering, escaped the judgment which they deserve. History also has its quota of individuals who, through pride or greed or lack of concern for the effects of their actions on other people, bring about the disasters which they subsequently seek to hide or blame on the innocent. Those who by ignorance, by malice, by deception and untruth, worked against the growth of peace, prosperity and security in India, should also be recognised for what they did. That, too, is one of the lessons of Amritsar.

Both these lessons need to be re-learned by every generation. In our time, the need for honesty, and unselfishness in the face of danger and the courage to maintain our standards in the face of malice still needs to be shown by individuals. How well those qualities were demonstrated on 9/11 in America and on 7/7 in London. How much they are still needed as we face the more subtle dangers of propaganda and untruth from those who claim to have our best interests at heart, while robbing us of our birthright and destroying our heritage.

# APPENDIX I

## ROWLATT LEGISLATION
### THE CRIMINAL LAW AMENDMENT BILL

A Bill to provide for the amendment of the Indian Penal Code and the Code of Criminal Procedure, 1898.

Whereas it is expedient to amend the Indian Penal Code and the Code of Criminal Procedure, 1898, in order to deal more effectively with certain acts dangerous to the State; it is hereby enacted is as follows:

1. This Act may be called the Indian Criminal Law (Amendment) Act 1919.

2. In Chapter VI of the Indian Penal Code after section 124A the following section shall be inserted, namely:

"124B. Whoever has in his possession any seditious document intending that the same shall be published or circulated shall, unless he proves that he had such document in his possession for a lawful purpose, be punishable with imprisonment which may extend to two years or with fine or with both."

*Explanation - For the purposes of this section the expression 'seditious document' means any document containing any words, signs or visible representations which instigate or .are likely to instigate whether directly or indirectly*

(a) The use of criminal force against His Majesty or the Government established by law in British India, or against public servants generally or any class of public servants or any individual public servant, or

(b) The commission or abetment of any thing, which is an offence against, sections 12I, 121A, 122 or 131

3. After section 196A of the Code of Criminal Procedure, 1898, hereinafter referred to as the said Act, the following section shall be inserted, namely:-

"196B. In the case of any offence referred to in section 196 or 196A, the District Magistrate or the Chief Presidency Magistrate may, notwithstanding anything contained in those sections or in any other part of this Code, order a 'preliminary inquiry by 'a police officer not below the rank of an Inspector in which case such police-officer shall have the powers referred to in section 155(3).

4. To section 343 of the said Code, the following proviso shall be added, namely:-

"Provided that promise of protection to an accused person against criminal force or any promise properly incidental to a promise of such protection shall not be deemed to be the use or influence within the meaning of this section."

5. After section 510 of the said Code, the following section shall be inserted, namely:-

"510A On the trial of an offence under Chapter VI of the Indian Penal Code, the following facts shall be relevant, namely:

(a) that the person accused has previously been convicted of an offence under that Chapter, and

(b) that such person has habitually and voluntarily associated with any person who has been convicted of an offence under that Chapter:

Provided that such facts shall nevertheless not be admissible in evidence under the provisions of this section, unless written notice of the intention to call evidence thereof has been served on he accused at least seven days before the commencement of the trial, together with reasonable particulars of the conviction or association intended to be proved."

# APPENDIX I

6. After section 565 of' the said Code, the following section shall be inserted, namely:

"565A(1) When any person is convicted of an offence punishable under Chapter VI of the Indian Penal Code, the Court may, if it thinks fit at the time of passing sentence on such person, order him, on his release after the expiration of such sentence, to execute a ' bond with sureties for his good behaviour so far as of offences under Chapter VI of the said Code are concerned, for such period not exceeding two years as it thinks fit."

(I) An order under sub-section (I) may also be made by an Appellate Court or by the High Court when exercising its powers of revision.

(3) If the Court makes an order under sub-section (1), it shall further direct that, until the person who is the subject of the order furnishes the required security, such person shall notify to the Local Government or to such officer as the Local Government may by general or special order appoint in this behalf, his residence and any change of residence after release for the period for which security is required.

(4) Where any person is under an obligation to notify, in accordance with the provisions of sub-section (3), his residence and any change of residence after release, the Local Government may by order in writing direct that such person:

(a) shall not enter, reside or remain in any area specified in the order.

(b) shall reside or remain in any area in British India so specified, and
(c) shall abstain from addressing public meetings for the furtherance or discussion of any subject likely to cause disturbance or public excitement, or of any political subject, or for the distribution of any writing or printed matter relating to any such subject.

(5) Any person refusing or neglecting to comply with any direction under sub-section (3) or any order under sub-section (4) shall be punishable as if he had committed an offence under section 176 of the Indian Penal Code.

(6) If the conviction is set aside on appeal or otherwise all orders made under the provisions of this section shall become void.

*"Explanation: - In this sub-section the expression 'public meeting' has the same meaning as is assigned to it by section 3 of the Prevention of Seditious Meetings Act 1911."*

In Schedule II of the said Code in the entries relating to Chapter VI, after the entry relating to section 124A, the entry contained in the Schedule shall be inserted.

## THE SCHEDULE

| 1 | 2 | 3 | 4 | 5 | 6 | 7 | 8 |
|---|---|---|---|---|---|---|---|
| Section | Offence | Whether Police may arrest without warrant or not | Whether warrant or summons shall ordinarily issue | Whether Bailable or not | Whether compoundable or not | Punishment | By what Court triable |
| 124B | Possession of Seditious Documents | Ditto | Ditto | Ditto | Ditto | Imprisonment for 2 years and fine | Ditto |

# THE MAIN ROWLATT BILL

The second Bill, which is intended to make provision in special circumstances to supplement the ordinary Criminal Law and for the exercise of emergency powers by Government, runs thus:

## BILL NO. II OF 1919

Whereas it is expedient to make provision that, in special circumstances, the ordinary criminal law should be supplemented and emergency powers should be exercisable by the Government; and whereas the previous approval of the Secretary of State in Council has been accorded to the making of this law; it is hereby enacted as follows:

1. (1) This Act may be called the Criminal La\v (Emergency Powers) Act, 1919.

    (2) It extends to the whole of British India.

2. (1) In this Act, unless there is anything repugnant in the subject or context,

    "Chief Justice" means the Judge of highest rank in a High Court;

    "The Code" means the Code of Criminal Procedure, 1898.

    "High Court" means the highest Court of Criminal appeal or revision for any local area.

"Offence against the State" means any offence under Chapter VI of the Indian Penal Code, and any attempt or conspiracy to commit, or any abetment of, any such offence, and

"Scheduled offence" means any offence specified, in the Schedule.

(2) All words and expressions used in this Act and defined in the Code, and not herein before defined, shall be deemed to have the meanings respectively attributed to them in the Code.

3. If the Governor General in Council is satisfied that scheduled offences are prevalent in the whole or any part of British India, and that it is expedient in the interests of the public safety to provide for the speedy trial of such offences, he may, by notification in the "Gazette of India, " make a declaration to that effect, and thereupon the provisions of this Part shall come into force in the area specified in the notification.

4 (1) Where the Local Government is of opinion that the trial of any person accused of a scheduled offence should be held in accordance with the provisions of this Part, it may order any Officer of Government to prefer a written information to the Chief Justice against such person.

(2) No order under sub-section (1) shall be made in respect of, or be deemed to include, any person who has been committed under the Code for trial before a High Court, but, save as aforesaid, an order under that sub-section may be made in respect of any scheduled offence whether such offence was committed before or after the issue of the notification under section 3.

(3) The information shall state the offence charged and so far as known the name, place of residence, and occupation of the accused, and the time and place when and where the offence is alleged to have been committed and such other facts within the knowledge of the prosecution as shall be reasonably sufficient to enable the accused to meet the accusation.

(4) The Chief Justice may by order require any information to be amended so as to supply further particulars of the offence charged to the accused, and shall direct a copy of the information, or the amended information as the case may be, to be served upon the accused in such manner as the Chief Justice may direct.

5. Upon such service being effected, and on application duly made to him, the Chief Justice shall nominate three of the High Court Judges (hereinafter referred to as the Court) for the trial of the information and shall fix a date for the commencement of the trial:

(b) with the consent of the Chief Justice of another High Court, persons who are Judges of that High court.

6. The Court may sit for the whole or any part of a trial at such place or places in the Province, as it may consider desirable.

Provided that the Governor General in Council, if he is satisfied that such a court is expedient in the interest of justice, may, by notification in the "Gazette of India", direct that the Court shall sit for the whole or any part of a trial at such place or places as may be specified in the notification.

7. The provisions of the Code shall apply to proceedings under this Part. in so far as they are not inconsistent with the provisions therein contained and such proceedings shall be deemed to be proceedings under the Code, and the Court shall have all the powers conferred by the Code on a Court of Sessions exercising original jurisdiction.

8. The trial shall be commenced by the reading of the information and thereafter the Court shall, subject to the provisions of this Part in trying the accused, follow the procedure prescribed by the Code for the trial of warrant cases by Magistrates.

9. If a charge is framed, the accused shall be entitled to ask for an adjournment for ten days or any less period that he may specify and the Court shall comply with his request.

10. The Court shall be required to make a memorandum only of the substance of the evidence of each witness examined and subject to the adjournment provided for by section 9, and shall not be bound to adjourn 'any trial for any purpose, unless such adjournment is in its opinion necessary in the interest of justice.

11. The Court, if it is of opinion that such a course is necessary in the public interest or for the protection of a witness, may prohibit or restrict in such way as it may direct, the publication or disclosure of its proceedings or any part of its proceedings.

12. (1) No question shall be put by the Court to the accused in the course of trial under this Part until the close of the case for the prosecution. Thereafter, and before the accused enters on his defence, the Court shall call upon him to state whether he intends to give evidence on oath or not, and shall at the same time inform him that if he does so,

he will be liable to cross-examination. Unless the accused then states that he intends to give evidence on oath, the Court may at any time thereafter question the accused generally on the case in accordance with the provisions of section 35.2 of the Code.

(2) If, when so called upon, the accused states that he intends to give evidence on oath, the Court shall not at any subsequent stage put any question to him, provided that if the accused does not so give evidence, then, after the witnesses for the defence have been examined, the Court may question the accused generally on the case in accordance with the provision of the said section.

(3) If the accused gives evidence on oath, the following rules shall be observed in regard to his cross-examination namely:

    (a) He may be asked any question in cross-examination notwithstanding that it would tend to criminate him as to the offence charged.

    (b) He shall not be asked, and if asked shall not be required to answer, any question tending to show that he has committed or been convicted of, or has been charged with, any offence other than that with which he is then charged, or has a bad character unless

        (i) proof that he has committed or been convicted of such other offence is admissible in evidence to show that he is guilty of the offence with which he is then charged, or

        (ii) witnesses for the prosecution have been cross examined with a view to establish his own good character, or he has given evidence of his character, or the nature of the conduct of the defence is such as to involve imputations on the character of the witnesses for the prosecution, or

        (iii) he has given evidence against any other person charged with the same offence.

13. If the accused or anyone of the accused calls and examines any witness, the right of final reply shall lie with the prosecution, but in all other cases with the accused, provided that the examination of an accused as a witness shall not of itself confer the right of final reply, on the prosecution.

14. In the event of any difference of opinion between the members of the Court, the opinion of the majority shall prevail.

15. If in any trial under this Part it is proved that the accused has committed any offence, whether a scheduled offence or not, the Court may convict the accused of that offence although he was not charged with it.

16.　　　The Court may pass upon any person convicted by it any sentence authorised by law for the punishment of the offence of which such person is convicted, and no order of confirmation shall be necessary in the case of any sentence passed by it.

17.　　　The judgment of the Court shall be final and conclusive and, notwithstanding the provisions of the Code or any other law for the time being in force, or of any thing having the force of law, by whatsoever authority made or done, there shall be no appeal from any order or sentence of the Court, and no High Court shall have authority to revise any such order or sentence to transfer any case from such Court, or to make any order under section 491 of the Code or have any jurisdiction of any kind in respect of any proceedings under this Part, provided that nothing in this section shall be deemed to affect the powers of the Governor General in Council or of the Local Government to make orders under section 401 or 402 of the Code in respect of any person sentenced by the Court.

18. (1)　Notwithstanding anything to the contrary contained in the Indian Evidence Act, 1872 where
   - (a) The statement of any person has been recorded by a Magistrate, and such statement has been read over and explained to the person making it, and has been signed by him, or
   - (b) the statement of any person has been recorded by the Court, but such person has not been cross-examined, such Statement may be admitted in evidence by the Court if the person making the same is dead or cannot be found or is incapable of giving evidence, and the Court is of opinion that such death, disappearance or incapacity has been caused in the interests of the accused.

(2)　Depositions recorded under section 512 of the Code may in the circumstances specified in that section, be given in evidence at the trial under this Part of an accused.

19.　　　The Chief Justice may from time to time make rules providing for:-
(1)　The appointment and powers of a President of the Court, and the procedures to be adopted in the event of any judge of the Court being prevented from attending throughout the trial of an accused.

(2)　Any matters which appear to him necessary for carrying into effect or supplementing the provision of this Part preliminary or ancillary to trials.

# PART II

20.　　　If the Governor General in Council is satisfied that movements which are in his opinion likely to lead to the commission of offences against the State are being extensively promoted in the whole or any part of

British India, he may by notification in the 'Gazette of India' make a declaration to that effect and thereupon the provisions of this Part shall come into force in the area specified in the notification.

21. (1) Where in the opinion of the Local Government, there are reasonable grounds for believing that any person is or has been actively concerned in such area in any movement of the nature referred to in section 20, the Local Government may, by order in writing containing a declaration to that effect, give all or any of the following directions, namely: that such person –
- (a) shall, within such period as may be specified in the order, execute a bond, with or without sureties, to be of good behaviour for such period not exceeding one year as may be so specified;
- (b) shall notify his residence and any change of residence to such authority as may be so specified;
- (c) shall remain or reside in any area in British India so specified, provided that, if the area so specified is outside the province, the concurrence of the Local Government of that area to the making of the order shall first have been obtained;
- (d) shall abstain from any act so specified which, in the opinion of the Local Government, is calculated to disturb the public peace or is prejudicial to the public safety, and
- (e) shall report himself to the police at such periods as may be so specified.

(2) Any order under clauses (b) to (e) may also be made to take effect upon default by the person concerned in complying with an order under clause (a).

22. An order made under section 21 shall be served on the person in respect of whom it is made in the manner provided in the Code for service of summons, and upon such service such person shall be deemed to have due notice thereof.

23. The Local Government and every officer of Government to whom a copy of any order made under section 21 may be directed, by or under the general or special authority of the Local Government, may use any and every means to enforce compliance with the same.

24. An order made under section 2.1 shall only continue in force for a period of one month, unless it is extended by the Local Government as hereinafter provided in this Part.

25. (1) When the Local Government makes an order under section 21, such Government shall, as soon as may be, forward to the investigating authority to be constituted under this Act, a concise statement in writing setting forth plainly the grounds on which the Government considered it necessary that the order should be made and shall lay before

(2) The investigating authority shall then hold an inquiry in camera for the purpose of ascertaining what, in its opinion, having regards to the facts and circumstances adduced by the Government, appears against the person in respect of whom the order has been made. Such authority shall, in every case, allow the person in question a reasonable opportunity of appearing before it at some stage of its proceedings and shall, if he so appears, explain to him the nature of the charge made against him and shall hear any explanation he may have to offer and may undertake such further investigation (if any such further investigation is considered by such authority) to be relevant and reasonable,

Provided that the investigating authority, shall not disclose to the person whose case is before it any fact the communication of which might endanger the public safety or the safety of any individual.

Provided further that nothing in this sub-section shall be deemed to entitle the person in question to appear or to be represented before the investigating authority by pleader nor shall the Local Government be so entitled.

(3) Subject to the provisions of sub-section (2), the inquiry shall be conducted in such manner as the investigating authority considers best suited to elicit the facts of the case, and in making the inquiry, such authority shall not be bound to observe the rules of the law of evidence.

(4) On the completion of the inquiry, the investigating authority shall report in writing to the Local Government the conclusions at which it has arrived.

(5) If the investigating authority has not completed the inquiry within the period for which the duration of the order is limited by section 24, such authority may recommend to the Local Government that the period of duration of the order shall be extended for such period as it may consider necessary, and on such a recommendation the Local Government may extend the duration of the order accordingly.

26. (1) On receipt of the report of the investigating authority, the Local Government may discharge the order made under section 21, or may pass any order which is authorised by the terms of that section.

Provided that:-
  (a) any order so passed shall recite the finding of the investigating authority; and
  (b) a copy of such order shall be furnished to that person in respect of whom it is made.

(2) No order made under subsection (1) shall continue in force for more than one year from the date on which it was made, but the Local

Government may, if it is satisfied that such a course is necessary in the interests of the public safety, on the expiry of any such order, again make any order in respect of the person to whom it related which is authorised by section 21.

(3) No order made under subsection (1) shall continue in force for more than one year from the date on which it was made, but on its expiry may be renewed by the Local Government for a further period not exceeding one year.

Provided that any order so made or renewed, may at any time, be discharged or may be altered by the substitution of any other order authorised by section 21 and in that case no further reference to the investigating authority shall be necessary.

27. If any person fails to comply with, or attempts to evade, any order (other than an order to furnish security) made under the provisions of section 21 or section 26, he shall be punishable with imprisonment for a term which may extend to six months, or with fine which may extend to one thousand rupees, or with both.

28. The provision of section 514 of the Code shall apply to bonds executed under the provisions of this Part, with this modification that, the powers conferred by that Section on the Court shall be exercisable by any District Magistrate or Chief Presidency Magistrate, on application made on behalf of the Local Government.

## The Investigating Authority

29. (1) The Local Government shall appoint one or more investigating authorities for the purpose of this Part.

(2) Every investigating authority shall be appointed by order in writing, and shall consist of three persons, of whom one shall be a person having held judicial office not inferior to that of a District and Sessions Judge, and one shall be a person not in the service of .the Crown in India.

(3) The Local Government may by a like order appoint persons to fill casual vacancies occurring by reason of death, resignation of office or otherwise on any investigating authority, but in so doing, shall observe the provisions of subsection (2).

30. The Local Government shall by order in writing appoint such persons as it thinks fit to the Visiting Committees, for the purposes of this Part and shall by rules prescribe the functions which these Committees shall exercise:-
Provided that, in making such rules, provisions shall be made for periodical visits to persons under the provisions of this Part. Provided further that a person in respect of whom an order has been made under section 21 or section

26 requiring him to abstain from any specified act, or to report himself to the police, shall not be deemed to be under restraint for the purposes of this section.

31. (1) The Local Government may make rules providing for the procedure to be followed, regarding the notification of residence and reports to the police by persons in respect of whom orders have been made under section 21 or section 26.

(2) All rules made under sub-section (1) shall be published in the local official Gazette, and on such publication shall have effect as if enacted in this Part.

# PART III

32. If the Governor General in Council is satisfied that scheduled offences have been or are being committed in the whole or any part of British India to such an extent as to endanger the public safety, he may by notification in the 'Gazette of India' make a declaration to that effect, and thereupon the provisions of this Part shall come into force in the area specified in the notification.

33. (1) Where in the opinion of the Local Government, there are reasonable grounds for believing that any person has been or is concerned in such area in any scheduled offence, the Local Government may make in respect of such person any order authorised by section 21 and may further by order in writing direct:

(a) the arrest of any such person without warrant;

(b) the confinement of any such person in such place and under such conditions and restrictions as it may specify; and

(c) the search of any place specified in the order which, in the opinion of the Local Government, has been, is being, or is about to be, used by any such person for any purpose prejudicial to the public safety.

(2) The arrest of any person in pursuance of an order under clause (a) of sub-section (1) may be effected at any place where he may be found by any police officer of Government to whom the order may be directed.

(3) An order for confinement under clause (b) or for search under clause (c) of sub-section 1 may be carried out by any officer of Government to whom the order may be directed, and such officer may use any and every means to enforce the same:

34. Any person making an arrest in pursuance of an order under clause (a) of section 33 (1) shall forthwith report the fact to the Local Government and, pending receipt of the orders of the Local Government, may by order in writing, commit any person so arrested to such custody as the Local Government may by general or special order specify in this behalf;

Provided that no person shall be detained in such custody for a period exceeding fifteen days.

35. An order for the search of any place issued under the search provision of clause (c) of section 33 (1) shall be deemed to be a warrant issued by the District Magistrate having jurisdiction in the place specified therein, and shall be sufficient authority for the seizure of anything found in such place which the person executing the' order has reason to believe is being used or is likely to be used for any purpose prejudicial to the public safety, and the provisions of the Code so far as they can be made applicable shall apply to searches made under the authority of any such order and to the disposal of any property seized in any such search.

36. Where an order (other than an order for arrest or search) has been made under section 33, the provisions of section 22 to 26 shall apply in the same way as if the order were an order made under section 21, save that on receipt of the report of the investigating authority, the Local Government may, subject to the conditions prescribed by section 26, make any order which is authorised by section 33, and sections 22 to 26 and 28 to 31 shall be deemed to be included in this Part.

37. If any person fails to comply with, or attempts to evade any order made under section 33 or section 36 other than an order to furnish security, he shall be punishable with imprisonment for a term which may extend to one year, or with fine, or with both.

# PART IV

38. (1) On the expiration of the Defence of India (Criminal Law Amendment) Act, 1915, every person in respect of whom an order under rule 3 of the Defence of India (Consolidation) Rules, 1915, was in force immediately before the expiration of that Act, and who has in the opinion of the Local Government been concerned in any scheduled offence, or who is, on such expiration in confinement in accordance with the provisions of the Bengal State prisoners Regulation, 1918, shall be deemed to be a person resident in an area in which a notification under section 33 is in force and the provisions of Part III shall apply to every such person accordingly, save that no reference to the investigating authority shall be necessary.

(3) On the expiration of the Ingress into India Ordinance,.1914, as continued in force by the Emergency Legislation Continuance Act, 1915, any person in respect of whom an order was in force immediately before such expiration under section 2 of the Ordinance read with clause (b) or clause (c) of sub-section (2) of section 3 of the Foreigners Ordinance, 1914, shall be deemed to be a person resident in an area in which a notification under section 30 is in force and the provisions of Part II shall apply to every such person accordingly, save that no reference to the investigating authority shall be necessary.

## PART V

39. When a notification issued under section 3 or sections 30 or section 32 is cancelled, such cancellation shall not affect any trial, investigation or order commenced or made under this Act, which may be continued or enforced, and on the completion of any such investigation, any order which might otherwise have been made may be made and enforced, as if such notification had not been cancelled.

40. (1) An order made under Part I or Part III directing a person to remain or reside in any area in British India outside the area in which such Part is in force shall be as valid and enforceable in like manner as if such Part were in force throughout British India.

Provided that, if the arrest is made outside the province of the Local Government which made the order, the report required by section 34 shall be made to that Local Government and the period of detention limited by proviso to that section shall be extended to thirty days.

41. No order under this Act shall be called in question in any Court, and no suit or prosecution or other legal proceeding shall lie against any person for anything which is in good faith done or intended to be done under this Act.

42. All powers given by this Act shall be in addition to, and not in derogation of, any other powers conferred by or under any enactment, and all such powers may he exercised in the same manner and by the same authority as if this Act had not been passed.

## THE SCHEDULE
### (SEE SECTION 2)

(1) Any offence under Chapter VI and section 131 and 132 of "the Indian Penal Code:

(2) Any of the following offences, if, in the opinion of Government, such offence is connected with any movement endangering the Safety of the State, namely:-
  - (a) any offence under sections 148, 153A, 302, 304, 307, 308, 236, 327, 329, 332, 333, 385, 386, 387, 392, 393, 394, 395, 396, 397, 398, 399, 400, 401, 402, 431, 435, 436, 437, 438, 440, 454, 455, 457, 458, 459, 460, and 506 of the Indian Penal Code;
  - (b) any offence under the Explosive Sub-sections Act, 1908;
  - (c) any offence under section 20 of the Indian Arms Act 1878

(3) Any attempt or conspiracy to commit or any abatement of any of the above offences.

# APPENDIX II

# "AMRITSAR"

**BY AN ENGLISHWOMAN. BLACKWOODS MAGAZINE, 20<sup>TH</sup> MARCH 1920**
**THE RALLYING POST**

I had arrived new to the country at the end of January; Amritsar was my 'station' and at the beginning of April, I was living with Mr. and Mrs. J. in one of a group of houses called Canal Bungalows. On the morning of Thursday, I thought for a moment of visiting the bazaar in the city, but I had only returned from Lahore the night before, and what I had seen there of the crowds at the Hartal (day of mourning) on the 6th had made me nervous. Moreover, the attitude of the shopkeepers in our own Hall bazaar, for some time past had been distinctly unfriendly and the last time I went there my bearer had warned me not to get out of my tonga. The extreme heat, which follows the extreme cold of the Punjab, was already beginning to be oppressive and I preferred the coolness of the bungalow to the heat and glare outside, so that fortunately for myself I changed my mind. I had just lain down under the punkah about one o'clock when a servant announced that a lady wished to see me. I rose reluctantly, annoyed with my bearer for admitting a visitor after my order that I was not to be disturbed, but before I could leave my room, a second knock announced the arrival of more visitors and my bearer poured forth a long story of which the only words I could catch were *"Badmash"* (scoundrels) and *"Bazaar"*. His voice was drowned by the shrill cries of babies in the next room and it flashed upon my memory that the house had been chosen as a rallying post for European women and children in the event of trouble. My suspicions were quickly confirmed when I came into a drawing room full of people I had never seen before, who paid no attention whatever to my entry. Fresh arrivals poured in every minute and from one or two acquaintances among them, I elicited the little that they knew of what had happened. A few minutes earlier, a wild crowd had burst over the Hall Bridge (which connects the City with the Civil Lines) driving back and stoning a small picket, which was posted there. No shots had then been fired but the howl of the mob could be heard a quarter of a mile away and the residents in the main thoroughfares were rapidly warned to leave their bungalows for the rallying posts. The crowd was close at hand and a moment's delay might prove fatal; but at this somnolent hour it was no small task to persuade the women to move and one of them persistently refused to move because her baby was asleep. As people left their bungalows a few shots were heard from the direction of the bridge, but nothing was then known of the course of events. From men passing on horseback, we gradually learned a few details and before long we saw smoke and flames rising from the City and heard that Europeans were being murdered. After a time it was known that banks and Government buildings were on fire and that the murdered men included three bank officials. The old Sikh cashier of the National Bank had seen his master beaten down and had fled to procure help, but before he could return, kerosene oil was poured onto the still living body and only one boot was left for identification of the remains. A few of the Europeans employed in the banks had succeeded in escaping to the Kotali or City Police Station and were still hemmed in there.

The afternoon passed slowly, with rumours and alarms, which increased the input of the many women who did not know where their husbands were. Those of us who had anything to do were too busy to think and three of the women and three of the babies were ill; but human nature is always the same and I was amused to see on returning to my room, that my dressing table had been depleted of everything that could be used as a cosmetic, as if a horde of locusts had settled on it, and we had to make peace between one or two who could not sit under the punkah and the majority who were prepared to faint if it was switched off.

About half an hour before sunset, news came that the fort was ready to receive us. Every possible conveyance had been secured and we packed ourselves in, making a picture like Epsom Road on Derby Day. Very few had brought anything with them, so we stripped the house of everything that could be used as bedding during the coming night.

The Fort

The Fort of Gobindgarh, which we were now to know so well, was built over a hundred years ago by the great Maharaja Ranjit Singh, to protect the treasure which he kept with the bankers of Amritsar, prosperous then as now. It is said that he employed an Italian engineer and traces of its exotic origin linger in the names of the different blocks and passages. To reach the Fort, we had to cross the railway line that our handful of troops had held all day against the hordes from the city, by the Rego Bridge. We set forth in some trepidation, but the arrival of some Ghurkha troops about this time enabled the road to be picketed and the way was safe. Men from the Central Follower's Depot, armed with staves, accompanied us and it was not long before we were driving through the winding entrances to the Fort.

Dusk was now falling and we had to make haste to prepare for the night. We found places where we could and most of us packed into the upper storey of the Cavalier Block which rises in the centre of the great quadrangle. The heat however, was stifling. There were not half a dozen fans in the whole Fort including those in the hospital and the canteen hall and so many people found it the lesser of two evils to spend that night on the ground outside. One or two had managed to get their bedding brought by their servants, but the rest were ill equipped for the conditions they had to face. We distributed the heavy clothing, blankets and rugs, which we had brought from the bungalow, but there would not have been enough to go round if the garrison had not given up some of their blankets. Our next thought was to find a meal for the many women and children who had eaten nothing since early morning. We had only scraps that we had brought away from the bungalow, but once again the soldiers came to the rescue and gave up half their bread ration. All these things were being done at once amid indescribable turmoil.

A roll call revealed 130 women and children besides babies. The civilian men who were not too old or sick had already been posted to defence duties round the Fort and made up another fifty. A number of servants had also come down before the gate closed at sundown and presented another problem, as they required native food. While they were being given their handful of grain to last them till the morning, a grey bearded old Sikh orderly, Sher Singh, proudly refused to take his share saying he had often had to go without food for two or three days on the field of battle. This man set a splendid example throughout and indeed all the servants behaved well under very trying circumstances.

It had long been-dark and we were working hard to get things straight and settle people down for the night, when I was suddenly drawn away by an officer who whispered a request for a lantern to bring in what was left of Mr. Thompson's body from one of the banks. Desperately afraid lest the news should spread, I secured the only lantern in the Fort for him and he went away. We learned afterwards that this was the body of Sergeant Rawlings, who had been beaten to death beneath the walls of the Fort and not Mr. Thompson's that had not then been recovered. When nothing more was left to be done, some of us went on to the ramparts for a few minutes quiet, and from the top of the Western wall, we saw the native city ablaze with electric light - a contrast to the darkness behind us.

At midnight we turned in but the daylight seemed to come before we had closed our eyes. The outlook was not pleasant, for women who had never known a day's hardship before they found themselves stripped of all the decencies and comforts they had come to look upon as necessities and surrounded by the miseries of dirt, heat and overcrowding. There was no sanitation; everything depended on the servants who had not yet been organised. There was no privacy and we had to hide under our beds to dress ourselves. Sixteen people shared one small room for the first three days and those who had no rooms were really better off. There were no beds, no proper bedding, no mosquito nets, no fans and hardly any lighting. No one had any small personal possessions or any change of clothing. We did not know when we could get supplies of fresh food or milk and as there were only twelve cups and about twenty plates, distribution of what food we had was difficult. One could summon up courage to face these conditions for oneself, but the presence of so many babies and children made the situation really serious. One had developed typhoid fever that morning and they all had requirements that could not be met.

Our numbers were swelling, for not everybody had managed to get to the rallying post. During the first night, three survivors who had escaped into the Police Station were brought out of the City in Indian clothes. They told us of the infuriated crowds that had swept through the City on that terrible afternoon, drunk with their victory over unarmed men and calling for 'white blood'. A Dutch merchant had hidden all day and had come out at night disguised in a 'burka' the all-enveloping white cloth used by purdah women. An English lady doctor had managed to conceal herself in her hospital while the crowd tried to find her and she, also, had escaped in the evening. Two Indian ladies, school teachers, who had driven out of the City in a closed carriage told us of the Sikh peasants who were pouring into the town with their iron-shod sticks. The booty from the National Bank had been carried out into the District as proof that the British rule was over and all the riff raff from miles around hurried in to be on the spot if looting began again. The residents of the railway quarters came in to us from the railway station, in which they had taken refuge. They brought news of how the crowd had swept through the station leaving behind them burning trucks and the hardly recognisable body of Guard Robinson. Everything was done to stop false reports. Under the conditions I have described, morale was of paramount importance, but the real truth was so often worse than anything rumour could invent that one realised the uses of censorship. It is not surprising that there was a certain amount of hysteria, but our people as a whole showed both courage and good sense.

During the first three days, every hour brought in some news from outside; of firing at Lahore, (only 20 miles away), of murders at Kasur, of trains de-railed and lines tom up, of telegraph wires cut and Government buildings and railway stations burnt, and we were very anxious about Europeans in the neighbourhood. The news was often vague, but with the breakdown in communications and our own experiences, we were left to imagine the worst and the native population had some excuse for their belief that the British Raj was over. The situation was so precarious and troops for defensive purposes so scarce, that it was decided to evacuate the Alexandra School just inside the Civil Lines, in which the Indian Christian Schoolchildren had been collected until now. It might be supposed by English readers, that these children would have been safe from their own countrymen, but on the day of the riots the crowd set fire to one school with the children inside and it was only the timely arrival of a small band of police that saved them. We were told how to receive them and when they arrived they brought our numbers up to about 400, a heavy strain on our resources, but they were grateful and worked splendidly.

An office was established in the Canteen Hall and all the civilian inhabitants of the Fort and their servants were registered. After a few days, passes were issued for going out of the Fort, but this was not allowed without an armed escort and everyone had to be back before sunset. The time at which the pass-holder was due to return was registered so that if he or she failed to report to the office by the hour named, a search party would be sent out immediately.

The days were monotonous and we had to keep very quiet for the sake of Miss Sherwood who was lying between life and death. Seizing her as she was cycling from house to house in the City, the crowd had beaten her down with iron bound sticks and left her for dead in the gutter. For many days, her life was in danger. After about a week it was considered safe for us to travel, and arrangements were made to remove all the women and children to the hills. Special trains were run, packed with refugees from Lahore and Amritsar. It was considered by the authorities that no women should be left behind and they decided that the Eurasians as well as Europeans should reside in hill stations for a time. The sight of the trains must have given residents in unaffected Districts some idea of what the riots meant, and yet it has been stated that there was no real insecurity and no .more trouble than the police could have dealt with. No European who was in Amritsar or Lahore doubts that, for some days, there was a very real danger of the entire European population being massacred and that General Dyer's action alone saved them.

# APPENDIX III

# EXTRACTS FROM MRS. GERARD WATHEN'S DIARY WRITTEN IN 1919

### (FROM THE PAGES IN THE POSSESSION OF RALEIGH TREVELYAN, QUOTED IN HIS BOOK)

We had a quiet spring though endless people to stay which is always nice ... the boys both go to classes with the Sikh boys – and every night a small team come to play some game in the garden – all a great success ... When we got back after Christmas, Gerard found for the first time a questioning about politics amongst the students ... in view of the sitting of Congress there next Christmas, he determined to meet the development in every possible way and gave up more of his spare time and his evenings than ever to talking to the students, explaining the Rowlatt Acts which are the present cry taken up by the seditionists – and listen to all their questions and their difficulties for which labour he was most doubly repaid when the trouble came.

In March, a hartal was proclaimed through the Province to take place each Sunday as a protest against the Rowlatt Act. Unbelievable lies were spread such as that if even five people seen speaking together, the police would take them to prison without trial. After that their marriage and burial rights would be interfered with. These lies were specially spread amongst the lower classes such as the tonga wallahs, sweepers and fruit sellers. By the beginning of April we realised things were nasty and Gerard and I went off shooting near Tarn Taran. Came in for the Great Mehla - a wonderful sight. All day from early dawn the crowd a moving mass as far as the eye could see, of gaily-dressed Sikhs and their families. On our way home we walked round the big tank of the Tauntroy [?] Golden Temple, so densely packed with Sikhs for the whole mile round that we could hardly move. Afterwards we met the Guilfords (missionaries) who spoke gravely and foretold a bad Sikh rising in the near future. The rising was correct but it was not the Sikhs. Nancy Barnes came to stay with us. I had been to the city fairly frequently, about the 5th April I took her to the Temple and found an unaccountable number of people moving about apparently with no particular object - in fact, for the first time I had an instinctive feeling of relief as I crossed the railway bridge out of the City. That Sunday a nasty crowd collected. We went to church, but the road was guarded and the soldiers wore ball cartridges. After that no Englishman could get a tonga. There was no doubt that clouds were gathering. The shops refused to serve us; a sais was beaten when he had been sent to fetch a tonga. I refused to let the horses go to the City.

On Wednesday 9th, Mr. Jarman came to lunch saying a plot had been discovered to murder all Europeans on 16th when Gandhi was expected. That Kitchlew and Satyapal were making most inflammatory speeches and things were in a very bad state. After he had gone I resolved to take the children away as soon as possible - and wired for my car on the 13th instead of the 25th - and so on and after tea Gerard and I drove round to see the Miles Irvings (Deputy-Commissioner) [*line crossed out and illegible, probably about opinion of Miles Irving*] Gerard heard serious rumours through his Professors though through all those weeks not one of his boys had observed Hartal- a great triumph as they were doing it freely at the Government College (Lahore). We found Miles Irving out but she was in [*dense crossing out*] ... they seemed not to have grasped the situation at all. She laughed at the people who were nervous - said someone had thought arrangements to go to the Fort if anything occurred, but nothing had been done and she didn't think they had remembered the people in the Khalsa College at all! We went away feeling thoroughly dissatisfied about things.

That night we dined with the Hexts (Supply and Transport). The Becketts were there. They were just back from Lahore where they had come in for a very nasty procession headed by Government College Students trying to force their way to Government House and demand withdrawal of the Rowlatt Acts. Fortunately there things were well in hand. Troops and police all prepared. The crowd got half way up the Mall, were fired on and a few fell and the rest departed. But though it subsided then it was by no means over - and yet this had not opened peoples' eyes. I spoke straight to the Becketts and Major Hext and Mr. Scott of the National Bank. They laughed - and Scott said it was ridiculous to be nervous with all our machine guns and airplanes. Poor man, he was dead within 15 hours, brutally murdered. I came away resolved to leave on Friday 11th at the earliest I could.

<u>April 10th, Thursday.</u> Our servants went to the bazaar early to buy flour and sugar - all was quiet – at 10 a.m. the D.C. sent for Kitchlew and Satyapal (the seditions leaders) and deported them in a motorcar with Mr. Rehill, to Dharamsala. At the same

time he summoned a committee; the A.C., Beckett, among them, to discuss what precautions to take. It was too late then to take any precautions except to place all the L.D.F. at their disposal within reach. This was done. They were posted in the Ram Bagh to await events, about a company all told - feeble and untrustworthy- some half a dozen gunners from the Fort were mounted and told to guard the bridges. At 10.30, Irving, the D.C. and A.C. rode round the City, finding 'all satisfactory' in the D.C.'s eyes though not in those of the A.C. Beckett, so unsatisfied was he that at 11.30 he rode back to the City only to meet a furious mob pouring out, headed by pleaders and shouting for Kitchlew and Satyapal. He tried to stop them telling them he would tell them all if they would go back into the City gates but they pushed him back on the Railway Bridge, making for Kuchery. At Madan's shop he found four mounted gunners. These he ordered to get the crowd back over the bridge but on no account to fire. Then he galloped to the D.C. When he got back to the bridge the gunners had got the crowd back over the bridge but at that moment D. galloped up from behind [*dense crossing out but some clear*] to say that he had been ordered with a handful of men to get in behind the crowd and disperse them. This he had tried to do by firing on them with the result that they went mad and he had to retire leaving the mob looting the National Bank and murdering every Englishman they could find and [*deletion*] wrecking the telegraph and telephone office.

All that morning we knew things were unquiet, but how bad we did not guess till we were at lunch and Beckett galloped up looking very wild, his horse covered with foam and blood, saying the crowd was in the station and coming to the civil lines.

I had everything in readiness since the morning as I felt things were bad - I now dressed the children in the most comfortable clothes they had, did up 3 small rolls of bedding that a man could easily carry and some food – got my khaki riding things and just waited expecting to have to fly to the Professors' quarters or some village at any moment. It was not pleasant at all. After that I walked round the college with Gerard. We were just coming home when we met Mr. Kitchin, the Commissioner from Lahore – motoring through with Donald the policeman and someone else ... Gerard got into their car and went off to the D.C.'s. It seemed hours till he came back ... I don't know that I even expected him back ... everything seemed at an end. At about 3 o'clock he appeared looking ghastly, to say that Stewart, Scott, Thompson and two others had been hideously murdered ... all Banks wrecked, the station wrecked, the telegraph office, a church and various other buildings and that but for an unexpected company of Ghurkhas who had just passed through, we would have been wiped out ... all communications cut and the lines below and above the station pulled up!

As we stood there a crowd of students and professors appeared ... here's the end I thought! But no ... they came to beg Gerard to let them guard us and the College through the night - not to send us to the Fort!!! It was a triumphant moment - after that my spirits rose a little. Meanwhile we sent some of our luggage and servants to Chakarta to' wait there till we could get a train through to Pindi. At 5.30 Gerard drove to the Ashford's house to see if we could help with the women and children who were going to the Fort... it was a tragic night ... never did I see horror so grimly written on any face except those who had come from the trenches - there were women and children all herded together - several not knowing if their husbands were dead or alive - some knew within an hour that they were dead - others were-not relieved of their suspense till after midnight. I uttered a heartfelt prayer of thankfulness as I drove home to my own house to sleep. There were over 400 people in the Fort with no provisions but bully beef and biscuits, four bathrooms and three rooms. The dust and glare and heat were ghastly and several people and children went in ill - so much for the forethought of our D.C. Miles, and yet <u>he must have known.</u>

That night we slept safely in the garden as usual and I even forgave the students when they demanded new hockey balls that they might see to play by moonlight - and when they did all through my flowerbeds most of the night!

After the mob had gone mad - they attacked the National. Bank - beat Mr. Stewart with lathis and then pouring oil on him when he was only half conscious, burnt him! They did the same to Mr. Scott, just piling the furniture on top of him.

Nothing was left of the Bank ... it was gutted - they then went to the Alliance Bank – Mr. Thomson defended himself and then ran upstairs and hid - but they found him - dropped him out - threw him out of the window - poured oil on him while he was alive and burnt him - they then burnt the Roman Catholic church - hunted and beat a Missionary, Miss Sherwood - saying she was English and must die - though she was eventually picked up unconscious and carried by an Indian into his house and safety - hunted Mr. Jarman who was rescued by Indians and another Thompson and another missionary lady - all of whom owed their lives to their clerks - and then pulled up the lines and wrecked the station - killing a goods inspector with lathis and trampling to death a Tommy whom they caught escaping to the Fort - it was just as they were marching to the Civil Lines that the Ghurkhas turned up - were detrained, fired on the mob and drove it back to the City and held it. At 7 p.m. an airplane at last arrived from Lahore. At midnight, .the Londons came from Jullundur. At 2 a.m. more British troops and an armoured train arrived from Lahore only then may we have been said to be in some safety.

<u>April 11th Friday.</u> At 7a.m., Gerard heard that the Commissioner and some soldiers were coming over with orders to march through the City - firing on anyone they saw - he dashed off to the station and found them already discussing it. For an hour he argued that it was political madness to do such a thing without warning - yesterday when the murdering was in swing, it would have been a different matter. At length he got the major on his side and finally got the Committee to say that the crowds should be given till 2 p.m. to bury their dead and disperse ... and he undertook to send his students and the maulvi into the City to warn the crowds. At 2 airplanes were to ascend and if the crowds still persisted, bombs were to be dropped - no European had so far, or could, enter the city.

Our feelings were intense all that morning. I packed the few remaining things. The butler returned from Chakarta station saying the luggage we sent down last night

## EXTRACTS FROM MRS. GERARD WATHEN'S DIARY WRITTEN IN 1919

was safe but that the crowds had locked all the rest of the station and had bribed them ... Gerard sent a guard of students to watch over our luggage until our train which we hoped to catch that evening passed through - I read "The Secret City" by Walpole, feverishly in between whiles - the more lurid questions about the riots in Petrograd being peculiarly in keeping - somewhat harrowing to one's nerves during those trying hours. Gerard came over occasionally reporting the students' behaviour was splendid. No news from the city. Mary and I managed to pack away all my favourite things that morning and afterwards as I lay for a few minutes on the sofa - nerves stretched to breaking point, she gave me a whisky and soda and I began to understand why people take to drink.

As the time drew on and 2 o'clock came nearer - the tension was intense ... at last the hour struck ... planes go up ... would they fire? Had the crowd dispersed? One, two, three minutes passed. Mary and I went onto the drive, breathless, to listen. Gerard came up - then old maulvi appeared ~ he had been to the mosques. At the one by the Hall Gate he had had some trouble to get a hearing, but he did so at last - and they listened to him and had gone to their homes. Still the planes hovered around - but no bombs were dropped - Gerard had saved the City and saved the Government from endless political difficulties in the future.

Gerard sat with me then - or we walked a little in the grounds. At 4 we all packed into the Tum-Tum and one tonga - with the Armstrongs with us and got down to the station with no mishaps though Gerard bicycling with us urged us to keep together. At the station the relief of finding oneself guarded by plenty of troops was immense, British and Ghurkhas, fully armed, guarded every inch of the place. In a siding stood the armoured train, machine guns ready and overhead droned the airplanes. Oh! The relief after the last four days. No one can imagine. We got some tea then with great difficulty, not a soul was on the platform except the D.C., and the Commissioner and the soldiers. Everything was hushed and expectant. I couldn't help having a sickening feeling at the thought of leaving Gerard ... and the journey before us, but I also felt the journey must be got through at all costs. The train was nearly four hours late, but she came in at last. All of us got into the carriage. The Armstrongs beastly dogs, some horrible Belgium [?] I doubt it - Cattle merchants were in our carriage come to buy at the big fair, they were most offensive and Gerard turned them out. At Chakarta there was a seething mob but our good students put our luggage in and thanks to them we lost nothing. It was dark now and as we passed through station after station and stopped at Arrari and Jallo with these dense crowds of restless angry looking peasants, I cannot think now why they did not attack us, as indeed they looked to doing all up the line the next day. Had they done so all would have been up. At Lahore it was a grim spectacle ... pickets of Sikhs up and down the platform, talk of 'strike' all down the line, processions, rioting, meetings in Lahore, grave looking soldiers, eating horrid meals in the refreshment rooms, ourselves the only civilians. Gerard took me in for a last meal. He was dressed in khaki with his collar open ... and like every other man looked as though he had had neither sleep nor rest for days, like all these men he wore the tense look - the look of constant expectation of what I or no one could tell. He said, "*We may never meet again, things are as bad as they have ever been in our history ... the whole country is ablaze ... we don't yet know what we are in for.*" And with almost these words - and very much these feelings, we parted. He standing there on that hot platform with its lurid half light in which soldiers stood in knots, they showed all that is best in our race, and so we passed out of the station; only one thing certain, that we were all in greater danger at that moment than ever in our lives, or than I hope we may ever be again..

I did not sleep much until the small hours of the morning when weariness came over me.

April 12th Saturday The Brian Bonham-Carters met us at Pindi, fed us and housed us that day, and got us cars. The Goodalls got to Kahalla and we to Murree, and how great was the relief to be out of danger no one who has not been through it, with children, can ever tell.

April 18th We got up without mishap. Mrs. Sykes had our tents ready but it was so horribly wet and cold, and the tents so badly pitched that many decided to go into houseboats. Accordingly, we hunted round and got two very nice ones, which we anchored by Gupkar beyond Gagribal point on the Dal Lake. Even here things are not too satisfactory, more from mismanagement by the Kashmir Government, but shortage of food and fuel may lead to rioting, and then ruffians once let loose, with Amritsar plunder in their minds, will not stay their hands when they come to the Europeans.

Today I got a letter from Gerard, he was in the grounds on the 13$^{th}$ when a young officer galloped up and ordered him and Armstrong and Hervey to go bag and baggage to the Camp.

It appears that orders had been given for no further meetings in the City - Martial Law was of course proclaimed on the 11$^{th}$ Dyer had sent out a Proclamation on the 13$^{th}$ (Sunday) that any meetings taking place would be dispersed by fire - his orders had been disobeyed up until then. He knew the country was in a state of rebellion afar and wide. He knew there was war in Afghanistan. He knew there was Bolshevik propaganda throughout the country, the time, he felt, had come to act.

That afternoon he heard, in spite of his Proclamation, there was to be a meeting in the Jalianwalla Bagh and the leaders were telling the people that the British would never fire. He went off with his troops, determined to teach them a lesson, fired 1600 rounds - the firing lasted 20 minutes in all, the people throwing themselves on the ground only to be shot as they rose, there were only two small exits for a crowd of over 20,000 ... and in one exit stood the soldiers. They estimated the kill at 1042.

When Gerard attacked him on this, saying India would never forget, Dyer said he had to make up his mind in a few seconds or his men would have been overpowered - he also said he meant to strike hard as a lesson. This was 2 p.m.

Gerard got to the Headquarters at about 6, to find a prevailing fear of the effect on the surrounding country, that the massacre might have the effect of setting it all ablaze - he discovered that only a cipher telegram stating that 'firing had taken place' was to be sent to the Lieutenant-Governor, no one was to be sent officially to tell him.

Gerard, seeing this was wrong argued the point and by 2 a.m., induced them to send Mr. Jacob, who had come to lecture to the College, to the Lieutenant Governor in his car, Gerard volunteering to go too.

They had a risky drive, well armed, for dacoits were ranging the countryside, but they got through safely. By 2 a.m. they had Sir Michael up to find the telegram had arrived indecipherable, so that he knew nothing of what had happened, he immediately held a council of war, tried to get into communication with Simla, of course failed, and evidently till that moment had never realised how bad things were at Amritsar. Then Gerard (as is his way) spoke his mind, he told Sir Michael that unless he wanted trouble in the future with the leaders and to stir up bitter political feeling both immediately and for years to come, he should immediately go to Amritsar himself, have Dyer replaced, and admit a mistake had been made; not in the actual firing but in the amount that was done. Sir Michael, probably disliking criticism refused to listen to what Gerard said. Instead sent a congratulatory message to Dyer through General Beynon, and afterwards sent word to Gerard through Mr. Kitchin, that he did not approve of Gerard speaking to him as he had!

From this time Martial Law came into force, no Indian might travel, and very few could get passes, all their bicycles and traps and cars were commandeered. No Indian might use a tonga and all water and electric light cut off, all shops forced to be opened, and life made as unpleasant for them as could be. This was both in Amritsar and Lahore. In Lahore the students had led the trouble. The D.A.V. in particular were bad, but so were the Government College, seems to have completely lost his head and knew so little of his students that he handed over many that were innocent, and convicted all he did convict on the word of the superintendents of the Boarding houses! And many of them after came to Gerard who never had anything to do with them, to get justice done, and Gerard managed to get things put right in some cases.

In Amritsar the great punishment was to the people who lived in the street where Miss Sherwood the missionary was nearly hammered to death. One end of the street was blocked; at the other end was a picket. Only people on urgent business were allowed up the street, they had to crawl on all fours all the way. This lasted some days. One Indian offered a Tommy a heavy bribe to let him walk up it; the Tommy replied that it was worth twice that money to see the man crawl. The order was General Dyer's and was in print.

Meanwhile the people, over 400, remained in the Fort for 10 days with most inadequate organisation, most of the time and for several days the Indians burned their dead and howled and wailed below the walls all night to annoy, but this was before Dyer's shooting, after that things began to take a turn.

We in Kashmir didn't feel altogether safe. I never felt really happy till I got to Gulmarg. Things in the state were unsatisfactory. there was a shortage of rice, a muddle over fuel, and so that many were starving and as Kashmiris were beginning to return from the looting of Amritsar, there was some cause to fear their influence might be brought to work and used as a further tool by the Bolsheviks. The authorities entirely recognised the danger and *every* day Mr. Glancy sent me word where we were encamped as to how things were going.

Otherwise we had a wonderful time, Mrs. Beckett was with us, we slept on the roof of our boat, watching marvellous nights and sunrises over the waters of the lake and the mountains all round.

I made friends with the Blunts and the Wards and the Andrews. Major Wigram and Mrs. Sykes and many others, and but for the horrid undercurrent of apprehension of trouble, should never have had a happier holiday.

On May 23$^{rd}$, we-went up to Gulmarg. Oh the beauty of that snow carpeted black forest up to Khulai, or streams, I never saw anything so beautiful, or such an exhilarating air.

We were in Mrs. McDonnell's and very comfortable we were. Really nothing of interest happened during those months. The boys did lessons with the Johnsons next door, with a Miss Mayer, which was a great success. Things began to settle down in the Punjab so that I was less anxious about Gerard. He went up to Simla at Easter and had a jolly week with the Barnes, and we sold Duiker to Captain Gordon Ives, one of the A.D.C.s, which nearly broke my heart and whose loss I seem to feel more and more as time goes on.

Sir Michael O'Dwyer came and said nice things about Gerard and the students and later Sir Edward Maclagan paid a private visit having tea with Gerard and meeting various Amritsar people there, and showing great interest in the whole thing, but from first to last no public recognition of all Gerard had done was ever put down. And this I account for entirely on the grounds of jealousy on the part of the civil authorities that could not bear the big part Gerard played in it all. Later his work was recognised he was given the C.I.E. for all that he had done, the youngest educationist to receive it, still feel joyous for the honour.

About July 10$^{th}$ Gerard came up to Gulmarg, the boys and I rode down to meet him and met him about three miles down. Then we had a glorious summer, the best I've ever had. Walking and climbing and rambling about, going into camp at Lion Knag for one jolly week. We could not go further afield because of the cholera so we took the boys with us for their last time. I really sat at my painting and managed to do over 200 different sorts worth publishing, but it was very hard work.

Gerard went down for a week in September, and then returned till the beginning of October. We followed him down on the 8$^{th}$ in tongas, a very easy pleasant journey. Mary had gone ahead in a motor so we saw her no more.

When I got down I found things fairly quiet but the Commission under Lord Hunter was beginning to rake up all the old feelings, which had really subsided. It was most unfortunate that the Home Government should have shown such complete distrust of the local Government. It not only criticised its actions most unfairly but also reversed all its sentences, which is absolutely bound to have a disastrous effect on the leaders and the people [*deletion*]. It is heartbreaking work. How can the Home people understand the situation or the people with whom they are dealing?

Our men in the Punjab are as fine a race as was ever bred, fair minded, with the highest sense of duty and working through sickness and in health for the good of the country, with literally never a thought for themselves, and with an understand and sympathy[?] unparalleled. There is no question but that they 'know more than the men at home, they should have been trusted through this but one of the worst errors in the history of our times in India has been perpetrated and with the action [*deletion of a whole line*] of the Home Government, the waning of our power has begun. The people now show an utter contempt for us and they know they can murder and rob and within a few hours of conviction by the local authorities - who do know, the India office - who can know nothing, will absolve them. Never have we made so great a blunder. Yet our men still stick loyally to their work and will do so.

I met several of the Commission. It's a thankless task - they know it. Sir Michael had made one mistake in not going over or seeing into everything himself the day after the shooting. Otherwise the sentences given, the laws made, were all that should have been meted out, and were neither malicious nor unjust. All they can find is that Dyer fired for too long, and that has been admitted. So why rake up all the bitter feeling that has subsided. Gandhi travels round the country with the Pandit Narayan, talking and stirring the people with lies, making them imagine horrors that never existed. They came to the College one day, Gerard showed them round. He was not [*deletion*] impressed by Gandhi, but found the Pandit intelligent and keen. That same day we had had two men from the Wild West, who gave an exhibition of lassoing. I was their 'victim' and it gave one an unpleasant feeling to be caught up short at full gallop with rope round one's waist, another over your horse's neck or leg. Later on the men on the sugar commission came in and we showed them around. Keen intelligent men thrilled with the possibilities of the place and the enormous influence the right men could have in it. Sunda Singh Megitia the ex-secretary brought them.

With the coming of the National Congress to Amritsar and Christmas, the knowledge of a coming railway strike, the ill feeling aroused by the sitting of the Hunter commission, and the news of the Bolshevist agents working through the Middle East, I began to feel I could not face any more trouble with the children and decided to go home as soon as we could get passages. Everyone was anxious. No one knew what we were in for, Turkish terms were hourly awaited and the fact of the delay was adding to the general unrest. I seldom drive in the City now, and when I did it was with a feeling that I dared not catch the eye of the men who now stared insolently at me in a way I had never experienced till last spring. One day as I went down the Ivory Market, two men ahead of me began to fight. In an instant, men collected from nowhere. Six sadhus were coming up the street behind me shouting and signing, the crowd grew, but many of them now were no longer interested in the fighters they were staring at and talking about me. I sat there quietly awaiting a chance and as soon as the fighters got into a side street I pushed though, and to my inexpressible relief met a mounted native superintendent of police and several men with him, he made way for me, followed me and did not leave me until I was safely in a broad street again. I had never experienced such a thing before and was more than relieved to get out of it. I had the children with me, and Nattu. Many Sikhs acknowledge me but there was no question whatsoever as to what the Mohammedans felt. At the Stations the atmosphere was the same. We felt it so electric that anything ... almost the dropping of a parcel, might set the whole thing ablaze. Our old servants were all right but new coolies in the garden were insolent and lazy - and even the boys who had only been a few months with us showed [*deleted*] a nasty insubordinate manner.

Amongst the better class Indians who professed loyalty but were doubtless all sitting on the fence, the change of manners in the last six months amazed me. They were openly off-hand, openly said things they would never have dreamt of last winter. Told Gerard straight out that the world was changing, the time had come for them to change too, we could not expect to govern India for ever, they did not want us any more and they meant to get rid of us. Syandi Gurbush Singh the secretary came to say goodbye, we taxed him with it:

*"Of course we want the country for ourselves"* but we said:

*"What will you do without our Army?"*

*"Mr. Wathen, within two days of your withdrawing the Afghans will be over the frontier and the Mohammedans all over the country will have looted our houses and carried off our women, it cannot be done"* (and in 1947 it happened).

That from an educated Indian who has spent years in England, and has now joined the progressives (secretly) attended Congress, helps in the organisation of it and is by way of being a barrister in Amritsar. They know they cannot do without our army. It is the question they have never faced. The question they will hide and avoid till it is dug out; and then they have but one answer:

*"We cannot do without you."*

Yet they do or will hide it so successfully that they will stir the people blindly against us till we shall be forced to either leave the country or hold it by force. There is one policy open that think, and many think, would bring them to their knees, to go now when Congress is assembled and say:

*"You do not want us here any more so we are going"* or the alternative –

*"We won you by the sword and by the sword we are going to hold you."*

Now is the time, even a few months later it will be too late, and then we shall drag on month by month with a dagger at our throats in an intolerable position, losing our best men by murder, and our best men too because they will not go to India under such conditions, till finally weakened beyond all hope we shall have to let the country go in the same state and a great deal worse than what Ireland is now.

# APPENDIX IV

# DISTRICT REPORTS

In the statement of the Bombay Government, a pattern was described which was seen in other places.

*"An outstanding feature of the rioting was the combination of Hindus and Mohammedans in attacking the police and the troops with showers of stones. The Mohammedans were deliberately incited by the Hindus, who spread the report that the Rowlatt Bills were intended to enable Government to coerce the Mohammedans and prevent them from giving trouble so as to facilitate the dismemberment of Turkey."*

The shouts of 'Hindu Mussulman ki jai' repeatedly raised by the crowd had this significance.

*"Forty-two rioters were arrested, and on conviction, received sentences varying from a fine of Rs. 2 to six months rigorous imprisonment. In connection with the damage done to the property of the Bombay Electric Supply and Tramways Company on the 10th and 11th April, proceedings were taken by the Chief Presidency Magistrate under section 45 of Act IV of 1902, who directed compensation to the amount of Rs. 4,552.8.0 to be recovered. Three police constables were seriously injured and taken to hospital. Many were slightly injured by stones. The squadron of cavalry suffered 16 casualties of whom 4 were severely injured and taken to hospital."*

In Ahmedabad and Kaira (where Home Rulers and Gandhi had taken up 'Passive Resistance' against the payment of Land revenue in 1918), the 'damage done to property was as follows:

Government Rs.    66,447,12.1
Municipal 24,420,0.0
Private      1,24,861.10.0
Total        2,15,729.6.1

That there was not a greater loss was probably due to the Deccan Infantry, whose detachments of from 25 up to one of 50 and one of 200, were despatched to guard the various Treasuries in the district. The number arrested was 132, of whom 51 were mill hands. The rest include almost every branch of employment - medical practitioners (1), teachers (1), cultivators (22) and barristers (2). Those arrested were also listed by caste and there were 17 Mussulmans, 39 Thakardas, 18 Banias and 1 Brahmin among a long list of others.

[Among the listed poems and inspirational runes are a number written, allegedly by Thoreau - so: Whom will you respect? Rowlatt Bills or the Truth. I see no necessity of teaching the virtue of respecting the law. As well as war cry poems inciting to kill the British there was one rhyme by 'Anarchist' at Dehra which advised the people clearly to kill the various officials.]

*"Har Har Mahadev* [Hindu War Cry]

*The English people are very tyrannical, they are perfidious and treacherous. They have disgraced India by enacting Black Acts.*

*In the war blood was freely shed (by Indian) and food money and valuable lives were given.*

*And as a reward thereof Black Acts and two stones of a grinding mill were given*

*Punjabi, Bengali, Decanni and Gujariti*

*Why have you been asleep you also rulers of the Native States. Post offices railways and telegraph offices must be destroyed first. Police must also be destroyed to ensure a positive success. Collectors Commissioners and Governors in particular,*

*Massacre them, only then will your (Indian) prestige be saved.*

*To slaughter the white people take up swords;*

*Brave men make haste- and do not delay;*

*If you spare them they will assume the tiger's form and will crush you all, even the Indian ruling chiefs.*

*Form plots and have courage but do not have at heart the slightest mercy. Then only will success be achieved understand, oh, India*

*Arjun too was given the same advice emphatically by Krishna;*

*You all too therefore act in the same way and victory in every way is attained.*

*Nothing will be achieved by taking to Satyagraha but by taking up arms victory will be had.*

*The English will fly and your object be served"* Anarchist.

# DISTRICT REPORTS

In the following paragraphs, we look at the successful economic situation due to good rains. In trade, merchandise into Bombay amounted to Rs. 2.30 crores during the first two weeks of July. This merchandise included cotton, wool and silk goods, kerosene oil, coal, dyes, motorcars, spirits and hardware.

[A fortnight later on 31st July, a report sent to the Home Member from the Punjab read as follows:]

Political:

The celebration of peace has been the great event of the past fortnight and has been almost universally characterised by real enthusiasm and friendliness. With the exception perhaps of one or two of the larger cites, the political situation is now satisfactory and opportunity was taken of the gala on the 19th to show the very real appreciation of the bulk of the people not only at the return of normal conditions with the hope of amelioration in the cost of living, but also at the return of the old relations between rulers and ruled. Liberal subscriptions were given by all classes for the purpose of illuminations and the feeding of the poor and almost every section of society took part. Many who had a few months ago been most energetic in promoting hartal were now equally to the fore in singing the praises of Government. This, as the Deputy Commissioner of Hoshiarpur remarks, is to be accepted as an apologia and no doubt betokens the hope that the hatchet is now to be buried. There is undoubtedly great anxiety among the loyal thinking Indians that there should be a return of normal conditions, particularly in respect of the relations between Europeans and the natives of the country. In Lahore, Ferozepore and in Gujranwala, where the intended levy of a fine of 5½ lakhs is much resented, there was a certain amount of captious and sullen criticism, but here, too, there is an improvement. Elsewhere, even where feeling had been very bitter, as at Multan, the occasion marked a most welcome rapprochement. In many places the coincidence of the long desired rain was considered a most happy augury. Rumours that the occasion would be marked by a complete political amnesty led many relatives of convicted persons to come to Lahore from Amritsar, Kasur and Gujranwala to await their release, but they went back disappointed.

The activities of the non-official committee of enquiry have temporarily ceased. Its place seems to have been taken by new Sewa Samities which have been or are being founded, nominally for relief work among the families of those who were killed in the disturbances or who have been convicted. The collection of funds is apparently continuing, but very little is forthcoming from this province. It is not yet generally known that the Privy Council had admitted the right to appeal against the Court Martial judgments, nor is the fact, even when known; likely to have any great effect. It is doubtful if anyone in a position to really know, expects any relief from the appeals and they are probably relying on Government's clemency.

Many of the old-fashioned wholehearted supporters of Government are quite unable to understand Government's attitude in permitting, almost welcoming, the criticism and judgement of its acts by those who have always been the sympathisers and supporters of those who are now convicted of waging war against the Government. As regards Gandhi, opinion is somewhat divided. There are those who consider it is for Government to protect the Punjab from his mischievous activities, whereas others think it would be a good thing to let him come to the Punjab and see how small is the influence he wields here. His abandonment of Satyagraha with the obvious intention of pressing Swadeshi will have little effect here. One Swadeshi store has been opened in Lahore, but it is probably no more than an effort to take advantage of a possible boom in Swadeshi products.

It seems certain that the Congress Reception Committee at Amritsar has no intention whatever of re-issuing the invitation to the Congress to meet at Amritsar this year, in spite of outside pressure and the efforts of a few irresponsible firebrands at Amritsar itself. It appears however that the Congress authorities are anxious to hold the Congress at Amritsar in spite of the absence of local assistance. The Government of India has accordingly been asked to sanction the extension of the Seditious Meetings Act for a further period after the expiry of the present term in October next and if this is sanctioned, it is proposed to draw the attention of the Congress authorities to the existence of the Act.

The municipal-elections at Hoshiarpur roused much excitement. The advanced Hindus and Mohammedans combined and secured two more seats for their party. There is not much interest taken in the Afghan war, and although the reported proceedings of the first day of the Peace Conference may revive discussion, the bazaar belief is that the negotiations will prove abortive: but there is now a general absence of the absurd and wild rumours of British defeats. Many consider indeed, that it will be a pity if peace results, before the Amir is made to realise his proper position. Soldiers returning from the front are said to be convinced that military measures will be taken in the autumn and that the Afghans will be suitably dealt with.

The unrest on the frontier is, so far as the Punjab is concerned, only affecting the Dera Ghazi Khan district. The company of Mangrotha had just been removed on the 15th when a lashkar of some 200-300 Sulieman Khels, Powindahs and Wazirs, appeared in the district. They burnt the Chittarwatta police post on the 16th and on the 17th were a few miles above Nilohar and on the 18th had entered the Vehoa nullah. They attacked Vehoa post, where a company of Indian Infantry was in place in addition to the Baluch Levy, on the night of the 18th and looted several houses on the outskirts, but were kept out of the main bazaar by a picket. The gang withdrew at about four in the morning, leaving one dead Waziri behind. From a hilltop, however, the gang is said to have been seen burying some of their dead companions. The casualties on our side were one sepoy and a Hindu killed and two sepoys wounded. The post was again threatened on the night of the 19th, but on the 20th, the gang crossed into the Kaura nullah by Jarwanga Tokh, taking with them much-looted cattle. By the 21st they had retreated to the upper end of the Kaura nullah beyond Mithakui. The

Officer Commanding the troops at Vehoa did not consider that he had sufficient force to follow up the lashkar and drive it out of the vicinity. The Bozdars in the Levy were doubtless considered suspect after the Dhanassar affair and the Kasranis had shown themselves quite ineffectual in preventing the lashkar going through their country. At the same time, another lashkar was reported to be making for Sanghar and the troops were consequently ordered back to Mangrotha. The cash and notes were removed from the Taunsa treasury to Dera Ghazi Khan and the records were kept ready to be moved into the shrine. On the night of the 21$^{st}$, this second lashkar of Sulieman Khels, Wazirs and Sheranis, was at Toisar, having come from Atal Kach. They gave out they were going to attack Musa Khel, but it was possible they would join with the first lashkar and again threaten Vehoa. On the 22$^{nd}$, information was received of this lashkar totalling 1,500 having been seen north of Fazla Kach, threatening Drug and Sanghar. An airplane was sent from Dera Ismail Khan to reconnoitre the Vehoa hills and arrangements were made to despatch the moveable column from Multan. On the 24$^{th}$, Vehoa was again attacked by about 1,500 enemy who were driven off with only one man wounded on our side. In the opinion of the Commissioner and the Officer Commanding, Multan Brigade, there are now sufficient troops in the neighbourhood to deal with any eventuality. It is satisfactory that, at any rate, so far, the Musa Khel have apparently remained loyal.

The young Khetran Sardar, Sardar Shah Ghazi Khan, surrendered to the Mazari Nawab, Sir Behram Khan, and is to be sent in-custody to Quetta. The postponed Shahi jirgas at Fort Monro are now to take place on the 23$^{rd}$ August, but it is not likely that Baluchistan will participate.

Economic.

Ample rain has at last been received all over the province with the exception of parts of the extreme west where, although the amounts of rain have been small, the canals and rivers are overflowing and parts of Jhelum and Shapur where it is possible that the position has improved since the reports were received. Lahore has had 10 inches in 24 hours. In Rawalpindi, where there has been great excess, the heavy soils are for the most part unworkable, but generally kharif ploughings are in full swing everywhere and the standing crops have been saved.

[The Resident, in the case of Baroda, one W.H. Wilkinson, sent the fortnightly reports that were sent from the Princely States to the Political Secretary of the Government of India. The States all had differing status and the Gaekwar of Baroda had a special connection with the Viceroy, being able to approach him direct without going through the Agent to the Governor-General - the latter being a system hotly criticised by Alwar, the 'cleverest' of the Princes according to Edwin Montagu, and the man who had most to hide in his psychopathic treatment of those in his power. It was from Baroda that the following fortnightly report came. It is to look ahead to the time of Lord Linlithgow, to see Gandhi creeping into every part of India including the States. It was the insidious infiltration of the Congress and Gandhi at that time that prevented the suspicious Princes from entering into the loosely knit Federation that Linlithgow was endeavouring to promote and which under Mountbatten, became their death knell when finally Congress and Nehru took over and wiped the Princes out. But this is still 1919 and we see Gandhi cautiously getting a hold on the Senior State, Baroda.]

Political and economic report for the first fortnight of August.

Economic.

Rainfall has been seasonable and satisfactory throughout the State. All standing crops are in excellent condition. A sixteen-anna harvest is expected and prices have fallen from 5 to 20 per cent.

Political.

The 10th of July was celebrated as a general holiday through out the State, all offices, schools and colleges being closed, a proclamation parade of Baroda forces was held at Baroda at which the terms of peace were read out. The Vahivatdars (Tahsildars) also read out the terms to the public and by the education authorities to the schoolchildren. The poor were fed in Baroda city. Prisoners were released and given remission of sentences on the scale adopted in British India. Thanksgiving services were held in all state aided temples and mosques. Public buildings were decorated and games were held in the Baroda public park, where a garden party was given by the State to which all European residents at the station were invited and the peace terms were read out.

Whether any deep impression was created is another matter. I think that even the educated people regard peace as having been established last November and that consequently further celebrations in the winter would fall so flat that it would hardly be worthwhile holding them at all.

As regards the peace with Afghanistan, I am told that the tendency among the people of Baroda is to persuade themselves that the Afghans have won, and that they point to the secrecy of the negotiations as a proof of this. They are also trying to believe that the Afghans were provoked into hostilities.

M.K. Gandhi accompanied by Sundaram Annuswami Aiyar and Bai Ganga of Vijapur, visited Vijapur, Kadi District on July 30th. On the 31st, he inspected the spinning factory and in the afternoon gave a lecture on Swadeshi, to which about 2,000 persons listened. A deputation from Maga Mahi Kantha waited on him with a request that he would pay their village a visit, but he said that he had no time. He put up at the house of Brahmin Javeri, Lallubhai Girdhar Sadasahib, and took his meals with Bhai Ganga.

On his way through Kalol on August 1st, he visited the Station Master's quarters, the handloom weaving factory and the gin of Vora Rasulbhai, where he lectured on Swadeshi. He was garlanded in the town by Jiwan Lal Gopal Bansal: two or three persons took the Swadeshi vow. There was nothing objectionable in either of the lectures and Gandhi did not touch on Satyagraha.

# DISTRICT REPORTS

K.G. Deshpande, who has been referred to in previous reports is at the head of a movement to revive home spinning in Baroda, in pursuance of the Swadeshi policy, by buying old spinning wheels and distributing them among the Mohammedan women of the city. The thread is to be woven into rough cloth that will be sold by a bookseller, Athavie, and the boys in the Lohana and Brahma Boarding Houses. It is said that the remnant of the capital of the India Spinning and weaving Company of Baroda, about Rs. 25,000 is to be used with the consent of Sardar Ghorpade who controls it, to finance the movement. Manckrao, the Akhado proprietor, is also interesting himself in the project. I do not think there is much political significance in this movement. Deshpande probably intends to use Gandhi's Swadeshi campaign for his own profit. This is obviously a good opportunity for a shrewd man with predatory instincts and no capital.

Dr. Madhavrao Suralkar distributed handbills about the observing of Tilak's birthday and also sold some photographs of Tilak; some State servants (Dekhnis) being among the purchasers. Only a few photographs were sold.

[The fortnightly report for the 15th August from the Punjab indicates yet again the way that Indian minds accepted the propaganda and the rumours about the rebellion, in this case the Afghan War part of it. There are those in this country who still do.]

Political.

The political situation continues to clear and the signature of peace with Afghanistan, so far only known in the towns, has been sincerely welcomed. Indians are quite as tired of war as are Englishmen. The braggadocio of Colonel Ali Ahmed led many, particularly in Rawalpindi, to believe that the Afghans were in an unassailably strong position. Their humble acceptance of a peace in which they did not receive a single concession, except perhaps the definition of Afghanistan as 'independent', has completely disabused those disaffected persons who were anxiously looking forward to a rebuff for Government. At the same time, there are those who consider it not impossible that the Afghans will renounce the Treaty, should the Turkish peace terms be unacceptable to them, and in any case, it is felt that there is bound to be civil war in Afghanistan sooner or later, owing to the impossibility of Amanullah making peace with the powerful interests he has already alienated. Near the frontier, it is devoutly hoped that the independent tribes will be severely punished for their actions, but it is feared that, as often before, they will not get as much as they deserve. The behaviour of Ali Ahmad Khan at Friday prayers at the Rawalpindi Jama Masjid on the 1st and 8th of August and at the garden party given in honour of the delegates after the signing of peace has been reported direct to the Government of India. On each occasion Ali Ahmad used language which was clearly intended to inflame Mohammedan religious feelings. The tact however, of Government officials who accompanied the delegates prevented any harm being done and indeed, to Ali Ahmed's ill concealed annoyance, rather turned the tables on him. [Sir Michael O'Dwyer apparently returned to India in time for the Delhi garden party.]

In internal politics, the chief interest has been in the reduction of sentences in the important conspiracy cases of Lahore, Amritsar and Gujranwala. Though European criticism is not absent, Government orders have been generally applauded by Indians as an act both of justice and of that clemency which the oriental associates with Government. Moderate opinion largely holds that the sentences were in fact savage and unjustified; extremists consider the remission, however welcome, to have been extorted by clamour and the fear of the coming enquiry and of a possible adverse verdict on the appeals now pending before the Privy Council. Scarcely anyone, as the Commissioner of Lahore points out, now realises how serious was the position in the middle of April.

[During the ensuing months the District Officers continued to work as usual; as the hot weather continued and as the fortnightly reports came in, the picture became clear.

Fortnightly reports had to be written by District Officers, sent to the Commissioners and from them to the Government of the Province involved, thence to the Government of India. It was from these reports that the Government of India derived the news. Failed crops through lack of rain or plenitude - economic and agricultural, industrial and political - all the information went to the Government to analyse and if necessary take action. So heavy was the workload that Eleanor Tolinton, on marrying her husband Phillip, a District Officer in the I.C.S., went into a home where the previous incumbent, having become ill under the pressure of work, had left 1,500 files to deal with. Finding her husband so busy that she never saw him, Eleanor went into his office and with the help of a chaprassi, went through the mounds of files, signing them on behalf of her husband. The chaprassi opened the file and she signed it, then he removed it for another file. What, I wondered, had all these files been about? They contained the detail of how India was run and how it was kept (comparatively) free of corruption. The strictest measures of control were in place just as in the army. The tail of a dead camel or a horse needing replacement had to be produced, to verify the need.

As Martial Law in the Punjab was removed with the success of the Afghan War, details from the Punjab and other areas came in to Government. The claims of the British and Indian journalists about Amritsar, that the Punjab Government were doing something prejudicial by not letting the pleaders from other Provinces come in to represent the people arrested, was not exceptional, it was something which was usual. Pleaders existed in throngs in the Punjab just as they did in other Provinces, but one of these men was Sir Chiminlal Setalvad, later a Member of the Hunter Commission.

From Delhi, Poona and Lahore, the fortnightly reports came in, indicating the build up of a movement that was to produce the transformation from Gandhi's apology to claims of the evils of Martial Law and the incorrect figures of the casualties in the Jallianwalla Bagh. Poona was the summer residence of the Government of

Bombay. From Delhi in July, came varied comments in the fortnightly report from C.E. Barron:]

> *"German peace had brought cheers from the City - prices had come down, although unfortunately only temporarily. Munshi Ram (Swami Shraddanand) had spent most of the fortnight since June, in Lahore and Amritsar, in company with various extremist leaders. I understand that he was not welcomed by some of his friends with the enthusiasm he expected! It is believed that besides making enquiries into the disturbances and the measures taken to suppress them, he is trying to arrange for a number of the Sewa Samitis to assist the sufferers from the riots and the relations of persons convicted for taking part in them."*

Ansari had applied for and been given a passport to go to England to join the Muslim League deputation. Difficulties had arisen from shortage of funds mentioned in the Pan Islamic Party correspondence.

Rumours, all adverse to Government, were current and the prolonged inactivity on the Afghan frontier was not understood. It was actually rumoured that the port of Karachi was to be one of the terms of peace with Afghanistan.

The Additional District Magistrate has completed the hearing of both the Shakarpur Railway case, and the Edward Park Riot case and hopes to deliver judgement in the latter in a few days. A curious and interesting, discovery, if true, has been made in the course of the railway strike enquiries, to the effect that the idea of calling a general strike originally emanated from Lahore on 11th April, some 30 hours before the Delhi telegrams were said to have been dispatched.

The 'Vijaya' newspaper had not had sufficiently discriminating a censor, a new appointment had led to the cessation of publication.

[From Poona and the districts that sent in their reports, July was covered by a report that took in the period from the 15th to the 31st.]

There was great relief when Gandhi announced his intention of postponing the resumption of his campaign. It is understood that this postponement will be for two or three months at least. From a telegram that was noticed in the censorship, Gandhi would appear to leave the question dependent on the success of a redoubled agitation for the repeal of the Rowlatt Act, which he anticipates the other leaders will now undertake. It was only with the greatest reluctance, however, that he gave in to the almost universal advice, not to restart the campaign, and he continues to express himself very strongly in regard to the heavy sentences passed in the Lahore and Amritsar cases. Both in his letter to the press notifying his intention and in a speech recently delivered at Bombay, he said that if he could only be sure that no untoward incident would arise he would not hesitate to restart his campaign to obtain redress in these cases. His reluctance to abandon his much-advertised campaign is also no doubt due to his consciousness that it will entail much loss of prestige and influence. 'Young

India' which he now, at least nominally, edits, and other local papers continue to publish the full .texts of the judgments in the various cases together with details and strongly worded criticisms and there is little doubt that feeling over the matter in Indian circles is very bitter. There was therefore much gratification evinced in these circles when it was known that the Privy Council had admitted appeals in these cases and this has also in a measure calmed the growing irritation at the delay in announcing the composition of the promised commission of enquiry into the recent disturbances. It is generally assumed that the Commission will examine the causes of the disorders as well as the measures adopted in dealing with each situation.

[Then there were the Tilak Birthday celebrations for his 64th birthday and the information that Rs. 210,000 were contributed and promised.]

A meeting of protest from all shades of opinion was held under the auspices of the Bombay Presidency Association, a one time moderate association. The attack was confined to Horniman's deportation having been carried out under the Defence of India Act rather than through the usual criminal processes. He had lost two of his main supports, S.R. Bomanji and Gandhi's friend Jamnadas Dwarkadas[63] and the first signatory to the Satyagraha pledge, as well as first member of the Satyagraha Committee. Horniman was allegedly involved with 'The Republic' which had been commented on unfavourably even by 'Young India'.

There were appreciations of the peace celebrations on the 19th (July) but unfavourable comments were made on the absence of amnesty releasing prisoners, particularly political prisoners. On the other hand the permission for Muslim soldiers to perform the Raj on their way home was favourably reported in Muslim papers.

'Young India' was now leading the way, with full reports of the Lahore and Amritsar cases, with unfavourable comment and Mr. Gandhi's denunciations of the Punjab Military Tribunals. 'Young India' hoped that the spirit shown by Lala Govindihahandas in the matter of his trial would permeate Indian society. The decision in the <u>Partap</u> case was declared to be a travesty of justice and a blot on the records of the Punjab Government and the judgments in the cases against Lala Harkishanlal and others were similarly denounced as specially directed against the anti-Rowlatt Act agitation, even the 'Servant of India', a moderate organ, remarking that the judges had failed completely to appreciate the doings of the Punjab leaders.

---

63    Jamnadas Dwarkadas was also the main speaker in the opening debate on the Punjab in Delhi in 1921.

# APPENDIX V

# GLOSSARY OF INDIAN WORDS

| | |
|---|---|
| Abhinav Bharat | Young India Society, secret revolutionary society |
| amaldar | official (police) |
| approver | informer, accuser |
| Arya Samaj | Hindu revolutionary movement with links to Theosophists |
| Ashram | A religious hermitage |
| ayah | native nursemaid |
| babu-log | petty bureaucrat class |
| Bahadur | The Brave |
| Baisakhi | Sikh Spring Festival and horse fair |
| Bande Mataram | Hindu Nationalist song |
| bearer | house valet |
| bibi-garh | site of slaughter of 206 women & children prisoners Cawnpore, 1857 |
| bussa, bhusa | animal fodder, hay |
| cantonment | permanent military station |
| Chalo | March! |
| chaprassi | doorkeeper, messenger |
| chowdhri | landowner |
| chowki | guard-hut |
| compounder | pharmacist |

| | |
|---|---|
| coolie | unskilled labourer |
| crore | ten million |
| cummerbund | broad pleated sash |
| dacoits | members of robber bands |
| dak | relay system in India, c.f. post system in England |
| Danda Fauj | Bludgeon Army |
| darshan | recognition of Divinity (Hindu) |
| Durbar | State Reception |
| feringhi | foreigner |
| firman | decree by a monarch |
| gaddi | throne cushion |
| Gandhi ki Jai | Long Live Gandhi |
| Garhwalis | Garhwal Rifles Regiment |
| Ghadr | The Mutiny Movement |
| goondas | ruffians |
| Great Mehla | Sikh pilgrimage |
| gulab jamans | Indian sweets |
| gusselkhana | latrine |
| hartal | a strike, a shutdown |
| izzat | respect, honour |
| jalabies | Indian sweets |
| Jihad | Holy War |
| Jemadar | Junior Viceroy's Commissioned Officer |
| jazail | Afghan home-made rifle |
| Jirga | Pashtu decision-making group of elders |
| Kamadhenu | Mother of all cows, hence, acme of perfection |
| Kamins | low caste villagers |
| Kardar | Afghan tribal name |
| khaira | Nobodies, persons of no note |
| kharif | Autumn crop |
| khudside | side of a ravine |
| Kotwali | Police Station |
| kraal | encampment |
| kshatrya raj | Hindu ancestral king |
| kukri | Ghurkha fighting knife |
| laddoo | ball-shaped Indian sweet |
| lakh | one hundred thousand |
| Lambardar | village headman |
| lashkar | army |
| lathi | 6' iron-shod bamboo staff, classed as a weapon |
| Mahasabha | Re-Conversion of Muslims to Hinduism |
| Mamlatdar | Land Tax collector |

## GLOSSARY OF INDIAN WORDS

| | |
|---|---|
| Manjha | District in Jullundur |
| Maro | Death! |
| Marwari | person from Marwar |
| maulvi | a Muslim teacher |
| melecha | barbarian |
| mullah | Muslim trained in Islamic law |
| munshi | Urdu, a teacher, a secretary |
| Nawab | Muslim prince or major landlord |
| Naib | Assistant |
| nullah | ravine or gulley |
| pagri | turban |
| Pandit | Brahmin scholar |
| Patwari | Land record clerk |
| pheta | Hindu-style turban |
| pleader | a legal advocate |
| postmaster | Afghan secret service chief |
| pukharo | seize |
| punkah | fan hung from the ceiling |
| purdah | lit. screen or veil, clothing to hide the body. |
| Raises | Chieftains |
| Ram Bagh | Garden on the site of former maharaja's palace |
| Risaldar | Viceroy-commissioned cavalry officer |
| rishi | divinely inspired poet or sage |
| Sadhu | a Hindu wandering holy man |
| sais, syce | a groom |
| sanad | cash reward |
| sangar | temporary fortified breastwork |
| sankhia | poisonous |
| sanyassi | Hindu wandering ascetic beggar |
| Sardar | Leader |
| Sirkar | Rule |
| satyagraha | lit. search for truth. Used by Gandhi as name for non-violent passive resistance, but also described violent anti-Government actions. |
| Satyagraha sabha | Passive resistance league |
| sepoys | Indian soldiers in the East India Company army. |
| Sewa Samitis | Voluntary help-groups |
| Shabash | Well done! |
| shigram | clumsy cart |
| solar topi | traditional Western pith helmet |
| sowar | mounted trooper |
| Subedar | Viceroy's Commissioned Officer |

| | |
|---|---|
| Subedar Major | Senior Viceroy's Commissioned Officer |
| Swadeshi | Gandhian 'charity begins at home' economics |
| Swami | Religious teacher |
| Swaraj | Self-rule |
| Tahsil | administrative district |
| Tahsildar | District officer for tax administration |
| tikka | forehead mark made by Hindus |
| tikka-gharri | hired tonga or cart |
| Tilak, Bal Gangadhur | Father of Indian unrest born 23 July 1856 |
| tonga | two-wheeled carriage |
| tonga-wallah | a tonga driver |
| Vakil | Attorney |
| wali | friend, kinsman |
| yakil | barrister |
| yogi | master of yoga philosophy |
| zamindar | village landowner |
| zareba | enclosure of bushes, stakes, etc. |
| zenana | part of the house reserved for women |

# BIBLIOGRAPHY NOTES

Case of General R.E.H. Dyer, 3rd July 1920, was the letter from Dyer to the Army Council, 3 copies of which were sent in to the House of Commons before the Debate on Amritsar on 8th July. Few Members were able to see them.

Short Biographies of Grand Duke Alexander Mikhailovitch and others were published in 1952 by The Foreign Languages Publishing House, Moscow.

The papers of Percy Marsden I.C.S. about Kasur, his later interview with Edwin Montagu in London and further papers appear in Cabinet Papers, held by The National Archives, Kew.

Anthony C Sutton's book, 'Wall Street and the Bolshevik Revolution', though not directly related to Montagu, links him with the background to the events in which he took a central part and which is made clear in the Cabinet papers. The paper of Sir Mark Sykes, who was poisoned (dying in Paris at the age of 49), together with the clear hints from Lord Ampthill in his speech in the Lords, when he said that Montagu was in deadly fear when he made his speech in the Commons damning Dyer and shocking Conservative Peers, provide links. The Labour/Liberal/Bolshevik links were clearly against General Dyer's action in putting down the rising with its Congress/Labour links; Labour being at that time, and for many years since, Bolshevik-funded and dancing to a tune which Sykes had traced to American Banking. Sutton brings together so much of Mark Sykes, not released at the time, that he also gives Nesta Webster, who relied on the Edgar Sisson Report, the validity it had in her writings. She traced back Bakunin's words, phrases and attitudes to Illuminism; and her writings can stand where they should have stood, and did in the mind of Churchill but have been carefully sneered at elsewhere.

Churchill, speaking in the House of Commons on November 5th 1919, was saying how Lenin headed the leading spirits of a formidable sect, the most formidable sect in the world of which he was the high priest and chief. Churchill did not then have the information which would have shown the background to the 1919 Rebellion in India. The clues that were available in 1918 were in the Sisson Report, published in America, which showed the links between Bolshevism and Germany. The Germans ran the Bolsheviks, American bankers backed the Bolsheviks and were closely linked with German bankers including those who later supported Hitler. These links are important since they are still the Illuminati inspiration from the 18th Century and continue in America's policy in Afghanistan today. If Dyer had not fired, with Montagu in the position he had been placed, India could have broken up at a time when the Congress has not sufficient power to save her from the results of their conspiracies. Gandhi tried again in 1920/21 in the Malabar rising. According to Mrs. Webster, the links are shown in the book by General Spiridovitch, 'The History of Bolshevism', a factual report made from Tsarist files not translated from the Russian, published four years after the Sisson Report. We therefore have on an ordinary open level, Ramsay Macdonald as the leader of the Labour Party, inspiring and possibly running Montagu, who manipulates the outcome of an important action in Indian History and with the gloss of propaganda, uses it to end our rule in India.

But it should not be overlooked that Montagu's partisan Indian friends were in direct touch with that international version of Germany's world rule policy – the C.U.P. Montagu may have been involved on account of his attitude to Zionism. The inference is made clearer when his position is looked at in terms of his friendship with Indians in this country. His was not a practical role such as that of Kemal Pasha, who could throw off the ideas in the needs of his country. Montagu's role was a political one, a matter of opinion rather than executive action. Whether he met Parvus or not (Parvus did spend time in London), that man's insidious and brilliantly subversive cleverness would have been handed about among the Labour people, the Morel men, and Montagu did not have the experience, insight or clarity of mind to analyse and refute the concepts with which his Indian friends were deeply imbued. By 1915, he was on the Privy Council and rubbing shoulders with that other persuasive German conspirator, Edgar Speyer.

Edwin Montagu played a central role in the political changes in India. He it was who made the speech which reduced General Dyer to the status of terrorist. He was involved in the new Indian Constitution and having believed Gandhi to be a saint, he realized in 1922 that Gandhi was a man who should be imprisoned, - this in the teeth of his fellow Jew, Lord Reading, the Viceroy of India, despite his original promise of the job to Lord Willingdon,. He lost his parliamentary seat and then for a year worked as a bullion dealer in South America. He also set up a wild life sanctuary in the Norfolk Broads. For his early life, any encyclopaedia has the facts of his going to Lancing College and then to London College daily; from thence to Trinity College, Cambridge.

After the Amritsar incident, he was instrumental in choosing the members of the Hunter Committee - the Indian Members being in favour of the Rebellion - although he had seen the Rowlatt Report on the widespread and dangerous conspiracy through India, partly funded by Germany and by the Bolsheviks. He spoke to Sir Sidney Rowlatt, whose legislation was the subject of the rebellion backed by Gandhi.

With the Rebellion over and India at peace, we have the correspondence between him and Lord Curzon, by then Foreign Secretary; the Congress Committee Report on which the present propaganda story is based and the careful comments by Colonel Sir John Hose, picking out the spins, twist and untruth on which the Congress report is based. The East India Company was made of people who had served in India and Hose therefore knew a great deal more about the subcontinent that did Montagu.

Nonetheless, with help from Churchill in correspondence, Montagu gave the speech almost entirely based on the Congress untruths. Prior to the speech, Dyer had sent into Parliament his letter of justification to the Army Council, who had refused to sack him, following a great deal of correspondence on the question of what to do with Dyer, whose family would suffer if he lost his pension.

Cabinet Papers in the National Archives show Montagu's anxiety to have Gandhi imprisoned after the Malabar Rebellion 1922. They also show the problems of his announcement of his ideas of India's wishes about the Treaty of Sevres on which he had to resign and with Hansard, show the desire finally to get rid of Montagu.

Newspapers: The Challenger, The Daily Telegraph, The Globe (various. articles).

Public Record Office papers in the India Office Library show the distress of Lady Willingdon and her husband, Freeman Thomas prior to his becoming a Marquis.

# BIBLIOGRAPHY
# PUBLISHED MATERIAL

| | |
|---|---|
| Alexander II, Czar | A Short Biography. Foreign Languages Publishing House 1952 |
| Andrus, J.R. & Mohammed, A.. | Trade Finance and Development in Pakistan. O.U.P. 1966 |
| Atkinson, Rodney | Treason and Maastricht. Computer Publishing 1994 |
| Bagehot, Walter | Literary Studies. Dent |
| Basham, A L | The Wonder That Was India. Orient Longmans 1953 |
| Bayley, Alice | Healing on the Seven Rays. 5 vols. Lucas Publishing 1953 |
| Bernstorff, Count von | Memoirs of. The Windmill Press 1936 |
| Bhutto, Benazair | 'Daughter of the East'. Hamilton 1988 |
| Birla, G.D. | In the Shadow of Mahatma. Orient Longmans 1953 |
| Blackwood | (Ed. Lt. Col. Bethell). Blackwood Tales from the Outposts 1941 |
| Brailsford, H.N. | Subject India. Left Book Club. Edition 1943 |
| Brook-Shepherd, Gordon | The Storm Petrels. The First Soviet Defectors. Collins 1977 |
| Brown, Dr. Judith M. | Modern India The Origins of an Asian Democracy O.U.P. 1994 |
| Brown, Dr. Judith M. | Prisoner of Hope. Yale University Press 1989 |
| Buchan, John | The Thirty-Nine Steps. First pub. 1915 |
| Buchan, John | Greenmantle. Penguin. First pub. 1916 |

| | |
|---|---|
| Burne, Sir Owen Tudor | Clyde and Strathnairn. Clarendon Press 1895 |
| Callwell, Maj. Gen. Sir C.E. | Various booklets. |
| Cameron, Roderick | Shadows from India. William Heinemann 1958 |
| Cecil, David | Lord Melbourne. Constable 1939 |
| Chaudhuri, Nirad | Thy Hand Great Anarch. Chatto and Windus 1987 |
| Chevenix-Trench, Charles | Viceroy's Agent. Jonathan Cape 1987 |
| Churchill, Winston S. | My Early Life. Thornton Butterworth 1930 |
| Colvin, Ian Duncan | Life of General Dyer. Blackwood 1929 |
| Connolly, Bernard | The Rotten Heart of Europe. Faber 1995 |
| Corbett, James | Man Eaters of Kumaon. Book Society and O.U.P. 1946 |
| Cotton, C.W.E. | Speeches As First Agent to the Governor General Madras States. Compiled and pub. with intro. by VRM Chohan, BA, LLB, Chief Court Vakil, Ernakulam. Printed at School Press 1929 |
| Crozier, Brian | Free Agent. The Unseen War. Harper Collins 1993 |
| Dale, Stephen Frederick | Islamic Society on the South Asian Frontier. The Mappilas of Malabar 1489-1922. Clarendon Press 1980 |
| Das, Durga | India from Curzon to Nehru and After. Collins 1969 |
| Denniston, Robert | Churchill's Secret War. Sutton 1997 |
| Desai, Mahadev | The Story of Bardoli. Navajivan Press. Ahmedabad 1929 |
| Disraeli, Benjamin | Coningsby. Heron Brooks. London. First pub. 1844 |
| Duncan, Ronald | The Writings of Gandhi. Faber 1951 |
| Dutt, R. Palme | India Today. Left Book Club. Victor Gollanz 1940 |
| Ferguson-Davie, C.J. | The Early History of Indians in Natal'. S. African Institute of Race Relations 1951 |
| Fischer, Louis | The Life of Mahatma Gandhi. Jonathan Cape 1951 |
| Forster, E.M. | The Hill of Devi. Edward Arnold 1953 |
| Forster, E.M. | A Passage to India. Edward Arnold 1924 |
| Furneaux, Rupert | Massacre at Amritsar. Allen and Unwin 1963 |
| Galpin, G.H. | Indians in South Africa Pietermaritzburg. Shuter and Shooter 1949 |

PUBLISHED MATERIAL

| | |
|---|---|
| Gandhi, M.K. | An Autiobiography The Story of My Experiments with Truth. First pub Navjivan Trust 1927 Penguin 1982 |
| Gandhi, M.K. | Selected Writings of Gandhi; ed. Ronald Duncan. Faber 1951 |
| Gandhi, M.K. | Hind Swaraj 1910 |
| Gaureschi, Giovanni | Comrade Don Camillo. Companion Book Club 1959 |
| Ghosh, Sudhir | Gandhi's Emissary. London Cresset Press 1971 |
| Gilbert, Sir Martin | Servant of India. Sir James Dunlop Smith. Longmans 1966 |
| Gilbert, Sir Martin | World in Torment. Winston Churchill 1917-1922. vols. iv & v 1923–1939 Minerva 1975 |
| Gilmour, David | Curzon. John Murray 1994 |
| Grant, James | Cassell's History of India 1898 |
| Graves, Robert | Lawrence and the Arabs. Jonathan Cape 1927 |
| Griffiths, Sir Percival | To Guard my People. A History of the Indian Police. Ernest Benn 1971 |
| Griffiths, Sir Percival | The British in India. Robert Hale 1946 |
| Gwynn, Charles W. | Imperial Policing. Macmillan 1936 |
| Hamid, Maj. Gen. Shahid | Disastrous Twilight. Leo Cooper 1986 |
| Hancock, W.H. | Smuts, The Sanguine Years' 1870 – 1919. C.U.P. 1962 |
| Harrer, Heinrich | Seven Years in Tibet. Rupert Hart-Davies 1953 |
| Heard, Gerald | These Hurrying Years. Chatto and Windus 1934 |
| Heyer, Georgette | The Spanish Bride. William Heinemann 1954 |
| Hilton, Adrian | The Principality and Power of Europe. Dorchester House. 1997 |
| Hitchock, R.H. | 'A History of the Malabar Rebellion 1921. First published 1925 as a confidential Government Report. Introduction by Robert Hardgrave, Jnr., Usha publications 1985 |
| Holman, Felice | The Wild Children. Scribner Book Co. 1983 |
| Hope, Lord John, Baron Glendevon | Viceroy at Bay; Lord Linlithgow in India'. Collins 1971 |
| Hopkirk, Peter | The Great Game. John Murray 1990 |

| | |
|---|---|
| Hunt, Roland and Harrison, Jn. | The District Officer in India 1930-47. Scholar Press 1980 |
| Hunt, Wray | Boy of the Indian Frontier. Moti Ram Bahadur. 1957. Penguin Books |
| Imperial War Museum | Indian Government 'India's Contribution to the Great War'. pub. 1923 |
| Indo British Review | Religious Traditions in South Asia. January 1974 |
| Ismay, Gen. the Lord | Memoirs. Heinemann |
| Judd, Denis | Lord Reading. Weidenfeld & Nicholson 1982 |
| Kaye, and Malleson, | History of the Indian Mutiny. Greenwood. Reprint 1971 |
| Keith, Prof. A.B. | Speeches on India Policy. 1750-1921. O.U.P. 1922. 2 vols. |
| Koestler, Arthur | The Case of the Midwife Toad. Hutchison. 1971 |
| Koestler, Arthur | The Heel of Achilles. Essays 1968-1973. Hutchison. 1974 |
| Kumar, C. & Puri, M. | Mahatma Gandhi. His Life and Influence. Heinemann 1982 |
| Kumar D. & Desai M. eds. | Cambridge Economic History of India. vol. 2 C1757 – 1970. C. U. P. 1983 Eds. Dharma Kumar and Meghnad Desai |
| Larousse | Encyclopaedia of Mythology. Intro: Robert Graves. Paul Hamlyn 1959 |
| Lawrence, T.E. | Letters of. ed. Malcolm Brown. J M Dent 1988 |
| Lawrence, T.E. | Seven Pillars of Wisdom. Jonathan Cape 1926 |
| Linklater, Eric | A year of Space. Macmillan 1953 |
| Llewellyn, Richard | At Sunrise the Rough Music. Michael Joseph 1978 |
| Lovett, Sir Verney | A History of the Indian Nationalist Movement Frank Cass 1968 |
| Lydall, Edward | Over the Hills. The Book Guild 1993 |
| Machiavelli, Niccolo | The Prince. Reprint 1940 |
| Mackenzie, Compton | The Windsor Tapestry. Rich and Cowan 1936 |
| Marco Polo | Travels. Dent 1905 |
| Marquand, Leo | The South African Way of Life. Heinemann 1953 |
| Marriott, J.A.R. | English Political Institutions. Clarendon Press 1910 |

# PUBLISHED MATERIAL

| | |
|---|---|
| Marsden, Percy | Papers on the 1919 Rebellion. Contemporary up to 1922 |
| Masani, Zareer | Indian Tales of the Raj. B.B.C. Books 1988 |
| Massie, Robert | Nicholas and Alexandra. 1967 |
| Masters, Anthony | The Man who was M. The Life of Maxwell Knight. Basil Blackwell. 1984 |
| Masters, John | Night Runners of Bengal. Michael Joseph 1951 |
| Masters, John | Himalayan Concerto. Michael Joseph 1976 |
| Mayo, Katherine | Mother India. Jonathan Cape. 1927 |
| Millin, Sarah Gertrude | The People of South Africa. Constable and Co London 1951 |
| Montagu, Edwin | An Indian Diary. ed. Venetia Montagu. William Heinemann 1930 |
| Moon, Sir Edward Penderel | The British Conquest and Dominion of India. Duckworth 1989 |
| Moon, Sir Edward Penderel | Gandhi and Modern India. E.U.P. 1968 |
| Moorhouse, Geoffrey | India Britannica. Collins 1983 |
| Morris, James | Pax Britannica. Faber 1978 3 vols. |
| Mosley, Diana | A Life of Contrasts. Hamish Hamilton 1977 |
| Murray, John | Letters of Queen Victoria. In 3 vols. 1911 |
| Naipaul, V.S. | India; A Thousand Mutinies Now. Minerva Press 1990 |
| Nair, Sir C. Sankaran | Gandhi and Anarchy. Tagore Publications Madras 1923 |
| Nair, Sir C. Sankaran | Autobiography. Lady Madhavan Nair pub. as Editor 1966 |
| Napier, Priscilla | Raven Castle. Charles Napier in India 1844-51. Russell. 1991 |
| Narayan, R.K. | Gods, Demons and Others. Heinemann 1965 |
| Nehru, Jawarharlal | An Autobiography. John Lane. The Bodley Head 1936 |
| Nichols, Beverley | Verdict on India. Jonathan Cape 1944 |
| O'Dwyer, Sir Michael | India As I Knew It. 1885-1925. London Constable & Co. 1925 |
| O.U.P. | Oxford History of Modern India 1740-1947. 1965 |
| Overstreet, Gene | Communism in India. University of California Press. Berkeley and Los Angeles 1959 |
| Parry, Benita | Delusions and Discoveries. On India. Allen Lane and the Penguin Press 1971 |

| | |
|---|---|
| Pearson, W.W. | Shantiniketan The Bolpur School of Rabindranath Tagore Macmillan 1918 |
| Perkins, Roger | Amritsar Legacy. Picton Publishing 1989 |
| Pickering, Carol | Goodbye India. Henry Martyn Centre archive |
| Piffer, The | Magazine of the Punjab Frontier Force |
| Potgieter, D.J. | Standard Encyclopaedia of Southern Africa. vol. 5 Nasou Ltd 1970 |
| Puri, M. & C. Kumar | Mahatma Gandhi. His Life and Influence. Heinemann 1982 |
| Raja Ram | Jallianwallah Bagh Massacre. Punjab University pubs. 1969 (A Premeditated Plan) |
| Reader's Digest | Chronicles of the 20th Century. |
| Ronaldshay, Lord | India. C. U. P. 1926 |
| Ronaldshay, Lord | The Life of Lord Curzon. Benn 1928 3 vols. |
| Ruskin, John | Sesame and Lilies. The True Path. Dent 1907 |
| Sanceau, Elaine | Indies Adventure. Alfonso de Albuquerque. Blackies 1936 |
| Soil Association | Mother Earth. 1963 |
| Solzhenitsyn, Alexander | Lenin in Zurich. arr. with Bodley Head. Book Club Ass. 1976 |
| Steiner, Rudolf | The Bhagavad-Gita. Anthroposophical Press. New York 1913 |
| Streatfield-James, Comdr. E.C. | In the Wake. (The Birth of the Indian and Pakistan Navies). Charles Skilton. Edinburgh 1983 |
| Stormer, John A. | None Dare Call It Treason. Liberty Bell Books 1964 |
| Storrs, Sir Ronald | Lawrence of Arabia. Zionism and Palestine. Penguin. Originally pub. As 'Orientations' 1937 |
| Stutley, Margaret & James | Hinduism. Routledge and Kegan Paul 1977 |
| Swinson, Arthur | Six Minutes to Sunset. London. Peter Dais. 1961 |
| Trotter, Lionel J. | The Bayard of India. The Life of Sir James Outram. Dent. 1909 |
| Tully, Mark | From Raj to Rajiv. BBC Books 1988 |
| Tully, Mark and Jacob, Satish | Amritsar. Pan Books. 1985 |
| Vittachi, Tarzie | The Brown Sahib. Andre Deutsch 1962 |
| Wavell, Field Marshal Lord | The Viceroy's Journal. ed. Penderel Moon O.U.P.1971 |
| Wavell, Field Marshal Lord | Diaries. pub. Penderel Moon 1973 |
| Webster, Nesta | Surrender of an Empire. Boswell 1931 |

| | |
|---|---|
| Webster, Nesta | The Socialist Network. Boswell 1926 |
| Wetherell, Violet | The Indian Question in South Africa. Unie Vollkspers Bpk 1946 |
| Willingdon Papers | British Library. Oriental and Asian Dept. |
| Woodruff, Philip | The Men Who Ruled India. 2 vols. Jonathan Cape 1954 |
| Woolacott, J.E. | India on Trial. Macmillan 1929 |
| Wright, Robert | Strewth So Help Me God. Wright 1994 |
| Wyatt, Sir Woodrow | Confessions of an Optimist. Collins 1985 |
| Yeats-Brown, B. | Martial India. Eyre and Spottiswood. 1945. |
| Ziegler, Philip | Mountbatten. William Collins 1985 |

## SOURCES FROM GOVERNMENT

1915 Defence of India Act
Case of General R E H Dyer. 3rd July 1920
1935 India Act
Debate on Martial Law. Delhi 1921 Legislative Assembly
Hansard 'Debates on the Punjab Disturbances' 1920 and generally
Hunter Committee Report – Secret Evidence
Hunter Committee Report Ahmedabad. Volume of Evidence. Secret Evidence
Report of the Montagu-Chelmsford Reforms
Rowlatt, Justice S.A.T. Committee Report 1919
Rowlatt Committee (Seditions) Report at the request of the Government of Bengal 1919
Secretary of State Despatch. May 26th 1920

## UNOFFICIAL REPORTS

Asiatic Review. April 1926.
British Assoc. for Cemeteries in South Asia.

| | |
|---|---|
| Congress Party | Report of the National Congress Meeting, Delhi 1918 |
| Congress Party | Report of the National Congress Meeting, Amritsar 1919 |
| The Challenger. | Various |
| The Daily Telegraph | Various |

| | |
|---|---|
| The Globe. | Various |
| The Times Law Report | 1924 |
| Tourist Guide of Agra | |

## UNPUBLISHED MATERIAL

| | |
|---|---|
| Beckett, R.B. | Biography (unpublished) |
| Montagu, Edwin | Papers, Trinity College Cambridge permission of M Gendell, Montagu's son-in-law |
| Wathen Diaries | |
| Beaumont, Christopher | I.C.S. In conversation. |

## PERSONAL COMMENTS & DISCUSSIONS

Various discussions with Bill Kennedy, I.C.S., Tom Rogers, I.C.S., Mollie Stanton, widow of Vernon Stanton I.C.S., Azim Hussain I.C.S., Sir Christopher Beaumont I.C.S. Sir Penderel Moon I.C.S. Sir Ian Scott I.C.S. and Lady Scott; Edward Lydall I.C.S., Elinor Tolinton, widow of Phillip Tolinton I.C.S., Philip Mason I.C.S., Major Edmund Marsden, Indian Army; Raymond Shingles Indian Army, Andrew Roy, Mark Wathen, Bappi Daw, Alan Arthur I.C.S., Lewis Percy Addison I.C.S., Leslie French I.C.S., other members of the Indian Police and Army, Mollie Hawkins, whose father was in the Carabiniers in South Africa at the time of Gandhi, Laurens van der Post, Jackie Smyth V.C.,M.P., Oliver Calder I.C.S. and Garwhalis, Mrs Shearer, daughter of James Dunnet I.C.S., Yunus Khan, Major General Shahid Hamid, Pakistan Army, Leghari Family, especially Attar Leghari I.C.S., Edward Eustace I.C.S., Louise Kennedy, Lady Susan Abell, widow of Sir George Abell, Viceroy's Secretary, Roger Perkins, author of Amritsar Legacy, Dr Stephen Ashton of the Commonwealth Institute, Dr Lawson, Indian Institute, Teddy Hopkins, Indian Policy, Dr Bingle, India Office Library and staff, Staff of the Indian Institute in Oxford, Trinity College (Cambridge) Librarian and Staff, Codrington Library at All Souls, Bodleian Library, and so on.

Made in the USA
Charleston, SC
03 January 2012